National Park Maps

Contents

Titus Canyon Road (Death Valley)

National Park Maps, First Edition
ISBN: 978-1-62128-078-1
Library of Congress Control Number (LCCN): 2022921547

Printed in the United States of America
Publisher: Stone Road Press
Author/Photographer/Designer: Michael Joseph Oswald

Cover and Full-Page Photo Details
Front Cover: Sunrise Park Road (Mount Rainier)
Back Cover: Arches National Park Road (near Skyline Arch),
Lower Cathedral Valley Trail (Capitol Reef)

Corrections/Contact
This guidebook has been researched and written with the greatest attention to detail in order to provide you with the most accurate and pertinent information. Unfortunately, information changes and mistakes happen. All errors are our own. If you'd like to contact us for any reason, please send an e-mail to mike@stoneroadpress.com.

Disclaimer
Your safety is important to us. If any activity is beyond your ability or threatened by forces outside your control, do not attempt it. The maps in this book, although accurate and to scale, are not intended for hiking. Serious hikers should purchase a detailed, waterproof, topographical map (or download them from USGS or NPS website). It is also suggested you write or call in advance to confirm information when it matters most. The primary purpose of this guidebook is to enhance our readers' national park experiences, but the author, editor, and publisher cannot be held responsible for any experiences while traveling.

Photo Credits
All photos are the author's with the exceptions of Glacier Bay, Wrangell-St. Elias, Lake Clark, Gates of the Arctic, Kobuk Valley, and American Samoa

White Rim Road (Canyonlands)

Your National Parks at a Glance

A lot of words are used to describe our National Parks. Magical. Special. Treasured. Sacred. They're all warranted. These are singular environments that have inspired and awed humans for as long as we've walked this land. My favorite descriptor is a possessive pronoun … yours. These are your national parks, preserved for the benefit and enjoyment of the people. And I want to make sure you have the right tools to make the most of your time in your national parks.

I've learned words and images only begin to describe national park experiences. There's the thrill of discovery. The joy of spotting wildlife in the wild. The awe of witnessing something beyond our imaginations. Like Yosemite's massive granite wall, El Capitan. Redwood's towering trees. The kaleidoscope of colors of Yellowstone's Grand Prismatic Spring. While words will never do these places justice, hopefully this book helps point you in the direction of many indescribable experiences.

BEST PARKS

1. Glacier
2. Yosemite
3. Yellowstone
4. Death Valley
5. Acadia
6. Big Bend
7. Canyonlands
8. Grand Canyon
9. Zion
10. Rocky Mountain
11. Mount Rainier
12. Grand Teton
13. Sequoia & Kings Canyon
14. Olympic
15. Joshua Tree

White Sands

BEST ATTRACTIONS

1. Yosemite Valley (Yosemite)
2. Grand Canyon of the Yellowstone
3. Stony Hill Overlook (Denali)
4. Upper Geyser Basin (Yellowstone)
5. Bryce Amphitheater (Bryce Canyon)
6. White Sands
7. Many Glacier (Glacier)
8. Mount Rainier
9. Crater Lake
10. Island in the Sky (Canyonlands)
11. The Teton Range (Grand Teton)
12. Grand Prismatic Spring (Yellowstone)
13. Johns Hopkins Inlet (Glacier Bay)
14. The Wall (Badlands)
15. Mesquite Flat Sand Dunes (Death Valley)

Lower New

BEST ADVENTURES

1. Raft the Grand Canyon
2. Drive/Bike White Rim Road (Canyonlands)
3. Climb Mount Rainier
4. See lava (Hawaii Volcanoes)
5. Raft the Tatshenshini/Alsek (Glacier Bay)
6. Hike rim-to-rim at the Grand Canyon
7. Climb Mount Whitney (Sequoia)
8. Go backpacking at Glacier
9. Climb Half Dome (Yosemite)
10. Paddle Channel Islands
11. Climb Longs Peak (Rocky Mountain)
12. Raft the Lower New (New River Gorge)
13. Wild Cave Tours (Mammoth Cave, Wind Cave)
14. Bike Denali Park Road
15. Float the Rio Grande (Big Bend)

High Peaks

BEST TRAILS

1. Grinnell Glacier (Glacier)
2. Skyline (Mount Rainier)
3. Precipice (Acadia)
4. Sky Pond (Rocky Mountain)
5. South Rim (Big Bend)
6. High Peaks Loop (Pinnacles)
7. Hidden Lake (Glacier)
8. Half Dome (Yosemite)
9. Old Rag (Shenandoah)
10. Observation Point (Zion)
11. Delicate Arch (Arches)
12. Queen's Loop (Bryce Canyon)
13. The Narrows (Zion)
14. Sliding Sands (Haleakala)
15. Lakes (Sequoia)

Denali Park Road

BEST DRIVES

1. Going-to-the-Sun Road (Glacier)
2. Denali Park Road (Denali, shuttles)
3. Badlands Loop Road (Badlands)
4. Glacier Point/Wawona Rd (Yosemite)
5. McCarthy Road (Wrangell–St. Elias)
6. US-101 (Redwood)
7. Trail Ridge Road (Rocky Mountain)
8. Crater Rim Drive (Crater Lake)
9. Skyline Drive (Shenandoah)
10. Teton Park Road (Grand Teton)
11. UT-24 (Capitol Reef)
12. Park Loop Road (Acadia)
13. UT-211 (Canyonlands)
14. Zion Canyon Scenic Drive (shuttle)
15. Park Boulevard (Joshua Tree)

Castle Geyser (Yellowstone)

BEST LODGES

1. Old Faithful Snow Lodge (Yellowstone)
2. Many Glacier Hotel (Glacier)
3. The Ahwahnee (Yosemite)
4. Grand Canyon Lodge (Grand Canyon)
5. El Tovar (Grand Canyon)
6. Le Conte Lodge (Great Smoky Mountains, hike in)
7. Jenny Lake Lodge (Grand Teton)
8. Crater Lake Lodge (Crater Lake)
9. Kalaloch Lodge (Olympic)
10. Phantom Ranch (Grand Canyon, hike/mule in)
11. Sperry/Granite Park Chalets (Glacier, hike in)
12. Paradise Inn (Mount Rainier)
13. Zion Lodge (Zion)
14. The Lodge at Bryce Canyon (Bryce Canyon)
15. Chisos Mountain Lodge (Big Bend)

Your Parks
from East to West

Penobscot Mountain

ACADIA
MAINE

A day-hikers' dreamland. Acadia features one of the best networks of short trails. Connect a few for an exciting loop or hike one-way and hop aboard the free Island Explorer Shuttle (exploreacadia.com). Take a leisurely walk along the coast or climb a 1,000-ft mountain with the help of metal rungs and rails. Acadia also boasts carriage roads for walking, biking, and carriage tours, as well as ample coastline for paddling, boat tours, and beachcombing.

Buttermilk Falls

CUYAHOGA VALLEY
OHIO

An urban oasis. Cuyahoga Valley possesses national park staples like wisp-y waterfalls, peculiar rocks, and an abundance of outdoor activity opportunities but it sets itself apart with an assortment of unique attractions. You'll find scenic train rides (cvsr.com), outdoor music concerts and theater performances, time-period exhibits, and even two ski hills. Cuyahoga Valley is loved deeply by the Greater Cleveland community, and there's a lot to love.

Old Rag

SHENANDOAH
VIRGINIA

An Appalachian escape. 105-mile Skyline Drive and colorful fall foliage receive most of the attention, but Shenandoah offers some of the best mountain hiking this side of the Mississippi River. From rocky ridges to meandering meadows, plummeting waterfalls to towering forests, there's hiking for all interests. You'll even find Rapidan Camp, Herbert Hoover's Summer White House, within park boundaries. Or simply enjoy the viewpoints along scenic Skyline Drive.

Long Point

NEW RIVER GORGE
WEST VIRGINIA

An old river and new national park. New River Gorge is the newest national park, and it's established around one of the world's oldest waterways, the New River. The region was developed around coal mines that powered the Industrial Revolution. Today, there's a new revolution, the era of tourism. This area is home to some of the nation's best whitewater rafting and rock climbing, and there's a whole lot of hiking and history mixed in.

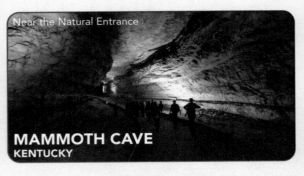
Near the Natural Entrance

MAMMOTH CAVE
KENTUCKY

An immense, nay, mammoth cave. Its name originates from the size of its rooms not the length of its passages, but its length is unmatched. Mammoth is the world's largest cave system. You can tour a few miles, ranging from short and easy walks to hours of crawling and squeezing through narrow rocky channels. Above ground are miles of trails for hikers, bikers, and horseback riders. Two rivers provide multitudes of paddling opportunities.

View from Clingman's Dome

GREAT SMOKY MOUNTAINS
TENNESSEE/NORTH CAROLINA

A wonderland of wildflowers and waterfalls. Great Smoky Mountains is the most visited national park. Location plays a part. Nearby tourist traps have a role. But the main reason more than 10 million people visit each year is the park's unbelievable beauty. It's brimming with beauty, wildlife, and outdoor activities. Hike to a wildflower-filled bald. Go tubing at Deep Creek. Pedal Cades Cove (there are motor-free time periods). Or ride a horse through the Smokies.

Boardwalk

CONGAREE
SOUTH CAROLINA

A swamp that's not a swamp. Congaree is a floodplain, meaning standing water isn't present most of the year. There's a primeval feel with Spanish moss, cypress knees, spiders, snakes, and mosquitoes. A more recent inhabitant stole the headlines. Synchronous fireflies perform each May/June. When conditions are right, you can paddle Cedar Creek. And anytime of year, as long as it isn't flooded, you can walk along the park's Boardwalk.

Boca Chita

BISCAYNE
FLORIDA

A park under water. More than 95% of the park is water. Much of the land is untethered islands, inaccessible to motorists. To explore this assortment of subtropical treats you'll need a boat or kayak. Or join Biscayne National Park Institute (biscaynenationalparkinstitute.org) on a tour. Popular destinations include Boca Chita, where you'll find a lighthouse, short trail, campground, and small beach or Totten and Old Rhodes Keys, which sandwich Jones Lagoon.

Pa-hay-okee

EVERGLADES
FLORIDA

A river of grass. Everglades offers a decent collection of hiking and biking paths, but with a maximum elevation of eight feet and variety of unique ecosystems, it delivers paddling and wildlife watching in spades. Paddlers can explore a labyrinth of mangrove-lined waterways, spending nights on elevated chickees. Alligators, crocodiles, and manatees call this area home. And more than 350 species of birds have been spotted. This is a special place for so many species.

Fort Jefferson

DRY TORTUGAS
FLORIDA

An abandoned fort/prison/quarantine station. Dry Tortugas is centered on Garden Key and its unfinished 19th-century fort. You can only reach it by boat or plane from Key West. You can't miss manmade (but never finished) Fort Jefferson. But the most interesting sites might be above and below these low-lying keys. Thousands of migratory birds visit in spring and colorful reefs are mere feet below the water's surface. It's a peculiar and refreshing place.

West Beach

INDIANA DUNES
INDIANA

Dunes with a view. Indiana Dunes is located along the Lake Michigan shoreline, an easy train ride from Chicago or South Bend. The coast and miles of trails offer a fresh breath of nature, often rewarding visitors with impressive views of the distant Chicago skyline. No national park displays humanity's contrasting needs better than Indiana Dunes. Sandy shoreline long used by weary workers is interrupted by steel mills, power plants, and a busy port.

Gateway Arch

GATEWAY ARCH
MISSOURI

A gateway to the West. Gateway Arch is a manmade monument, not something you'd expect to find mingling with natural wonders like the Grand Canyon and Yosemite Valley. The national park designation is much less about the land the arch is built on but what the arch symbolizes. It's a symbol of Jefferson's Louisiana Purchase and America's push west, making all those national parks we love today possible. And the tram to the top is pretty neat.

Rock Harbor Trail

ISLE ROYALE
MICHIGAN

An isolated island for moose, wolf, and backpacker. It may come as a surprise that Isle Royale is the only national park closed during winter. This is because the remote island in Lake Superior can only be reached by ferry or seaplane. While daytrips are possible, the necessary transportation logistics make overnight stays (backpacking or paddling) more practical ways to visit. Regardless, it's a magical moose-filled wilderness.

Namakan Lake

VOYAGEURS
MINNESOTA

A paddler's paradise. This isn't your typical motorist's park. Voyageurs consists of five large freshwater lakes and the Kabetogama Peninsula. Four of the lakes span the Canada-U.S. border. Paddling is popular but with so much water, a motorboat or even houseboat remains the more practical option to explore this vast expanse. In winter, the lakes freeze and motorists drive across their icy surface to fish, ski, or even camp.

Big Badlands Overlook

BADLANDS
SOUTH DAKOTA

A photographer's favorite. Badlands is most often treated as a brief detour from I-90. But if you take your time, hike a few trails, watch some wildlife, and venture further into this colorful collection of spires, pinnacles, and walls, you'll find these Badlands to be one of Mother Nature's greatest masterpieces, similarly striking as the hoodoos of Bryce Canyon or Zion Canyon's red rock walls. While it may be tough living over here, Badlands is definitely worth a visit.

Natural Entrance Tour

WIND CAVE
SOUTH DAKOTA

Boxwork below, bison above. Wind Cave contains more than 95% of the world's known boxwork cave formations, named because it resembles an array of post office boxes. With few stalagmites and stalactites, boxwork is the cave's most notable formation (although pure darkness is fun too). Come for the cave. Stay for the wildlife. Bison, elk, and pronghorn roam the open grass prairies. And then there are prairie dogs. Lots and lots of prairie dogs.

Beef Corral Bottom

THEODORE ROOSEVELT
NORTH DAKOTA

A Rough Rider's retreat. Theodore Roosevelt consists of three distinct units connected by the meandering Little Missouri River. South and North Unit scenic drives are the most popular activity, but you'll also find exceptional hiking and horseback riding (with your own horse). The South Unit features petrified forests. Both protect a wealth of wildlife, including bison, pronghorn, elk, wild horses, and (unofficially) the greatest collection of prairie dogs in the U.S.

Moulton Barn

GRAND TETON
WYOMING

An iconic landscape. Thanks to their abrupt rise from the flat floor of Jackson Hole, the Tetons are one of the world's most recognizable mountain ranges. And they're more than just mountains. This is a playground for adults. No matter what your interest, Grand Teton has something to offer. Hiking. Backpacking. Mountaineering. Biking. Driving. Floating. Fishing. Horseback Riding. Each activity has top notch options. It's even great in winter!

The bison roam in Yellowstone

YELLOWSTONE
WYOMING

Where it all began. The first national park. And there may not be a more worthy place. The magic of Yellowstone cannot be conveyed through words or even images. It's beyond the limit of the wildest imagination and outside the realm of anything you've seen. Yellowstone features predictable geysers, golden canyons, colorful hot springs, towering falls, and so much more. It is one of the few places you must see to believe, and even then you may have doubts.

Wild Goose Island

GLACIER
MONTANA

A layered landscape. Few settings deliver more drama than Glacier's majestic mountains. And it isn't their size—none reaching 11,000 feet—it's prominence, precipitousness, and abundance setting them apart. With great mountains comes great hiking. Glacier is unquestionably one of the best hiking, backpacking, and sightseeing destinations on the planet. And there's more. You can bike, fish, boat, raft, even ride a horse into these magnificent mountains.

The Promenade

HOT SPRINGS
ARKANSAS

A memory of a bygone era. Hot Springs hearkens back to a time when mobsters ran the streets and the only crimes you could get to stick were tax evasion. Bathhouse Row was built up during the late 19th century to compete with the extravagant European baths. Receiving "traditional therapy" at Buckstaff Baths (buckstaffbaths.com) is probably the oddest NPS-approved thing you can do in a national park, but there's also outdoor activities like hiking and camping.

River Road

BIG BEND
TEXAS

A big ol' bend in the Rio Grande. Big Bend is one of the more pleasant surprises in the entire collection of national parks. It takes some effort to reach this remote mountain desert at the southern border. But the rewards are great. You can float through or hike along spectacular canyons. Soak in hot springs. Or crawl across miles of rugged 4x4 roadways. And the Chisos Mountains become a pleasant oasis once things begin to swelter in summer.

Devil's Hall

GUADALUPE MOUNTAINS
TEXAS

Home to the highest peak in Texas. While you can't overlook the Guadalupe Mountains when you're in their vicinity, they are often overlooked by national park enthusiasts. The park is small and trails are sparse. But there are many quality options like Guadalupe Peak, Devil's Hall, and McKittrick Canyon. It also hosts a rich history of colorful characters, challenging commerce, and native-pioneer confrontations. It's at least worth a pit-stop if not an extended stay.

Lower Cave Tour

CARLSBAD CAVERNS
NEW MEXICO

A subterranean cathedral of nature's delicate artwork. Carlsbad is one of the more beautiful commercialized caverns. You can tour a few miles of it on your own, walking through the natural entrance or descending into the Big Room via an elevator from the Visitor Center. The cave is cool but ranger-guided tours (and bat flight program) make a trip here really fun. Come for the cave. Stay for the bats. And enjoy a little time beneath the earth's surface.

Alkali Trail

WHITE SANDS
NEW MEXICO

A sea of shimmering sand. White Sands is one of the most beautiful places on the planet. That isn't hyperbole. All the music videos, album covers, and movie sets back it up. And visitors agree. However, there are complications. The park is small. It closes overnight. And it regularly opens late for missile testing. Alkali Flat Trail is wonderful but the real fun is playing/sledding in the dunes or simply absorbing all that stunning scenery.

Giant Logs

PETRIFIED FOREST
ARIZONA

Trees of stone. A painted desert. Ancient petroglyphs. Petrified Forest offers many interesting sites. Historic Route 66 even passed through. Perhaps in its spirit, Petrified Forest is treated as a drive-thru attraction by most visitors. The park closes at dusk and lacks overnight accommodations. Contributing factors for sure, but camping is allowed in the backcountry. You can still have some kicks out here but now they're found at Petrified Forest.

SAGUARO
ARIZONA

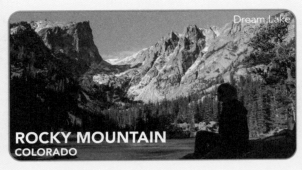
ROCKY MOUNTAIN
COLORADO

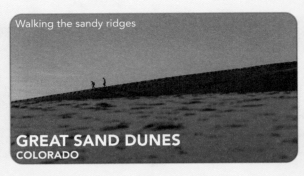
GREAT SAND DUNES
COLORADO

A symbol of the Sonoran Desert. Saguaro, cacti and park, are found in the midst of Tucson's urban sprawl. The park is two units, east and west, both formed around a prominent mountain range. Hiking, birdwatching, biking, and horseback riding are common activities. And the quirky cacti add a considerable amount of character to the setting. Hundreds of prickly and oddly welcoming cacti line the mountains' slopes as if waiting to greet you.

A rocky retreat. Rocky Mountain is one of those parks that has it all. Alpine lakes and imposing summits. A scenic drive crossing the continental divide. A wealth of wildlife and waterfalls. Activities for every season and interest. It has just about everything, and everyone knows it. If it has one problem, that's it. Rocky Mountain hosts just about as many visitors as Yellowstone (which also gets busy in summer) but it's roughly one-eighth the size.

A sea in a storm. Great Sand Dunes dunefields go up and down, the tallest rising more than 700 feet. While the dunes immediately draw your attention, the Sangre de Cristo Mountains stand quietly in the back. They compliment each other nicely. Play in the sand, sledding, sandboarding, or camping, one day. Hike to a lake at the base of a 13,000-ft mountain the next. Just know you'll want a 4WD vehicle to reach most mountain trailheads.

BLACK CANYON OF THE GUNNISON
COLORADO

MESA VERDE
COLORADO

ARCHES
UTAH

An impassable canyon. Black Canyon of the Gunnison was a site of serious frustration for fur traders and frontiersmen. It remains an imposing obstacle to visitors, but visiting is the primary intent for just about everyone who sets eyes on it these days. Trails lead guests above and below the rim. Experienced adventurers climb these 2,000-foot walls and paddle the wild water below them. It isn't a particularly popular park, but it is a beautiful one.

A collection of mysterious cultural ruins. Mesa Verde is unique in that it isn't about the landscape. It's about how past people used the land to help them survive, building dwellings beneath undercut cliffs. It's unclear what drove Puebloans to construct complicated cliff dwellings nearly 1,000 years ago, but you can tour several of them (including 100-room Cliff Palace) and satisfy your own curiosities. Mesa Verde is different but not less interesting.

2,000 natural sandstone arches. Arches is an easy park to visit but it's hard to explain. Seriously, what conditions were required to form these peculiar red-rock arches? And how long did it take? One stands more than ten stories high. Another spans the length of a football field. It's a weird place. A quirky place. A very fun place, where you can hike through the Fiery Furnace, hike to Delicate Arch (above), or drive off-road to less popular parcels.

CANYONLANDS
UTAH

CAPITOL REEF
UTAH

BRYCE CANYON
UTAH

A cacophony of colorful canyons carved by the Green and Colorado Rivers. Among an unmatched assortment of unreal landscapes, Canyonlands might be the most weirdly wonderful of them all. While roads lead to viewpoints and trails ramble to strange rock formations, it isn't an easy park to explore. You need a 4x4 or mountain bike. A raft or kayak would help too. But once you get a taste of Canyonlands' wilder side, you'll be coming back for more.

A mix of southern Utah's finest red rock formations. Capitol Reef is no one-trick pony. Slot canyons and arches are mixed among the awe-inspiring geology visitors expect to see in this part of the planet. There's excellent hiking, backpacking, off-roading, and camping. Heck, you can even pick fruit in Fruita when it's in season. There are many reasons Capitol Reef should slide out of the shadow cast by the other four Utah national parks.

An indescribable amphitheater. Bryce Canyon's amphitheater, lined with stony sentinels called hoodoos, is one of the most striking landscapes on earth. Unfortunately, most people simply view this enigmatic wilderness from the rim and move on. It's true, Bryce is somewhat limited, especially compared to large parks like Yellowstone or Death Valley, but you're doing yourself an extreme disservice if you don't hike among the red rock columns (or take a horse!).

ZION
UTAH

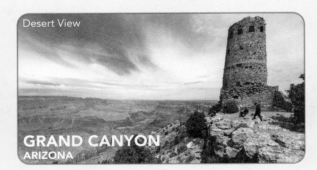
GRAND CANYON
ARIZONA

GREAT BASIN
NEVADA

Yosemite in color. The view of Zion Canyon from Angel's Rest or Observation Point (above) is not one you'll soon forget. The Virgin River has carved one of the most mind-bogglingly beautiful canyons known to man. The Narrows and Angel's Landing draw all the headlines, but you'll find a quieter corner at Kolob Canyons, and challenging (if not technical) terrain at sites like The Subway. Zion means "holy sanctuary" in Arabic. Sounds about right to me.

A grand canyon. I'm not sure any park features more extreme variance in visitor experiences than Grand Canyon. For most of the year, visitors are rafting raucous rapids of the Colorado River. Others are looking down on it from above aboard a sightseeing plane or helicopter. Some see the canyon from above and below, hiking rim-to-rim, perhaps sleeping at Phantom Ranch. Most simply enjoy the canyon's glory from a few canyon-top viewpoints.

Ancient trees, snow-capped mountains, and an ornate cave. Great Basin is often an oversight of the western national parks. It isn't for lack of beauty. Wheeler Peak provides a strenuous hike. Lehman Cave is open for tours. Bristlecone groves are home to some of the oldest known organisms, some were even alive before ancient Egyptians began work on the pyramids. And then, when the sun sets, the skies are some of the darkest in the country.

JOSHUA TREE
CALIFORNIA

CHANNEL ISLANDS
CALIFORNIA

PINNACLES
CALIFORNIA

A tale of two deserts. Weird and wacky only begin to describe the oddities of this extremely peculiar desert landscape. It's covered in piles of massive boulders, strewn about as if they fell from the sky. In their midst you'll find forests of appropriately-spaced Joshua trees, allowing their roots room to soak up enough water in the arid climate (they grow maybe an inch or two each year). If you like deserts, you'll love Joshua Tree. It's quite special.

An island escape. The Channel Islands sit a mere 100 miles from more than 18 million people living in Greater Los Angeles. Water separating this sea of humanity and these picturesque islands teems with whales, dolphins, seals, and much more marine life. The Channel Islands aren't just an escape, they're filled with adventures. You can paddle through arches and sea caves, snorkel or SCUBA in kelp forests, and backpack across uninhabited wilderness.

A jumble of volcanic rocks. Pinnacles is small by national park standards. But its trails traversing across High Peaks and through talus caves are some of the best hikes maintained by the National Park Service. It's also a favorite destination among rock climbers. And then there's the California condor, the largest flying bird in North America. Once the rarest bird on the planet, they're enjoying a resurgence in numbers thanks to a laborious and costly effort.

DEATH VALLEY
CALIFORNIA

SEQUOIA & KINGS CANYON
CALIFORNIA

YOSEMITE
CALIFORNIA

An inconceivable environment. Death Valley might rouse the wrong impression. Lead with the fact it can reach 130+ degrees at Furnace Creek and you might wonder why anyone would come here. The reason is, it's spectacular. There are sand dunes, salt flats, canyons, and mountains galore. Badwater Basin is the lowest point in North America. Across the valley is 11,000-ft Telescope Peak. Contradictions like these are everywhere at wildly magnificent Death Valley.

Eternal trees and transcendent trails. Sequoia and Kings Canyon, two parks under one management. Both possess some of the world's most massive lifeforms, the giant sequoia, but it's the park's backcountry—the ever-impressive Sierra Nevada—that steals the show. Pacific Crest and John Muir Trails lead to the park's pinnacle and the tallest peak in the Lower 48, Mount Whitney, but there are many spectacular sites with awe-inspiring mountain scenery.

A granite icon. Our national parks contain some of the world's most special and spectacular natural environments. Yosemite stands out among them. For many devout visitors a trip here is a spiritual experience, coming to commune with the trees, summits, wildlife, and waterfalls. While the park is much more than Yosemite Valley, upon seeing this sacred setting for the first time there's a very good chance you may feel you've died and gone to heaven.

LASSEN VOLCANIC
CALIFORNIA

REDWOOD
CALIFORNIA

CRATER LAKE
OREGON

A miniature Yellowstone. Lassen Volcanic is home to towering volcanoes, simmering hydrothermal areas, alpine lakes, and even a massive lava bed. Before it was a park, Lassen Peak's eruption captivated the nation. More recently, the nation's gaze returned to this remote section of California, this time as wildfires razed much of the forested landscape. Both events show the dynamic forces of nature and how they help shape the places we love.

Skyscrapers of wood. Redwood protects the world's tallest trees—some towering more than 370 feet. Stand next to them for a humbling experience. And the coast is no slouch. Whales pass through these waters. Bluffs provide the perfect vantage point to watch for flukes, spouts, and breaches. Inland you'll find trails for hiking, biking, and horseback riding. The Pacific Coast suffers an embarrassment of outdoor riches and Redwood is one of its gems.

A brilliant blue lake. Crater Lake is all about the 1,943-foot-deep lake filling a volcano that collapsed into itself during a cataclysmic eruption some 8,000 years ago. The park is something of a one-hit wonder, but that hit has been near the top of the charts since long before prospectors scaled these slopes. Still, there's much to do. You can board a boat and cruise to Wizard Island (above). There's plenty of hiking and in winter you can camp along the crater's rim.

MOUNT RAINIER
WASHINGTON

OLYMPIC
WASHINGTON

NORTH CASCADES
WASHINGTON

A beacon of the Pacific Northwest. On a clear day Mount Rainier can be seen from 100 miles in each direction, some days it can even be seen from Canada. It's the anti-lighthouse. When visible, people heed the mountain's call to explore its trails and enjoy witnessing its majesty. Rainier serves as proving ground for aspiring mountaineers. At 14,410 feet, its summit is heavily glaciated and a formidable challenge for the fittest climbers.

A diverse wilderness. Olympic features an extreme variety of ecosystems. In one day you can view a distant glacier from a mountain ridge, paddle a freshwater lake, tidepool along the Pacific Coast, and stroll through a primeval rain forest. And that's only the beginning. There are hot springs, waterfalls, exceptional backpacking opportunities, world record trees, paddling, biking, camping, and miles and miles of Pacific coastline.

A mountaineer's dreamscape. North Cascades is premier mountain country. While most of the mountains can only be reached by a small subset of the park's visitors, there's plenty for everyone. You can ferry to remote Stehekin Village, paddle to secluded campsites, or hike a few trails beginning along North Cascades Scenic Highway. It isn't the most user-friendly park, but if you know where to go, it's mountains are sure to wow you!

GLACIER BAY
ALASKA

Glacier Tour

A land of calving glaciers and spouting whales. Glacier Bay can only be reached by boat or plane. Most guests arrive aboard massive cruise liners. Others fly into Gustavus, stay at Glacier Bay Lodge (there are alternatives, even camping) and enjoy small boat tours, sea kayak adventures (for experienced paddlers), and hiking opportunities. And then there are those who raft the Alsek-Tatshenshini Rivers, one of the world's best rafting adventures.

WRANGELL-ST. ELIAS
ALASKA

Kennecott Mill

America's Alps. Wrangell-St. Elias is one of the most visually remarkable landscapes on the planet. It's also enormous, the largest national park at more than 13 million acres, covering more than 150 miles of undeveloped coastline; inland you'll find nine of the sixteen tallest mountains in the United States. Extreme is the place to start when describing this wild wilderness. Air is the best way to explore the park, but two roads penetrate its interior.

DENALI
ALASKA

Wonder Lake

The High One. Denali, at 20,320 feet, is the tallest mountain in North America. When it isn't obscured by clouds, it cannot be ignored. Even if it isn't out, Denali has much to offer. Most visitors explore the park via 92-mile Denali Park Road. Its first 15 miles are open to personal vehicles, the rest is left for park-operated buses. Along the way you'll see many of the park's inhabitants: grizzlies, caribou, moose, Dall's sheep, and wolves.

KENAI FJORDS
ALASKA

Pedersen Glacier

Rivers of ice. Kenai Fjords possesses more than 400 miles of jagged coastline. Glaciers carved these fjords. Many remain, but most are receding back to their source, Harding Icefield, a 300-square-mile, mile-high mass of ice. Visitors can hike to the impressive icefield, paddle near tidewater glaciers, or patrol the coastal waters, watching for whales or fishing for the catch of the day. In a state filled with inconceivable wonders, Kenai Fjords features some of its best.

LAKE CLARK
ALASKA

Chinitna Bay

"One Man's Wilderness." The inspiration for many Lake Clark visitors stems from one man, Dick Proenneke. He lived along the shore of Twin Lakes for 30 years, building a log cabin with hand tools, living an ascetic life documenting wildlife and weather. Things aren't that different from when Dick lived here. Today, more visitors hunt the preserve and watch grizzlies at sites like Chinitna Bay. That's summer. The rest of the year it may feel like your own wilderness.

KATMAI
ALASKA

Brooks Falls

Fishing bears and smoking valleys. Katmai was established after the Novarupta Volcano eruption in 1912, when an observer referred to the area as the "valley of 10,000 smokes." Today, the surrounding volcanoes and valleys—still buried in volcanic ash—remain impressive, but its grizzly bears fishing for sockeye salmon at Brooks Falls that draw photographers from around the globe every July and September when they're most active.

GATES OF THE ARCTIC
ALASKA

Above the Arctic Circle

Unsurpassed solitude. Gates of the Arctic is 8.5 million acres of undeveloped wilderness. No roads. No trails. Absolutely no campgrounds, lodges, or motorists. The park is best explored by water, floating free-flowing rivers. Most features remain nameless. There are exceptions. Gates of the Arctic refers to Frigid Crags and Boreal Mountain, one on each side of the Koyukuk River. Arrigetch Peaks, another prominent site, rise above the Kobuk River.

KOBUK VALLEY
ALASKA

Home of the Caribou

An alluring Arctic wilderness. Kobuk Valley is similar to Gates of the Arctic. Both reside entirely above the Arctic Circle. Both are best explored via river (or bush plane). The land is unspoiled, undeveloped, consisting mostly of nameless wilderness. Still, some half-a-million caribou migrate across the park's southern reaches twice a year, leaving tracks across Great Kobuk Sand Dunes, the largest active dunefield in the Arctic.

U.S. VIRGIN ISLANDS

Trunk Bay

A tropical paradise. U.S. Virgin Islands is not your typical park. Most park enthusiasts expect to hike long days, sleep in a tent, maybe even work up a sweat from exertion. Here, you can sleep in a tent, but days are spent relaxing on the beach or frolicking in the Caribbean. You may sweat, but that's because it's 80 degrees and sunny. The white sand beaches and turquoise waters are a welcome change of pace for many.

HALEAKALA
HAWAII

Sliding Sands

A sleeping volcano and a lively rain forest. Haleakala is a bit of a paradox. The summit area looks more like Martian land explored by Perseverance, not the lush jungle of Hawaiian vacation dreams. The park's other region, Kipahulu, begins at the Pacific, continuing up the 10,023-ft volcano's eastern flank through dense rain forest, accented with towering waterfalls. An image congruous to our idea of Hawaii, but both worlds are equally fascinating.

HAWAII VOLCANOES
HAWAII

Kilauea

A dynamic landscape. Hawaii Volcanoes is constantly changing. In the last decade lava spilled through Pahoa, buried Kapoho Tide Pools, poured into the Pacific, and spawned a sometimes-explosive lake of lava at Halemaumau Crater. When the lava lake is full, it lights up the night sky, letting you know Madame Pele is stirring. And when we went to print, Mauna Loa, the world's most massive mountain was rumbling!

AMERICAN SAMOA

Rainmaker

A remote island chain in the South Pacific. Due to its isolated location, sitting in the South Pacific nearly 5,000 miles from the West Coast of the United States, there's no park with more unique culture and geography. Many Samoans face a difficult impasse, how to hold onto their traditions and culture and embrace the ways of the West. The park may be a place to soften such an extreme dichotomy, and visitors are sure to enjoy the tropical beaches.

Delta Lake (Grand Teton)

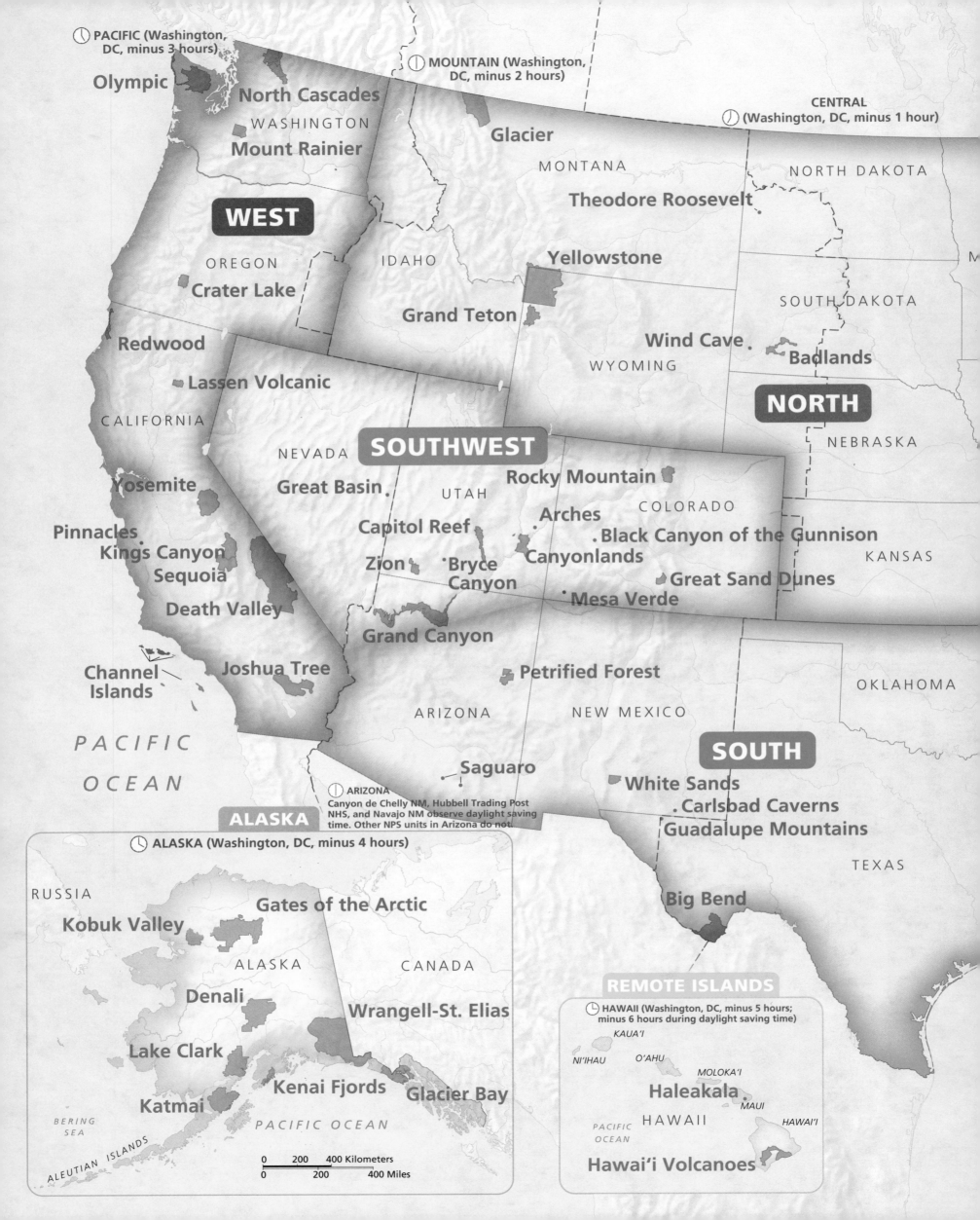

PACIFIC (Washington, DC, minus 3 hours)

MOUNTAIN (Washington, DC, minus 2 hours)

CENTRAL (Washington, DC, minus 1 hour)

Olympic

North Cascades

WASHINGTON

Mount Rainier

Glacier

MONTANA

NORTH DAKOTA

Theodore Roosevelt

WEST

OREGON

IDAHO

Crater Lake

SOUTH DAKOTA

Yellowstone

Grand Teton

Wind Cave

Badlands

Redwood

WYOMING

NORTH

Lassen Volcanic

CALIFORNIA

NEBRASKA

Yosemite

NEVADA

SOUTHWEST

Great Basin

Rocky Mountain

UTAH

COLORADO

Pinnacles

Arches

Black Canyon of the Gunnison

Kings Canyon

Capitol Reef

KANSAS

Sequoia

Canyonlands

Zion

Bryce Canyon

Great Sand Dunes

Death Valley

Mesa Verde

Grand Canyon

Channel Islands

Joshua Tree

Petrified Forest

OKLAHOMA

PACIFIC

OCEAN

ARIZONA

NEW MEXICO

SOUTH

ARIZONA
Canyon de Chelly NM, Hubbell Trading Post NHS, and Navajo NM observe daylight saving time. Other NPS units in Arizona do not.

Saguaro

White Sands

Carlsbad Caverns

Guadalupe Mountains

ALASKA

ALASKA (Washington, DC, minus 4 hours)

TEXAS

Big Bend

RUSSIA

Gates of the Arctic

Kobuk Valley

ALASKA

CANADA

Denali

Wrangell-St. Elias

REMOTE ISLANDS

HAWAII (Washington, DC, minus 5 hours; minus 6 hours during daylight saving time)

Lake Clark

KAUA'I

NI'IHAU

O'AHU

MOLOKA'I

Katmai

Kenai Fjords

Glacier Bay

Haleakala

MAUI

BERING SEA

PACIFIC OCEAN

PACIFIC OCEAN

HAWAII

HAWAI'I

ALEUTIAN ISLANDS

Hawai'i Volcanoes

0   200   400 Kilometers
0   200   400 Miles

Eastern Driving Distances

Much is made of the amount of driving required to visit Western parks. The East, although densely populated, is also vast.

Acadia ←→ Cuyahoga Valley — 14 hours / 920 miles
Cuyahoga Valley ←→ Shenandoah — 5.5 hours / 320 miles
Shenandoah ←→ New River Gorge — 4 hours / 230 miles
New River Gorge ←→ Mammoth Cave — 6 hours / 370 miles
Mammoth Cave ←→ Great Smoky Mtns — 4.5 hours / 240 miles
Great Smoky Mtns ←→ Congaree — 4.5 hours / 250 miles
Congaree ←→ Biscayne — 10 hours / 660 miles
Biscayne ←→ Everglades — 0.5 hours / 20 miles
Everglades ←→ Dry Tortugas — 3.5 hours / 130 miles (+ flight or ferry)

EASTERN (Washington, DC)

EAST

NORTHEAST

BOSTON AREA
Adams NHP
Boston African American NHS
Boston Harbor Islands NRA
Boston NHP
Frederick Law Olmsted NHS
John Fitzgerald Kennedy NHS
Longfellow House–Washington's Headquarters NHS
Minute Man NHP
Salem Maritime NHS
Saugus Iron Works NHS

NEW YORK CITY AREA
African Burial Ground NM
Castle Clinton NM
Federal Hall N MEM
Gateway NRA (also NJ)
General Grant N MEM
Governors Island NM
Hamilton Grange N MEM
Saint Paul's Church NHS
Statue of Liberty NM
Stonewall NM
Theodore Roosevelt Birthplace NHS

PHILADELPHIA AREA
Edgar Allan Poe NHS
Hopewell Furnace NHS
Independence NHP
Thaddeus Kosciuszko N MEM
Valley Forge NHP

BALTIMORE AREA
Fort McHenry NM and Historic Shrine
Hampton NHS

NATIONAL CAPITAL

DISTRICT OF COLUMBIA
Belmont-Paul Women's Equality NM
Carter G. Woodson Home NHS
Constitution Gardens
Ford's Theatre NHS
Franklin Delano Roosevelt Memorial
Frederick Douglass NHS
Korean War Veterans Memorial
Lincoln Memorial
Lyndon Baines Johnson Memorial Grove
Martin Luther King, Jr. Memorial
Mary McLeod Bethune Council House NHS
National Capital Parks
National Mall
Pennsylvania Avenue NHS
Rock Creek Park
Theodore Roosevelt Island
Thomas Jefferson Memorial
Vietnam Veterans Memorial
Washington Monument
White House
World War I Memorial
World War II Memorial

MARYLAND
Antietam NB
Catoctin Mountain Park
Chesapeake and Ohio Canal NHP (also DC and WV)
Clara Barton NHS
Fort Washington Park
Greenbelt Park
Monocacy NB
Piscataway Park
Potomac Heritage NST (also PA, VA, and DC)

VIRGINIA
Arlington House, The Robert E. Lee Memorial
George Washington Memorial PKWY (also MD)
Manassas NBP
Prince William Forest Park
Wolf Trap National Park for the Performing Arts

North

0   100   200   300   400 Kilometers
0   100   200   300   400 Miles

THE EAST

Acadia Basics
(207) 288-3338 | nps.gov/acad
Entrance Fee: $30/car
Lodging: None
Camping: Blackwoods*, Seawall*, Schoodic Woods*, Duck Harbor*

*reserve at recreation.gov

Otter Cliffs

Acadia Driving Distances
With three distinct regions it's a good idea to know how much time (ignoring traffic) to allot to reach one from the other. There is a seasonal passenger ferry from Bar Harbor and Winter Harbor (among several other ferries), and you'll need to book fare with the Mail Boat to reach Isle au Haut from Stonington.

Bar Harbor	←16 minutes / 6 miles→	Cadillac Mtn
Bar Harbor	←12 minutes / 5 miles→	Sand Beach
Bar Harbor	←16 minutes / 7 miles→	Jordan Pond
Bar Harbor	←30 minutes / 18 miles→	Bass Harbor
Bar Harbor	←75 minutes / 49 miles→	Schoodic Peninsula
Bar Harbor	←85 minutes / 58 miles→	Stonington, ME
Stonington, ME	←100 minutes / 67 miles→	Schoodic Peninsula

Why Visit Acadia?
- Exceptional hiking!
- Bike, hike or ride (horse-drawn carriages!) along Rockefeller's carriage roads
- Water activities (swimming, boat tours, ferries, and paddling)
- Rock climbing
- Fall foliage (Sept/Oct)
- Lighthouses
- The park (and MDI in particular) is a very unique place with an interesting mix of human history and recreational opportunities
- Hiking! It needed to be repeated as Acadia is one of the best hiking destinations.

Precipice

Acadia Favorites
Easy Hikes: Bar Island (1.4 miles), Ocean Path (4.4), Summit Path (0.3), Great Meadow (2)
Moderate Hikes: Gorham Mtn (1.8), Bubble Rock (1, steep)
Strenuous Hikes: Giant Slide (2.8), Penobscot (3.7), Sargent Mountain (varies), Pemetic Northwest (varies)
Extreme (Ladder) Hikes: Precipice (2.1), Beehive (1.6), Ladder/Dorr (3.3), Jordan Cliffs (3.7)
Views: Cadillac Mountain, Sand Beach, Bass Harbor Head Lighthouse, Jordan Pond House, Schoodic Point
Carriage Roads: Bike/hike to the top of Day Mountain or around Eagle Lake

Long Pond

What You Need to Know About Acadia
- Visitation peaks in July/August.
- The Island Explore Shuttle (exploreacadia.com) is a great free resource available from June through mid-October. You won't have to worry about parking and it opens up many one-way hiking possibilities.
- Precipice Trail is awesome (and extreme) but it's typically closed from mid-March to mid-August.
- Fall foliage typically peaks in early October.
- For "thunder" at Thunder Hole, try to arrive between high and low tides.
- In summer, a permit (recreation.gov) is required to drive to the summit of Cadillac Mountain. It's a popular destination all day long, but it's known as the spot to watch the sunrise as it receives the first rays of light on the East Coast for part of the year.
- Even if you missed out on a Cadillac permit, don't sleep in. There are many good sunrise spots along Ocean Path, including Sand Beach, Thunder Hole, Boulder Beach, and Gorham Mountain.
- If you like guided tours, Acadia has plenty. Outfitters will take you paddling in Frenchman's Bay or Somes Sound. You can learn to rock climb, join a bicycle tour, explore the ocean on scenic and/or educational cruises, and there are carriage tours along the park's famed carriage roads. You can also book a scenic flight from Bar Harbor airport.
- If you'd like a uniquely primitive and quiet camping experience at Isle au Haut's Duck Harbor, try to reserve (recreation.gov) one of the five sites as soon as they become available (typically early April).
- Most visitors reach Isle au Haut aboard the Mail Boat (isleauhaut.com) out of Stonington.

Ocean Path Sunrise

How Much Time Do You Have?
1 Day: You'll want to spend your day on Mount Desert Island. And make it count by taking in the sunrise atop Cadillac Mountain (reservation required in summer via recreation.gov) or along Ocean Path. Stop at Jordan Pond House for tea and a popover and join a carriage tour. Spend the rest of your time hiking. If you're visiting during peak season, you may be tempted to venture over to the quiet side of MDI (west of Somes Sound) but the busy side is busy for a reason. Traffic can be troublesome but the Island Explorer Shuttle (exploreacadia.com) makes it bearable. It also allows you to make a bunch of short one-way hiking routes.

2 Days: Stick with the 1-day plan staying around Park Loop Road. If you're tired from hiking, rent a canoe or kayaks to paddle Eagle Lake, Long Pond, or Jordan Pond. You can also paddle out into Frenchman Bay from Bar Harbor.

3 Days: Now you can start thinking about heading over to Isle au Haut or Schoodic Peninsula (a passenger ferry travels from Bar Harbor to Winter Harbor in about the same amount of time it takes to drive). With that said there are plenty of exceptional hikes to spend more than three days on MDI. Check out the favorites lists for a few ideas.

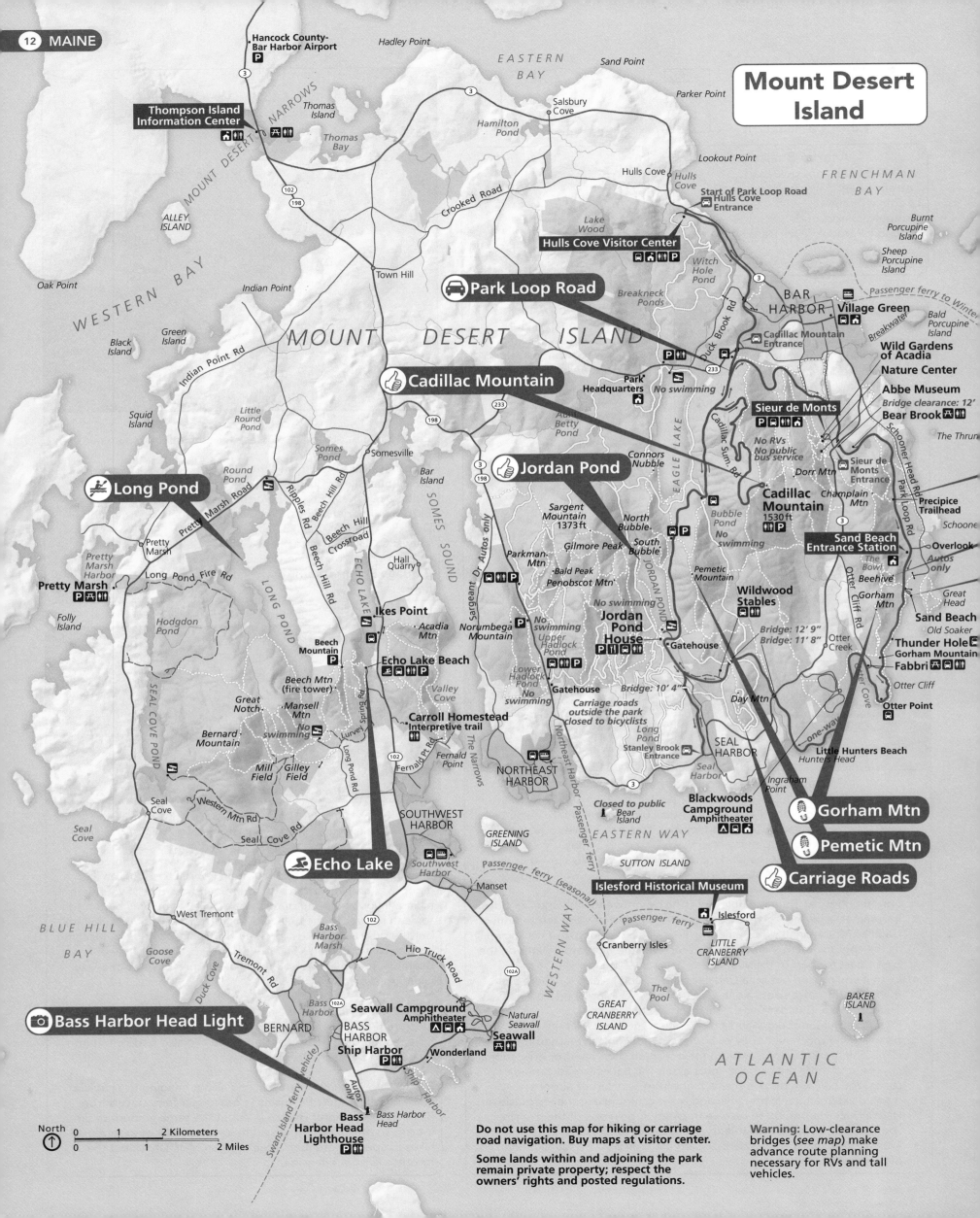

Mount Desert Island

Thompson Island Information Center

EASTERN BAY

FRENCHMAN BAY

WESTERN BAY

ALLEY ISLAND

Oak Point

Salsbury Cove

Hamilton Pond

Parker Point

Lookout Point

Hulls Cove

Start of Park Loop Road
Hulls Cove Entrance

Hulls Cove Visitor Center

🚗 **Park Loop Road**

MOUNT DESERT ISLAND

BAR HARBOR

Village Green

Passenger ferry to Winter

Burnt Porcupine Island

Sheep Porcupine Island

Bald Porcupine Island

Breakwater

Wild Gardens of Acadia
Nature Center

Abbe Museum
Bridge clearance: 12'
Bear Brook

Black Island

Green Island

Squid Island

Little Round Pond

Town Hill

Indian Point

Crooked Road

Lake Wood

Witch Hole Pond

Breakneck Ponds

Duck Brook Rd

Park Headquarters

No swimming

Sieur de Monts

No RVs
No public bus service

The Thrum

👍 **Cadillac Mountain**

Aunt Betty Pond

Connors Nubble

Dorr Mtn

Sieur de Monts Entrance

👍 **Jordan Pond**

Sargent Mountain 1373ft

North Bubble
South Bubble

Cadillac Mountain 1530ft

Champlain Mtn

Precipice Trailhead

🚣 **Long Pond**

Round Pond

Somes Pond

Somesville

Bar Island

Gilmore Peak

Pemetic Mountain

Bubble Pond
No swimming

Sand Beach Entrance Station

Schooner

Pretty Marsh Harbor

Pretty Marsh

Hall Quarry

Parkman Mtn

Bald Peak Penobscot Mtn

No swimming

Wildwood Stables

Overlook
Autos only

Beehive

Great Head

Pretty Marsh

Long Pond Fire Rd

Ikes Point

Acadia Mtn

Norumbega Mountain

Upper Hadlock Pond

Jordan Pond House

Bridge: 12' 9"
Bridge: 11' 8"

Gorham Mtn

Sand Beach
Old Soaker

Thunder Hole
Gorham Mountain
Fabbri

Folly Island

Hodgdon Pond

Beech Mountain

Echo Lake Beach

Beech Mtn (fire tower)

Valley Cove

Lower Hadlock Pond
No swimming

Gatehouse

Bridge: 10' 4"

Otter Cliff Rd

Otter Cliff

Otter Point

Great Notch

Mansell Mtn

No swimming

Carroll Homestead
Interpretive trail

Carriage roads outside the park closed to bicyclists

Day Mtn

Little Hunters Beach

Bernard Mountain

Mill Field Gilley Field

Lurvey

Fernald Pt Rd

Fernald Point

Gatehouse

Long Pond
Stanley Brook Entrance

SEAL HARBOR

👟 **Gorham Mtn**

Seal Cove Pond

Seal Cove

Western Mtn Rd

Seal Cove Rd

SOUTHWEST HARBOR

GREENING ISLAND

NORTHEAST HARBOR

EASTERN WAY

Seal Harbor

Ingraham Point

Hunters Head

👟 **Pemetic Mtn**

👍 **Carriage Roads**

Blackwoods Campground
Amphitheater

one-way

SUTTON ISLAND

Closed to public
Bear Island

Echo Lake

Southwest Harbor

Manset

Passenger ferry (seasonal)

Islesford Historical Museum

West Tremont

BLUE HILL BAY

Goose Cove

Bass Harbor Marsh

Tremont Rd

Hio Truck Road

WESTERN WAY

Passenger ferry

Cranberry Isles

Islesford

LITTLE CRANBERRY ISLAND

GREAT CRANBERRY ISLAND

The Pool

BAKER ISLAND

📷 **Bass Harbor Head Light**

BERNARD

Bass Harbor

BASS HARBOR

Seawall Campground
Amphitheater

Natural Seawall

Seawall

Ship Harbor

Wonderland

ATLANTIC OCEAN

Swans Island ferry (vehicle)

Autos only

Duck Cove

Ship Harbor

Bass Harbor Head Lighthouse

North 0 1 2 Kilometers
0 1 2 Miles

Bass Harbor Head

Do not use this map for hiking or carriage road navigation. Buy maps at visitor center.

Some lands within and adjoining the park remain private property; respect the owners' rights and posted regulations.

Warning: Low-clearance bridges (see map) make advance route planning necessary for RVs and tall vehicles.

Hancock County-Bar Harbor Airport

Hadley Point

Thomas Island

Thomas Bay

MOUNT DESERT NARROWS

Indian Point Rd

Ripples Rd

Beech Hill Rd

Beech Hill Crossroad

Echo Lake

SOMES SOUND

Sargent Dr Autos only

Eagle Lake

Cadillac Sum. Rd

Jordan Pond

Otter Creek

Py Bounds

Long Pond Rd

The Narrows

Northeast Harbor Passenger ferry

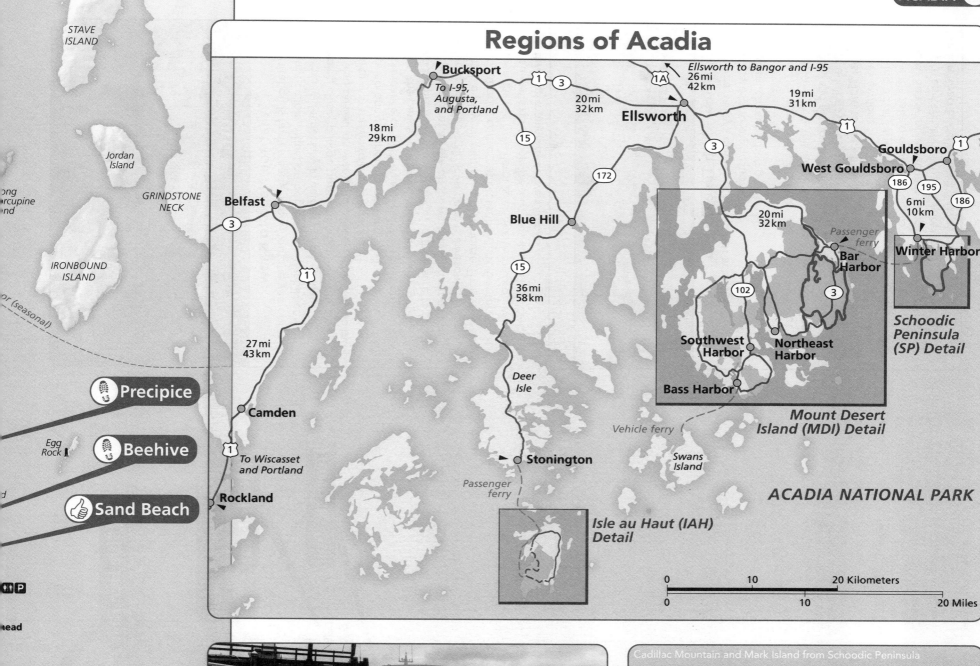

Regions of Acadia

Bucksport
To I-95, Augusta, and Portland
1 3
20 mi / 32 km
Ellsworth
1A Ellsworth to Bangor and I-95 — 26 mi / 42 km
18 mi / 29 km
15
172
19 mi / 31 km
1
Gouldsboro
West Gouldsboro
186 195
186
Belfast
3
1
Blue Hill
15
3
20 mi / 32 km
Passenger ferry
Bar Harbor
102
3
6 mi / 10 km
Winter Harbor
Schoodic Peninsula (SP) Detail
36 mi / 58 km
Southwest Harbor
Northeast Harbor
Camden
1
Deer Isle
Bass Harbor
Mount Desert Island (MDI) Detail

Precipice
Beehive
Sand Beach

Egg Rock
Vehicle ferry
1
To Wiscasset and Portland
Stonington
Swans Island
ACADIA NATIONAL PARK
Rockland
Passenger ferry
Isle au Haut (IAH) Detail

0 10 20 Kilometers
0 10 20 Miles

Legend
- Acadia National Park
- Park Loop Road
- Unpaved road
- Carriage road
- Hiking trail
- Locked gate
- Ranger station
- Picnic area
- Campground
- Swimming (seasonal)
- Boat launch
- Restrooms
- Lighthouse
- Food service
- Parking
- Bus stop
- Ferry to park areas
- Park Loop Road Entrance

The Mail Boat

Isle au Haut

Passenger ferry Stonington to Town Landing, Isle au Haut (year-round)
Town Landing
KIMBALL ISLAND
Isle au Haut
Thorofare
ISLE AU HAUT
Turnip Yard
Passenger ferry to Duck Harbor Landing (seasonal)
Moore Harbor
Long Pond
Boom Beach
Duck Harbor Landing
Deep Cove
Barred Harbor
Head Harbor
Eastern Head

0 1 2 Kilometers
0 1 2 Miles

Cadillac Mountain and Mark Island from Schoodic Peninsula

Schoodic Peninsula

Winter Harbor
Birch Harbor
Schoodic Woods Campground Amphitheater
Winter Harbor
Day-use Parking
Mosquito Harbor
Frazer Point
Begin one-way traffic Autos only
Birch Harbor
Bunkers Harbor
Park Exit End one-way traffic
Passenger ferry to Bar Harbor (seasonal)
Mark Island
SCHOODIC PENINSULA
Schoodic Harbor
Rolling Island
Pond Island
Bike path
Horses are prohibited on the bike paths on Schoodic Peninsula.
Schoodic Institute and Welcome Center
Schoodic Point
Little Moose Island
Blueberry Hill
Schoodic Island

0 0.5 1 Kilometer
0 0.5 1 Mile

Brandywine Falls

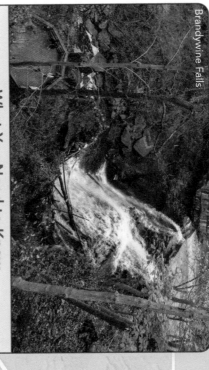

What You Need to Know

- Visitation is fairly steady throughout the year, with a noticeable reduction between November and February (especially in January and February).

- Being close to large population centers, the park is also busiest on weekends. Escape the crowds by visiting in the middle of the week.

- Spring brings supercharged waterfalls and an abundance of wildflowers. Fall foliage is great too.

- Yes, the park's waterfalls, hiking and biking trails, and waterways are wonderful, but be sure to take advantage of all the unconventional offerings you'll find here. The train (cvsr.com) is awesome! You can catch a play or musical at Porthouse Theatre or enjoy an outdoor concert at Blossom Music Center. And then there's Hale Farm & Village (wrhs.org), where you can experience life as it was in the 19th century through many interactive exhibits.

How Much Time Do You Have?

Cuyahoga Valley's diverse collection of activities complicates trip suggestions (in a good way because there's much more than great hiking).

1 Day: The mandatory activities are taking a look at Brandywine Falls, hiking to Blue Hen Falls, exploring Ledges, and riding Cuyahoga Valley Scenic Railroad. That's a full day!

2 Days: Time to start thinking about bringing (or renting) bikes to explore Towpath Trail (you can pedal one-way by taking advantage of the train). Check out Hale Farm & Village. It'll take a couple hours to walk the property.

3 Days: See what events are happening at Porthouse Theatre and Blossom Music Center, and hike around Station Road Bridge and/or Frazee House

Hale Farm

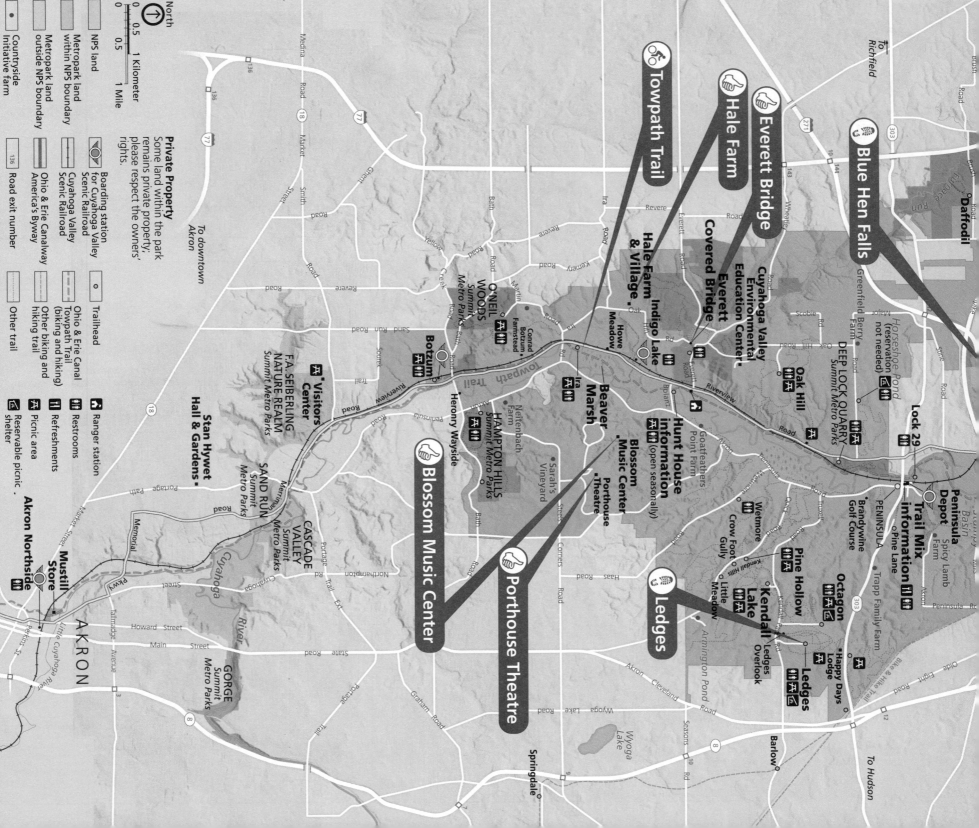

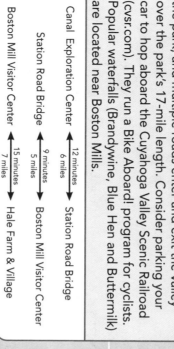

Ledges

Cuyahoga Valley Basics

(440) 717-3890 | nps.gov/cuva
Entrance Fee: None
Lodging: Inn at Brandywine Falls (innatbrandywinefalls.com) and Stanford House (conservancyforcvnp.org)
Camping: None

Why Visit Cuyahoga Valley?

- Waterfalls!
- Cuyahoga Valley Scenic Railroad (cvsr.com)
- The Arts! Regular events are held at Blossom Music Center and Porthouse Theatre
- Biking the railroad runs a Bike Aboard! program)
- Rich history found at Hale Farm & Village (wrhs.org), along Towpath Trail, and the park's visitor centers)
- Skiing, snowboarding, sledding, and snow-tubing!!

Cuyahoga Valley Driving Distances

Cuyahoga Valley is confusing for its small size. There are many noteworthy attractions and trailheads throughout the park, and multiple roads enter and exit the valley over the park's 17-mile length. Consider parking your car to hop aboard the Cuyahoga Valley Scenic Railroad (cvsr.com). They run a Bike Aboard! program for cyclists. Popular waterfalls (Brandywine, Blue Hen and Buttermilk) are located near Boston Mills.

Canal Exploration Center	12 minutes	Station Road Bridge
	6 miles	
Station Road Bridge	9 minutes	Boston Mill Visitor Center
	5 miles	
Boston Mill Visitor Center	15 minutes	Hale Farm & Village
	7 miles	

Station Road Bridge

Cuyahoga Valley Favorites

Easy Hikes: Brandywine Falls (0.3 mile), Bridal Veil Falls (0.25), Towpath Trail (varies, good starting points: Boston, Ira, and Station Road Bridge)
Moderate Hikes: Ledges (2.2), Blue Hen Falls/Buttermilk Falls (3/4.3), Haskell Run (0.5)
Views: Ledges Overlook, Brecksville Station, Boston Mills, Everett Covered Bridge, Kendall Lake, Hale Farm & Village, Beaver Marsh (Towpath Trail)

What You Need to Know About Shenandoah

- Visitation peaks in October for fall foliage, subsides for winter, and begins to pick up in March.

- With heavy weekend visitation, this is another good park to plan a mid-week trip.

- There's nearly unlimited lodging and camping around the park but in-park accommodations are priced fairly and save a ton of time. The only problem is how difficult it is to show up and secure a campsite or room (particularly on weekends). However, you can receive twice-daily first-come, first served campsite availability by texting SHENCAMP to 888777.

- Starting in 2022, a day-use ticket (recreation.gov) is required to hike Old Rag to curb over-crowding and overuse.

- Old Rag is demanding, requiring a fair amount of scrambling. Wear shoes with good grip. Do the 9.2-mile loop. You'll enjoy the more leisurely return trip along Weakley Hollow Fire Road.

- Rapidan Camp (Hoover's summer White House) is interesting but it's only accessible during ranger-guided tours. You can hike to it any time via Mill Prong Trail (4 miles).

Riprap

Humans aren't the only ones who enjoy the views

How Much Time Do You Have?

1 Day: If you're here to hike Old Rag, reserve a ticket (recreation. gov) and get after it. It's somewhere between a half- and full-day activity for most visitors. Everyone else should head to Skyline Drive. Focus most of your time around Skyland and Big Meadows.

2 Days: Shenandoah may be best known for peeping leaves, but the hiking here is no slouch. Just remember almost all of the trails originating from Skyline Drive descend into hollows and runs, and you'll have to hike back out.

3 Days: With a little more time it's a good idea to look into joining a ranger tour of Rapidan Camp, booking a trail ride or rock climbing lesson, or else there will be plenty of great hiking opportunities left.

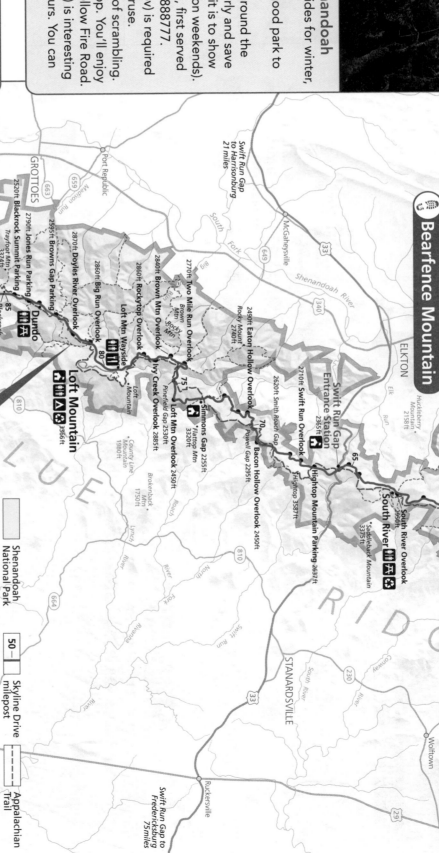

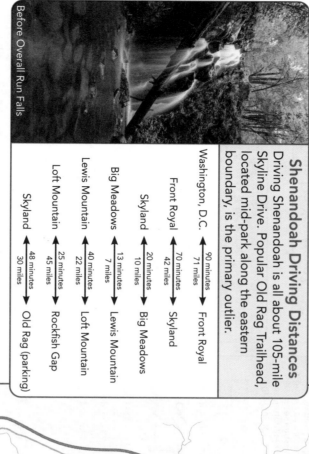

Skyline Drive from Stony Man

Shenandoah Basics

(540) 999-3500 | nps.gov/shen

Entrance Fee: $30/car
Lodging*: Big Meadows Lodge, Skyland Resort, Lewis Mountain
Camping: Big Meadows#, Mathews Arm#, Lewis Mtn, Loft Mtn#

*reserve at goshenandoah.com
#reserve at recreation.gov

Shenandoah Driving Distances

Driving Shenandoah is all about 105-mile Skyline Drive. Popular Old Rag Trailhead, located mid-park along the eastern boundary, is the primary outlier.

Washington, D.C.	90 minutes / 71 miles	Front Royal
Front Royal	70 minutes / 42 miles	Skyland
Skyland	20 minutes / 10 miles	Big Meadows
Big Meadows	13 minutes / 7 miles	Lewis Mountain
Lewis Mountain	40 minutes / 22 miles	Loft Mountain
Loft Mountain	25 minutes / 45 miles	Rockfish Gap
Skyland	48 minutes / 30 miles	Old Rag (parking)

Before Overall Run Falls

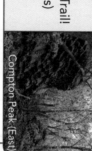

Compton Peak (East)

Why Visit Shenandoah?

- Waterfalls, hiking, and Appalachian Trail!
- Horseback riding (including trail rides)
- Rock climbing (goshenandoah.com)
- Top notch fall foliage

Shenandoah Favorites

Easy Hikes: Stony Man (0.9 mile), Black Rock Summit (0.8), Frazier Discovery (1.4), Limberlost (1.3), Hickerson Hollow (2.2)
Moderate Hikes: Passamaquoddy (3.4), Mary's Rock (2.8), Compton Peak (2.4), Hawksbill Mountain (2.1), Dark Hollow Falls (1.4)
Strenuous Hikes: Riprap/Wildcat Loop (9.8), Little Devil Stairs (7.7), Doyle's River Falls (3.2)
Extreme Hikes: Old Rag (5.6 out-and-back, 9.2 loop)
Views: Hazletop Ridge (mile 54.5), The Point (55.5), Pinnacles (35), Thorofare Mountain (40.5)

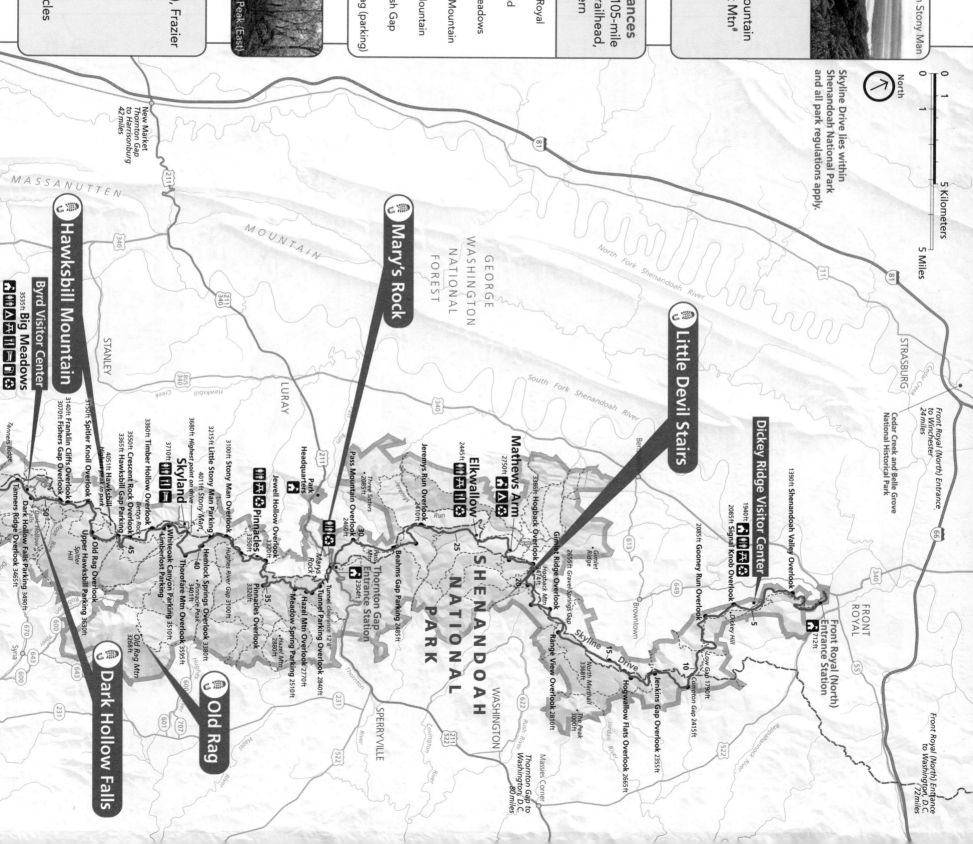

North
0 1 5 Kilometers
0 1 5 Miles

Skyline Drive lies within Shenandoah National Park and all park regulations apply.

Map labels

MASSANUTTEN
MOUNTAIN
GEORGE WASHINGTON NATIONAL FOREST
SHENANDOAH NATIONAL PARK
WASHINGTON

New Market to Harrisonburg 42 miles
STRASBURG
Front Royal (North) to Winchester 24 miles
Cedar Creek and Belle Grove National Historical Park

Little Devil Stairs

Dickey Ridge Visitor Center
1940ft Shenandoah Valley Overlook
2085ft Gooney Run Overlook
2085ft Signal Knob Overlook

1390ft Shenandoah Valley Overlook

FRONT ROYAL
Front Royal (North) Entrance Station 712ft

Front Royal (North) Entrance to Washington, D.C. 72 miles

Mathews Arm 2750ft
Elkwallow 2445ft
Jeremys Run Overlook 2085ft
2410ft
Three Sisters
338ft Hogback Overlook
474ft Hogback Mtn
Gimlet Ridge Overlook
Range View Overlook 2465ft
2810ft Hogwallow Flats Overlook 2665ft
2665ft North Marshall 3368ft
The Peak 3001ft
Jenkins Gap Overlook 2355ft
2415ft Compton Gap
Low Gap 1790ft
Browntown
Skyline Drive
15
10
5

Mary's Rock
Park Headquarters
211
Jewell Hollow Overlook
Pass Mountain Overlook 2460ft
Marys Rock
Tunnel (clearance 12'8")
Thornton Gap Entrance Station 2304ft
Tunnel Parking Overlook 2840ft
Hazel Mtn Overlook 2770ft
Meadow Spring Parking 2510ft
2880ft

Skyland
Highest point on drive 3680ft
Timber Hollow Overlook 3360ft
Crescent Rock Overlook 3550ft
Hawksbill Gap Parking 3365ft
Betsy Rock
4051ft Hawksbill Mtn
Stony Man Overlook 3100ft
Little Stony Man Parking 3215ft
4011ft Stony Man
3710ft
Franklin Cliffs Overlook 3140ft
Fishers Gap Overlook 3070ft
Spitler Knoll Overlook 3140ft
Upper Hawksbill Parking 3630ft
Hughes River Gap Parking 3100ft

Pinnacles
Pinnacles Overlook 3320ft
Hemlock Springs Overlook 3380ft
Thorofare Mtn Overlook 3595ft
Whiteoak Canyon Parking 3510ft
Limberlost Parking
Old Rag Overlook
3268ft Old Rag Mtn
45
40
35

Hawksbill Mountain
Big Meadows 3535ft
Byrd Visitor Center
Naked Creek Overlook 3250ft
Milam Gap Parking 3230ft
Dark Hollow Falls Parking 3490ft
Tanners Ridge Overlook 3465ft
Tanners Ridge
Rapidan Camp
Doubletop Mountain
50

Old Rag

Dark Hollow Falls

LURAY
STANLEY
SPERRYVILLE
Banco
Syria
South Fork Shenandoah River
North Fork Shenandoah River
Thornton Gap to Washington, D.C. 80 miles
Massies Corner
211
340
81
66
55
522
211
340

What You Need to Know About

The Gauley!

- The park receives strong visitation from March through November, peaking in June/July.

- Whitewater rafting is the headliner. The easiest run is the upper New River, which is great for families (especially in summer when the weather and water are warm) with Class I-III rapids. Things pick up on the Lower New with two Class IV+ rapids. If you have some experience and want the most extreme whitewater try the lower New in spring or visit during the Gauley River's short season in late September/early October. The upper Gauley is considered the wildest water with nearly non-stop named rapids. There are many rafting outfitters, but reservations remain a good idea, especially for the Gauley.

- One neat thing about the New is it flows from the south, providing uncommonly warm water.

- There's much more than whitewater rafting. It's a beloved destination for experienced rock climbers. There are a few mountain biking trails. And you'll find a handful of exceptional hiking trails (Long Point topping that list).

- Adrenaline junkies jump off the famous New River Gorge Bridge on Bridge Day (mid-October), when they open the bridge to these maniacs and spectators alike.

- Fayette Station Road is great but narrow, winding, and mostly one-way. Access it from the Canyon Rim Visitor Center side of the bridge.

How Much Time Do You Have?

How much time you need depends on how much rafting you plan on doing. Even though the park is small, exploring its depths requires at least one day.

1 Day: Go rafting, hike Long Point, and try to catch sunrise at Grandview and sunset at Canyon Rim (and drive one-way Fayette Station Road while you're there). You'll need a long summer's day to fit all that in.

2 Days: If you like to raft, go rafting again. Maybe level up to the lower New or Gauley? Otherwise check out historic mining sites. Thurmond is a site you drive to. Kaymoor is a great mine site, but it's a steep hike to reach it, including 821 stairs to the bottom. But it begins near a nice waterfall.

3 Days: Take another trip down the river! Stop at Sandstone Falls. Hike Endless Wall (2 ladders lead to a lower section of trail).

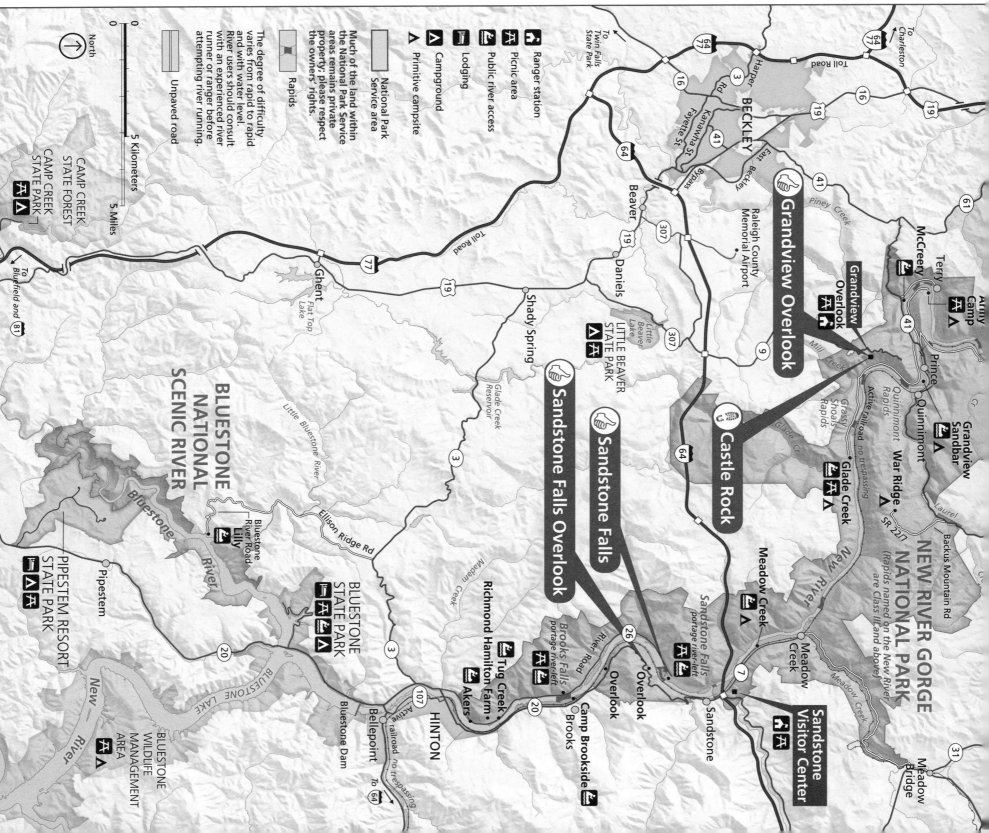

New River Gorge Basics

(304) 465-0508 | nps.gov/neri
Entrance Fee: None
Lodging: None
Camping: 8 small, free, primitive campgrounds (first-come, first-served)

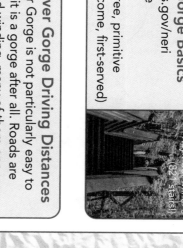

Kaymoor Miner's (82 stairs)

New River Gorge Driving Distances

New River Gorge is not particularly easy to navigate, it is a gorge after all. Roads are narrow and winding, many of them one-way. Regions are disjointed, most with a single access point. Canyon Rim, Grandview, and Sandstone Falls are the easiest sites to reach.

Charleston, WV	↔ 70 minutes / 53 miles ↔	Canyon Rim
Canyon Rim	↔ 50 minutes / 42 miles ↔	Grandview
Grandview	↔ 50 minutes / 35 miles ↔	Sandstone Falls

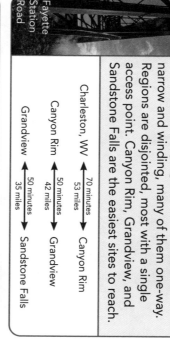

Fayette Station Road

Why Visit New River Gorge?

- Raft the wildest water in the country!
- Climb some vertical cliffs!
- Let it rip mountain biking
- Hike to wondrous waterfalls and scenic views
- Bridge jumping! (Bridge Day (Oct)
- Learn about mining history
- Fall foliage and spring wildflowers

Canyon Rim

New River Gorge Favorites

Easy Hikes: Tunnel (0.5 mile), Canyon Rim (0.1), Boardwalk/Island Loop (0.75)
Moderate Hikes: Long Point (3.2), Castle Rock (1.2), Kaymoor (8.6), Endless Wall (2.9), Butchers Branch (1.6), Glade Creek (11.2), Grandview Rim (3.2)
Strenuous Hikes: Kaymoor Miner's (2), Big Branch (2)
Views: Canyon Rim, Grandview, Sandstone Falls Overlook, Turkey Spur

Endless Wall

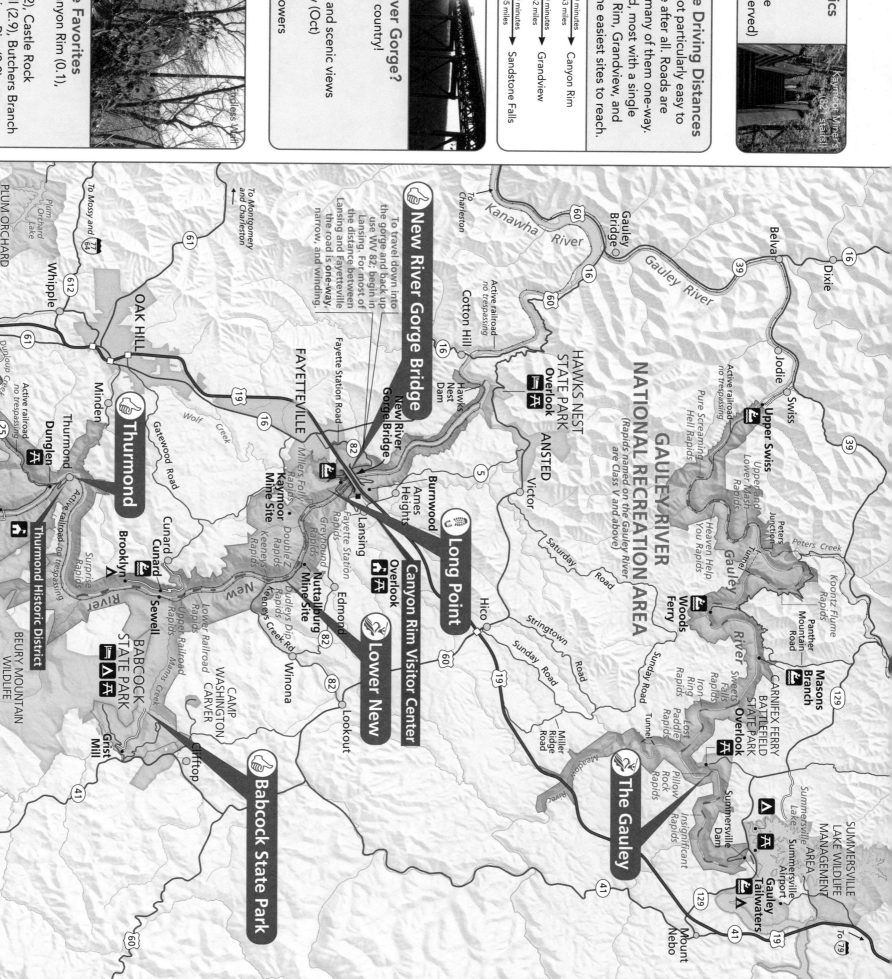

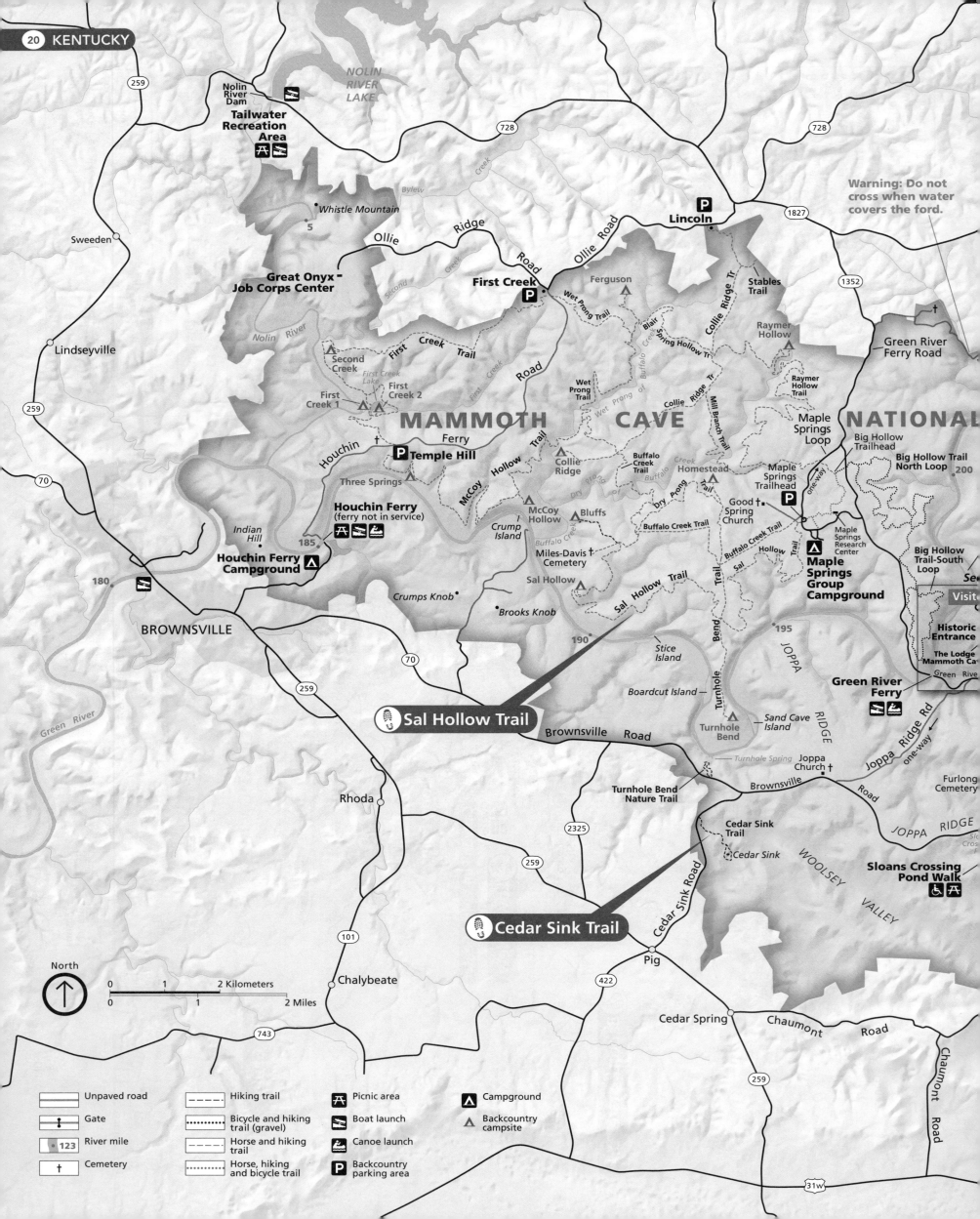

NOLIN RIVER LAKE

(259)

Nolin River Dam
Tailwater Recreation Area

Whistle Mountain
5

Sweeden

Ollie Ridge Road

(728)

(728)

(1827)

Warning: Do not cross when water covers the ford.

P Lincoln

Great Onyx - Job Corps Center

First Creek P

Ferguson

Ollie Road

(1352)

Lindseyville

Second Creek

First Creek Lake

First Creek 1

First Creek 2

Nolin River

First Creek Trail

Wet Prong Trail

Blair

Spring Hollow Tr

Collie Ridge Tr

Stables Trail

Raymer Hollow

Raymer Hollow Trail

Green River Ferry Road

(259)

(70)

MAMMOTH

Houchin Ferry

Temple Hill P

Three Springs

Houchin Ferry (ferry not in service)

185

Houchin Ferry Campground

Indian Hill

180

BROWNSVILLE

McCoy Hollow

McCoy Hollow Trail

Crump Island

Miles-Davis Cemetery

Collie Ridge

Wet Prong Trail

Wet Prong of Buffalo

CAVE

Collie Ridge Tr

Buffalo Creek Trail

Homestead

Dry Prong

Mill Branch Trail

Buffalo Creek Trail

NATIONAL

Big Hollow Trailhead

Maple Springs Loop

Maple Springs Trailhead P

Good Spring Church

Big Hollow Trail North Loop

200

Big Hollow Trail-South Loop

Se

McCoy Hollow

Bluffs

Sal Hollow

Crumps Knob

Brooks Knob

190

Dry Prong of Buffalo Creek

Buffalo Creek Trail

Sal Hollow Trail

Maple Springs Research Center

Maple Springs Group Campground

Visito

🥾 **Sal Hollow Trail**

Stice Island

Boardcut Island

Brownsville Road

Turnhole Bend

Turnhole Spring

Turnhole Bend Nature Trail

Sand Cave Island

JOPPA

195

RIDGE

Historic Entrance

The Lodge Mammoth Ca

Green Rive

Green River Ferry

Joppa Ridge Rd one-way

Furlong Cemetery

Rhoda

Brownsville Road

(2325)

Joppa Church

JOPPA RIDGE

Cedar Sink Trail

Cedar Sink

WOOLSEY VALLEY

Sl Cro

Sloans Crossing Pond Walk

(259)

🥾 **Cedar Sink Trail**

(101)

Chalybeate

Cedar Sink Road

Pig

(422)

Cedar Spring

Chaumont Road

North ↑

0   1   2 Kilometers
0   1   2 Miles

(743)

(259)

Chaumont Road

(31w)

	Unpaved road	⌐ ⌐ ⌐	Hiking trail	🏕	Picnic area	⛺	Campground
	Gate	•••••	Bicycle and hiking trail (gravel)	🛶	Boat launch	△	Backcountry campsite
•123	River mile	— — —	Horse and hiking trail	🚣	Canoe launch		
†	Cemetery	•••••	Horse, hiking and bicycle trail	P	Backcountry parking area		

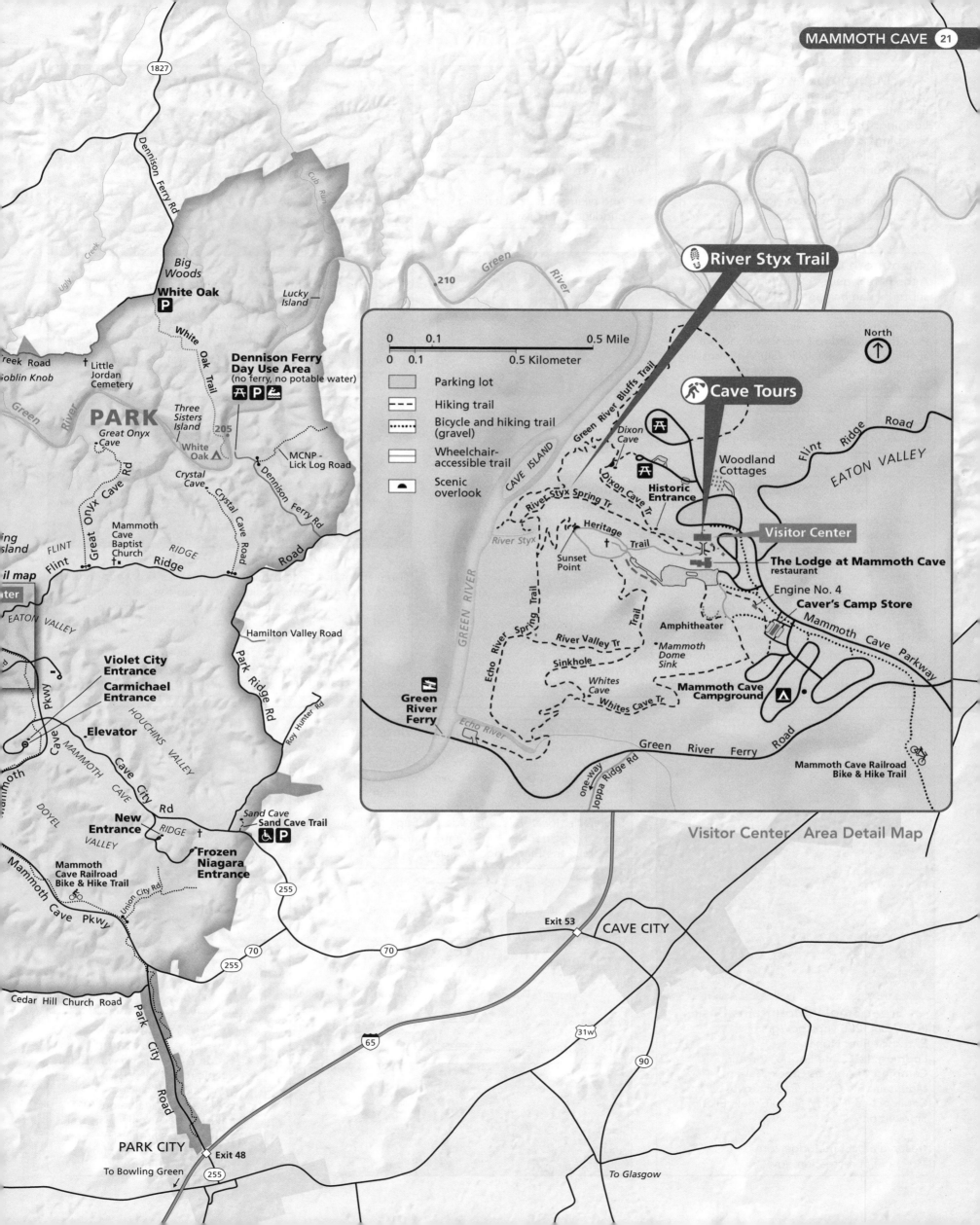

1827

Dennison Ferry Rd

Cub Run

Big Woods

White Oak
P

Lucky Island

Creek Road

Little Jordan Cemetery
†

Goblin Knob

White Oak Trail

Dennison Ferry Day Use Area
(no ferry, no potable water)

Green River

PARK

Great Onyx Cave

Three Sisters Island

205

White Oak

Dennison Ferry Rd

MCNP - Lick Log Road

Great Onyx Cave Rd

Crystal Cave

Crystal Cave Road

ng Island

FLINT

Flint

RIDGE

Ridge

Road

Mammoth Cave Baptist Church
†

il map

ter

EATON VALLEY

Hamilton Valley Road

Park Ridge Rd

Violet City Entrance

Carmichael Entrance

HOUCHINS VALLEY

Mammoth Cave City Rd

Roy Hunter Rd

Pkwy

Cave

Elevator

MAMMOTH

CAVE

DOYEL

VALLEY

New Entrance

RIDGE

Union City Rd

Sand Cave
Sand Cave Trail

P

Frozen Niagara Entrance
†

Mammoth Cave Railroad Bike & Hike Trail

Mammoth Cave Pkwy

255

Cedar Hill Church Road

Park City Road

PARK CITY   Exit 48

255

To Bowling Green

70

255

70

65

Exit 53

CAVE CITY

31w

90

To Glasgow

River Styx Trail

Cave Tours

North
↑

0   0.1   0.5 Mile
0 0.1   0.5 Kilometer

Parking lot

- - - Hiking trail

······· Bicycle and hiking trail (gravel)

═══ Wheelchair-accessible trail

Scenic overlook

210

Green River

Green River Bluffs Trail

Dixon Cave

Woodland Cottages

Flint Ridge Road

EATON VALLEY

CAVE ISLAND

Dixon Cave Tr

Historic Entrance

River Styx Spring Tr

Heritage

Visitor Center

GREEN RIVER

River Styx

Sunset Point

Trail

†

The Lodge at Mammoth Cave
restaurant

Engine No. 4

Caver's Camp Store

Echo River Spring Trail

River Valley Tr

Sinkhole

Mammoth Dome Sink

Amphitheater

Trail

Mammoth Cave Parkway

Whites Cave

Whites Cave Tr

Green River Ferry

Echo River

Mammoth Cave Campground

Joppa Ridge Rd

one-way

Green River Ferry Road

Mammoth Cave Railroad Bike & Hike Trail

Visitor Center Area Detail Map

Mammoth Cave Basics

(270) 758-2180 | nps.gov/maca
Entrance Fee: None
Lodging: The Lodge*
Camping**: Mammoth Cave, Houchin's Ferry, Maple Springs
Cave Tours**: Year Round

*reserve at mammothcavelodge.com
**reserve at recreation.gov

Domes and Dripstones Tour

Why Visit Mammoth Cave?
- Cave tours!
- And hiking, horseback riding, paddling, and biking

Booth's Amphitheater (Gothic Avenue)

Mammoth Cave Driving Distances

A trip here requires exploring the subterranean passages of Mammoth Cave. All tours depart from the Visitor Center. Beyond that, driving Flint Ridge Road to Park Ridge Road to Cave City Road is a scenic loop (especially in fall). And crossing the Green River via Green River Ferry is always fun.

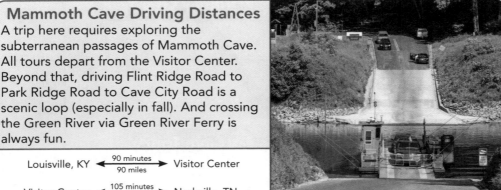

Louisville, KY	90 minutes / 90 miles	Visitor Center
Visitor Center	105 minutes / 95 miles	Nashville, TN

Green River Ferry

Mammoth Cave Favorites

Moderate Hikes: River Styx Spring (0.6 mile), Cedar Sink (1), Green River Bluffs (1.1)
Cave Tours: Wild Cave (strenuous, 6 hours), Broadway (moderate, 2 hours), Gothic (Avenue (moderate, 2 hours) Frozen Niagara (easy, 1.25 hours), Violet City (moderate, lit by lanterns, 3 hours), River Styx (moderate, 2.5 hours)

What You Need to Know About Mammoth Cave

- Tour offerings are provided to meet demand, paring back the menu in winter and weekdays. Reservations are a good idea, especially for less-frequent offerings like Wild Cave, Intro to Caving, Trog (kids only), River Styx, Violet City. You can usually show up and join a tour without reservations but that was not the case during the pandemic.
- Wild Cave is great but it is difficult. You will exit the cave dirty. You must wear hiking boots and have a chest/hip measurement of less than 42 inches. All Wild Cave participants must be at least 16 years old.
- Coin-operated showers are available near Mammoth Cave Campground.
- Broadway, Gothic Avenue, Historic, Discovery, Star Chamber, Violet City, River Styx, and Trog Tours all begin at the cave's Natural Entrance.
- The cave is always cool, so summer visitors may want to hike/paddle in the morning/evening, and tour the cave in the afternoon when it's hottest.

The Natural Entrance

How Much Time Do You Have?

Time spent at Mammoth Cave is almost entirely dependent on cave tours for most visitors. Refer to the park website for tour details (and schedule) and figure out which one(s) you'd like to join. They're all priced reasonably and rangers add a lot to the experience. If you wanted to extend your trip backpacking or packrafting the Green and/or Nolin Rivers, that's an option. You're even allowed to camp on islands and alongside the river (with a free permit).

Chimney Tops

Great Smoky Mountains Basics

(865) 436-1200 | nps.gov/grsm
Entrance Fee: None
Lodging: Le Conte Lodge* (hike-in)
Camping**: Abrams Creek, Balsam Mountain, Big Creek, Cades Cove, Cataloochee, Cosby, Deep Creek, Elkmont, Smokemont

*reserve at lecontelodge.com
**reserve at recreation.gov

Great Smoky Mountains Driving Distances

This is the most visited national park. Expect roads to be busy, especially if you're visiting in summer or during peak foliage. Cades Cove, Roaring Fork Motor Nature Trail, Newfound Gap, and Clingman's Dome are particularly popular. Gatlinburg, Pigeon Forge, and Sevierville, located just outside the Sugarlands area, are huge tourist traps. If you're entering or exiting from the east, take the Blue Ridge Parkway.

Knoxville, TN	60 minutes / 43 miles	Gatlinburg, TN
Gatlinburg, TN	12 minutes / 4 miles	Sugarlands Visitor Center
Sugarlands Visitor Center	75 minutes / 30 miles	Cades Cove Visitor Center
Sugarlands Visitor Center	45 minutes / 20 miles	Clingman's Dome
Clingman's Dome	40 minutes / 23 miles	Oconaluftee Visitor Center
Oconaluftee Visitor Center	80 minutes / 40 miles	Cataloochee
Oconaluftee Visitor Center	63 minutes / 90 miles	Asheville, NC (Blue Ridge)

A baby owl spotted hiking to Gregory Bald

Tom Branch Falls (Deep Creek)

Why Visit Great Smoky Mountains?
- Grade-A hiking and waterfalls!
- Scenic roads
- Fantastic fall foliage
- Backpacking, including 70 miles of the Appalachian Trail
- Synchronous fireflies!
- Le Conte Lodge (hike in)
- Horseback riding

The view from Shuckstack (Appalachian Trail)

Great Smoky Mountains Favorites

Easy Hikes: Indian Creek (1.6 miles), Laurel Falls (2.6), Mingo Falls (0.4)
Moderate Hikes: Charlie's Bunion (8.1), Andrew's Bald (3.5), Grotto Falls (2.8), Clingman's Dome (0.5), Mouse Creek Falls (4), Little Cataloochee (6), Rainbow Falls (5.4), Hen Wallow Falls (4.4)
Strenuous Hikes: Alum Cave (4.6), Chimney Tops (4), Gregory Bald (11.3+), Ramsay Cascades (8), Rocky Top (13.9), Mount Cammerer (12)
Activities: Spend the night at Le Conte Lodge, take a hay or carriage ride at Cades Cove, go tubing at Deep Creek, ride a horse at Smokemont or Cades Cove, see the synchronous fireflies (mid-June, ticket from recreation.gov required), you'll also find whitewater rafting outfitters all around the park

What You Need to Know About Great Smoky Mountains

- Great Smoky Mountains is the most visited national park, and the next closest entry is well under half the annual visitation. I'm not exactly sure how they come to these numbers, but they often feel right (unless you visit in winter (which isn't a terrible idea).
- You may have to pay for parking in the future (it's being discussed).
- Crowds congregate in a few places. #1 is Cades Cove. A line often forms before the gate opens at sunrise, but early morning is your best bet for a less congested experience. If you arrive later and aren't enjoying it, two bisecting roads allow you to evacuate the one-way loop early.
- Another option is to bike Cades Cove Loop Road. Every Wednesday from mid-June through September the road is closed to motorists. It's a pilot program, so it may not stick around for long. Bike rentals are available at Cades Cove Campground Store. While the elevation change of Cades Cove Loop Road is not extreme, I wouldn't call the 11-mile loop easy. There are some pretty steady grades you'll have to climb (and then descend).
- One of the main draws to Cades Cove is the chance to see black bears (and other wildlife). If it's at all possible, please pull off to the side of the road to view wildlife.
- Roaring Fork Motor Nature Trail isn't quite as busy as Cades Cove but traffic can back up (especially if there's wildlife). You'll find a few popular trails like Grotto Falls and Rainbow Falls, and trailhead parking areas fill most of the year.
- The park is busy, and it's best to make a plan, a backup plan, and a backup to the backup plan for every activity you plan to do. Parking can also be hard to come by at Alum Cave, Chimney Tops, Newfound Gap, Clingman's Dome, and Laurel Falls.
- Due to the park's popularity, it's a good idea to camp inside it. If hiking is your primary activity (not all the touristy things found in Gatlinburg, Pigeon Forge, and Sevierville) and you don't mind roughing it a little bit, it's a no brainer. Plus, you can often hike right out of the campground.
- The Smoky Mountain Synchronous Fireflies is another popular spectacle. It isn't a trendy new folk group, they're real-life fireflies lighting up in sync, typically for two weeks in the middle of June. To enjoy the show, you'll have to win a lottery (recreation.gov) to park (fee) at Sugarlands and then be shuttled to Elkmont to enjoy the light extravaganza. Be courteous by using a red or green light, pointing it toward the ground. Don't disturb or capture the fireflies. Pack out everything you brought.
- Many family's favorite memories are simply playing in the abundance of roadside streams. Choose a spot and have fun. I like the picnic area on the Little River near the Wears Valley Entrance.

How Much Time Do You Have?

It's not hyperbole to say there's something for people of all interests in this area of the country. Sevierville, Pigeon Forge, and Gatlinburg represent some of the most gaudy tourist traps known to man. And, believe it or not, they're fun. Then there's the park with all kinds of hiking, driving, and historical attractions. If you are a little bit of an adrenaline junkie, you'll find plenty of whitewater rafting, ziplining, and even skydiving. History buffs will find sites like the Old Mill outside the park, and Cable Mill (and all the other Cades Cove sites), Mingus Mill, and Oconaluftee fascinating. Then there's hiking. Waterfalls, mountains, and balds, oh my!

1 Day: First, one day isn't nearly enough time to spend in the park, not to mention get a taste of the unlimited supply of entertainment opportunities found around the park. But, if it's all the time you have, I'd forget about Cades Cove, unless you can get an early start. If it's spring/summer and the balds are blooming, Gregory Bald is a great albeit strenuous hiking choice for a day hike, with a trailhead located beyond Cades Cove. Drive Newfound Gap Road, stop at Newfound Gap (hike the Appalachian Trail to Charlie's Bunion and back), and continue to Clingman's Dome (the parking lot will probably be full but space turns over fairly quickly). Continue on to Mingus Mill and Oconaluftee. Exit via the Blue Ridge Parkway to take in the sunset.

2 Days: With another day, you can get an early (or late) start and drive Roaring Fork Motor Nature Trail to do some waterfall hikes (like Grotto or Rainbow Falls), or catch the sunrise/sunset in the park at Clingman's Dome (and then hike to Andrews Bald if you have time).

3 Days: Hikers should consider moving around the park, spending time in Big Creek, Cataloochee, and Deep Creek. There's some great hiking in these areas. You'll almost always find a semblance of peace and quiet a few miles into the wilderness, but the traffic is less overwhelming here as well. Whether you're a family, couple, or traveling solo, three days will go by in a flash at the Smokies.

Charlie's Bunion

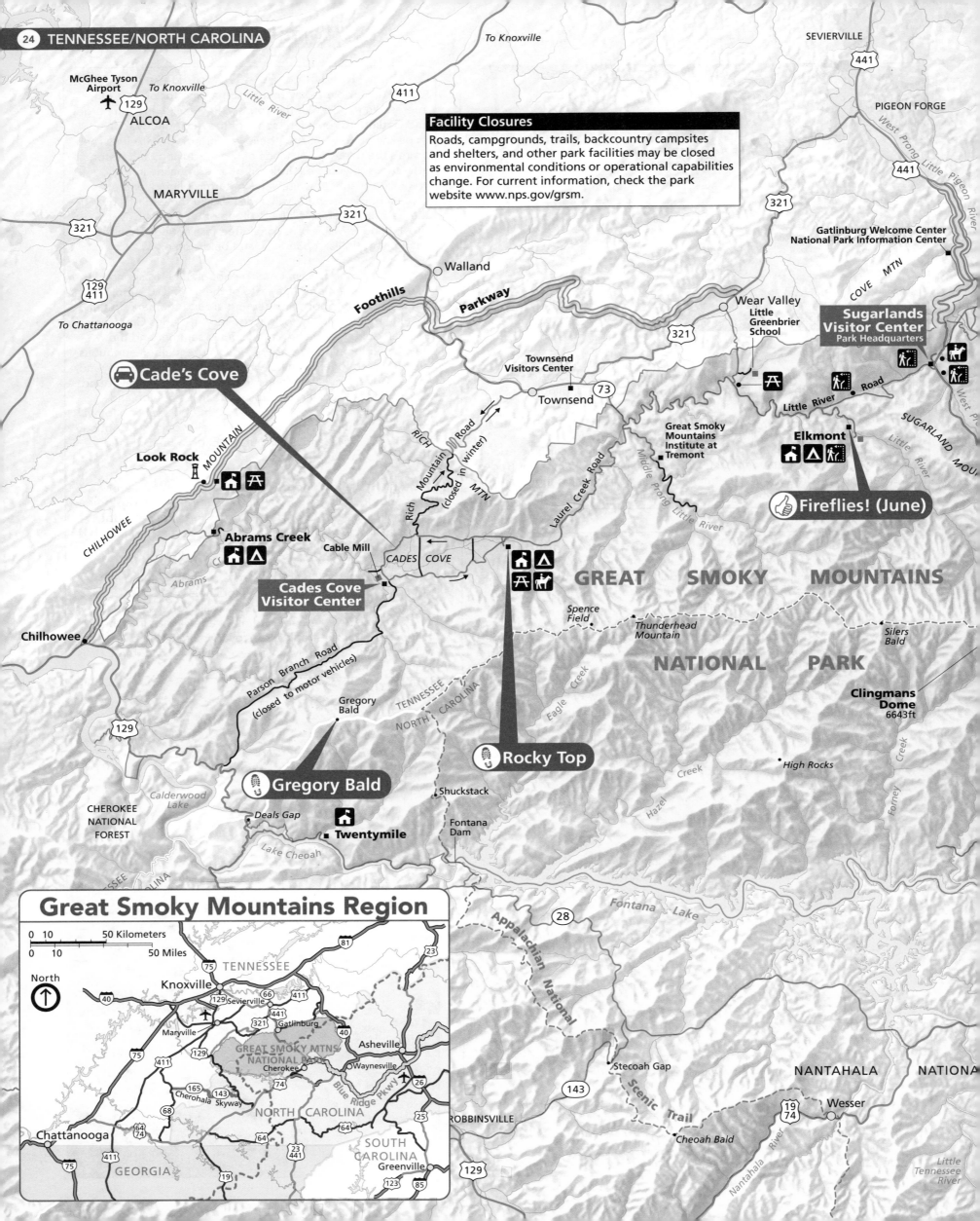

McGhee Tyson Airport
To Knoxville
ALCOA
129
411
MARYVILLE
321
129
411
To Chattanooga

To Knoxville
411
Walland

Foothills Parkway
321

Townsend Visitors Center
Townsend
73

SEVIERVILLE
441
PIGEON FORGE
441

Gatlinburg Welcome Center
National Park Information Center

Wear Valley
Little Greenbrier School

COVE MTN

Sugarlands Visitor Center
Park Headquarters

Facility Closures
Roads, campgrounds, trails, backcountry campsites and shelters, and other park facilities may be closed as environmental conditions or operational capabilities change. For current information, check the park website www.nps.gov/grsm.

Little River Road

Great Smoky Mountains Institute at Tremont

Elkmont

Fireflies! (June)

Little River

SUGARLAND MOUN

WEST P

Cade's Cove

Look Rock

CHILHOWEE MOUNTAIN

Abrams Creek

Cable Mill

CADES COVE

RICH Mountain Road (closed in winter)

RICH MTN

Laurel Creek Road

Middle Prong Little River

Cades Cove Visitor Center

Chilhowee

Abrams

GREAT SMOKY MOUNTAINS

Spence Field
Thunderhead Mountain
Silers Bald

NATIONAL PARK

Clingmans Dome 6643ft

Parson Branch Road (closed to motor vehicles)

Gregory Bald

129

Calderwood Lake

CHEROKEE NATIONAL FOREST

Deals Gap

Gregory Bald

Lake Cheoah

TENNESSEE
NORTH CAROLINA

Eagle Creek

Rocky Top

Shuckstack

Fontana Dam

Twentymile

Hazel Creek

High Rocks

Forney Creek

Appalachian National

28

Fontana Lake

Great Smoky Mountains Region

0 10   50 Kilometers
0 10   50 Miles

North

81
75 TENNESSEE
Knoxville
40
129 Sevierville
66 411
441
321 Gatlinburg
Maryville
40
75
411
129
165
143 Cherohala Skyway
68
64 74
Chattanooga
411
75
19
GEORGIA
NORTH CAROLINA
Cherokee
74
Asheville
Waynesville
Blue Ridge Pkwy
26
25
64
23 441
64
SOUTH CAROLINA
Greenville
129
123 85
23

ROBBINSVILLE

143

Stecoah Gap

Scenic Trail

Cheoah Bald

Nantahala River

NANTAHALA NATIONA

19 74 Wesser

Little Tennessee River

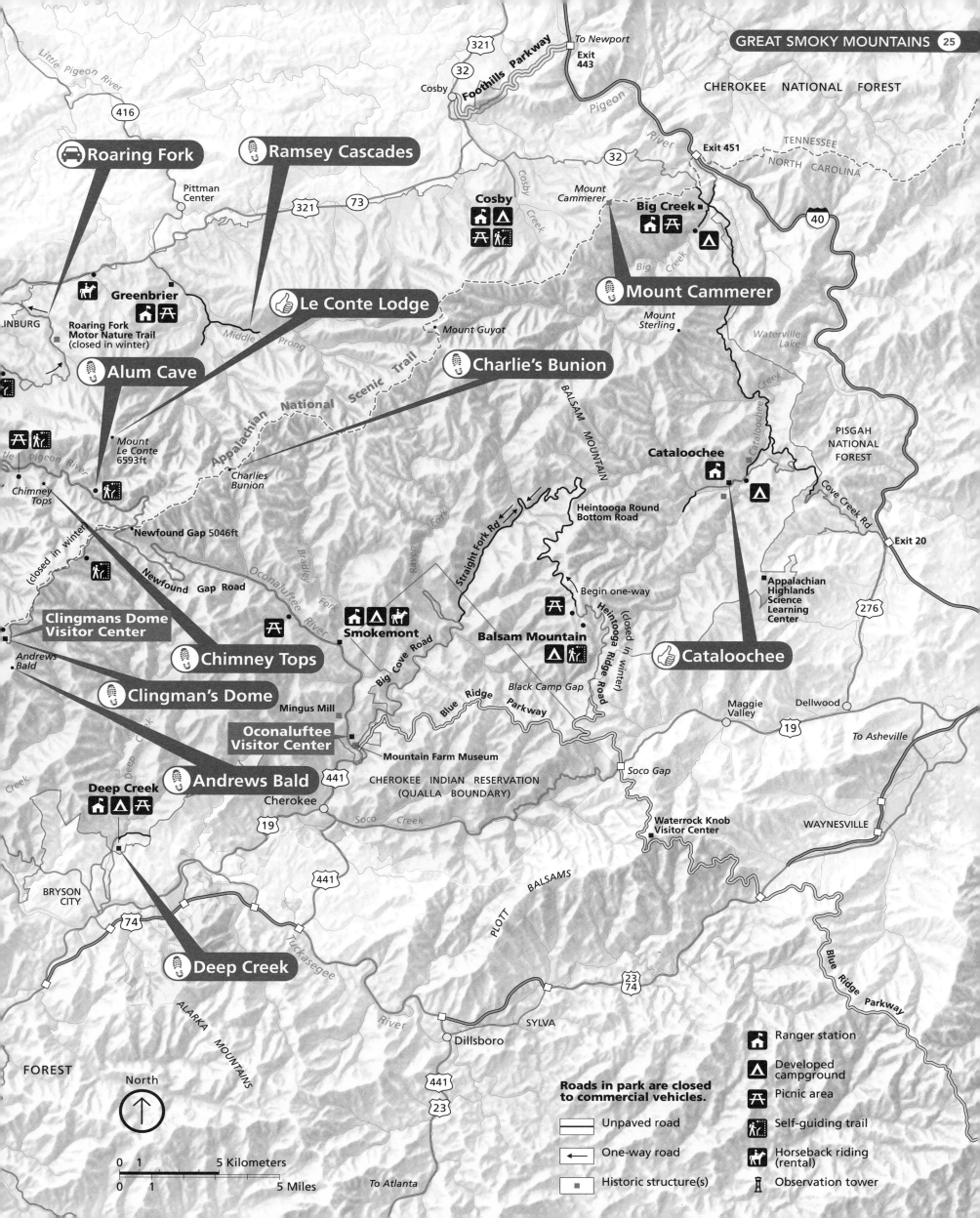

Roaring Fork

Ramsey Cascades

CHEROKEE NATIONAL FOREST

To Newport
Exit 443

321

32

Cosby

Foothills Parkway

Pigeon River

Exit 451

TENNESSEE
NORTH CAROLINA

40

Pittman Center

321   73

Cosby

Mount Cammerer

Big Creek

Greenbrier

Roaring Fork Motor Nature Trail (closed in winter)

Le Conte Lodge

Mount Guyot

Mount Cammerer

Mount Sterling

Waterville Lake

Alum Cave

Charlie's Bunion

Appalachian National Scenic Trail

Mount Le Conte 6593ft

Charlies Bunion

Cataloochee

PISGAH NATIONAL FOREST

Cove Creek Rd

Chimney Tops

Newfound Gap 5046ft

Heintooga Round Bottom Road

Balsam Mountain

Exit 20

(closed in winter)

Newfound Gap Road

Oconaluftee River

Bradley Fork

Straight Fork Rd

Begin one-way

Appalachian Highlands Science Learning Center

276

Clingmans Dome Visitor Center

Smokemont

Balsam Mountain

Heintooga Ridge Road

Cataloochee

Chimney Tops

Andrews Bald

Clingman's Dome

Oconaluftee Visitor Center

Mingus Mill

Black Camp Gap

Blue Ridge Parkway

Maggie Valley

Dellwood

19

To Asheville

Andrews Bald

Deep Creek

Mountain Farm Museum

441

CHEROKEE INDIAN RESERVATION (QUALLA BOUNDARY)

Soco Gap

Cherokee

19

Soco Creek

Waterrock Knob Visitor Center

WAYNESVILLE

Deep Creek

BRYSON CITY

441

74

Tuckasegee

PLOTT BALSAMS

23 74

Blue Ridge Parkway

ALARKA MOUNTAINS

River

SYLVA

FOREST

Dillsboro

North

441

23

To Atlanta

Roads in park are closed to commercial vehicles.

Ranger station

Developed campground

Picnic area

Self-guiding trail

Horseback riding (rental)

Historic structure(s)

Observation tower

Unpaved road

One-way road

0 1   5 Kilometers
0 1   5 Miles

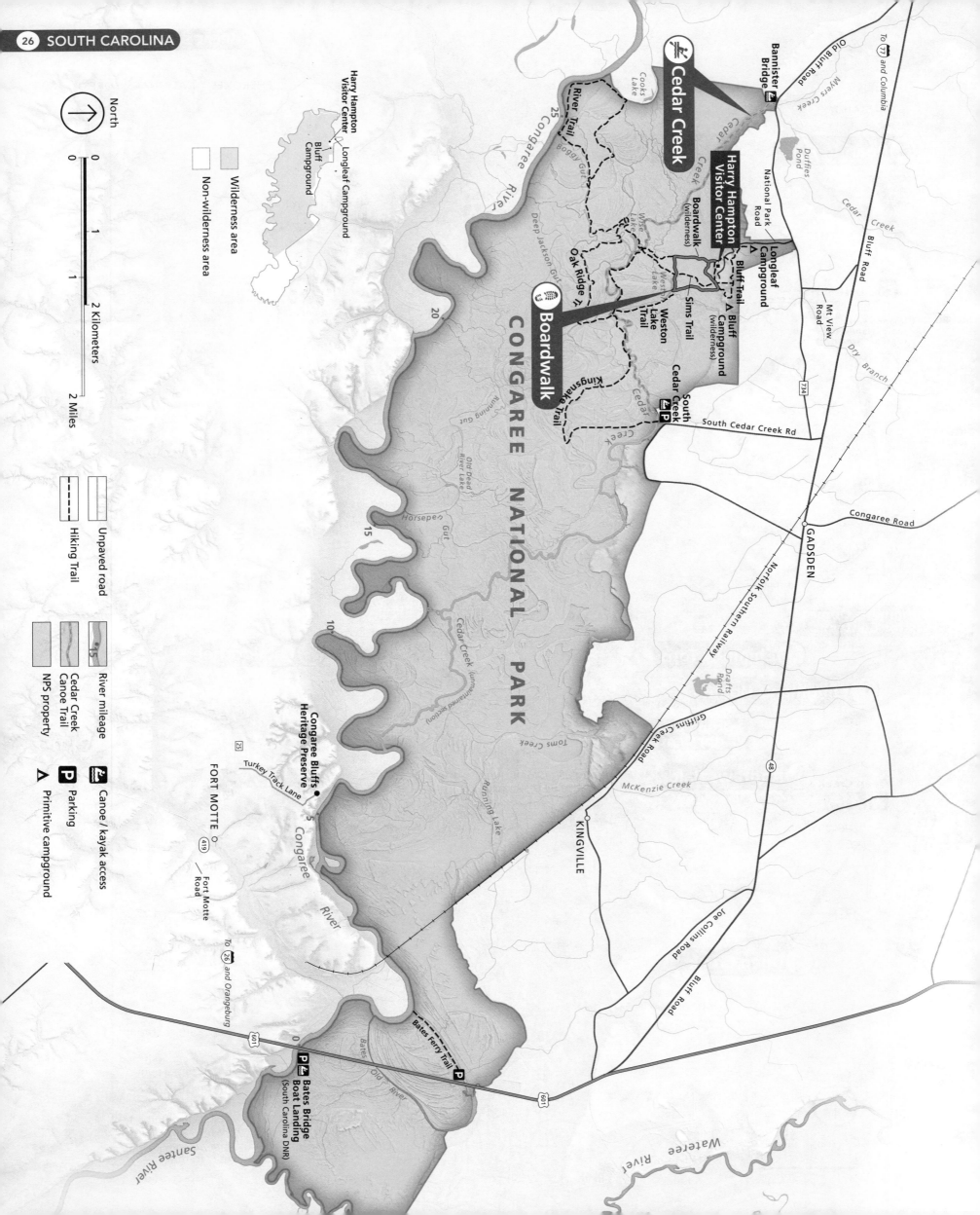

Congaree Basics
(803) 776-4396 | nps.gov/cong
Entrance Fee: None
Lodging: None
Camping*: Long Leaf, Bluff

*reserve at recreation.gov (required)

Boardwalk

Congaree Driving Distances
Congaree is pretty simple. All trails (except a short trek down to the Congaree River from US-601) begin at Harry Hampton Visitor Center. There are landings on each end of the park for paddlers.

| Columbia, SC | 35 minutes / 20 miles | Harry Hampton VC |
| Harry Hampton VC | 150 minutes / 150 miles | Savannah, GA |

Cedar Creek

Why Visit Congaree?
- Walk among giants (Big trees!)
- Paddle through a primeval forest (Cedar Creek)
- Fireflies and owls!

Congaree Favorites
Hikes: Boardwalk (easy, 2.6 miles), River (easy, 10)
Activities: Paddle Cedar Creek, join a park ranger on an Owl Prowl or Big Tree Hike

What You Need to Know About Congaree
- It used to be named Congaree Swamp but it's actually a floodplain. The fact it is a floodplain is important as it floods, typically in winter, so you'll want to check water level at the park website before making plans. Sections of The Boardwalk can be underwater and impassable at times.
- Campers must reserve sites online (recreation.gov). Cell coverage is spotty but there is wi-fi at the visitor center.
- Check the park website for up-to-date information about current ranger programs. Big Tree Hike, Owl Prowl, and Guided Canoe Tour require reservations.
- Synchronous fireflies have been performing for some time at Great Smoky Mountains…they're a more recent phenomenon here. It's different each year, but the show usually begins sometime in May and lasts a week or two. Congaree puts on a Firefly Festival for the duration.

Boardwalk

Wise Lake

How Much Time Do You Have?
Congaree is a small park. It's well worth a stop but you don't need to plan a whole lot of time for a visit. If you're arriving in late May/early June, check to see if the fireflies are in sync. You won't want to miss that. While planning, also refer to the park website for a schedule of ranger programs (Big Tree Hike, Owl Prowl, Canoe Tour) during your travel dates. Beyond that, stop in, hike The Boardwalk, and continue on River Trail if you have the time and energy. Paddling is peaceful too.

Biscayne Basics
(305) 230-1114 | nps.gov/bisc
Entrance Fee: None
Lodging: None
Camping: Boca Chita (restrooms, no showers), Elliott Key (restrooms, cold showers)

Boca Chita Key

Biscayne Favorites
Activities: Biscayne National Park Institute's Boca Chita Tour, Snorkel and Island Visit (departs from Dinner Key Marina), Jones Lagoon Eco-Adventure, and Stiltsville Guided Tour (Dinner Key Marina); with your own boat you could explore several shipwrecks or camp at Elliott or Boca Chita Keys; view Stiltsville from Bill Baggs Cape Florida State Park

Boca Chita

Biscayne Driving Distances
Biscayne is next door to Everglades and Miami and there's really only one point to drive to, Convoy Point, where you'll find Dante Fascell Visitor Center and the park's concessioner, Biscayne National Park Institute (biscaynenationalparkinstitute.org). The rest of the park is islands, water, or mangrove shoreline.

| Miami, FL | 50 minutes / 35 miles | Dante Fascell VC |
| Dante Fascell VC | 170 minutes / 135 miles | Key West, FL |

Where does the sky end and water begin?

What You Need to Know About Biscayne
- Visitation is steady year-round. Warm winters draw northern vacationers. And the ocean is welcoming in the summer heat. But hurricane season is June through November.
- Make sure you book boat tours (biscaynenationalparkinstitute.org) prior to arrival. You probably don't need to make them months in advance like camping/lodging reservations at flagship parks, but a week or two ahead is a good idea.
- With a group of five or six, think about booking a charter. You'll get more time exploring the park's water. It will be a more intimate experience. And you'll probably have a better snorkeling experience (as long as you're comfortable doing it on your own). There are wrecks out there like the *Mandalay* that you don't need SCUBA equipment to investigate.
- Stiltsville is quite the oddity. You'll have to book a charter or boat tour to see it up close, but you can get a good look at it from the beach at Bill Baggs Cape Florida State Park (which is pretty great in its own right).

Stiltsville

Why Visit Biscayne?
- Explore long forgotten Shipwrecks!
- Paddle Jones Lagoon
- Ponder the decadence of Stiltsville in its heyday
- Hike Elliott Key's Spite Highway

How Much Time Do You Have?
Most visitors don't spend much time here. The usual itinerary is book a tour with Biscayne Institute, peruse the visitor center while you wait for departure, go on the tour, and leave. Honestly, there isn't much more to it unless you have your own boat. You could bring or rent kayaks and paddle the coast. Experienced paddlers could cross about 9 miles of open water to get to Boca Chita or Elliott Keys.

Boat tours

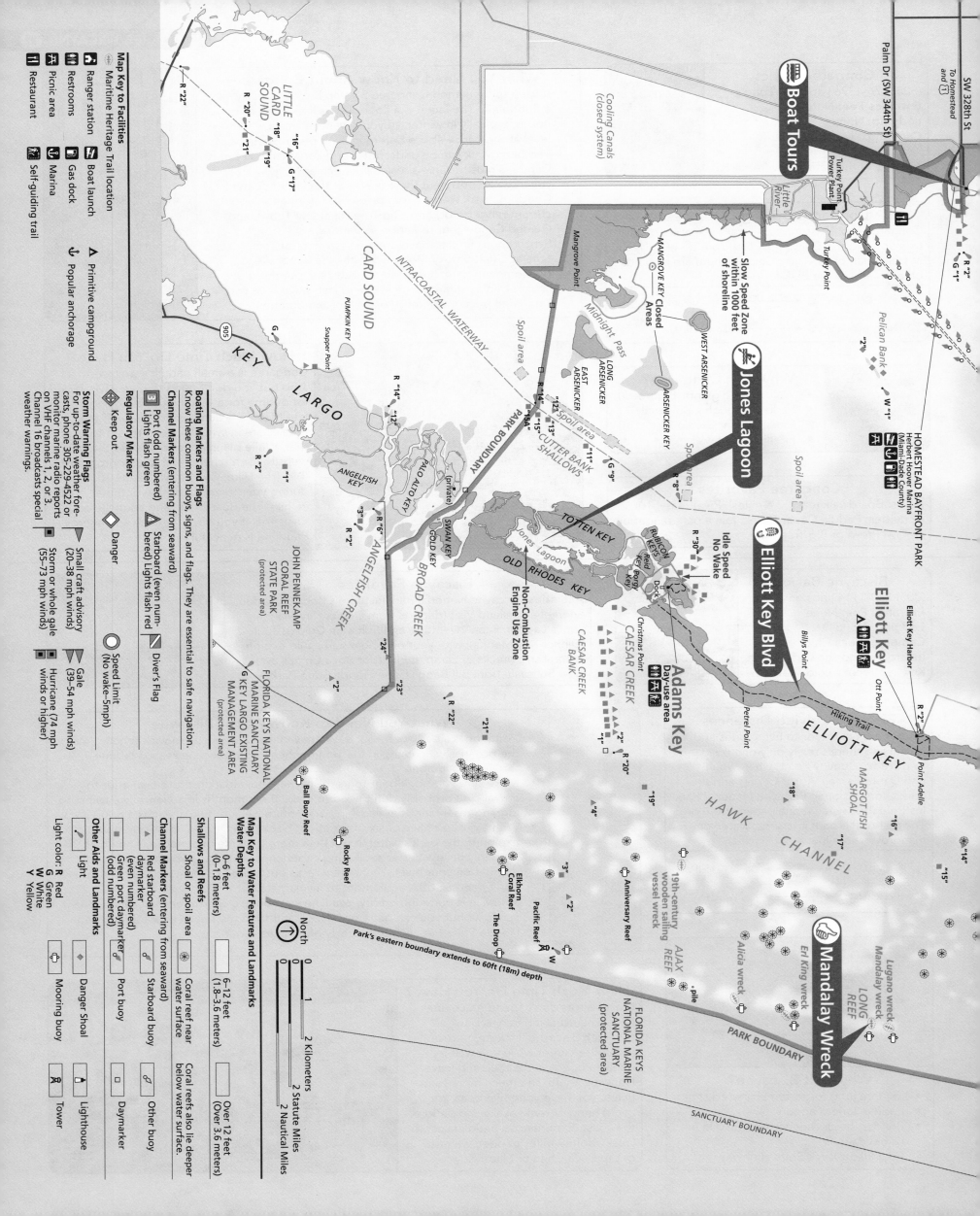

Map Key to Facilities

- 🏢 Ranger station
- 🚻 Restrooms
- ⛽ Gas dock
- 🏖️ Picnic area
- ⚓ Marina
- 🍴 Restaurant
- 🚤 Boat launch
- Δ Primitive campground
- ⚓ Popular anchorage
- ⛵ Self-guiding trail

Maritime Heritage Trail location

Boating Markers and Flags

Know these common buoys, signs, and flags. They are essential to safe navigation.

Regulatory Markers

- ◇ Keep out
- ◇ Danger
- △ Diver's Flag
- ○ Speed Limit (No wake–5mph)

Channel Markers (entering from seaward)

- ▢ Port (odd numbered) Lights flash green
- △ Starboard (even numbered) Lights flash red

Storm Warning Flags

For up-to-date weather forecasts, phone 305-229-4522 or monitor marine radio reports on VHF channels 1, 2, or 3. Channel 16 broadcasts special weather warnings.

- ▽ Small craft advisory (20–38 mph winds)
- ▽▽ Gale (39–54 mph winds)
- ▣ Storm or whole gale (55–73 mph winds)
- ▣▣ Hurricane (74 mph winds or higher)

Map Key to Water Features and Landmarks

Water Depths

- ▢ 0–6 feet (0–1.8 meters)
- ▢ 6–12 feet (1.8–3.6 meters)
- ▢ Over 12 feet (Over 3.6 meters)

Shallows and Reefs

- ▢ Shoal or spoil area
- ❋ Coral reef near water surface
- ▢ Coral reefs also lie deeper below water surface.

Channel Markers (entering from seaward)

- ◣ Red starboard daymarker
- ◢ Starboard buoy
- ▢ Green port daymarker (odd numbered)
- ▢ Port buoy

Other Aids and Landmarks

- ▪ Danger
- ◆ Danger Shoal
- ⬭ Other buoy
- ◻ Daymarker
- ⌖ Mooring buoy
- ⊡ Lighthouse
- ⚓ Tower

Light color: R Red
- G Green
- W White
- Y Yellow
- / Light

North ⟶

Scale: 0 1 2 Kilometers
0 1 2 Statute Miles
0 1 2 Nautical Miles

Park's eastern boundary extends to 60ft (18m) depth

Map labels

SW 328th St

To Homestead and US 1

Palm Dr (SW 344th St)

Turkey Point, Power Plant

Cooling Canals (closed system)

Little River

Turkey Point

Boat Tours

Slow Speed Zone within 1000 feet of shoreline

Mangrove Point

MANGROVE KEY Closed Areas

WEST ARSENICKER

LONG ARSENICKER

EAST ARSENICKER

ARSENICKER KEY

Spoil area

Midnight Pass

Pelican Bank

W "1"

"2"

R "2"
G "1"

HOMESTEAD BAYFRONT PARK
Herbert Hoover Marina
(Miami-Dade County)

Spoil area

Spoil area

Jones Lagoon

R "8"

G "9"

R "14"
"12½"
"13"
"15"
"11"
18A

PARK BOUNDARY

"CUTTER BANK SHALLOWS"

LITTLE CARD SOUND

R "22"
R "20"
R "21"
R "18"
"16"
G "17"
"19"

KEY LARGO

CARD SOUND

INTRACOASTAL WATERWAY

905

G

PUMPKIN KEY

Snapper Point

SWAN KEY
GOLD KEY

R "14"
R "12"
R "2"
"1"

ANGELFISH KEY

PALO ALTO KEY

JOHN PENNEKAMP CORAL REEF STATE PARK (protected area)

ANGELFISH CREEK

R "6"
R "2"
R "3"

BROAD CREEK

"24"

FLORIDA KEYS NATIONAL MARINE SANCTUARY
G KEY LARGO EXISTING MANAGEMENT AREA (protected area)

"23"

"2"

TOTTEN KEY

Jones Lagoon

OLD RHODES KEY

Non-Combustion Engine Use Zone

RUBICON KEYS
Reid Key
Porgy Key

R "30"

Idle Speed No Wake

Elliott Key Blvd

Elliott Key

Elliott Key Harbor

Billys Point

Ott Point

R "2"

Petrel Point

Point Adelle

ELLIOTT KEY

Hiking Trail

Adams Key
Day-use area

Christmas Point

CAESAR CREEK BANK

CAESAR CREEK

R "20"
R "2"
"1"
"2"
"3"

"19"

"18"

"16"

"17"

"15"

"14"

HAWK CHANNEL

MARGOT FISH SHOAL

AJAX REEF

Alicia wreck

Lugano wreck
Mandalay wreck

LONG REEF

Erl King wreck

FLORIDA KEYS NATIONAL MARINE SANCTUARY (protected area)

Mandalay Wreck

PARK BOUNDARY

SANCTUARY BOUNDARY

Ball Buoy Reef

Rocky Reef

"21"
"22"

"4"

Anniversary Reef

Elkhorn Coral Reef

Pacific Reef

The Drop

W

pile

19th-century wooden sailing vessel wreck

Dante Fascell Visitor Center

Convoy Point
Park Headquarters

SW 304th St

SW 107th Ave

Florida's Turnpike (toll)

821

Coconut Palm Dr (SW 248th St)

CUTLER RIDGE

SW 87th Ave

Old Cutler Road

SW 184th St

SW 168th St

Coral Reef Dr (SW 152nd St)

SW 144th St

KENDALL

Don Shula Expy 874

Palmetto Expy 826

874

Ludlum Rd (SW 67th Ave)

SOUTH MIAMI

SW 57th Ave

Old Cutler Road

1

Goulds Canal

Black Creek

Fender Point

Breakwater

Black Point

BLACK POINT PARK (Miami-Dade County)

R "2"

Slow Speed Zone within 1000 feet of shoreline

DEERING ESTATE AT CUTLER (Miami-Dade County)

Cutler Power Plant

CHICKEN KEY

R "2"

Shoal Point

Fairchild Tropical Botanic Garden

MATHESON HAMMOCK PARK (Miami-Dade County)

G "1"

R "2"

BISCAYNE BAY

PARK BOUNDARY

Black Ledge

R "2"

Y "C"

Spoil area

W

W

Non-Combustion Engine Use Zone

R "6"

"4"

G "3"

"5"

FEATHERBED BANK

"X"

W "5"

INTRACOASTAL WATERWAY

R "2"

"1"

W

G "1B"

B I S C A Y N E   N A T I O N A L   P A R K

Idle Speed No Wake

University Dock

"4"

"2"

G "3"

harbor

ornamental lighthouse

RAGGED KEYS (private)

SANDS KEY

SANDS CUT

BOWLES BANK

LEWIS CUT

Boca Chita Key

SOLDIER KEY @Closed Area

SAFETY VALVE

Y "b"

Stiltsville

G "1A"

G "1"

G "21"

"19"

R "3"

"1"

Y "A"

R "4"

"2"

G "17"

"18" "20"

"16"

"15"

"14" "12"

"13"

STILTSVILLE

BISCAYNE CHANNEL

"11"

"10"

"8"

G "7"

Bill Baggs State Park

KEY BISCAYNE

BILL BAGGS CAPE FLORIDA STATE PARK

W

R "6"

"4"

G "3"

G "1"

W

R "2"

Boundary marker

"N"

Do Not Use This Map For Navigation Zones and regulations are subject to change. For safe boating, Use National Ocean Survey charts are indispensable. Use chart 11451 (purchase at visitor center) or charts 11462, 11463, and 11465.

BACHE SHOAL

G "11 BS"

"13"

"g"

R "8"

"7"

"9"

"4"

"2"

"3"

FOWEY ROCKS

Arratoon Apcar wreck

BREWSTER REEF

STAR REEF

Triumph Reef

Restricted Area

LEGARE ANCHORAGE

W "2TR"

LEWIS CUT

Everglades National Park Map

To Naples 25 mi

Big Cypress Bend

Carnestown

Big Cypress Swamp Welcome Center

Ochopee

H.P. Williams Roadside Park

Burns Lake

Turner Trail

Gulf Coast Visitor Center

Everglades City

Halfway Creek Canoe Tr

Tamiami Trail

Monument Lake

Kirby Storter Roadside Park

Oasis Visitor Center

Florida National Scenic Trail

Midway

Monroe Station

Air Boat Tours

Water Conservation Area 3A

Chokoloskee

Crooked Creek Chickee

Tiger Key

Picnic Key

Gator Hook Trail

BIG CYPRESS NATIONAL PRESERVE

Miccosukee Cultural Center

Tamiami Tr

Jewell Key

Lopez River

CYPRESS

Loop Rd (scenic drive)

Tree Snail Hammock

Pinecrest

Everglades Safari Park Gator Park

Rabbit Key

Sweetwater Bay Chickee

PINELAND

Mitchell Landing

Miccosukee Reserve Area

Shark Valley Visitor Center

Boat Tours

The Watson Place

Darwins Place

GULF OF MEXICO

Bobcat Boardwalk
Otter Cave Hammock Trail
Bicycles allowed on tram trail

Recent construction of bridges along this port of Tamiami Trail is designed to deliver more sheet flow of water into the park.

Mormon Key

New Turkey Key

Plate Creek Bay Chickee

Turkey Key

Lostmans Five Bay

Tram Tours

Observation Tower

HARDWOOD HAMMOCK

Hog Key

Wilderness Waterway

Willy Willy

FRESHWATER SLOUGH

Anhinga Trail

Chekika (closed)

South Florida National Parks

Lake Okeechobee

Big Cypress National Preserve

EVERGLADES NATIONAL PARK

Dry Tortugas National Park

Biscayne National Park

Rodgers River Bay Chickee

EVERGLADES NATIONAL PARK

FRESHWATER MARL PRAIRIE

Highland Beach

Camp Lonesome

Pa-hay-okee

Pa-hay-okee Overlook

Rock Reef Pass

Pinelands

Long Pine Key

Park Head

Broad River

Harney River Chickee

Canepatch

Pine Glades Lake

Long Pine Key Trail

Robertson Building

Ernest Visitor

Wilderness Waterway

A well–marked inland water route runs from Flamingo to Everglades City. Sequentially numbered markers guide you along its 99 miles (160 kilometers). Boats over 18 feet (6 meters) long or with high cabins and windshields should not attempt the route because of narrow channels.

and overhanging foliage in some areas. The route takes a minimum of six hours with an outboard motor or seven days by canoe. One-day round trips are not advised. Campsites are available on the route; backcountry permits are required.

COASTAL MARSH

Graveyard Creek

Shark River Chickee

Sisal Pond

Hole in the Donut wetlands restoration area

Nike Missile Base Historic Area
Daniel Beard Center

Ficus Pond

Royal Palm

Anhinga Trail
Gumbo Limbo T

PONCE DE LEON BAY

Little Shark River

Watson River Chickee

North River Chickee

Mahogany Hammock

Old Ingraham Hwy

Oyster Bay Chickee

Oyster Creek

Roberts River Chickee

Sweet Bay Pond

CYPRESS

Coe Visitor Center to Areas in the Park

Royal Palm	4mi	6km
Long Pine Key	6mi	10km
Pinelands	7mi	11km
Pa-hay-okee Overlook	13mi	21km
Mahogany Hammock	20mi	32km
Paurotis Pond	24mi	39km
Nine Mile Pond	27mi	43km
West Lake	31mi	50km
Flamingo Visitor Center	38mi	61km
Florida Bay Ranger Station	38mi	61km
Chekika	26mi	42km
Shark Valley Visitor Center	50mi	80km
Gulf Coast Visitor Center	92mi	148km

MANGROVE

Mud Bay

Joe River Chickee

WHITEWATER BAY

Lane Bay Chickee

Paurotis Pond

Hells Bay Canoe Tr

Nine Mile Pond

Pearl Bay Chickee

Hells Bay Chickee

Nine Mile Pond Canoe Trail

Lard Can

Noble Hammock Canoe Tr

TAYLOR SLOUGH

Coe Visitor Center to Other Areas

Homestead	11mi	18km
Miami International Airport	45mi	72km
Key West	135mi	217km

Northwest Cape

South Joe River Chickee

CAPE SABLE

Tarpon Creek

Wilderness Waterway

West Lake Restrooms

West Lake Canoe Trail

Long Lake

Nike Missile Base

Coot Bay Pond

Alligator Creek

Shark Pt Chickee

North N

Message to Boaters

Do not use this map for navigation. For safe boating, National Ocean Survey charts are indispensable. Charts 11430, 11432, 11433, 11451 are for sale at the Coe Visitor Center, Flamingo, and in the Everglades City area. Keys and beaches in Florida Bay

are closed to landings unless otherwise designated. Commercial fishing is prohibited in the park. Recreational fishing requires a license in both freshwater and saltwater. Where backcountry camping is allowed, a camping permit is required.

Middle Cape Canal

Bear Lake Canoe Trail

Homestead Canal

Mud Lake Canoe Trail

Buttonwood Canal

POLE/TROLL ZONE

Snake Bight Trail

Mrazek Pond

Rowdy Bend Trail

West Lake

East Cape

East Cape Canal

Clubhouse Beach

Eco Pond

Flamingo

Coastal Prairie Trail

Christian Point Trail

COASTAL PRAIRIE

Eco Pond

Johnson Key Chickee

Flamingo Visitor Center

North 0 1   5   10 Kilometers
0 1   5   10 Miles

FLORIDA BAY

Boat Tours

Little Rabbit Key

Everglades Ecosystems

Marine and Estuarine — Coastal Marsh

Freshwater Slough — Mangrove

Hardwood Hammock — Pineland

Freshwater Marl Prairie — Cypress

Coastal Prairie

Water Depths

0-3 feet (0-1 meter)

3-6 feet (1-2 meters)

Over 6 feet (Over 2 meters)

Hiking trail

Unpaved road

Wilderness Waterway and canoe trail

Pumping station

Lighted marker

Canal and gate

Wildlife protection area (limited access)

Water detention area

NPS Campground

Private campground

Interpretive trail

Bike trail

Tram tour

Airboat tour

Boat tour

NPS primitive campsite

Picnic area

Marina

Boat launch

Gas station

Lodging

Food service

Lignumvitae Key State Aquatic Preserve

Islamorada

Florida Keys National Marine Sanctuary

To Key West 70 mi

Intracoastal Waterway

Anne's Beach

Long Key

Everglades Basics

(305) 242-7700 | nps.gov/ever
Entrance Fee: $30/car
Lodging: A lodge* is coming soon
Camping: Long Pine Key, Flamingo

*reserve at flamingoeverglades.com

Everglades Driving Distances

Everglades is 1.5 million acres of freshwater prairie, mangrove forest, coastal marsh, and saltwater. While Ernest F. Coe Visitor Center serves as the park's information hub, most activity occurs at Flamingo, Shark Valley, and Gulf Coast Visitor Center. It takes some time to visit them all.

Flamingo	⟷ 45 minutes / 38 miles ⟷	Coe VC
Coe VC	⟷ 70 minutes / 49 miles ⟷	Shark Valley VC
Shark Valley VC	⟷ 55 minutes / 45 miles ⟷	Gulf Coast VC
Miami, FL	⟷ 60 minutes / 45 miles ⟷	Coe VC
Miami, FL	⟷ 50 minutes / 41 miles ⟷	Shark Valley VC

Why Visit Everglades?

- To see alligators, crocodiles and manatees in their natural habitats!
- Birds! There are many nesting and migratory birds.
- To paddle through a maze of mangrove forests
- To rent a houseboat and explore Whitewater Bay
- To paddle the 99-mile Wilderness Waterway
- To explore Shark Valley by foot, bike, or tram (with a guide)
- To join a boat tour from Flamingo or Gulf Coast Visitor Center

Shark Valley Tower

Everglades Favorites

Hikes: Anhinga (easy, 0.8 mile), Shark Loop Road (moderate, 15, bikes allowed, tram rides available)
Activities: Paddle West Lake Canoe Trail, paddle Turner River, Shark Valley Tram Tour, paddle Hells Bay Canoe Trail, tour a Nike Missile Site (ranger-led tours, December through March), rent a houseboat at Flamingo, ride an air boat near Shark Valley, take a boat tour at Flamingo or Gulf Coast

Look at all those little gators

What You Need to Know About Everglades

- If you're #1 goal is to see alligators, drive Tamiami Trail (US-41). Take the tram tour at Shark Valley and you're almost guaranteed to see a few. Otherwise stop at Oasis Visitor Center and drive Loop Road, where you'll find some (although this is Big Cypress National Preserve). Down by Coe Visitor Center, your best bet is usually Anhinga Trail. Gators need freshwater. If water is low, they'll be farther north or hiding out in a gator hole.
- Paddling is different here. Yes, there's unique wildlife (alligators and invasive Burmese pythons!) but they don't pose much of a problem to you. Rapids? You won't face those either. The maximum elevation in the park is eight feet and water flows into Florida Bay at roughly 0.25 mile per day. The difficulty is navigation. Some areas are maze-like. Others are huge open mangrove-lined expanses like Whitewater Bay. Both can be difficult to gain your bearings. Trails have markers. Follow them. There are platforms called chickees for overnight trips. Some were upgraded in 2022. Use them.
- Everglades is an important bird habitat, and thus a good place for birders. Favorite spots are Anhinga Trail, Christian Point, and Eco Pond.
- Vultures have taken up residence in the Anhinga Trail parking area. They're there to eat rubber seals found in vehicles. The best solution for now has been to wrap your car in tarp.

How Much Time Do You Have?

1 Day: With just one day, I'd start at Shark Valley. Take the tram or rent a bike and complete the 15-mile loop. Be sure to look carefully into the surrounding ditches—lots of little gators lurking in there! If you have some more time, head down toward Coe Visitor Center to hike Anhinga Trail.

2 Days: With another day, spend some time on the water. Boat tours at Flamingo (up into Whitewater Bay) and out of Gulf Coast (you'll probably see dolphins) are good. For a little more adventure, rent kayaks and paddle Turner River (near Gulf Coast) or West Lake. West Lake Trail is 7.7 miles one-way and will take a full day at a casual pace.

3 Days: An Everglades oddity is a Nike Missile Site not far from Long Pine Key Campground. It's only accessible with a ranger, so you'll have to check online for availability during your travel dates. Rangers also offer guided canoe trips (you must bring your own watercraft). Another great option is to rent a boat from Flamingo to explore the backcountry or Florida Bay. You'll see all kinds of birds and maybe a manatee or two.

Touring Buttonwood Canal

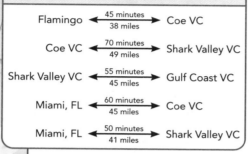

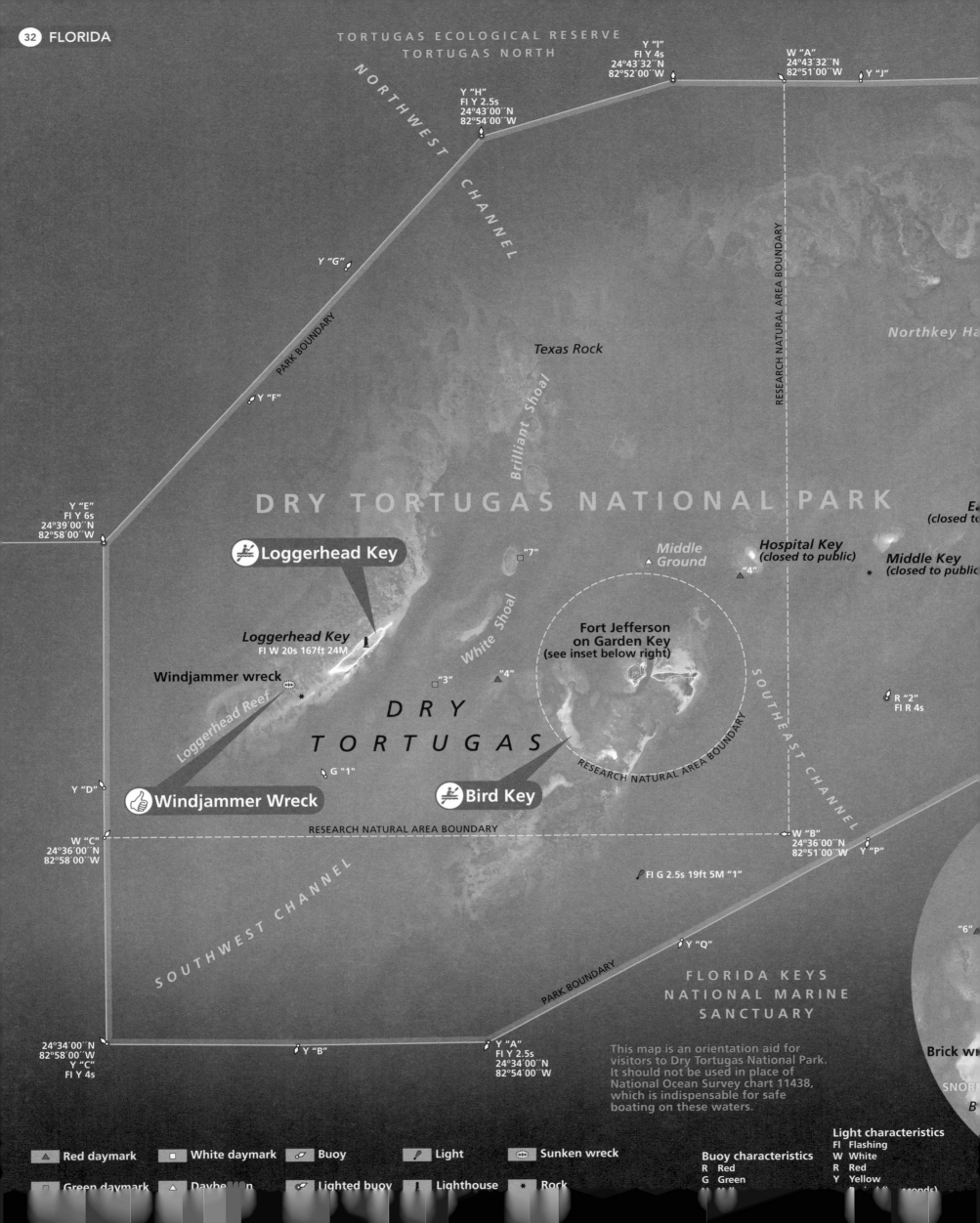

TORTUGAS ECOLOGICAL RESERVE
TORTUGAS NORTH

N O R T H W E S T

C H A N N E L

Y "I"
Fl Y 4s
24°43´32´´N
82°52´00´´W

W "A"
24°43´32´´N
82°51´00´´W

Y "J"

Y "H"
Fl Y 2.5s
24°43´00´´N
82°54´00´´W

PARK BOUNDARY

Y "G"

RESEARCH NATURAL AREA BOUNDARY

Northkey Ha

Texas Rock

Brilliant Shoal

Y "F"

D R Y   T O R T U G A S   N A T I O N A L   P A R K

E
(closed to

Y "E"
Fl Y 6s
24°39´00´´N
82°58´00´´W

Loggerhead Key

"7"

Middle
Ground

Hospital Key
(closed to public)

Middle Key
(closed to public

"4"

Loggerhead Key
Fl W 20s 167ft 24M

White Shoal

Fort Jefferson
on Garden Key
(see inset below right)

Windjammer wreck

"3"

"4"

Loggerhead Reef

R "2"
Fl R 4s

D R Y
T O R T U G A S

S O U T H E A S T   C H A N N E L

Y "D"

G "1"

Windjammer Wreck

Bird Key

RESEARCH NATURAL AREA BOUNDARY

W "C"
24°36´00´´N
82°58´00´´W

RESEARCH NATURAL AREA BOUNDARY

W "B"
24°36´00´´N
82°51´00´´W

Y "P"

Fl G 2.5s 19ft 5M "1"

S O U T H W E S T   C H A N N E L

"6"

Y "Q"

PARK BOUNDARY

F L O R I D A   K E Y S
N A T I O N A L   M A R I N E
S A N C T U A R Y

Brick wr

24°34´00´´N
82°58´00´´W
Y "C"
Fl Y 4s

Y "B"

Y "A"
Fl Y 2.5s
24°34´00´´N
82°54´00´´W

This map is an orientation aid for
visitors to Dry Tortugas National Park.
It should not be used in place of
National Ocean Survey chart 11438,
which is indispensable for safe
boating on these waters.

SNOR

B

▲ Red daymark   □ White daymark   Buoy   Light   Sunken wreck

□ Green daymark   △ Daybeacon   Lighted buoy   Lighthouse   * Rock

Buoy characteristics
R   Red
G   Green

Light characteristics
Fl   Flashing
W   White
R   Red
Y   Yellow

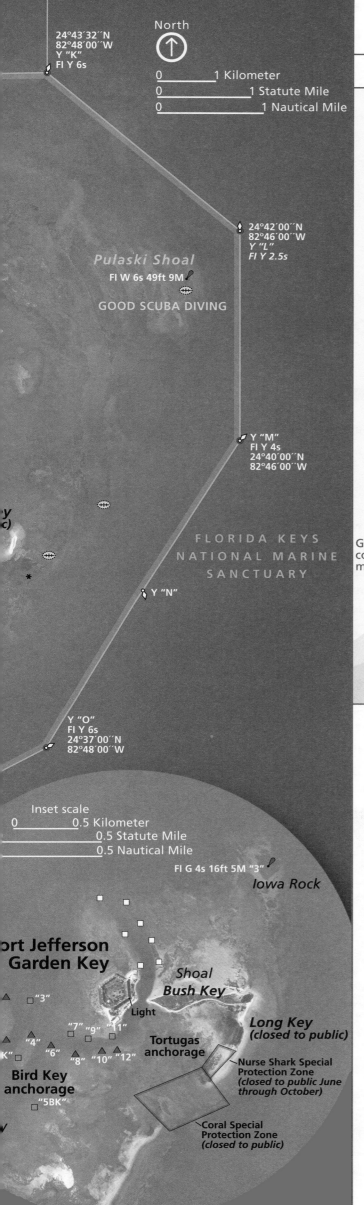

24°43'32''N
82°48'00''W
Y "K"
FI Y 6s

North
↑

0 _____ 1 Kilometer
0 _____ 1 Statute Mile
0 _____ 1 Nautical Mile

24°42'00''N
82°46'00''W
Y "L"
FI Y 2.5s

Pulaski Shoal
FI W 6s 49ft 9M

GOOD SCUBA DIVING

Y "M"
FI Y 4s
24°40'00''N
82°46'00''W

FLORIDA KEYS
NATIONAL MARINE
SANCTUARY

Y "N"

Y "O"
FI Y 6s
24°37'00''N
82°48'00''W

Inset scale
0 _____ 0.5 Kilometer
_____ 0.5 Statute Mile
_____ 0.5 Nautical Mile

FI G 4s 16ft 5M "3"

Iowa Rock

Fort Jefferson
Garden Key

Shoal
Bush Key

Light

"3"

"7" "9" "1"
"4"
"6" "8" "10" "12"

**Tortugas
anchorage**

*Long Key
(closed to public)*

Bird Key
anchorage

"5BK"

Nurse Shark Special
Protection Zone
*(closed to public June
through October)*

Coral Special
Protection Zone
(closed to public)

Fort Jefferson

0 100 200 Feet

0 100 200 Meters

North
↑

GARDEN
KEY

Good snorkeling

North
coaling
dock ruins

Swimming
area

Good snorkeling

MOAT

Magazine

Officers'
Quarters

Soldiers'
Barracks

Visitor
Center

Good snorkeling

Cistern

Park
Headquarters

Magazine

Harbor light

Seaplane
beach

Boat pier

Dockhouse

👍 Fort Jefferson

Swimming
area

Dinghy
beach

Good snorkeling off
coaling docks and
moat walls

South coaling
dock ruins

Good snorkeling

Visible ruin
🏕 Picnic area
🚻 Restrooms
⛺ Primitive campground

ANCHORAGE AREA

■ "11"

Dry Tortugas Basics
(305) 242-7700 | nps.gov/drto
Entrance Fee: $15/person
Lodging: None
Camping: Primitive camping
on Garden Key

Dry Tortugas Driving Distances
You can't reach Dry Tortugas by car,
and, quite frankly, that's a nice change
of pace. From Key West, you can reach
Garden Key by ferry (drytortugas.com) or
seaplane (keywestseaplanecharters.com).

Miami, FL ← 220 minutes → Key West, FL
170 miles

Why Visit Dry Tortugas?
- Spend the night and have
  an island almost entirely to
  yourself!
- Come for the birds, 10s of
  thousands of birds!
- Bring kayaks and paddle
  to Loggerhead Key and
  your own private snorkel!
- Tour a massive 19th-
  century fort

Dry Tortugas Favorites
Activities: Snorkel the
coaling docks and moat wall,
tour Fort Jefferson, paddle/
snorkel Loggerhead Key,
watch the birds, take the
seaplane (early or late) or
camp to have the park almost
entirely to yourself for a while

What You Need to Know About Dry Tortugas
- The park is open year-round and a couple thousand visitors arrive each month. Most people
  see April and May as the best time to visit but there's no bad time (except during a hurricane).
- You can't drive here. Visitors arrive aboard the *Yankee Freedom* (drytortugas.com) or seaplane
  (keywestseaplanecharters.com).
- Campsites are booked with a ferry ticket. You'll want to reserve them months in advance.
- Campers, be sure to keep your food and scented items in an animal-resistant food cannister
  (rats!). There are poles to hang your food but they aren't 100% rat-proof.
- *Yankee Freedom* has room for kayaks (for a fee). If you're comfortable in the open water and
  plan on spending the night, bring them along!
- Ferry passengers receive complimentary snorkel equipment. It's not bad, but if you have your
  own mask, bring that too.
- Serious birders come for spring and fall migration. Nearly 100,000 sooty turns nest on Bush
  Key each year, typically arriving in winter and departing in summer

How Much Time Do You Have?
It's more about how much time you
get. Chances are you'll arrive aboard
the *Yankee Freedom*. Their passengers
get five hours on the island. They lead
a one-hour tour of the fort (worth
joining). Lunch is served aboard the
boat. The rest of the time is at your
leisure (snorkeling, sunbathing, or
taking a longer look around Fort
Jefferson). Campers get an additional
24 hours. You can get a little alone
time by taking the early or late plane.

Fort Jefferson

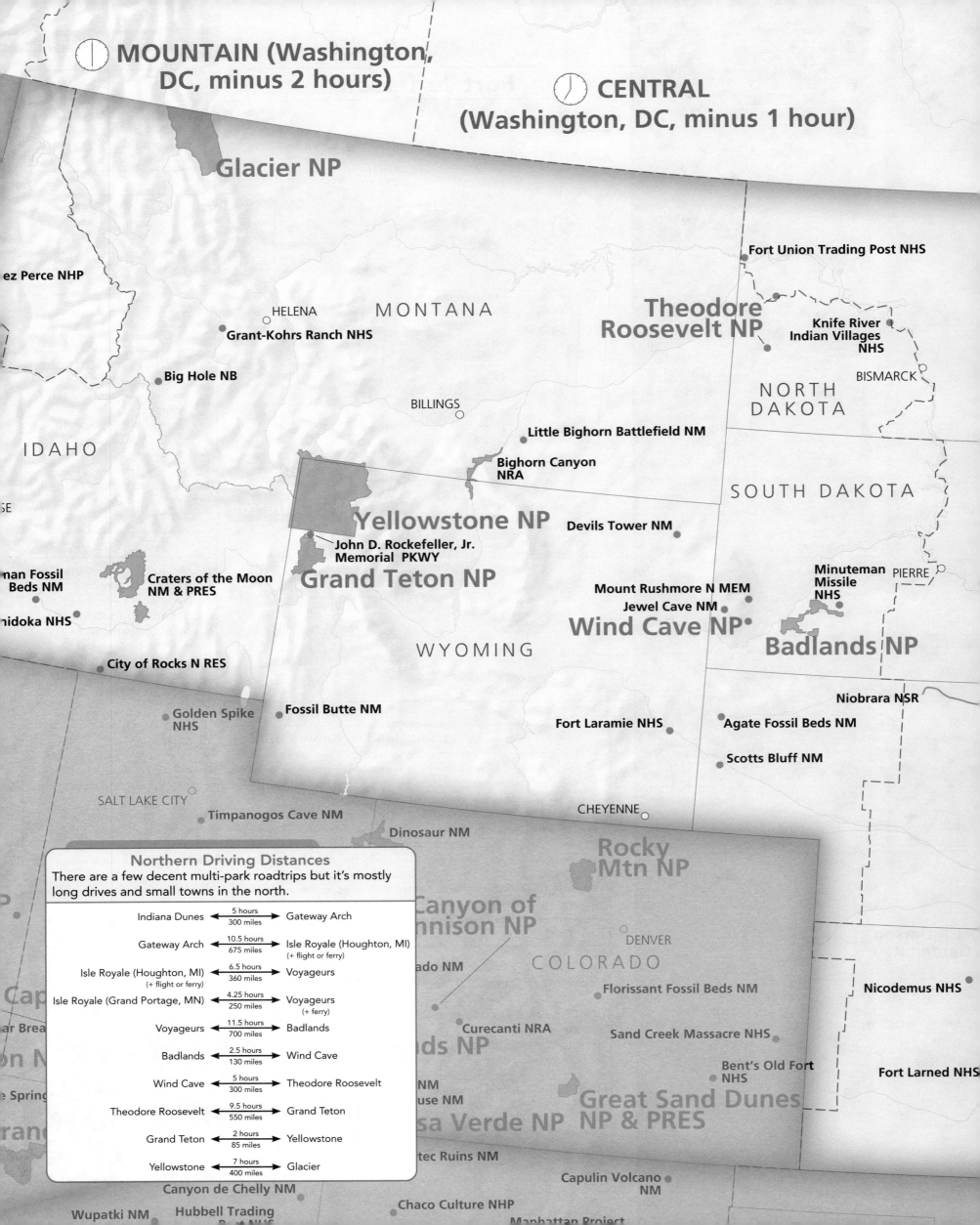

Glacier NP

Fort Union Trading Post NHS

ez Perce NHP

MONTANA

HELENA

Grant-Kohrs Ranch NHS

Big Hole NB

BILLINGS

IDAHO

Theodore Roosevelt NP

Knife River Indian Villages NHS

BISMARCK

NORTH DAKOTA

Little Bighorn Battlefield NM

Bighorn Canyon NRA

SOUTH DAKOTA

Yellowstone NP

John D. Rockefeller, Jr. Memorial PKWY

Devils Tower NM

nan Fossil Beds NM

Craters of the Moon NM & PRES

Grand Teton NP

Minuteman Missile NHS

PIERRE

hidoka NHS

Mount Rushmore N MEM

Jewel Cave NM

Wind Cave NP

Badlands NP

WYOMING

City of Rocks N RES

Niobrara NSR

Fossil Butte NM

Fort Laramie NHS

Agate Fossil Beds NM

Golden Spike NHS

Scotts Bluff NM

SALT LAKE CITY

Timpanogos Cave NM

CHEYENNE

Dinosaur NM

Rocky Mtn NP

Northern Driving Distances
There are a few decent multi-park roadtrips but it's mostly long drives and small towns in the north.

Indiana Dunes	←→ 5 hours / 300 miles	Gateway Arch
Gateway Arch	←→ 10.5 hours / 675 miles	Isle Royale (Houghton, MI) (+ flight or ferry)
Isle Royale (Houghton, MI) (+ flight or ferry)	←→ 6.5 hours / 360 miles	Voyageurs
Isle Royale (Grand Portage, MN)	←→ 4.25 hours / 250 miles	Voyageurs (+ ferry)
Voyageurs	←→ 11.5 hours / 700 miles	Badlands
Badlands	←→ 2.5 hours / 130 miles	Wind Cave
Wind Cave	←→ 5 hours / 300 miles	Theodore Roosevelt
Theodore Roosevelt	←→ 9.5 hours / 550 miles	Grand Teton
Grand Teton	←→ 2 hours / 85 miles	Yellowstone
Yellowstone	←→ 7 hours / 400 miles	Glacier

Canyon of nnison NP

DENVER

COLORADO

ado NM

Florissant Fossil Beds NM

Nicodemus NHS

ds NP

Curecanti NRA

Sand Creek Massacre NHS

Bent's Old Fort NHS

Fort Larned NHS

NM

use NM

Great Sand Dunes NP & PRES

sa Verde NP

Cap

ar Brea

n N

e Spring

rand

tec Ruins NM

Capulin Volcano NM

Canyon de Chelly NM

Chaco Culture NHP

Wupatki NM   Hubbell Trading

Manhattan Project

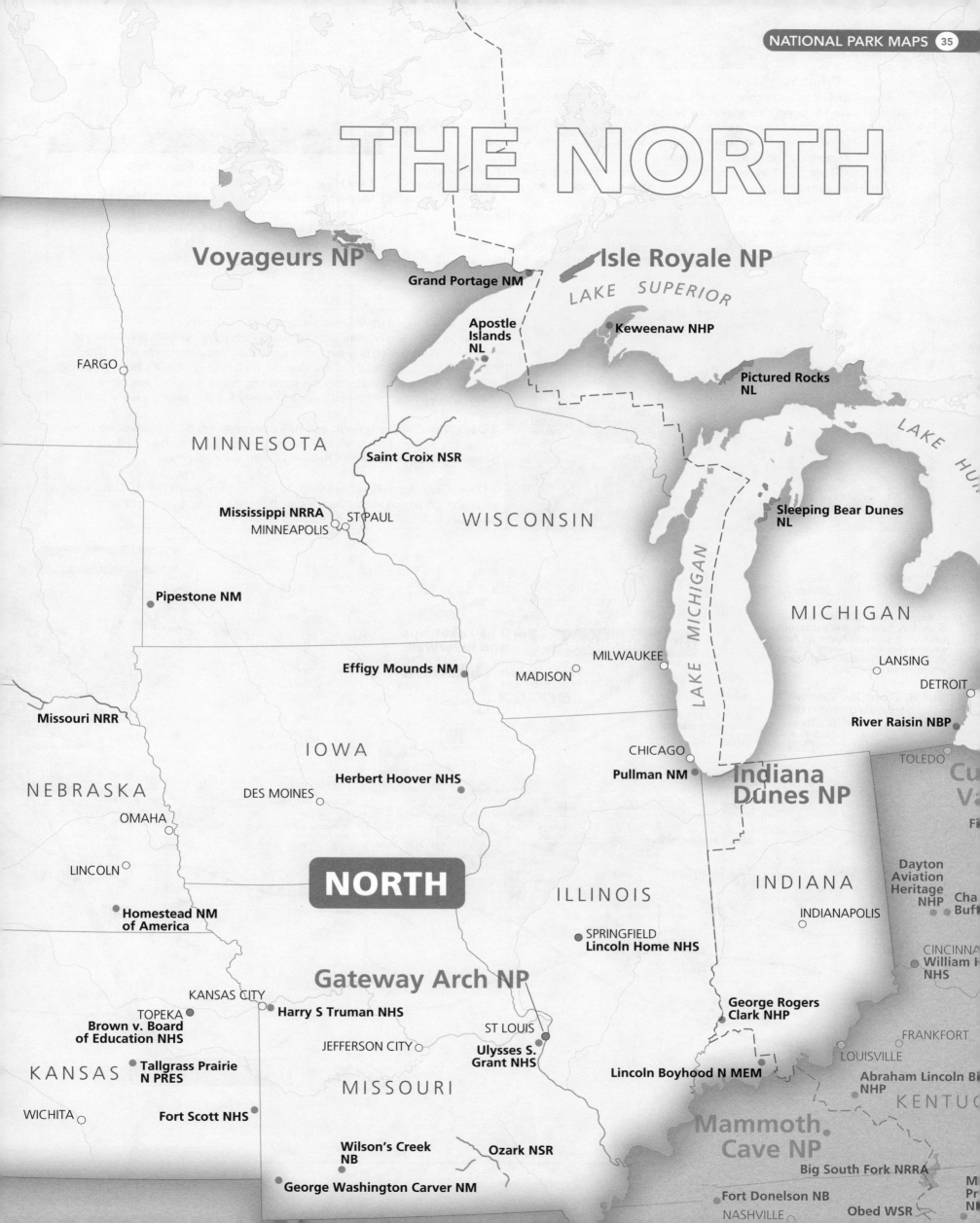

THE NORTH

Voyageurs NP

Isle Royale NP

Grand Portage NM

LAKE SUPERIOR

Apostle Islands NL

Keweenaw NHP

FARGO

Pictured Rocks NL

MINNESOTA

LAKE HU

Saint Croix NSR

Mississippi NRRA
ST PAUL

MINNEAPOLIS

WISCONSIN

Sleeping Bear Dunes NL

Pipestone NM

LAKE MICHIGAN

MICHIGAN

LANSING

DETROIT

MILWAUKEE

Effigy Mounds NM

MADISON

Missouri NRR

River Raisin NBP

IOWA

CHICAGO

TOLEDO

Cu
Va

Pullman NM

Indiana Dunes NP

Herbert Hoover NHS

NEBRASKA

DES MOINES

Fi

OMAHA

INDIANA

Dayton Aviation Heritage NHP

Cha
Buff

NORTH

ILLINOIS

LINCOLN

Homestead NM of America

INDIANAPOLIS

SPRINGFIELD
Lincoln Home NHS

CINCINNA
**William H
NHS**

Gateway Arch NP

KANSAS CITY

George Rogers Clark NHP

FRANKFORT

Harry S Truman NHS

TOPEKA

ST LOUIS

LOUISVILLE

Brown v. Board of Education NHS

JEFFERSON CITY

Ulysses S. Grant NHS

**Abraham Lincoln B
NHP**

KANSAS

Tallgrass Prairie N PRES

MISSOURI

Lincoln Boyhood N MEM

KENTUC

WICHITA

Fort Scott NHS

Wilson's Creek NB

Ozark NSR

Mammoth Cave NP

Big South Fork NRRA

George Washington Carver NM

Fort Donelson NB

M
Pr

Obed WSR

NASHVILLE

What You Need to Know About Indiana Dunes

- Indiana Dunes can be enchanting any time of year but summer is the most inviting (even if Lake Michigan's temperature first peaks at about 70°F in August).
- About half all visitors arrive between June and August.
- Being close to Chicago and South Bend, it's a popular weekend destination. Planning a weekday trip is a good idea.
- The South Shore Line (mysouthshoreline.com) connects the park with Chicago and South Bend by rail. You'll want a car at the park. The park is fairly disjointed so you'll want a car, but the train's a good way to visit Chicago.
- The park offers a unique mix of ranger programs. Be sure to check the official website or Facebook page to see what's happening.
- The national park brackets Indiana Dunes State Park. Here you'll find expansive beach, the Devil's Slide (a big sand dune), good hiking (3 Dunes Challenge), and year-round camping.

View from West Beach

Indiana Dunes Favorites

Easy Hikes: West Beach (1.2 miles), Riverwalk (0.9)
Moderate Hikes: Dune Succession (1), Mount Baldy (1.1, ranger tour required to scale dune), Pinhook Bog (2.1, ranger tour only), Paul H. Douglas (3.2)
Strenuous Hikes: Cowle's Bog (4.7)
Views: West Beach, Lake View, Bailly Homestead, Chellberg Farm, Portage Lakefront

Kemil Beach (with Dunbar and Lake View in the distance)

How Much Time Do You Have?

1 Day: Spend most of your time on the beach (especially if you're visiting in summer). West Beach is great but it's popular. You can also reach it by hiking Paul H. Douglas (formerly Miller Woods) Trail. Hiking Cowle's Bog, stopping at Mount Baldy, and watching the sunset from the lakefront are more good ideas, and you can get that all done in a very full day (with an early start).

2 Days: Visit Chellberg Farm and Bailly Homestead. Better yet, bring bikes and utilize some of the park's 37 miles of bike trails. Calumet Trail, running between Mount Baldy and Chellberg Farm, is a good choice.

3 Days: Consider taking the train into Chicago (or South Bend). Otherwise you can't go wrong with a beach day. If there's a ranger tour of Pinhook Bog, join it. Indiana Dunes State Park is very nice too!

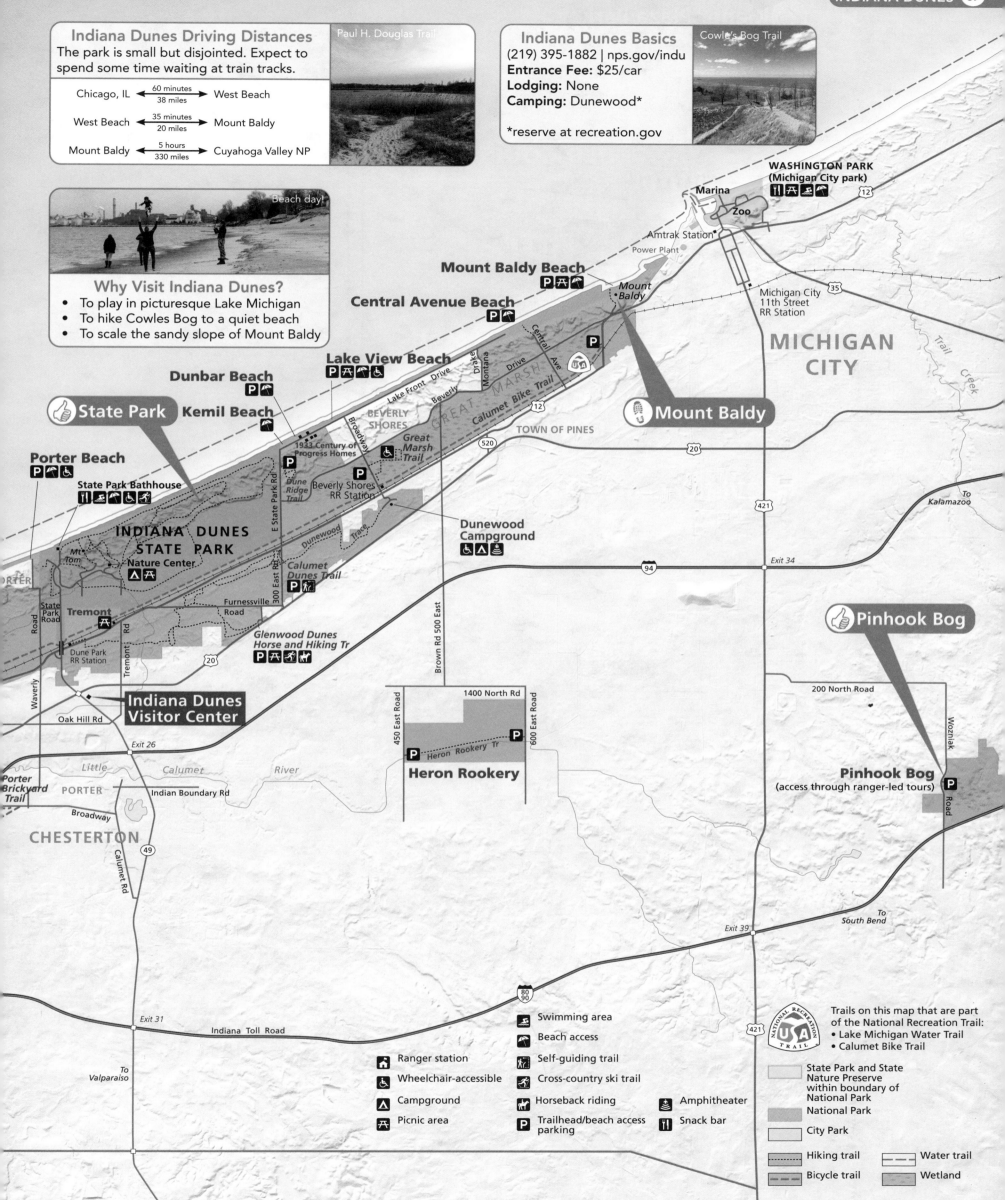

Indiana Dunes Driving Distances
The park is small but disjointed. Expect to spend some time waiting at train tracks.

Chicago, IL	60 minutes / 38 miles	West Beach
West Beach	35 minutes / 20 miles	Mount Baldy
Mount Baldy	5 hours / 330 miles	Cuyahoga Valley NP

Paul H. Douglas Trail

Indiana Dunes Basics
(219) 395-1882 | nps.gov/indu
Entrance Fee: $25/car
Lodging: None
Camping: Dunewood*

*reserve at recreation.gov

Cowle's Bog Trail

Beach day!

Why Visit Indiana Dunes?
- To play in picturesque Lake Michigan
- To hike Cowles Bog to a quiet beach
- To scale the sandy slope of Mount Baldy

WASHINGTON PARK
(Michigan City park)

Marina

Zoo

Amtrak Station

Power Plant

Mount Baldy Beach

Michigan City
11th Street
RR Station

Central Avenue Beach

Mount
Baldy

MICHIGAN
CITY

Lake View Beach

GREAT MARSH

Mount Baldy

Dunbar Beach

State Park

Kemil Beach

1933 Century of
Progress Homes

Great
Marsh
Trail

TOWN OF PINES

Calumet Bike Trail

BEVERLY
SHORES

Lake Front Drive

Porter Beach

State Park Bathhouse

Dune
Ridge
Trail

Beverly Shores
RR Station

Dunewood
Campground

To
Kalamazoo

INDIANA DUNES
STATE PARK

Mt
Tom

Nature Center

Dunewood Trace

Calumet
Dunes Trail

Furnessville
Road

Pinhook Bog

Tremont

Glenwood Dunes
Horse and Hiking Tr

Dune Park
RR Station

Waverly

State
Park
Road

Indiana Dunes
Visitor Center

200 North Road

Oak Hill Rd

Exit 26

1400 North Rd

Little Calumet River

Porter
Brickyard
Trail

PORTER

Indian Boundary Rd

Broadway

Heron Rookery Tr

Heron Rookery

Pinhook Bog
(access through ranger-led tours)

CHESTERTON

Exit 39

To
South Bend

Exit 31

To
Valparaiso

Indiana Toll Road

Trails on this map that are part of the National Recreation Trail:
- Lake Michigan Water Trail
- Calumet Bike Trail

Legend
- Swimming area
- Beach access
- Ranger station
- Wheelchair-accessible
- Campground
- Picnic area
- Self-guiding trail
- Cross-country ski trail
- Horseback riding
- Trailhead/beach access parking
- Amphitheater
- Snack bar

State Park and State Nature Preserve within boundary of National Park

National Park

City Park

Hiking trail
Bicycle trail
Water trail
Wetland

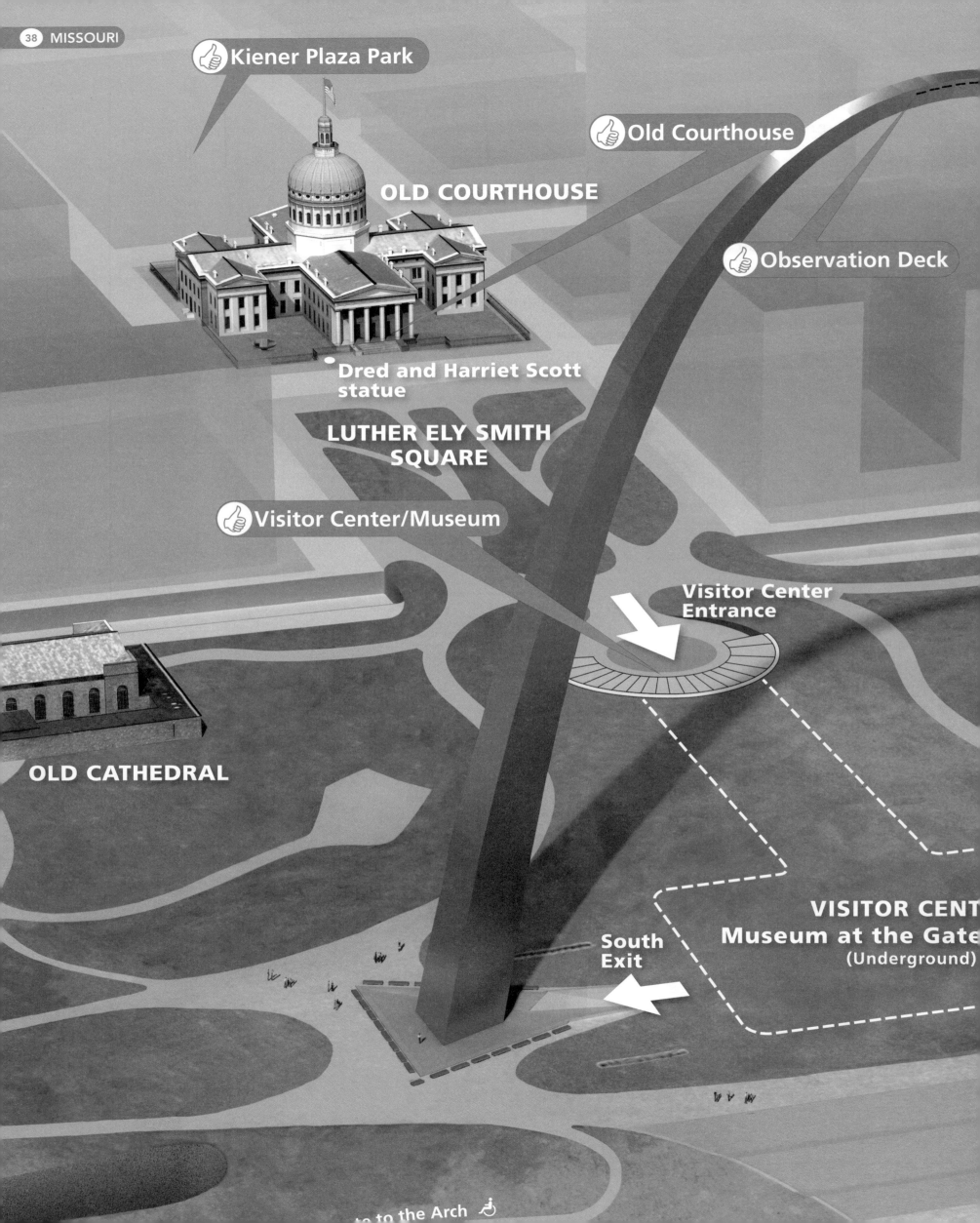

Gateway Arch Basics

(314) 655-1600 | nps.gov/jeff
Entrance Fee*: $3/person

*Additional fees for Tram Tour, Movie, River Cruise, and Helicopter Tour

Top-of-the-Arch View

Gateway Arch Driving Distances

The park is less than 100 acres and located in St. Louis. You navigate it on foot.

Chicago, IL ⟷ 5 hours / 300 miles ⟷ Gateway Arch

Gateway Arch ⟷ 4 hours / 250 miles ⟷ Kansas City

Gateway Arch ⟷ 5 hours / 300 miles ⟷ Nashville, TN

Gateway Arch Favorites

The center-piece is a massive stainless steel arch. Walk around the small urban park for different perspectives. Don't skip the museum and Top-of-the-Arch.

Views: Kiener Plaza Park, Top-of-the-Arch, in front of the Museum, by the legs, Mississippi Overlook in Illinois

Why Visit Gateway Arch?

- To see the one park that isn't like all the others
- And to admire the Arch from all the angles

Kiener Plaza Park

What You Need to Know About Gateway Arch

- About half all visitors arrive between June and August but summer isn't exactly the best time to visit. It's hot. The underground museum and riverboats are air conditioned. Spring, when trees are in bloom, is beautiful. Or, if you can catch a little snow on the ground, you're in for a real treat.
- Parking can be difficult to find. The most reliable nearby options are two parking garages on 4th Street, just north of the Arch.
- The museum is great and it's a good idea to take the tram to the top.
- You can reserve tram tickets in advance (gatewayarch.com) but make sure you arrive with enough time to pass through the airport-style security checkpoint. Allow at least 30 minutes. If there isn't a line, you can get a head start on browsing the informative exhibits. Reservations aren't required most days, but you may have to wait an hour or two to get to the top, particularly in summer.
- I prefer taking the tram in the morning when the sun is east of the city, but it's pretty good any time of day, even after dark.
- The museum's movie is interesting but it's a little pricey.
- The Old Courthouse features a few dated exhibits. Begin at the Legacy of Courage exhibit (about Dred Scott) and see how long the place holds your interest.
- Most people prefer being on the riverboat's top deck unless it's a sweltering hot summer's day.

To the North Gateway →

North Exit

Accessible Route to the Arch →

Mississippi Overlook

How Much Time Do You Have?

1 Day: You don't need more than a day to explore Gateway Arch (unless you have grander plans in St. Louis, like catching a baseball game). The whole park is under 100 acres. Check out the museum. Ride the tram. Walk around the grounds. Mississippi Overlook (on the other side of the river) is a good place to watch the sunset. Riverboat cruises (booked within the museum or at gatewayarch.com) or helicopter tours (gatewayhelicoptertours.com) are available. If you did everything, and very casually perused the Old Courthouse and Museum, you could conceivably stretch a Gateway Arch trip into an active three days.

ay Arch

HE GRAND
STAIRCASE

To Lewis and Clark statue

Isle Royale Basics

(906) 482-0984 | nps.gov/isro
Entrance Fee*: $7/person per day
Lodging: Rock Harbor Lodge** and Windigo Camper Cabins
Camping: 36 small primitive backcountry campgrounds

*please pay in advance at pay.gov
**reserve at rockharborlodge.com

Moose near Lookout Louise

Isle Royale Driving Distances

You can't get here by car. Ferries depart from Grand Portage, MN and Houghton and Copper Harbor in Michigan. You can also hop on a seaplane out of Houghton.

Minneapolis, MN	←5 hours / 300 miles→	Grand Portage, MN
Grand Portage, MN	←7 hours / 365 miles→	Houghton, MI
Houghton, MI	→70 minutes / 47 miles→	Copper Harbor, MI
Milwaukee, WI	←5.5 hours / 325 miles→	Houghton, MI
Detroit, MI	←9 hours / 600 miles→	Houghton, MI

Why Visit Isle Royale?

- To watch for moose and listen for wolves
- To get away from it all (Isle Royale is one of the least visited national parks and cars cannot reach the islands)

Isle Royale Favorites

Isle Royale is one-of-a-kind. While there is a lodge at Rock Harbor and camper cabins at Windigo, it's a park for backpackers and paddlers. With that in mind, we're just going to list a few favorite backcountry camps.

Camps: Lane Cove, Moskey Basin, Little Todd, McCargoe Cove, Siskiwit Bay

Near Minong Mine

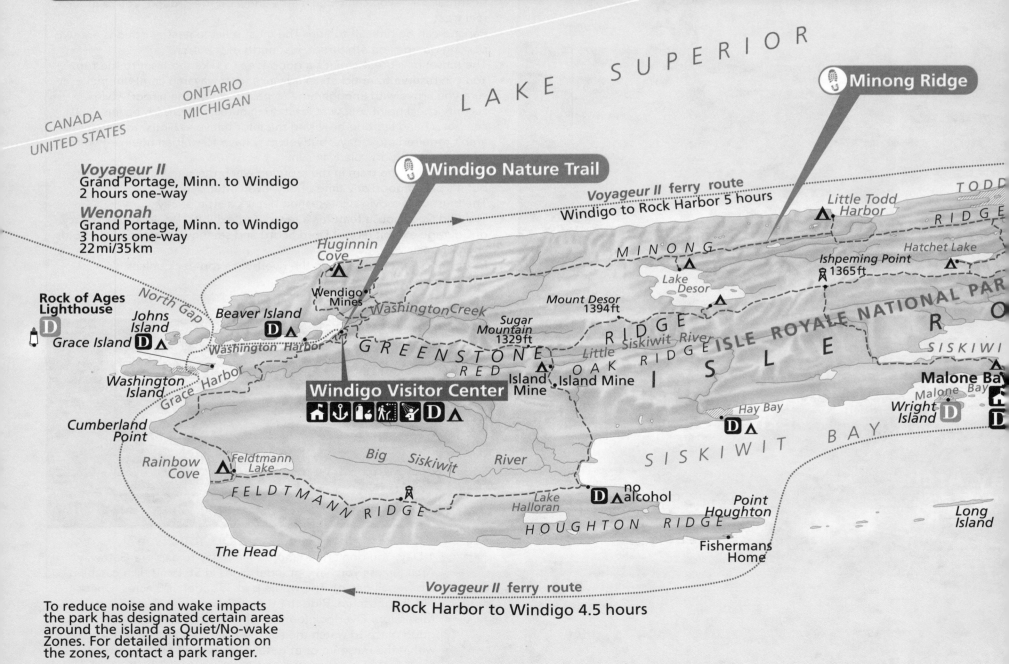

Voyageur II
Grand Portage, Minn. to Windigo
2 hours one-way

Wenonah
Grand Portage, Minn. to Windigo
3 hours one-way
22mi/35km

LAKE SUPERIOR

CANADA / UNITED STATES
ONTARIO / MICHIGAN

Minong Ridge

Windigo Nature Trail

Voyageur II ferry route
Windigo to Rock Harbor 5 hours

Little Todd Harbor

TODD RIDGE

MINONG

Hatchet Lake

Ishpeming Point 1365ft

Lake Desor

Mount Desor 1394ft

RIDGE

ISLE ROYALE NATIONAL PARK

Huginnin Cove

Rock of Ages Lighthouse

Johns Island

Grace Island

Beaver Island

Wendigo Mines

Washington Creek

Sugar Mountain 1329ft

RED

OAK RIDGE

Little Siskiwit River

ISLE RO

SISKIWI

North Gap

Washington Harbor

GREENSTONE

Island Mine

Island Mine

Malone Bay

Malone Bay

Washington Island

Grace Harbor

Windigo Visitor Center

Hay Bay

Wright Island

Cumberland Point

Rainbow Cove

Feldtmann Lake

Big Siskiwit River

SISKIWIT BAY

no alcohol

FELDTMANN RIDGE

Lake Halloran

Point Houghton

Long Island

The Head

HOUGHTON RIDGE

Fishermans Home

Voyageur II ferry route
Rock Harbor to Windigo 4.5 hours

To reduce noise and wake impacts the park has designated certain areas around the island as Quiet/No-wake Zones. For detailed information on the zones, contact a park ranger.

The Isle Royale National Park boundary extends 4.5 miles into Lake Superior from Isle Royale and the outer islands, or to the international boundary.

- - - - -	Trail
▨	Quiet/no wake zones

▲	Campsite
🗼	Lookout tower
🛢	Lighthouse

D	Overnight dock
D	Day-use only dock
⚓	Marina

What You Need to Know About Isle Royale

- Isle Royale is the only national park that closes for winter (November through mid-April). August is typically the best time to visit. It's warm, bugs are waning, and blueberries should be ripe for the picking.
- To reach the island you'll need to take a ferry or seaplane. Ferries depart from Grand Portage, MN (isleroyaleboats.com), Houghton, MI (nps.gov/isro), and Copper Harbor, MI (isleroyale.com). Seaplanes fly out of Houghton (isleroyaleseaplanes.com).
- You can daytrip to the island by taking the *Queen Royale IV* out of Copper Harbor, *Seahunter III* out of Grand Portage, or a seaplane out of Houghton, but you'll only have a few hours on the island, and you'll miss out on most of its charming aspects.
- Isle Royale is a backpacking/paddling destination. And, even though this is a remote, undeveloped destination, you should be fine as long as you have a little camping/backpacking/paddling experience and are fairly comfortable being uncomfortable. Still, planning is key. You'll want to call the park and scour its website (or purchase a more thorough guidebook), in order to be properly prepared.
- The *Voyageur II* (out of Grand Portage) makes several stops as it circumnavigates the island, allowing you to make one-way backpacking routes.
- There are a lot of moose on the island, and often times they're seen where most people are, Rock Harbor and Windigo. I've had best success using my ears. Listen for them sloshing in water, or passing your campsite early in the morning. If you hear something, take a look (safely, of course).
- By Isle Royale Standards, Daisy Farm, Three Mile, and Washington Creek are busy sites.

M.V. Sandy and Ranger III

How Much Time Do You Have?

If you're daytripping via seaplane, the *Queen Royale IV* (Copper Harbor), or *Seahunter II* (Grand Portage), your activities are going to be limited to exploring the area where you dock.

Backpacking from Rock Harbor, Three Mile to Lane Cove to Rock Harbor is a moderate 3-night trip. An extra night or earlier start and you could hike to Moskey Basin, McCargoe Cove, Daisy Farm, and back to Rock Harbor.

From Windigo, loop to Feldtmann Lake, Siskiwit Bay, and Island Mine.

Of course, you can spend more time or use *Voyageur II* to reach even more remote regions.

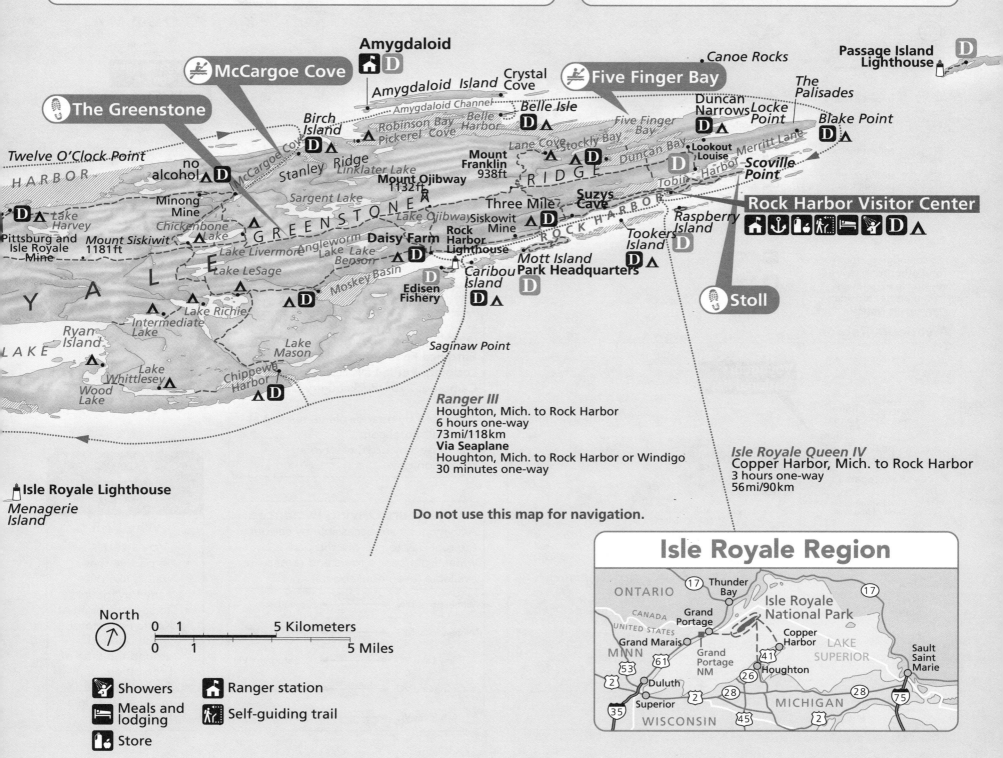

Ranger III
Houghton, Mich. to Rock Harbor
6 hours one-way
73mi/118km
Via Seaplane
Houghton, Mich. to Rock Harbor or Windigo
30 minutes one-way

Isle Royale Queen IV
Copper Harbor, Mich. to Rock Harbor
3 hours one-way
56mi/90km

Do not use this map for navigation.

Isle Royale Region

North

0 1   5 Kilometers
0 1   5 Miles

Showers
Meals and lodging
Store
Ranger station
Self-guiding trail

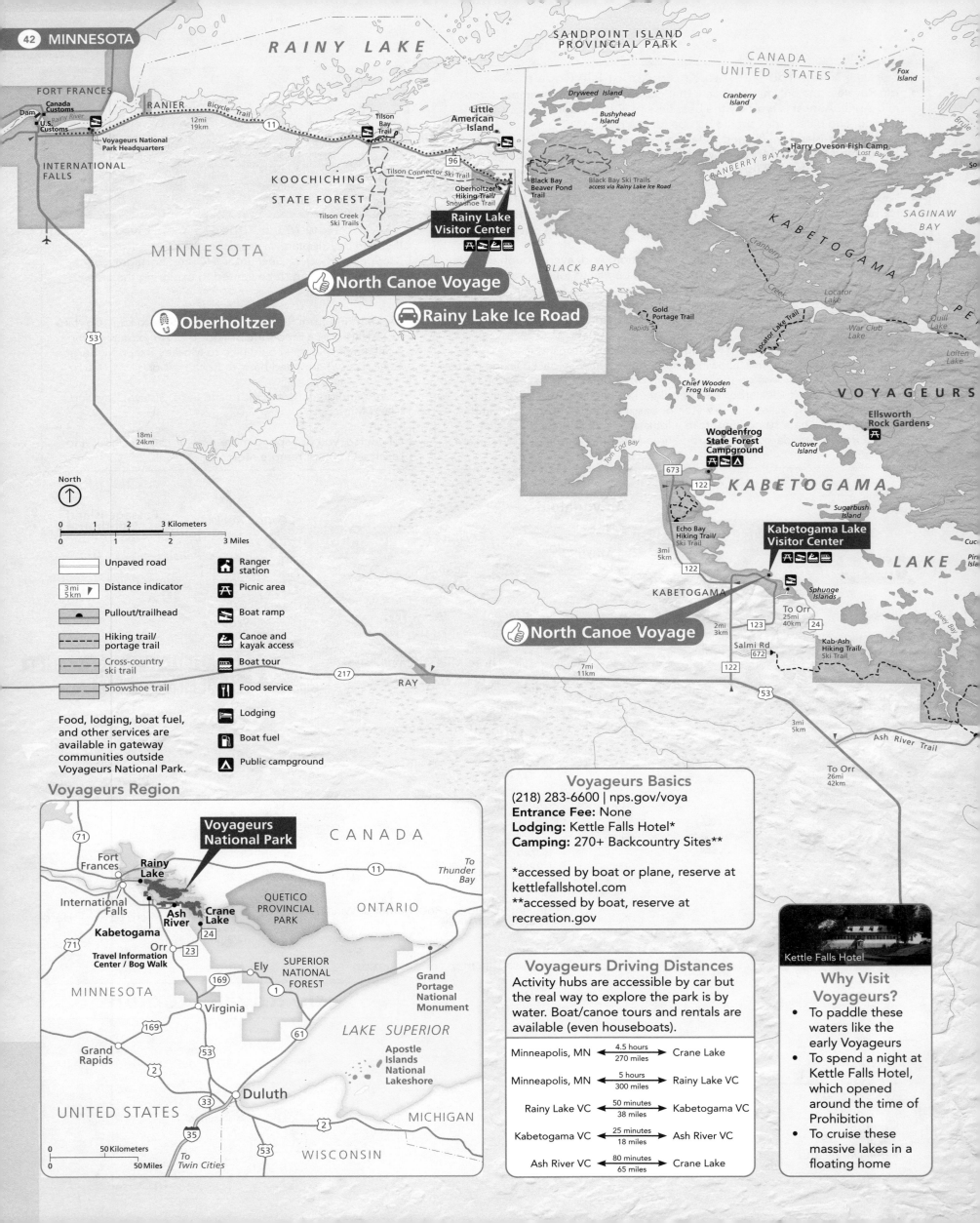

RAINY LAKE

SANDPOINT ISLAND PROVINCIAL PARK

CANADA
UNITED STATES

FORT FRANCES

Canada Customs

Dam
Rainy River
U.S. Customs

RANIER
Bicycle Trail
12mi
19km
11

Voyageurs National Park Headquarters

INTERNATIONAL FALLS

53

Tilson Bay Trail

Little American Island

96

Tilson Connector Ski Trail

KOOCHICHING STATE FOREST

Tilson Creek Ski Trails

Oberholtzer Hiking Trail/ Snowshoe Trail

Black Bay Beaver Pond Trail

Black Bay Ski Trails
access via Rainy Lake Ice Road

Dryweed Island

Bushyhead Island

Cranberry Island

Fox Island

Harry Oveson Fish Camp
Lost Bay

CRANBERRY BAY

SAGINAW BAY

KABETOGAMA

Rainy Lake Visitor Center

MINNESOTA

👍 **North Canoe Voyage**

👣 **Oberholtzer**

🚗 **Rainy Lake Ice Road**

BLACK BAY

Gold Portage Trail

Rapids

Cranberry Creek

Locator Lake

Locator Lake Trail

War Club Lake

Quill Lake

Loiten Lake

Chief Wooden Frog Islands

V O Y A G E U R S

Ellsworth Rock Gardens

Cutover Island

Tom Cod Bay

Woodenfrog State Forest Campground

673

122

K A B E T O G A M A

Sugarbush Island

Echo Bay Hiking Trail/ Ski Trail

3mi
5km

122

Kabetogama Lake Visitor Center

L A K E

KABETOGAMA

123

122

Salmi Rd

672

Kab-Ash Hiking Trail/ Ski Trail

Sphunge Islands

To Orr
25mi
40km

24

Daisy Bay

2mi
3km

7mi
11km

RAY

217

53

👍 **North Canoe Voyage**

3mi
5km

Ash River Trail

To Orr
26mi
42km

North
↑

0 1 2 3 Kilometers	
0 1 2 3 Miles	

▭	Unpaved road	🏛	Ranger station
[3 mi / 5 km]	Distance indicator	🍴	Picnic area
▬●	Pullout/trailhead	🚤	Boat ramp
┈┈	Hiking trail/ portage trail	🛶	Canoe and kayak access
┄┄	Cross-country ski trail	⛴	Boat tour
▭▭	Snowshoe trail	🍴	Food service
		🏨	Lodging
		⛽	Boat fuel
		⛺	Public campground

Food, lodging, boat fuel, and other services are available in gateway communities outside Voyageurs National Park.

Voyageurs Region

Voyageurs National Park

71

Fort Frances

Rainy Lake

CANADA

To Thunder Bay

11

International Falls

Ash River

Crane Lake

QUETICO PROVINCIAL PARK

ONTARIO

Kabetogama

71

Orr

Travel Information Center / Bog Walk

23

24

169

Ely

1

SUPERIOR NATIONAL FOREST

Grand Portage National Monument

MINNESOTA

169

Virginia

61

Grand Rapids

2

53

33

Duluth

35

UNITED STATES

WISCONSIN

To Twin Cities

LAKE SUPERIOR

Apostle Islands National Lakeshore

2

MICHIGAN

0 50 Kilometers	
0 50 Miles	

Voyageurs Basics

(218) 283-6600 | nps.gov/voya
Entrance Fee: None
Lodging: Kettle Falls Hotel*
Camping: 270+ Backcountry Sites**

*accessed by boat or plane, reserve at kettlefallshotel.com
**accessed by boat, reserve at recreation.gov

Voyageurs Driving Distances

Activity hubs are accessible by car but the real way to explore the park is by water. Boat/canoe tours and rentals are available (even houseboats).

Minneapolis, MN	←4.5 hours / 270 miles→	Crane Lake
Minneapolis, MN	←5 hours / 300 miles→	Rainy Lake VC
Rainy Lake VC	←50 minutes / 38 miles→	Kabetogama VC
Kabetogama VC	←25 minutes / 18 miles→	Ash River VC
Ash River VC	←80 minutes / 65 miles→	Crane Lake

Kettle Falls Hotel

Why Visit Voyageurs?

- To paddle these waters like the early Voyageurs
- To spend a night at Kettle Falls Hotel, which opened around the time of Prohibition
- To cruise these massive lakes in a floating home

What You Need to Know About Voyageurs

- Staying on land can be an underwhelming experience. Oberholtzer and Blind Ash Bay are nice trails, but they hardly emote the park's essence.
- Most visitors arrive in summer, when the lakes are most welcoming to the bevy of paddlers and boaters.
- To join a North Canoe Voyage, check the park website for a current schedule and call the respective visitor center to make reservations.
- Boat tours depart from Rainy Lake Visitor Center and Kabetogama Lake Visitor Center. Tickets can be reserved through recreation.gov.
- There are endless paddling opportunities. Without a water taxi your best bet is to depart from Ash River and paddle north into Lost Bay or east into Blind Indian Narrows. Neither name is too reassuring for easy navigation. And it isn't. Come prepared with map, compass, and GPS.
- You can cover much more water by boat. Still the distances are daunting. For example to reach Kettle Falls Hotel from either Rainy Lake or Crane Lake, you're looking at about a 30-mile boat trip. It's closer from Kabetogama, maybe 8 or 9 miles. Add another 12 miles to that from Ash River.
- If you don't plan on bringing your own boat, rentals are available. Select a boat with some speed and some size, to cover distance quickly and not be worried when the lakes get choppy (remember this is big open water). A depth finder with GPS is a big-time benefit.
- Houseboat rental is available. They're slow. They're big. You have to rent and tow a smaller boat (in case of emergency). But it's comfortable and some outfitters will even ferry food and fuel out to you so you don't have to deviate from your itinerary for provisions.
- Most of the lakes are very deep so you rarely have to worry about hitting bottom but there are several narrows (some with blind corners) where you must use caution and be courteous of other boaters. Houseboats need to look out for speedboats, and vice versa.
- Don't forget your passport if you plan to visit Canada or fish in its waters.
- If you'd like to have an entire park almost to yourself, visit in winter. About 85% of all guests arrive between May and September. Once the lakes freeze over (typically January), a few bundled up snowmobilers, fishermen, and motorists (via ice roads) take to the park to enjoy its icy wonders.

Driving the ice roads

Voyageurs Favorites

Hikes: Anderson Bay (moderate, 1.8 miles), Cruiser Lake (strenuous, 9.5), Blind Ash Bay (moderate, 1.2)

Activities: Cruising to Grassy Bay Cliffs, sleeping at the park's remote campsites, joining a North Canoe Voyage Ranger Program, driving the ice roads in the depths of winter

Grassy Bay Cliffs

House-boating

How Much Time Do You Have?

More than one-third of the park is water, so to get to know it, you'll need to leave your vehicle behind. If you aren't comfortable boating or paddling on your own, be sure to join a boat tour (recreation.gov) or North Canoe Voyage. Plan at least two nights, if you're going to boat it yourself, and plan your trip very carefully. There's a whole lot of water out there, and it's fairly easy to get disoriented.

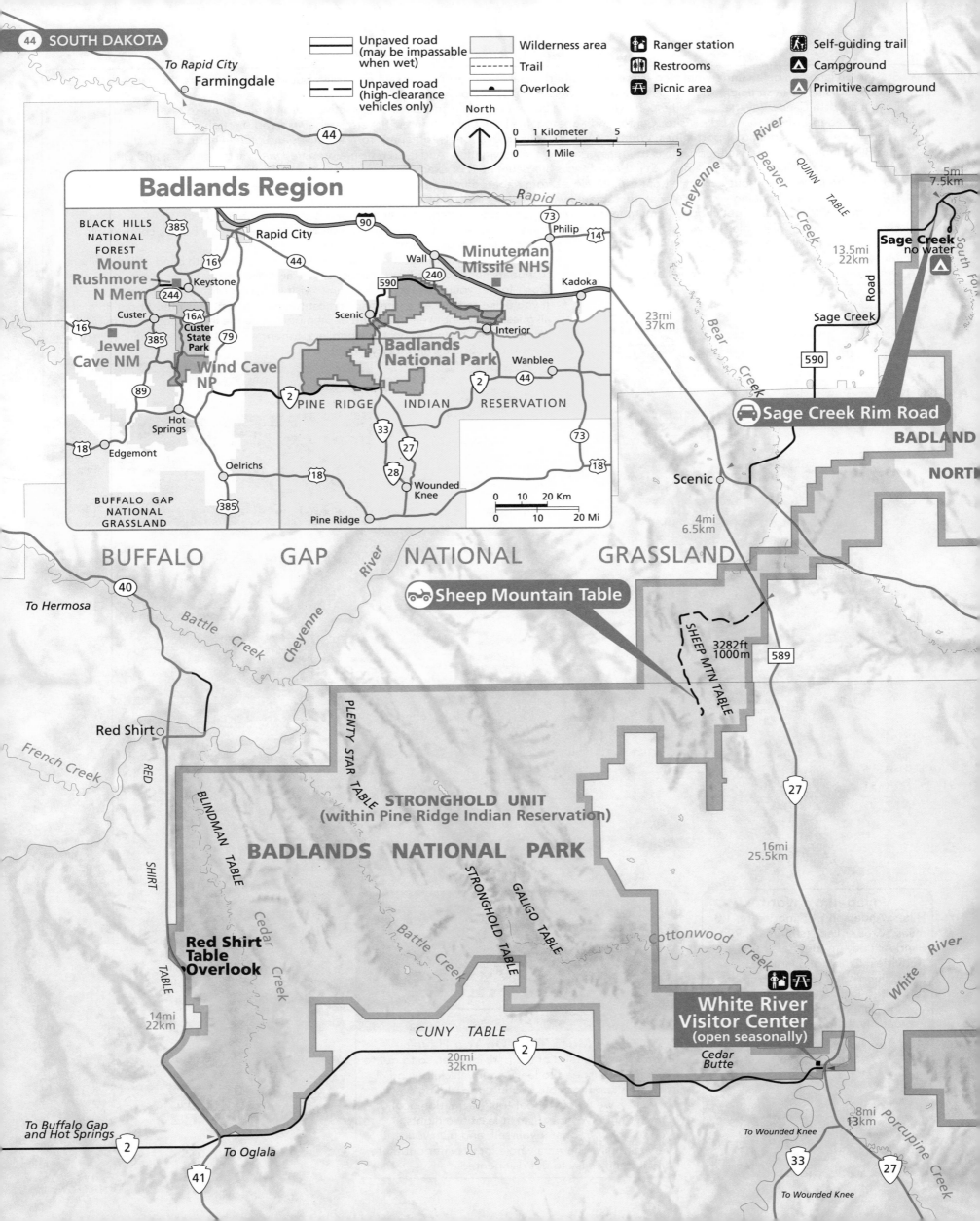

44 SOUTH DAKOTA

Legend:
- Unpaved road (may be impassable when wet)
- Unpaved road (high-clearance vehicles only)
- Wilderness area
- Trail
- Overlook
- Ranger station
- Restrooms
- Picnic area
- Self-guiding trail
- Campground
- Primitive campground

North

0 — 1 Kilometer — 5
0 — 1 Mile — 5

To Rapid City
Farmingdale

Badlands Region

BLACK HILLS NATIONAL FOREST

Mount Rushmore N Mem

Keystone

Rapid City

Wall

Philip

Minuteman Missile NHS

Kadoka

Custer

Jewel Cave NM

Custer State Park

Scenic

Interior

Badlands National Park

Wanblee

Wind Cave NP

Hot Springs

PINE RIDGE   INDIAN   RESERVATION

Edgemont

Oelrichs

Wounded Knee

BUFFALO GAP NATIONAL GRASSLAND

Pine Ridge

0 — 10 — 20 Km
0 — 10 — 20 Mi

5mi
7.5km

Sage Creek
no water

13.5mi
22km

Sage Creek

590

Sage Creek Rim Road

BADLAND

NORTH

23mi
37km

Scenic

4mi
6.5km

BUFFALO   GAP   NATIONAL   GRASSLAND

To Hermosa

40

Sheep Mountain Table

SHEEP MTN TABLE
3282ft
1000m

589

Red Shirt

French Creek

Battle Creek

Cheyenne River

16mi
25.5km

27

PLENTY STAR TABLE

STRONGHOLD UNIT
(within Pine Ridge Indian Reservation)

BLINDMAN TABLE

BADLANDS   NATIONAL   PARK

RED SHIRT TABLE

Cedar Creek

STRONGHOLD TABLE

GALIGO TABLE

Battle Creek

Cottonwood Creek

White River

Red Shirt Table Overlook

14mi
22km

CUNY TABLE

20mi
32km

2

Cedar Butte

White River Visitor Center
(open seasonally)

To Buffalo Gap and Hot Springs

2

41

To Oglala

33

27

8mi
13km

Porcupine Creek

To Wounded Knee

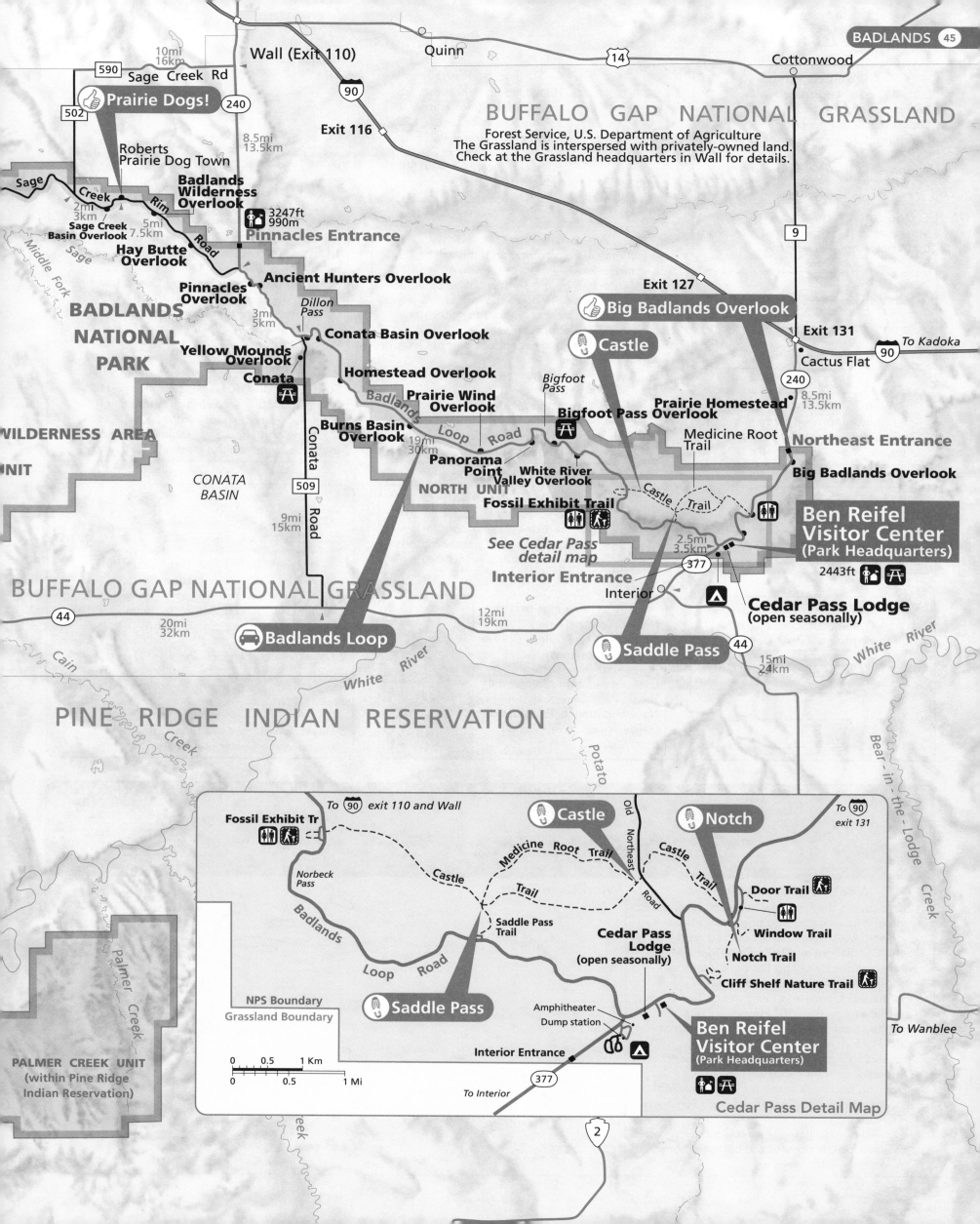

Badlands Basics

(605) 433-5361 | nps.gov/badl
Entrance Fee: $30/car
Lodging: Cedar Pass Lodge*
Camping: Cedar Pass*, Sage Creek

*reserve at cedarpasslodge.com

Badlands Driving Distances

Most visitors just drive-thru. I guess that's better than driving by.

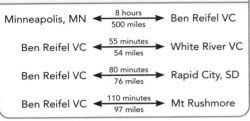

Minneapolis, MN	8 hours / 500 miles	Ben Reifel VC
Ben Reifel VC	55 minutes / 54 miles	White River VC
Ben Reifel VC	80 minutes / 76 miles	Rapid City, SD
Ben Reifel VC	110 minutes / 97 miles	Mt Rushmore

Why Visit Badlands?

- To photograph and hike among some of the most beautiful rock formations on the planet!

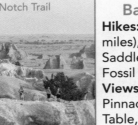
Notch Trail

Badlands Favorites

Hikes: Notch (moderate, 1.5 miles), Castle (moderate, 10), Saddle Pass (strenuous, 0.25), Fossil Exhibit (easy, 0.25)
Views: Big Badlands Overlook, Pinnacles Overlook, Red Shirt Table, Hay Butte Overlook

What You Need to Know

- Summer is most popular, but it will be hot and trails are almost entirely exposed. Winter can be unbearably cold, but snow really makes the badlands formations pop. Spring can be wet and muddy. Storms are typically brief but intense.
- The park is nearly abandoned from October through April.
- If you're just driving through, it's about an hour-long detour from I-90.
- Sheep, bison, and prairie dogs are commonly seen.
- If the campground is full, there's BLM land north of the Pinnacles Entrance.

Big Badlands Overlook

How Much Time Do You Have?

1 Day: A full day can be just enough to get a good look of Badlands. Drive Badlands Loop Road and hike Notch Trail and Castle Trail (shorten the hike by parking on Old Northeast Road). With more time, continue along unpaved Sage Creek Rim Road, stopping at Robert's Prairie Dog Town.

2 Days: With another day, head over to the Stronghold Unit. A 4x4 unlocks the road to Sheep Mountain Table, which is fantastic. You can hike or bike (or camp) up there too. Continue on to Red Shirt Table Overlook and explore at your leisure. It's beautiful country.

Wind Cave Basics

(605) 745-4600 | nps.gov/wica
Entrance Fee: None
Lodging: None
Camping: Elk Mountain

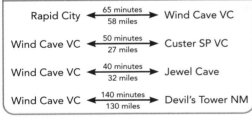
Bison

Why Visit Wind Cave?

- Come for the cave, stick around for the bison, prairie dogs, and elk!
- It's a great wildlife park, with tons to do in the surrounding area

Wind Cave Driving Distances

The park is small but there's a lot to see in this corner of South Dakota.

Rapid City	65 minutes / 58 miles	Wind Cave VC
Wind Cave VC	50 minutes / 27 miles	Custer SP VC
Wind Cave VC	40 minutes / 32 miles	Jewel Cave
Wind Cave VC	140 minutes / 130 miles	Devil's Tower NM

Wind Cave Favorites

Hikes: Highland Creek (strenuous, 17.2 miles), Cold Brook Canyon (easy, 2.8), East Bison Flats (moderate, 7.4), Lookout Point (moderate, 4.4)
Tours: Wild Cave, Candlelight, Natural Entrance, Fairgrounds, Garden of Eden (they're all pretty great!)

Cave Opening

NPS-5

How Much Time Do You Have?

1 Day: Take a cave tour. Natural Entrance is a good choice. If you're looking to crawl around, go for Wild Cave. And then look for animals. Prairie dogs are everywhere. So are bison.

2 Days: Nearby Black Elk Peak Trail is a good choice. East Bison Flat or Cold Brook Canyon or Rankin Ridge are nice in-park options. NPS-5 is a decent drive too.

3 Days: Spend the extra time at nearby attractions like Custer State Park.

Did prairie dogs excavate the caves? Well, no, but it's great prairie dog country!

What You Need to Know

- The cave is the big draw here, so you should go in it (unless you won't be comfortable down there). Reservations are required for the Candlelight and Wild Cave Tours. Make reservations by calling the park. All other tours are first-come, first-served.
- Natural Entrance and Fairgrounds Tours include more than 300 stairs.
- While I think the Wild Cave Tour is a great deal of fun, many people won't enjoy spending a couple hours crawling around in the dark on their hands and knees.
- You can backpack in the park, but only in the northwest corner (Centennial Trail, Sanctuary Trail, etc.)
- Driving around you're sure to find bison and prairie dogs. It's one of the better national parks for wildlife viewing.

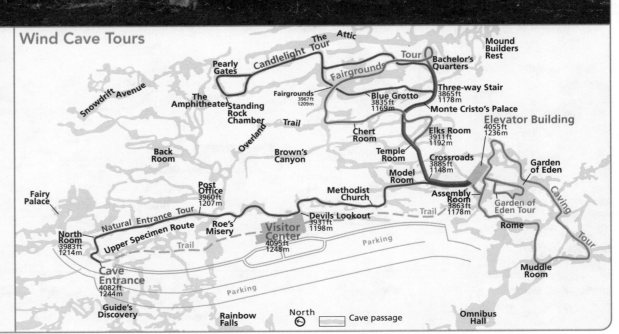

Wind Cave Tours

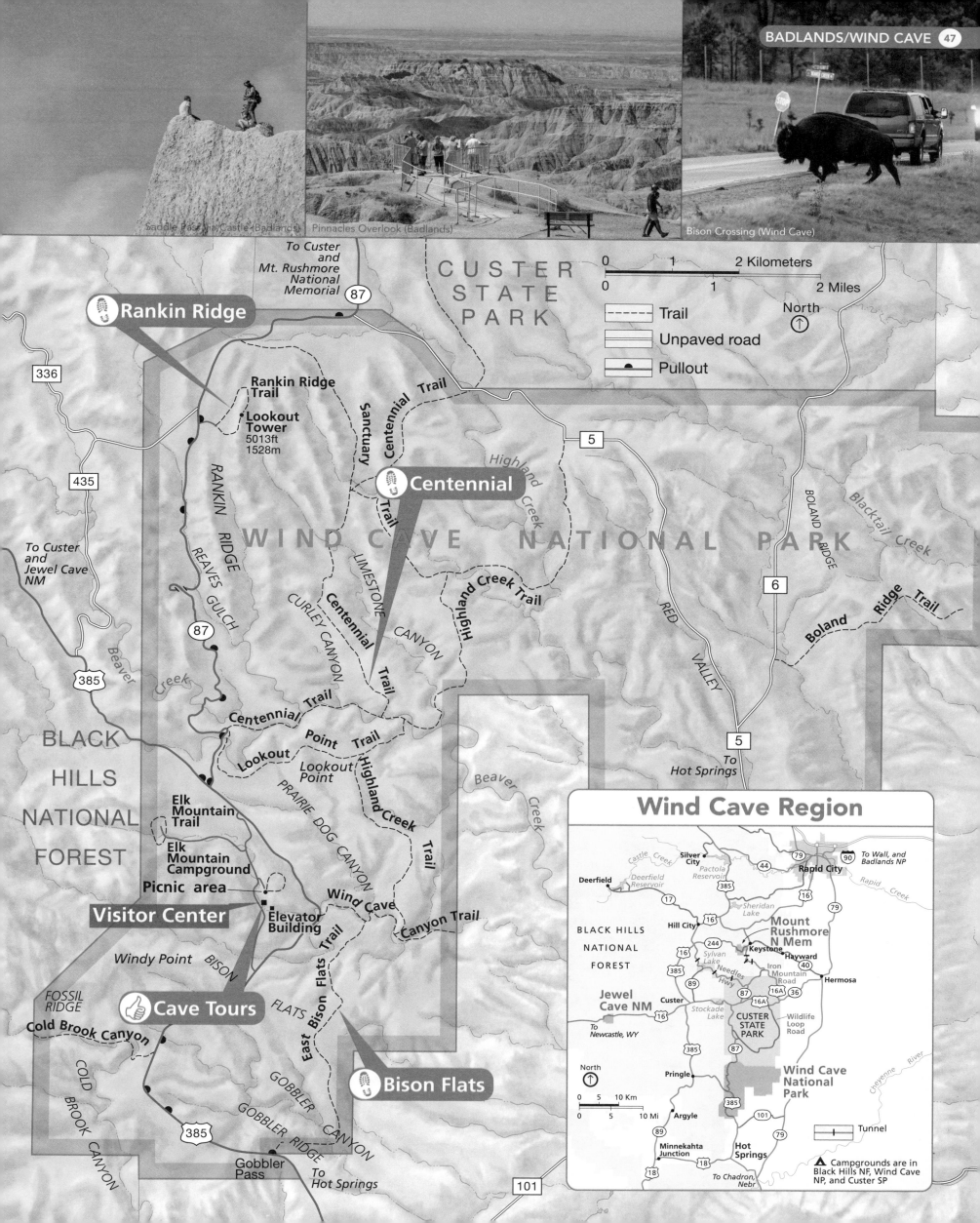

Saddle Pass via Castle (Badlands)   Pinnacles Overlook (Badlands)

Bison Crossing (Wind Cave)

To Custer and Mt. Rushmore National Memorial 87

C U S T E R
S T A T E
P A R K

0   1   2 Kilometers
0   1   2 Miles

North

- - - - - Trail
═══════ Unpaved road
●━━━━━ Pullout

Rankin Ridge

336

435

Rankin Ridge Trail

Lookout Tower 5013ft 1528m

Centennial Trail

5

Sanctuary Trail

Centennial

Highland Creek

W I N D   C A V E   N A T I O N A L   P A R K

6

BOLAND RIDGE

Blacktail Creek

To Custer and Jewel Cave NM

385

RANKIN RIDGE

REAVES GULCH

87

CURLEY CANYON

Centennial Trail

LIMESTONE CANYON

Highland Creek Trail

RED VALLEY

Boland Ridge Trail

Beaver Creek

Centennial Trail

Lookout

Lookout Point

Point Trail

Highland Creek Trail

5

To Hot Springs

BLACK HILLS NATIONAL FOREST

Elk Mountain Trail

Elk Mountain Campground

Picnic area

PRAIRIE DOG CANYON

Beaver Creek

Visitor Center

Elevator Building

Wind Cave

Highland Creek Trail

Wind Cave Region

Canyon Trail

Windy Point

BISON FLATS

FOSSIL RIDGE

Cave Tours

Cold Brook Canyon

COLD BROOK CANYON

385

East Bison Flats Trail

Bison Flats

GOBBLER CANYON

GOBBLER RIDGE

Gobbler Pass

To Hot Springs

101

Wind Cave Region

Castle Creek

Silver City

Deerfield Reservoir

Pactola Reservoir

Deerfield

44

79

90 **To Wall, and Badlands NP**

Rapid City

Rapid Creek

BLACK HILLS NATIONAL FOREST

17

385

Hill City

16

Sheridan Lake

16

Mount Rushmore N Mem

79

Jewel Cave NM

244

Keystone

Hayward

40

Custer

16

385

89

Sylvan Lake

Needles Hwy

Iron Mountain Road

87

16A

36

Hermosa

To Newcastle, WY

385

Stockade Lake

CUSTER STATE PARK

Wildlife Loop Road

North

Pringle

Wind Cave National Park

Cheyenne River

0   5   10 Km
0   5   10 Mi

385

Argyle

101

89

Minnekahta Junction

18

79

Hot Springs

═╪═ Tunnel

▲ Campgrounds are in Black Hills NF, Wind Cave NP, and Custer SP

18

To Chadron, Nebr

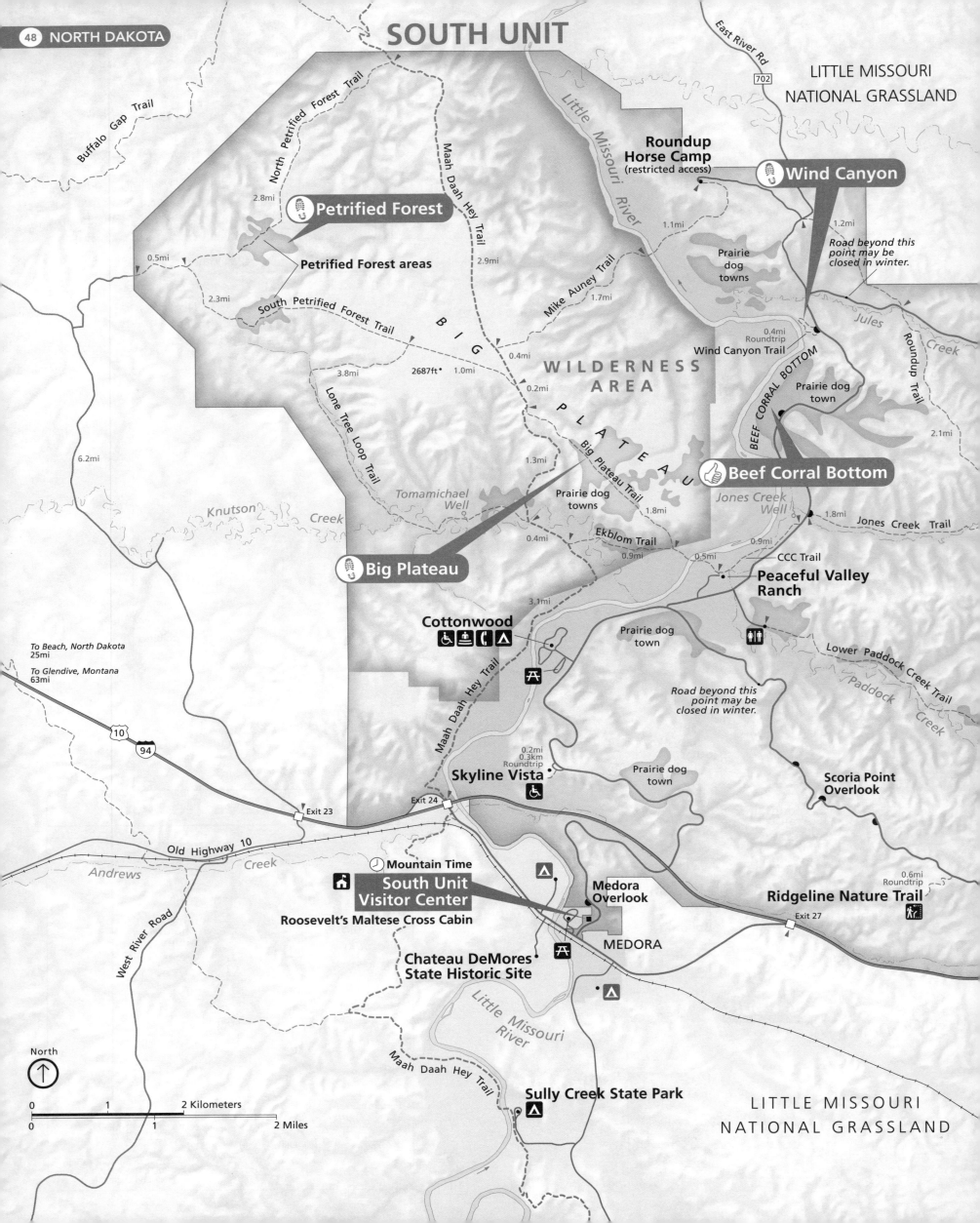

SOUTH UNIT

LITTLE MISSOURI
NATIONAL GRASSLAND

Buffalo Gap Trail

North Petrified Forest Trail

2.8mi

👣 **Petrified Forest**

Petrified Forest areas

0.5mi

2.3mi

South Petrified Forest Trail

Maah Daah Hey Trail

2.9mi

B I G

3.8mi   2687ft•   1.0mi

Lone Tree Loop Trail

Knutson   Creek

Tomamichael
Well

0.4mi

WILDERNESS
AREA

P L A T E A U

1.3mi

Big Plateau Trail

Prairie dog
towns

6.2mi

0.4mi

👣 **Big Plateau**

Ekblom Trail   1.8mi

0.9mi

3.1mi

Cottonwood
♿ ⛵ 🚻 ⛺

🏕

**Roundup
Horse Camp**
(restricted access)

👟 **Wind Canyon**

East River Rd

702

1.1mi

Prairie dog
towns

1.2mi

Road beyond this
point may be
closed in winter.

Mike Auney Trail   1.7mi

Jules

0.4mi
Roundtrip

Wind Canyon Trail

BEEF CORRAL BOTTOM

Prairie dog
town

Creek

Roundup Trail

2.1mi

👍 **Beef Corral Bottom**

Jones Creek
Well

1.8mi   Jones Creek Trail

0.9mi

0.5mi   CCC Trail

**Peaceful Valley
Ranch**
🚻

Prairie dog
town

Lower Paddock Creek Trail

Paddock Creek

Road beyond this
point may be
closed in winter.

To Beach, North Dakota
25mi

To Glendive, Montana
63mi

10

94

Exit 23

Exit 24

Old Highway 10

Andrews   Creek

West River Road

🕐 **Mountain Time**

🏠 **South Unit
Visitor Center**

Roosevelt's Maltese Cross Cabin

🏕

**Chateau DeMores
State Historic Site**

🏕

Medora
Overlook

MEDORA

🏕

0.2mi
0.3km
Roundtrip

Skyline Vista ♿

Prairie dog
town

Prairie dog
town

Scoria Point
Overlook

0.6mi
Roundtrip

Ridgeline Nature Trail
🚶

Exit 27

Little
Missouri
River

Maah Daah Hey Trail

Sully Creek State Park
🏕

North
↑

| 0 | | 1 | | 2 Kilometers |

| 0 | 1 | 2 Miles |

LITTLE MISSOURI
NATIONAL GRASSLAND

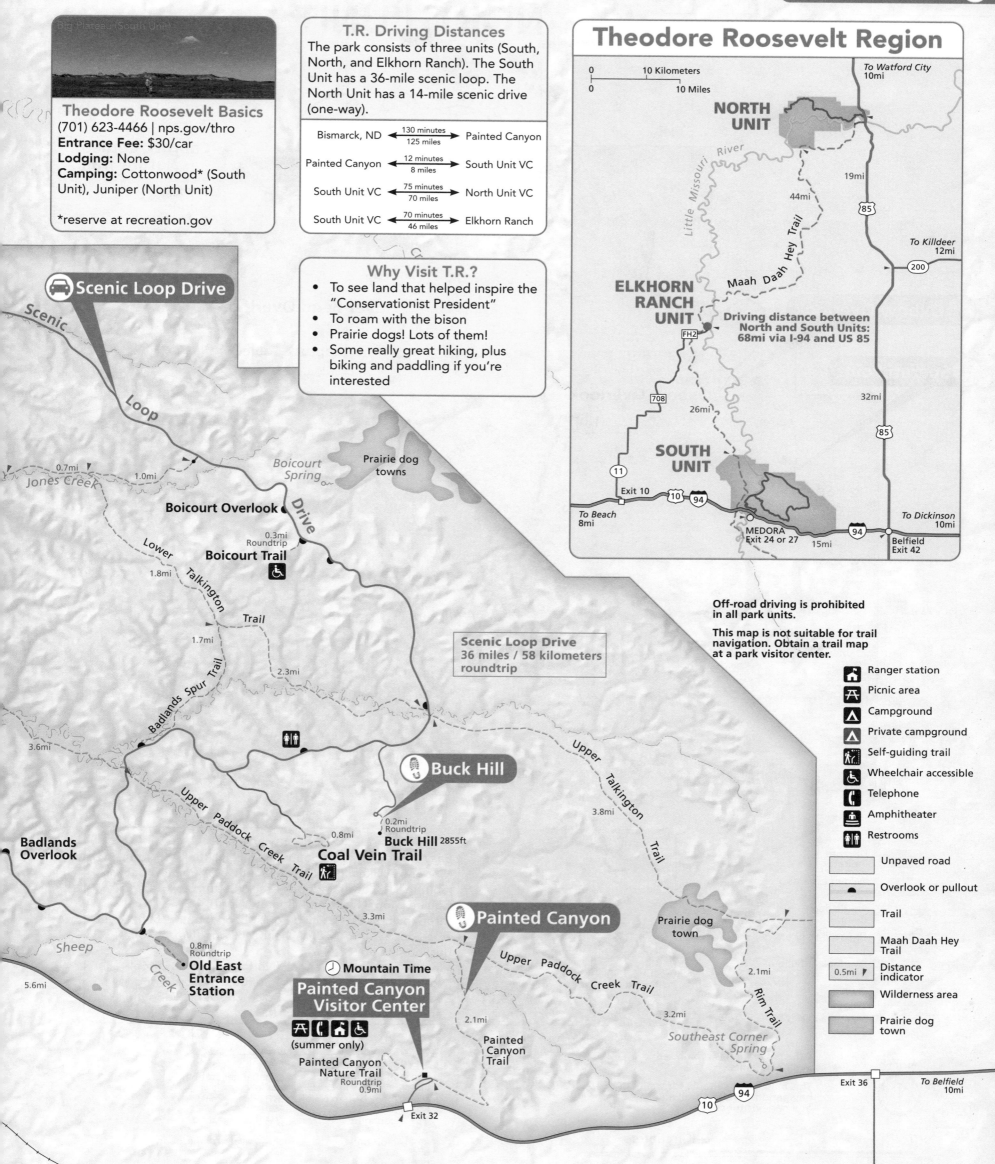

Theodore Roosevelt Basics

(701) 623-4466 | nps.gov/thro
Entrance Fee: $30/car
Lodging: None
Camping: Cottonwood* (South Unit), Juniper (North Unit)

*reserve at recreation.gov

T.R. Driving Distances

The park consists of three units (South, North, and Elkhorn Ranch). The South Unit has a 36-mile scenic loop. The North Unit has a 14-mile scenic drive (one-way).

Bismarck, ND	130 minutes / 125 miles	Painted Canyon
Painted Canyon	12 minutes / 8 miles	South Unit VC
South Unit VC	75 minutes / 70 miles	North Unit VC
South Unit VC	70 minutes / 46 miles	Elkhorn Ranch

Why Visit T.R.?

- To see land that helped inspire the "Conservationist President"
- To roam with the bison
- Prairie dogs! Lots of them!
- Some really great hiking, plus biking and paddling if you're interested

Theodore Roosevelt Region

0   10 Kilometers
0   10 Miles

To Watford City 10mi

NORTH UNIT

Little Missouri River

19mi

44mi

US 85

To Killdeer 12mi

200

Maah Daah Hey Trail

ELKHORN RANCH UNIT

FH2

Driving distance between North and South Units: 68mi via I-94 and US 85

708

26mi

32mi

85

SOUTH UNIT

11

Exit 10

10   94

To Beach 8mi

MEDORA Exit 24 or 27

15mi

94

To Dickinson 10mi

Belfield Exit 42

Off-road driving is prohibited in all park units.

This map is not suitable for trail navigation. Obtain a trail map at a park visitor center.

Scenic Loop Drive

Scenic Loop

Drive

0.7mi   1.0mi

Jones Creek

Boicourt Spring

Prairie dog towns

Boicourt Overlook

0.3mi Roundtrip
Boicourt Trail ♿

Lower Talkington Trail

1.8mi

1.7mi

Badlands Spur Trail

2.3mi

3.6mi

Scenic Loop Drive
36 miles / 58 kilometers roundtrip

Upper Talkington Trail

3.8mi

Buck Hill

Upper Paddock Creek Trail

0.8mi

0.2mi Roundtrip
Buck Hill 2855ft
Coal Vein Trail

Badlands Overlook

Painted Canyon

Prairie dog town

3.3mi

Upper Paddock Creek Trail

2.1mi

Sheep Creek

0.8mi Roundtrip
Old East Entrance Station

5.6mi

🕐 **Mountain Time**

Painted Canyon Visitor Center

🛈 🚻 🏠 ♿

(summer only)

Painted Canyon Nature Trail
Roundtrip 0.9mi

2.1mi

Painted Canyon Trail

3.2mi

Southeast Corner Spring

Rim Trail

Exit 32

Exit 36

To Belfield 10mi

10   94

Legend

🏠 Ranger station
🏕 Picnic area
⛺ Campground
△ Private campground
🚶 Self-guiding trail
♿ Wheelchair accessible
☎ Telephone
🎭 Amphitheater
🚻 Restrooms

Unpaved road

● Overlook or pullout

Trail

Maah Daah Hey Trail

0.5mi ▸ Distance indicator

Wilderness area

Prairie dog town

NORTH UNIT

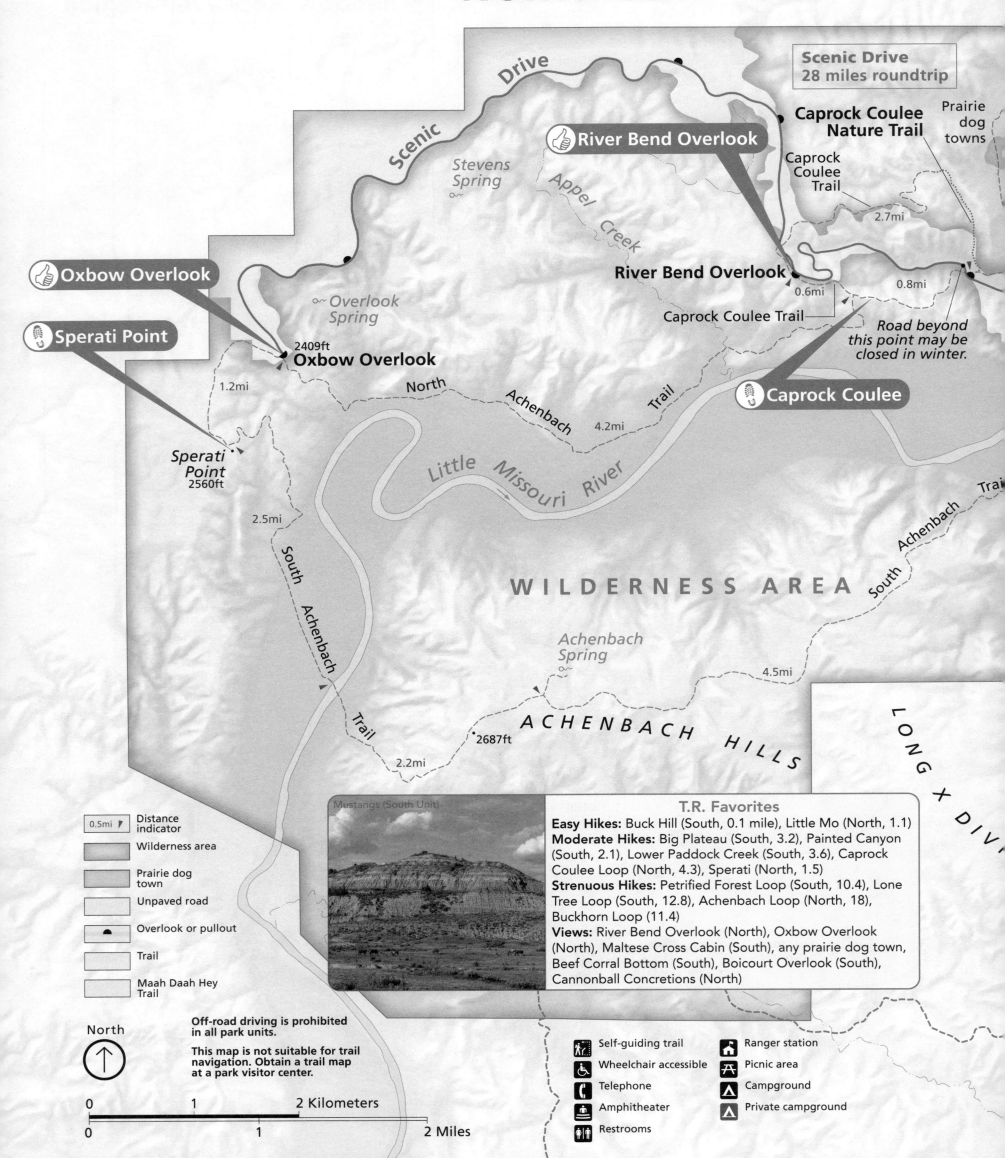

Scenic Drive

Scenic Drive
28 miles roundtrip

Prairie dog towns

👍 River Bend Overlook

Caprock Coulee Nature Trail

Stevens Spring

Caprock Coulee Trail

Appel Creek

2.7mi

👍 Oxbow Overlook

River Bend Overlook

0.6mi

0.8mi

Overlook Spring

2409ft
Oxbow Overlook

Caprock Coulee Trail

Road beyond this point may be closed in winter.

👢 Sperati Point

North Achenbach Trail

1.2mi

4.2mi

👢 Caprock Coulee

Sperati Point 2560ft

Little Missouri River

2.5mi

South Achenbach

WILDERNESS AREA

South Achenbach Trail

Achenbach Spring

4.5mi

Trail

2.2mi

•2687ft

A C H E N B A C H   H I L L S

L O N G   X   D I V

Mustangs (South Unit)

T.R. Favorites
Easy Hikes: Buck Hill (South, 0.1 mile), Little Mo (North, 1.1)
Moderate Hikes: Big Plateau (South, 3.2), Painted Canyon (South, 2.1), Lower Paddock Creek (South, 3.6), Caprock Coulee Loop (North, 4.3), Sperati (North, 1.5)
Strenuous Hikes: Petrified Forest Loop (South, 10.4), Lone Tree Loop (South, 12.8), Achenbach Loop (North, 18), Buckhorn Loop (11.4)
Views: River Bend Overlook (North), Oxbow Overlook (North), Maltese Cross Cabin (South), any prairie dog town, Beef Corral Bottom (South), Boicourt Overlook (South), Cannonball Concretions (North)

0.5mi ▸ Distance indicator

Wilderness area

Prairie dog town

Unpaved road

Overlook or pullout

Trail

Maah Daah Hey Trail

North
↑

Off-road driving is prohibited in all park units.

This map is not suitable for trail navigation. Obtain a trail map at a park visitor center.

🚶 Self-guiding trail
♿ Wheelchair accessible
☎ Telephone
🎭 Amphitheater
🚻 Restrooms

🏠 Ranger station
⛲ Picnic area
⛺ Campground
⛺ Private campground

0   1   2 Kilometers
0   1   2 Miles

LITTLE MISSOURI NATIONAL GRASSLAND

Cannonball Concretions (North Unit)

What You Need to Know About Theodore Roosevelt

- About four out of every five visitors arrive between May and September, making Teddy Roosevelt a great shoulder-season destination if you're looking for solitude (without having to backpack for it).
- Wild horses are a popular draw in the South Unit. I've seen them all over but more commonly between Beef Corral Bottom and Coal Vein. That's a huge area, but I feel pretty confident if you're looking, you will find them. Don't forget to ask a ranger about recent wildlife sightings.
- Chances are you'll see more wildlife in the South Unit. The bison herd is twice the size and it's more accessible (more road), creating more encounters.
- Maltese Cross Cabin is accessible with a ranger in summer and self-guided touring for the rest of the year.

Squaw

Buckhorn

Trail   5.9mi

Hagen Spring

WILDERNESS AREA

85

Buckhorn Trail

Creek

1.6mi

Juniper

Prairie dog town

North Unit Visitor Center

Central Time

Cannonball Concretions Pullout

Scenic Drive

Buckhorn

2.1mi

Trail

1.8mi

Long X Bridge

Little Missouri River

Group Camp

Little Mo Nature Trail
Short Loop 0.7mi
Long Loop 1.4mi

CCC Campground
US Forest Service

Buck Hill (South Unit)

How Much Time Do You Have?

1 Day: It's conceivable to drive through the North and South Units in a day but you're better off spending (at least) one day at each. Trying to do them both, stop at Beef Corral Bottom, Buck Hill, and the Visitor Center (to tour Maltese Cross Cabin) at the South Unit. (Painted Canyon is a pretty good spot for sunrise or sunset, too.) Drive to the North Unit and stop at River Bend Overlook (sunset or sunrise) and Oxbow Overlook.

2 Days: Hike to the South Unit's Petrified Forest. You can cross the Little Mo via Ekblom Trail (be mindful of the water level) and then up to the petrified forest via Big Plateau (which is also great). Drive up to the North Unit. The trails here are big loops, so either you backpack or turn around when you feel like it. Good sunset choices are Caprock Coulee Loop (which provides stunning views of River Bend Overlook) and Sperati Point.

3 Days: With another day, you could head over to Elkhorn Ranch. It's right on the Little Mo, so there's some scenic value but the ranch is ruins without much to see. You could also drive around to the western trailhead for the Petrified Forest Loop. There's a pretty good chance of seeing wildlife and 100% chance of seeing some oil-drilling operations. Personally, I'd spend the extra day hiking the South Unit.

85

Maah   Daah   Hey   Trail

Summit Campground
US Forest Service

LITTLE MISSOURI NATIONAL GRASSLAND

To Belfield
and 94
48mi

Lake Solitude

Phelps Lake

Amphitheater Lake

Delta Lake

Moulton Barn

Schwabacher Landing

Craig Thomas Discovery and Visitor Center

Jenny Lake Visitor Center

Jenny Lake Lodge

CARIBOU-TARGHEE NATIONAL FOREST

TETON

JEDEDIAH SMITH WILDERNESS

BRIDGER-TETON NATIONAL FOREST

JACKSON

HOLE

NATIONAL ELK REFUGE

BRIDGER-TETON NATIONAL FOREST

GROS VENTRE WILDERNESS

BRIDGER-TETON NATIONAL FOREST

Teton Pass
8431ft
2570m

Wilson

Fish Creek Road

PHILLIPS RIDGE

Rendezvous Peak

Teton Village
Jackson Hole Mountain Resort

Rendezvous Mountain
10450ft
3185m

Aerial Tramway

Moose-Wilson Road

WEST GROS VENTRE BUTTE

EAST GROS VENTRE BUTTE

To Pinedale

River access

Snake River

Granite Canyon Entrance

Granite Canyon Trailhead

Laurance S. Rockefeller Preserve

Death Canyon Trailhead

Phelps Lake

Prospectors Mountain

Mount Hunt

Static Peak

OPEN CANYON

GRANITE CANYON

DEATH CANYON

ALASKA BASIN

Mount Wister

Buck Mountain
11938ft
3639m

Mount Meek

AVALANCHE CANYON

Nez Perce

South Teton
12514ft
3814m

Middle Teton
12804ft
3902m

Grand Teton
13770ft
4197m

Mount Owen
12928ft
3940m

Teewinot Mountain
12325ft
3756m

GARNET CANYON

CASCADE CANYON

Mount St John

Rockchuck Peak

String Lake Trailhead

Cathedral Group Turnout

North Jenny Lake Junction

Jenny Lake

Inspiration Point

Hidden Falls

Cascade Canyon Turnout

Jenny Lake Overlook

South Jenny Lake Junction

Jenny Lake Trailhead

Lupine Meadows Trailhead

Teton Glacier Turnout

Climbers Ranch

Bradley Lake

Taggart Lake

Taggart Lake Trailhead

Cottonwood Creek

Menors Ferry Historic District

Chapel of the Transfiguration

Moose Entrance

Moose Junction

Park Headquarters

Dornans

Antelope Flats Rd

Mormon Row

Mormon Row Historic District

Moulton Barns

Glacier View Turnout

Teton Point Turnout

Schwabacher Landing

ANTELOPE FLATS

Snake River Overlook

River Road (4-wheel-drive rec)

THE POTHOLES

Cunningham Cabin Historic Site

Deadmans Bar Road

River access

Triangle X Ranch

SHADOW MOUNTAIN

Ditch Creek

Teton Science Schools

Kelly Warm Spring

Kelly

Gros Ventre

Gros Ventre River

Gros Ventre Road

Gros Ventre Slide

Lower Slide Lake

Atherton Creek

Crystal Creek

Flat Creek

Curtis Canyon

National Museum of Wildlife Art

Jackson National Fish Hatchery

Park Entrance Turnout

Gros Ventre Junction

Jackson Hole Airport

Moose Ranch

Snow King Resort

JACKSON

Jackson Hole and Greater Yellowstone Visitor Center

Refuge sleigh rides (winter only)

Moose Creek

Fox Creek

Coal Creek

Darby Creek

Teton Creek

Grand Targhee Resort

Teton Canyon

Schoolroom Glacier

Table Mountain

Alaska Basin

Crest Trail

DEATH CANYON

8 mi
13 km

8 mi
13 km

18 mi
29 km

Road closed to trucks, RVs and trailers

Map legend / scale

5 mi
8 km

Trail

Multi-use pathway

Distance indicator

Unpaved road (4-wheel-drive recommended)

Turnout or overlook

Ranger station

Self-guiding trail

Horseback riding

Marina

Food service

Picnic area

Store

Gas station

Lodging

Campground

Medical clinic

Tent-only campground

North

0   1   5 Kilometers

0   1   5 Miles

Do not use this map for backcountry hiking. Topographic maps available at visitor centers.

WINEGAR HOLE WILDERNESS

CARIBOU-TARGHEE NATIONAL FOREST

Ashton - Flagg Ranch Road

JEDEDIAH SMITH WILDERNESS

YELLOWSTONE

Survey Peak

Grassy Lake Reservoir

Grassy Lake Road

Road not recommended for trailers or RVs.

To West Thumb
South Entrance

JOHN D. ROCKEFELLER, JR. MEMORIAL PARKWAY

Glade Creek Trailhead

Glade Creek

Steamboat Mountain
7872ft
2399m

Berry Creek

Owl Creek

Snake River

8 mi
13 km

River access

Sheffield

Headwaters Lodge & Cabins at Flagg Ranch

Flagg Ranch Information Station

River access

R A N G E

Moose Mountain

MORAN CANYON

MOOSE BASIN

North Moran Creek

Moran Creek

WEBB CANYON

GRAND

TETON

NATIONAL

PARK

Ranger Peak
11355ft
3461m

Eagles Rest Peak
11258ft
3431m

COLTER CANYON

WATERFALLS CANYON

LEIGH CANYON

LEIGH LAKE

Mount Moran
12605ft
3842m

Triple Glaciers

Skillet Glacier

Falling Ice Glacier

Trapper Lake

Bearpaw Lake

Bivouac Peak

CANYON

Moran Bay

Spalding Bay

ELK ISLAND

JACKSON LAKE
Surface elevation
6772ft
2064m

Lizard Creek

Jackson Lake Overlook

Arizona Island

191
287

89

Arizona Creek

16 mi
26 km

Arizona Lake

Colter Bay Visitor Center

UW-NPS Research Center
AMK Ranch

Leeks Marina

Hermitage Point Trailhead

Colter Bay

Heron Pond

Swan Lake

Hermitage Point

Half Moon Bay

Donoho Pt.

Jackson Lake Lodge

Chapel of the Sacred Heart

Jackson Lake Junction

Signal Mountain Lodge

12 mi
19 km
Road

Potholes

Signal Mountain Rd.

Jackson Lake Dam

River access

Willow Flats Overlook

Colter Bay Village

Pilgrim Creek

Signal Mountain
7727ft
2355m

River access

Christian Pond

Oxbow Bend Turnout

Cattleman's Bridge

EMMA MATILDA LAKE

Grand View Point
7586ft
2312m

TWO OCEAN LAKE

Two Ocean Lake Trailhead

Pacific Creek Road

Moran Entrance

Moran Junction

River access

191
26
89

River

5 mi
8 km

5 mi
8 km

Pacific Creek

BRIDGER-TETON NATIONAL FOREST

TETON WILDERNESS

Pacific Creek

Buffalo Fork

Buffalo Valley Rd.

26
287

2 mi
3 km

Hatchet

Grand Teton Basics

(307) 739-3399 | nps.gov/grte
Entrance Fee: $35/car
Lodging: Dornan's Spur Ranch (dornans.com), AAC Climber's Ranch (americanalpineclub.org), Jenny Lake Lodge (gtlc.com), Signal Mountain Lodge (signalmountainlodge.com), Jackson Lake Lodge (gtlc.com), Triangle X Ranch (trianglex.com), Colter Bay Cabins (gtlc.com), Headwaters Lodge & Resort (gtlc.com)
Camping: Gros Ventre (gtlc.com), Jenny Lake (gtlc.com), Signal Mountain (signalmountainlodge.com), Colter Bay Campground & RV Park (gtlc.com), Lizard Creek (signalmountainlodge.com), Headwaters at Flagg Ranch (gtlc.com)

Cunningham Cabin

Grand Teton Driving Distances

There are a few unpaved roads to explore here, but most visitors stick to Teton Park Road and US-191. Both run parallel to the Teton Range.

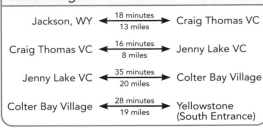

Jackson, WY	18 minutes / 13 miles	Craig Thomas VC
Craig Thomas VC	16 minutes / 8 miles	Jenny Lake VC
Jenny Lake VC	35 minutes / 20 miles	Colter Bay Village
Colter Bay Village	28 minutes / 19 miles	Yellowstone (South Entrance)

Why Visit Grand Teton?

- To admire one of the most iconic mountains on earth, the Teton Range
- To float the Snake River as Grand Teton looms in the distance
- To experience a real-life Dude Ranch!
- To enjoy exceptional mountain hiking
- To bike the multi-use pathway

Schwabacher Landing

Grand Teton Favorites

Easy Hikes: Jenny Lake Loop (7.1 miles), Leigh Lake (1.8), Menor's Ferry (0.3), Taggart Lake (3)
Moderate Hikes: Phelps Lake Loop (6.3), Hidden Falls (5.2), Bearpaw Lake (8)
Strenuous Hikes: Delta Lake (Extreme, ~9), Lake Solitude Loop (19.2), Surprise & Amphitheater Lakes (10.1), Table Mountain (12), Garnet Canyon (8.4), Death Canyon (varies)
Activities: Ride a horse, float the Snake, climb Grand Teton, bike the paths
Views: Schwabacher Landing, Moulton Barns, Chapel of the Transfiguration, Glacier View, Snake River Overlook, Cunningham Cabin

Moulton Barn

What You Need to Know About Grand Teton

- The park gets busy. While it's open year-round, 95% of all visitors arrive between May and October.
- In summer, wake up early to secure parking or expect to wait for parking at sites like Laurence S. Rockefeller Reserve (where one car parks when one car leave) or to park quite a ways away like at Lupine Meadows or Jenny Lake (where you can park alongside the road as well).
- Grand Teton and Yellowstone form a classic national park combo vacation. Yellowstone warrants plenty of vacation time but Grand Teton is no slouch. Do more than a daytrip.
- The loop to Lake Solitude is great. You can hike it either way but many prefer starting up Paintbrush Canyon in the morning. It's prettier, so having the sun at your back puts it in the best light. It also gets you to Lake Solitude earlier in the day. And then you hike out Cascade Canyon (and decide if you have enough time for the spur trails to Hidden Falls and Inspiration Point).
- Surprise Lake and Amphitheater Lake are wonderful too. But the real show-stopper is Delta Lake, accessed via a spur trail along the way to these alpine lakes. It isn't marked. It isn't maintained by the park. It's fairly treacherous. But it is truly special.
- The Tetons are iconic but head down to Jackson Lake to ogle Mount Moran too.
- Schwabacher Landing is well known by photographers. There are two parking areas near the end of the road. Both lead to reflective views.
- If you bring your own watercraft (even SUP or kayaks), you'll need to get a permit and complete an Aquatic Invasive Species inspection. There are several places to rent water toys, even boats at Signal Mountain Marina.

How Much Time Do You Have?

1 Day: Start early. Maybe sunrise at Moulton Barns (it'll be busy in summer) and then hustle over to Schwabacher Landing. Then head over to Phelps Lake (do the loop and you'll find a big rock people like to jump off). If you have time, head to Jenny Lake before returning to some of the Overlooks along US-191 for sunset.

2 Days: Float the Snake or join a horse ride. If that isn't for you, there's plenty more hiking opportunities. Paddling String Lake is another good option (kayak and SUP rentals available). Or rent a boat at Signal Mountain Marina and cruise Jackson Lake.

3 Days: Excuse me for being repetitive but there's plenty of great hiking. There are also a few dirt roads worth a look, like River Road or heading up into Antelope Flats.

Yellowstone Basics

(307) 344-7381 | nps.gov/yell
Entrance Fee: $35/car
Lodging*: Canyon Lodge, Grant Village, Lake Lodge, Lake Hotel, Mammoth Hot Springs Hotel, Old Faithful Lodge, Old Faithful Inn, Old Faithful Snow Lodge, Roosevelt Lodge
Camping: Bridge Bay*, Canyon*, Fishing Bridge (RV)*, Grant Village*, Madison*, Indian Creek**, Lewis Lake**, Mammoth**, Norris, Pebble Creek**, Slough Creek**, Tower Fall

*reserve at
yellowstonenationalparklodges.com
**reserve at recreation.gov

Yellowstone Driving Distances

The park's Grand Loop Road makes a giant figure-8. The top half is 70 miles, connecting developed areas like Mammoth Hot Springs, Tower-Roosevelt, Canyon Village, and Norris. The bottom half is 96 miles, connecting Norris, Canyon Village, Lake Village, West Thumb, and Old Faithful.

Bozeman, MT	100 minutes / 83 miles	Mammoth Hot Springs (North Entrance)
Billings, MT	3.5 hours / 195 miles	Tower Roosevelt (Northeast Entrance)
Cody, WY	110 minutes / 80 miles	Lake Village (East Entrance)
Jackson, WY	140 minutes / 97 miles	Old Faithful (South Entrance)
West Yellowstone	55 minutes / 32 miles	Old Faithful (West Entrance)

Grand Prismatic Spring

Why Visit Yellowstone?

- To see geysers, hot springs, mud pots, and all the geothermal features
- To witness one of the closest things to a safari in the Americas
- Waterfalls like Upper and Lower Falls of Grand Canyon of the Yellowstone
- To stare in awe of the sublime colors of Grand Prismatic Spring

What You Need to Know About Yellowstone

- The park is massive (2+ million acres) but most visitors congregate around a few select locations (Old Faithful, Grand Prismatic Spring, Mammoth Hot Springs, Grand Canyon of the Yellowstone, and Lake Village), making it feel much smaller than it is.
- Consider a wintertime visit if you'd like a more intimate and much more magical Yellowstone experience (and it's awfully magical in summer!).
- The park doesn't close for winter but most of its roads do. North and Northeast Entrance provide the only year-round access to wheeled vehicles. The remainder of the park can be reached by snowmobile or snowcoach.
- Driving around the Grand Loop's figure-8, you won't notice an overwhelming amount of mountainous terrain. This is because you're within the supervolcanoe's caldera (for the lower half). Drive in/out of the Northeast or East Entrance and you'll find some dramatic topography. There are also towering mountains in the northwestern corner of the park.
- The busiest section of the Grand Loop tends to be the leg between West Yellowstone and Old Faithful. I strongly recommend spending a night in/near Old Faithful for easier visitation during peak season. There's much more to see than Old Faithful, and it's easy to spend a day walking among the geyser basin.
- Rangers update eruption prediction times on dry erase boards at the reliable geysers but your geyser viewing will be much more efficient if you check predictions online at the park website before exploring the geyser basins.
- Everyone wants to know about wildlife. Well, you're probably going to see some. Bison are common in Lamar Valley, Hayden Valley and the Central Plateau. Elk are widespread and commonly seen along the Madison and Yellowstone rivers, as well as Mammoth Hot Springs. Grizzlies continue to expand their territory, but they're most commonly seen at Fishing Bridge, Hayden Valley, and Lamar Valley. Wolves are commonly seen at Lamar Valley (look for groups of people with spotting scopes) or along the Madison River.
- Grand Canyon of the Yellowstone is magnificent, but it's better early, when the sun is east of the waterfalls. Artist Point and Uncle Tom's Trail on the South Rim, and Lookout Point and Red Rock Point on the North Rim, are my favorite viewing locations.
- The parking lot for Midway Geyser Basin gets a little crowded in summer. The good news is there's a large parking area south of the basin. Here you'll find the trail to Fairy Falls and an overlook with the best views of Grand Prismatic Spring. You may be tempted to come here early in the morning to secure a parking space, but the spring is best seen when the sun is high above the horizon. That's when the spring's kaleidoscope of colors really pop.
- Each geyser basin offers something different. Upper has the most geyser action. Midway has Grand Prismatic Spring. West Thumb is along the shore of Yellowstone Lake, which is pretty neat. Mammoth Hot Springs Terrace is incredibly unique. Norris Geyser Basin has a different feel, smell, and look than all the others. And there are more. Monument Geyser Basin, Biscuit Basin, Black Sand Basin. Each one has its charm.
- You can soak in bodies of water fed by run-off from hydrothermal features. The two most popular sites are Boiling River (north of Mammoth Hot Springs but closed when we went to print) and a swimming area just south of Firehole Falls on Firehole Canyon Drive.
- Cascade Corner takes some effort to reach, but if you're a hiker/backpacker, the rewards are huge. It's named for an abundance of waterfalls like Dunanda, Ouzel, and Union, just to name a few. Don't go out here on a whim. There are creek crossings, preferred campsites, and all sorts of other useful details you should know before arriving.

Old Faithful

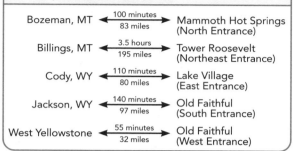
Cave Falls

Yellowstone Favorites

Easy Hikes: Fairy Falls (6.7 miles), Wraith Falls (1), Lone Star Geyser (4.8), Boiling River (1), Storm Point (2.3), Trout Lake (1.2)
Moderate Hikes: Dunanda Falls (16 miles from Bechler), Union Falls (multiple long options), Bunsen Peak (4.6), Osprey Falls (8)
Strenuous Hikes: Avalanche Peak (4.2), Mount Washburn (5), Hellroaring (6.2)
Extreme Hikes: Electric Peak (18)
Activities: Yellowstone Lake boat tour, watch for wolves, photo tour, trail ride near Tower Fall
Views: Artist's Point, Grand Prismatic Spring Overlook, the geysers of Upper Geyser Basin, Mammoth Hot Springs, Tower Fall, Hayden Valley, Gibbon Falls, Lamar Valley, Norris Geyser Basin, Undine Falls, Firehole Falls, West Thumb Geyser Basin

How Much Time Do You Have?

I'm sure it's possible to race around Grand Loop Road in a single day but it's a terrible idea. There's so much to see at Yellowstone. Plan at least three days, but the park is huge, and there are remote regions to consider like Cascade Corner (and trailheads in the Absaroka and Gallatin Ranges).

3 Days: It's easy to spend an entire day (or more) at Upper Geyser Basin (where you'll find Old Faithful and many more geysers). While there, you'll want to check out Midway Geyser Basin (Grand Prismatic Spring), as well as Firehole Lake Drive and Firehole Canyon Drive. Spend a day (or more) at Canyon Village. Similarly, you could easily spend all your daylight hours at Grand Canyon of the Yellowstone. Instead you'll want to hustle down to Lake Village/Fishing Bridge and Hayden Valley. Spend another day at Mammoth Hot Springs or Tower Roosevelt. Lamar Valley, Mount Washburn, and Mammoth Terraces are primary stops.

West Yellowstone to Bozeman, MT
90 mi
145 km

West Yellowstone to Big Sky, MT
48 mi
77 km

GALLATIN

Gallatin River

CUSTER - GALLATIN NATIONAL FOREST

Old Yellowstone Trail

Gardiner to Livingston, MT
52 mi
84 km
Gardiner to Bozeman, MT
84 mi
135 km

Jardine

Specimen Creek

Fan Creek

Sportsman Lake

Electric Peak
10969 ft
3343 m

89

no water

Gardiner

Bear Creek

LEE METCALF WILDERNESS

RANGE

Roosevelt Arch

North Entrance
5314 ft
1620 m

Road between Gardiner and Cooke City is open all year

5 mi
8 km

191

Mammoth Hot Springs

Albright Visitor Center

Mammoth Hot Springs Terraces

Park Headquarters

Mount Everts
7841 ft
2390 m

Yellowstone

one-way

Forces of the Northern Range

Blacktail Pond

Phantom *on*

CUSTER-GALLATIN NATIONAL FOREST

Little Quadrant Mountain
9885 ft
3013 m

Road closed from early November to mid-April

Bunsen Peak
8564 ft
2610 m

Golden Gate

👍 **Mammoth Terrace**

GARDNERS HOLE

Gardner River

Swan Lake

Undine Falls

Wraith Falls

BLACKTAIL DEER PLATEAU

Blacktail Plate

👍 **Wraith Falls**

Quadrant Mountain
9944 ft
3031 m

Panther Creek

Sheepeater Cliff

Indian Creek

👣 **Bunsen Peak**

Prospect Peak
9525 ft
2903 m

WASHBURN

31 mi
50 km

Antler Peak
10023ft
3055 m

Indian Creek

WILLOW PARK

21 mi
34 km

Dome Mountain
9894 ft
3016 m

Winter Creek

Beaver Lake

Obsidian Cliff
7383 ft
2250 m

Road between Tower Fall and Canyon Village is closed mid-October to late May

Mount Holmes
10336 ft
3150 m

Grizzly Lake

Observation Peak
9397 ft
2864 m

RANGE

West Yellowstone, MT to Earthquake Lake Visitor Center
28 mi
45 km

Gneiss Creek

Roaring Mountain

Twin Lakes

Museum of the National Park Ranger

Grebe Lake

Cascade Lake

287

Hebgen Lake

Straight Creek

Nymph Lake

Norris
7526 ft 2311 m

Wolf Lake

191

287

Hebgen Lake

MADISON VALLEY

Museum and Information Station

NORRIS GEYSER BASIN
Steamboat Geyser

Ice Lake

Gibbon River

12 mi
19 km

👍 **Firehole Falls**

👍 **Norris Basin**

Artists Paintpots

Virginia Cascade

West Yellowstone, MT to Ashton, ID
60 mi
97 km

20

West Yellowstone

West Entrance
6667 ft
2032 m

Monument Geyser Basin

Beryl Spring

👍 **Gibbon Falls**

Otter Creek

Two Ribbons

14 mi
23 km

14 mi
23 km

YELLOWSTONE

West Yellowstone Visitor Information Center

Road closed from early November to mid-April

Madison River

Gibbon River

Gibbon Falls
84 ft
26 m

Alum Creek

HAYD

Mount Haynes
8235 ft
2510 m

National Park Mountain
7500 ft
2286 m

Madison
6806 ft 2074 m

Information Station

Mary Lake

CENTRAL PLATEAU

Firehole Falls

Firehole Canyon Drive

Firehole R

Fountain Flat Drive

Nez Perce Creek

Fairy Creek

👍 **Grand Prismatic Spring**

LOWER GEYSER BASIN
Fountain Paint Pot

Firehole Lake Drive
Great Fountain Geyser

Beach Lake

Fairy Falls

Goose Lake

👍 **West Thumb Geyser Basin**

MONTANA

IDAHO

MIDWAY GEYSER BASIN
Grand Prismatic Spring

16 mi
26 km

CONTINENTAL DIVIDE

MADISON

Biscuit Basin

Little Firehole River

Firehole River

Mallard Lake

De Lacy Lakes

Mystic Falls

UPPER GEYSER BASIN

Black Sand Basin

Black Sand Basin

Old Faithful Geyser

MONTANA
WYOMING

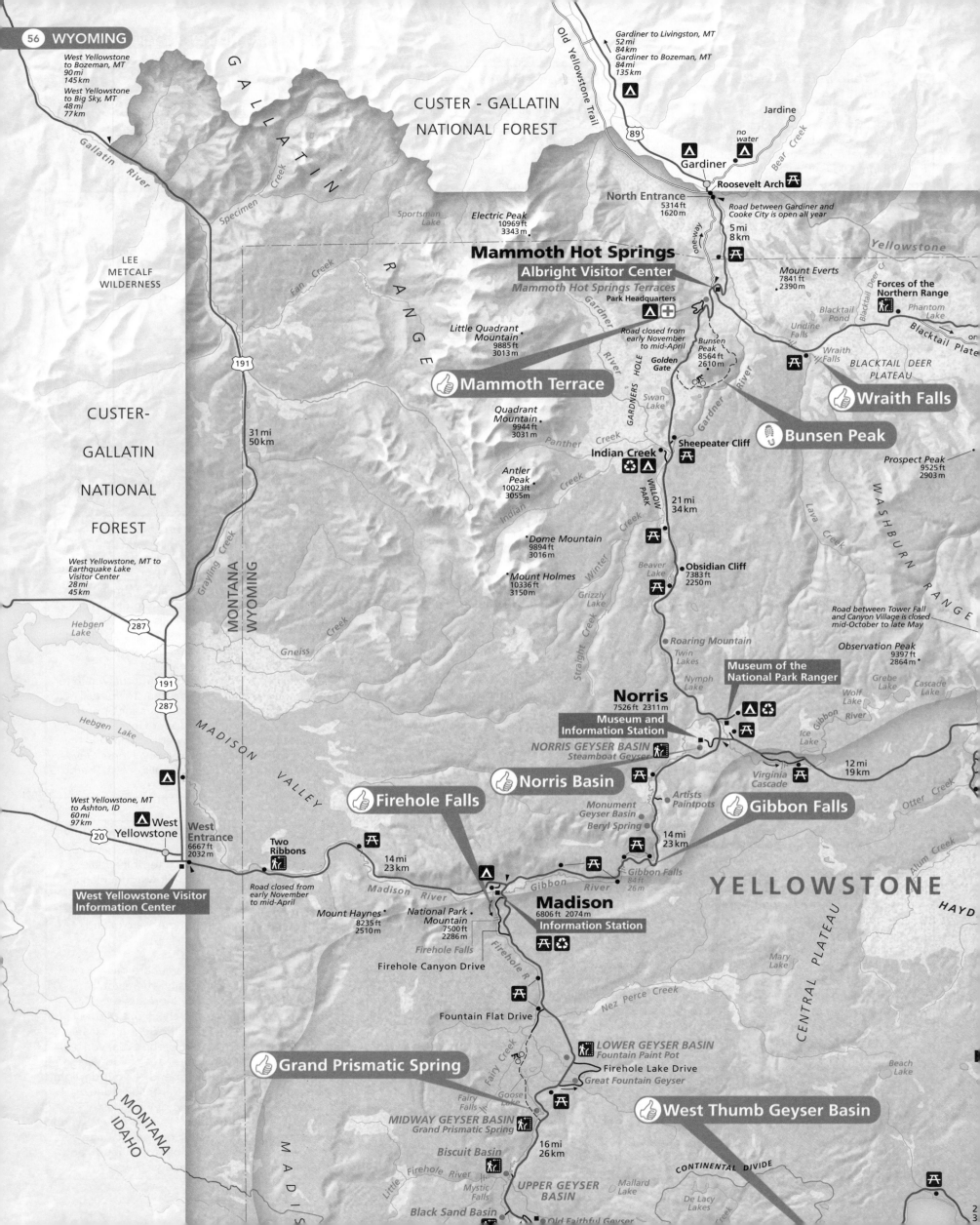

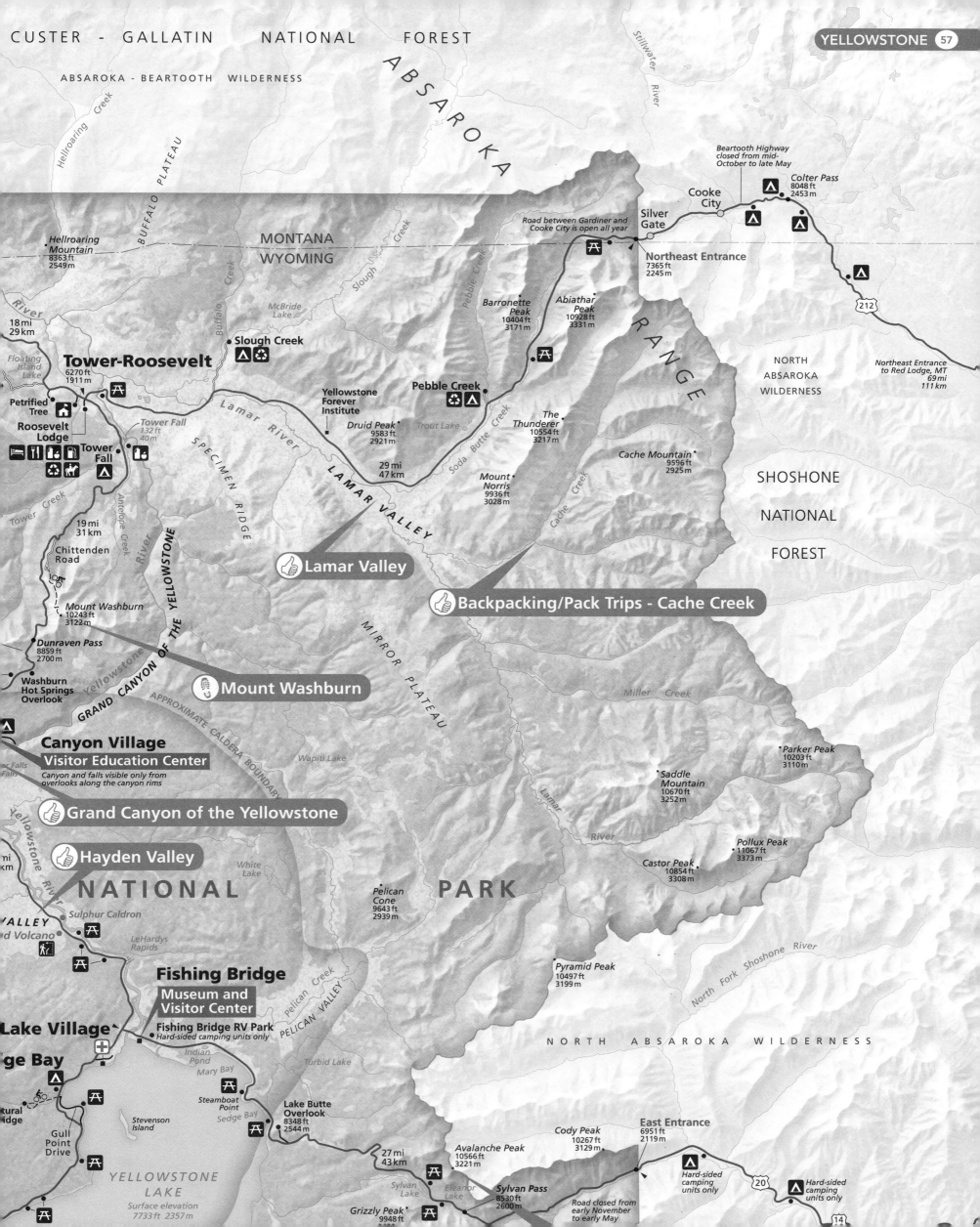

ABSAROKA - BEARTOOTH WILDERNESS

ABSAROKA

Stillwater River

MONTANA
WYOMING

Beartooth Highway closed from mid-October to late May

Colter Pass
8048 ft
2453 m

Cooke City

Silver Gate

Road between Gardiner and Cooke City is open all year

Northeast Entrance
7365 ft
2245 m

*Northeast Entrance to Red Lodge, MT
69 mi
111 km*

212

*Hellroaring Mountain
8363 ft
2549 m*

BUFFALO PLATEAU

Hellroaring Creek

McBride Lake

Slough Creek

*Barronette Peak
10404 ft
3171 m*

*Abiathar Peak
10928 ft
3331 m*

RANGE

NORTH
ABSAROKA
WILDERNESS

Floating Island Lake

18 mi
29 km

River

Tower-Roosevelt
6270 ft
1911 m

Slough Creek

Yellowstone Forever Institute

Pebble Creek

*Druid Peak
9583 ft
2921 m*

Trout Lake

*The Thunderer
10554 ft
3217 m*

*Cache Mountain
9596 ft
2925 m*

SHOSHONE

NATIONAL

FOREST

Petrified Tree

Roosevelt Lodge

*Tower Fall
132 ft
40 m*

Tower Fall

Lamar River

LAMAR VALLEY

29 mi
47 km

Soda Butte Creek

*Mount Norris
9936 ft
3028 m*

Cache Creek

SPECIMEN RIDGE

Antelope Creek

19 mi
31 km

Tower Creek

Chittenden Road

River

GRAND CANYON OF THE YELLOWSTONE

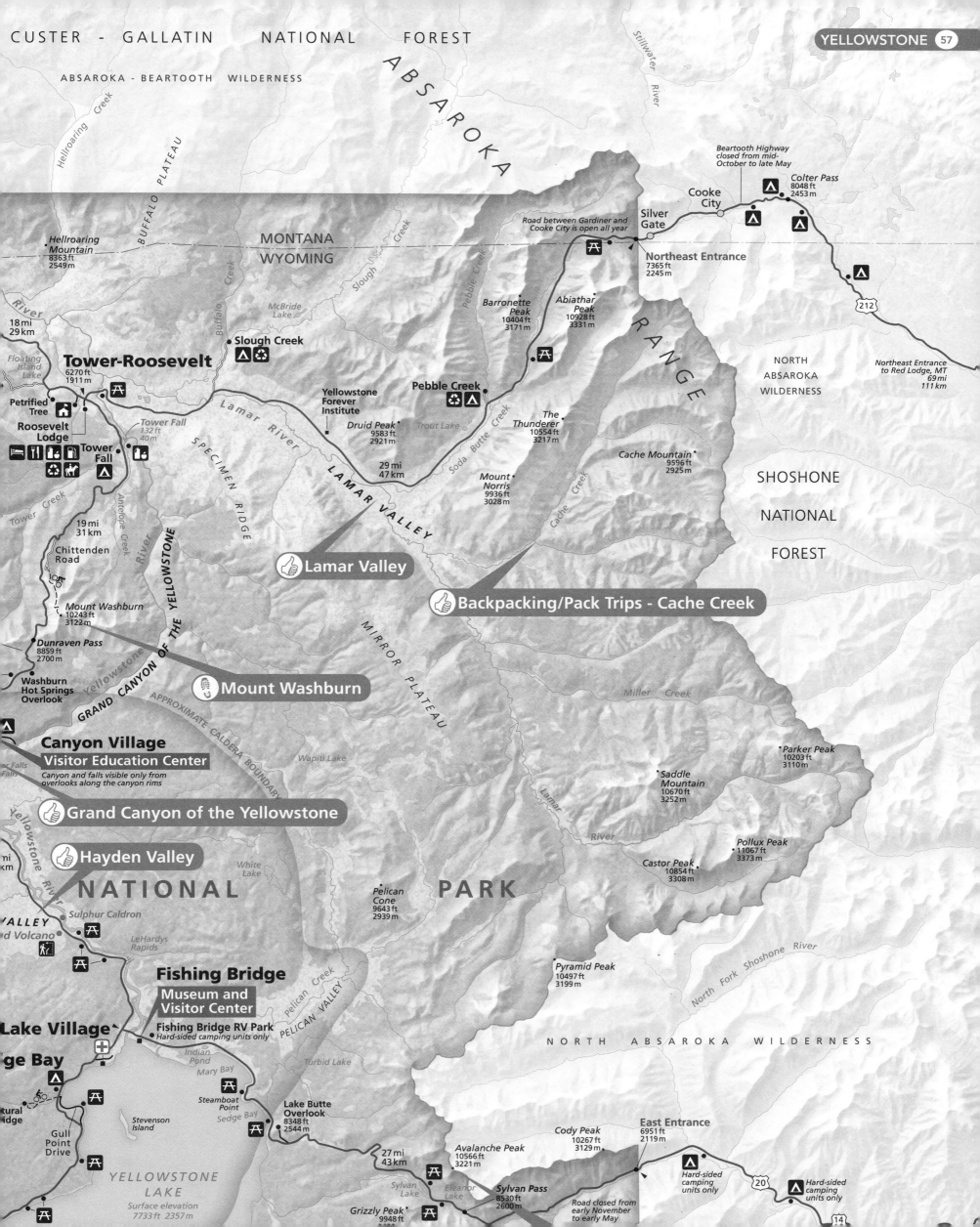 **Lamar Valley**

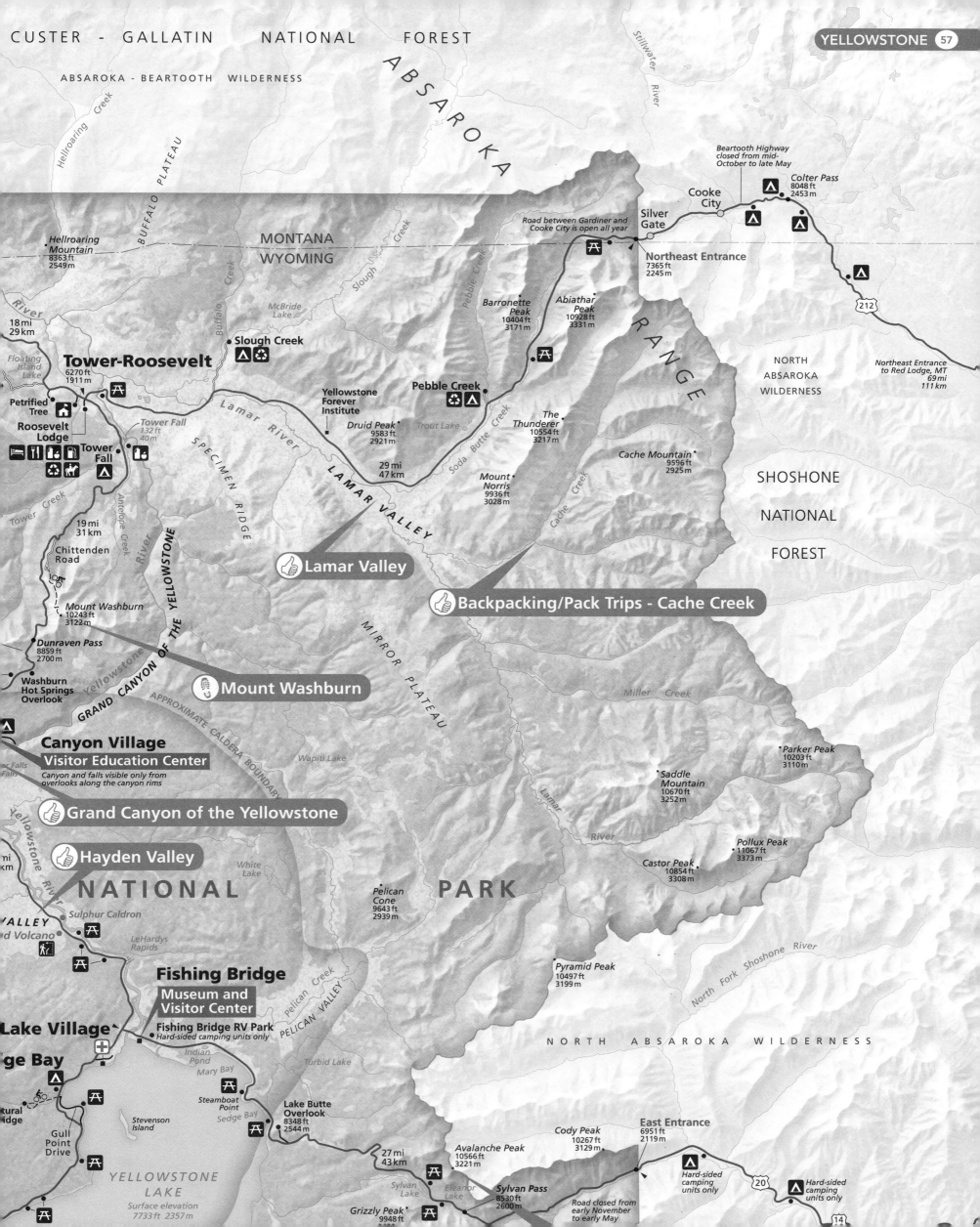 **Backpacking/Pack Trips - Cache Creek**

*Mount Washburn
10243 ft
3122 m*

*Dunraven Pass
8859 ft
2700 m*

APPROXIMATE CALDERA BOUNDARY

MIRROR PLATEAU

Miller Creek

Washburn Hot Springs Overlook

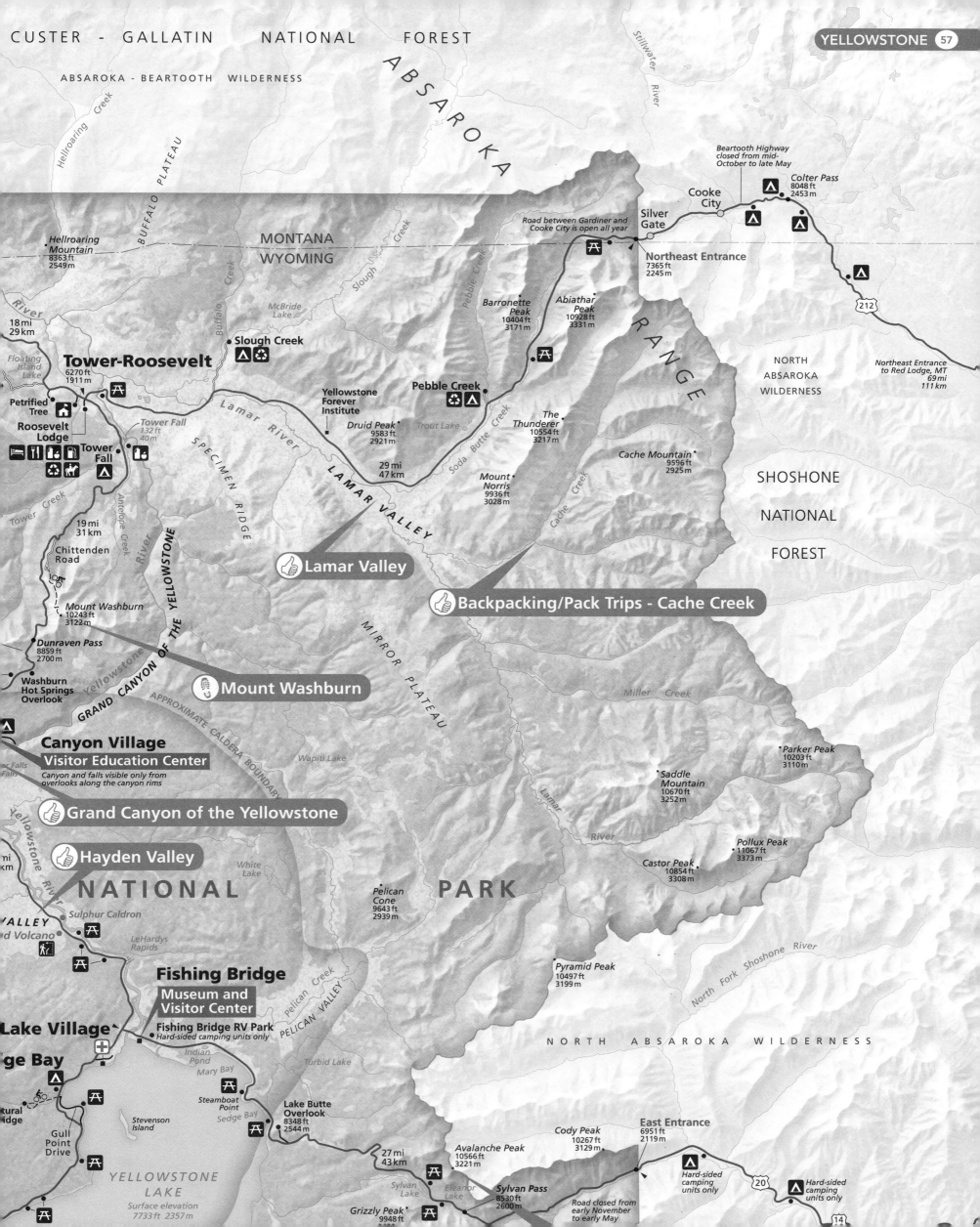 **Mount Washburn**

*Parker Peak
10203 ft
3110 m*

Canyon Village
Visitor Education Center
Canyon and falls visible only from overlooks along the canyon rims

Wapiti Lake

*Saddle Mountain
10670 ft
3252 m*

*r Falls
Falls*

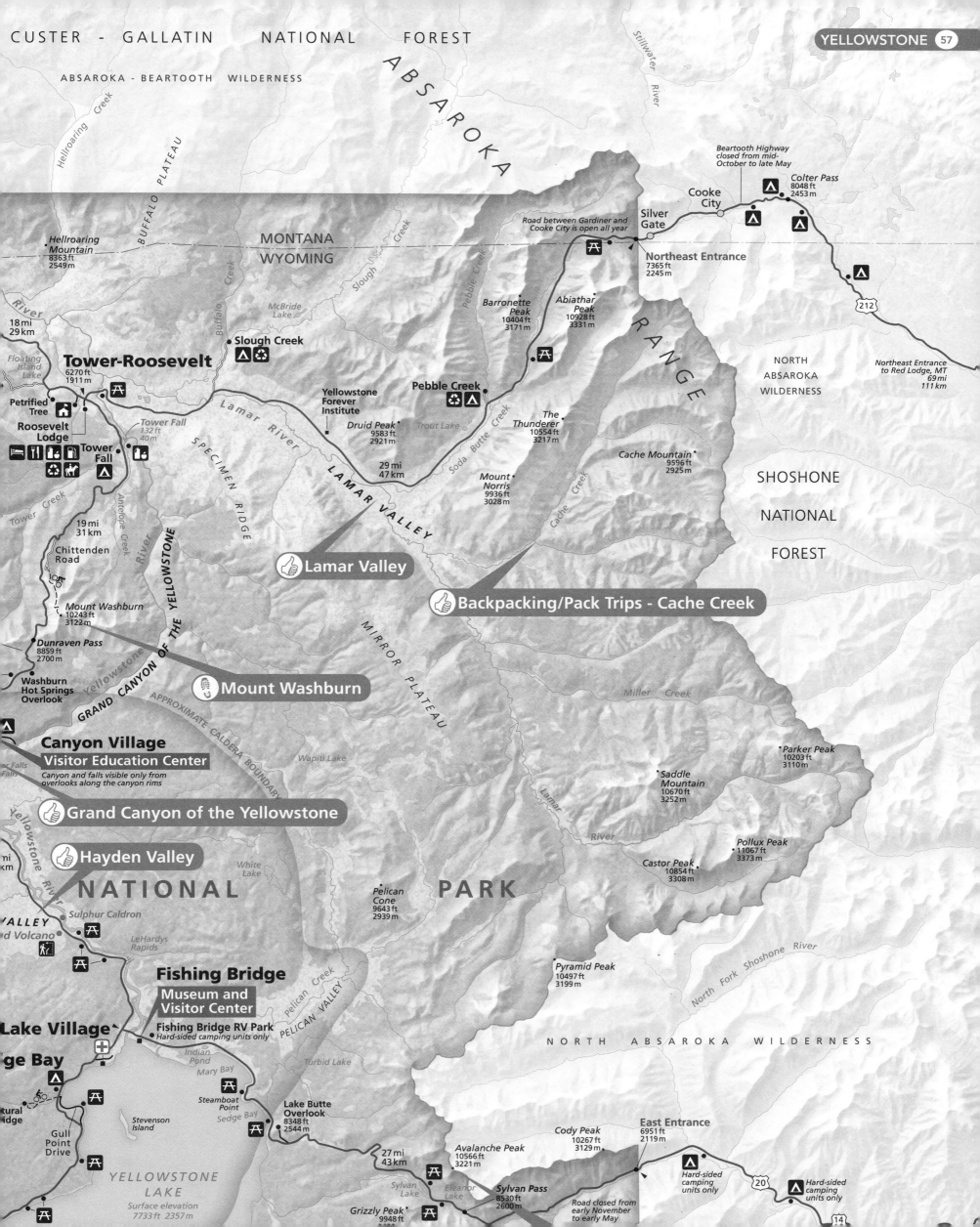 **Grand Canyon of the Yellowstone**

*Pollux Peak
11067 ft
3373 m*

Yellowstone River

 Hayden Valley

White Lake

NATIONAL

PARK

Lamar River

*Castor Peak
10854 ft
3308 m*

mi
km

Sulphur Caldron

*Pelican Cone
9643 ft
2939 m*

**ALLEY
d Volcano**

LeHardys Rapids

*Pyramid Peak
10497 ft
3199 m*

North Fork Shoshone River

Fishing Bridge

Pelican Creek

Museum and Visitor Center

Fishing Bridge RV Park
Hard-sided camping units only

PELICAN VALLEY

Lake Village

*Indian Pond
Mary Bay*

Turbid Lake

NORTH ABSAROKA WILDERNESS

ge Bay

*Steamboat Point
Sedge Bay*

Stevenson Island

*Cody Peak
10267 ft
3129 m*

East Entrance
6951 ft
2119 m

Gull Point Drive

Lake Butte Overlook
8348 ft
2544 m

Hard-sided camping units only

20

Hard-sided camping units only

tural idge

27 mi
43 km

*Avalanche Peak
10566 ft
3221 m*

YELLOWSTONE LAKE

Sylvan Lake

Eleanor Lake

Sylvan Pass
8530 ft
2600 m

Road closed from early November to early May

*Grizzly Peak
9948 ft*

Surface elevation
7733 ft 2357 m

14

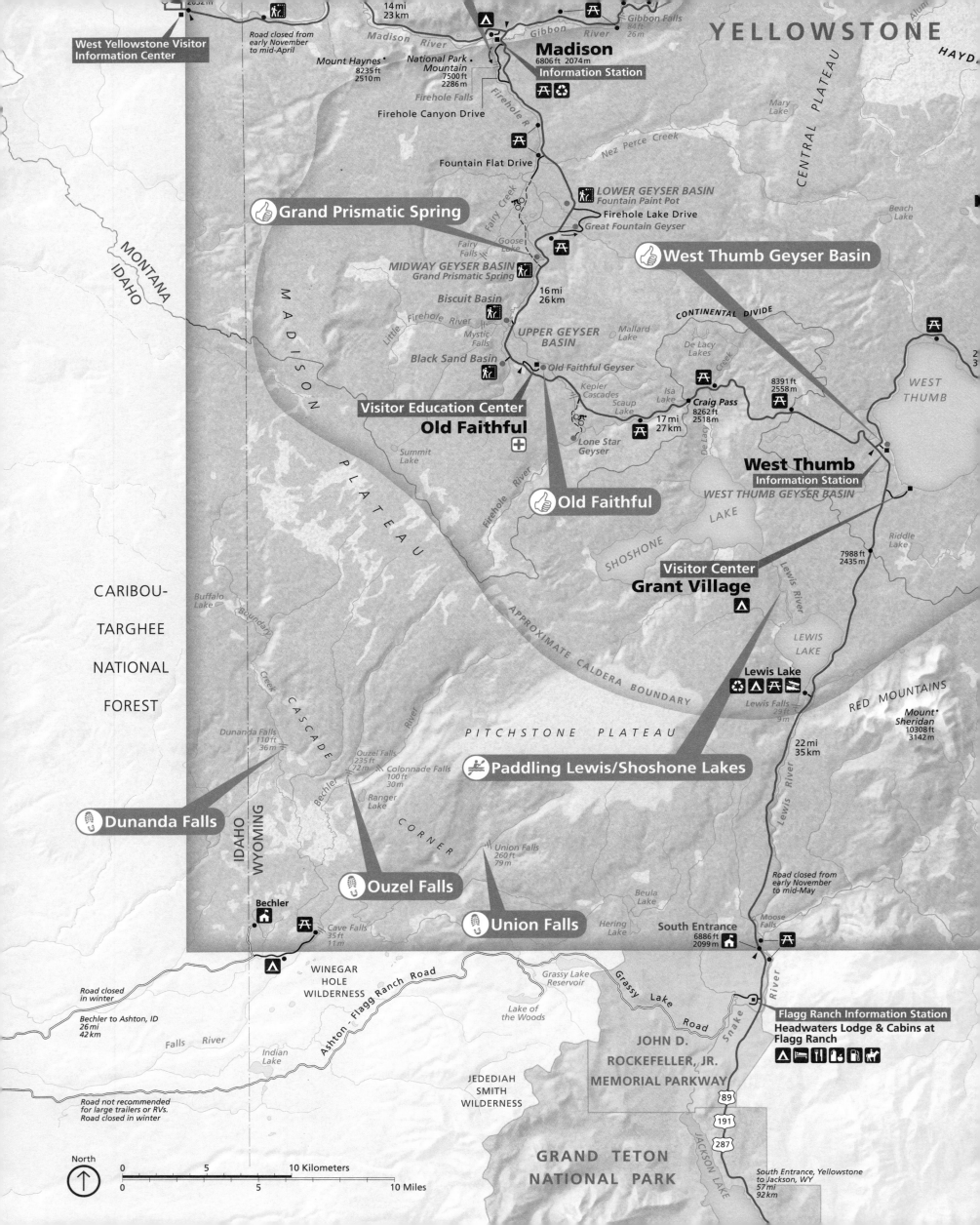

West Yellowstone Visitor
Information Center

Road closed from
early November
to mid-April

14 mi
23 km

Gibbon Falls
84 ft
26 m

Gibbon *River*

Madison
6806 ft 2074 m
Information Station

Madison River

Mount Haynes
8235 ft
2510 m

National Park
Mountain
7500 ft
2286 m

Firehole Falls

Firehole Canyon Drive

Firehole R.

CENTRAL PLATEAU

HAYD

Mary
Lake

Beach
Lake

Nez Perce Creek

LOWER GEYSER BASIN
Fountain Paint Pot

Fountain Flat Drive

Firehole Lake Drive
Great Fountain Geyser

👍 **Grand Prismatic Spring**

👍 **West Thumb Geyser Basin**

CONTINENTAL DIVIDE

Fairy Creek

Goose
Lake

Fairy Falls

16 mi
26 km

MIDWAY GEYSER BASIN
Grand Prismatic Spring

Biscuit Basin

Little Firehole River

Mystic
Falls

UPPER GEYSER
BASIN

Mallard
Lake

De Lacy
Lakes

8391 ft
2558 m

WEST
THUMB

2
3

Black Sand Basin

◄ *Old Faithful Geyser*

Visitor Education Center
Old Faithful
✚

Kepler
Cascades

Scaup Lake

Isa
Lake

Craig Pass
8262 ft
2518 m

17 mi
27 km

Firehole River

Summit
Lake

👍 **Old Faithful**

Lone Star
Geyser

De Lacy Creek

West Thumb
Information Station
WEST THUMB GEYSER BASIN

LAKE

SHOSHONE

Visitor Center
Grant Village
⛺

7988 ft
2435 m

Lewis River

Riddle
Lake

LEWIS
LAKE

MONTANA
IDAHO

MADISON PLATEAU

Buffalo
Lake

Boundary Creek

CARIBOU-

TARGHEE

NATIONAL

FOREST

CASCADE

APPROXIMATE CALDERA BOUNDARY

PITCHSTONE PLATEAU

Lewis Lake
♻ ⛺ 🛶

Lewis Falls
29 ft
9 m

RED MOUNTAINS

Mount
Sheridan
10308 ft
3142 m

Dunanda Falls
110 ft
36 m

Ouzel Falls
235 ft
72 m

Colonnade Falls
100 ft
30 m

Ranger
Lake

👣 **Dunanda Falls**

IDAHO
WYOMING

Bechler River

CORNER

🛶 **Paddling Lewis/Shoshone Lakes**

Union Falls
260 ft
79 m

22 mi
35 km

Lewis River

👣 **Ouzel Falls**

👣 **Union Falls**

Road closed from
early November
to mid-May

Beula
Lake

Hering
Lake

Bechler
🏠

⛺

Cave Falls
35 ft
11 m

⛺

South Entrance
6886 ft
2099 m

Moose
Falls

🏠

Snake River

Road closed
in winter

Bechler to Ashton, ID
26 mi
42 km

WINEGAR
HOLE
WILDERNESS

Ashton - Flagg Ranch Road

Grassy Lake
Reservoir

Grassy Lake Road

Lake of
the Woods

JOHN D.

ROCKEFELLER, JR.

MEMORIAL PARKWAY

Flagg Ranch Information Station
Headwaters Lodge & Cabins at
Flagg Ranch
⛺ 🛏 🍴 ⛽ 🏪 🐴

Falls River

Indian Lake

Road not recommended
for large trailers or RVs.
Road closed in winter

JEDEDIAH
SMITH
WILDERNESS

89
191

287

GRAND TETON
NATIONAL PARK

Jackson Lake

South Entrance, Yellowstone
to Jackson, WY
57 mi
92 km

North
⬆

0   5   10 Kilometers

0   5   10 Miles

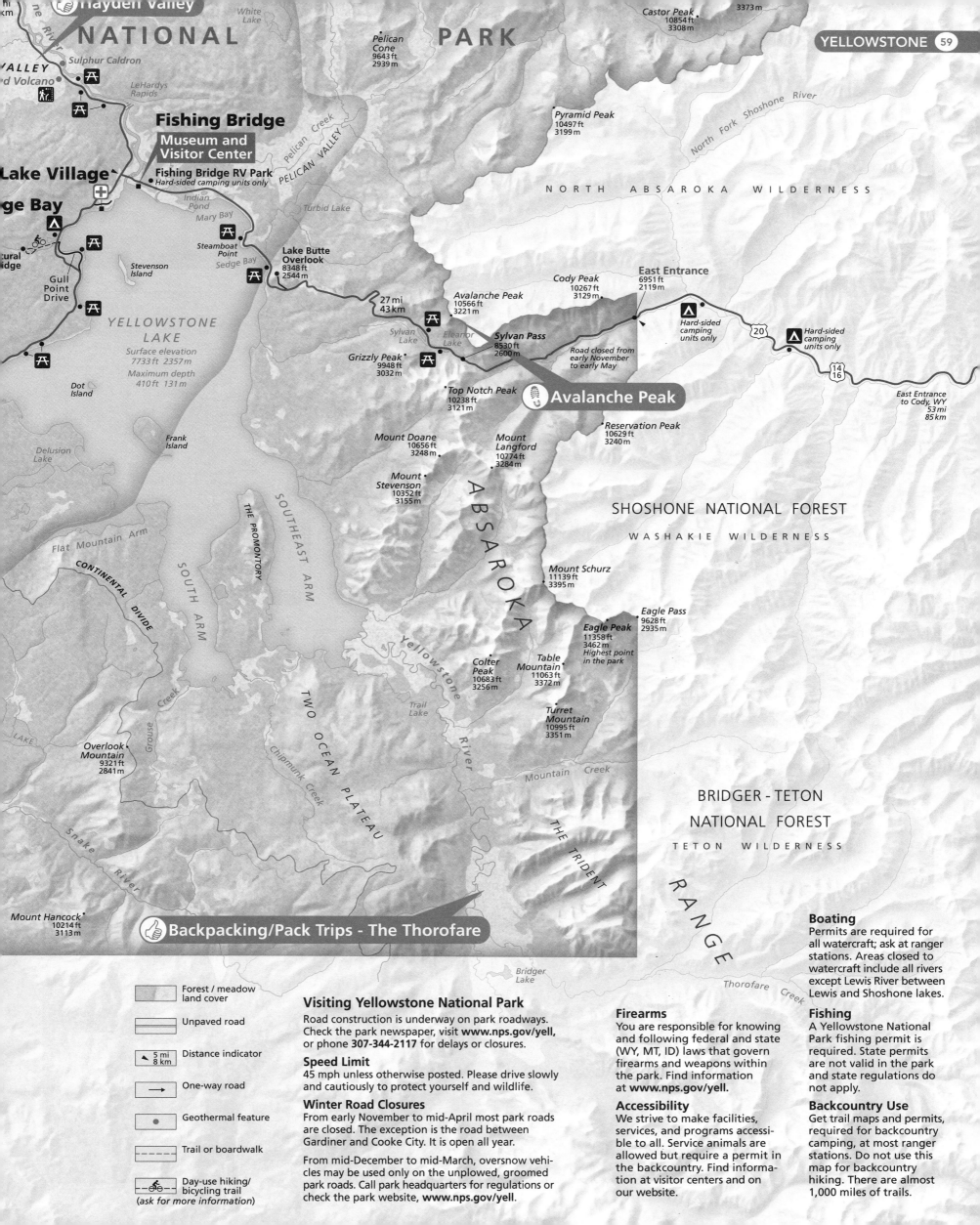

Hayden Valley

N A T I O N A L   P A R K

VALLEY

Sulphur Caldron

'd Volcano

White Lake

Pelican Cone
9643 ft
2939 m

Castor Peak
10854 ft
3308 m

3373 m

Fishing Bridge
Museum and
Visitor Center

LeHardys
Rapids

Pyramid Peak
10497 ft
3199 m

N O R T H   A B S A R O K A   W I L D E R N E S S

Lake Village

ge Bay

Fishing Bridge RV Park
Hard-sided camping units only

Indian
Pond

Mary Bay

Pelican Creek

PELICAN VALLEY

Turbid Lake

Steamboat
Point

Sedge Bay

Lake Butte
Overlook
8348 ft
2544 m

Cody Peak
10267 ft
3129 m

East Entrance
6951 ft
2119 m

20

Hard-sided
camping
units only

Hard-sided
camping
units only

cural
idge

Gull
Point
Drive

Stevenson
Island

27 mi
43 km

Avalanche Peak
10566 ft
3221 m

Sylvan
Lake

Eleanor
Lake

Sylvan Pass
8530 ft
2600 m

Road closed from
early November
to early May

14
16

YELLOWSTONE
LAKE

Surface elevation
7733 ft   2357 m

Maximum depth
410 ft   131 m

Grizzly Peak
9948 ft
3032 m

Top Notch Peak
10238 ft
3121 m

👣 **Avalanche Peak**

East Entrance
to Cody, WY
53 mi
85 km

Dot
Island

Delusion
Lake

Frank
Island

Mount Doane
10656 ft
3248 m

Mount
Stevenson
10352 ft
3155 m

Mount
Langford
10774 ft
3284 m

Reservation Peak
10629 ft
3240 m

S H O S H O N E   N A T I O N A L   F O R E S T

W A S H A K I E   W I L D E R N E S S

A
B
S
A
R
O
K
A

Mount Schurz
11139 ft
3395 m

Flat Mountain Arm

CONTINENTAL DIVIDE

THE PROMONTORY

SOUTHEAST ARM

SOUTH
ARM

Yellowstone

Eagle Pass
9628 ft
2935 m

Eagle Peak
11358 ft
3462 m
Highest point
in the park

LAKE

Grouse

Creek

TWO OCEAN PLATEAU

Trail Lake

Chipmunk Creek

Yellowstone
River

Colter
Peak
10683 ft
3256 m

Table
Mountain
11063 ft
3372 m

Turret
Mountain
10995 ft
3351 m

Mountain   Creek

B R I D G E R - T E T O N

N A T I O N A L   F O R E S T

T E T O N   W I L D E R N E S S

Overlook
Mountain
9321 ft
2841 m

Snake

River

THE TRIDENT

R
A
N
G
E

Mount Hancock
10214 ft
3113 m

👍 **Backpacking/Pack Trips - The Thorofare**

Bridger
Lake

Thorofare   Creek

Boating
Permits are required for
all watercraft; ask at ranger
stations. Areas closed to
watercraft include all rivers
except Lewis River between
Lewis and Shoshone lakes.

Legend

	Forest / meadow land cover
	Unpaved road
5 mi / 8 km	Distance indicator
→	One-way road
•	Geothermal feature
┄	Trail or boardwalk
🚲	Day-use hiking/ bicycling trail (ask for more information)

Visiting Yellowstone National Park
Road construction is underway on park roadways.
Check the park newspaper, visit www.nps.gov/yell,
or phone **307-344-2117** for delays or closures.

Speed Limit
45 mph unless otherwise posted. Please drive slowly
and cautiously to protect yourself and wildlife.

Winter Road Closures
From early November to mid-April most park roads
are closed. The exception is the road between
Gardiner and Cooke City. It is open all year.

From mid-December to mid-March, oversnow vehicles may be used only on the unplowed, groomed
park roads. Call park headquarters for regulations or
check the park website, **www.nps.gov/yell.**

Firearms
You are responsible for knowing
and following federal and state
(WY, MT, ID) laws that govern
firearms and weapons within
the park. Find information
at **www.nps.gov/yell.**

Accessibility
We strive to make facilities,
services, and programs accessible to all. Service animals are
allowed but require a permit in
the backcountry. Find information at visitor centers and on
our website.

Fishing
A Yellowstone National
Park fishing permit is
required. State permits
are not valid in the park
and state regulations do
not apply.

Backcountry Use
Get trail maps and permits,
required for backcountry
camping, at most ranger
stations. Do not use this
map for backcountry
hiking. There are almost
1,000 miles of trails.

Mammoth Terraces (Yellowstone)

Beehive Geyser (Yellowstone)

Grand Canyon of the Yellowstone

West Thumb (Yellowstone)

Dunanda Falls

Hidden Lake (Glacier)

Cracker Lake (Glacier)

Lake McDonald (Glacier)

Bowman Lake (Glacier)

Grinnell Glacier Trail (Glacier)

Heavens Peak from Crystal Point (Glacier)

Looking out from Ptarmigan Tunnel (Glacier)

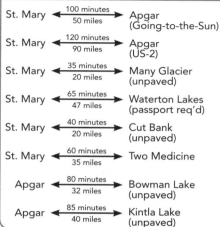

Glacier Basics

(406) 888-7800 | nps.gov/glac
Entrance Fee: $35/car
Timed-Entry Permits*: required in summer
Lodging: Glacier Park Lodge#, St. Mary Lodge#, Apgar Village Lodge#, West Glacier Motel#, Motel Lake McDonald#, Grouse Mountain Lodge#, Prince of Wales Hotel#, Many Glacier Hotel***, Swiftcurrent Motor Inn**, Rising Sun Motor Inn**, Lake McDonald Lodge**, Village Inn at Apgar**, Cedar Creek Lodge**
Camping: St. Mary*, Rising Sun, Avalanche Creek, Sprague Creek, Apgar*, Two Medicine, Cut Bank, Many Glacier*, Fish Creek*, Logging Creek, Quartz Creek, Bowman Lake, Kintla Lake

*reserve at recreation.gov
#reserve at glacierparkcollection.com
**reserve at glaciernationalparklodges.com

Many Glacier Hotel

Glacier Driving Distances

Going-to-the-Sun Road has become synonymous with Glacier National Park, but it usually first opens completely in late June. Fortunately, US-2 remains open year-round allowing visitors to switch sides of the Rockies.

From	Time	Distance	To
St. Mary	100 minutes	50 miles	Apgar (Going-to-the-Sun)
St. Mary	120 minutes	90 miles	Apgar (US-2)
St. Mary	35 minutes	20 miles	Many Glacier (unpaved)
St. Mary	65 minutes	47 miles	Waterton Lakes (passport req'd)
St. Mary	40 minutes	20 miles	Cut Bank (unpaved)
St. Mary	60 minutes	35 miles	Two Medicine
Apgar	80 minutes	32 miles	Bowman Lake (unpaved)
Apgar	85 minutes	40 miles	Kintla Lake (unpaved)

Granite Park Chalet

Why Visit Glacier?

- To hike among some of the world's most dramatic mountain scenery
- Some of the most exceptional backpacking in the country
- To spend a night or two at Granite Park or Sperry Chalet
- To join a boat or Red Jammer tour, go whitewater rafting, or giddy-up into the park's wilderness

Glacier Favorites

Easy Hikes: Grinnell Lake (6.8 miles), Apikuni Falls (2), St Mary's Falls (1.6), Running Eagle Fall (0.6), Virginia Falls (3.6), Baring Falls (0.6), Sun Point (1.6), Aster Park (4), Twin Falls (7)
Moderate Hikes: Grinnell Glacier (10.6), Hidden Lake Overlook (2.8), Cracker Lake (12.8), Lake Francis (12.4), Avalanche Lake (4.6), Redgap Pass (12.8), Bowman Lake (14.2), Iceberg Lake (9.6), Quartz Lake (12), Piegan Pass (16.6), Cobalt Lake (11.6), Lincoln Lake (16), Apgar Lookout (7.2)
Strenuous Hikes: Highline Trail (15.2), Ptarmigan Tunnel (10.6), Gunsight Pass (18.4), Dawson Pass (13), Swiftcurrent Pass (13.6), Sperry Chalet (12.6), Pitamakan Pass (15.2), Siyeh Pass (11)
Activities: Take a boat tour from Many Glacier, go whitewater rafting, take a Red Jammer tour, go horseback riding
Views: Hidden Lake Overlook, Many Glacier, Two Medicine, Crystal Point, Wild Goose Island Overlook, Apgar, Logan Pass, Sun Point, Jackson Glacier Overlook

Iceberg Lake (the icebergs aren't the coolest thing, it's the setting you don't see in this image)

What You Need to Know About Glacier

- When Going-to-the-Sun Road (GTSR) fully opens in late June/early July, tourists flood into the park. Remember it's open the rest of the year, and, as long as there isn't a snowstorm, lower portions of GTSR are open year-round (providing access to many popular attractions) and you can circle the park via US-2 (which is also quite scenic).
- With that said, many attractions are only accessible in summer. The hike to Grinnell Glacier usually fully opens in mid-July. Shuttles and Red Jammers and boats start up in June. Trail rides and whitewater rafting are summer-only. So, you have to decide what's important to you. Smaller crowds and easier driving/parking or big crowds and more activities.
- Parking is often difficult in summer. Some days, you have to get to Logan Pass by 8 am to get a space. It's also incredibly difficult to park at Avalanche Lake. The free shuttle is great. Use it if it's running. You won't have to compete for parking and everyone can enjoy the views. Park at Apgar or St. Mary, if you aren't spending the night in the park.
- It's a good idea to have a plan, a backup plan, and a backup to the backup plan. This isn't strictly because you might strike out due to limited parking. Things change. Weather changes. Trails occasionally close for grizzly activity. The nice thing is that most of the hiking trails here are truly marvelous. There's no wrong choice.
- Now, if there are a few trails you have your heart set on (like Hidden Lake, Avalanche Lake, or Grinnell Glacier), make them a priority, wake up early, and enjoy the heck out of it when you're out there (regardless of the weather).
- Demand is high for campsites and lodging. For sites at Many Glacier, you need to be logged in to recreation.gov and ready to make your reservation within minutes of them becoming available (six months in advance). This frenzy has another side effect…increased cancellations. It never hurts to check online for a canceled site.
- You can get a warm meal and comfortable night's rest in the park's backcountry by making reservations at Granite Park Chalet (graniteparkchalet.com) or Sperry Chalet (sperrychalet.com). Granite Park Chalet has multiple access routes, but it's nestled not far from one of the most stunning vistas in the park, Grinnell Glacier Overlook. Just be warned, it's a pretty steep hike up to the overlook. Sperry Chalet is in a similarly beautiful location with the added benefit of having the option to ride a horse to the chalet.
- Boat tours are available at Lake McDonald, Two Medicine, St. Mary Lake, and Swift Current Lake and Lake Josephine (Many Glacier) from June through Labor Day. They're great experiences (especially for the family). Boat tickets, including a ride to Goat Haunt from Waterton Lakes National Park in Canada, can be reserved at watertoncruise.com.
- Red Jammer Tours explore the park's roadways. There are quite a few options and pickup/drop-off locations. Reserve online at glaciernationalparklodges.com.
- Trail rides are available at Many Glacier, Lake McDonald, and Apgar. If you're comfortable in the saddle for a couple of hours, I'd go with the full-day ride to Cracker Lake out of Many Glacier. Reservations can be made at swanmountainglacier.com.
- If crowds are getting you down, look into the trailheads located along US-2.

Two Medicine

How Much Time Do You Have?

Glacier is a hiker's paradise. Spend at least three full days. In a perfect world a trip here would include two nights at Many Glacier and two nights at Sprague Creek (camping) or two nights at Lake McDonald (lodging).

3 Days: The problem with Glacier is a good one: it's so darn beautiful. You could spend three full days hiking at Many Glacier and want more. You could spend three full days exploring Going-to-the-Sun Road and want more. You could spend three full days at Apgar and want more. Two Medicine is incredible. You can do some great backpacking at Bowman/Kintla Lake. You can drive up to Waterton Lakes National Park in Canada and boat to Goat Haunt (another great idea) or hike to Crypt Lake (it's awesome!). And there's more in the Canadian Rockies (Banff, Jasper, Kootenai, and Yoho national parks).

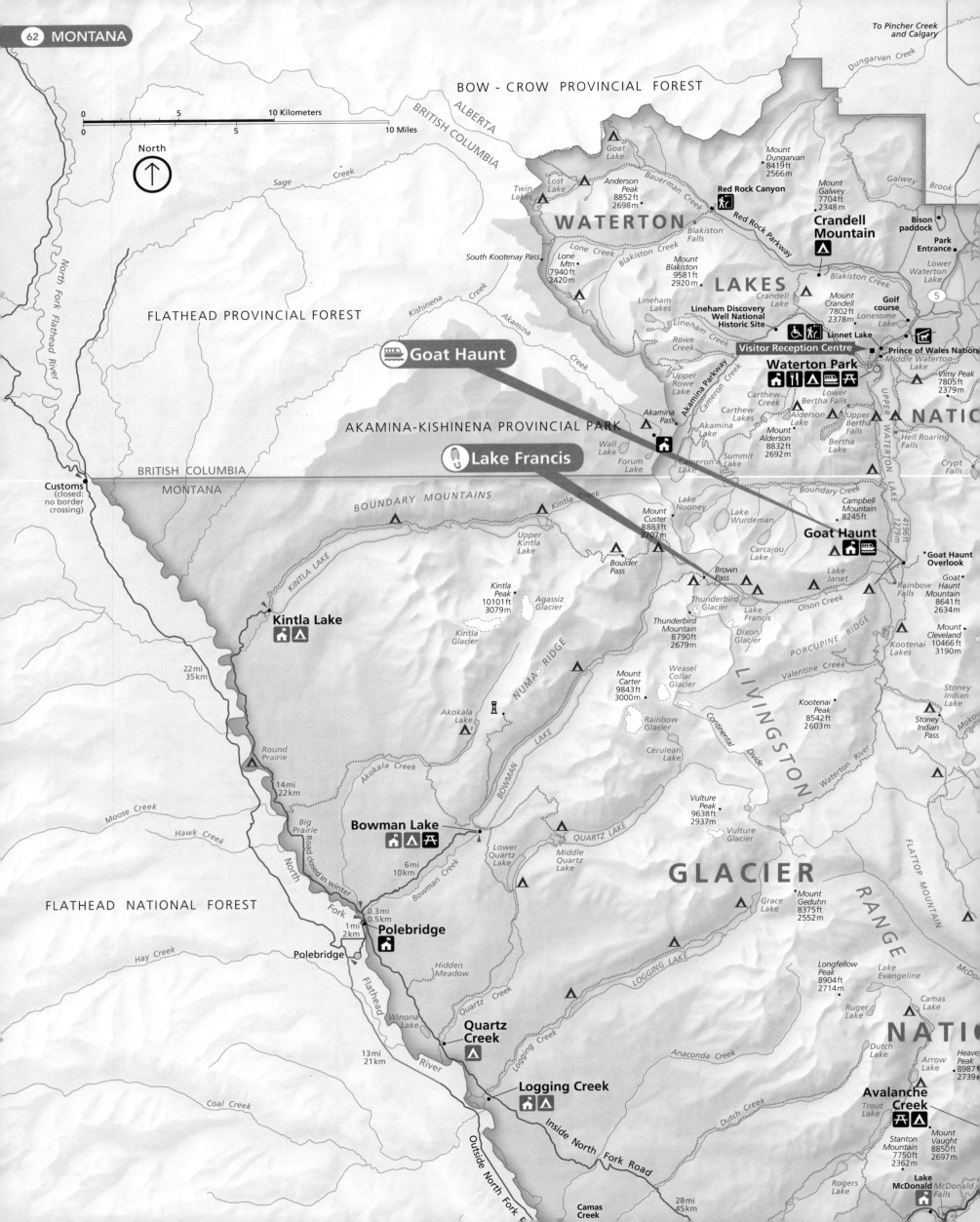

BOW - CROW PROVINCIAL FOREST

BRITISH COLUMBIA
ALBERTA

To Pincher Creek
and Calgary

Dungarvan Creek

0   5   10 Kilometers
0   5   10 Miles

North

Sage   Creek

FLATHEAD PROVINCIAL FOREST

North Fork Flathead River

Twin Lakes

Lost Lake

Goat Lake

Anderson Peak
8852 ft
2698 m

Bauerman Creek

Mount Dungarvan
8419 ft
2566 m

Mount Galwey
7704 ft
2348 m

Galwey Brook

Red Rock Canyon

Red Rock Parkway

WATERTON

Crandell Mountain

Bison paddock

Park Entrance

South Kootenay Pass

Lone Mtn •
7940 ft
2420 m

Blakiston Falls

Blakiston Creek

Mount Blakiston
9581 ft
2920 m

LAKES

Crandell Lake

Mount Crandell
7802 ft
2378 m

Blakiston Creek

Golf course

Lineham Lakes

Lineham Creek

Lineham Discovery
Well National
Historic Site

Lower Waterton Lake

5

Lonesome Lake

Kishinena

Akamina

Creek

Rowe Creek

Upper Rowe Lake

Akamina Parkway

Cameron Creek

Visitor Reception Centre

Prince of Wales Nation

Middle Waterton Lake

Goat Haunt

Waterton Park

Vimy Peak
7805 ft
2379 m

AKAMINA-KISHINENA PROVINCIAL PARK

Akamina Pass

Carthew-Creek

Carthew Lakes

Akamina Lake

Lower Bertha Falls

Upper Bertha Falls

Bertha Lake

NATIO

Lake Francis

Wall Lake

Forum Lake

Cameron Lake

Summit Lake

Mount Alderson
8832 ft
2692 m

UPPER WATERTON LAKE

Hell Roaring Falls

Crypt Falls

Customs
(closed: no border crossing)

BRITISH COLUMBIA
MONTANA

BOUNDARY MOUNTAINS

Kintla Creek

Boundary Creek

Lake Nooney

Lake Wurdeman

Campbell Mountain
8245 ft

4196 ft
1279 m

Goat Haunt

Goat Haunt Overlook

Mount Custer
8883 ft
2707 m

Upper Kintla Lake

Boulder Pass

Carcajou Lake

Lake Janet

Rainbow Falls

Goat Haunt Mountain
8641 ft
2634 m

Kintla Peak
10101 ft
3079 m

Agassiz Glacier

Brown Pass

Thunderbird Glacier

Lake Francis

Olson Creek

KINTLA LAKE

Kintla Glacier

Thunderbird Mountain
8790 ft
2679 m

Dixon Glacier

PORCUPINE RIDGE

Kootenai Lakes

Mount Cleveland
10466 ft
3190 m

Kintla Lake

Akokala Lake

NUMA RIDGE

Mount Carter
9843 ft
3000 m

Weasel Collar Glacier

Rainbow Glacier

Cerulean Lake

LIVINGSTON

Valentine Creek

Kootenai Peak
8542 ft
2603 m

Continental Divide

Waterton River

Stoney Indian Lake

Stoney Indian Pass

22 mi
35 km

Round Prairie

14 mi
22 km

Akokala Creek

BOWMAN LAKE

Big Prairie

Bowman Lake

6 mi
10 km

Lower Quartz Lake

Middle Quartz Lake

QUARTZ LAKE

GLACIER

Mokow

Moose Creek

Hawk Creek

North Fork

Bowman Creek

Vulture Peak
9638 ft
2937 m

Vulture Glacier

RANGE

FLATTOP MOUNTAIN

FLATHEAD NATIONAL FOREST

0.3 mi
0.5 km

1 mi
2 km

Polebridge

Polebridge

Hidden Meadow

Quartz Creek

Quartz Creek

Logging Lake

Grace Lake

Mount Geduhn
8375 ft
2552 m

Longfellow Peak
8904 ft
2714 m

Lake Evangeline

Camas Lake

McD

Hay Creek

Flathead River

Winona Lake

Quartz Creek

Logging Creek

Ruger Lake

Dutch Lake

Arrow Lake

Heavens Peak
8987 ft
2739 m

13 mi
21 km

Logging Creek

Anaconda Creek

Dutch Creek

NATIO

Trout Lake

Avalanche Creek

Coal Creek

Inside North Fork Road

Outside North Fork R

Camas Creek

28 mi
45 km

Stanton Mountain
7750 ft
2362 m

Mount Vaught
8850 ft
2697 m

Lake McDonald

McDonald Falls

Rogers Lake

To Calgary 2 5 To Lethbridge

Cardston
Alberta-Remington
Carriage Centre

Mountain View 5

26mi
42km

16mi
25km

BLOOD
INDIAN
RESERVE

👣 Crypt Lake

Sofa
Mountain
8252ft
2515m

Belly River ⛺

Customs
(summer only) 6

PARK

North Fork Belly River

30mi
47km

Chief Mountain International Highway

CANADA
UNITED STATES

Customs

ALBERTA
MONTANA

👣 Margaret Lake

Kaina
Mountain
9489ft
2892m

Belly River ⛺🏠

Gable
Pass

Chief
Mountain
9080ft
2767m

89

10mi
16km

Saint Mary River

Cosley
Lake

Glenns
Lake

Gable
Mountain
9262ft
2823m

Slide
Lake

Otatso Creek

17

Mokowanis
Lake

Elizabeth
Lake

👣 Swiftcurrent Lookout

Kennedy Creek

4mi
6km

DUCK LAKE

Old Sun
Glacier

Redgap
Pass

👣 Iceberg Lake

Poia
Lake

Margaret
Lake

Ptarmigan
Tunnel

Apikuni
Mountain
9068ft
2764m

👟 Grinnell Glacier

Babb

Duck   Lake   Road

464

Ipasha
Lake

Ahern
Glacier

Kennedy
Lake

Swiftcurrent
Ridge Lake

👣 Highline

Swiftcurrent Creek

Helen
Lake

Ptarmigan
Falls

Many
Glacier
Entrance

12mi
19km

Iceberg
Lake

Many Glacier
Information 🍴⛺🏠

Apikuni
Falls

LAKE SHERBURNE

Redrock
Falls

Swiftcurrent
Nature Trail 🏕️🎋

🚻🍴🦌

White
Park
Inlet

Bullhead
Lake

Swiftcurrent
Lake

Lake Josephine

Napi Point

👍 St. Mary Lake

Lower Saint Mary Lake

9mi
14km

Hudson Bay Divide

Swiftcurrent
Pass

Grinnell
Lake
Grinnell
Glacier

Cataract
Creek

Dry Canyon Cr

St. Mary ⛺

Saint Mary Visitor Center
Saint Mary Entrance

The Loop

GARDEN WALL

Mt Gould
9553ft
2911m

Cracker
Lake

Mount Siyeh
10014ft
3052m

Going-to-the-Sun Road

Saint Mary 🍴

Packers
Roost

Weeping
Wall

Piegan Pass

🏠

BLACKFEET

Triple Arches
Mt Oberlin
8180ft
2493m

Otokomi
Lake

Rose Creek

Rising Sun

18mi
29km

4484ft
1366m

INDIAN RESERVATION

To
Browning

Trail of
the Cedars
Nature Trail ♿🚻

Clements Mtn
8760ft
2670m

Logan Pass
Visitor Center
6646ft/2025m

Going-to-the-Sun Mtn
9642ft
2939m

Goat
Lake

Sun Point
Nature Trail 🏕️🎋🖼️

🚗 Going-to-the-Sun Road

89

Hidden Lake
Nature Trail 🚶

Siyeh
Bend

Sunrift
Gorge

SAINT   MARY   LAKE

Jackson
Glacier
Overlook

Going-to-the-
Sun Road

St Mary River

Baring Falls

Reynolds Mtn
9125ft
2781m

Florence
Falls

St Mary
Falls

Virginia
Falls

Red Eagle
Lake

Divide
Mountain
8665ft
2641m

20mi
32km

Avalanche
Lake

Mount
own
665ft
510m

Hidden
Lake

Avalanche Creek

Hidden Creek

PARK

EAST FLATTOP MOUNTAIN

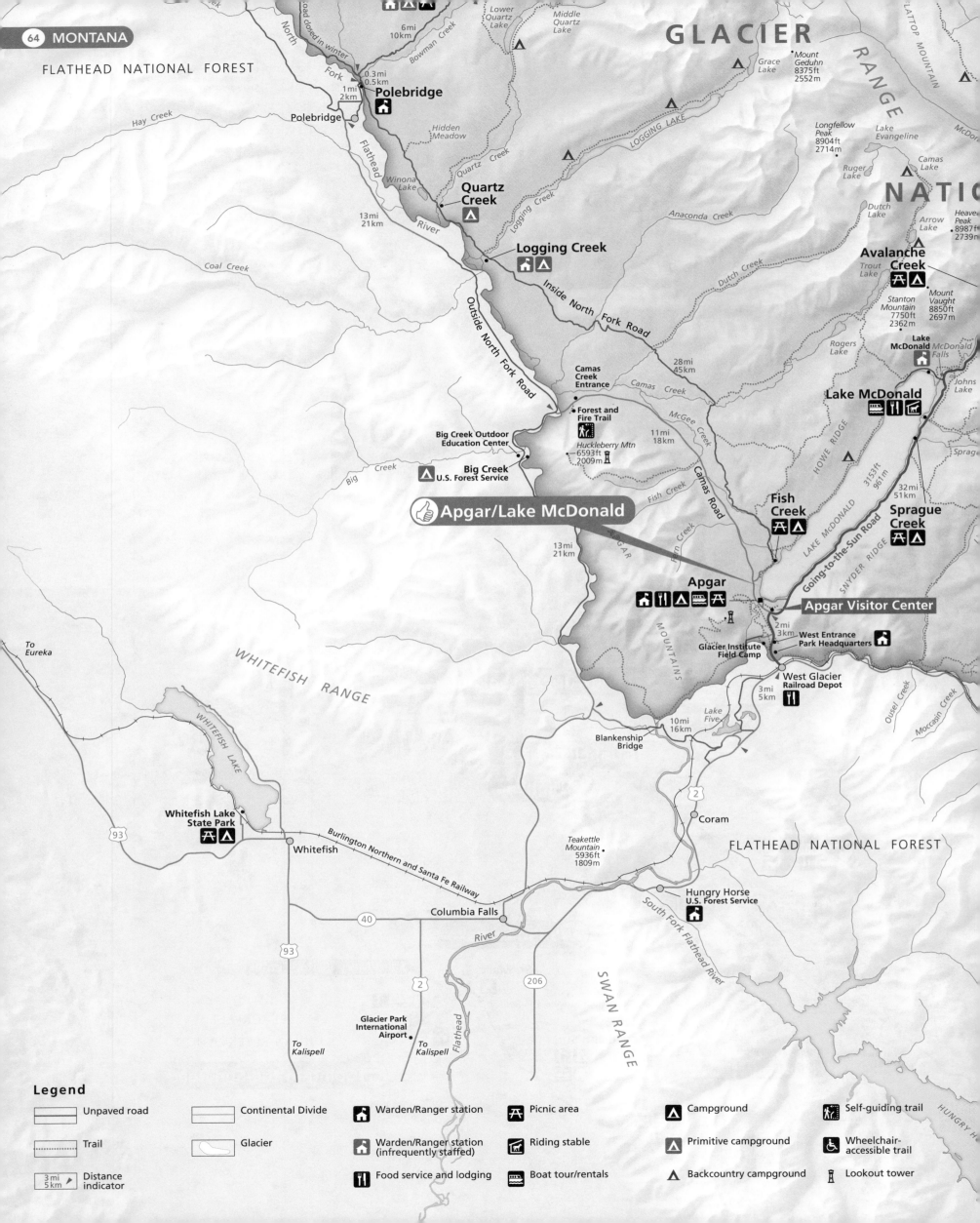

GLACIER

NATIO

FLATHEAD NATIONAL FOREST

Road closed in winter

6mi
10km

Polebridge
0.3mi
0.5km
1mi
2km

Polebridge

Lower
Quartz
Lake

Middle
Quartz
Lake

Hidden
Meadow

Winona
Lake

North Fork

Flathead

River

Hay Creek

Coal Creek

13mi
21km

**Quartz
Creek**

Quartz   Creek

Logging Creek

Bowman Creek

LOGGING LAKE

Grace
Lake

Mount
Geduhn
8375ft
2552m

Longfellow
Peak
8904ft
2714m

Lake
Evangeline

Camas
Lake

Logging Creek

Inside North Fork Road

Anaconda Creek

Dutch Creek

Ruger
Lake

Dutch
Lake

Arrow
Lake

Heaven's
Peak
8987ft
2739m

**Avalanche
Creek**

Trout
Lake

Stanton
Mountain
7750ft
2362m

Mount
Vaught
8850ft
2697m

Rogers
Lake

Lake
McDonald

McDonald
Falls

Camas Creek

Camas
Creek
Entrance

28mi
45km

McGee Creek

Lake McDonald

Johns
Lake

**Forest and
Fire Trail**

11mi
18km

Big Creek Outdoor
Education Center

Big   Creek

*Huckleberry Mtn
6593ft
2009m*

Fish Creek

Camas Road

Camas Road

Big Creek
U.S. Forest Service

👍 **Apgar/Lake McDonald**

13mi
21km

APGAR
MOUNTAINS

**Fish
Creek**

HOWE RIDGE

3153ft
961m

LAKE McDONALD

32mi
51km

**Sprague
Creek**

Going-to-the-Sun Road

SNYDER RIDGE

Sprague

Apgar

Apgar Visitor Center

2mi
3km

Glacier Institute
Field Camp

**West Entrance
Park Headquarters**

To
Eureka

WHITEFISH   RANGE

WHITEFISH LAKE

**West Glacier
Railroad Depot**

3mi
5km

10mi
16km

Lake
Five

Blankenship
Bridge

Ousel Creek

Moccasin Creek

**Whitefish Lake
State Park**

93

Whitefish

Burlington Northern and Santa Fe Railway

*Teakettle
Mountain
5936ft
1809m*

FLATHEAD NATIONAL FOREST

2

Coram

Hungry Horse
U.S. Forest Service

South Fork Flathead River

40

Columbia Falls

River

206

SWAN   RANGE

93

2

*Glacier Park
International
Airport*

*To
Kalispell*

*To
Kalispell*

Flathead

HUNGRY

Legend

▭ Unpaved road	▭ Continental Divide	🏠 Warden/Ranger station	🟤 Picnic area	⛺ Campground	🚶 Self-guiding trail
┅ Trail	◡ Glacier	🏠 Warden/Ranger station (infrequently staffed)	🏇 Riding stable	△ Primitive campground	♿ Wheelchair-accessible trail
3mi / 5km ▶ Distance indicator		🍴 Food service and lodging	🚃 Boat tour/rentals	△ Backcountry campground	🗼 Lookout tower

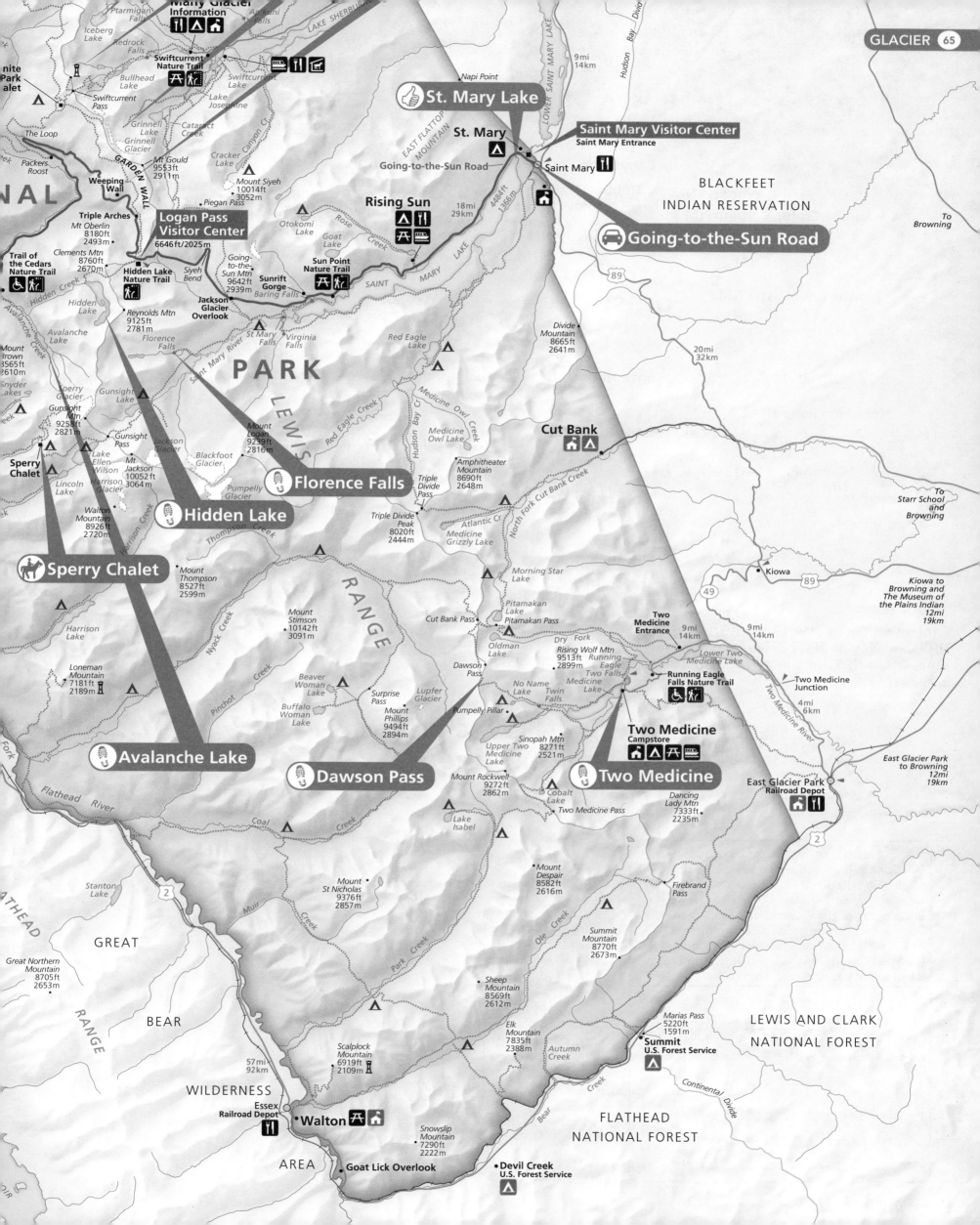

BLACKFEET
INDIAN RESERVATION

To
Browning

9mi
14km

20mi
32km

To
Starr School
and
Browning

Kiowa to
Browning and
The Museum of
the Plains Indian
12mi
19km

9mi
14km

9mi
14km

Kiowa

Two Medicine
Junction

4mi
6km

East Glacier Park
to Browning
12mi
19km

👍 St. Mary Lake

Saint Mary Visitor Center
Saint Mary Entrance

St. Mary

Going-to-the-Sun Road

Saint Mary

🚗 Going-to-the-Sun Road

Many Glacier
Information

Swiftcurrent
Nature Trail

Swiftcurrent

Iceberg
Lake

Ptarmigan
Falls

Redrock
Falls

Apikuni
Falls

LAKE SHERBURNE

Napi Point

nite
Park
alet

Bullhead
Lake

Swiftcurrent
Lake

Lake
Josephine

Grinnell
Lake

Grinnell
Glacier

Cataract
Creek

Cracker
Lake

Mount Siyeh
10014ft
3052m

Piegan Pass

EAST FLATTOP
MOUNTAIN

Rising Sun

18mi
29km

4484ft
1366m

The Loop

Packers
Roost

Weeping
Wall

Mt Gould
9553ft
2911m

GARDEN WALL

Triple Arches
Mt Oberlin
8180ft
2493m

Logan Pass
Visitor Center
6646ft/2025m

Clements Mtn
8760ft
2670m

Trail of
the Cedars
Nature Trail

Hidden Lake
Nature Trail

Siyeh
Creek

Siyeh Bend

Going-to-the-
Sun Mtn
9642ft
2939m

Sunrift
Gorge

Baring Falls

Sun Point
Nature Trail

Otokomi
Lake

Rose
Creek

Goat
Lake

Hidden Creek

Hidden
Lake

Avalanche
Creek

Avalanche
Lake

Mount
Brown
8565ft
2610m

Reynolds Mtn
9125ft
2781m

Florence
Falls

St Mary
Falls

Virginia
Falls

Jackson
Glacier
Overlook

SAINT
MARY
LAKE

Red Eagle
Lake

Divide
Mountain
8665ft
2641m

PARK

LEWIS

PARK

Snyder
Lakes

Sperry
Glacier

Gunsight
Lake

Gunsight
Mtn
9258ft
2821m

Gunsight
Pass

Lake
Ellen
Wilson

Mt
Jackson
10052ft
3064m

Jackson
Glacier

Blackfoot
Glacier

Pumpelly
Glacier

Florence Falls 👣

Mount
Logan
9239ft
2816m

Red Eagle Creek

Medicine
Owl
Creek

Medicine Owl
Lake

Cut Bank

Amphitheater
Mountain
8690ft
2648m

Sperry
Chalet

Lincoln
Lake

Harrison
Glacier

Harrison Creek

Walton
Mountain
8926ft
2720m

👣 Hidden Lake

Thompson Creek

Triple
Divide
Pass

Triple Divide
Peak
8020ft
2444m

Atlantic Cr

Medicine
Grizzly Lake

North Fork Cut Bank Creek

Sperry Chalet 🧗

Harrison
Lake

Mount
Thompson
8527ft
2599m

Nyack Creek

RANGE

Mount
Stimson
10142ft
3091m

Cut Bank Pass

Morning Star
Lake

Pitamakan
Lake

Pitamakan Pass

Two
Medicine
Entrance

Loneman
Mountain
7181ft
2189m

Pinchot Creek

Beaver
Woman
Lake

Surprise
Pass

Mount
Phillips
9494ft
2894m

Lupfer
Glacier

Oldman
Lake

Dawson
Pass

Rising Wolf Mtn
9513ft
2899m

Running
Eagle
Two Falls
Medicine

Lower Two
Medicine Lake

Running Eagle
Falls Nature Trail

👣 Avalanche Lake

Buffalo
Woman
Lake

No Name
Lake

Twin
Falls

Twin
Lakes

Two
Medicine
Lake

Two Medicine
Campstore

Flathead River

👣 Dawson Pass

Pumpelly Pillar

Upper Two
Medicine
Lake

Sinopah Mtn
8271ft
2521m

👣 Two Medicine

Two Medicine River

North Fork
Flathead
River

Coal Creek

Mount
Rockwell
9272ft
2862m

Cobalt
Lake

Two Medicine Pass

Dancing
Lady Mtn
7333ft
2235m

East Glacier Park
Railroad Depot

Stanton
Lake

Lake
Isabel

Mount
Despair
8582ft
2616m

Firebrand
Pass

GREAT

Mount
St Nicholas
9376ft
2857m

Summit
Mountain
8770ft
2673m

Great Northern
Mountain
8705ft
2653m

BEAR

Park Creek

Muir Creek

Sheep
Mountain
8569ft
2612m

Ole Creek

Elk
Mountain
7835ft
2388m

Autumn
Creek

Marias Pass
5220ft
1591m

Summit
U.S. Forest Service

LEWIS AND CLARK

NATIONAL FOREST

WILDERNESS

Scalplock
Mountain
6919ft
2109m

57mi
92km

Continental Divide

Essex
Railroad Depot

Walton

Snowslip
Mountain
7290ft
2222m

Bear Creek

FLATHEAD

AREA

Goat Lick Overlook

Devil Creek
U.S. Forest Service

NATIONAL FOREST

89

89

49

2

2

ADHEAD

RANGE

Zion NP

Glen Canyon NRA

Natural Bridges NM

Hovenweep NM

Yucca House NM

Pipe Spring NM

Great Sand NP & PRES

LAS VEGAS

Grand Canyon NP

Rainbow Bridge NM

Navajo NM

Mesa Verde NP

e Mead NRA

Aztec Ruins NM

Capulin Volcano NM

Canyon de Chelly NM

Chaco Culture NHP

Wupatki NM

Hubbell Trading Post NHS

Valles Caldera N Pres

Manhattan Project NHP

Sunset Crater Volcano NM

Bandelier NM

Fort Union NM

Walnut Canyon NM

SANTA FE

Pecos NHP

Tuzigoot NM

El Morro NM

Petroglyph NM

Petrified Forest NP

Montezuma Castle NM

Petroglyph NM

ALBUQUERQUE

A R I Z O N A

El Malpais NM

N E W   M E X I C O

PHOENIX

Tonto NM

Salinas Pueblo Missions NM

Hohokam Pima NM

Casa Grande Ruins NM

Gila Cliff Dwellings NM

Organ Pipe Cactus NM

Saguaro NP

White Sands NP

Fort Bowie NHS

Chiricahua NM

Carlsbad Caverns NP

Tumacacori NHP

Coronado N MEM

🕐 **ARIZONA**

EL PASO

Guadalupe Mtns NP

Canyon de Chelly NM, Hubbell Trading Post NHS, and Navajo NM observe daylight saving time. Other NPS units in Arizona do not.

Chamizal N MEM

🕐 **MOUNTAIN (Washington, DC, minus 2 hours)**

Fort Davis NHS

Rio Grande WSR

Southern Driving Distances

Hot Springs is an outlier. Big Bend isn't close to anything. Petrified Forest can just as easily be mixed in with Arches in Utah or Mesa Verde in Colorado or the Grand Canyon in Arizona. But you can make a pretty nice roadtrip out of El Paso, combining Guadalupe Mountains, Carlsbad Caverns and White Sands. Add Big Bend to it if you can. It's incredible.

Big Bend NP

THE SOUTH

Hot Springs	← 13 hours / 860 miles →	Big Bend
Big Bend	← 4.5 hours / 270 miles →	Guadalupe Mountains
Guadalupe Mountains	← 45 minutes / 42 miles →	Carlsbad Caverns
Carlsbad Caverns	← 3.5 hours / 188 miles →	White Sands
White Sands	← 6.5 hours / 410 miles →	Petrified Forest
Petrified Forest	← 5 hours / 280 miles →	Saguaro
White Sands	← 5 hours / 325 miles →	Saguaro

's Old Fort

Fort Larned NHS

Tallgrass Prairie
N PRES

MISSOURI

Ulysses S.
Grant NHS

WICHITA

Fort Scott NHS

Wilson's Creek
NB

Ozark NSR

George Washington Carver NM

Pea Ridge NMP

Lake Meredith
NRA

TULSA

Buffalo NR

Washita Battlefield NHS

Fort Smith NHS

Alibates Flint
Quarries NM

OKLAHOMA CITY

ARKANSAS

OKLAHOMA

Hot Springs NP

LITTLE ROCK
Little Rock Central
High School NHS

Br

Chickasaw NRA

Arkansas Post N MEM

SOUTH

President William
Jefferson Clinton
Birthplace Home NHS

M

FT WORTH

DALLAS

Poverty Point NM

Vicksb
NMP

LOUISIANA

Cane River
Creole NHP

TEXAS

Waco Mammoth NM

Natchez N

BATON
ROUGE

Big Thicket
N PRES

NEW ORLEANS

Lyndon B. Johnson NHP

AUSTIN

New Orleans Jazz NHP

HOUSTON

Jean Lafitte
NHP & PRES

Amistad NRA

SAN ANTONIO
San Antonio Missions NHP

**CENTRAL
(Washington, DC, minus 1 hour)**

Padre Island
NS

GULF OF MEXICO

Palo Alto Battlefield
NHP

Hot Springs Basics

(501) 620-6715 | nps.gov/hosp
Entrance Fee: None
Bathhouses: Buckstaff and Quapaw
Lodging: Hotel Hale*
Camping: Gulpha Gorge**

*reserve at hotelhale.com
**reserve at recreation.gov

Hot Springs Driving Distances

You can walk most of the park. From Bathhouse Row, you can walk the Grand Promenade, and then take Peak Trail (steep) up to Hot Springs Mountain Tower. Drives are quick. It's about two miles from Bathhouse Row to Gulpha Gorge Campground. The loop around Hot Springs Mountain is less than four miles. The parking area for Sunset Trail on Black Snake Road (Whittington) is three miles from the Fordyce Bathhouse.

Balanced Rock

Why Visit Hot Springs?

- To receive "traditional therapy" at Buckstaff Baths
- To tour Bathhouse Row and historic Fordyce Bathhouse
- To walk the Grand Promenade
- To look down on Hot Springs from the Mountain Tower

Hot Springs Favorites

Hikes: Grand Promenade (easy, 1 mile), Goat Rock (moderate, 2.2), Balanced Rock (easy, 1.6+), Hot Springs Mountain (moderate, 3.4), Sunset (moderate, 10+)
Views: Hot Springs Mountain Tower

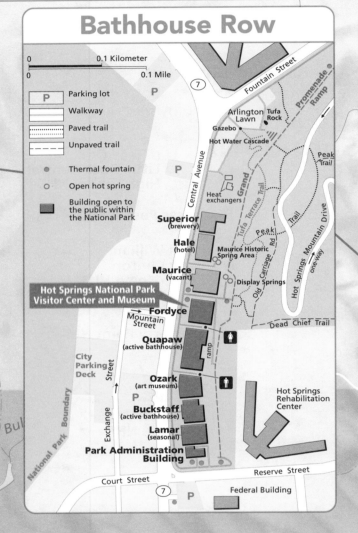

Bathhouse Row

0   0.1 Kilometer
0   0.1 Mile

P Parking lot
Walkway
Paved trail
Unpaved trail

● Thermal fountain
○ Open hot spring
■ Building open to the public within the National Park

Fountain Street

Promenade Ramp

Central Avenue

Arlington Tufa Lawn Rock
Gazebo
Hot Water Cascade

Peak Trail

Heat exchangers

Grand

Tufa Terrace Trail

Superior (brewery)

Hale (hotel)
Maurice Historic Spring Area

Peak Trail

Old Carriage Rd

Hot Springs Mountain Drive one-way

Maurice (vacant)
Display Springs

Hot Springs National Park Visitor Center and Museum

Fordyce
Mountain Street

Dead Chief Trail

Quapaw (active bathhouse)
ramp

City Parking Deck

Exchange Street

Ozark (art museum)

Hot Springs Rehabilitation Center

Buckstaff (active bathhouse)

Park Street

Lamar (seasonal)

Park Administration Building

National Park Boundary

Court Street
Reserve Street

7
P
Federal Building

Balanced Rock

Cedar Glades Road

To Lake Ouachita State Park

Balanced Rock

🥾 **Balanced Rock**

1209ft

SUGARLOAF MOUNTAIN

Sunset Trail

Dangerous curves
Drive with caution

Black Snake Road

Whittington Avenue

Park Maintenance Area • **Whittington Spring**

City Park

Whittington Creek

Mountain Top Trail

West

West

Sunset Trail

MUSIC MOUNTAIN

1100ft West

West

Mtn Top Trail

•1405ft
Highest Point in Park

WEST MOUNTAIN

Sunset Trail

1260ft

North

•1179ft

0   0.5   1 Kilometer
0   0.5   1 Mile

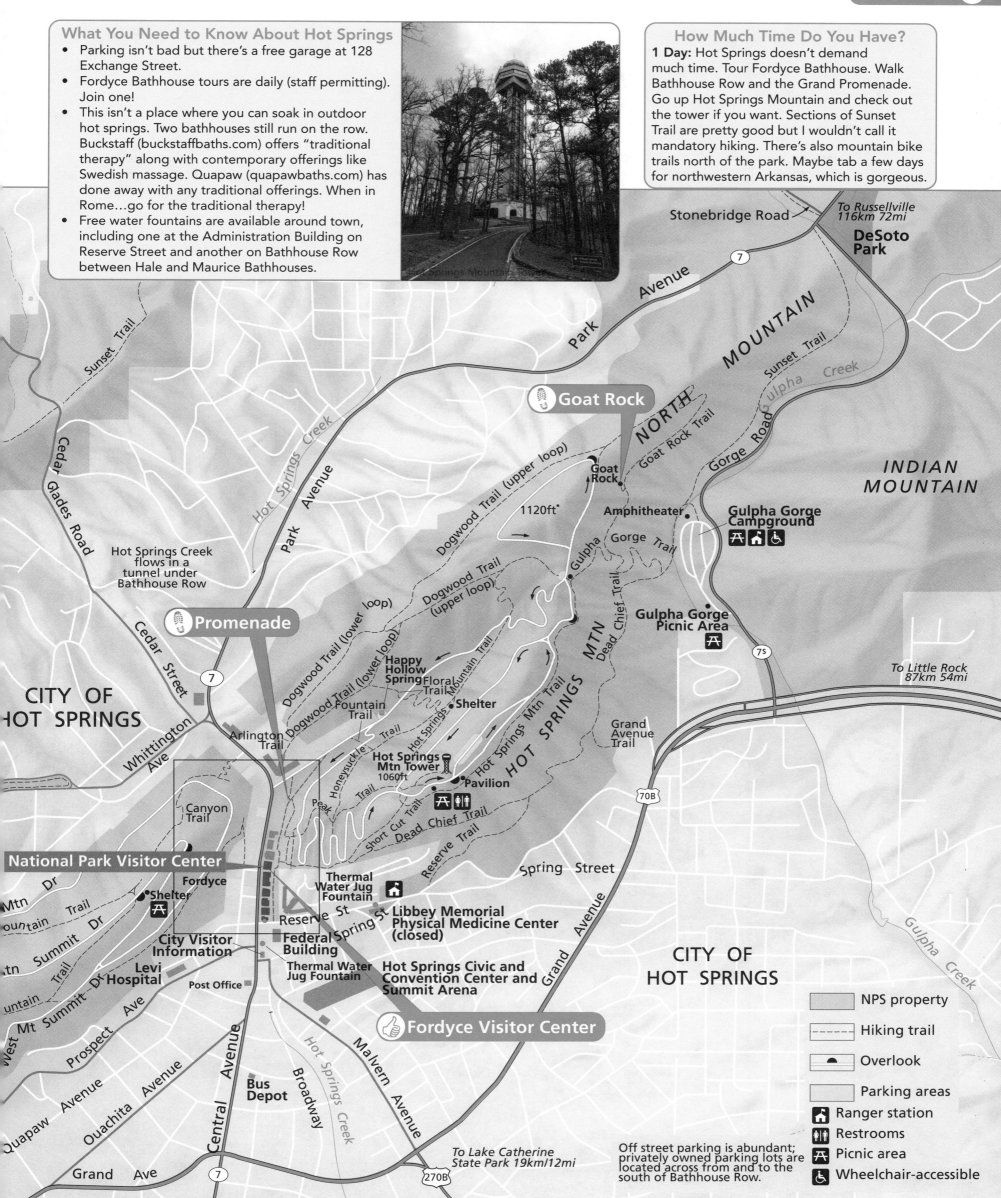

What You Need to Know About Hot Springs

- Parking isn't bad but there's a free garage at 128 Exchange Street.
- Fordyce Bathhouse tours are daily (staff permitting). Join one!
- This isn't a place where you can soak in outdoor hot springs. Two bathhouses still run on the row. Buckstaff (buckstaffbaths.com) offers "traditional therapy" along with contemporary offerings like Swedish massage. Quapaw (quapawbaths.com) has done away with any traditional offerings. When in Rome…go for the traditional therapy!
- Free water fountains are available around town, including one at the Administration Building on Reserve Street and another on Bathhouse Row between Hale and Maurice Bathhouses.

How Much Time Do You Have?

1 Day: Hot Springs doesn't demand much time. Tour Fordyce Bathhouse. Walk Bathhouse Row and the Grand Promenade. Go up Hot Springs Mountain and check out the tower if you want. Sections of Sunset Trail are pretty good but I wouldn't call it mandatory hiking. There's also mountain bike trails north of the park. Maybe tab a few days for northwestern Arkansas, which is gorgeous.

Stonebridge Road

To Russellville
116km 72mi

DeSoto Park

7

Park Avenue

NORTH MOUNTAIN

Gulpha Creek

Sunset Trail

INDIAN MOUNTAIN

Goat Rock

Goat Rock Trail

Dogwood Trail (upper loop)

1120ft

Goat Rock

Amphitheater

Gulpha Gorge Campground

Gulpha Gorge Trail

Dogwood Trail (upper loop)

Gulpha Gorge Road

Gulpha Gorge Picnic Area

7S

To Little Rock
87km 54mi

Promenade

Cedar Street

Hot Springs Creek flows in a tunnel under Bathhouse Row

Park Avenue

Hot Springs Creek

Dogwood Trail (lower loop)

Dogwood Trail (lower loop)

Dead Chief Trail

HOT SPRINGS MTN

7

CITY OF HOT SPRINGS

Whittington Ave

Arlington Trail

Happy Hollow Spring

Floral Trail

Fountain Trail

Hot Springs Mountain Trail

Shelter

Hot Springs Mtn Trail

Grand Avenue Trail

Honeysuckle Trail

Canyon Trail

Peak Trail

Hot Springs Mtn Trail

Hot Springs Mtn Tower
1060ft

Pavilion

70B

National Park Visitor Center

Mtn Dr

Trail

Fordyce

Shelter

Mountain Summit Dr

West Mt Summit Dr

Short Cut Trail

Dead Chief Trail

Reserve Trail

Spring Street

CITY OF HOT SPRINGS

Gulpha Creek

Thermal Water Jug Fountain

Libbey Memorial Physical Medicine Center (closed)

Reserve St

Spring St

City Visitor Information

Levi Hospital

Prospect Ave

Post Office

Thermal Water Jug Fountain

Federal Building

Hot Springs Civic and Convention Center and Summit Arena

Grand Avenue

Quapaw Avenue

Ouachita Avenue

Central Avenue

Broadway

Bus Depot

Hot Springs Creek

Fordyce Visitor Center

Malvern Avenue

Grand Ave

7

270B

To Lake Catherine State Park 19km/12mi

Off street parking is abundant; privately owned parking lots are located across from and to the south of Bathhouse Row.

Legend

- NPS property
- - - - - Hiking trail
- Overlook
- Parking areas
- Ranger station
- Restrooms
- Picnic area
- Wheelchair-accessible

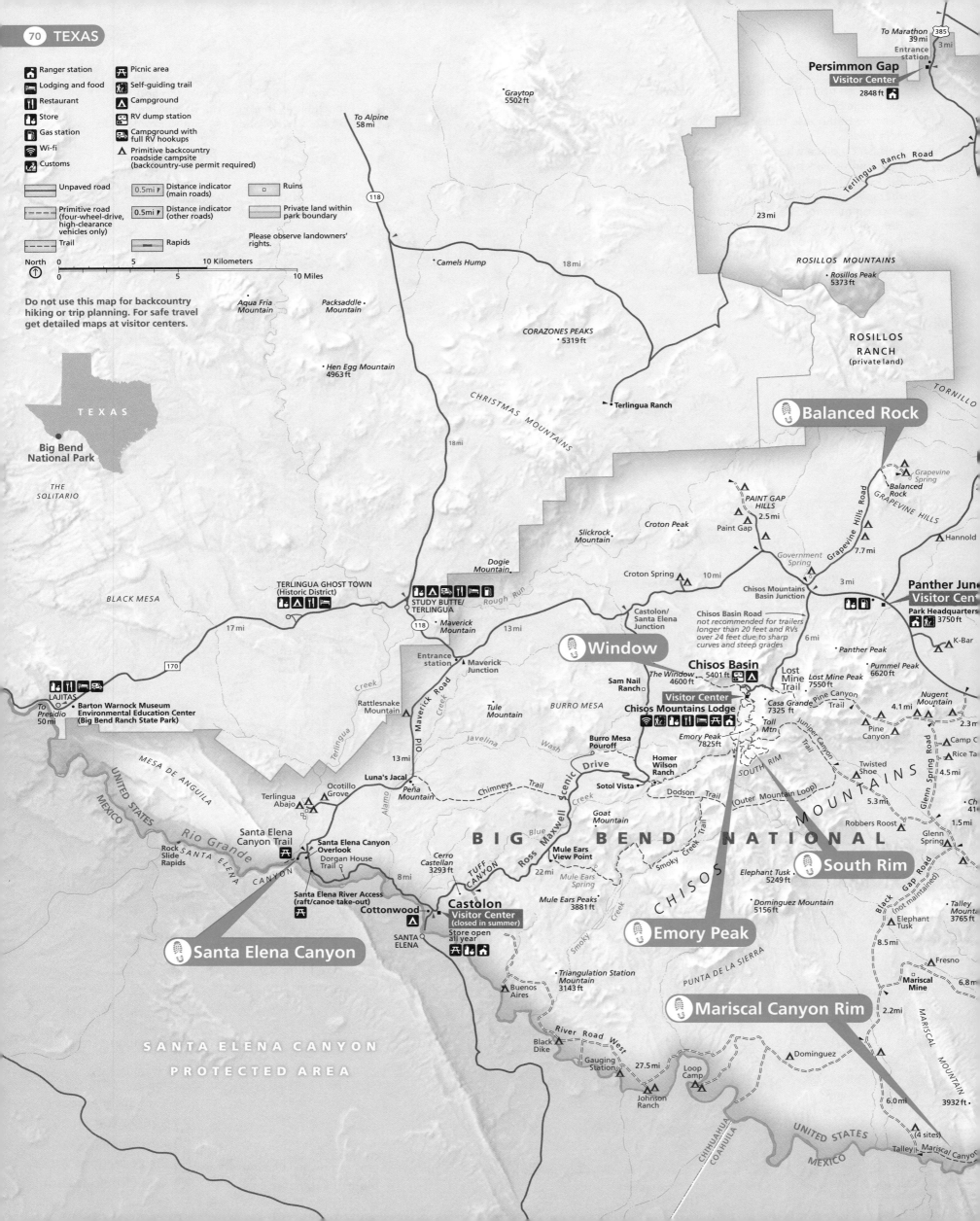

Map Legend

- 🏠 Ranger station
- 🛏️ Lodging and food
- 🍴 Restaurant
- 🏪 Store
- ⛽ Gas station
- 📶 Wi-fi
- 🛃 Customs

- 🏕️ Picnic area
- Self-guiding trail
- ⛺ Campground
- RV dump station
- Campground with full RV hookups
- ▲ Primitive backcountry roadside campsite (backcountry-use permit required)

- Unpaved road
- Primitive road (four-wheel-drive, high-clearance vehicles only)
- Trail
- 0.5mi ▸ Distance indicator (main roads)
- 0.5mi ▸ Distance indicator (other roads)
- Rapids
- □ Ruins
- Private land within park boundary

Please observe landowners' rights.

North ⊕

0   5   10 Kilometers
0   5   10 Miles

Do not use this map for backcountry hiking or trip planning. For safe travel get detailed maps at visitor centers.

TEXAS

Big Bend National Park

THE SOLITARIO

To Alpine 58 mi

118

Graytop 5502 ft

Camels Hump

18 mi

Aqua Fria Mountain

Packsaddle Mountain

CORAZONES PEAKS 5319 ft

CHRISTMAS MOUNTAINS

Hen Egg Mountain 4963 ft

18 mi

Terlingua Ranch

To Marathon 39 mi 385
3 mi
Entrance station

Persimmon Gap
Visitor Center
2848 ft 🏠

Terlingua Ranch Road

23 mi

ROSILLOS MOUNTAINS

Rosillos Peak 5373 ft

ROSILLOS RANCH (private land)

TORNILLO

Balanced Rock 👣

BLACK MESA

TERLINGUA GHOST TOWN (Historic District)

STUDY BUTTE/ TERLINGUA

118

Maverick Mountain

13 mi

17 mi

170

LAJITAS

To Presidio 50 mi

Barton Warnock Museum Environmental Education Center (Big Bend Ranch State Park)

Entrance station

Rattlesnake Mountain

Old Maverick Road

Maverick Junction

Dogie Mountain

Rough Run

Slickrock Mountain

Croton Peak

PAINT GAP HILLS

2.5 mi

Paint Gap

7.7 mi

Government Spring

Grapevine Spring

Balanced Rock

GRAPEVINE HILLS

*Hannold

Grapevine Hills Road

Croton Spring

10 mi

Chisos Mountains Basin Junction

3 mi

Panther Junction
Visitor Center
Park Headquarters 🏠 3750 ft

Castolon/ Santa Elena Junction

Chisos Basin Road not recommended for trailers longer than 20 feet and RVs over 24 feet due to sharp curves and steep grades

6 mi

Window 👣

Maverick Mountain

Sam Nail Ranch

BURRO MESA

The Window 4600 ft

Chisos Basin
Visitor Center
Chisos Mountains Lodge

Panther Peak

K-Bar

Pummel Peak 6620 ft

Emory Peak 7825 ft

Casa Grande 7325 ft

Lost Mine Trail

Lost Mine Peak 7550 ft

Pine Canyon Trail

4.1 mi

Nugent Mountain

2.3 m

Creek

MESA DE ANGUILA

Terlingua Abajo

Ocotillo Grove

Luna's Jacal

Peña Mountain

Chimneys Trail

Tule Mountain

Javelina

Wash

Burro Mesa Pouroff

Homer Wilson Ranch

Sotol Vista

Maxwell Scenic Drive

Goat Mountain

Dodson Trail

SOUTH RIM

Juniper Canyon Trail

Emory Peak 7825ft

Toll Mtn

CHISOS MOUNTAINS

(Outer Mountain Loop)

Twisted Shoe

Camp C

Rice Ta

4.5 mi

5.3 mi

Glenn Spring Road

UNITED STATES
MEXICO

Rio Grande

SANTA ELENA

Rock Slide Rapids

CANYON

Santa Elena Canyon Trail

Santa Elena Canyon Overlook

Dorgan House Trail

Santa Elena River Access (raft/canoe take-out)

13 mi

Terlingua

Alamo

Cerro Castellan 3293 ft

TUFF CANYON

Ross Maxwell

Blue

Mule Ears View Point

Mule Ears Spring

22 mi

Smoky Creek Trail

Mule Ears Peaks 3881 ft

B I G   B E N D   N A T I O N A L

Elephant Tusk 5249 ft

Dominguez Mountain 5156 ft

Robbers Roost

1.5 m

Glenn Spring

Black Gap Road (not maintained)

Elephant Tusk

South Rim 👣

8 mi

Cottonwood

Castolon
Visitor Center
(closed in summer)
Store open all year

SANTA ELENA

Santa Elena Canyon 👣

Triangulation Station Mountain 3143 ft

Buenos Aires

Smoky

Creek

Emory Peak 👣

PUNTA DE LA SIERRA

8.5 mi

Talley Mount 3765 ft

Fresno

Mariscal Mine

6.8 m

SANTA ELENA CANYON
PROTECTED AREA

River Road West

Black Dike

Gauging Station

27.5 mi

Mariscal Canyon Rim 👣

2.2mi

MARISCAL MOUNTAIN

Loop Camp

Dominguez

Johnson Ranch

6.0 mi

3932 ft

UNITED STATES
MEXICO

CHIHUAHUA
COAHUILA

(4 sites)

Talley

Mariscal Canyo

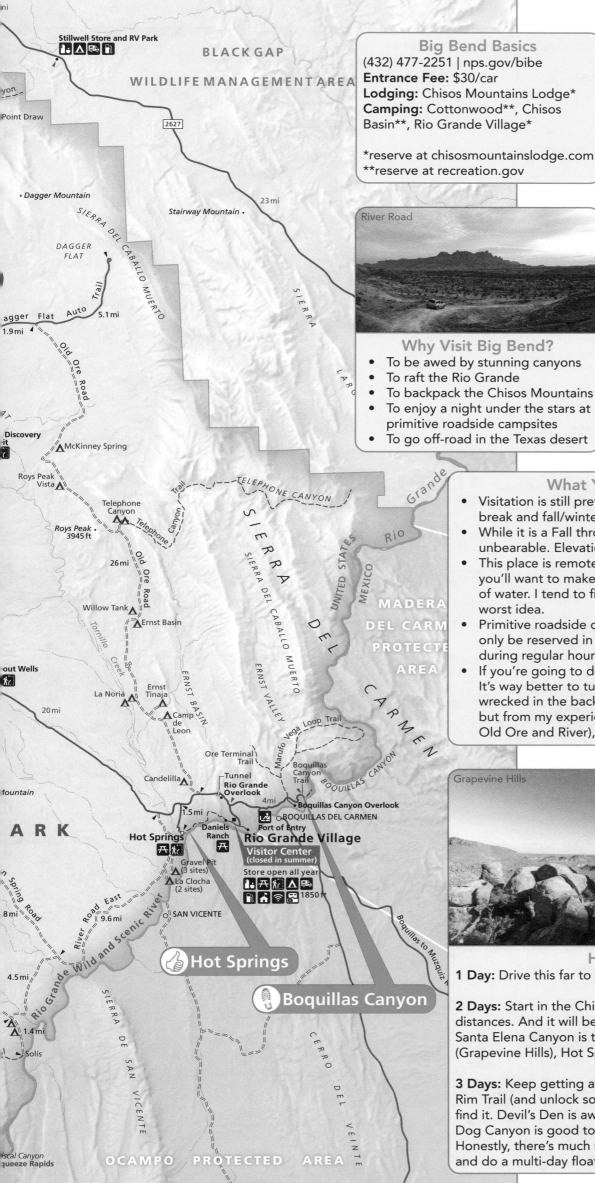

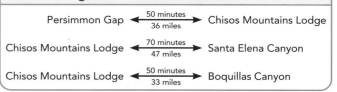

Big Bend Basics
(432) 477-2251 | nps.gov/bibe
Entrance Fee: $30/car
Lodging: Chisos Mountains Lodge*
Camping: Cottonwood**, Chisos Basin**, Rio Grande Village*

*reserve at chisosmountainslodge.com
**reserve at recreation.gov

Why Visit Big Bend?
- To be awed by stunning canyons
- To raft the Rio Grande
- To backpack the Chisos Mountains
- To enjoy a night under the stars at primitive roadside campsites
- To go off-road in the Texas desert

Big Bend Driving Distances
Big Bend is not an easy place to reach. Chisos Mountains Lodge is more than five hours from El Paso, the nearest large city. And, if you're coming from the east, the drive across Texas is a real chore. However, Big Bend is well worth the effort.

Persimmon Gap	⟵ 50 minutes / 36 miles ⟶	Chisos Mountains Lodge
Chisos Mountains Lodge	⟵ 70 minutes / 47 miles ⟶	Santa Elena Canyon
Chisos Mountains Lodge	⟵ 50 minutes / 33 miles ⟶	Boquillas Canyon

Big Bend Favorites
Easy Hikes: Santa Elena Canyon (1.7 miles), Ward Spring (3.6), Ernst Tinaja (1.4), Hot Springs (1.4)
Moderate Hikes: Window (5.6), Dog Canyon (4) & Devil's Den (5.6), Lost Mine (4.8), Boquillas Canyon (1.4), Grapevine Hills (2.2)
Strenuous Hikes: South Rim (varies), Mariscal Canyon (6.5), Emory Peak (10.5)
Activities: Paddling the Rio Grande, off-roading River Road, backpacking South Rim
Views: Santa Elena Canyon, Hot Springs, Boquillas Canyon Overlook, Mule Ears Viewpoint, Sam Nail Ranch, Window Overlook

What You Need to Know About Big Bend
- Visitation is still pretty light at Big Bend, but things pick up around spring break and fall/winter holidays.
- While it is a Fall through Spring park, summer in the Chisos Mountains isn't unbearable. Elevation and regular storms keep the mountains cool(ish).
- This place is remote. There are a few small camp stores with essentials, but you'll want to make sure you pack everything you need and always carry plenty of water. I tend to fill up at every opportunity. That's a bit excessive but not the worst idea.
- Primitive roadside campsites are awesome! You'll need a permit, and they can only be reserved in person at Panther Junction or Chisos Basin Visitor Centers during regular hours. Not all sites require a high-clearance 4x4.
- If you're going to do some off-roading. Don't go beyond your comfort level. It's way better to turn around and drive another day than to get stuck or wrecked in the backcountry. It'll be a very expensive tow. Conditions change, but from my experience road conditions are worst at the middle of roads (like Old Ore and River), where they're driven least (and farthest from humanity).

How Much Time Do You Have?
1 Day: Drive this far to stay one measly day? No. Spend a couple nights.

2 Days: Start in the Chisos Mountains. You'll find hikes of all difficulties and distances. And it will be refreshingly cool, if you're visiting around summer. Santa Elena Canyon is the one place you have to see. Mule Ears, Balanced Rock (Grapevine Hills), Hot Springs, and Boquillas Canyon are also worth checking out.

3 Days: Keep getting after the trails. With a 4x4, you can get to Mariscal Canyon Rim Trail (and unlock some special camping sites). If you want more hiking, you'll find it. Devil's Den is awesome (but you have to be a good cairn spotter). Nearby Dog Canyon is good too. Ward Spring is great. Sam Nail Ranch is interesting. Honestly, there's much more than three days of fun at Big Bend. Maybe come back and do a multi-day float trip on the Rio Grande?

NEW MEXICO
TEXAS

Guadalupe Mountains Basics
(915) 828-3251 | nps.gov/gumo
Entrance Fee: $10/person
Lodging: None
Camping: Pine Springs, Dog Canyon

The lonely road to Guadalupe Peak

Why Visit Guadalupe Mtns?
- To hike to the highest point in Texas, Guadalupe Peak
- To pass through the Devil's Hall
- To explore Pratt Cabin and the Grotto at McKitrrick Canyon
- To enjoy Salt Basin Dunes

Guadalupe Mountains Driving Distances
Not in accordance with Texas standards, it's a fairly small park. To compensate, it possesses the state's highest peak and it's just two hours from El Paso.

Pine Springs VC	⟷ 60 minutes / 48 miles	Salt Basin Dunes
Pine Springs VC	⟷ 18 minutes / 12 miles	McKittrick Canyon (day use only)
McKittrick Canyon	⟷ 130 minutes / 100 miles	Dog Canyon
Pine Springs VC	⟷ 90 minutes / 15 miles	Williams Ranch (unpaved, 4x4)

Guadalupe Mountains Favorites
Moderate Hikes: Devil's Hall (4.2 miles), McKittrick Canyon (4.8), El Capitan (11.3)
Strenuous Hikes: Guadalupe Peak (8.4), Lost Peak (6.4), The Bowl (9.1), Permian Reef (8.4)
Views: stops along US-62/180 or Salt Basin Dunes (it's often windy south and west of the mountains)

Salt Basin Dunes day use only 🅰 🅿

Williams Road
To Dell City 9miles 15km | Gate

No vehicles beyond this point

GYPSUM SAND DUNES

👍 **Salt Basin Dunes**

Butterfield

GUADALUPE MOUNTAINS
NATIONAL PARK

WILDERNESS

👣 **Devil's Hall**

👣 **Shumard Canyon**

Stage

Route

👣 **Guadalupe Peak**

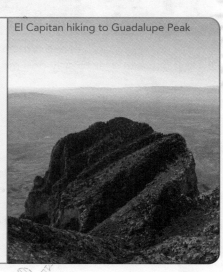
The path to Devils Hall

What You Need to Know
- Guadalupe Mountains isn't an extremely popular destination but it gets busy around spring break and again in fall when leaves change color.
- There are several access roads. Pine Springs is the activity hub, but you can also go to Salt Basin Dunes (day use only), McKittrick Canyon (day use only), Williams Ranch (day use only, 4x4, you must get a key from the visitor center, and occasionally the road is closed due to poor conditions), Frijole Ranch, and Dog Canyon. The park is small, but, if you want to visit every location, it takes some time.
- If you're thinking of day-tripping Guadalupe Mountains, it works pretty well to stay near Carlsbad Caverns (Whites City). There aren't many alternatives. Roll White Sands into this trip as well.

How Much Time Do You Have?
1 Day: There are two primary trails. Guadalupe Peak and Devil's Hall. With an early start, an ambitious hiker could do them both in a day. Or do one and enjoy a drive to Salt Basin Dunes or wander around Frijole Ranch for a bit.

2 Days: With another day you could keep hiking in the Pine Springs area or head up to McKittrick Canyon to hike to the Grotto or up Permian Reef. They're both good options. With a 4x4, you could make the arduous drive to Williams Ranch (be sure to get the gate key from the visitor center), but you can also hike/backpack there via El Capitan Trail.

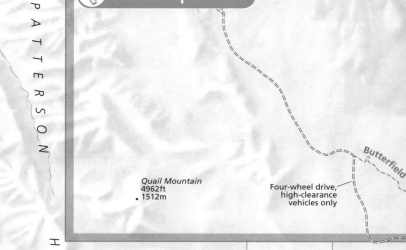
El Capitan hiking to Guadalupe Peak

PATTERSON HILLS

Quail Mountain 4962ft 1512m

Four-wheel drive, high-clearance vehicles only

Cone Peak 5017ft 1529m

NPS property

To Dell City 32miles (51km) and El Paso 99miles (159km)

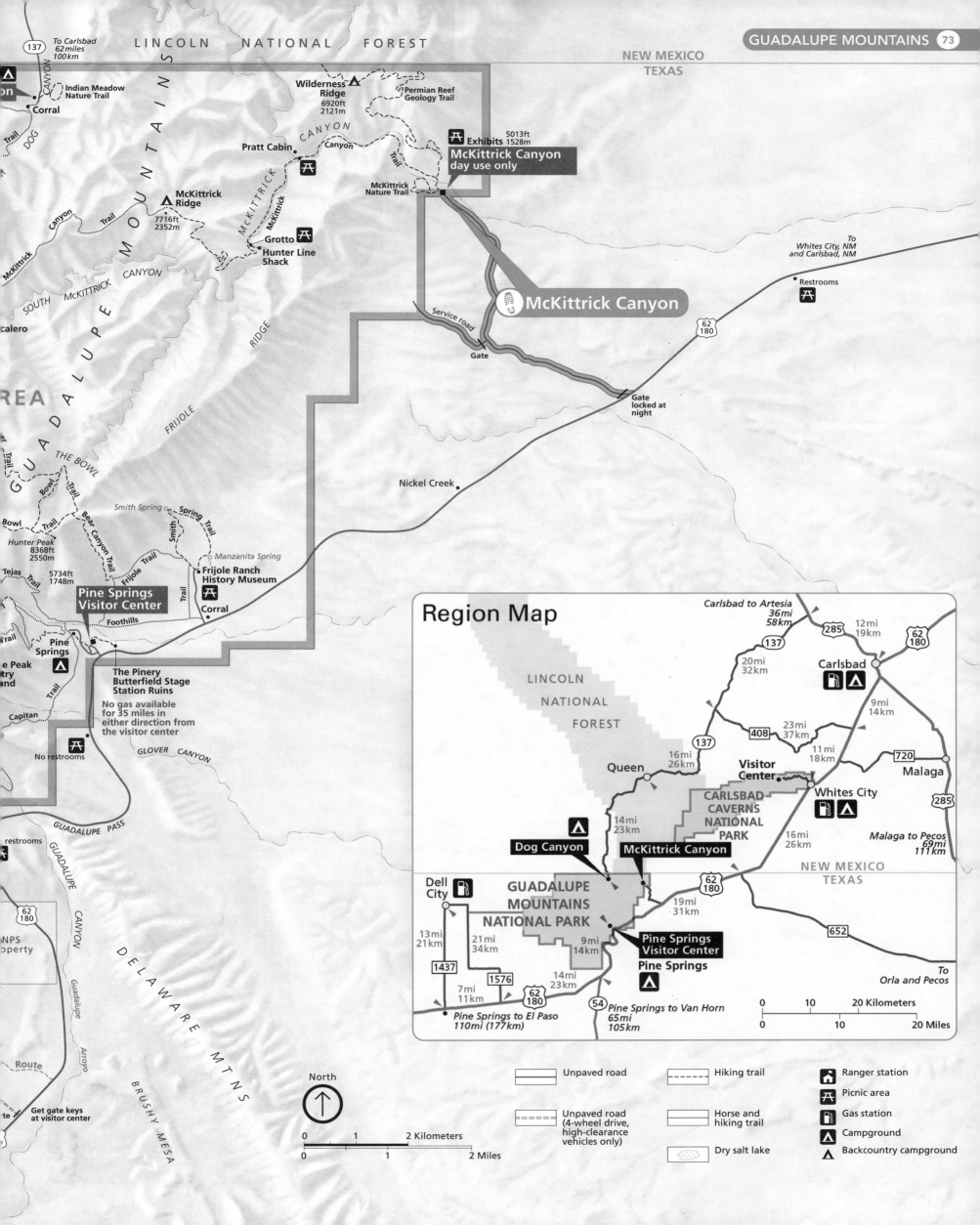

LINCOLN NATIONAL FOREST

NEW MEXICO
TEXAS

(137) To Carlsbad
62 miles
100km

Indian Meadow
Nature Trail

Corral

DOG CANYON

Trail

McKittrick Canyon

Wilderness
Ridge
6920ft
2121m

Permian Reef
Geology Trail

Pratt Cabin

Canyon

McKittrick
Ridge
7716ft
2352m

Grotto
Hunter Line
Shack

SOUTH McKITTRICK CANYON

McKittrick

Trail

Exhibits 5013ft
1528m

McKittrick Canyon
day use only

McKittrick
Nature Trail

To
Whites City, NM
and Carlsbad, NM

Restrooms

McKittrick Canyon

Service road

Gate

Gate
locked at
night

62
180

FRIJOLE RIDGE

THE BOWL

Smith Spring

Spring Trail

Bear Canyon Trail

Manzanita Spring

Hunter Peak
8368ft
2550m

5734ft
1748m

Frijole Trail

Smith Trail

Frijole Ranch
History Museum

Corral

Tejas

Trail

Nickel Creek

AREA

GUADALUPE MOUNTAINS

Bowl Trail

Bowl

Capitan

Pine Springs
Visitor Center

Foothills

Pine
Springs

Pine Springs

The Pinery
Butterfield Stage
Station Ruins

No gas available
for 35 miles in
either direction from
the visitor center

GLOVER CANYON

No restrooms

GUADALUPE PASS

62
180

GUADALUPE CANYON

NPS
property

Get gate keys
at visitor center

Route

DELAWARE MTNS

BRUSHY MESA

Arroyo

restrooms

Region Map

Carlsbad to Artesia
36mi
58km

Carlsbad to Artesia
36mi
58km

285

12mi
19km

62
180

LINCOLN

NATIONAL

FOREST

137

20mi
32km

Carlsbad

408

23mi
37km

9mi
14km

137

16mi
26km

Queen

Visitor
Center

11mi
18km

720

Malaga

14mi
23km

CARLSBAD
CAVERNS
NATIONAL
PARK

Whites City

285

Dog Canyon

McKittrick Canyon

16mi
26km

Malaga to Pecos
69mi
111km

NEW MEXICO
TEXAS

Dell
City

GUADALUPE
MOUNTAINS
NATIONAL
PARK

62
180

19mi
31km

652

13mi
21km

21mi
34km

9mi
14km

Pine Springs
Visitor Center

Pine Springs

To
Orla and Pecos

1437

1576

14mi
23km

0   10   20 Kilometers

7mi
11km

62
180

54

Pine Springs to Van Horn
65mi
105km

0   10   20 Miles

Pine Springs to El Paso
110mi (177km)

North

0   1   2 Kilometers

0   1   2 Miles

	Unpaved road		Hiking trail		Ranger station
	Unpaved road (4-wheel drive, high-clearance vehicles only)		Horse and hiking trail		Picnic area
	Dry salt lake				Gas station
					Campground
					Backcountry campground

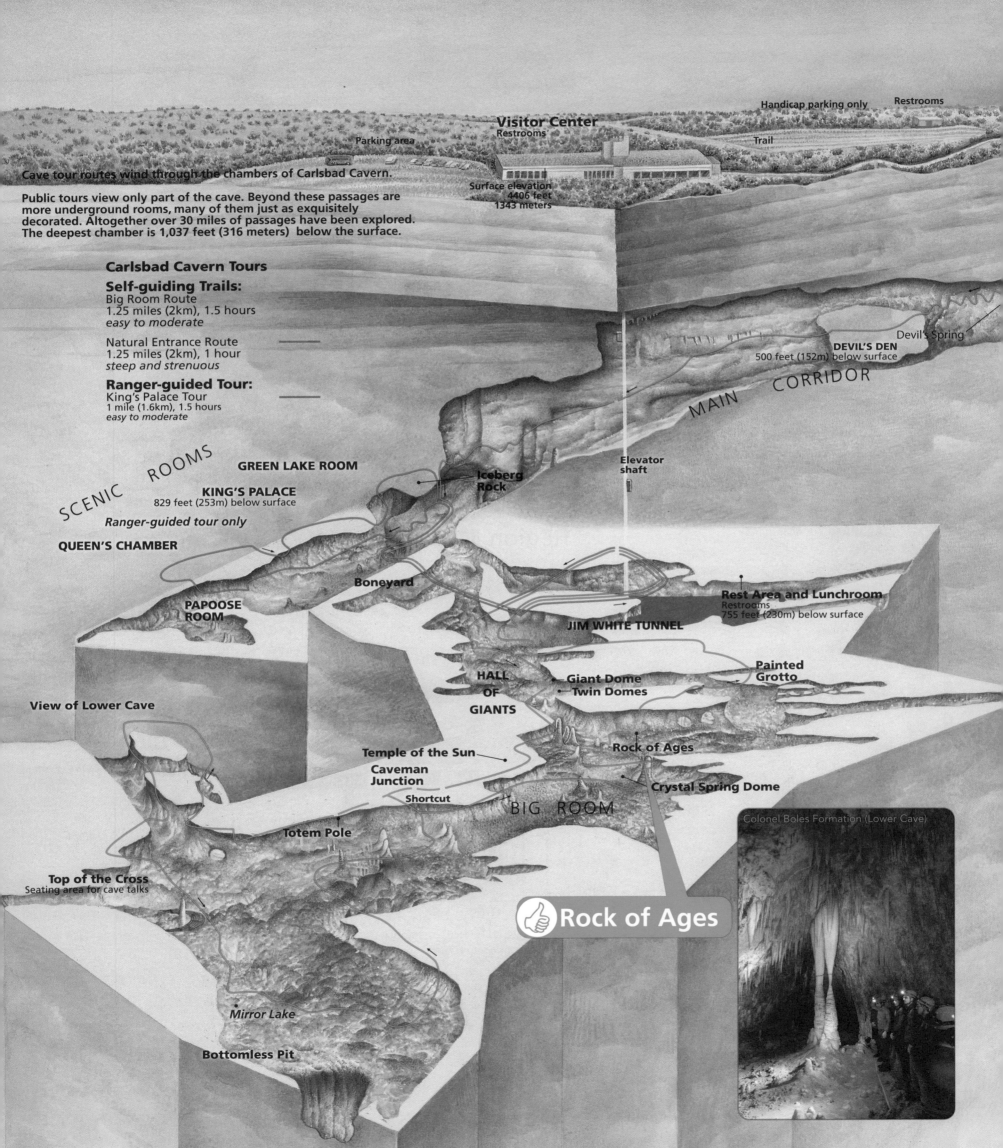

Cave tour routes wind through the chambers of Carlsbad Cavern.

Public tours view only part of the cave. Beyond these passages are more underground rooms, many of them just as exquisitely decorated. Altogether over 30 miles of passages have been explored. The deepest chamber is 1,037 feet (316 meters) below the surface.

Carlsbad Cavern Tours

Self-guiding Trails:
Big Room Route
1.25 miles (2km), 1.5 hours
easy to moderate

Natural Entrance Route
1.25 miles (2km), 1 hour
steep and strenuous

Ranger-guided Tour:
King's Palace Tour
1 mile (1.6km), 1.5 hours
easy to moderate

Handicap parking only   Restrooms

Visitor Center
Restrooms

Parking area   Trail

Surface elevation
4406 feet
1343 meters

Devil's Spring

DEVIL'S DEN
500 feet (152m) below surface

MAIN   CORRIDOR

Elevator
shaft

SCENIC   ROOMS   **GREEN LAKE ROOM**

Iceberg
Rock

KING'S PALACE
829 feet (253m) below surface

Ranger-guided tour only

QUEEN'S CHAMBER

Boneyard

Rest Area and Lunchroom
Restrooms
755 feet (230m) below surface

**PAPOOSE
ROOM**

JIM WHITE TUNNEL

Painted
Grotto

**HALL
OF
GIANTS**

Giant Dome
Twin Domes

View of Lower Cave

Rock of Ages

Temple of the Sun

Crystal Spring Dome

Caveman
Junction

Shortcut   BIG   ROOM

Totem Pole

Colonel Boles Formation (Lower Cave)

Top of the Cross
Seating area for cave talks

👍 Rock of Ages

Mirror Lake

Bottomless Pit

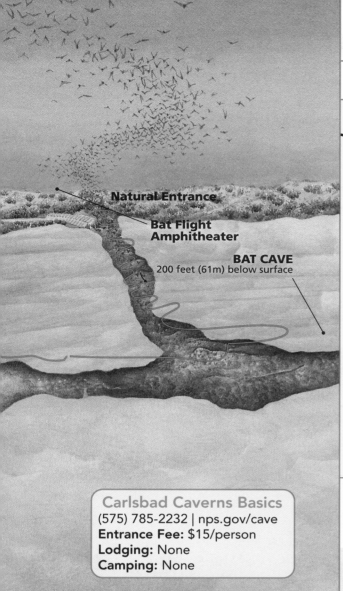

Natural Entrance

Bat Flight
Amphitheater

BAT CAVE
200 feet (61m) below surface

Carlsbad Region

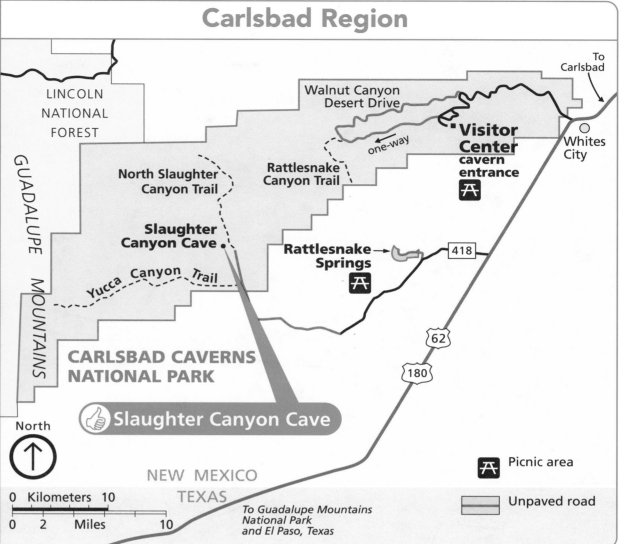

LINCOLN
NATIONAL
FOREST

Walnut Canyon
Desert Drive

To
Carlsbad

one-way

**Visitor
Center**
cavern
entrance

Whites
City

North Slaughter
Canyon Trail

Rattlesnake
Canyon Trail

GUADALUPE MOUNTAINS

**Slaughter
Canyon Cave**

**Rattlesnake
Springs**

418

Yucca Canyon Trail

**CARLSBAD CAVERNS
NATIONAL PARK**

62

180

👍 Slaughter Canyon Cave

North
↑

NEW MEXICO

TEXAS

0 Kilometers 10

0 2 Miles 10

To Guadalupe Mountains
National Park
and El Paso, Texas

🅰 Picnic area

▢ Unpaved road

Carlsbad Caverns Basics
(575) 785-2232 | nps.gov/cave
Entrance Fee: $15/person
Lodging: None
Camping: None

Carlsbad Caverns Driving Distances
All cave tours begin at the Visitor Center. From
there you can drive a scenic 9.5-mile loop. The
closest lodging and camping is in Whites City
and there's plenty more in Carlsbad.

Carlsbad, NM ⟷ Whites City, NM
25 minutes / 20 miles

Whites City, NM ⟷ Visitor Center
12 minutes / 7 miles

Visitor Center ⟷ Slaughter Canyon Cave
40 minutes / 24 miles

Why Visit Carlsbad Caverns?
- To see the swarm of bats as they
  exit/enter the cave
- To explore the last great
  terrestrial unknown...a cave!

Hall of the White Giant

Carlsbad Caverns Favorites
Hall of the White Giant is the most
adventurous cave tour.
Lower Cave Tour leads to Colonel Boles
Formation. It requires a rope-aided descent.
Slaughter Canyon Cave is awesome. The trail
to the cave is more strenuous than the tour.
Left Hand Tunnel Tour is lit by hand-held
lanterns. Have some fun in the dark!
And **King's Palace** is the park's standard tour.

What You Need to Know About Carlsbad Caverns
- Kings Palace and Left Hand Tunnel tours are offered daily. Reservations (recreation.gov) are
  a good idea regardless of tour.
- For the Hall of the White Giant Tour, keep your phone in a running belt or fannypack. You'll
  be crawling around, sometimes on your belly, so you do not want it in your pocket. Or else
  leave it behind. (Read and follow the tour requirements.)
- You don't have to tour the cave with a park ranger. You'll find 2.5 miles of self-guided trail
  between Carlsbad's Natural Entrance (long, gradual descent) and its Big Room. The tours
  are great, but the self-guided portion alone is worth a visit.
- Baby strollers are not permitted in the cave. Babies are. Canes and walking sticks are okay in
  the Big Room, Natural Entrance, or King's Palace (if medically necessary). Flash photography
  is allowed (just pay attention to others).
- Bring a flashlight or headlamp. While a light source isn't necessary, there are plenty of fun
  things obscured by darkness.
- Water is the only food or drink allowed in the cave. There is a snack bar near the elevator.
- The park's Bat Flight Program is great but it needs bats to proceed. They're typically
  occupying the cave from mid-April through October but that changes. If your heart is set on
  it, confirm bat activity prior to departure.
- Explore the above-ground park. You may spot non-native Barbary sheep along Walnut
  Canyon Desert Drive (Desert Loop Road). And the canyons are pretty fun.
- There's no in-park lodging, but you'll find an RV park and hotel nearby in White's City.
  There's also dispersed camping at nearby BLM land.

How Much Time Do You Have?
It's all about the cave tours. Check online
(recreation.gov), make reservations, and then plan short
hikes at Carlsbad in between. Guadalupe Mountains
(Pine Springs Visitor Center) is about a half an hour drive
from Whites City. It's a good destination if you want to
do multiple cave tours and they aren't on consecutive
days. Hall of the White Giant and Slaughter Canyon
Cave aren't offered as frequently as the rest, and they're
my favorite tours of the bunch. You'll often have to
travel on a weekend for them too. Don't forget to add
Guadalupe Mountains and White Sands to your itinerary.

Slaughter Canyon Cave

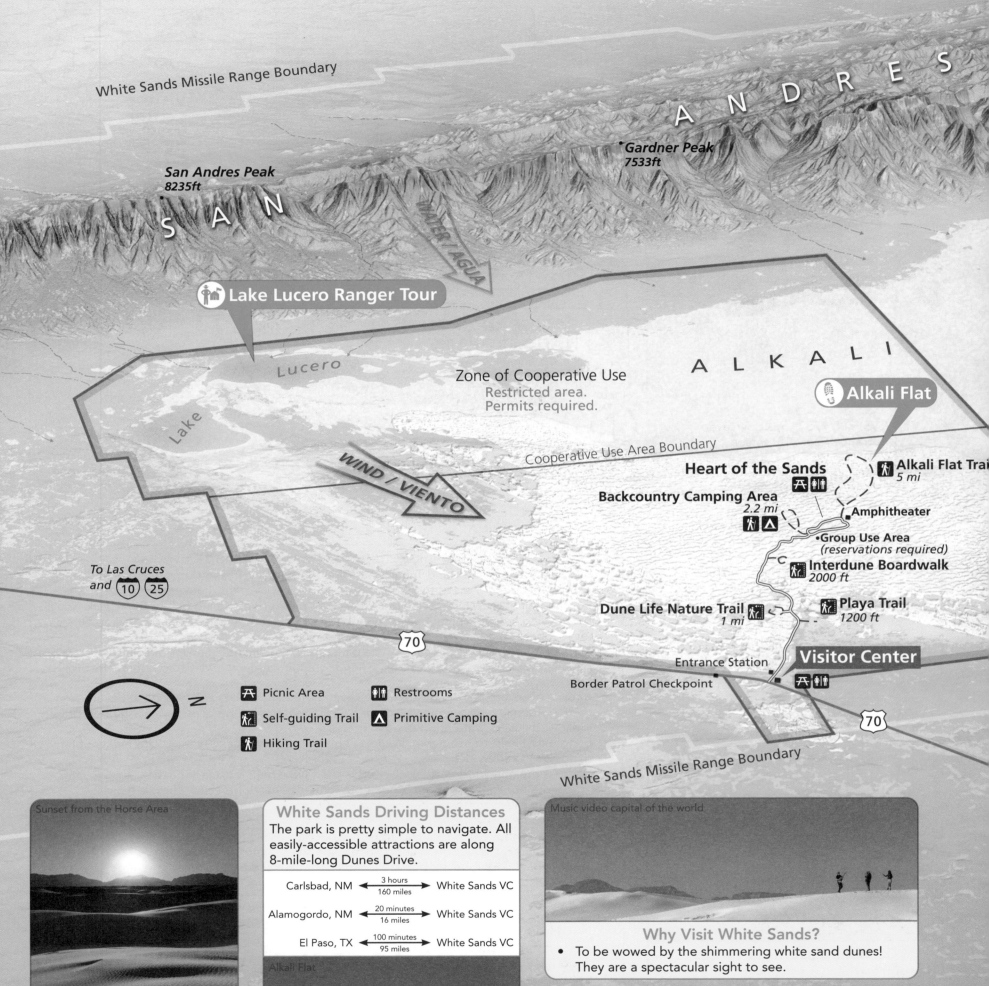

White Sands Missile Range Boundary

S A N A N D R E S

Gardner Peak
7533ft

San Andres Peak
8235ft

AGUA / WATER

Lake Lucero Ranger Tour

Lucero

A L K A L I

Zone of Cooperative Use
Restricted area.
Permits required.

Lake

Alkali Flat

Cooperative Use Area Boundary

Heart of the Sands

Alkali Flat Trail
5 mi

Backcountry Camping Area
2.2 mi

WIND / VIENTO

Amphitheater

Group Use Area
(reservations required)

Interdune Boardwalk
2000 ft

To Las Cruces
and 10 25

Dune Life Nature Trail
1 mi

Playa Trail
1200 ft

70

Entrance Station

Visitor Center

Border Patrol Checkpoint

70

White Sands Missile Range Boundary

N

🏕 Picnic Area   🚻 Restrooms

Self-guiding Trail   🔺 Primitive Camping

🥾 Hiking Trail

Sunset from the Horse Area

White Sands Driving Distances
The park is pretty simple to navigate. All
easily-accessible attractions are along
8-mile-long Dunes Drive.

Carlsbad, NM	3 hours / 160 miles	White Sands VC
Alamogordo, NM	20 minutes / 16 miles	White Sands VC
El Paso, TX	100 minutes / 95 miles	White Sands VC

Music video capital of the world

Why Visit White Sands?
• To be wowed by the shimmering white sand dunes!
  They are a spectacular sight to see.

Alkali Flat

White Sands Basics
(575) 479-6124 | nps.gov/whsa
Entrance Fee: $25/car
Lodging: None
Camping: 10 backcountry sites

White Sands Favorites
Hikes: Alkali Flat (moderate, 5 miles)
Activities: Lake Lucero Ranger Tour, photography in the
dunes (just be careful of flying sand if it's windy), sledding
Views: West Filming Area, Horse Area, Backcountry
Camping Loop, Yucca Picnic Area

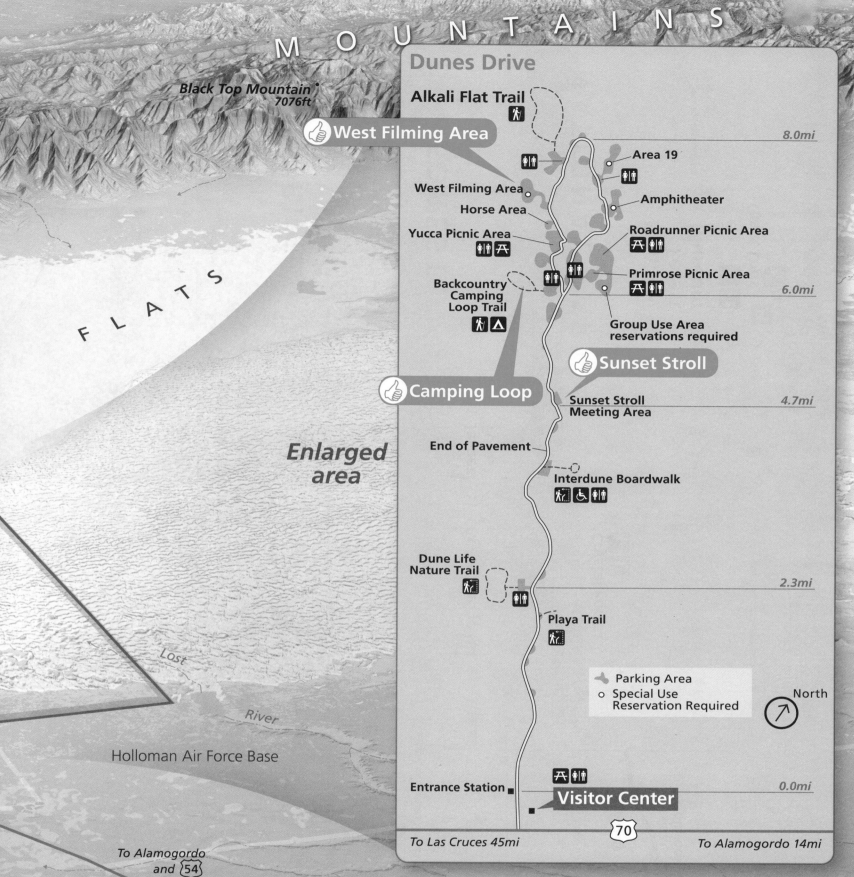

Dunes Drive

MOUNTAINS

Alkali Flat Trail 🚶

👍 **West Filming Area**

Black Top Mountain
7076ft

West Filming Area ○

Horse Area

Yucca Picnic Area 🚻 🏕

Backcountry Camping Loop Trail 🚶 ⛺

👍 **Camping Loop**

FLATS

Enlarged area

Area 19 🚻

Amphitheater

Roadrunner Picnic Area 🏕 🚻

Primrose Picnic Area 🏕 🚻

Group Use Area reservations required

👍 **Sunset Stroll**

Sunset Stroll Meeting Area — 4.7mi

End of Pavement

Interdune Boardwalk 🚶 ♿ 🚻

Dune Life Nature Trail 🚶

🚻 — 2.3mi

Playa Trail 🚶

Lost

River

Holloman Air Force Base

8.0mi

6.0mi

🛩 Parking Area
○ Special Use Reservation Required

North ↗

Entrance Station ■

🏕 🚻

Visitor Center ■ — 0.0mi

🛣 70

To Las Cruces 45mi   To Alamogordo 14mi

To Alamogordo and 54

What You Need to Know About White Sands

- The park is open from 7am until sunset, although you can pay for an Early Entry or Stay Late permit if you have some photography or filming ideas.
- Check the park website to see about missile testing closures. They usually only delay opening an hour or two, but they occur about twice a week.
- Every day (except Christmas) the park offers a Sunset Stroll. All you have to do is show up at the Sunset Stroll Meeting Area (4.7 miles from the entrance station) about an hour before sunset.
- Waxed plastic saucers work best for sledding. They sell them in the gift shop but you may want to call and check availability before arriving.
- There are ten backcountry camping sites available on a first-come, first-served basis at the entrance booth. For obvious reasons, backcountry camping is not available the night before missile testing.
- If you're traveling in summer, be prepared for the heat. Sun reflects off the gypsum dunes. Carry plenty of water. Hike early in the morning if you can.
- The picnic areas are some of the best in the park system. Use them.

Sledding at Roadrunner Picnic Area

How Much Time Do You Have?

White Sands is a strange place to plan for. You can hike the nine miles of trails in a day, no problem. But I could spend days here and never tire of the sight of these stunning dunes!

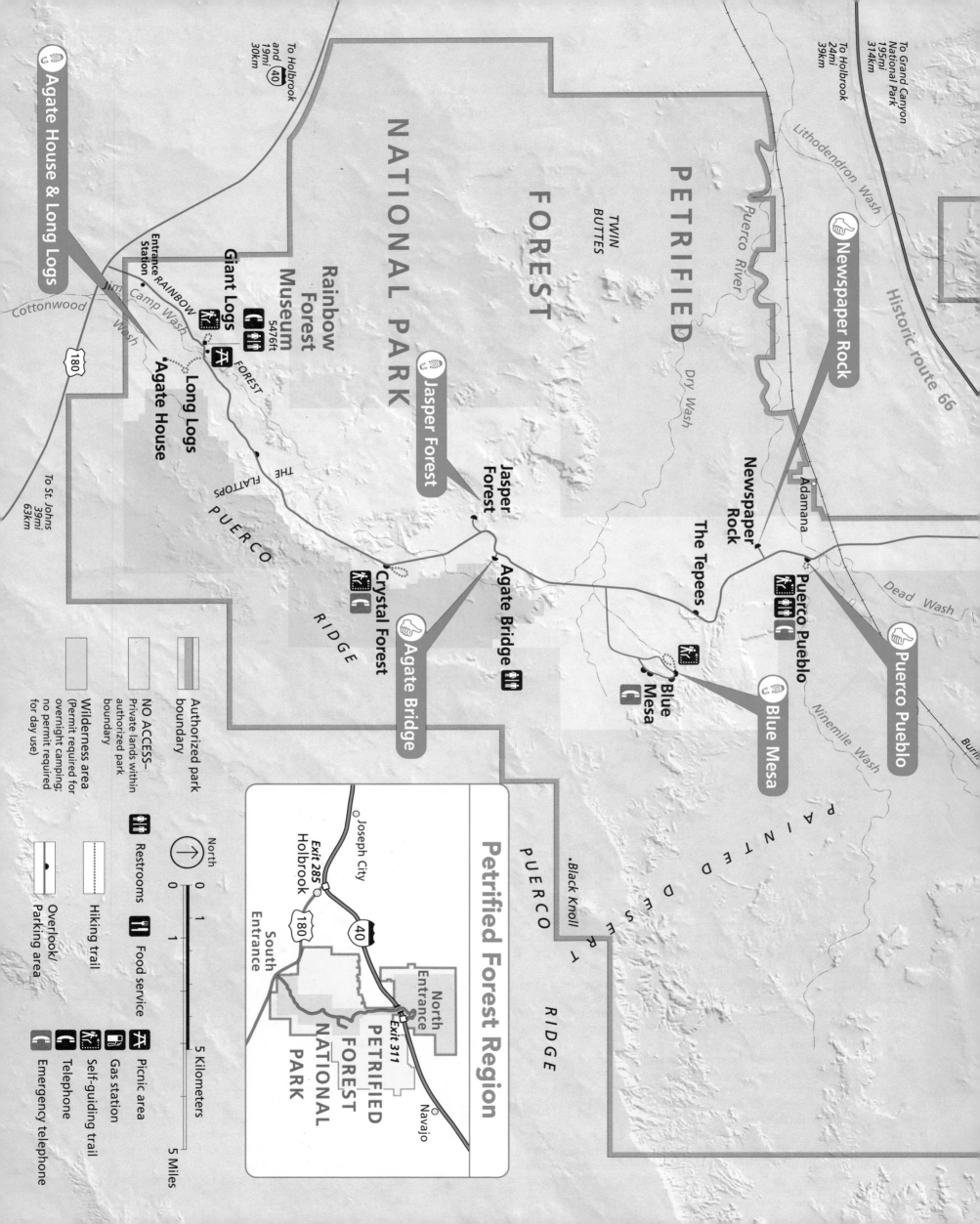

Petrified Forest Region

Map Labels

To Grand Canyon National Park 195mi 314km
To Holbrook 24mi 39km

Historic route 66

Lithodendron Wash

Newspaper Rock

Newspaper Rock

Adamana

Puerco River

Dry Wash

PETRIFIED

FOREST

TWIN BUTTES

NATIONAL PARK

To Holbrook 19mi 30km

To St. Johns 39mi 63km

Cottonwood

Jim Camp Wash

Entrance Station

RAINBOW

Agate House & Long Logs

Giant Logs

Rainbow Forest Museum 5476ft

Long Logs Agate House

FOREST

THE FLATTOPS

PUERCO

RIDGE

Jasper Forest

Jasper Forest

Crystal Forest

Agate Bridge

Agate Bridge

The Tepees

Puerco Pueblo

Puerco Pueblo

Blue Mesa

Blue Mesa

Dead Wash

Ninemile Wash

Burnt

PAINTED DESERT

PUERCO RIDGE

Black Knoll

Inset Map: Petrified Forest Region

Joseph City

Exit 285 Holbrook

180

40

South Entrance

North Entrance

Exit 311

PETRIFIED FOREST NATIONAL PARK

Navajo

North

0   1   5 Miles
0   1   5 Kilometers

Legend

Authorized park boundary

NO ACCESS— Private lands within authorized park boundary

Wilderness area (Permit required for overnight camping; no permit required for day use)

Hiking trail

Overlook/ Parking area

Restrooms

Food service

Picnic area

Gas station

Self-guiding trail

Telephone

Emergency telephone

Newspaper

Petrified Forest Basics

(928) 524-6228 | nps.gov/pefo
Entrance Fee: $25/car
Lodging: None
Camping: None

Petrified Forest Driving Distances

It's a drive-thru park. Most visitors don't venture far beyond the 28-mile Park Road.

Albuquerque, NM	3.5 hours	210 miles
Painted Desert VC	40 minutes	26 miles
Rainbow Forest VC	2 hours	110 miles

Painted Desert VC → Painted Desert VC
Rainbow Forest VC → Rainbow Forest VC
Flagstaff, AZ

Why Visit Petrified Forest?

- To see some old, rocky logs (which doesn't sound exciting but the science behind them is fascinating)
- To explore the colorful Painted Desert and Blue Mesa

Blue Mesa

Petrified Forest Favorites

Easy Hikes: Long Logs/Agate House (1.6/2 miles), Painted Desert Rim (1), Crystal Forest (0.8)
Moderate Hikes: Blue Mesa (1), Jasper Forest (2.5)
Views: Chinde Point, Kachina Point, Newspaper Rock, Old Faithful (log), Route 66 Landmark

How Much Time Do You Have?

It's a drive-thru park to most. A typical trip includes driving the park road, doing some hiking (Blue Mesa, Agate House, Giant Logs), checking out the museum, and then returning to I-40. This is perfectly fine but you will find some interesting things in the park's wilderness areas with a little bit of hiking.

Long Logs

Agate House

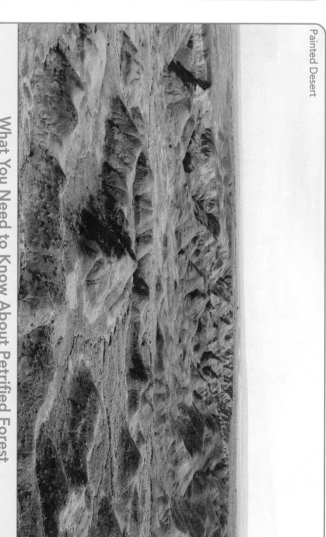
Painted Desert

What You Need to Know About Petrified Forest

- The only way to spend the night is in the backcountry. Park hours change by season, but they basically correlate to open from sun up to sun down. Backpackers require a free wilderness permit.
- Easily accessible petrified logs are found at Rainbow Forest Museum and nearby Long Logs Trail. It's much more difficult to find at the other end of the park road, so plan accordingly.
- Ranger programs are awesome here. Join one if you can or else Petrified Forest Field Institute (petrifiedforestfieldinstitute.org) offers classes and custom trips.
- Don't take the petrified wood. It's been here for 200 million years. Let's keep it around for a few more.

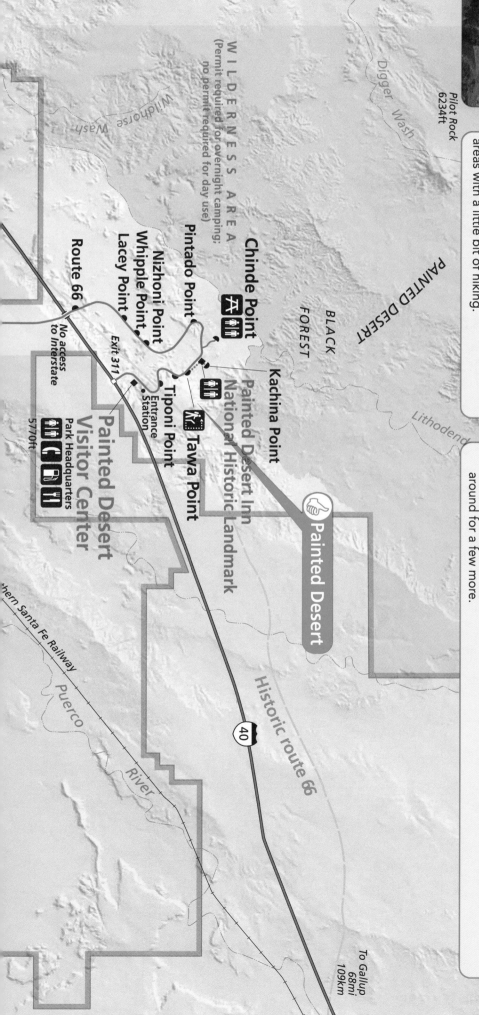

WILDERNESS AREA
(Permit required for overnight camping; no permit required for day use)

Wildhorse Wash

Digger Wash

Pilot Rock
6235ft

PAINTED DESERT

BLACK FOREST

Lithodendron Wash

Chinde Point 🅰

Pintado Point

Nizhoni Point
Whipple Point
Lacey Point

Exit 311

Route 66

No access to Interstate

Kachina Point

Painted Desert Inn
National Historic Landmark

Tiponi Point
Tawa Point

Entrance Station

🖐 Painted Desert

Painted Desert Visitor Center

Park Headquarters
5770ft

Historic route 66

40

Puerco River

thern Santa Fe Railway

To Gallup
68mi
109km

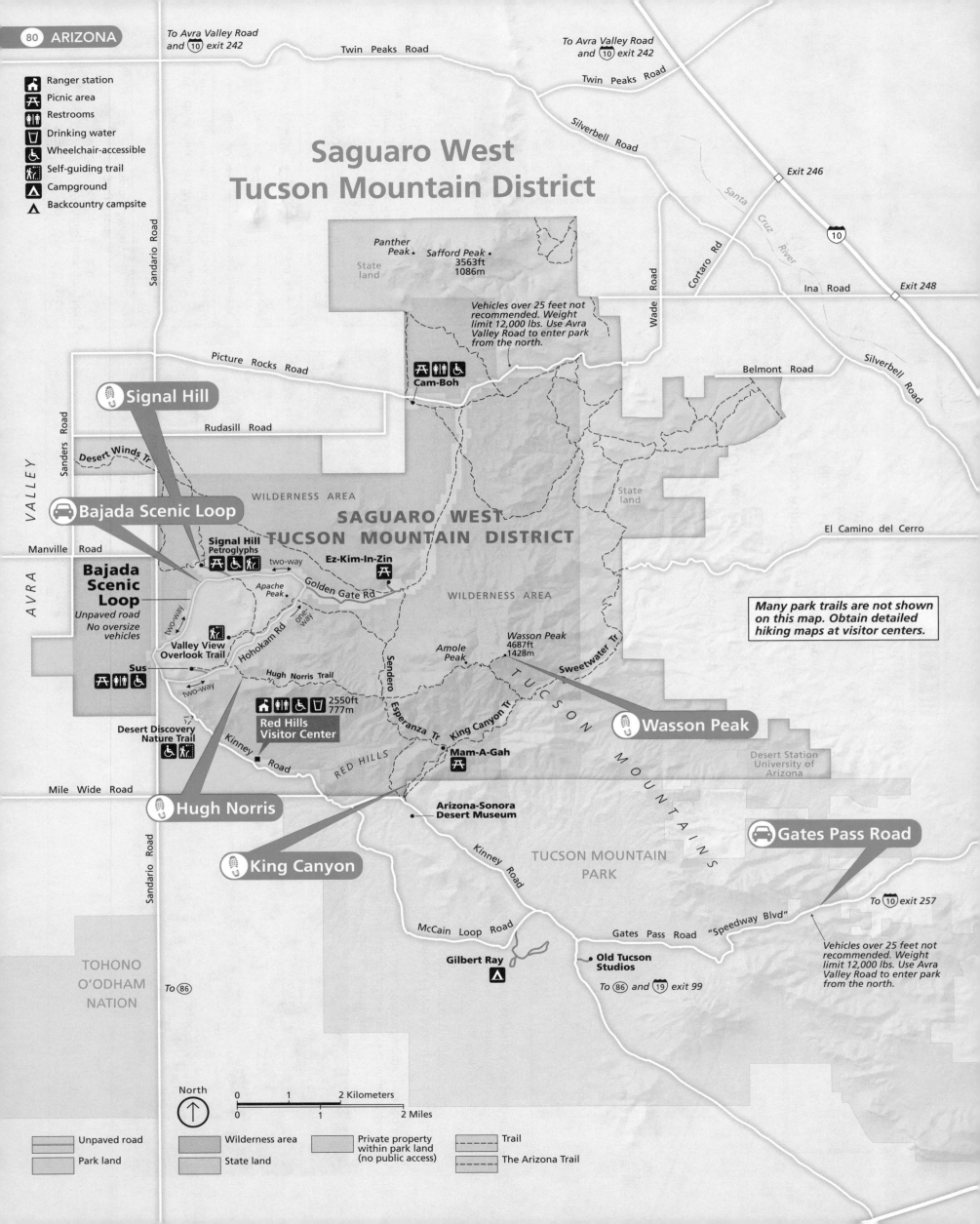

Saguaro West
Tucson Mountain District

Ranger station
Picnic area
Restrooms
Drinking water
Wheelchair-accessible
Self-guiding trail
Campground
Backcountry campsite

To Avra Valley Road
and 10 exit 242

Twin Peaks Road

To Avra Valley Road
and 10 exit 242

Twin Peaks Road

Silverbell Road

Santa Cruz River

Exit 246

10

Panther Peak
Safford Peak
3563ft
1086m

State land

Wade Road

Cortaro Rd

Ina Road

Exit 248

Vehicles over 25 feet not
recommended. Weight
limit 12,000 lbs. Use Avra
Valley Road to enter park
from the north.

Picture Rocks Road

Belmont Road

Silverbell Road

Cam-Boh

Signal Hill

Rudasill Road

Desert Winds Tr

WILDERNESS AREA

State land

Bajada Scenic Loop

El Camino del Cerro

Manville Road

Bajada Scenic Loop
Unpaved road
No oversize vehicles

Signal Hill Petroglyphs

two-way

Ez-Kim-In-Zin

**SAGUARO WEST
TUCSON MOUNTAIN DISTRICT**

Apache Peak

Golden Gate Rd

WILDERNESS AREA

Many park trails are not shown
on this map. Obtain detailed
hiking maps at visitor centers.

two-way

Valley View
Overlook Trail

Hohokam Rd

one-way

Wasson Peak
4687ft
1428m

Amole Peak

Sweetwater Tr

Sus

Hugh Norris Trail

Sendero Esperanza Tr

2550ft
777m

King Canyon Tr

Wasson Peak

Desert Discovery
Nature Trail

Kinney Road

**Red Hills
Visitor Center**

RED HILLS

Mam-A-Gah

TUCSON MOUNTAINS

Desert Station
University of
Arizona

Mile Wide Road

Hugh Norris

King Canyon

Arizona-Sonora
Desert Museum

Kinney Road

TUCSON MOUNTAIN
PARK

Gates Pass Road

Sandario Road

To 10 exit 257

McCain Loop Road

Gates Pass Road

"Speedway Blvd"

TOHONO
O'ODHAM
NATION

To 86

Gilbert Ray

Old Tucson
Studios

To 86 and 19 exit 99

Vehicles over 25 feet not
recommended. Weight
limit 12,000 lbs. Use Avra
Valley Road to enter park
from the north.

North

0   1   2 Kilometers
0   1   2 Miles

Unpaved road
Park land
Wilderness area
State land
Private property
within park land
(no public access)
Trail
The Arizona Trail

Sanders Road
AVRA VALLEY

Saguaro Basics

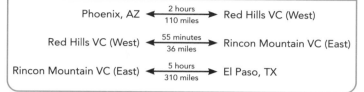
Great birding park

(520) 733-5153 | nps.gov/sagu
Entrance Fee: $25/car
Lodging: None
Camping: None

Saguaro Driving Distances

The park consists of two units located on the east and west outskirts of Tucson. The east unit offers an 8-mile loop drive. There's a 5-mile loop in the west.

Phoenix, AZ ←→ Red Hills VC (West)
2 hours / 110 miles

Red Hills VC (West) ←→ Rincon Mountain VC (East)
55 minutes / 36 miles

Rincon Mountain VC (East) ←→ El Paso, TX
5 hours / 310 miles

Wasson Peak

Why Visit Saguaro?
- To hike to the top of Wasson Peak
- To pose with as many saguaro cactus as you can
- To backpack to Manning Camp (Saguaro East)

Saguaro Favorites

Easy Hikes (West): Cactus Wren (3 miles), Signal Hill (0.5), Cactus Garden (0.1)
Easy Hikes (East): Desert Ecology (0.3), Freeman Homestead (1)
Moderate/Strenuous Hikes (West): Hugh Norris (9.8), King Canyon (7 miles to Wasson Peak, just doing the short hike through the wash is enjoyable as well), Valley View Overlook (0.8)
Moderate/Strenuous Hikes (East): Tanque Verde (18), Rincon Peak (3.3), Douglas Spring (varies)
Views: Gates Pass Scenic Lookout (outside West District), Ez-Kim-In-Zin Picnic Area (West), Javelina (East)

What You Need to Know About Saguaro
- Each district is open daily roughly from sunrise to sunset. And most visitors arrive between October and May, when weather is most comfortable.
- Saguaros bloom nocturnally in May/June.
- Be prepared for heat any time of year. Particularly in summer, it's a good idea to hike/bike early in the morning. Be sure to carry plenty of water.
- Backpackers should be prepared for the cold. Manning Camp is at close to 8,000 feet elevation, where the temperature is about 20 degrees cooler. Nights get cold, even in summer.
- There are no campgrounds or lodges within the park, but you aren't short on overnight (or activity or food and drink) options in Tucson.

How Much Time Do You Have?

1 Day: Driving each scenic loop road and hiking a trail or two is possible in a day. I prefer the west district for sunset but as long as you have a saguaro cactus and a good view of the horizon, you're all set.

2 Days: A little more time is better because you can hike up to Wasson Peak (West). And then you'll have more time hiking in the east district too, maybe hit a few trails beginning from Broadway Boulevard.

King Canyon

Saguaro East - Rincon Mountain District

Map labels:

CORONADO NATIONAL FOREST

Tanque Verde Road

Speedway Boulevard

Broadway Boulevard

Houghton Road

22nd St

Old Spanish Tr

Escalante Road

Freeman Road

TUCSON

Tanque Verde Wash

Douglas Spring Trail

Douglas Spring

Douglas Spring 4694ft 1431m

Italian Spring Trail

North Slope

Mica Mountain Highest point in park 8666ft 2641m

Spud Rock

Helens Dome

Reef Rock

WILDERNESS AREA

Cow Head Saddle

Cow Head Saddle

7941ft 2420m

Manning Camp

Spud Rock 7359ft 2243m

Turkey Creek Trail

Deer Valley

Garwood

Carrillo

Pink Hill

Mica View

Loma Verde

Squeeze Pen

Desert Ecology Trail

WILDHORSE CANYON

Cactus Forest Loop

Cactus Forest Loop Drive
Paved road
No oversize vehicles

Cactus Forest Trail

Rincon Mountain Visitor Center
3090ft 942m

one-way

two-way

TANQUE VERDE RIDGE

Tanque Verde Peak 7049ft 2148m

5286ft 1611m

Grass Shack

Juniper Basin 6010ft 1832m

CHIMENEA CANYON

MADRONA CANYON

Manning Camp Trail

RINCON MOUNTAINS

Heartbreak Ridge Tr

Tanque Verde Ridge Trail

BOX CANYON

Javelina

Freeman Homestead Trail

Tanque Verde

SAGUARO EAST RINCON MOUNTAIN DISTRICT

Quilter Trail

Backpack/Manning Camp

Miller Creek Tr

Happy Valley Saddle 6117ft 1864m

Deer Camp (historic site)

Ridge View Trail

Hope Camp Trail

Ruiz Trail

Hope Camp (historic site)

State land

Private land

Private land

Rincon Creek Trail

Rincon Peak Trail

WILDERNESS AREA

Rincon Peak 8482ft 2585m

Old Spanish Trail

Camino Loma Alta

Rincon Creek

Arizona Nat'l Scenic Tr

RINCON VALLEY

North

0 1 2 Kilometers
0 1 2 Miles

To Colossal Cave Mountain Park

CORONADO NATIONAL FOREST

Southwestern Driving Distances

The American Southwest is unreal. You can make some great combos. Well known is Utah's Mighty 5, but you can also mix in Mesa Verde or Black Canyon of the Gunnison. And then the North Rim of the Grand Canyon is reasonably close to Zion. Great Basin isn't out of the question either (and it's a lot less busy). Regardless, spend some time in the Southwest and you'll be itching to return immediately (and there's much more to it than national parks).

Rocky Mountain	← 5.5 hours / 275 miles →	Great Sand Dunes
Great Sand Dunes	← 4 hours / 200 miles →	Black Canyon of the Gunnison
Black Canyon of the Gunnison	← 3 hours / 155 miles →	Mesa Verde
Mesa Verde	← 2.5 hours / 130 miles →	Arches
Arches	← 0.5 hours / 30 miles →	Canyonlands
Canyonlands	← 2.5 hours / 150 miles →	Capitol Reef
Capitol Reef	← 2.5 hours / 120 miles →	Bryce Canyon
Bryce Canyon	← 2 hours / 85 miles →	Zion
Zion	← 7.5 hours / 430 miles →	Grand Canyon (North Rim)
Zion	← 4.5 hours / 250 miles →	Grand Canyon (South Rim)
Grand Canyon (North Rim)	← 4 hours / 210 miles →	Grand Canyon (South Rim)
Grand Canyon (South Rim)	← 7.5 hours / 430 miles →	Great Basin

World War II ... in the Pacific NM
...e Lake)

Hagerman Fossil Beds NM

Craters of the ... NM & PRES

Minidoka NHS

City of Rocks N RES

Golden Spike NHS

SALT LAKE CITY

Timpanogos Cave NM

NEVADA

UTAH

Great Basin NP

SOUTHWEST

...vils Postpile NM

...yon NP

...a NP

Manzanar NHS

Bryce Canyon NP

Capitol Reef NP

Cedar Breaks NM

Zion NP

Glen Canyon NRA

Tule Springs Fossil Beds NM

LAS VEGAS

Pipe Spring NM

Rainbow Bridge NM

...eath Valley NP

Grand Canyon N?

Navajo NM

NM

Castle Mountains NM

Lake Mead NRA

Canyo...

Santa Monica Mountains NRA

Mojave N PRES

Wupatki NM

Hubb...

Sunset Crater Volcano NM

Walnut Cany...

John D. Rockefeller, Jr.
Memorial PKWY

Grand Teton NP

THE
SOUTHWEST

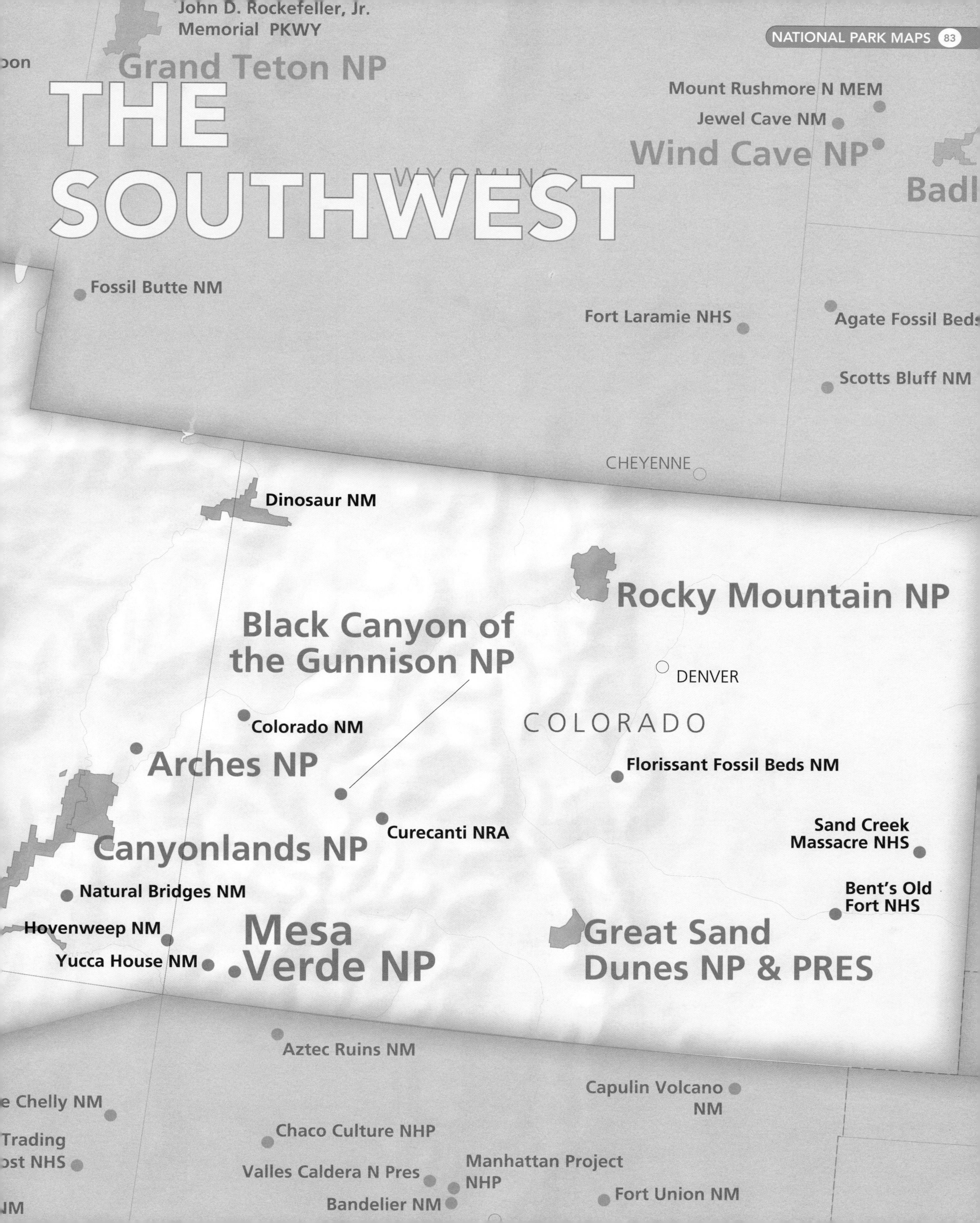

Mount Rushmore N MEM

Jewel Cave NM

Wind Cave NP

WYOMING

Badl

Fossil Butte NM

Fort Laramie NHS

Agate Fossil Beds

Scotts Bluff NM

CHEYENNE

Dinosaur NM

Rocky Mountain NP

Black Canyon of
the Gunnison NP

DENVER

COLORADO

Colorado NM

Florissant Fossil Beds NM

Arches NP

Curecanti NRA

Sand Creek
Massacre NHS

Canyonlands NP

Natural Bridges NM

Bent's Old
Fort NHS

Hovenweep NM

Mesa
Verde NP

Great Sand
Dunes NP & PRES

Yucca House NM

Aztec Ruins NM

Capulin Volcano
NM

e Chelly NM

Trading
ost NHS

Chaco Culture NHP

Manhattan Project
NHP

Valles Caldera N Pres

Fort Union NM

Bandelier NM

NM

RAWAH
WILDERNESS
COLORADO

To Fort Collins

NEOTA
WILDERNESS

ROOSEVELT
NATIONAL FOREST

To Walden

Cameron Pass

STATE FOREST

Long Draw Road

Corral Creek Trailhead

NPS/USFS

Long Draw

LONG DRAW RESERVOIR

Flatiron Mountain
12335ft
3760m

Mummy Pass

Hague

ROUTT

NATIONAL FOREST

Lake Agnes

Michigan Lakes

Snow Lake

Thunder Pass

Thunder Mountain
12070ft
3679m

BOX CANYON

Mount Richthofen
12940ft
3944m

Tepee Mountain
12568ft
3831m

SKELETON

Lead Mountain
12537ft
3821m

Mount Cirrus
12797ft
3901m

Lake of the Clouds

Howard Mountain
12810ft
3904m

Divide

Mount Cumulus
12725ft
3879m

Red Mountain
11605ft
3537m

Red Mtn Trail

Mount Nimbus
12706ft
3873m

Mount Stratus
12480ft
3804m

Continental

Baker Mountain
12397ft
3779m

Parika Lake

NEVER

SUMMER

WILDERNESS

Bowen Mountain
12524ft
3817m

Blue Lake

Mineral Point
11488ft
3502m

BAKER GULCH

Bowen Lake

BLUE RIDGE

ARAPAHO

NATIONAL FOREST

Skeleton Gulch

La Poudre Pass

GRAND DITCH

LITTLE YELLOWSTONE

Site of Lulu City

SHIPLER PARK

COLORADO RIVER TRAIL

Trail Ridge Road

Specimen Mountain
12489ft
3807m

12mi
19km

Poudre Lake

Milner Pass
10758ft
3279m

Lake Irene

Colorado River Trailhead

Road closed from here east to Many Parks Curve mid-October to Memorial Day

Beaver Ponds

Timber Creek

Holzwarth Historic Site

GRAND DITCH

Farview Curve

Timber Lake Trailhead

Timber Lake Trail

Jackstraw Mountain
11704ft
3567m

Timber Lake

KAWUNEECHE VALLEY

Bowen/Baker Trailhead

Coyote Valley Trailhead

Continental Divide National Scenic Trail

BOWEN GULCH

8mi
13km

Onahu Creek

Onahu Trailhead

Green Mountain Trail

Green Mountain Trailhead

Green Mtn
10313ft
3143m

Poudre River Trail (WILD AND SCENIC RIVER)

Cache la Poudre River

Chapin Creek

Medicine Bow Curve

Fall River Pass

Alpine Ridge Trail

Chapin Creek Trailhead

Mount Chapin
12454ft
3796m

Trail Ridge Road

Ute Trail

Gore Range

Highest point on road
12183ft
3713m

Alpine Visitor Center

Seasonal Snack bar

11796ft
3595m

9mi
14km

One-way up only. Road

Old Fall

Lava Cliffs

Iceberg Pass

Tundra Communities Trailhead

Rock Cut

Sundance
12466ft
3800m

Continental Divide

Beaver Creek

Arrowhead Lake

Gorge Lakes

Azure Lake

Inkwell Lake

Doughnut Lake

Terra Tomah Mountain
12718ft
3876m

Forest Lake

Thompson River

Forest Canyon

Mount Ida
12880ft
3926m

Highest Lake

Mount Julian
12928ft
3940m

Julian Lake

ROCKY MOUNTAIN

Hayden Lake

Haynach Lake

Nakai Peak
12216ft
3723m

Tonahutu Creek

Lonesome Lake

Stones Peak
12922ft
3939m

Sprague Glacier

Rainbow Lake

Granite Falls

National Trail

BIG MEADOWS

Continental Divide

Big Meadows Creek

Scenic Trail

BIGHORN FLATS

Snowdrift Peak
12274ft
3741m

Mount Patterson
11424ft
3482m

NATIONAL PARK

Ptarmigan Lake

Bench Lake

Inlet

ARAPAHO

NATIONAL FOREST

BLUE RIDGE

Continental Divide National Scenic Trail

BOWEN GULCH

CHE

Onahu Trailhead

8mi
13km

Onahu Creek Trail

Green Mountain Trail

Green Mountain Trailhead

VALLEY

Colorado River

491

492

Harbison Meadows

34

491

49

Grand Lake Entrance Station

BIG MEADOWS

Tonahutu Creek Trail

Granite Falls

Snowdrift Peak
12274ft
3741m

Ptarmigan Lake

Mount Patterson
11424ft
3482m

Green Mtn
10313ft
3143m

8720ft/2658m
Open all year

Kawuneeche
Visitor Center

Tonahutu Spur Trail

Tonahutu/
North Inlet
Trailheads

Cascade Falls

Summerland Park

Pettingell Lake

Bench Lake

North Inlet Trail

NATIONAL PARK

BIGHORN FLATS

National Scenic Trail

Apiatan Mountain
10319ft
3145m

Colorado River

Supply Creek

GRAND
LAKE

GRAND LAKE
8367ft
2550m

East Shore Trailhead

West Portal

Lookout tower

Ptarmigan Mountain
12324ft
3756m

Alva B. Adams Tunnel
(water diversion structure)

East Inlet Trailhead

East Inlet

Adams Falls

Lake Nokoni

Lake Nanita

Andrews Peak
12565ft
3830m

Pine Beach

SHADOW
MOUNTAIN
LAKE

Shadow Mtn Trail

Shadow Mountain
10155ft
3095m

Lone Pine Lake

Lake Verna

East Inlet Trail

Shadow Mountain

Shadow Mountain Dam

Green Ridge

Continental Divide National Scenic Trail

Colorado River

Mount Bryant
11034ft
3363m

Mount Craig
12007ft
3660m

PARADISE PARK

Cutthroat Bay
(group campground)

GREEN RIDGE

Columbine Creek

Mount Adams
12121ft
3694m

Adams Lake

Stillwater

Mount Acoma
10508ft
3203m

ARAPAHO NATIONAL RECREATION AREA

Watanga Mountain
12375ft
3772m

TABLE MOUNTAIN

Willow Creek Reservoir

Sunset Point

Granby Dam

Rainbow Bay

Knight Ridge

Twin Peaks
11957ft
3644m

Willow Creek

Willow Creek

Pump Canal

Quinette Point

Rainbow Bay

LAKE GRANBY

Knight Ridge Trail

Roaring Fork

INDIAN

Willow Creek

34

Colorado River

Arapaho Bay

Arapaho Bay-Roaring Fork Loop
Knight Ridge Trailhead

Arapaho Bay-Moraine Loop

Arapaho Bay-Big Rock Loop

ARAPAHO

NATIONAL FOREST

Strawberry Lake

Monarch Lake

Continental Divide National Scenic Trail

To Granby and 40

North

0   1   2   3 Kilometers
0   1   2   3 Miles

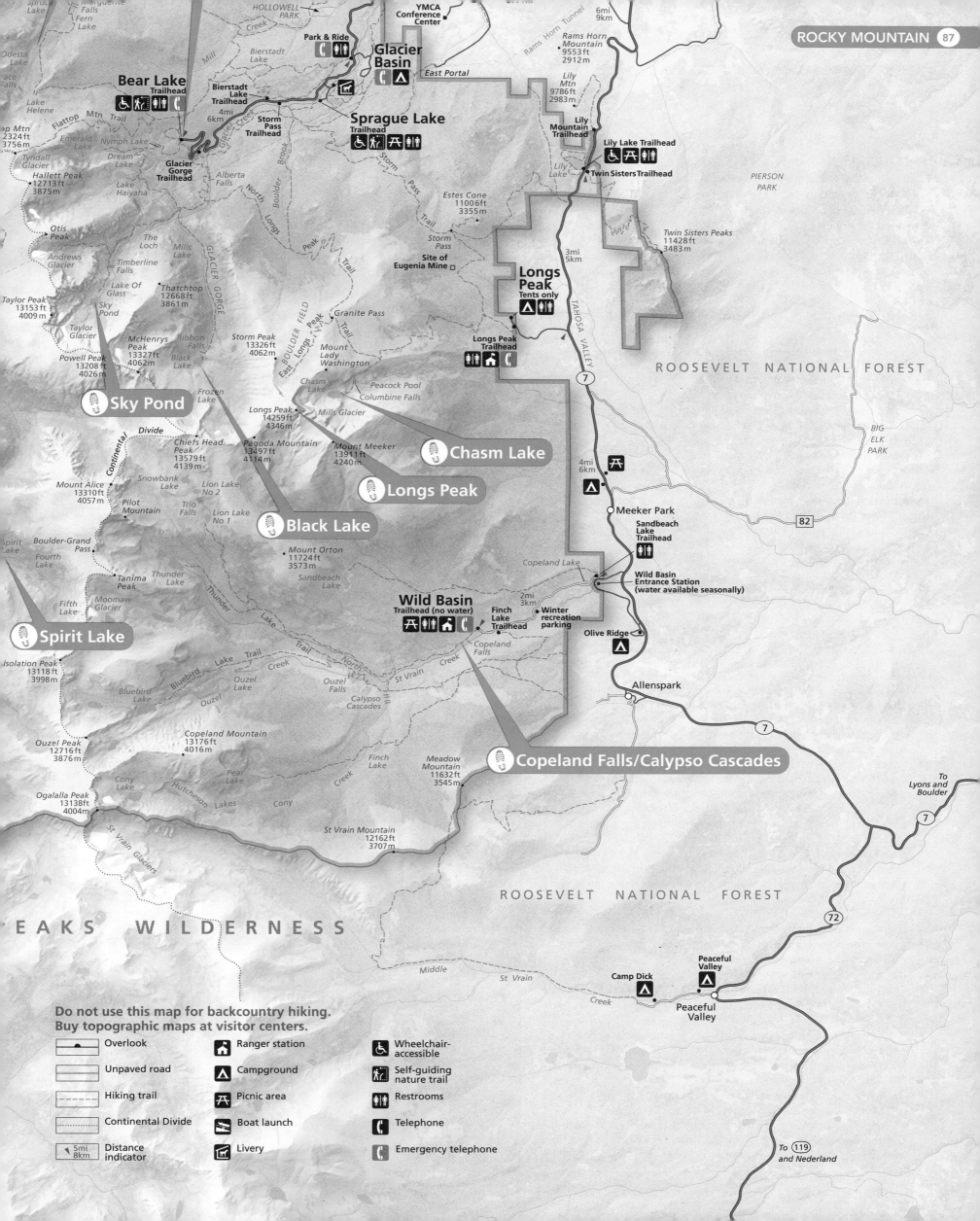

Map Labels

Bear Lake Trailhead

Glacier Basin

Park & Ride

Bierstadt Lake Trailhead

Storm Pass Trailhead

Glacier Gorge Trailhead

Sprague Lake Trailhead

YMCA Conference Center

East Portal

Rams Horn Tunnel

6mi 9km

Rams Horn Mountain 9553ft 2912m

Lily Mtn 9786ft 2983m

Lily Mountain Trailhead

Lily Lake Trailhead

Twin Sisters Trailhead

PIERSON PARK

Spruce Lake

Fern Lake

Odessa Lake

Lake Helene

Lake Haiyaha

Emerald Lake

Tyndall Glacier

Hallett Peak 12713ft 3875m

Otis Peak

Andrews Glacier

Timberline Falls

Lake Of Glass

Sky Pond

Taylor Peak 13153ft 4009m

Taylor Glacier

Powell Peak 13208ft 4026m

McHenrys Peak 13327ft 4062m

Frozen Lake

Sky Pond

Mount Alice 13310ft 4057m

Pilot Mountain

Chiefs Head Peak 13579ft 4139m

Pagoda Mountain 13497ft 4114m

Mount Meeker 13911ft 4240m

Longs Peak 14259ft 4346m

Chasm Lake

Longs Peak

Black Lake

Snowbank Lake

Lion Lake No 2

Lion Lake No 1

Trio Falls

Boulder-Grand Pass

Spirit Lake

Fourth Lake

Fifth Lake

Tanima Peak

Thunder Lake

Moomaw Glacier

Spirit Lake

Isolation Peak 13118ft 3998m

Bluebird Lake

Ouzel Lake

Ouzel Falls

St Vrain

Calypso Cascades

Mount Orton 11724ft 3573m

Sandbeach Lake

Wild Basin Trailhead (no water)

Finch Lake Trailhead

Copeland Falls

Copeland Lake

Winter recreation parking

2mi 3km

Meeker Park

Sandbeach Lake Trailhead

Wild Basin Entrance Station (water available seasonally)

Olive Ridge

Allenspark

Ouzel Peak 12716ft 3876m

Copeland Mountain 13176ft 4016m

Finch Lake

Pear Lake

Meadow Mountain 11632ft 3545m

Copeland Falls/Calypso Cascades

Ogalalla Peak 13138ft 4004m

Cony Lake

Hutcheson Lakes

St Vrain Mountain 12162ft 3707m

ROOSEVELT NATIONAL FOREST

BIG ELK PARK

ROOSEVELT NATIONAL FOREST

Storm Pass

Estes Cone 11006ft 3355m

Site of Eugenia Mine

Longs Peak Tents only

Longs Peak Trailhead

Twin Sisters Peaks 11428m 3483m

TAHOSA VALLEY

3mi 5km

4mi 6km

Storm Peak 13326ft 4062m

Mount Lady Washington

Peacock Pool

Columbine Falls

Chasm Lake

Mills Glacier

Granite Pass

BOULDER FIELD

Mills Lake

The Loch

Dream Lake

Nymph Lake

Bierstadt Lake

Alberta Falls

North Longs Peak Trail

East Longs Peak Trail

Glacier Gorge

Black Lake

Ribbon Falls

Thatchtop 12668ft 3861m

Lake Of Glass

St Vrain Glaciers

EAKS WILDERNESS

Middle St Vrain

Camp Dick

Peaceful Valley

Peaceful Valley

To Lyons and Boulder

To 119 and Nederland

Do not use this map for backcountry hiking. Buy topographic maps at visitor centers.

- Overlook
- Unpaved road
- Hiking trail
- Continental Divide
- Distance indicator 5mi 8km
- Ranger station
- Campground
- Picnic area
- Boat launch
- Livery
- Wheelchair-accessible
- Self-guiding nature trail
- Restrooms
- Telephone
- Emergency telephone

Sheep near Rock Cut

Rocky Mountain Basics

(970) 586-1206 | nps.gov/romo
Entrance Fee: $25/car
Timed-Entry Permits* required in summer
Lodging: None
Camping: Apsenglen*, Glacier Basin*, Longs Peak, Moraine Park*, Timber Creek

*reserve at recreation.gov

Rocky Mountain Driving Distances

The park isn't overwhelmingly huge like Yellowstone but there are several distinct regions. You'll need some time to see them all.

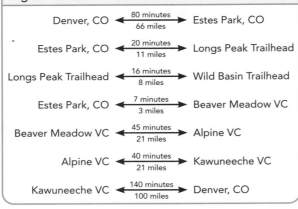

From	Time / Distance	To
Denver, CO	← 80 minutes / 66 miles →	Estes Park, CO
Estes Park, CO	← 20 minutes / 11 miles →	Longs Peak Trailhead
Longs Peak Trailhead	← 16 minutes / 8 miles →	Wild Basin Trailhead
Estes Park, CO	← 7 minutes / 3 miles →	Beaver Meadow VC
Beaver Meadow VC	← 45 minutes / 21 miles →	Alpine VC
Alpine VC	← 40 minutes / 21 miles →	Kawuneeche VC
Kawuneeche VC	← 140 minutes / 100 miles →	Denver, CO

Trail riding the Rockies

Why Visit Rocky Mountain?

- To drive Trail Ridge Road, the highest continuous paved road in the country
- To hike a wide variety of splendid mountain trails
- To join a Rocky Mountain trail ride
- To spot sheep, and moose, and elk!

Rocky Mountain Favorites

Easy Hikes: Dream Lake (2.2 miles), Sprague Lake (0.5), Tundra Communities (1), Calypso Cascades (3.6), Adams Falls (0.6), Bear Lake (0.5), Lily Lake (0.7)
Moderate Hikes: Bluebird Lake (12), Odessa Lake (8.2), Deer Mountain (6), Alluvial Fan (0.4)
Strenuous Hikes: Sky Pond (9.8), Chasm Lake (8.4), Black Lake (10), Hallet Peak (10), Ypsilon Lake (9)
Extreme Hike: Longs Peak (16)
Activities: Ride a horse, climb some rocks, fishing, sledding
Views: Sprague Lake, Forest Canyon Overlook, Gore Range Overlook, Rainbow Curve, Many Parks Curve, Moraine Park, Hollowell Park

Sky Pond

What You Need to Know About Rocky Mountain

- During peak season visitors are required to reserve a timed-entry permit to access Trail Ridge Road (between 9am and 3pm) and/or Bear Lake (between 5am and 6pm) through recreation.gov.
- Estes Park is remarkably busy in summer, especially weekends. And crowds don't thin out until October. The park is great in winter. Just dress for the weather and make sure you have traction devices for your boots.
- Pencil acclimating to elevation into your itinerary. Even if you're incredibly fit, you probably can't come here and day-hike Longs Peak like it's no big deal. It's a pretty big deal. As are the other summits. Simply driving Trail Ridge Road can take your breath away. You want the scenery to leave you breathless, not the elevation.
- Allow a full day to explore Trail Ridge Road. Even though there aren't a bunch of trails fanning off of it. There are quite a few viewpoints, a visitor center, and you may want to relax and enjoy the quieter west side of the mountains once you get there (or spend a few nights).
- Old Fall River Road is an alternative route into the heart of the Rockies. It's pretty exposed at places. It's gravel. Most of it is one-way. But it isn't that intimidating.
- If you want to hike to Longs Peak or Chasm Lake, secure a campsite or get there very very early. Most Longs Peak day hikers leave well before the sun rises. And the parking lot fills accordingly.
- It's also hard to park at Bear Lake in summer, but there are free shuttles, greatly increasing accessibility (while decreasing frustration). Shuttles connect Estes Park Visitor Center, Beaver Meadows Visitor Center, and Moraine Park and Glacier Park campgrounds with Bear Lake.

How Much Time Do You Have?

1 Day: Catch sunrise at Sprague Lake or get an early start on Trail Ridge Road and watch it from Rainbow Curve. Pick a few trails to hike. Bear Lake is the busiest area for a reason. It's stunning. My choice for a hike would be Sky Pond but it's fairly long and difficult. Do Sky Pond for the adventurous in your group, Black Lake for those looking for a medium adventure, and Dream Lake for anyone looking for a casual walk.

2 Days: Get back into the heart of the Rockies but this time take Fall River Road (it's one-way and gravel but nothing too treacherous for most motorists). Stick to the Bear Lake Area or head over to the west side of the park where things are a bit quieter.

3 Days: Acclimated to the elevation, consider hiking to Chasm Lake or spend the night out in the boulder field to get up to Longs Peak the next day if you're feeling extreme. Otherwise you could continue to the southeast corner of the park and hike at Wild Basin.

Old Fall River Road

Lots of wildlife in the Rockies

Great Sand Dunes Region

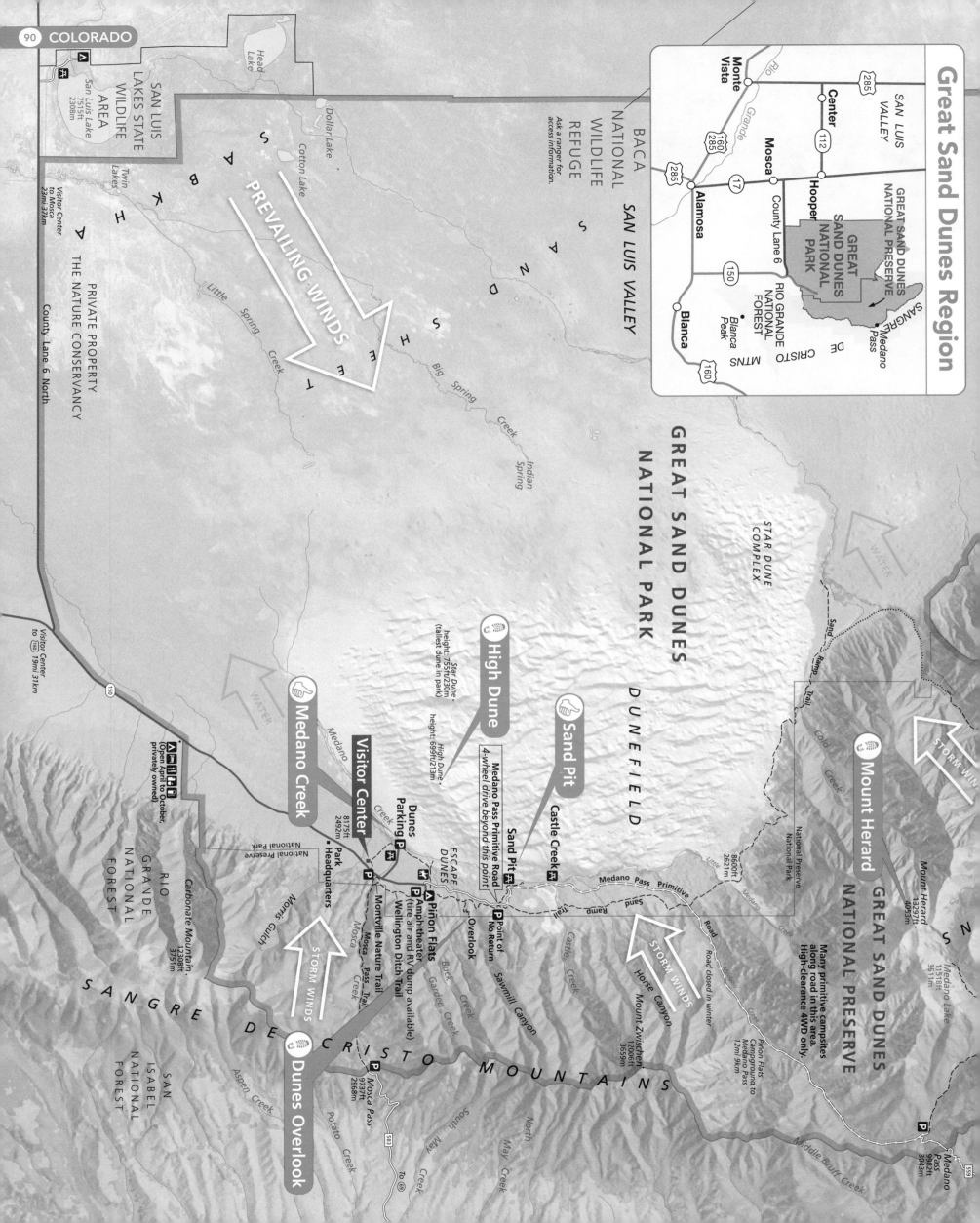

SAN LUIS LAKES STATE WILDLIFE AREA

San Luis Lake
7515ft
2308m

Head Lake

Twin Lakes

Visitor Center to Mosca 23mi 37km

County Lane 6 North

PRIVATE PROPERTY
THE NATURE CONSERVANCY

Dollar Lake

Cotton Lake

Little Spring Creek

Big Spring Creek

Indian Spring

SABKHA

PREVAILING WINDS

BACA NATIONAL WILDLIFE REFUGE

Ask a ranger for access information.

SAN LUIS VALLEY

DUNES

Inset map

Great Sand Dunes Region

SAN LUIS VALLEY

Monte Vista

285

Rio Grande

Center

112

Mosca

17

Hooper

County Lane 6

285

GREAT SAND DUNES NATIONAL PRESERVE

GREAT SAND DUNES NATIONAL PARK

Alamosa

160
285

150

RIO GRANDE NATIONAL FOREST

SANGRE DE CRISTO MTNS

Blanca

Blanca Peak

Medano Pass

160

GREAT SAND DUNES NATIONAL PARK

STAR DUNE COMPLEX

DUNEFIELD

High Dune
Star Dune •
height: 755ft/230m
(tallest dune in park)
High Dune •
height: 699ft/213m

Sand Pit
Castle Creek
Sand Pit

Medano Pass Primitive Road
4-wheel drive beyond this point

Visitor Center to Mosca 19mi 31km

150

WATER

Medano Creek

Medano Creek

Visitor Center
8175ft
2492m
Dunes Parking

Park Headquarters

(Open April to October; privately owned)

National Preserve National Park

Montville Nature Trail

Mosca Creek

Morris Gulch

Mosca Pass Trail

Amphitheater
(tire air and RV dump available)
Wellington Ditch Trail

Piñon Flats

Overlook

Point of No Return

ESCAPE DUNES

Medano Pass Primitive

Sand Ramp Trail

Buck Garden Creek

Sawmill Canyon

Castle Creek

Cold Creek

Little Medano Creek

National Preserve National Park

8600ft
2621m

Mount Herard
Mount Herard
13297ft
4053m

Medano Lake
11518ft
3511m

STORM WINDS

GREAT SAND DUNES NATIONAL PRESERVE

Many primitive campsites along road in this area. High-clearance 4WD only.

Piñon Flats Campground to Medano Pass 12mi 9km

WATER

STORM WINDS

RIO GRANDE NATIONAL FOREST

Carbonate Mountain
12308ft
3751m

SANGRE DE CRISTO MOUNTAINS

Aspen Creek

Potato Creek

SAN ISABEL NATIONAL FOREST

Dunes Overlook

STORM WINDS

Mosca Pass
9737ft
2968m

Mosca Creek

150

North May Creek

South May Creek

To 69

Horse Canyon

Mount Zwischen
12006ft
3659m

Road closed in winter

Road

Medano Pass
9982ft
3043m

Middle Braff Creek

160

Ridgelines

...is not alone with the dunes

A sea of sand

Great Sand Dunes Basics

(719) 378-6395 | nps.gov/grsa
Entrance Fee: $25/car
Lodging: None
Camping: Pinon Flats*

*reserve at recreation.gov

Great Sand Dunes Driving Distances

A high-clearance 4x4 unlocks some beautiful areas but most people stick to the main road along the east flank of the dunefield.

From	Time	Distance	To
Denver, CO	3.5 hours / 175 miles		Music Pass
Denver, CO	4 hours / 250 miles		Visitor Center
Visitor Center	2 hours / 33 miles		Mosca Pass
Visitor Center	55 minutes / 12 miles		Medano Pass (unpaved, 4x4)

Legend:
- Unpaved road
- 4-wheel-drive road
- Unimproved road
- Hiking trail
- Unimproved trail

- P Parking/trailhead
- ⛺ Picnic area
- ▲ Campground
- Lodging
- 🍴 Food service
- F Store
- ⛽ Gas station
- 🐴 Horse trailer parking

North

0   1   2 Kilometers
0   1   2 Miles

Why Visit Great Sand Dunes?

- To play in the great big sand box at the foot of the Sangre de Cristo Mountains

What You Need to Know

- Visitation peaks when Medano Creek flows at maximum volume (typically late May/early June). Expect the park to be extremely crowded during this time. Pack your patience and travel during the week if it's possible.
- Most years the creek begins to retreat in late June/July. Wear footwear in the dunes during summer. The sand gets awfully hot.
- The park is surprisingly remote. Great Sand Dunes Oasis, located near the main entrance, is the only restaurant within 25 miles, so pack enough food for the duration of your stay.
- This is another high elevation park. The western flats are above 7,500 feet above sea level. The surrounding mountains max out above 13,000 feet.
- There aren't marked trails in the dunes but there will be footprints. It's easiest to follow the ridgelines. It's fun to bound down them. But then it's difficult to get back to the top.
- To reach High Dune, most people begin from Dunes Parking Area, cross Medano Creek, and climb the main ridgeline to the east. Work your way up, and then follow ridgelines (and footprints) to the west and north. High Dune is fairly obvious.
- Unless you're comfortable on a board, sledding is the way to go!
- Camping in the dunes (permit required) can be great, but you're going to get sand everywhere (especially if it's windy). There are also designated campsites along Medano Pass Road.

How Much Time Do You Have?

1 Day: Plenty of time to hike in the dunes and enjoy Medano Creek (if it's running). Hike to Dunes Overlook and you can call it a day or head just outside the park and hike to Zapata Falls.

2 Days: The dunes are entertaining enough for a few days, but if you have a 4x4, drive up Medano Pass Road for some mountain hiking. It'll take all day.

3 Days: There's more than enough hiking for a few more days, but I'd move on to your next destination after two nights here.

Great Sand Dunes Favorites

Hikes: High Dune (moderate, 2.5 miles), Medano Lake (strenuous, 7.4), Music Pass (strenuous, 2), Dunes Overlook (moderate, 2.3), Star Dune (strenuous, ~8)

Activities: Sled or snowboard down the dunes, go off-roading up Medano Pass Road, sleep among the dunes, ride horses at Zapata Ranch (ranchlands.com)

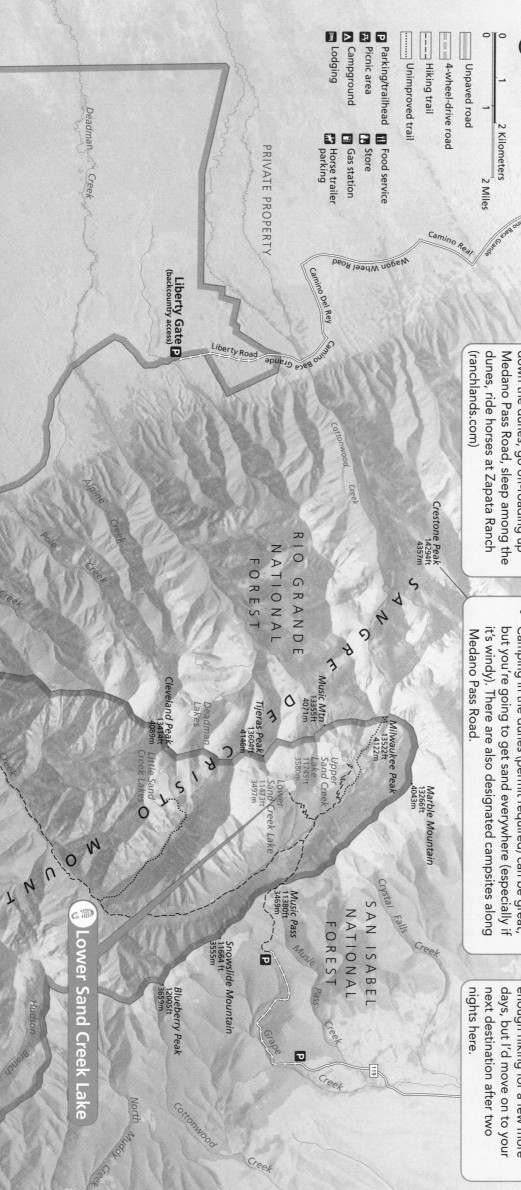

Lower Sand Creek Lake

Crestone Peak
14294ft
4357m

RIO GRANDE NATIONAL FOREST

S A N G R E   D E   C R I S T O   M O U N T A I N S

Cottonwood Creek

Pole Creek

Alpine Creek

Deadman Creek

Deadman Lakes

Cleveland Peak
14043ft
4280m

Little Sand Creek Lakes

Music Mtn
13355ft
4071m

Milwaukee Peak
13522ft
4122m

Tijeras Peak
13604ft
4146m

Upper Sand Creek Lake
11745ft
3580m

Lower Sand Creek Lake
11473ft
3497m

Marble Mountain
13266ft
4043m

Crystal Falls

Creek

Music Pass
11380ft
3469m

SAN ISABEL NATIONAL FOREST

Snowslide Mountain
11664ft
3555m

Blueberry Peak
12005ft
3659m

Grape Creek

Music Pass Creek

Hudson Branch

North Creek

North Muddy Creek

Cottonwood Creek

119

PRIVATE PROPERTY

Liberty Gate (backcountry access)

Liberty Road

Camino Baca Grande

Camino Del Rey

Wagon Wheel Road

Camino Real

Colorado Road T

To 17

Crestone

Black Canyon of the Gunnison Driving Distances

A paved road follows the South Rim (along with East Portal Road, which descends steeply to the Gunnison). An unpaved road follows the North Rim.

Denver, CO	←— 6.5 hours / 250 miles —→	North Rim
North Rim	←— 2 hours / 80 miles —→	South Rim VC
South Rim VC	←— 3.5 hours / 180 miles —→	Moab, UT

Black Canyon of the Gunnison Basics

(970) 641-2337 x205 | nps.gov/blca
Entrance Fee: $30/car
Lodging: None
Camping: South Rim*, East Portal, North Rim

*reserve at recreation.gov

Gunnison Point

BLACK CANYON

OF THE GUNNISON

NATIONAL PARK

North Vista

8563ft
2610m

North Vista

Exclamation Point
7702ft
2348m

Serpent Point
7922ft
2415m

Painted

WILDERNESS
AREA

PAINTED WALL

Cedar Point

Dragon Point

Why Visit Black Canyon of the Gunnison?

- To enjoy a relatively quiet park for this corner of the country with a deep, dark canyon
- To try some pretty gnarly inner-canyon hiking trails

Painted Wall

Warner Point

Red Rock Canyon

Warner Point

PRIVATE
PROPERTY

Warner
Point

Warner Point

Sunset View

V E R N A

Black Canyon of the Gunnison Favorites

Hikes: Warner Point (moderate, 1.5 miles), Rim Rock/Oak Flat (strenuous, 2), Long Draw (strenuous, 2), North Vista (moderate, 3), Gunnison Route (strenuous, 3)
Views: Painted Wall/Cedar Point (South), Gunnison Point (South), Chasm View (North), Chasm View (South), Pulpit Rock (South), Island Peaks (North), The Narrows View (North), Kneeling Camel (North)

Painted Wall/Chasm View

High Point
(no fires)
8289ft
2523m

PRIVATE
PROPERTY

GUNNISON GORGE

NAL CONSERVATION AREA

JONES   DRAW

B O S T W I C K

What You Need to Know About Black Canyon of the Gunnison

- South Rim is open every day of the year but South Rim Road closes beyond Gunnison Point in winter. East Portal Road and the North Rim are seasonal, closing each winter.
- Like most parks, hiking is the primary activity. Rock climbing and kayaking are possible, but they're reserved for people who take those hobbies very seriously.
- You can drive into the canyon via East Portal Road. It's steep (16% grade).
- You can hike into the canyon via any one of seven inner canyon trails (steep and rocky).
- Another way to see the canyon from its floor is to join a ranger-led boat tour at Curecanti National Recreation Area (nps.gov/cure).
- The road to the North Rim is unpaved but it's usually accessible to regular vehicles. North Rim is great, as is the drive there from Gunnison.

East   Lateral   Vernal   Mesa   Ditch

Bostwick Park Road

Bostwick Park Road

Irrigation   Ditch

B O S T W I C K   P A R K

▄▄	Overlook
- - -	Hiking trail
═══	Unpaved road

🏠	Ranger station	⛺	Campground	👣	Self-guiding trail	🎭	Amphitheater
⛱	Picnic area	🚻	Restrooms	♿	Wheelchair-accessible		
🛶	River rafting	🚶	Trailhead	🐎	Horseback riding		

North
↑

0   0.5   1 Kilometer
0   0.5   1 Mile

Black Canyon of the gunnison Region

Hotchkiss
Delta
Gunnison Gorge
National Conservation Area
Crawford
**Black Canyon
of the Gunnison
National Park**
Gunnison

Montrose

Curecanti
National
Recreation
Area

Ridgway

To Telluride
Ouray
Lake City

North

0   10   20 Kilometers
0   10   20 Miles

50
92
135
347
92
50
550
149
114
62
145

GRIZZLY GULCH

Black Canyon Road (closed in winter)

North Rim
Ranger Station

North Rim
Campground

Chasm View

Chasm View

The Narrows
View

Devils
Lookout

Balanced
Rock
View

Rock
Point

MESA INCLINADO

Big Island
7915ft
2413m

Big Island
View

Cross Fissures
View

Island Peaks View

Island
Peaks
7631ft
2326m

PRIVATE
PROPERTY

Pulpit Rock
Overlook

Kneeling Camel View

Deadhorse Trail

*Closed to vehicles in
winter from Gunnison
Point to High Point*

WILDERNESS
AREA

GRIZZLY

RIDGE

PRIVATE
PROPERTY

Poison Spring Hill
9040ft
2755m

Oak Flat Trail

Gunnison
Point

MESA

South Rim Road

**South Rim
Visitor Center**

Uplands Trail

Rock Trail

Tomichi Point

PRIVATE
PROPERTY

Rim Rock Trail

👍 **Gunnison Point**

South Rim
Campground
8320ft
2536m

Jones Summit
8266ft
2519m

Entrance
Station

Gunnison

River

WILDERNESS
AREA

Deadhorse Trail

DEADHORSE GULCH

*Vehicles longer than
22 feet prohibited on
East Portal Road.*

East Portal Road (closed in winter)

PRIVATE
PROPERTY

East
Portal
6547ft
1996m

Gunnison
Diversion Dam

CURECANTI NATIONAL
RECREATION
AREA

To Montrose 15.2mi (24.5km)
To 50 7.0mi (11.3km)

Gunnison Tunnel

**BLACK CANYON
OF THE GUNNISON
NATIONAL PARK**

dead end road

Crystal
Reservoir   Crystal Dam

Kneeling Camel (North Rim)

How Much Time Do You Have?

1 Day: The typical visitor only visits the
South Rim. Unless you plan on hiking
into the canyon, one day is plenty to
drive the rim, enjoy the viewpoints, and
hike a trail or two (like Warner Point or
Oak Flat Loop).

2 Days: With another day, head over to
the North Rim for more viewpoints and
hiking.

3 Days: Unless you're going to do a
few inner canyon trails, Black Canyon
doesn't require a whole lot of time.
However, you could go to Red Rock
Canyon. It requires a permit, available
through online lottery from the park
website. It's the longest (6.8 miles) and
easiest way into the canyon.

Mesa Verde Basics

(970) 529-4465 | nps.gov/meve
Entrance Fee: $30/car
Lodging: Far View Lodge*
Camping: Morefield*

*reserve at visitmesaverde.com

Mesa Verde Driving Distances

There are three primary destinations: the visitor center (buy tour tickets), Wetherill Mesa (Long House) and Chapin Mesa (Cliff Palace, Spruce Tree House, Balcony House). There are two separate loops at Chapin Mesa (Mesa Top Loop and Cliff Palace Loop).

Santa Fe, NM	4.5 hours / 250 miles	Visitor Center
Visitor Center	60 minutes / 27 miles	Wetherill Mesa
Visitor Center	45 minutes / 22 miles	Cliff Palace
Visitor Center	2.5 hours / 124 miles	Moab, UT

Mesa Verde Favorites

Hikes: Petroglyph Point (moderate, 2.4 miles), Point Lookout (moderate, 2.2), Prater Ridge (moderate, 7.8)
Activities: Cliff Palace Tour, Long House Tour, Balcony House Tour, Step House Tour
Views: Cliff Palace Overlook, Square Tower House, Sun Point View (a different view of Cliff Palace), Sunset House, Soda Canyon Overlook (Balcony House)

Why Visit Mesa Verde?

- To learn all about the culture of the Puebloans
- To tour remarkable cliff dwellings, true marvels of ancient architecture

Interesting tours

How Much Time Do You Have?

A trip here doesn't require a whole lot of time. With a little planning, you should be able to tour the three main cliff dwellings (Cliff Palace, Balcony House, and Long House) and hike Petroglyph Point in two days. Of course, if you love this sort of stuff, there are enough cultural exhibits to keep you occupied for days.

Cliff Palace

What You Need to Know About Mesa Verde

- The park is open year-round, but most of its notable attractions close for the off-season (November–April). Wetherill Mesa Road is open from May through September (weather permitting).
- It's a good idea to reserve cliff dwelling tour tickets in advance through recreation.gov. Otherwise get tickets at the visitor center upon entering the park. It's the only place tickets are sold. You do not want to drive an hour into the park, only to have to turn around for tickets. Unfortunately, I wouldn't consider any of the cliff dwelling tours easy. Cliff Palace is the easiest, but there still are a few stairs. The dwellings are built into the side of a cliff after all.
- Spruce Tree House has been closed for quite awhile due to stability concerns. It's a good idea to check its status before arriving.
- Take your time. Walk around and imagine what it was like living in these cliff dwellings. Think about why they built them? Think about what made them leave?
- The park offers a few special backcountry hikes. They can also be reserved in advance at recreation.gov.

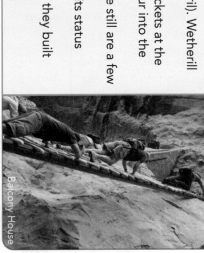
Balcony House

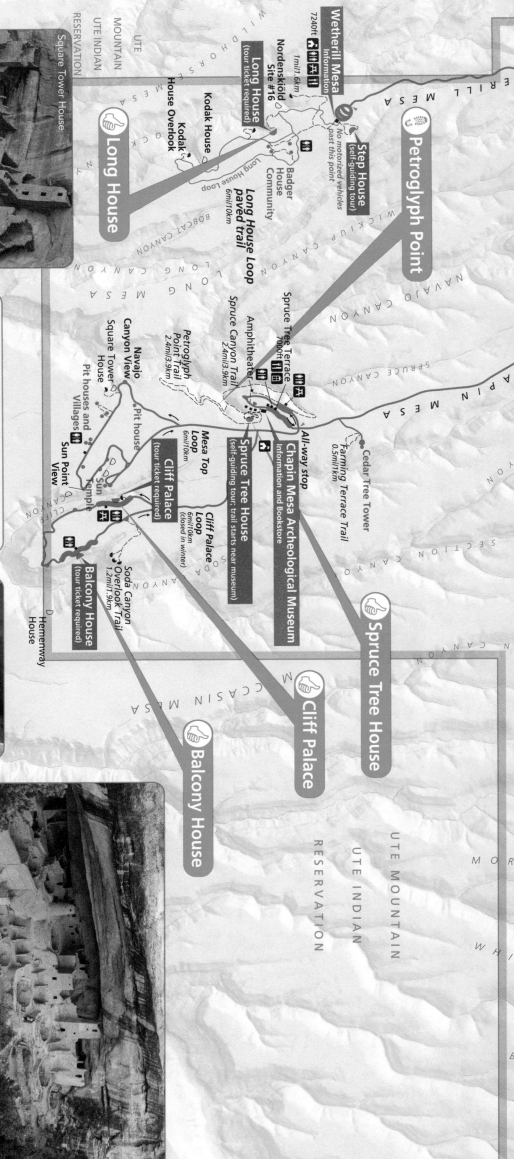

Wetherill Mesa
Information
7240ft

Nordenskiöld Site #16

Long House
(tour ticket required)
1mi/1.6km

Step House
(self-guiding tour)

No motorized vehicles past this point

Kodak House Overlook

Kodak House

Badger House Community

Long House Loop
paved trail
6mi/10km

Square Tower House

WILDHORSE MESA

UTE MOUNTAIN UTE INDIAN RESERVATION

WICKIUP CANYON

BOBCAT CANYON

LONG MESA

NAVAJO CANYON

SPRUCE CANYON

Spruce Tree Terrace
7000ft

Amphitheater

Spruce Canyon Trail
2.4mi/3.9km

Petroglyph Point Trail
2.4mi/3.9km

Chapin Mesa Archeological Museum
Information and Bookstore

All-way stop

Farming Terrace Trail
0.5mi/1km

Cedar Tree Tower

CHAPIN MESA

Navajo Canyon View
Square Tower House

Pit houses and Villages

Pit house

Spruce Tree House
(self-guiding tour; trail starts near museum)

Mesa Top Loop
(self-guiding tour)
6mi/10km

Sun Point View

Sun Temple

Cliff Palace
(tour ticket required)

Cliff Palace Loop
6mi/10km
(closed in winter)

Soda Canyon Overlook Trail
1.2mi/1.9km

Balcony House
(tour ticket required)

Hemenway House

SODA CANYON

CLIFF CANYON

MOCCASIN MESA

MORE SECTION CANYON

UTE MOUNTAIN UTE INDIAN RESERVATION

Petroglyph Point
(self-guiding tour)

Long House

Spruce Tree House

Cliff Palace

Balcony House

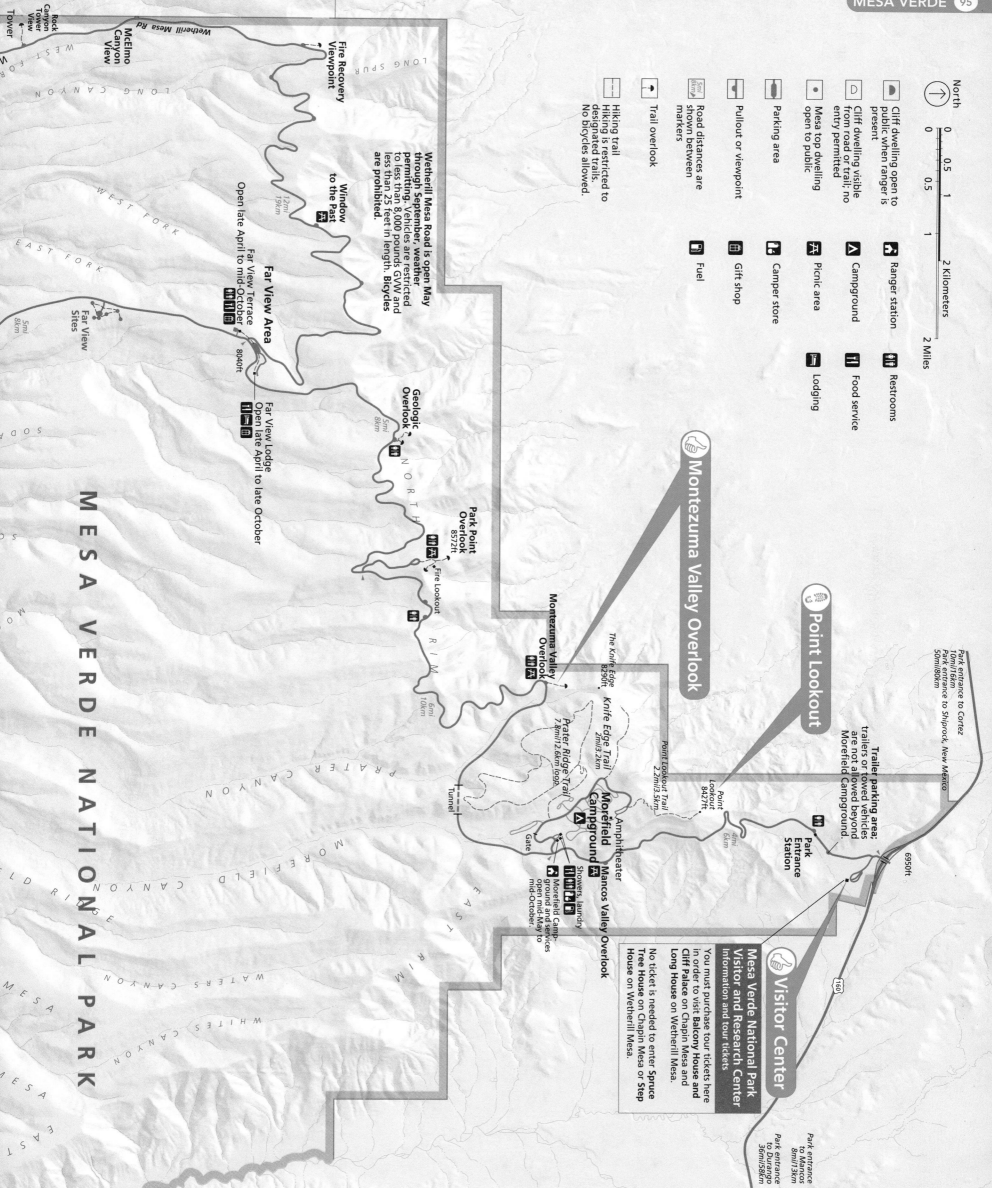

North

0   0.5   1   2 Kilometers
0   0.5   1   2 Miles

▲ Cliff dwelling open to public when ranger is present

▲ Cliff dwelling visible from road or trail; no entry permitted

D Mesa top dwelling open to public

Road distances are shown between markers

→ Trail overlook

Hiking trail
Hiking is restricted to designated trails. No bicycles allowed.

Ranger station
Restrooms
Campground
Food service
Picnic area
Parking area
Camper store
Gift shop
Lodging
Fuel

MESA VERDE NATIONAL PARK

MESA VERDE NATIONAL PARK

Rock Canyon Tower View
McElmo Canyon View
Fire Recovery Viewpoint

WEST FORK
LONG CANYON
EAST FORK
WEST FORK
SODA

Wetherill Mesa Rd
LONG SPUR

Window to the Past

Wetherill Mesa Road is open May through September, weather permitting. Vehicles are restricted to less than 8,000 pounds GVW and less than 25 feet in length. Bicycles are prohibited.

Far View Sites
5mi/8km

Far View Terrace
Open late April to mid-October
8040ft

Far View Area

Far View Lodge
Open late April to late October

Geologic Overlook
5mi/8km

NORTH RIM

Park Point Overlook
8572ft
Fire Lookout

Montezuma Valley Overlook
6mi/10km

PRATER CANYON
MOREFIELD CANYON
EAST RIM
WATERS CANYON
WHITES CANYON
MESA

The Knife Edge
8290ft
Knife Edge Trail
2mi/3.2km

Prater Ridge Trail
7.8mi/12.6km loop

Tunnel
Gate
Amphitheater

Morefield Campground
Showers, laundry
Morefield Campground and services open mid-May to mid-October.

Mancos Valley Overlook

Point Lookout Trail
2.2mi/3.5km
Point Lookout
8427ft

Trailer parking area; trailers or towed vehicles are not allowed beyond Morefield Campground.

Park entrance to Cortez
10mi/16km
Park entrance to Shiprock, New Mexico
50mi/80km

4mi/6km

Park Entrance Station

6950ft

160

Park entrance to Mancos
8mi/13km

Park entrance to Durango
36mi/58km

Montezuma Valley Overlook

Point Lookout

Visitor Center
Mesa Verde National Park Visitor and Research Center
Information and tour tickets

You must purchase tour tickets here in order to visit **Balcony House** and **Cliff Palace** on Chapin Mesa and **Long House** on Wetherill Mesa.

No ticket is needed to enter **Spruce Tree House** on Chapin Mesa or **Step House** on Wetherill Mesa.

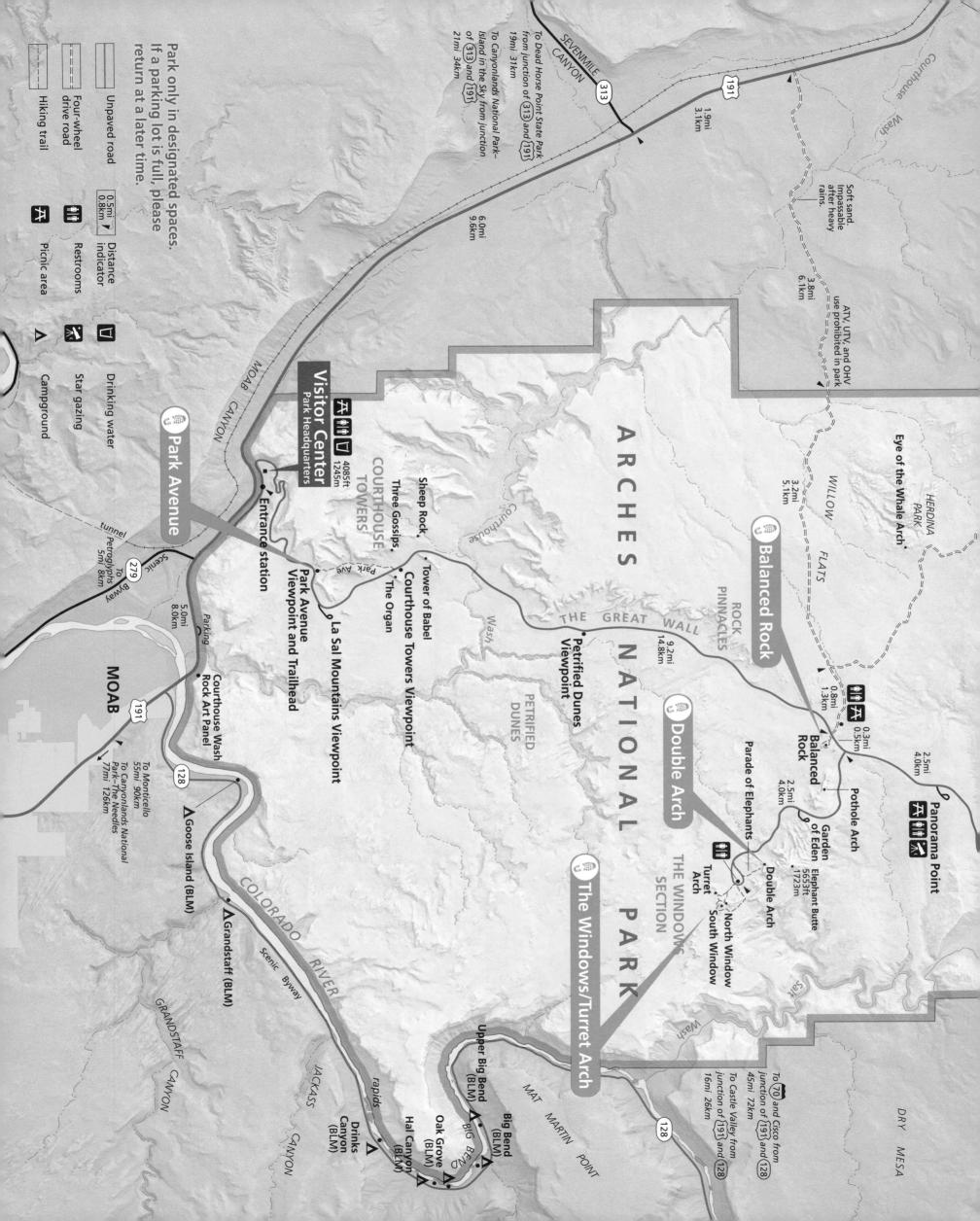

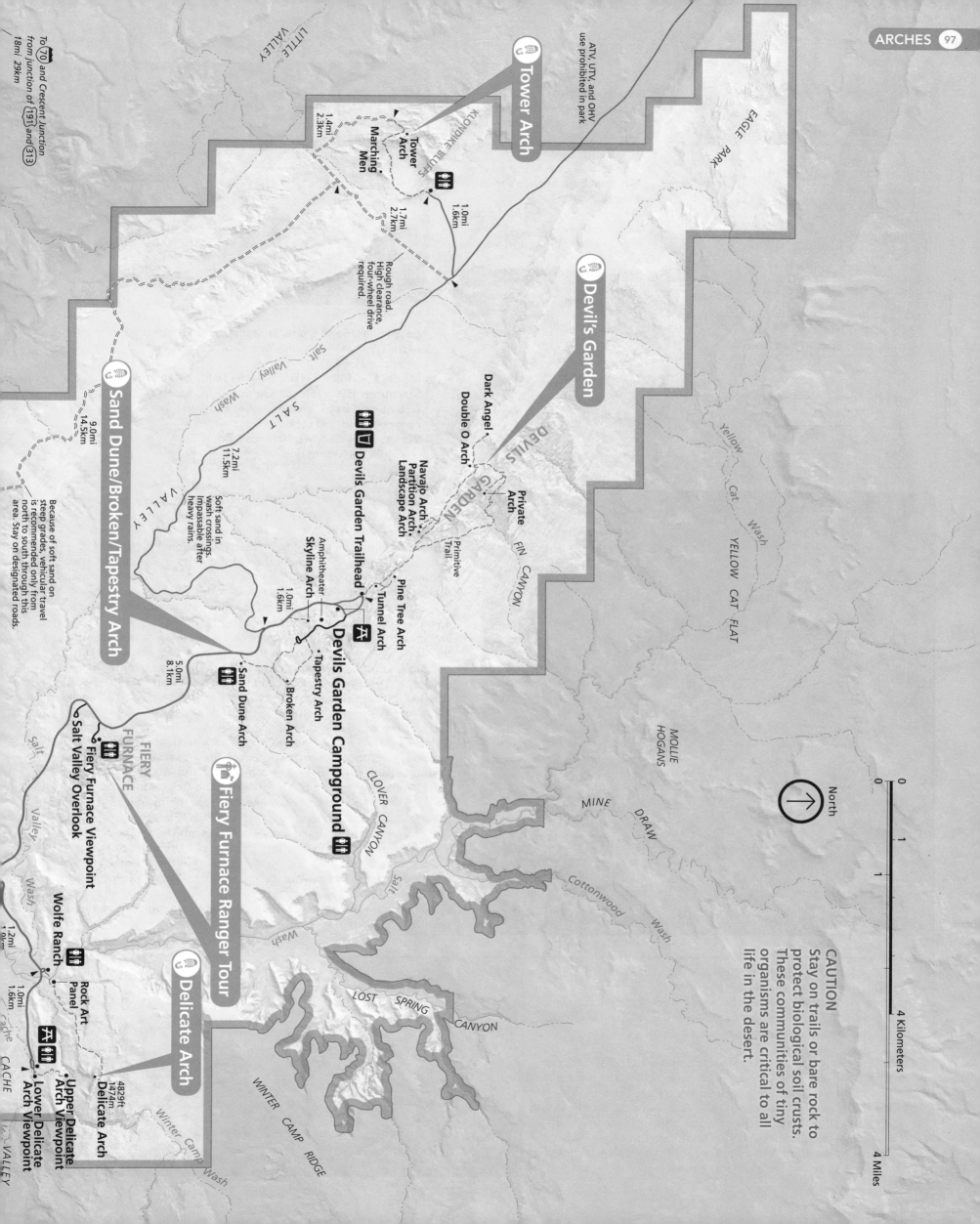

Tower Arch

To 70 and Crescent Junction from Junction of 191 and 313
18mi 29km

ATV, UTV, and OHV use prohibited in park

Marching Men

Tower Arch

1.4mi 2.3km

1.7mi 2.7km

1.0mi 1.6km

Rough road. High clearance, four-wheel drive required.

KLONDIKE BLUFFS

LITTLE VALLEY

EAGLE PARK

Devil's Garden

Dark Angel

Double O Arch

Navajo Arch
Partition Arch
Landscape Arch

Private Arch

Primitive Trail

DEVILS

GARDEN

FIN CANYON

Yellow Cat Wash

YELLOW CAT FLAT

MOLLIE HOGANS

MINE DRAW

North

0

0

1

1

4 Kilometers

4 Miles

CAUTION
Stay on trails or bare rock to protect biological soil crusts. These communities of tiny organisms are critical to all life in the desert.

Devils Garden Trailhead

Pine Tree Arch

Tunnel Arch

7.2mi 11.5km

Devils Garden Campground

Sand Dune/Broken/Tapestry Arch

9.0mi 14.5km

Soft sand in wash crossings impassable after heavy rains.

Amphitheater

Skyline Arch

1.0mi 1.6km

Tapestry Arch

Broken Arch

Sand Dune Arch

5.0mi 8.1km

Because of soft sand on steep grades, vehicular travel is recommended only from north to south through this area. Stay on designated roads.

SALT VALLEY

SALT VALLEY WASH

CLOVER CANYON

Fiery Furnace Ranger Tour

FIERY FURNACE

Fiery Furnace Viewpoint

Salt Valley Overlook

Wolfe Ranch

Salt Valley

Salt Wash

Cottonwood Wash

Delicate Arch

Rock Art Panel

1.2mi
1.0mi

1.0mi 1.6km

4829ft 1474m

Upper Delicate Arch Viewpoint

Lower Delicate Arch Viewpoint

Delicate Arch

LOST SPRING CANYON

WINTER CAMP RIDGE

Winter Camp Wash

CACHE VALLEY

Devil's Garden

Arches Basics

(435) 719-2299 | nps.gov/arch
Entrance Fee: $30/car
Timed-Entry Permits*: required spring through fall
Lodging: None
Camping: Devil's Garden*

*reserve at recreation.gov

Arches Driving Distances

The main road is short and one way.

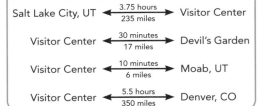

Salt Lake City, UT	← 3.75 hours / 235 miles →	Visitor Center
Visitor Center	← 30 minutes / 17 miles →	Devil's Garden
Visitor Center	← 10 minutes / 6 miles →	Moab, UT
Visitor Center	← 5.5 hours / 350 miles →	Denver, CO

Why Visit Arches?

- To see some of the 2,000+ sandstone arches that took a few million years to come into existence
- To hike to Delicate Arch (undeniably one of the National Park Service's best short hikes)
- To explore the Fiery Furnace with a park ranger
- To spend the night and see the stars

Tower Arch

Landscape Arch

Arches Favorites

Easy Hikes: Sand Dune/Broken/Tapestry Arch (3), Landscape Arch (1.9 miles), Double Arch (0.5), Skyline Arch (0.4), Balanced Rock (0.3)
Moderate Hikes: Delicate Arch (3), Park Avenue (1)
Strenuous Hikes: Devil's Garden (7.8), Tower Arch (2.6)
Activities: Fiery Furnace Ranger Program, 4x4, photography, canyoneering and rock climbing
Views: The Windows, Balanced Rock, Skyline Arch, Turret Arch, La Sal Mountains

North Window

What You Need to Know About Arches

- During peak season, you'll need a timed-entry permit available online at recreation.gov.
- For better or worse, I don't think there's a national park town that's developed more rapidly than Moab in the past decade. It's a popular place, with sprawling hotels, restaurants, and shops.
- Arches is busy from March through October, peaking in summer (even though it's often uncomfortably hot in the middle of the day). If you're crowd-averse, consider visiting in winter.
- Precipitation is light year-round, but it's something to pay attention to, especially if you plan to leave the pavement for some 4x4 fun.
- Parking is limited. The park is small and traffic turns over fairly quickly, but you'll want to get an early (or late) start for ultra-popular sites like Devil's Garden and Delicate Arch Trailhead (Wolfe Ranch).
- If you only want to drive through the park, that'll take about two hours (but it will depend on the line/wait at the entrance station).
- Campers should make reservations as early as possible (typically six months in advance) via recreation.gov. They go fast.
- With that said, you'll find more camping at and around Canyonland's Island in the Sky and on BLM land along the Colorado River.
- Balanced Rock is kind of neat. I like it best in the evening light from the picnic area just across the road (on Willow Flats Road).
- You can get neat photos of Delicate Arch from Upper Delicate Arch Viewpoint, but only with a pretty long lens (200mm or so). Also, the climb to the viewpoint is nearly as steep as the toughest part of Delicate Arch Trail from Wolf Ranch. Skip the distant viewpoint and hike to the arch if you can.
- Fiery Furnace is great. Tours (recreation.gov) are typically offered from May through September.

How Much Time Do You Have?

1 Day: The popular spots are Delicate Arch, Devil's Garden (Landscape Arch), the Windows, Balanced Rock, Park Avenue, and Sand Dune Arch (continue the lollipop loop if you have time). You can do them all in a fun-filled day, no problem.

2 Days: With another day, go off-roading and hike to Tower Arch in the park's backcountry (you can also reach the trailhead via a maintained unpaved road). If you can book a Fiery Furnace Tour, great, go for it! If not, check out Skyline Arch or complete the entire Devil's Garden Loop. Beyond that, I wouldn't spend much more time here as there's so much fun stuff to do around Moab (like Canyonlands!). However, Arches is a great photography destination. You may want to return for a few more mornings/evenings.

Balanced Rock

Joint Trail

Canyonlands Basics

(435) 719-2313 | nps.gov/cany
Entrance Fee: $30/car
Lodging: None
Camping: Willow Flat (Island in the Sky), Squaw Flat (Needles District)*

*reserve at recreation.gov

Canyonlands Driving Distances

Judging from its name you can already guess this park is complex. There are many deep, impenetrable canyons formed by the Green and Colorado Rivers. Still, there's much to see by car, foot, and mountain bike. Island in the Sky is the most popular region, followed by Needles.

From	Time / Distance	To
Salt Lake City, UT	4 hours / 250 miles	Island in the Sky VC
Island in the Sky VC	21 minutes / 12 miles	Grand View Point
Island in the Sky VC	19 minutes / 11 miles	Upheaval Dome
Island in the Sky VC	2.5 hours / 130 miles	Horseshoe Canyon TH
Horseshoe Canyon TH	1.5 hours / 26 miles	Hans Flat Ranger Station
Island in the Sky VC	2 hours / 107 miles	Needles VC
Needles VC	15 minutes / 7 miles	Big Spring Canyon

Why Visit Canyonlands?

- To drive (4x4) or bike White Rim Road and admire this incredibly quirky environment
- To see some of the most other-worldly views on the planet
- To see Canyonlands from its floor rafting Cataract Canyon just beyond the confluence of the Green and Colorado Rivers
- To navigate the rocky labyrinth known as The Maze
- To enjoy millions and millions of stars from your tent

Biking White Rim Road

What You Need to Know About Canyonlands

- Summers are hot during the day. Winters are cold over night. It snows occasionally but it rarely sticks, however it causes complications for off-roading. Spring and fall are ideal.
- The campgrounds are small and popular. Try to reserve a site at Squaw Flat (Needles) if you can, otherwise get to either campground early and hope you get lucky securing a site. If you get one, you're in for a real treat at night (and during the day)!
- Joint Trail is great! You can get there on a long day hike from Squaw Flat or Elephant Hill or you can take a long 4x4 ride to the trailhead (permit required).
- A permit is required for White Rim Road (even day trips). You'll want to get these early through recreation.gov.
- Shafer Road (access to White Rim Road near Island in the Sky Visitor Center) is steep and winding, with considerable exposure. You can also access it via Potash Road (near Moab) or Mineral Road (via UT-313). You'll miss a lot of Colorado River scenery, but I'd take Shafer Road down. It just spares you from a whole lot of bouncing around in your vehicle.
- Make sure you start with a full tank of gas, plenty of water, and a tow strap.
- You won't encounter anything really technical but there are a few steep/rocky sections. You won't encounter many other humans out here, but always watch ahead for other 4x4s and mountain bikers. There are a few spots you really don't want to encounter a vehicle traveling the other direction.
- Camping White Rim Road, Taylor and Candlestick are great sites. Labyrinth and Murphy are pretty darn good too. There's no wrong answer here.
- You'll find a few 4x4 tours in the area. For White Rim Road they typically enter via Potash Road and go to Lathrop Canyon (this stretch of road is unrelenting in its ruggedness). It'll be slow (~5mph or so) and long. You'll also probably find a pretty long muddy stretch at the potash ponds as well.
- Mountain bike tours typically spend time on the other end (Mineral/Horse Thief Road), where the road is much better. However, this section is more susceptible to flooding since it travels along the Green River for a stretch.
- If you want to paddle on your own, you'll need a permit. They're available through recreation.gov, too.
- There are no gas stations in the park. The park isn't overwhelmingly large, but it takes some driving to reach its remote corners. Be sure to fill up, especially before heading out on a long off-road trip.
- Water is available at Island in the Sky and Needles visitor centers. Be sure to carry more water than you'll need too.
- False Kiva is an interesting hike. It's a kiva of unknown origins situated in an alcove with a view. Ask Island in the Sky rangers about the trailhead as accessibility may change.
- There are a several 4x4 rental and tour agencies in Moab. They're worth looking into if you'd like to rip around the red rock a bit. There are also side-by-side tours. Moab has a lot going on.

Canyonlands Favorites

IS = Island in the Sky, N = Needles
Easy Hikes: Joint (N, 3 miles, 4x4 required), Grand View Point (IS, 2 miles), Moses and Zeus (IS, 1), Murphy Point (IS, 3.6), Mesa Arch (IS, 0.5)
Moderate Hikes: Whale Rock (IS, 1)
Strenuous Hikes: Chesler Park (N, 11, including Joint Trail), Syncline Loop (IS, 8.3), Peekaboo (N, 10), Lost Canyon (N, 8.7), Druid Arch (N, 11), Confluence Overlook (N, 10)
Activities: Raft the weird, wonderful world of Canyonlands, off-roading, mountain biking, rock climbing, stargazing
Views: Grand View Point, Green River Overlook, Dead Horse Point State Park (outside Island in the Sky)

Sunset at Candlestick

How Much Time Do You Have?

1 Day: Spend more time. A 4x4 unlocks lots of fun. And if you can get a permit to drive/bike White Rim Road, that'll take a couple days (you could probably drive it in a day, but it won't be too enjoyable). Float the river? There's a lot to do here. If you only have one day, get an early start and head to Island in the Sky, Mesa Arch is a very popular sunrise destination or stop at Dead Horse Point State Park. Continue on to Grand View Point Overlook. Stop at Green River Overlook. There are a bunch of good hikes in the area. My first choice would be Syncline Loop around Upheaval Dome. Check out the Shafer switchbacks and start thinking about what you want to do for a return trip!

2 Days: Head to Needles. Similarly, it possesses a wealth of hiking and off-roading opportunities. Elephant Hill is great but not particularly easy hiking. The trail network is fairly dense, creating a variety of loops/lollipop routes. For a very long and ambitious day, start at Elephant Hill, hike to Elephant Canyon (EC1 campsite), hike up to Devil's Kitchen, over to Devil's Pocket, take a short stretch along a 4x4 road to Joint Trail, then work your way around Chesler Park back to Elephant Hill (add the spur to Druid Arch, time and energy permitting). With Druid Arch, the total distance is about 18 miles.

3 Days: You could head over to the Maze (4x4 required) or Horseshoe Canyon. I would spend an extra day at Island in the Sky or Needles to cross off a few more trails.

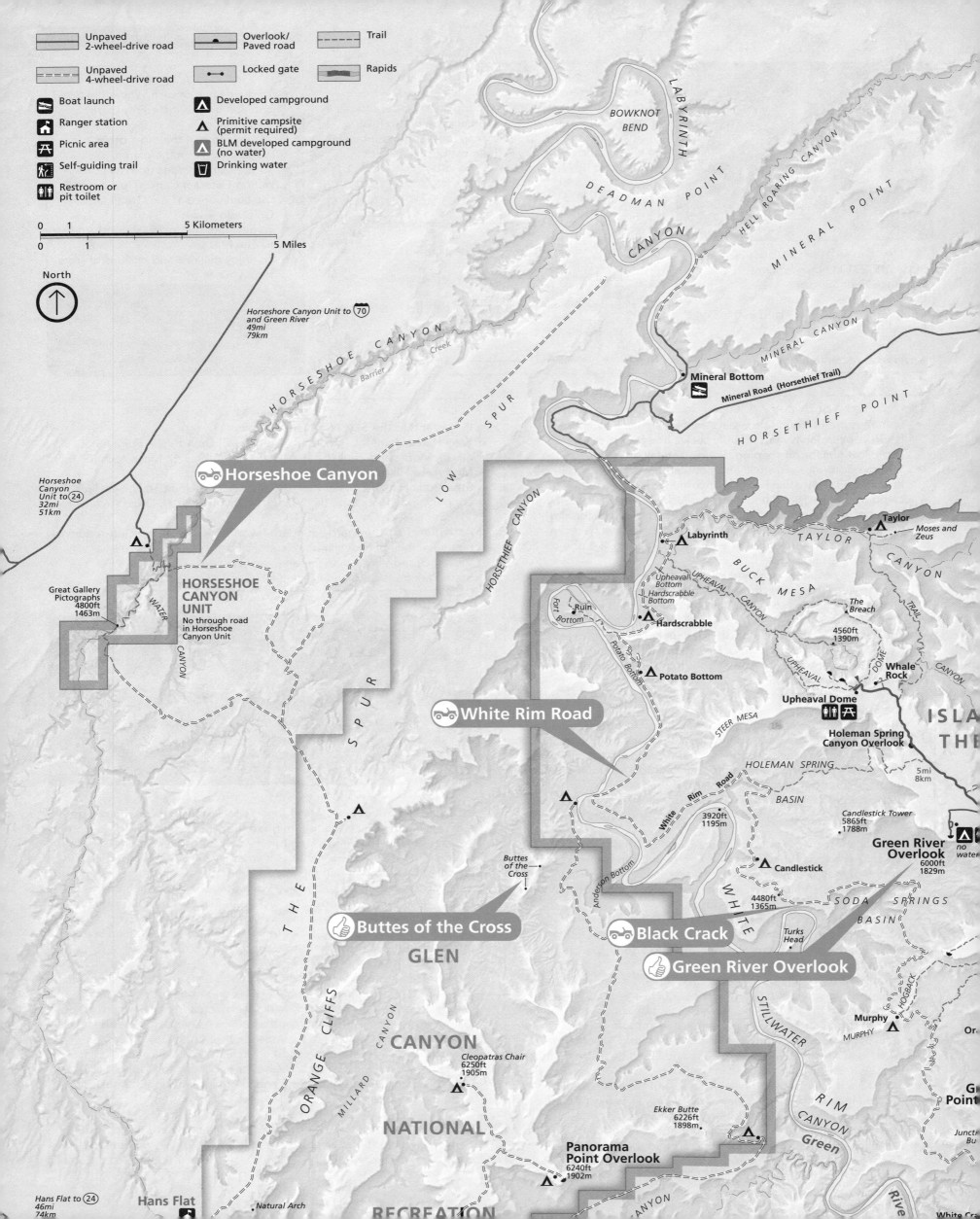

Legend

Unpaved 2-wheel-drive road	Overlook/Paved road
Unpaved 4-wheel-drive road	Locked gate
	Trail
	Rapids

- Boat launch
- Ranger station
- Picnic area
- Self-guiding trail
- Restroom or pit toilet
- △ Developed campground
- ▲ Primitive campsite (permit required)
- △ BLM developed campground (no water)
- Drinking water

0 1 5 Kilometers
0 1 5 Miles

North
↑

BOWKNOT BEND

LABYRINTH CANYON

DEADMAN POINT

HELL ROARING CANYON

MINERAL POINT

MINERAL CANYON

Horseshore Canyon Unit to 70 and Green River 49mi 79km

HORSESHOE CANYON

Barrier Creek

LOW SPUR

HORSETHIEF CANYON

Mineral Bottom
Mineral Road (Horsethief Trail)

HORSETHIEF POINT

Horseshoe Canyon Unit to 24 32mi 51km

Taylor
Moses and Zeus

Labyrinth

TAYLOR CANYON

BUCK MESA

HORSESHOE CANYON

HORSESHOE CANYON UNIT
No through road in Horseshoe Canyon Unit

Great Gallery Pictographs 4800ft 1463m

WATER CANYON

Upheaval Bottom
Hardscrabble Bottom

UPHEAVAL CANYON

The Breach

Fort Bottom
Ruin

Hardscrabble

4560ft 1390m

Potato Bottom

Whale Rock

DOME

UPHEAVAL

Upheaval Dome

ISLA
THE

WHITE RIM ROAD

White Rim Road

STEER MESA

Holeman Spring Canyon Overlook

HOLEMAN SPRING BASIN

5mi 8km

THE SPUR

Buttes of the Cross

△

3920ft 1195m

Candlestick Tower 5865ft 1788m

Green River Overlook 6000ft 1829m

no wate

BUTTES OF THE CROSS

Anderson Bottom

Candlestick

WHITE

4480ft 1365m

SODA SPRINGS BASIN

GLEN

Black Crack

Green River Overlook

Turks Head

STILLWATER

HOGBACK

Murphy

MURPHY

CANYON

ORANGE CLIFFS

Cleopatras Chair 6250ft 1905m

RIM CANYON

G
Point

MILLARD

NATIONAL

Ekker Butte 6226ft 1898m

Green

Junct
Bu

Panorama Point Overlook 6240ft 1902m

Hans Flat to 24 46mi 74km

Hans Flat

Natural Arch

RECREATION

White Cr

River

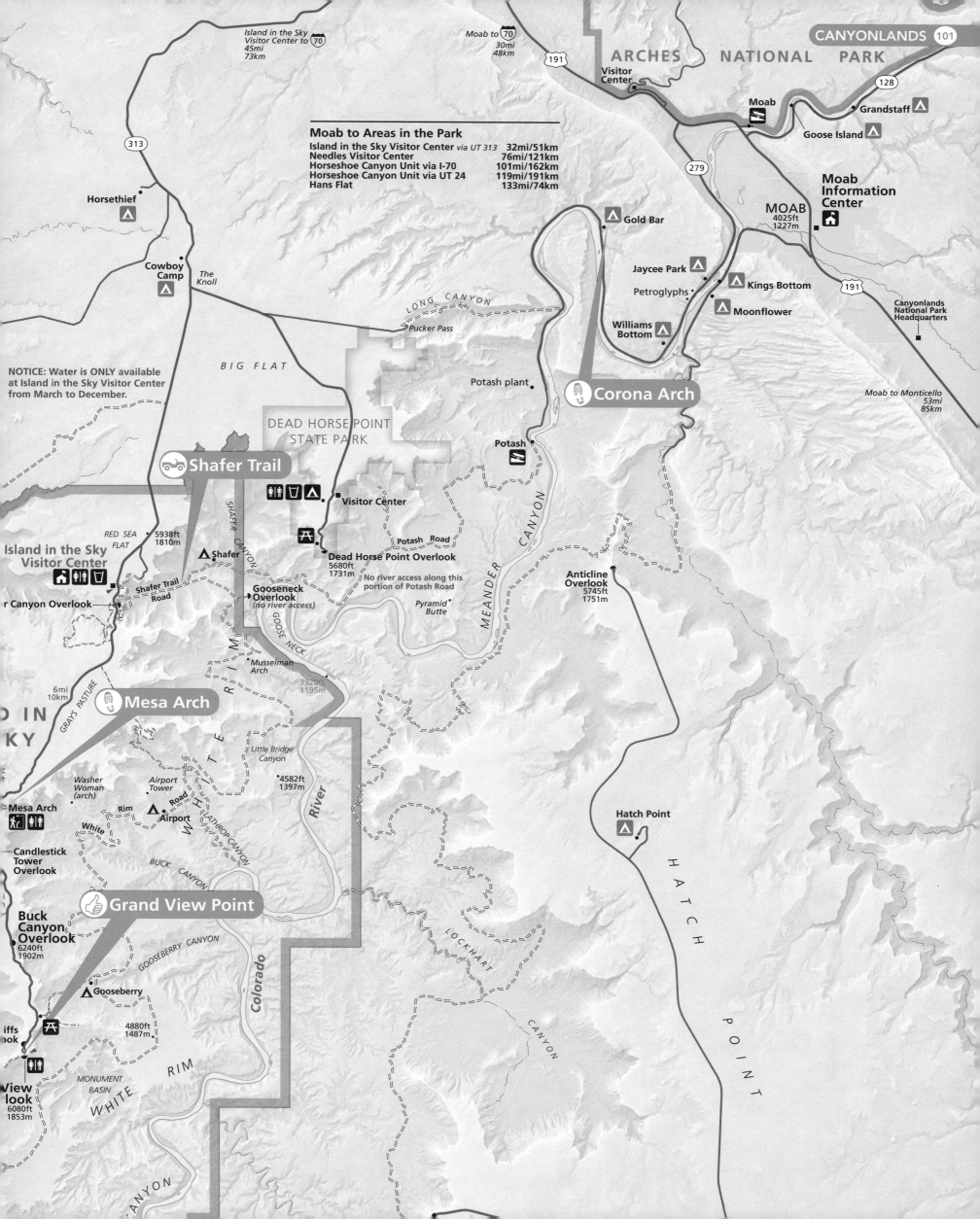

ARCHES NATIONAL PARK

Visitor Center

Moab

Grandstaff

Goose Island

Moab Information Center

MOAB
4025ft
1227m

Island in the Sky
Visitor Center to 70
45mi
73km

Moab to 70
30mi
48km

Gold Bar

Jaycee Park

Petroglyphs

Kings Bottom

Moonflower

Williams Bottom

Canyonlands National Park Headquarters

Moab to Areas in the Park
Island in the Sky Visitor Center *via UT 313*   32mi/51km
Needles Visitor Center   76mi/121km
Horseshoe Canyon Unit via I-70   101mi/162km
Horseshoe Canyon Unit via UT 24   119mi/191km
Hans Flat   133mi/74km

Horsethief

Cowboy Camp

The Knoll

LONG CANYON

Pucker Pass

BIG FLAT

DEAD HORSE POINT STATE PARK

Potash plant

Corona Arch

Potash

NOTICE: Water is ONLY available at Island in the Sky Visitor Center from March to December.

Shafer Trail

Visitor Center

RED SEA FLAT

5938ft
1810m

Shafer

Island in the Sky Visitor Center

Dead Horse Point Overlook
5680ft
1731m

Potash   Road

No river access along this portion of Potash Road

Anticline Overlook
5745ft
1751m

Moab to Monticello
53mi
85km

r Canyon Overlook

Shafer Trail Road

Gooseneck Overlook
(no river access)

Pyramid Butte

MEANDER CANYON

6mi
10km

GRAYS PASTURE

Musselman Arch

3920ft
1195m

Mesa Arch

Little Bridge Canyon

Washer Woman (arch)

Airport Tower

Rim   Road

Airport

4582ft
1397m

Mesa Arch

Hatch Point

Candlestick Tower Overlook

White

LATHROP CANYON

River

Grand View Point

Buck Canyon Overlook
6240ft
1902m

BUCK CANYON

GOOSEBERRY CANYON

Gooseberry

4880ft
1487m

Colorado

LOCKHART CANYON

HATCH POINT

iffs
ook

View ook
6080ft
1853m

MONUMENT BASIN

WHITE RIM

CANYON

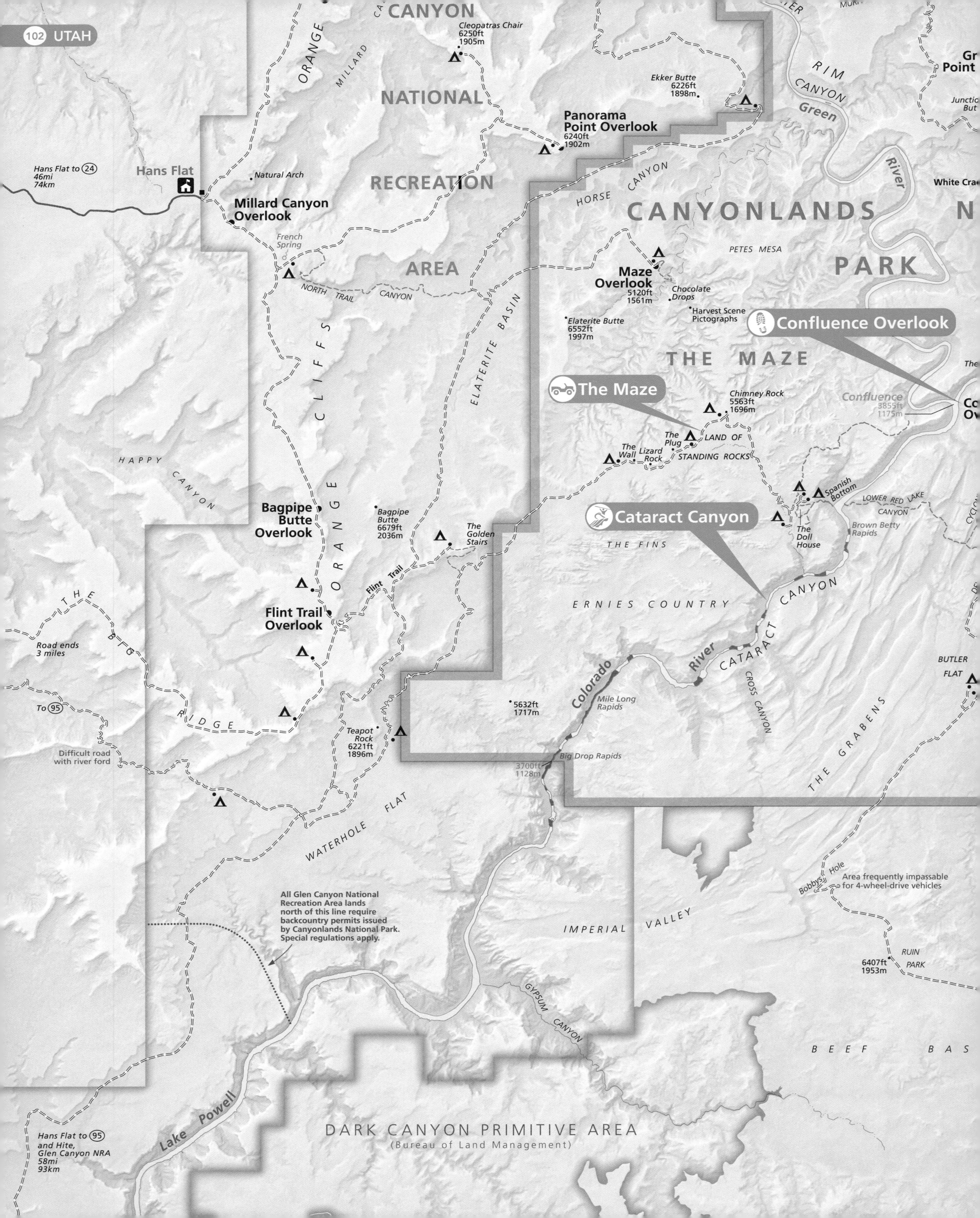

CANYON

Cleopatras Chair
6250ft
1905m

Ekker Butte
6226ft
1898m

RIM
CANYON

Gr
Point

NATIONAL

Green

Junctio
But

**Panorama
Point Overlook**
6240ft
1902m

CANYONLANDS

N

White Cra

HORSE

CANYON

PETES MESA

RECREATION

Hans Flat

• Natural Arch

**Millard Canyon
Overlook**

ORANGE

MILLARD

French
Spring

AREA

NORTH TRAIL CANYON

**Maze
Overlook**
5120ft
1561m

Chocolate
• Drops

• Harvest Scene
Pictographs

Confluence Overlook

Confluence
3855ft
1175m

Co
Ov

THE MAZE

ELATERITE BASIN

• Elaterite Butte
6552ft
1997m

The Maze

Chimney Rock
5563ft
1696m

HAPPY

CANYON

The Wall

C
L
I
F
F
S

ORANGE

The
Plug

Lizard
Rock

LAND OF

STANDING ROCKS

**Bagpipe
Butte
Overlook**

• Bagpipe
Butte
6679ft
2036m

• The
Golden
Stairs

Cataract Canyon

Spanish
Bottom

LOWER RED LAKE

CANYON

• The
Doll
House

Brown
Betty
Rapids

THE FINS

Flint Trail

**Flint Trail
Overlook**

ERNIES COUNTRY

CATARACT CANYON

THE

Road ends
3 miles

BIG

• 5632ft
1717m

Colorado

Mile Long
Rapids

CROSS CANYON

BUTLER
FLAT

To (95)

RIDGE

River

Difficult road
with river ford

Teapot
Rock
6221ft
1896m

Big Drop Rapids

3700ft
1128m

THE GRABENS

WATERHOLE

FLAT

All Glen Canyon National
Recreation Area lands
north of this line require
backcountry permits issued
by Canyonlands National Park.
Special regulations apply.

IMPERIAL

VALLEY

Bobbys
Hole

Area frequently impassable
for 4-wheel-drive vehicles

6407ft
1953m

RUIN
PARK

BEEF
BAS

GYPSUM
CANYON

Lake
Powell

DARK CANYON PRIMITIVE AREA
(Bureau of Land Management)

View
erlook
6080ft
1853m

MONUMENT
BASIN

WHITE

RIM

CANYON

TIONAL

THE
LOOP

MEANDER

**Needles
Overlook**
6295ft
1919m

Indian

Creek

**Colorado River
Overlook**
4880ft
1487m

Lower
Jump

Salt

Hamburger Rock
⛺

Needles Overlook to [191]
*22mi
35km*

ence
ook

**Big Spring
Canyon Overlook**
4880ft
1487m

Slickrock
👣

Creek

Needles Outpost
(private)
⛺

**Creek
Pasture**
⛺

**The Needles
Visitor Center**
4960ft
1512m

Pothole Point
👣

🏕

Roadside Ruin
👣

10mi
16km

Cave Spring
👣

ELEPHANT

one-way

one-way

BIG

SPRING

**Wooden
Shoe Arch
Overlook**

Permit required
for vehicle entry

Area frequently impassable
for 4-wheel-drive vehicles

⛺

Superbowl

POCKET

ELEPHANT
HILL

Permit required
for vehicle entry

*Wooden Shoe
Arch*

**North Sixshooter
Peak**
6374ft
1943m

Devils
Kitchen

CANYON

SQUAW

CANYON

*Paul
Bunyans
Potty*

**South Sixshooter
Peak**
6132ft
1869m

J.B. HILL

LOST

CANYON

*Peekaboo
Spring*

🏕

•Tower Ruin

CHESLER
PARK

Salt

Creek

CANYON

THE NEEDLES

Gothic Arch•

HORSE

Joint Trail

•Druid Arch

Chesler Park

👣 **Joint**

👣 **Chesler Park**

*Castle
Arch•*

DAVIS

CANYON

👣 **Druid Arch**

•Fortress Arch

•Angel Arch

Upper Jump

👣 **Angel Arch**

•Caterpillar Arch

Permit required
for vehicle entry

LAVENDER

[211]

To Moab

•Natural Arch

Cedar Mesa
6987ft
2130m

*Cleft
Arch•*

Creek

North

Cottonwood

*Needles
Visitor Center
to* [191]
*35mi
56km*

**Cathedral
Point**
7120ft
2170m

Newspaper Rock
Petroglyphs

To Monticello

Cathedral Butte
7940ft
2420m

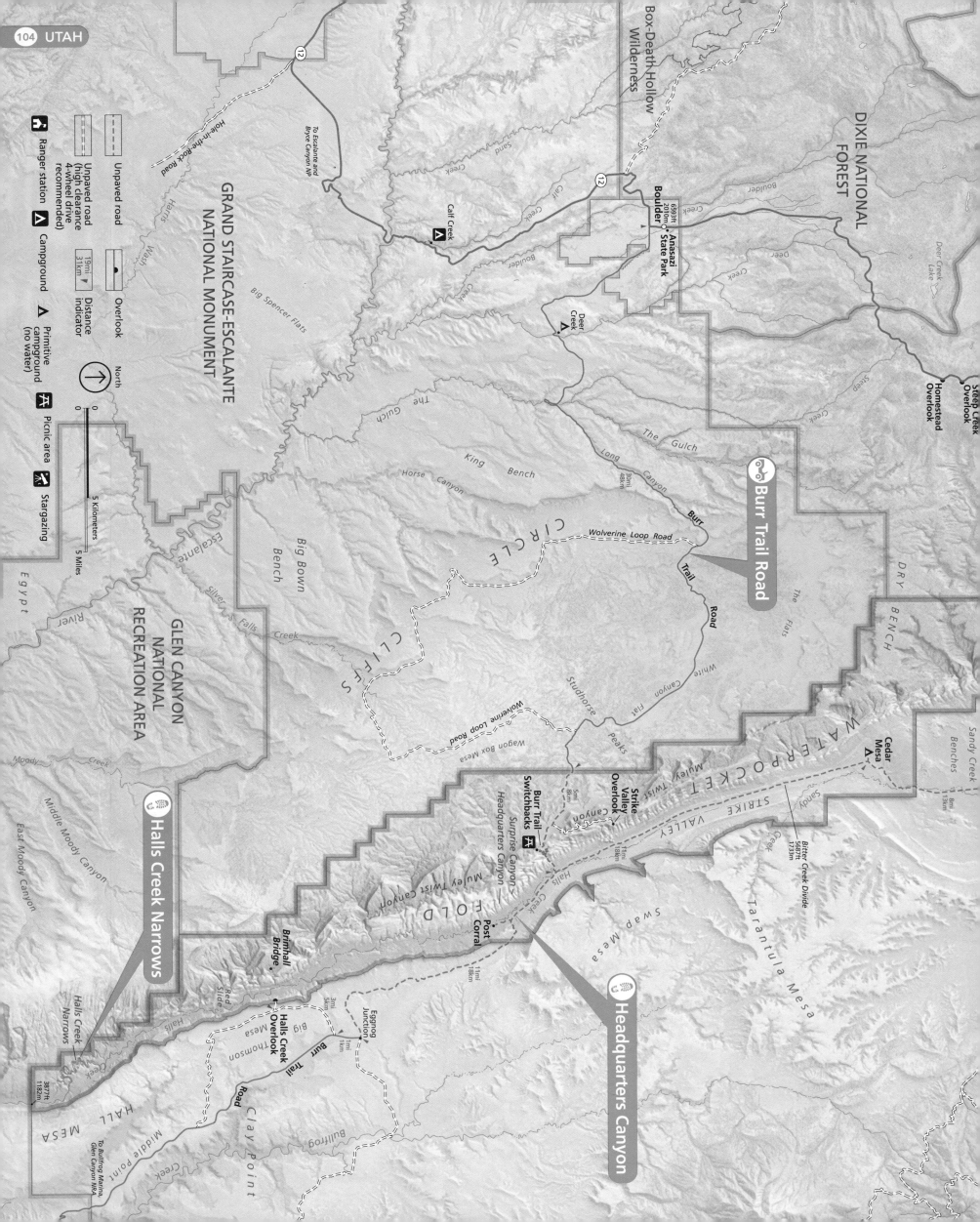

GRAND STAIRCASE-ESCALANTE NATIONAL MONUMENT

Legend

- Unpaved road
- Unpaved road (high clearance 4-wheel drive recommended)
- Overlook
- Distance indicator | 19mi 31km ▼
- ⬢ Ranger station
- ▲ Campground
- △ Primitive campground (no water)
- ⛺ Picnic area
- ✦ Stargazing

North

0
5 Kilometers
5 Miles

DIXIE NATIONAL FOREST

Box-Death Hollow Wilderness

12

To Escalante and Bryce Canyon NP

Hole-in-the-Rock Road

12

Sand Creek

Calf Creek △

Boulder
6993ft 2010m ◉
Anasazi State Park ▲

Deer Creek

Deer Creek △

Homestead Overlook
Steep Creek Overlook

Big Spencer Flats

Harris Wash

The Gulch

King Bench

Horse Canyon

Long Canyon
The Gulch
30mi 48km

Burr Trail Road

Burr Trail Road

CIRCLE

Wolverine Loop Road

DRY BENCH

The Flats

Egypt

Escalante River

Big Bown Bench

Silver Falls Creek

Creek

GLEN CANYON NATIONAL RECREATION AREA

CLIFFS

Wolverine Loop Road

Wagon Box Mesa

Studhorse Peaks

White Canyon

Studhorse Flat

WATERPOCKET

Cedar Mesa △

Bitter Creek Divide 5687ft 1733m

Sandy Creek Benches

8mi 13km

Moody Creek

Middle Moody Canyon

East Moody Canyon

Halls Creek Narrows

Halls Creek Narrows

Surprise Canyon
Headquarters Canyon ⛺
Burr Trail Switchbacks
5mi 8km

Strike Valley Overlook

STRIKE VALLEY

Muley Twist Canyon
11mi 18km

FOLD

Muley Twist Canyon

Swap Mesa

Tarantula Mesa

Brimhall Bridge

Halls Creek

Post Corral

Big Thomson Mesa

Red Slide

Halls Creek Overlook
3mi 5km

Eggnog Junction
1mi 1km

11mi 18km

Burr Trail Road

Clay Point

Bullfrog Creek

HALL MESA

Middle Point

3877ft 1182m

Headquarters Canyon

To Bullfrog Marina, Glen Canyon NRA

Goosenecks & Sunset Point

Spring Canyon/Chimney Rock

Lower Cathedral Valley

Fruita

Cassidy Arch

Temple of the Sun/Moon

FISHLAKE NATIONAL FOREST

BOULDER MOUNTAIN

FISHLAKE NATIONAL FOREST

FISHLAKE NATIONAL FOREST

11129ft 3392m

Donkey Reservoir

Blind Lake

Oak Creek

Larb Hollow Overlook

37mi 60km

9600ft

Singletree

Pleasant Creek

Lower Browns Reservoir

Oak Creek

Extremely rough unmaintained 4WD road

Pleasant Creek

Miners Mountain

Grover

Teasdale

Torrey
6843ft 2085m

Panorama Point
Goosenecks Overlook

Orientation Pullout

Twin Rocks

Sunset Point

Chimney Rock

SEE DETAIL MAP

Fruita
5500ft 1676m
Gifford House

Visitor Center

Cassidy Arch
Scenic Drive

8mi 13km

Ferns Nipple

Golden Throne

Grand Wash

Capitol Gorge

9mi 14km

Behunin Cabin

Orientation Pullout

South Draw

Sheets Gulch

Cottonwood Wash

Sandy Creek

Notom

Notom-Bullfrog

14mi 23km

Burro Wash

10mi 16km

To Bicknell and

To Fremont and

Thousand Lake Mtn 11306ft 3446m

Neff Reservoir

Big Lake

Polk Creek Road

Road closed during winter

Elkhorn Road

Elkhorn Road

Elkhorn

9256ft 2821m

Cathedral Junction

Cathedral Valley

MONOLITHS

Gypsum Sinkhole

Upper Cathedral Valley Overlook

Upper South Desert Overlook

Hartnet Junction

Hartnet Road

5mi 8km

14mi 23km

Baker Ranch Rd

Oil Well Bench Road

Little Black Mountains

9mi 14km

THE SOUTH

WATERPOCKET

FOLD

Spring Canyon

Deep Creek

DESERT

Temple of the Sun

Temple of the Moon

Lower South Desert Overlook

Hartnet Road

15mi 24km

14mi 23km

Polk Creek

Black Mountain 6308ft 1923m

CATHEDRAL VALLEY

MIDDLE DESERT

Morrell Slopes

North Blue Flats

Deep Creek

Red Desert

River ford

3mi 5km

7mi 11km

Caineville

Caineville Wash

N Caineville Mesa

NORTH CAINEVILLE REEF

Salt Wash

Caineville 4600ft 1402m

S Caineville Mesa

Thompson Mesa

Upper Blue Hills

Fremont River

Chimney Rock Canyon

To Henry Mountains
Extremely rough 4WD roads

19mi 31km

Muddy Creek

FISHLAKE NATIONAL FOREST

Temple of the Sun and Moon

Capitol Reef Basics

(435) 425-3791 | nps.gov/care
Entrance Fee: $20/car
Lodging: None
Camping: Fruita*, Cathedral Valley, Cedar Mesa

*reserve at recreation.gov

Capitol Reef Driving Distances

The park is a mix of paved, unpaved, and high-clearance 4x4 roads. Most people stick to Scenic Drive but there are many wonders beyond the comfort of smooth pavement.

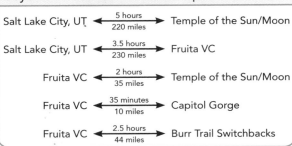

From	Time/Distance	To
Salt Lake City, UT	5 hours / 220 miles	Temple of the Sun/Moon
Salt Lake City, UT	3.5 hours / 230 miles	Fruita VC
Fruita VC	2 hours / 35 miles	Temple of the Sun/Moon
Fruita VC	35 minutes / 10 miles	Capitol Gorge
Fruita VC	2.5 hours / 44 miles	Burr Trail Switchbacks

Why Visit Capitol Reef?

- It's a little bit of Zion, Bryce Canyon, Arches, and Canyonlands wrapped in one less-visited park!
- Great off-road (and off-trail) adventures!

Capitol Reef Favorites

Easy Hikes: Grand Wash (4.4 miles), Capitol Gorge (2), Goosenecks (0.2)
Moderate Hikes: Lower Cathedral Valley (2.5), Spring Canyon/Chimney Rock (varies), Cohab Canyon (3.4), Headquarters Canyon (2), Hickman Bridge (1.8)
Strenuous Hikes: Cassidy Arch (3.4), Sulphur Creek (5.8), Golden Throne (4), Rim Overlook (4.6)
Activities: It's a great place for horseback riding but no outfitters offer rides
Views: UT-24, Scenic Drive, Sunset Point, Burr Trail Switchbacks, Goosenecks Overlook, Hall Creek Overlook

What You Need to Know

- Spring and fall tend to be the best seasons to visit. Summer is busiest. Fruit can be picked in Fruita between June and October. Flash floods are most common from July through September. Stay out of slot canyons when rain is predicted.
- Look over the park map carefully. Pavement crosses the Waterpocket Fold at Fruita via UT-24. Scenic Drive heads up to Capitol Gorge and down to Notom. Burr Trail and Notom Bullfrog are well-maintained and accessible to most vehicles. Things are a little dicier around Cathedral Valley. Take your time. Come prepared. And enjoy your time in this wonderland.
- Before driving some of the park's unpaved roads, it's a good idea to check road conditions by calling (435) 425-3791 (press 1 then 4).
- Cathedral Valley Road to Temple of the Moon/Sun is pretty nice from UT-24. It becomes increasingly more rugged the closer you get to Cathedral Valley Camp, then Hartnet Road is pretty nice all the way to the River Ford (where there's an abundance of sand, but again, not anything that's too overwhelming). To reach Hartnet Road (and the river ford) from UT-24, I like to take the unmarked road to the east. It's a direct shot down a rocky road, but you won't have to deal with a mix of public and private sandy roads to reach the ford. The sandy area is a pretty bad place to meet oncoming traffic. Be mindful of what's ahead. It's also a good idea to download the river ford map from the nps.gov/care. Under normal conditions the river crossing is nothing to be afraid of, but you should arrive with an idea of what you're going to encounter while out there. There's a steady flow of off-roaders in this area, but you should still be prepared for self rescue.
- Accommodations are limited in the area. If you aren't a camper, there are a few nice options in (and around) Torrey. And, as is the case in most of this region of Utah, there are people free camping all over the place.

How Much Time Do You Have?

1 Day: If you're willing to take on some of the unpaved/4x4 roads, you're going to want more than a day. If you stick to pavement, one or two days should suffice. Hike Chimney Rocks/Canyon (you can actually do a less-than-10-miles one-way hike to UT-24 via Chimney and Spring Canyon if you arrange a ride). Spend some time in Fruita. Pick fruit if in season. Hike to Cassidy Arch (or Cohab Canyon or Grand Wash, whatever suits you). Drive out through Hanksville. UT-24 is awesome.

2 Days: Drive to Temple of the Moon/Sun. This is a full day and it's better if you spend the night at the primitive campground (although the road is pretty rugged climbing up to it). Lower Cathedral Valley Trail (on Hartnet Road) leads to two saddles with views of Temple of the Moon and Sun from above.

3 Days: Drive Notom-Bullfrog and Burr Trail roads. Again, this is a full day, especially if you plan to do some hiking (which you should). Fortunately, there's another primitive campground at Cedar Mesa. Muley Twist or Headquarters Canyon are fun.

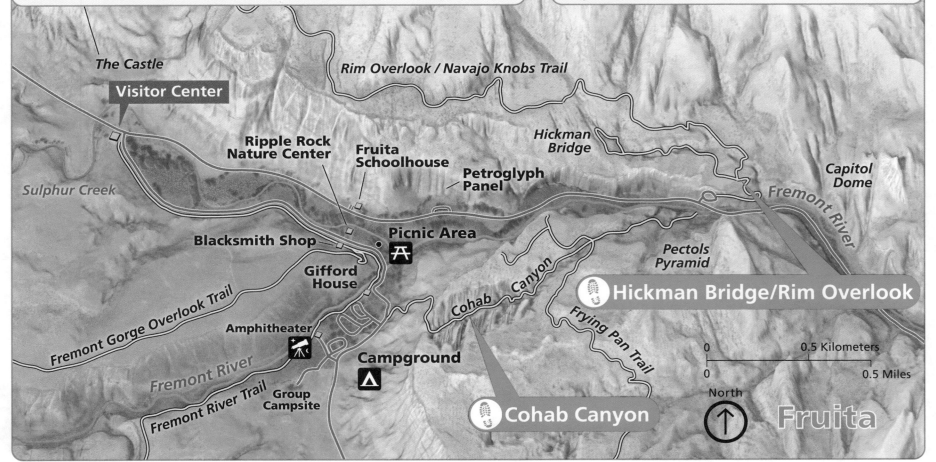

The Castle
Rim Overlook / Navajo Knobs Trail
Visitor Center
Ripple Rock Nature Center
Fruita Schoolhouse
Petroglyph Panel
Hickman Bridge
Capitol Dome
Fremont River
Sulphur Creek
Blacksmith Shop
Picnic Area
Pectols Pyramid
Gifford House
Cohab Canyon
Hickman Bridge/Rim Overlook
Fremont Gorge Overlook Trail
Amphitheater
Frying Pan Trail
Fremont River Trail
Campground
Group Campsite
Cohab Canyon
North
Fruita

0   0.5 Kilometers
0   0.5 Miles

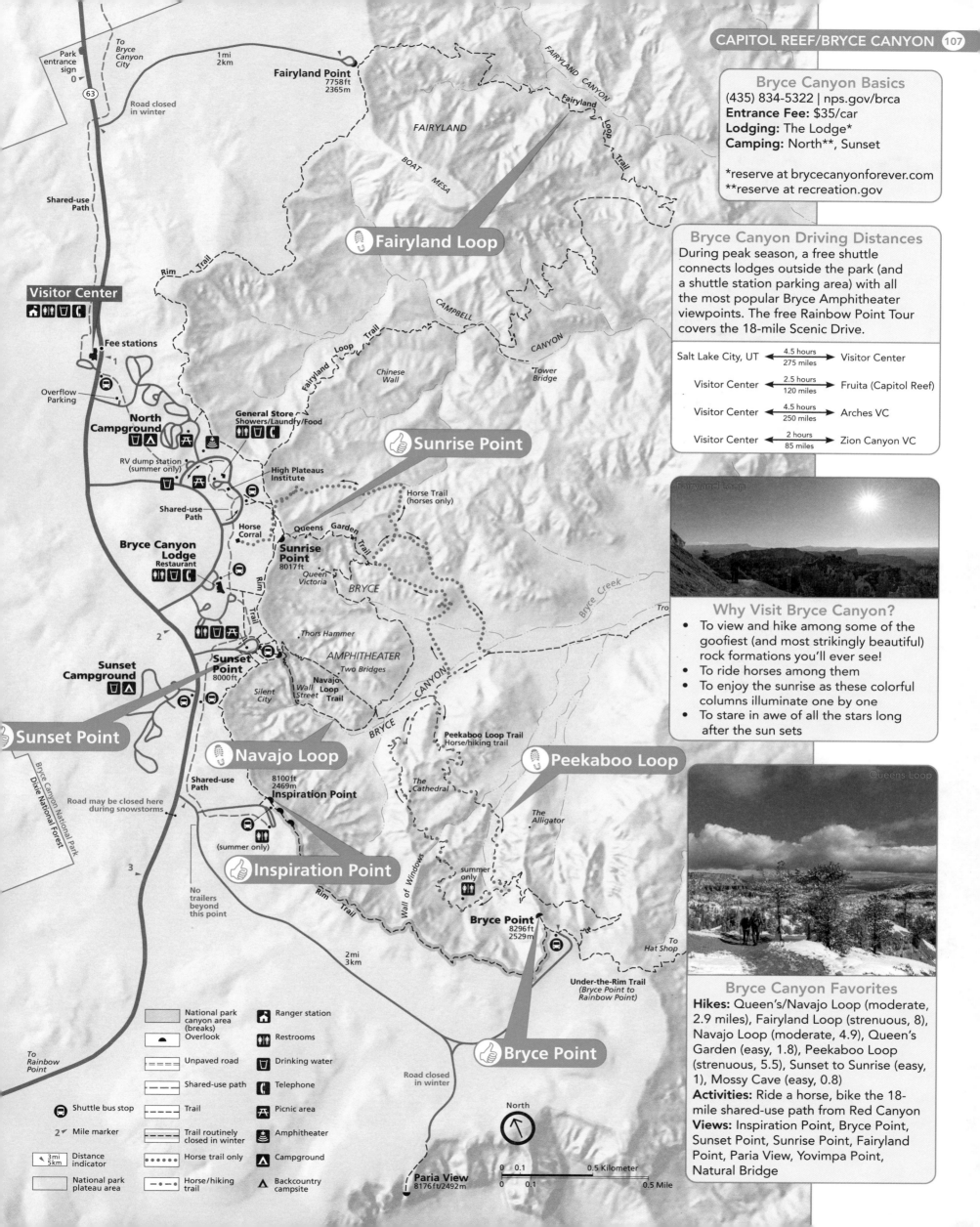

To Bryce Canyon City

Park entrance sign

63

Road closed in winter

0
1mi
2km

Shared-use Path

Fairyland Point
7758ft
2365m

FAIRYLAND

FAIRYLAND CANYON

BOAT MESA

Fairyland Loop Trail

Fairyland Loop

Visitor Center

Fee stations

1

Overflow Parking

CAMPBELL CANYON

Chinese Wall

Tower Bridge

Sunrise Point

RV dump station (summer only)

North Campground

General Store
Showers/Laundry/Food

High Plateaus Institute

Horse Trail (horses only)

Shared-use Path

Horse Corral

Queens Garden Trail

Bryce Canyon Lodge
Restaurant

Sunrise Point
8017ft

Queen Victoria

Queen's Garden Trail

BRYCE

Bryce Creek

2

Thors Hammer

AMPHITHEATER
Two Bridges

Sunset Point

Sunset Point
8000ft

Sunset Campground

Navajo Loop Trail

Silent City

Wall Street

BRYCE CANYON

Navajo Loop

Shared-use Path

8100ft
2469m
Inspiration Point

The Cathedral

Peekaboo Loop Trail
Horse/hiking trail

Peekaboo Loop

Road may be closed here during snowstorms

(summer only)

The Alligator

Inspiration Point

No trailers beyond this point

3

summer only

Wall of Windows

Rim Trail

Bryce Point
8296ft
2529m

To Hat Shop

Bryce Point

Under-the-Rim Trail
(Bryce Point to Rainbow Point)

Bryce Canyon National Park

Dixie National Forest

To Rainbow Point

2mi
3km

Legend

National park canyon area (breaks)

Overlook

Unpaved road

Shared-use path

Trail

Trail routinely closed in winter

Horse trail only

Horse/hiking trail

Shuttle bus stop

2 Mile marker

3mi
5km Distance indicator

National park plateau area

Ranger station

Restrooms

Drinking water

Telephone

Picnic area

Amphitheater

Campground

Backcountry campsite

Road closed in winter

North

Paria View
8176ft/2492m

0 0.1   0.5 Kilometer
0 0.1   0.5 Mile

Bryce Canyon Basics

(435) 834-5322 | nps.gov/brca
Entrance Fee: $35/car
Lodging: The Lodge*
Camping: North**, Sunset

*reserve at brycecanyonforever.com
**reserve at recreation.gov

Bryce Canyon Driving Distances

During peak season, a free shuttle connects lodges outside the park (and a shuttle station parking area) with all the most popular Bryce Amphitheater viewpoints. The free Rainbow Point Tour covers the 18-mile Scenic Drive.

Salt Lake City, UT	←4.5 hours / 275 miles→	Visitor Center
Visitor Center	←2.5 hours / 120 miles→	Fruita (Capitol Reef)
Visitor Center	←4.5 hours / 250 miles→	Arches VC
Visitor Center	←2 hours / 85 miles→	Zion Canyon VC

Why Visit Bryce Canyon?

- To view and hike among some of the goofiest (and most strikingly beautiful) rock formations you'll ever see!
- To ride horses among them
- To enjoy the sunrise as these colorful columns illuminate one by one
- To stare in awe of all the stars long after the sun sets

Bryce Canyon Favorites

Hikes: Queen's/Navajo Loop (moderate, 2.9 miles), Fairyland Loop (strenuous, 8), Navajo Loop (moderate, 4.9), Queen's Garden (easy, 1.8), Peekaboo Loop (strenuous, 5.5), Sunset to Sunrise (easy, 1), Mossy Cave (easy, 0.8)
Activities: Ride a horse, bike the 18-mile shared-use path from Red Canyon
Views: Inspiration Point, Bryce Point, Sunset Point, Sunrise Point, Fairyland Point, Paria View, Yovimpa Point, Natural Bridge

How Much Time Do You Have?

1 Day: If you only have a day, start early (dressed in layers) and head into the Amphitheater. Queen's/Navajo Loop is a good choice. You could probably knock out Fairyland Loop in the same day. If you're into photography, plan on spending a lot of time snapping photos.

2 Days: Unless you're backpacking or want a very leisurely trip, you don't need a bunch of time here. One night is great. It gives you a day to explore the Amphitheater (I wouldn't blame you if you go back in—maybe hike Peekaboo Loop!) and a day to explore Scenic Drive and hike Mossy Cave or Fairyland Loop.

3 Days: With another day, take a long trail ride (if you're comfortable on a horse). Or in three days you could backpack Under-the-Rim trail (and thanks to the Rainbow Point Tour you won't need to cache a car for a one-way hike).

Navajo Loop

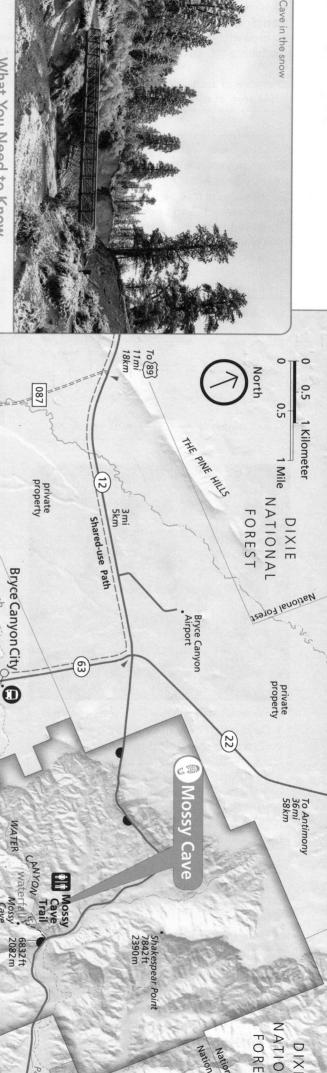

Mossy Cave in the snow

What You Need to Know

- The park is open year-round. It's at higher elevation than the other Utah national parks, so it will be cooler. But it's also pretty darn cool covered in snow. Still, the elevation shortens its primary tourism season to May through September.

- The Lodge and its restaurant are typically open from March through October. A few rooms stay open for November and December. North Campground is open year-round. Sunset closes for winter.

- The free shuttle is a blessing. It runs from April through October, connecting various points outside the park with all the popular Bryce Amphitheater viewpoints.

- There's also a free shuttle from Ruby's Inn to Rainbow Point (all 18 miles of Scenic Drive), called the Rainbow Point Tour. It operates from mid-April to mid-September.

- Do not miss Bryce Amphitheater. People have visited only to motor down Scenic Drive and exit wondering what all the fuss was about. The fuss is primarily about Bryce Amphitheater.

- Visitation is fairly intense from May through September, but most stays are short, so the turnover is quick.

- Wall Street closes for winter but most other trails remain open. Come with traction devices for your boots and enjoy a peaceful winter trip in a rocky paradise. Cross-country skiing and snowshoeing are also options in winter as snow is fairly common from November through March (even with day-time highs in the 40s°F).

- With limited time for a visit, spend all of it at Bryce Amphitheater.

- Hiking among the hoodoos is best in the morning light (the amphitheater opens up to the east. The amphitheater's rim blocks late evening light. Remember, mornings will be chilly.

- For Scenic Drive, all the viewpoints are on the east side of the road. Drive to Rainbow Point, noting interesting viewpoints along the way, and then stop at them on your way back to the park entrance. Those right turns are much easier for everyone.

Zion Basics

(435) 772-3256 | nps.gov/zion
Entrance Fee: $35/car
Lodging: Zion Lodge*
Camping: South**,
Watchman**, Lava Point

*reserve at zionlodge.com
**reserve at recreation.gov

Zion Favorites

Easy Hikes: Pa'rus (3.5 miles)
Moderate: Watchman (3.3), Canyon Overlook (1), Taylor Creek (5)
Strenuous: Observation Point (8), Mouth of the Narrows (9.4), Left Fork/Subway (9), East Rim (10.8), West Rim (14.2), Kolob Arch (14)
Extreme: Narrows (16), Angel's Landing (5.4), Hidden Canyon (2.5)
Activities: Ride a horse beneath the towering red rocks, play in the slots if you have the knowledge and skills to do it
Views: Court of the Patriarchs, Lava Point, Kolob Canyons Overlook

Zion Driving Distances

Zion Canyon is where most recreating takes place. Most of the year, it's only accessible by free shuttle, bike, foot, and guests of Zion Lodge. Zion's Upper Trailhead is where hikers begin to thru-hike the Narrows. Kolob Terrace Road leads to Lava Point Campground and a few good trailheads. Kolob Canyons is the quiet corner of the park.

From	Time / Distance	To
Salt Lake City, UT	7 hours / 315 miles	Zion Canyon VC
Zion Canyon VC	60 minutes / 35 miles	Zion Narrows Upper Trailhead
Zion Canyon VC	60 minutes / 35 miles	Lava Point
Zion Canyon VC	50 minutes / 40 miles	Kolob Canyons VC
Zion Canyon VC	3 hours / 170 miles	Las Vegas, NV

Why Visit Zion?

- To see if it lives up to its billing, Yosemite in color!
- To hike the famous Angel's Landing and Zion Narrows
- To witness ephemeral waterfalls

Watchman Trail

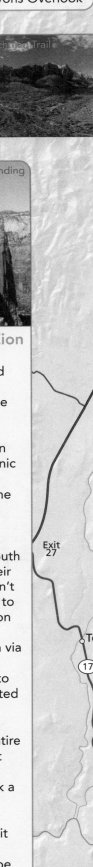
Angel's Landing

What You Need to Know About Zion

- Zion is quite busy almost year-round, only slowing down a bit in January and February.
- Winter/early spring can be a great time to visit, when snowmelt powers a few stunning ephemeral waterfalls.
- Motorists (unless you're staying at Zion Lodge) cannot enter Zion Canyon Scenic Drive when free shuttles are running (mid-March through October, and some weekends in February, March, and November).
- There's an additional shuttle loop between Springdale and the park's South Entrance, allowing visitors to leave their vehicles in Springdale. Even if you aren't staying in Springdale, it's a good idea to catch a shuttle here. Parking fills at Zion Canyon Visitor Center too.
- You can walk or bike into Zion Canyon via Pa'rus Trail.
- Starting in 2022, a permit is required to hike Angel's Landing. They're distributed via lottery at recreation.gov.
- Due to Zion Canyon's popularity, it's a good idea to plan on spending the entire day in the canyon. Food is available at Zion Lodge (where you might want to avoid normal meal-time hours) or pack a lunch.
- Zion Narrows (beyond Big Springs) and Subway hikes also require a permit (available through the park website). They're difficult trails and should not be taken lightly. You spend a fair amount of time in water hiking the Narrows.
- Observation Point is a great spot. There's been a period of time where access from Zion Canyon has been limited due to a rockfall years ago, but there are other ways to reach it (i.e. East Mesa and East Rim trails).

Narrows in October

How Much Time Do You Have?

1 Day: If you only have a day here, you're probably going to spend it in Zion Canyon. You don't need to hike to have a good time. Simply watching the play of light and shadow as the sun translates across the sky is a joy. Still, you should hike. Angel's Landing, Zion Narrows, Observation Point are all great choices.

2 Days: If you want to hike the full Narrows that's an overnight trip or a long day. Angel's Landing (permit required) is a relatively short hike, but it's strenuous and you'll want to spend some time enjoying the view. Observation Point, depending on how you get there, is close to a full day too. The Subway. Yeah, that's a full day. Days fill up fast here.

3 Days: With three days or more, think about hopping on a horse, driving to Kolob Canyons or maybe even looking into hikes outside the park like Spooky Gulch, The Wave, or Kanarra Falls.

To Cedar City, Cedar Breaks National Monument, and Salt Lake City

Gas station — Exit 42

15

Exit 40

Kolob Canyons Visitor Center
5074ft

Taylor Creek — Taylor Creek
Kolob Canyons Rd
Middle Fork — PARIA POINT
Lee Pass Trailhead
Nagunt Mesa

Kolob Canyons Viewpoint

Timber Creek Overlook Trail
La Verkin Creek Trail

8055ft
TIMBER TOP

To St George and Las Vegas, Nevada

HURRICANE CLIFFS

La Verkin Creek

Exit 27

Toquerville

17

HURRICANE MESA

La Verkin Creek

9

La Verkin

Virgin
3550ft

9 — 15
To 15 exit 16, St George, and Las Vegas, Nevada

Springdale/Zion Canyon Shuttle and Zion-Mount Carmel Highway tunnel information

Hurricane 59
To Pipe Spring National Monument and Grand Canyon National Park

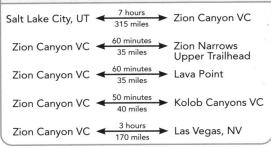

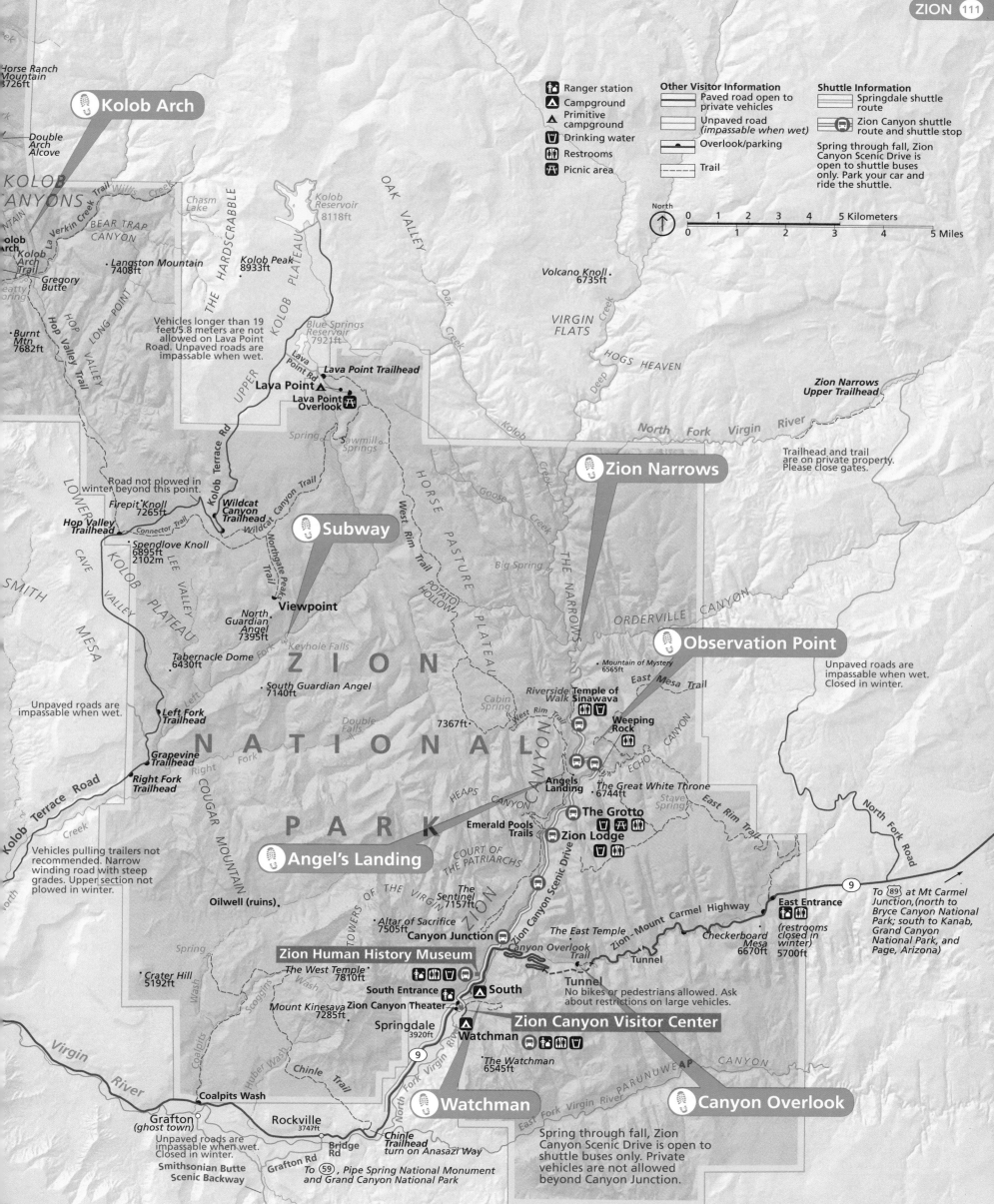

VIRGIN

Grand Canyon Basics

(928) 638-7888 | nps.gov/grca

Entrance Fee: $35/car

South Rim Lodging: Bright Angel Lodge*, El Tovar*, Kachina Lodge*, Thunderbird Lodge*, Maswik Lodge*, Yavapai Lodge*

South Rim Camping: Mather**, Trailer Village**, Desert View

North Rim Lodging: Grand Canyon Lodge#

North Rim Camping: North Rim**

*reserve at visitgrandcanyon.com
**reserve at recreation.gov
#reserve at grandcanyonforever.com

Grand Canyon Driving Distances

Driving from the South Rim to North Rim is 3.5 hours. Along the way, you'll pass nearby Page, AZ (Horseshoe Bend, Glen Canyon National Recreation Area, Antelope Canyon, etc.). And then there's paradise on earth, Havasu Falls, which is a solid 3.5-hour drive from the South Rim (plus a difficult overnight hike to the waterfalls).

Las Vegas, NV	← 4.5 hours / 280 miles →	Grand Canyon VC (South Rim)
Grand Canyon VC	← 40 minutes / 22 miles →	Desert View VC (South Rim)
Desert View VC	← 3.5 hours / 188 miles →	North Rim VC

UINKARET PLATEAU

Pima Point

Why Visit Grand Canyon?

- To raft the Colorado River
- To spend a night at the canyon's floor at Phantom Ranch
- To be awed by its massive size (277 miles long, up to 18 miles wide, and 1+ mile deep) from the rim, from the air, or from the back of a mule

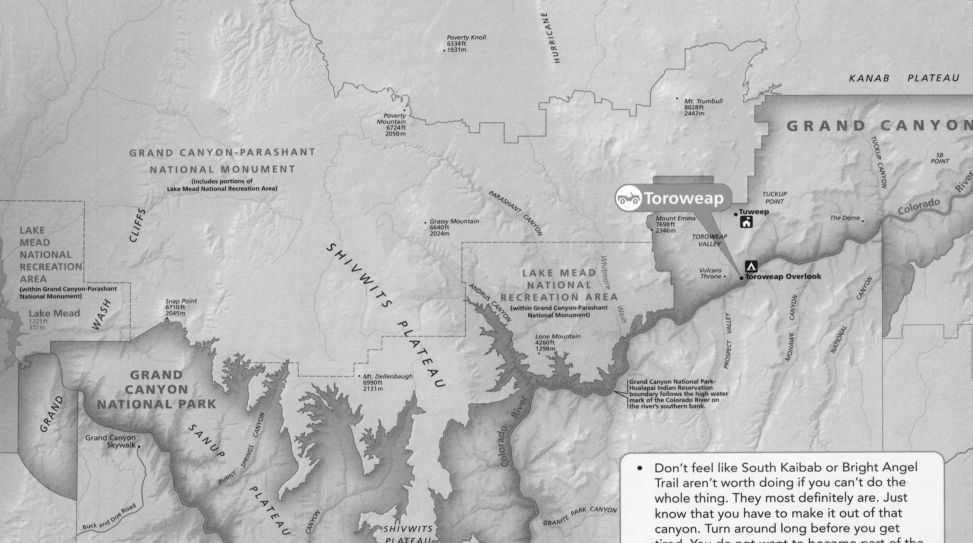

Poverty Knoll
6334ft
1931m

HURRICANE CLIFFS

KANAB PLATEAU

Mt. Trumbull
8028ft
2447m

GRAND CANYON

TUCKUP CANYON

SB POINT

Poverty Mountain
6724ft
2050m

GRAND CANYON-PARASHANT NATIONAL MONUMENT
(includes portions of Lake Mead National Recreation Area)

PARASHANT CANYON

Toroweap

TUCKUP POINT

Tuweep

Mount Emma
7698ft
2346m

TOROWEAP VALLEY

The Dome

Colorado River

LAKE MEAD NATIONAL RECREATION AREA
(within Grand Canyon-Parashant National Monument)

CLIFFS

Grassy Mountain
6640ft
2024m

S H I V W I T S   P L A T E A U

Whitmore Wash

LAKE MEAD NATIONAL RECREATION AREA
(within Grand Canyon-Parashant National Monument)

Vulcans Throne

Toroweap Overlook

NATIONAL CANYON

MOHAWK CANYON

PROSPECT VALLEY

WASH

Snap Point
6710ft
2045m

ANDRUS CANYON

Lone Mountain
4260ft
1298m

Grand Canyon National Park-Hualapai Indian Reservation boundary follows the high water mark of the Colorado River on the river's southern bank.

LAKE MEAD NATIONAL RECREATION AREA
(within Grand Canyon-Parashant National Monument)

Lake Mead
1221ft
372m

GRAND CANYON NATIONAL PARK

Mt. Dellenbaugh
6990ft
2131m

Colorado River

GRAND

SANUP

Grand Canyon Skywalk

BURNT SPRINGS CANYON

PLATEAU

GRANITE PARK CANYON

SHIVWITS PLATEAU

Grand Canyon National Park-Hualapai Indian Reservation boundary follows the high water mark of the Colorado River on the river's southern bank.

Buck and Doe Road

LOWER GRANITE GORGE

SURPRISE CANYON

To Meadview

HORSE FLAT CANYON

LOWER GRANITE GORGE

1500 ft
457m

- Don't feel like South Kaibab or Bright Angel Trail aren't worth doing if you can't do the whole thing. They most definitely are. Just know that you have to make it out of that canyon. Turn around long before you get tired. You do not want to become part of the park's rescue statistics.
- The North Rim receives about 10% the visitation of the South Rim but there are also fewer visitor accommodations. So, it's a good idea to make reservations well in advance. You won't regret it. There's great hiking on the North Rim as well as some striking viewpoints with features you can't spot from the South.
- A high-clearance 4x4 unlocks Toroweap, a memorable North Rim viewpoint, well-worth the long journey. There are campsites there too (permit required). Call about road conditions before heading out.

What You Need to Know

- The South Rim is open all year, the North Rim typically closes from late October/early November until mid-May. Rafting trips are offered from April through October.
- Temperature on the South Rim is typically 7°F warmer than the North Rim. The canyon floor is about 20°F warmer than the South Rim. So, dress in layers, especially if you plan on going Rim-to-Rim.
- Grand Canyon is busy most of the year. Escaping the crowds is best done by hiking away from popular viewpoints, but you could also visit the North Rim (closed winter) or stop at the South Rim in winter.
- Four free shuttle loops help ease congestion at the South Rim. Use them (you have to at Hermit Road).

Yavapai Point Sunset

H U A L A P A I   I N D I A N   R E S E R V A T I O N

(Permit required for off-highway travel)

66

To Seligman and 40

To Kingman and 40   PEACH SPRINGS

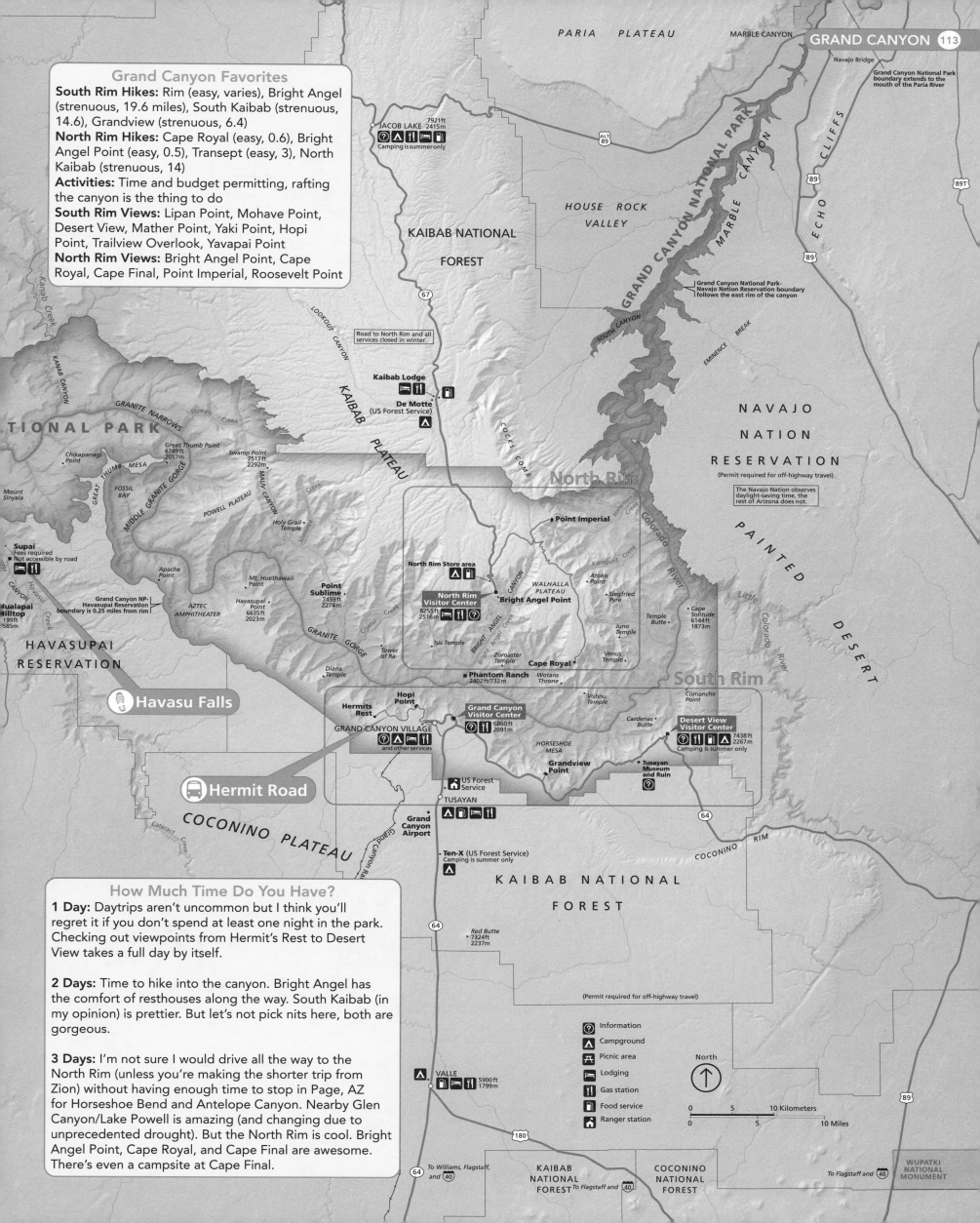

Grand Canyon Favorites

South Rim Hikes: Rim (easy, varies), Bright Angel (strenuous, 19.6 miles), South Kaibab (strenuous, 14.6), Grandview (strenuous, 6.4)

North Rim Hikes: Cape Royal (easy, 0.6), Bright Angel Point (easy, 0.5), Transept (easy, 3), North Kaibab (strenuous, 14)

Activities: Time and budget permitting, rafting the canyon is the thing to do

South Rim Views: Lipan Point, Mohave Point, Desert View, Mather Point, Yaki Point, Hopi Point, Trailview Overlook, Yavapai Point

North Rim Views: Bright Angel Point, Cape Royal, Cape Final, Point Imperial, Roosevelt Point

How Much Time Do You Have?

1 Day: Daytrips aren't uncommon but I think you'll regret it if you don't spend at least one night in the park. Checking out viewpoints from Hermit's Rest to Desert View takes a full day by itself.

2 Days: Time to hike into the canyon. Bright Angel has the comfort of resthouses along the way. South Kaibab (in my opinion) is prettier. But let's not pick nits here, both are gorgeous.

3 Days: I'm not sure I would drive all the way to the North Rim (unless you're making the shorter trip from Zion) without having enough time to stop in Page, AZ for Horseshoe Bend and Antelope Canyon. Nearby Glen Canyon/Lake Powell is amazing (and changing due to unprecedented drought). But the North Rim is cool. Bright Angel Point, Cape Royal, and Cape Final are awesome. There's even a campsite at Cape Final.

Legend

- Information
- Campground
- Picnic area
- Lodging
- Gas station
- Food service
- Ranger station

North

0   5   10 Kilometers
0   5   10 Miles

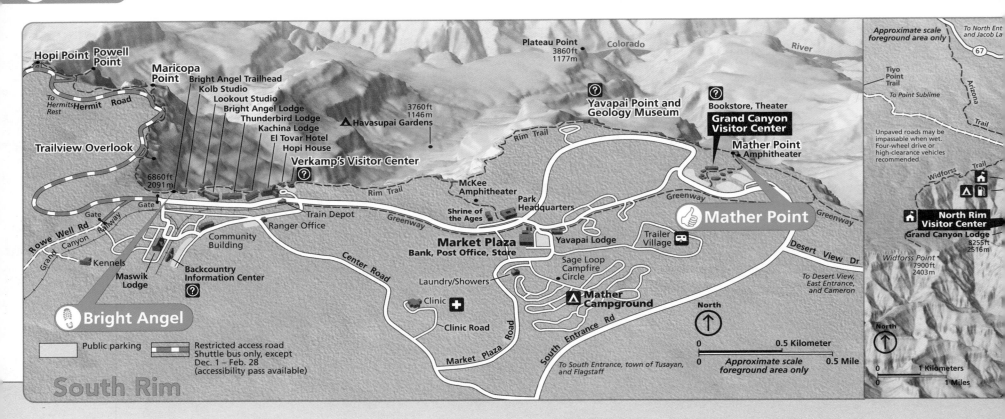

Hopi Point
Powell Point
Maricopa Point
Bright Angel Trailhead
Kolb Studio
Lookout Studio
Bright Angel Lodge
Thunderbird Lodge
Kachina Lodge
El Tovar Hotel
Hopi House
Verkamp's Visitor Center

Trailview Overlook

To Hermits Rest / Hermit Road

Rowe Well Rd

Gate
Gate
Railway
Grand Canyon

6860ft
2091m

Rim Trail

Kennels

Maswik Lodge

Community Building

Backcountry Information Center

Train Depot
Ranger Office

Center Road

Greenway

Market Plaza
Road

Market Plaza

3760ft
1146m
△ Havasupai Gardens

McKee Amphitheater

Shrine of the Ages

Rim Trail

Park Headquarters

Market Plaza
Bank, Post Office, Store

Laundry/Showers

Clinic +

Clinic Road

Yavapai Lodge

Sage Loop Campfire Circle

△ Mather Campground

South Entrance Rd

Yavapai Point and Geology Museum

Bookstore, Theater

Grand Canyon Visitor Center

Mather Point
Amphitheater

Greenway

👍 **Mather Point**

Trailer Village

Greenway

Desert View Dr

To Desert View, East Entrance, and Cameron

👟 **Bright Angel**

To South Entrance, town of Tusayan, and Flagstaff

Plateau Point
3860ft
1177m
Colorado River

Approximate scale foreground area only

Tiyo Point Trail

To North Ent and Jacob La
67

Arizona Trail

Unpaved roads may be impassable when wet. Four-wheel drive or high-clearance vehicles recommended.

Widforss Trail

🏠 🧍 **North Rim Visitor Center**
Grand Canyon Lodge
8255ft
2516m

Widforss Point
7900ft
2403m

Public parking
Restricted access road
Shuttle bus only, except Dec. 1 – Feb. 28 (accessibility pass available)

North ↑

0   0.5 Kilometer
Approximate scale foreground area only
0   0.5 Mile

North ↑

0   1 Kilometers
0   1 Miles

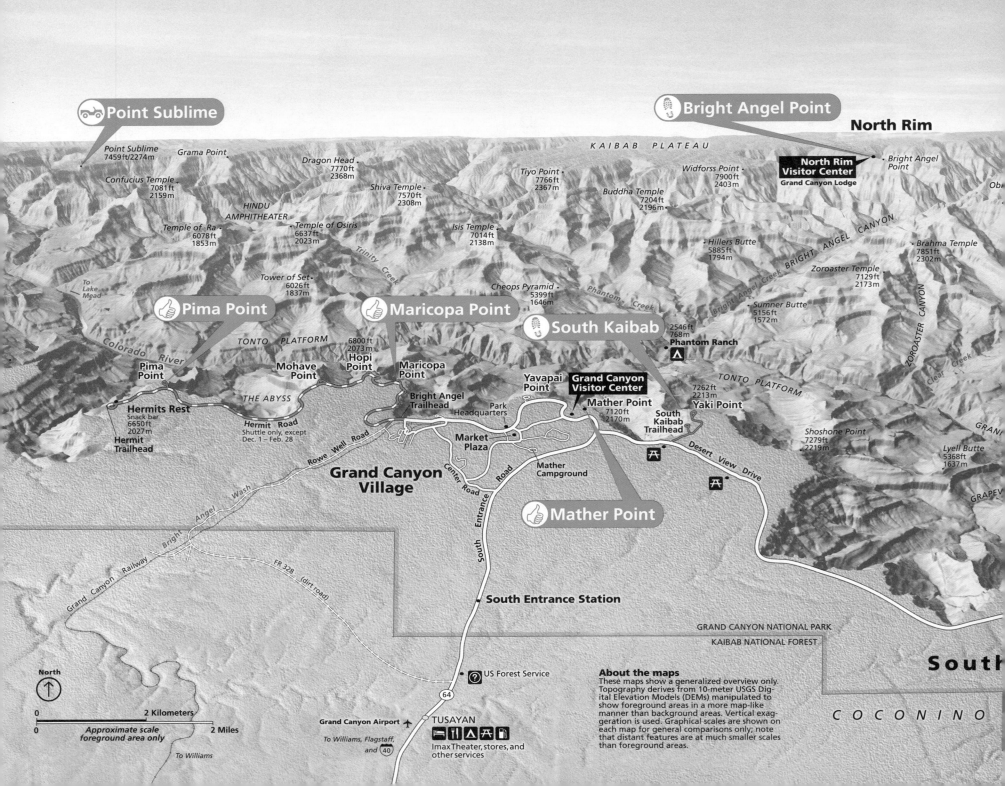

🚙 **Point Sublime**

👟 **Bright Angel Point**

North Rim

KAIBAB PLATEAU

Point Sublime
7459ft/2274m
Grama Point

Confucius Temple
7081ft
2159m

Dragon Head
7770ft
2368m

Shiva Temple
7570ft
2308m

HINDU AMPHITHEATER

Temple of Ra
6078ft
1853m

Temple of Osiris
6637ft
2023m

Isis Temple
7014ft
2138m

Tiyo Point
7766ft
2367m

Widforss Point
7900ft
2403m

Buddha Temple
7204ft
2196m

Bright Angel Point

North Rim Visitor Center
Grand Canyon Lodge

Hillers Butte
5885ft
1794m

BRIGHT ANGEL CANYON

Brahma Temple
7851ft
2302m

👍 **Pima Point**

👍 **Maricopa Point**

Trinity Creek

Tower of Set
6026ft
1837m

Cheops Pyramid
5399ft
1646m

Phantom Creek

Zoroaster Temple
7129ft
2173m

ZOROASTER CANYON

Colorado River

TONTO PLATFORM

Pima Point

Mohave Point

6800ft
2073m
Hopi Point

Maricopa Point

Sumner Butte
5156ft
1572m

👟 **South Kaibab**

2546ft
768m
Phantom Ranch
△

Clear Creek

THE ABYSS

Bright Angel Trailhead

Yavapai Point

Grand Canyon Visitor Center

TONTO PLATFORM

7262ft
2213m
Yaki Point

Hermits Rest
Snack bar
6650ft
2027m

Hermit Trailhead

Hermit Road
Shuttle only, except Dec. 1 – Feb. 28

Rowe Well Road

Center Road

Park Headquarters

Mather Point
7120ft
2170m

South Kaibab Trailhead

Shoshone Point
7279ft
2219m

GRAN

Lyell Butte
5368ft
1637m

GRAPEV

Bright Angel Wash

Grand Canyon Village

Market Plaza

South Entrance Road

Mather Campground

👍 **Mather Point**

Desert View Drive

Grand Canyon Railway

FR 328 (dirt road)

South Entrance Station

GRAND CANYON NATIONAL PARK
KAIBAB NATIONAL FOREST

South

North ↑

0   2 Kilometers
0   2 Miles
Approximate scale foreground area only

To Williams

🔵 US Forest Service

64

Grand Canyon Airport ✈

TUSAYAN
🏨🍴△🏕🅿

To Williams, Flagstaff, and 40

Imax Theater, stores, and other services

About the maps
These maps show a generalized overview only. Topography derives from 10-meter USGS Digital Elevation Models (DEMs) manipulated to show foreground areas in a more map-like manner than background areas. Vertical exaggeration is used. Graphical scales are shown on each map for general comparisons only; note that distant features are at much smaller scales than foreground areas.

C O C O N I N O

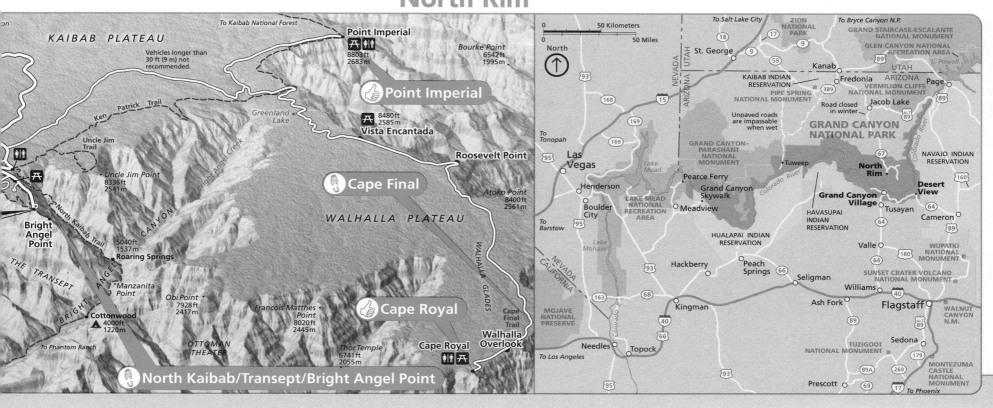

KAIBAB PLATEAU

To Kaibab National Forest

Vehicles longer than 30 ft (9 m) not recommended.

Point Imperial
8803ft
2683m

Bourke Point
6542ft
1995m

Ken Patrick Trail

Greenland Lake

👍 Point Imperial

Uncle Jim Trail

🅰 8480ft
2585m
Vista Encantada

Uncle Jim Point
8336ft
2541m

Roosevelt Point

🅰

Bright Angel Point

Roaring Springs

5040ft
1537m

👣 Cape Final

Atoko Point
8400ft
2561m

WALHALLA PLATEAU

"Manzanita" Point

THE TRANSEPT

Obi Point
7928ft
2417m

Francois Matthes Point
8020ft
2445m

👍 Cape Royal

WALHALLA GLADES

▲ Cottonwood
4000ft
1220m

OTTOMAN THEATER

Cape Final Trail

To Phantom Ranch

Thor Temple
6741ft
2055m

Cape Royal

Walhalla Overlook

👣 North Kaibab/Transept/Bright Angel Point

North
⬆

0   50 Kilometers
0   50 Miles

To Salt Lake City

ZION NATIONAL PARK

To Bryce Canyon N.P.

GRAND STAIRCASE-ESCALANTE NATIONAL MONUMENT

GLEN CANYON NATIONAL RECREATION AREA

St. George

NEVADA / UTAH

Kanab

UTAH
ARIZONA

Fredonia

VERMILION CLIFFS NATIONAL MONUMENT

Page

KAIBAB INDIAN RESERVATION

PIPE SPRING NATIONAL MONUMENT

Road closed in winter

Jacob Lake

L. Powell

Las Vegas

Henderson

GRAND CANYON-PARASHANT NATIONAL MONUMENT

Unpaved roads are impassable when wet

GRAND CANYON NATIONAL PARK

North Rim

NAVAJO INDIAN RESERVATION

Tuweep

Boulder City

Meadview

Pearce Ferry

Grand Canyon Skywalk

LAKE MEAD NATIONAL RECREATION AREA

Lake Mead

Colorado River

Grand Canyon Village

Desert View

To Tonopah

To Barstow

HAVASUPAI INDIAN RESERVATION

Tusayan

Grand View

Cameron

To Los Angeles

Lake Mohave

HUALAPAI INDIAN RESERVATION

Valle

WUPATKI NATIONAL MONUMENT

Hackberry

Peach Springs

Seligman

Williams

SUNSET CRATER VOLCANO NATIONAL MONUMENT

MOJAVE NATIONAL PRESERVE

Colorado

Kingman

Ash Fork

Flagstaff

WALNUT CANYON N.M.

Needles

Topock

TUZIGOOT NATIONAL MONUMENT

Sedona

Prescott

MONTEZUMA CASTLE NATIONAL MONUMENT

To Phoenix

KAIBAB PLATEAU

👣 Point Imperial

Point Imperial
8803ft
2683m

Vista Encantada
8480ft
2585m

Chuar Butte
6394ft
1949m

Cape Solitude
6144ft
1873m

Little Colorado River

Francois Matthes Point
8020ft
2445m

👣 Cape Royal

WALHALLA PLATEAU

Cape Final
7916ft
2413m

Jupiter Temple
7081ft
2158m

Temple Butte
5308ft
1618m

From Lake Powell

PALISADES OF THE DESERT

Thor Temple
6741ft
2055m

Walhalla Overlook
7998ft
2438m

Cape Royal
7865ft
2398m

Freya Castle
7299ft
2225m

Venus Temple
6257ft
1907m

Espejo Butte

OTTOMAN AMPHITHEATER

Wotans Throne
7633ft
2327m

Vishnu Temple
7829ft
2386m

Apollo Temple

Comanche Point
7073ft
2156m

Angels Gate

Krishna Shrine
6615ft
1864m

Rama Shrine
6411ft
1954m

TANNER CANYON

...kins Butte

Colorado River

Cardenas Butte
6269ft
1911m

Newberry Butte
5105ft
1556m

Sheba Temple

Solomon Temple
5670ft
1545m

👍 Lipan Point

Stores (campground and gas station closed in winter)

Navajo Point

Desert View
7438ft
2267m

👣 Grandview

HANCE CANYON

Lipan Point
7360ft
2243m

Papago Point

Pinal Point

East Entrance Station

To Cameron
64

Horseshoe Mesa
5238ft
1597m

RED CANYON

Zuni Point
7278ft
2219m

Desert View Drive

Tusayan Museum and Ruin

👍 Desert View

Grandview Trailhead
7399ft
2256m

👣 Grandview Point

Coronado Butte
7108ft
2167m

Moran Point
7160ft
2182m

GRAND CANYON NATIONAL PARK

KAIBAB NATIONAL FOREST

Sinking Ship
7344ft
2239m

🅰 Buggeln

im

PLATEAU

To Arizona Trail

Restricted access road
No private vehicles

Restricted access road
Shuttle bus only, except
Dec. 1 – Feb. 28
(accessibility pass available)

Trail

Paved road

Unpaved road
High-clearance
vehicles recommended

? Information

🅰 Picnic area

Trailer camping

Campground

Backcountry campsite

Lodging

Food service

Gas station

First aid

Restrooms

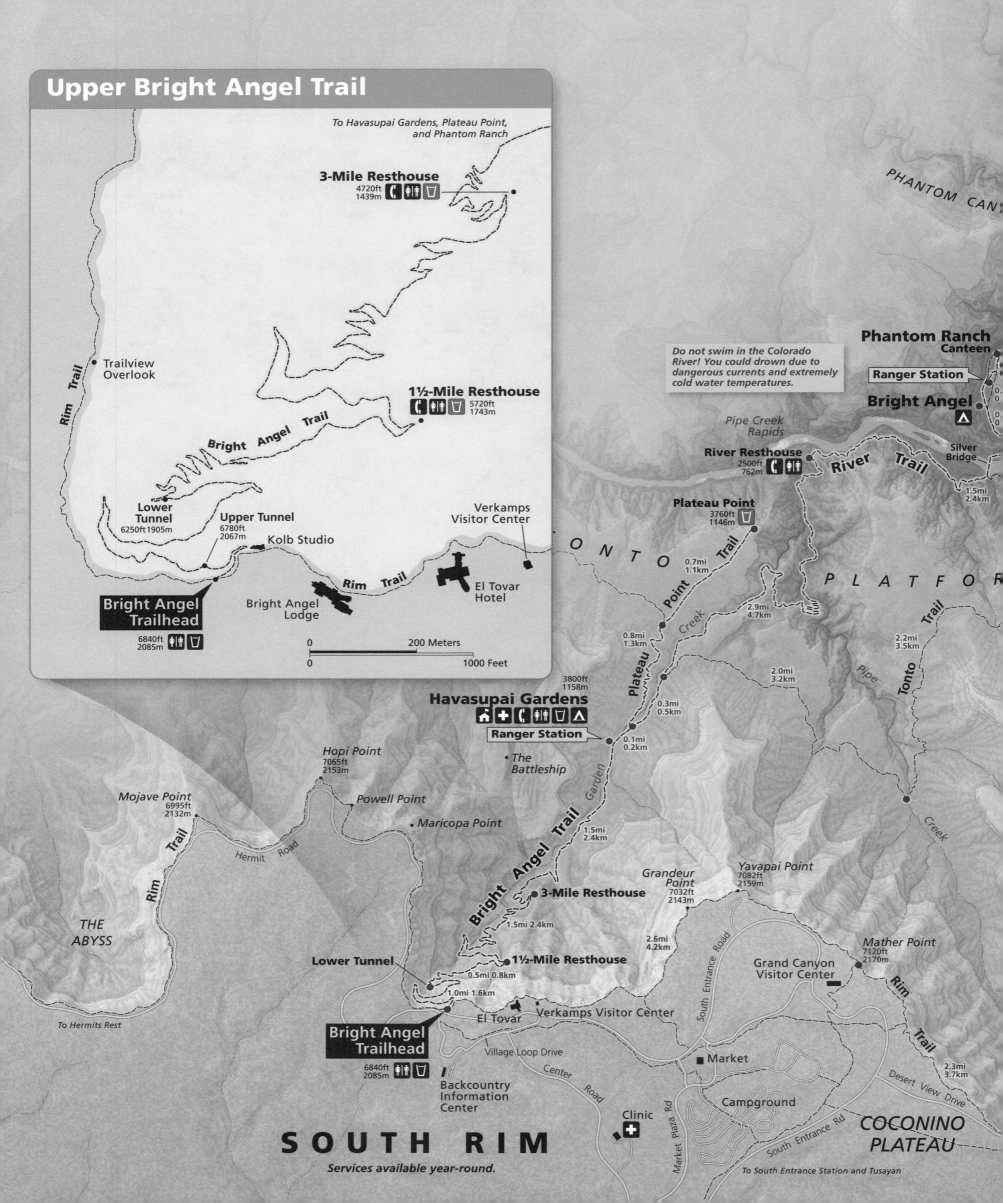

Upper Bright Angel Trail

To Havasupai Gardens, Plateau Point,
and Phantom Ranch

3-Mile Resthouse
4720ft
1439m

1½-Mile Resthouse
5720ft
1743m

Trailview
Overlook

Rim Trail

Bright Angel Trail

Lower
Tunnel
6250ft 1905m

Upper Tunnel
6780ft
2067m

Kolb Studio

Rim Trail

**Bright Angel
Trailhead**
6840ft
2085m

Bright Angel
Lodge

El Tovar
Hotel

Verkamps
Visitor Center

0   200 Meters
0   1000 Feet

Do not swim in the Colorado
River! You could drown due to
dangerous currents and extremely
cold water temperatures.

Phantom Ranch
Canteen

Ranger Station

Bright Angel

Silver
Bridge

Pipe Creek
Rapids

River Resthouse
2500ft
762m

River   Trail

1.5mi
2.4km

Plateau Point
3760ft
1146m

T O N T O

P L A T F O R

Plateau   Point   Trail

0.7mi
1.1km

2.9mi
4.7km

2.2mi
3.5km

Tonto   Trail

Pipe

0.8mi
1.3km

Plateau

2.0mi
3.2km

3800ft
1158m

Havasupai Gardens

Ranger Station

0.3mi
0.5km

0.1mi
0.2km

Garden

Creek

• *The
Battleship*

Hopi Point
7065ft
2153m

Powell Point

Mojave Point
6995ft
2132m

Maricopa Point

Rim   Trail

Hermit   Road

Bright   Angel   Trail

1.5mi
2.4km

*Grandeur
Point*
7032ft
2143m

Yavapai Point
7082ft
2159m

Creek

*THE
ABYSS*

3-Mile Resthouse

1.5mi 2.4km

2.6mi
4.2km

Mather Point
7120ft
2170m

South Entrance Road

Lower Tunnel

1½-Mile Resthouse

0.5mi 0.8km

Grand Canyon
Visitor Center

Rim   Trail

To Hermits Rest

1.0mi 1.6km

**Bright Angel
Trailhead**
6840ft
2085m

El Tovar

Verkamps Visitor Center

Village Loop Drive

Backcountry
Information
Center

Center   Road

Market Plaza Rd

Market

Campground

Clinic

2.3mi
3.7km

Desert View Drive

S O U T H   R I M
Services available year-round.

South Entrance Rd

*COCONINO
PLATEAU*

To South Entrance Station and Tusayan

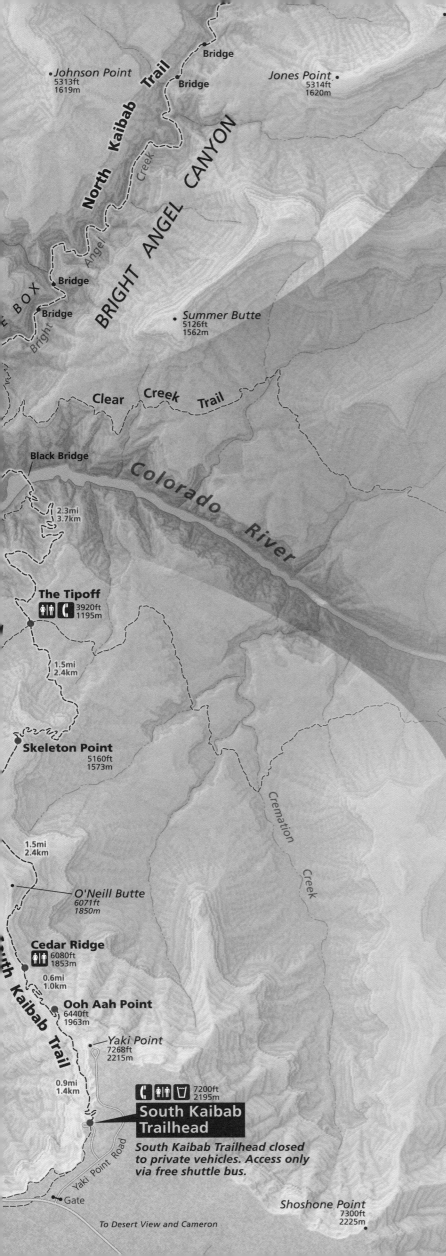

• Johnson Point
5313ft
1619m

Bridge

• Jones Point
5314ft
1620m

Bridge

NORTH KAIBAB TRAIL

BRIGHT ANGEL CANYON

E BOX

Bridge

Bridge

Summer Butte
5126ft
1562m

Clear Creek Trail

Black Bridge

Colorado River

2.3mi
3.7km

The Tipoff
3920ft
1195m

1.5mi
2.4km

Skeleton Point
5160ft
1573m

Cremation Creek

1.5mi
2.4km

O'Neill Butte
6071ft
1850m

Cedar Ridge
6080ft
1853m

0.6mi
1.0km

SOUTH KAIBAB TRAIL

Ooh Aah Point
6440ft
1963m

Yaki Point
7268ft
2215m

0.9mi
1.4km

7200ft
2195m

South Kaibab Trailhead

South Kaibab Trailhead closed to private vehicles. Access only via free shuttle bus.

Yaki Point Road

Gate

Shoshone Point
7300ft
2225m

To Desert View and Cameron

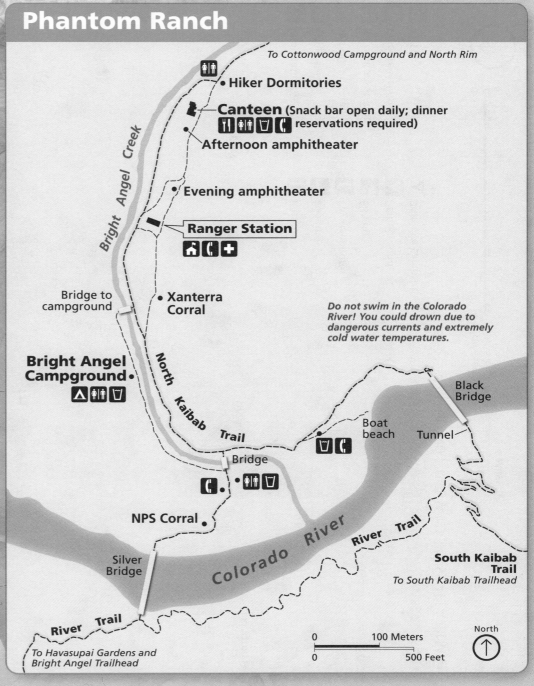

Phantom Ranch

To Cottonwood Campground and North Rim

• **Hiker Dormitories**

Canteen (Snack bar open daily; dinner reservations required)

• **Afternoon amphitheater**

• **Evening amphitheater**

Ranger Station

Bright Angel Creek

Bridge to campground

• **Xanterra Corral**

Bright Angel Campground •

North Kaibab Trail

Black Bridge

Boat beach

Tunnel

Do not swim in the Colorado River! You could drown due to dangerous currents and extremely cold water temperatures.

Bridge

NPS Corral •

Silver Bridge

Colorado River

River Trail

South Kaibab Trail
To South Kaibab Trailhead

River Trail

To Havasupai Gardens and Bright Angel Trailhead

0   100 Meters
0   500 Feet

North ↑

Legend

Drinking Water: Year-Round *Always carry backup water purification*		**Ranger Station: Year-round**	
Drinking Water: Seasonal; check availability		**Ranger Station: Seasonal**	
Emergency phone		**Toilet**	
First aid		**Campground** *Camp in designated sites only; permit required*	
Food service			

Featured trail

Other trail

Road

North ↑

0   0.5   1 Kilometer
0   0.5   1 Mile

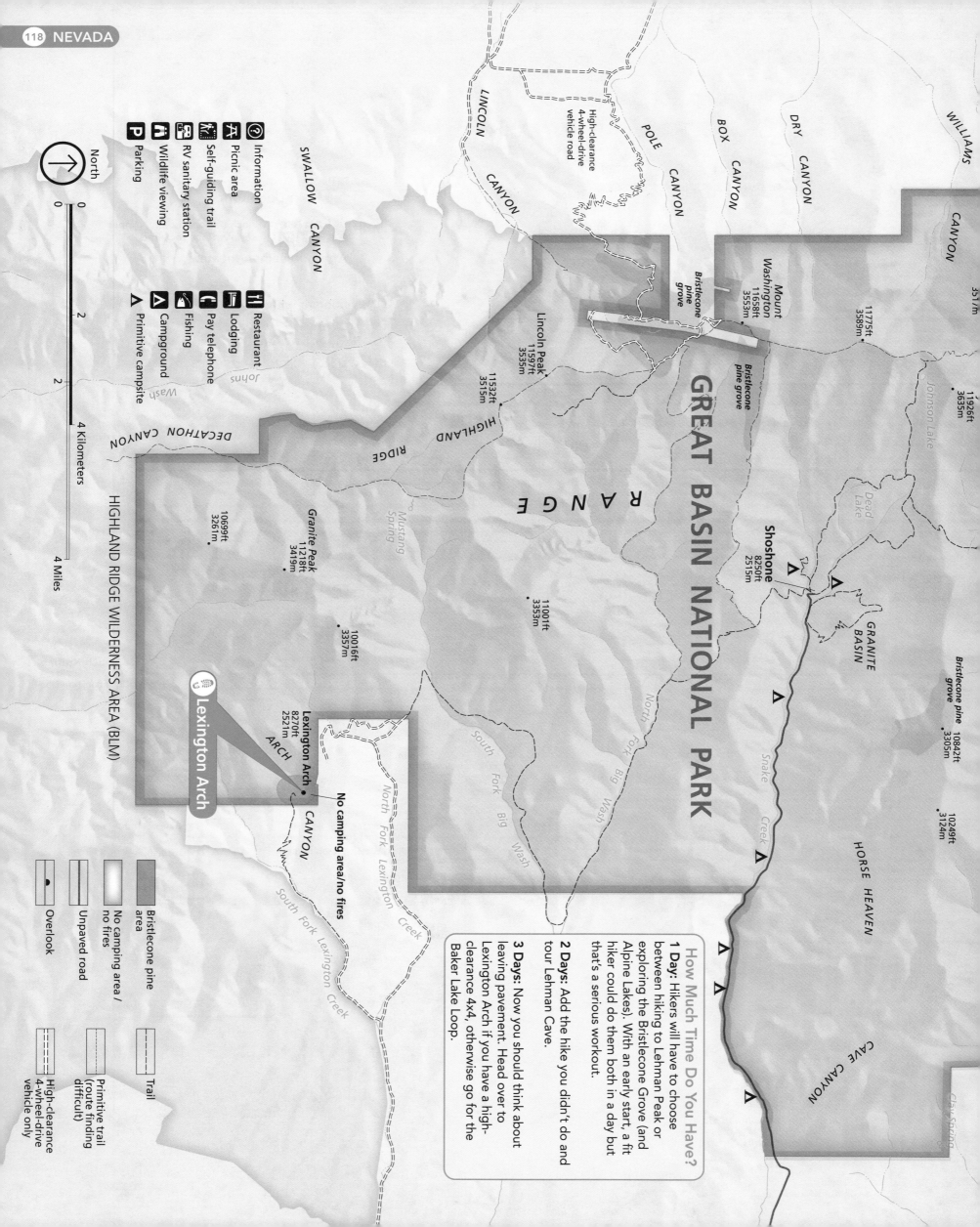

GREAT BASIN NATIONAL PARK

RANGE

North

0 0
0
2
2
2
4 Kilometers
4 Miles

Information
Picnic area
Self-guiding trail
RV sanitary station
Wildlife viewing
P **Parking**

Restaurant
Lodging
Fishing
Pay telephone
Campground
▲ **Primitive campsite**

Overlook
Unpaved road
No camping area / no fires
Bristlecone pine area
High-clearance 4-wheel-drive vehicle road only
Primitive trail (route finding difficult)
Trail

SWALLOW CANYON

LINCOLN CANYON

POLE CANYON

BOX CANYON

DRY CANYON

WILLIAMS CANYON

CANYON

351/m

Mount Washington
11658ft
3553m

11926ft
3635m

11775ft
3589m

Bristlecone pine grove

Bristlecone pine grove

Lincoln Peak
11597ft
3535m

11532ft
3515m

HIGHLAND RIDGE

Johns Wash

DECATHON CANYON

10699ft
3261m

Granite Peak
11218ft
3419m

Mustang Spring

11001ft
3353m

Shoshone
8250ft
2515m

Dead Lake

Johnson Lake

GRANITE BASIN

Bristlecone pine grove
10842ft
3305m

10249ft
3124m

North Fork Big Wash

South Fork Big Wash

Snake Creek

HORSE HEAVEN

CAVE CANYON

Clay Spring

10016ft
3357m

Lexington Arch

Lexington Arch
8270ft
2521m

ARCH CANYON

North Fork Lexington Creek

South Fork Lexington Creek

No camping area/no fires

HIGHLAND RIDGE WILDERNESS AREA (BLM)

High-clearance 4-wheel-drive vehicle road

How Much Time Do You Have?

1 Day: Hikers will have to choose between hiking to Lehman Peak or exploring the Bristlecone Grove (and Alpine Lakes). With an early start, a fit hiker could do them both in a day but that's a serious workout.

2 Days: Add the hike you didn't do and tour Lehman Cave.

3 Days: Now you should think about leaving pavement. Head over to Lexington Arch if you have a high-clearance 4x4, otherwise go for the Baker Lake Loop.

Alpine Lakes Trail

Glacier Trail

Great Basin Basics

(775) 234-7331 | nps.gov/grba

Entrance Fee: None.

Lodging: None

Camping: Upper* and Lower* Lehman Creek, Wheeler Peak*, Baker Creek, Grey Cliffs*

*reserve at recreation.gov

Great Basin Driving Distances

In perhaps the most park-dense region of the country, Great Basin remains isolated.

Salt Lake City, UT	3.75 hours → 230 miles	Great Basin VC		
Great Basin VC	9 minutes → 6 miles	Lehman Caves VC		
Lehman Caves VC	30 minutes → 13 miles	Wheeler Peak		
Great Basin VC	4.75 hours → 290 miles	Las Vegas, NV		

What You Need to Know About Great Basin

- Visitation is light by national park standards, but campgrounds and cave tours fill frequently.
- The park is open all year, but the final nine miles of Wheeler Park Scenic Drive usually close from November through May.
- There are a few remote regions. Unpaved roads lead to Strawberry Creek, Baker Creek, and Shoshone. 4x4 roads penetrate a few canyons and lead to Lexington Arch Trailhead.
- Great Basin sparked an interest in trees. It's pretty wild thinking about how some of those bristlecones were living during construction of Giza's Pyramids.
- Make the most of your mornings. Most activity occurs on the mountain's eastern flank, best viewed in the morning light.
- Make the most of your nights. You'll be treated to very dark skies here, and the park occasionally hosts astronomy programs.

Lehman Caves Visitor Center to:
Ely 68mi 109km
Pioche 121mi 195km

Why Visit Great Basin?

- To stand among some of the world's oldest lifeforms, the bristlecone pines
- To hike to the top of imposing Wheeler Peak

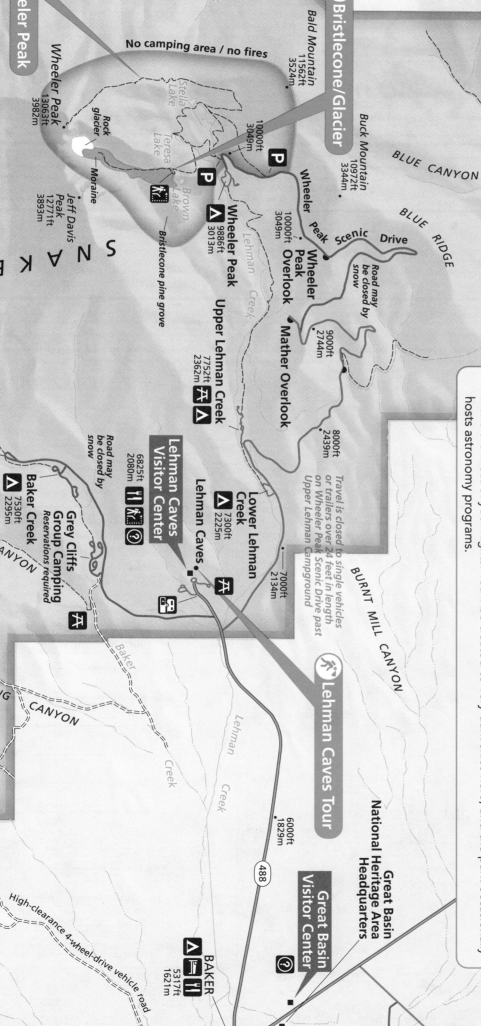

Windy Peak
10144ft
3092m

Wheeler Peak

No camping area / no fires

Bald Mountain
11562ft
3524m

Baker Peak
12298ft
3748m

Wheeler Peak
13063ft
3982m

12305ft
375m

Jeff Davis Peak
12771ft
3893m

11456ft
3492m

Rock glacier

Moraine

Stella Lake

Teresa Lake

Brown Lake

Bristlecone pine grove

Bristlecone/Glacier

Buck Mountain
10972ft
3344m

BLUE CANYON

BLUE RIDGE

P

P

10000ft
3049m

Wheeler Peak Scenic Drive

10000ft
3049m

Wheeler Peak
9886ft
3013m

Wheeler Peak Overlook

Mather Overlook

9000ft
274m

Road may be closed by snow

8000ft
2439m

Upper Lehman Creek
7752ft
2362m

S N A K E

Lehman Creek

Baker Creek

South Fork Baker Cr.

Timber Creek

Shingle Creek

Pine Creek

Ridge Creek

Board Creek

Willard Creek

BURNT MILL CANYON

Lehman Caves Tour

Road may be closed by snow

6825ft
2080m

Lehman Caves Visitor Center

Grey Cliffs Group Camping
Reservations required

Baker Creek
7530ft
2295m

POLE CANYON

Lower Lehman Creek
7300ft
2225m

Lehman Caves

7000ft
2134m

Travel is closed to single vehicles or trailers over 24 feet in length on Wheeler Peak Scenic Drive past Upper Lehman Campground

CAN YOUNG CANYON

KIOUS BASIN

YOUNG CANYON

MAHOGANY CANYON

High-clearance 4-wheel-drive vehicle road

6000ft
1829m

488

Lehman Creek

Baker Creek

Great Basin National Heritage Area Headquarters

Great Basin Visitor Center

BAKER
5317ft
1621m

6 50

6 50

Great Basin Favorites

Hikes: Bristlecone (moderate, 2.8 miles), Wheeler Peak (strenuous, 8.6), Alpine Lakes (easy, 2.7), Lexington Arch (moderate, 5.4)

Activities: Tour Lehman Cave, stay up for the stars

Lehman Cave

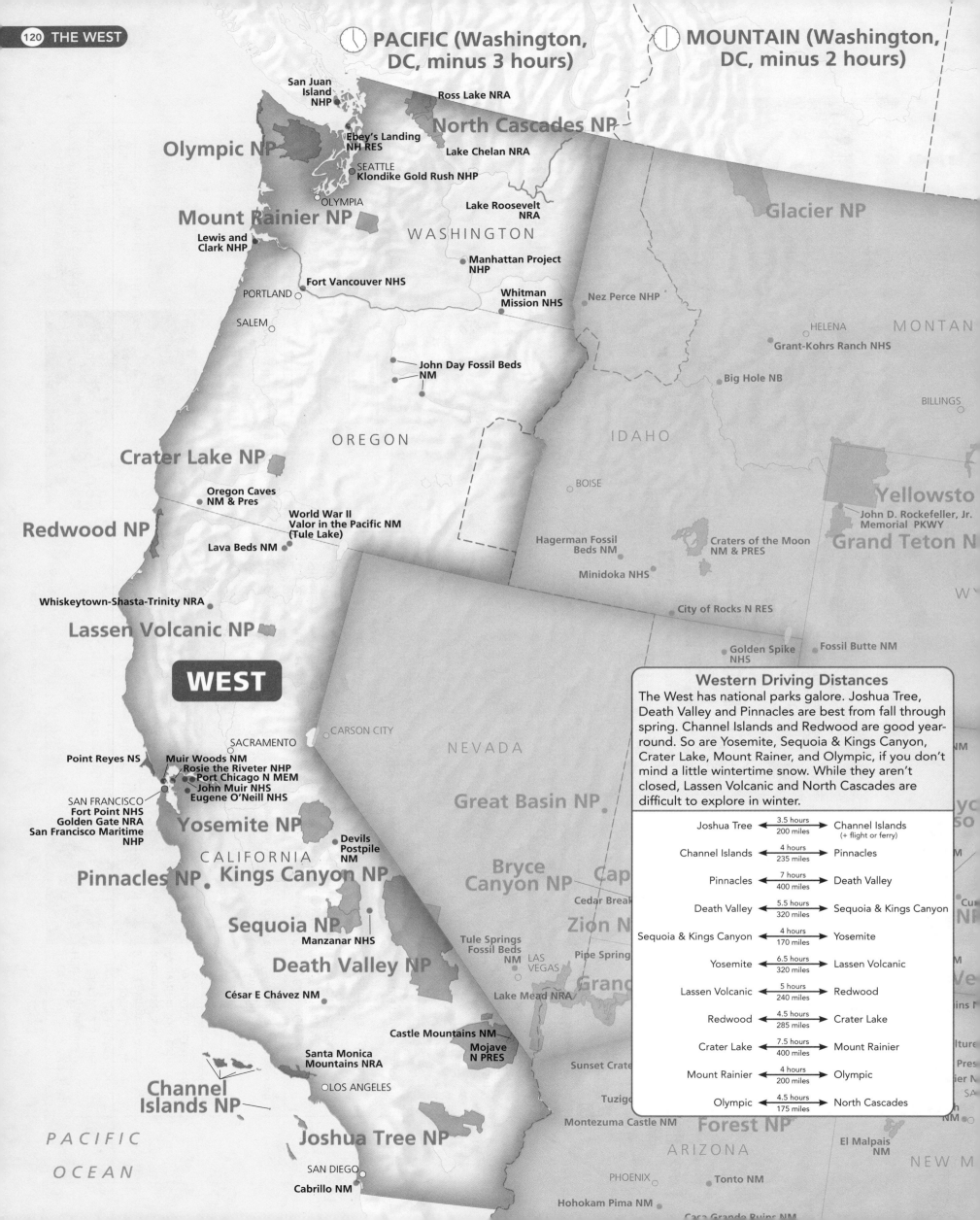

PACIFIC (Washington, DC, minus 3 hours)

MOUNTAIN (Washington, DC, minus 2 hours)

San Juan Island NHP

Ross Lake NRA

North Cascades NP

Olympic NP

Ebey's Landing NH RES

Lake Chelan NRA

SEATTLE

Klondike Gold Rush NHP

OLYMPIA

Lake Roosevelt NRA

Mount Rainier NP

WASHINGTON

Lewis and Clark NHP

Manhattan Project NHP

Fort Vancouver NHS

PORTLAND

Whitman Mission NHS

Nez Perce NHP

Glacier NP

SALEM

HELENA

MONTANA

Grant-Kohrs Ranch NHS

John Day Fossil Beds NM

Big Hole NB

BILLINGS

OREGON

IDAHO

Crater Lake NP

BOISE

Yellowstone

Oregon Caves NM & Pres

John D. Rockefeller, Jr. Memorial PKWY

Redwood NP

World War II Valor in the Pacific NM (Tule Lake)

Hagerman Fossil Beds NM

Craters of the Moon NM & PRES

Grand Teton

Lava Beds NM

Minidoka NHS

Whiskeytown-Shasta-Trinity NRA

City of Rocks N RES

Lassen Volcanic NP

Golden Spike NHS

Fossil Butte NM

WEST

CARSON CITY

NEVADA

Point Reyes NS

SACRAMENTO

Muir Woods NM

Rosie the Riveter NHP

Port Chicago N MEM

John Muir NHS

Eugene O'Neill NHS

SAN FRANCISCO

Fort Point NHS

Golden Gate NRA

San Francisco Maritime NHP

Great Basin NP

Yosemite NP

Devils Postpile NM

CALIFORNIA

Pinnacles NP

Kings Canyon NP

Bryce Canyon NP

Cap

Cedar Break

Zion N

Sequoia NP

Manzanar NHS

Tule Springs Fossil Beds NM

LAS VEGAS

Pipe Spring

Death Valley NP

César E Chávez NM

Lake Mead NRA

Grand

Castle Mountains NM

Mojave N PRES

Santa Monica Mountains NRA

Sunset Crate

Channel Islands NP

LOS ANGELES

Joshua Tree NP

Montezuma Castle NM

Forest NP

ARIZONA

NEW M

PACIFIC OCEAN

SAN DIEGO

Cabrillo NM

PHOENIX

Tonto NM

El Malpais NM

Hohokam Pima NM

Western Driving Distances

The West has national parks galore. Joshua Tree, Death Valley and Pinnacles are best from fall through spring. Channel Islands and Redwood are good year-round. So are Yosemite, Sequoia & Kings Canyon, Crater Lake, Mount Rainer, and Olympic, if you don't mind a little wintertime snow. While they aren't closed, Lassen Volcanic and North Cascades are difficult to explore in winter.

Joshua Tree	← 3.5 hours / 200 miles →	Channel Islands (+ flight or ferry)
Channel Islands	← 4 hours / 235 miles →	Pinnacles
Pinnacles	← 7 hours / 400 miles →	Death Valley
Death Valley	← 5.5 hours / 320 miles →	Sequoia & Kings Canyon
Sequoia & Kings Canyon	← 4 hours / 170 miles →	Yosemite
Yosemite	← 6.5 hours / 320 miles →	Lassen Volcanic
Lassen Volcanic	← 5 hours / 240 miles →	Redwood
Redwood	← 4.5 hours / 285 miles →	Crater Lake
Crater Lake	← 7.5 hours / 400 miles →	Mount Rainier
Mount Rainier	← 4 hours / 200 miles →	Olympic
Olympic	← 4.5 hours / 175 miles →	North Cascades

THE WEST

Lucky Boy Vista

Joshua Tree Basics

(760) 367-5522 | nps.gov/jotr
Entrance Fee: $30/car
Lodging: None
Camping: Cottonwood*, White Tank, Belle, Jumbo Rocks*, Sheep Pass*, Ryan*, Hidden Valley, Indian Cove*, Black Rock*

*reserve at recreation.gov

Joshua Tree Driving Distances

Pavement crosses the park in the shape of a 'y', with a few unpaved (mostly high-clearance) roads reaching more remote regions.

From	Time / Distance	To
Los Angeles, CA	← 165 minutes / 145 miles →	Joshua Tree VC
Joshua Tree VC	← 30 minutes / 14 miles →	Hidden Valley
Hidden Valley	← 12 minutes / 7 miles →	Keys View
Hidden Valley	← 30 minutes / 20 miles →	Oasis VC
Oasis VC	← 4 hours / 235 miles →	Death Valley
Oasis VC	← 52 minutes / 38 miles →	Cottonwood VC
Cottonwood VC	← 3.5 hours / 230 miles →	Phoenix, AZ

Joshua Tree Sunset

Why Visit Joshua Tree?

- Because every visit you'll find (and fall in love with) some new, weird, totally wacky thing
- To hike to Wonderland of Rocks
- To take in some of the most magical sunsets and sunrises you'll ever experience
- To climb some rocks!
- To tour Keys Ranch (ticket required)

Park Boulevard - It's definitely a landscape that won't appeal to everyone

What You Need to Know About Joshua Tree

- Summer days are hot, but mornings can be pleasant and the park will be quiet. Visitation is extremely heavy from November through April (especially around spring break and holidays).
- The park is experienced in many ways. Most like to drive around, stopping when a Joshua Tree or uniquely weird rock formation draws their gaze and forces a quick pit-stop. Others come with a detailed itinerary, bang out some hiking trails, and call it a trip. Rock climbers and scramblers have a few lifetime's worth of routes to choose from. It's a fun place, with something for everyone.
- Be prepared for the heat. Water is only available at Cottonwood, Black Rock, Indian Cove Ranger Station, West Entrance Station, and Oasis Visitor Center.
- Most easily-accessible Joshua trees are found between the intersection of Pinto Basin Road and Park Boulevard and the Joshua Tree (West) Entrance Station. It's also where you'll find most of the goofy rocks.
- Joshua Tree (West) Entrance is the busiest. You may want to enter at Twentynine Palms (North) during peak season.
- Cholla Cactus Garden is regarded as a great sunrise/sunset destination but the magic happens when the sun is just above the surrounding mountains. Low-angled light makes the prickly cactus glow. This is great, because you'll have time to enjoy the actual sunrise/sunset up the road with some Joshua trees.
- Boy Scout Trail is amazing from either trailhead, but the show-stopper is Wonderland of Rocks (via Willow Hole Trail). It's a shorter trek to Willow Hole by using the trailhead on Park Boulevard.
- Indian Cove is great too. It has its own access road, so you have to go there with intent.
- A few good hikes begin near Cottonwood Visitor Center. If you don't plan on doing them, skip the South Entrance and Pinto Basin Road altogether (except for sunrise/sunset at Cholla Cactus Garden and Arch Rock).

Joshua Tree Favorites

Cholla Cactus Garden

Easy Hikes: Hidden Valley (1 mile), Split Rock (2), Arch Rock (0.8), Skull Rock (1.7), Keys View (0.3), Cap Rock (0.4), Cholla Cactus Garden (0.3), Barker Dam (1.1)
Moderate Hikes: Willow Hole via Boy Scout (7), Lost Palms Oasis (7.5), Lost Horse Mine (4)
Strenuous Hikes: Boy Scout Trail/Willow Hole (16+), Ryan Mountain (3), Mastodon Peak (3)
Activities: Rock climbing!
Views: Keys View, go find some Joshua Trees or peculiar rocks

How Much Time Do You Have?

1 Day: Make it a full day to get a morning hike in (maybe Ryan Mountain), then hike Boy Scout Trail to Willow Hole. If you can get tickets (recreation.gov) for a Keys Ranch Tour, do it. There are tons of great sunset spots along Park Boulevard, Desert Queen Mine Road, and Queen Valley Road.

2 Days: Head up to Indian Cove. The north end of Boy Scout Trail is great or there's an interesting scramble at Rattlesnake Canyon. You could spend the whole day at Indian Cove or head over to Fortynine Palm Oasis. If you're still energized, head back to the Hidden Valley Area for sunset.

3 Days: There are plenty of 4x4 options, like Bedoo Canyon Road. Or explore some of the rock areas. Hall of Horrors, Jumbo Rocks, White Tank, Hidden Valley, Cap Rock, Skull Rock, they're all fun. At Skull Rock in particular, most of the fun is in the surrounding area, not the Skull Rock viewpoint.

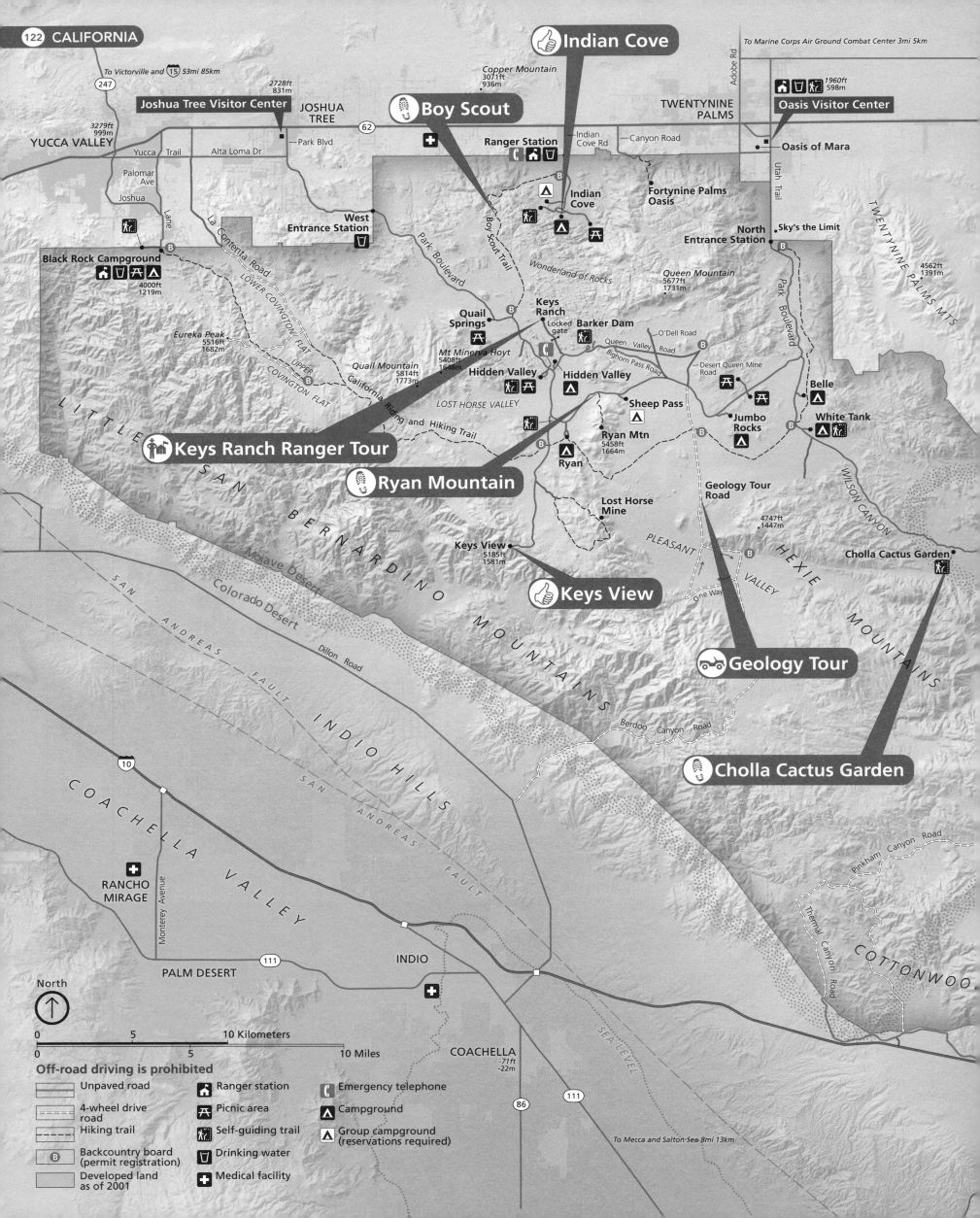

To Victorville and 15 53mi 85km

247

YUCCA VALLEY

3279ft
999m

Palomar Ave

Joshua

Yucca Trail

Lane

Alta Loma Dr

2728ft
831m

Joshua Tree Visitor Center

JOSHUA TREE

Park Blvd

62

Copper Mountain
3071ft
936m

👍 Indian Cove

👣 Boy Scout

Ranger Station

TWENTYNINE PALMS

To Marine Corps Air Ground Combat Center 3mi 5km

Adobe Rd

1960ft
598m

Oasis Visitor Center

Canyon Road

Oasis of Mara

Indian Cove Rd

Indian Cove

Fortynine Palms Oasis

West Entrance Station

Boy Scout Trail

Wonderland of Rocks

North Entrance Station

Sky's the Limit

Utah Trail

4562ft
1391m

TWENTYNINE PALMS MTS

Black Rock Campground

4000ft
1219m

La Contenta Road

LOWER COVINGTON FLAT

UPPER COVINGTON FLAT

B

Eureka Peak
5516ft
1682m

Quail Mountain
5814ft
1773m

California Riding and Hiking Trail

Quail Springs

Keys Ranch

Locked gate

Barker Dam

O'Dell Road

Queen Valley Road

Bighorn Pass Road

Desert Queen Mine Road

Queen Mountain
5677ft
1731m

Park Boulevard

Belle

Mt Minerva Hoyt
5408ft
1648m

Hidden Valley

Hidden Valley

LOST HORSE VALLEY

Sheep Pass

Ryan Mtn
5458ft
1664m

Ryan

Jumbo Rocks

White Tank

🧍 Keys Ranch Ranger Tour

👣 Ryan Mountain

LITTLE SAN BERNARDINO MOUNTAINS

Lost Horse Mine

Geology Tour Road

4747ft
1447m

Mojave Desert

Keys View
5185ft
1581m

👍 Keys View

PLEASANT

HEXIE MOUNTAINS

Cholla Cactus Garden

Colorado Desert

One Way

VALLEY

WILSON CANYON

SAN ANDREAS FAULT

Dillon Road

🚙 Geology Tour

Berdoo Canyon Road

👣 Cholla Cactus Garden

COACHELLA VALLEY

10

INDIO HILLS

SAN ANDREAS FAULT

Pinkham Canyon Road

COTTONWOO

RANCHO MIRAGE

Monterey Avenue

Thermal Canyon Road

111

PALM DESERT

INDIO

North

↑

COACHELLA

-71ft
-22m

86

111

SEA LEVEL

To Mecca and Salton Sea 8mi 13km

0   5   10 Kilometers
0   5   10 Miles

Off-road driving is prohibited

▬▬ Unpaved road	🏠 Ranger station
▭▭ 4-wheel drive road	🌲 Picnic area
▭ ▭ Hiking trail	🚶 Self-guiding trail
B Backcountry board (permit registration)	🚰 Drinking water
▭ Developed land as of 2001	✚ Medical facility

☎ Emergency telephone
⛺ Campground
🏕 Group campground (reservations required)

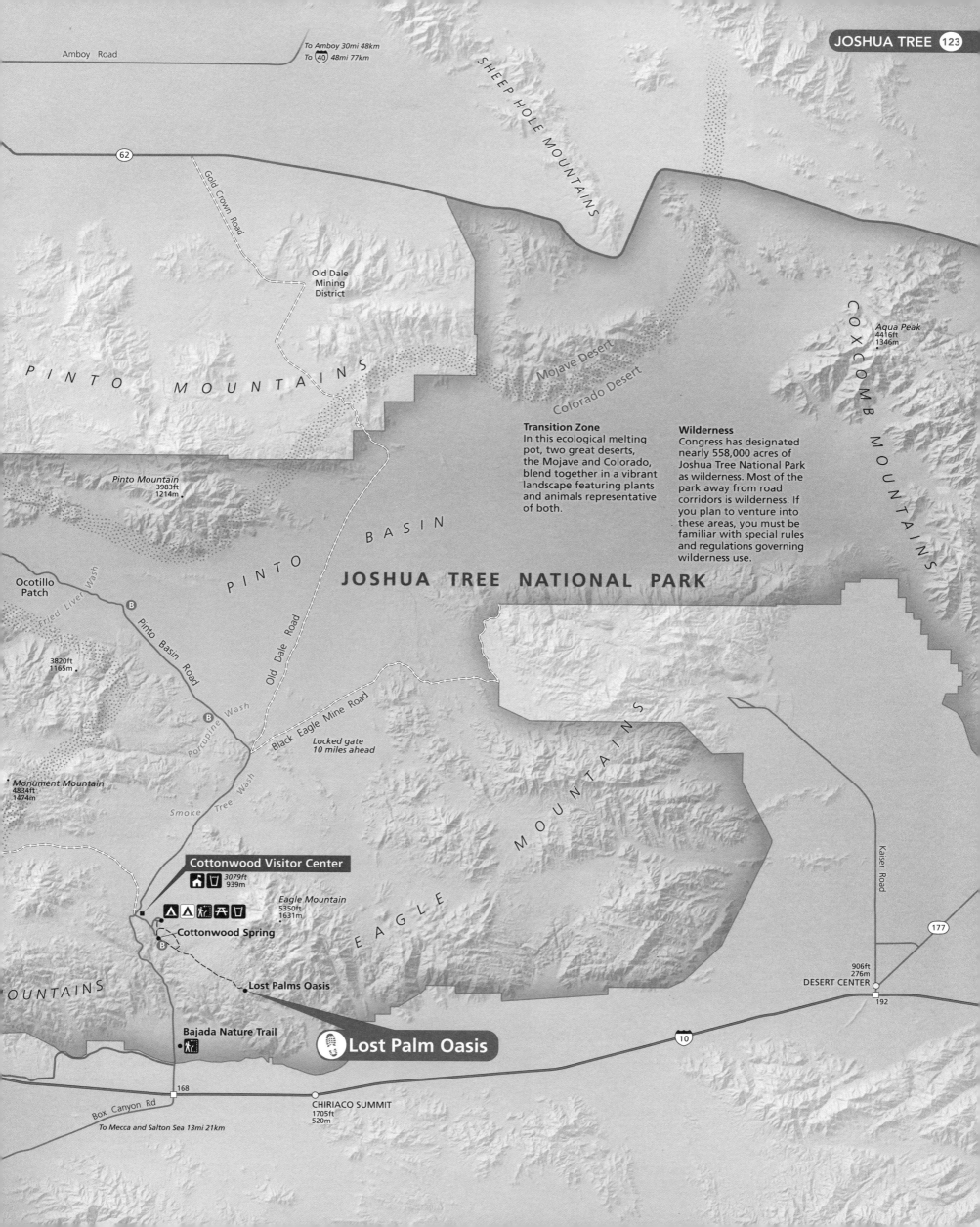

Amboy Road

To Amboy 30mi 48km
To 40 48mi 77km

62

Gold Crown Road

SHEEP HOLE MOUNTAINS

Old Dale
Mining
District

COXCOMB MOUNTAINS

Aqua Peak
4416ft
1346m

P I N T O   M O U N T A I N S

Mojave Desert

Colorado Desert

Transition Zone
In this ecological melting
pot, two great deserts,
the Mojave and Colorado,
blend together in a vibrant
landscape featuring plants
and animals representative
of both.

Wilderness
Congress has designated
nearly 558,000 acres of
Joshua Tree National Park
as wilderness. Most of the
park away from road
corridors is wilderness. If
you plan to venture into
these areas, you must be
familiar with special rules
and regulations governing
wilderness use.

Pinto Mountain
3983ft
1214m

P I N T O   B A S I N

JOSHUA TREE NATIONAL PARK

Ocotillo
Patch

Fried Liver Wash

B

Pinto Basin Road

Old Dale Road

3820ft
1165m

Porcupine Wash

B

Black Eagle Mine Road

Locked gate
10 miles ahead

Monument Mountain
4834ft
1474m

Smoke Tree Wash

Kaiser Road

177

Cottonwood Visitor Center

🏠 🚻 3079ft
         939m

△ △ 🚶 🍽 🚻

Cottonwood Spring

B

Eagle Mountain
5350ft
1631m

E A G L E   M O U N T A I N S

Lost Palms Oasis

906ft
276m
DESERT CENTER

192

Bajada Nature Trail
🚶

👣 **Lost Palm Oasis**

10

168

CHIRIACO SUMMIT
1705ft
520m

Box Canyon Rd

To Mecca and Salton Sea 13mi 21km

Santa Cruz's rugged landscape

Channel Islands Basics
(805) 658-5730 | nps.gov/chis
Entrance Fee: None
Lodging: None
Camping*: Two primitive campgrounds on Santa Cruz, one on all other islands

*reserve at recreation.gov

Channel Islands Driving Distances
This isn't a drive-in park. You'll need to take a ferry (islandpackers.com) or seaplane (flycia.com) to reach the islands.

Painted Cave

Los Angeles, CA	←→ 80 minutes / 67 miles	Channel Islands VC
Channel Islands VC	←→ 46 minutes / 33 miles	Santa Barbara VC
Santa Barbara VC	←→ 6 hours / 315 miles	San Francisco, CA

Why Visit Channel Islands?
- To witness the bountiful marine life
- To enjoy a remote and undeveloped wilderness
- To kayak through water-carved sea caves

Prisoner's Harbor

Channel Islands Favorites
Hikes: Each island has a few miles of trails but Santa Cruz and Santa Barbara are best for hiking
Solitude: They're all pretty isolated but San Miguel and Santa Rosa are the quietest of these already quiet islands
Activities: Kayak the sea caves, snorkel with kelp, backpack these unoccupied islands

SANTA   BARBARA   CHAN

-1998ft
-609m

SANTA   BARBARA   BASIN

CHANNEL   ISLANDS   NA

Richardson Rock

Wilson Rock

SAN MIGUEL ISLAND

Harris Point

Cuyler Harbor

Prince Island

Castle Rock

San Miguel Hill
831ft
253m

Point Bennett

Tyler Bight

Cabrillo Monument
Lester Ranch site

Crook Point

Sandy Point

SAN MIGUEL PASSAGE

West Point

SANTA ROSA ISLAND

Carrington Point

Vail and Vickers Ranch

Bechers Bay

Skunk Point

Torrey Pines

Soledad Peak
1574ft
480m

East Point

Johnsons Lee

South Point

SANTA CRUZ CHANNEL

SANTA

👍 Seals/Sea Lions

What You Need to Know About Channel Islands
- The park is open all year. Weather—albeit unpredictable—is usually comfortable. High winds, fog, and rain can complicate camping and kayaking but it rarely alters island transportation.
- In the unlikely event your travel is delayed, there's more than enough non-park things to keep you occupied on the mainland.
- You have two ways of reaching the islands. Island Packers (islandpackers.com) runs regular ferry service from two different harbors in the area. Be sure to check your ticket to confirm departure point. Channel Islands Aviation (flycia.com) provides year-round air transportation to Santa Rosa and San Miguel. Regardless of transportation, you end up with a couple hours on the island.
- Most of Island Packers tours are full-day affairs, but they also offer a few half-day express tours.
- Or you can camp. When making plans, be sure to check camping reservations (recreation.gov) at the same time as ferry service (islandpackers.com). Campsites go quickly for summer.
- Food storage boxes are provided at campsites. Use them or pack your food and scented items in an animal-proof container to keep rodents out.
- Watch for marine life. While the islands are special, a good whale sighting is often the highlight of any trip.

Whale!

How Much Time Do You Have?
Channel Islands isn't a park you can visit on a whim. You need to learn about the islands, plan what you'd like to do, and reserve ferry or plane tickets (and campgrounds if necessary). Anacapa is the standard trip. You see an arch. There are a few short trails. You'll likely spot marine life. And there will probably be plenty of seagulls. It's brief but enjoyable. Santa Cruz is another option. You can book a paddle trip or stay on Island Packers' boat to check out Painted Cave. Then you'll be free to hike or possibly join a guided hike through Conservancy land. Snorkeling is also available in summer. San Miguel is known for its huge seal and sea lion populations, as well as caliche forest. Santa Rosa is the site of a few important archaeological discoveries. Santa Barbara is the smallest island (and a fair distance southeast of the other Channel Islands).

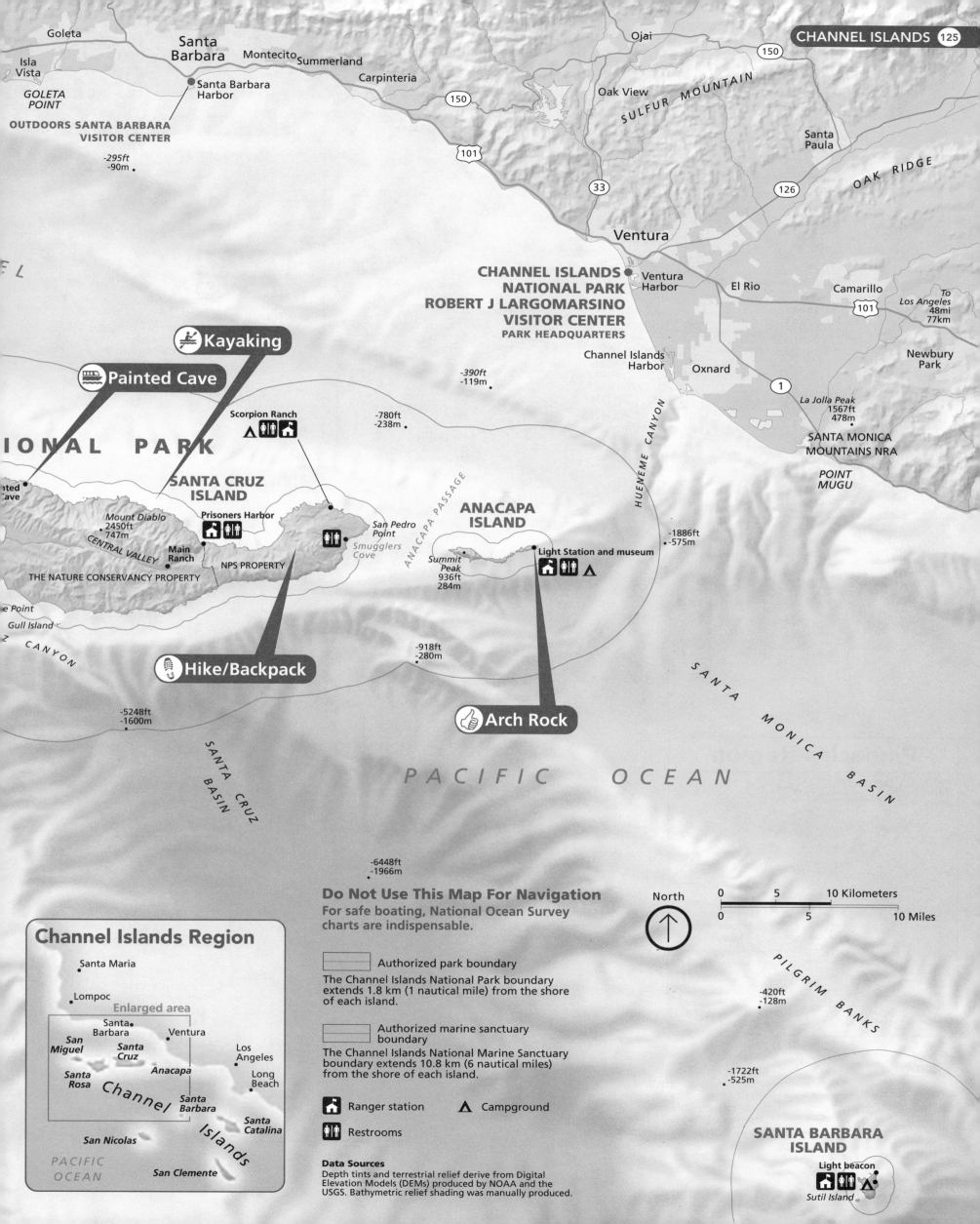

Goleta

Santa Barbara

Montecito Summerland

Carpinteria

Ojai

Oak View

SULFUR MOUNTAIN

150

Santa Paula

OAK RIDGE

Isla Vista

GOLETA POINT

OUTDOORS SANTA BARBARA VISITOR CENTER

Santa Barbara Harbor

150

101

33

101

126

Ventura

CHANNEL ISLANDS NATIONAL PARK ROBERT J LARGOMARSINO VISITOR CENTER PARK HEADQUARTERS

Ventura Harbor

El Rio

Camarillo

To Los Angeles 48mi 77km

-295ft -90m

Channel Islands Harbor

Oxnard

101

Newbury Park

🚣 **Kayaking**

🚐 **Painted Cave**

Scorpion Ranch
🏕 🚻 🏠

-390ft -119m

-780ft -238m

La Jolla Peak 1567ft 478m

1

SANTA MONICA MOUNTAINS NRA

NATIONAL PARK

SANTA CRUZ ISLAND

Prisoners Harbor
🏠 🚻

San Pedro Point

Smugglers Cove

ANACAPA ISLAND

POINT MUGU

nted ave

Mount Diablo 2450ft 747m

Main Ranch

CENTRAL VALLEY

THE NATURE CONSERVANCY PROPERTY

NPS PROPERTY

🚻

ANACAPA PASSAGE

Summit Peak 936ft 284m

Light Station and museum
🏠 🚻 🏕

-1886ft -575m

e Point

Gull Island

🥾 **Hike/Backpack**

-918ft -280m

SANTA MONICA BASIN

Z CANYON

-5248ft -1600m

👍 **Arch Rock**

SANTA CRUZ BASIN

PACIFIC OCEAN

HUENEME CANYON

-6448ft -1966m

Do Not Use This Map For Navigation
For safe boating, National Ocean Survey charts are indispensable.

North
⬆

0   5   10 Kilometers

0   5   10 Miles

Authorized park boundary
The Channel Islands National Park boundary extends 1.8 km (1 nautical mile) from the shore of each island.

Authorized marine sanctuary boundary
The Channel Islands National Marine Sanctuary boundary extends 10.8 km (6 nautical miles) from the shore of each island.

🏠 Ranger station   🏕 Campground

🚻 Restrooms

PILGRIM BANKS

-420ft -128m

-1722ft -525m

Channel Islands Region

Santa Maria

Lompoc

Enlarged area

Santa Barbara

Ventura

San Miguel

Santa Cruz

Santa Rosa

Anacapa

Channel

Islands

Santa Barbara

Los Angeles

Long Beach

Santa Catalina

San Nicolas

PACIFIC OCEAN

San Clemente

Data Sources
Depth tints and terrestrial relief derive from Digital Elevation Models (DEMs) produced by NOAA and the USGS. Bathymetric relief shading was manually produced.

SANTA BARBARA ISLAND

Light beacon
🏠 🚻 🏕

Sutil Island

PINNACLES NATIONAL PARK

See detail map

Willow Spring

West Fork Chalone Creek

BALCONIES

Balconies Cave Trail

1401ft
427m
Chaparral Parking Area

Machete Ridge

Jawbone Parking Area
1447ft
441m

Old Pinnacles Trailhead Parking

Pinnacles Visitor Center
1000ft
305m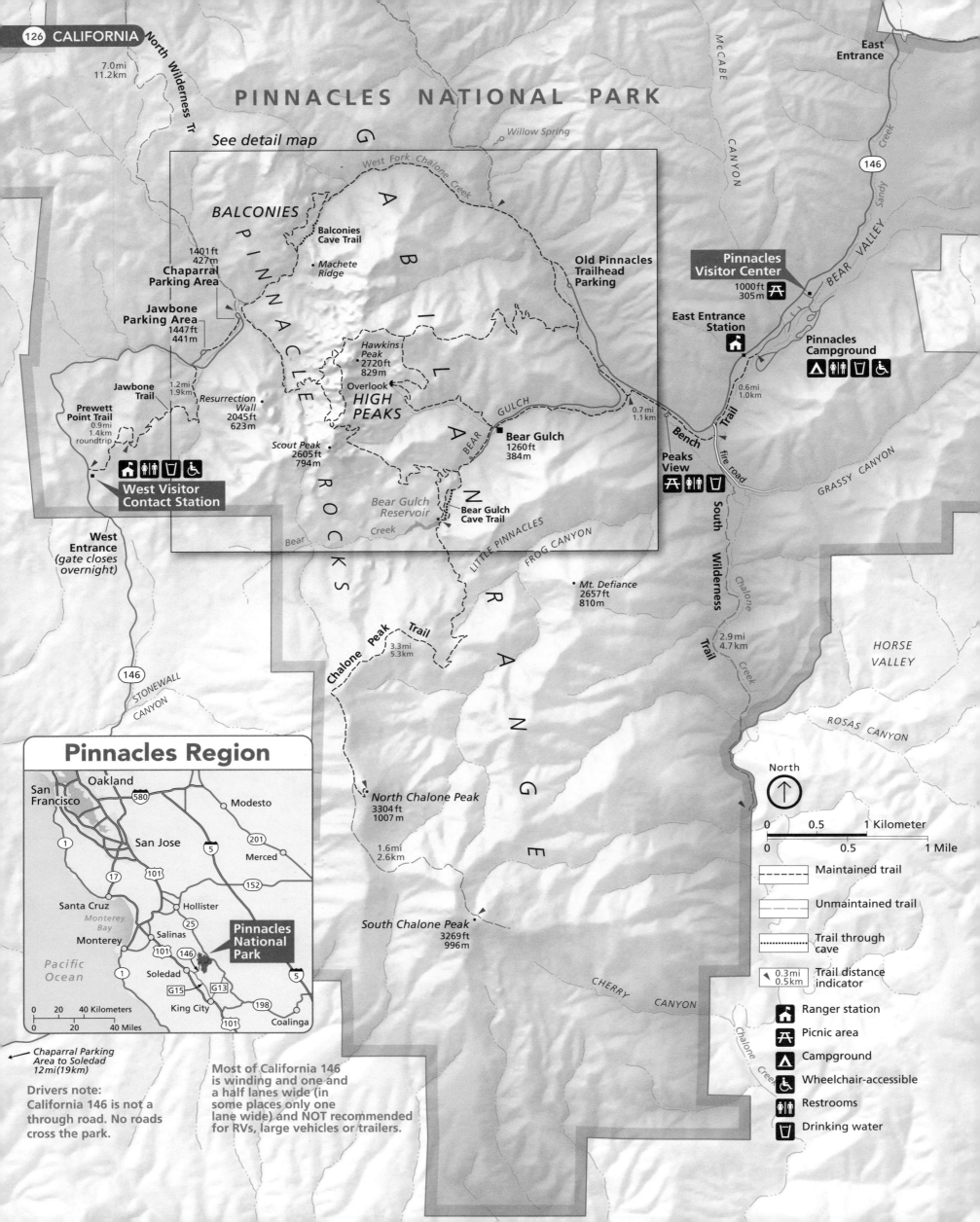

East Entrance Station

Pinnacles Campground

Jawbone Trail
1.2mi
1.9km

Resurrection Wall
2045ft
623m

Hawkins Peak
2720ft
829m
Overlook
HIGH PEAKS

0.6mi
1.0km

Overlook

Prewett Point Trail
0.9mi
1.4km
roundtrip

Scout Peak
2605ft
794m

BEAR GULCH

■ **Bear Gulch**
1260ft
384m

0.7mi
1.1km

Bench

Peaks View

West Visitor Contact Station

Bear Gulch Reservoir

Bear Gulch Cave Trail

fire road

Trail

West Entrance
(gate closes overnight)

Bear Creek

LITTLE PINNACLES

FROG CANYON

South Wilderness

2.9mi
4.7km

• *Mt. Defiance*
2657ft
810m

HORSE VALLEY

ROSAS CANYON

Chalone Peak Trail
3.3mi
5.3km

Trail

Pinnacles Region

San Francisco
Oakland
Modesto
San Jose
Merced
Santa Cruz
Hollister
Monterey Bay
Salinas
Monterey
Soledad
Pinnacles National Park
Pacific Ocean
King City
Coalinga

0   20   40 Kilometers
0   20   40 Miles

*Chaparral Parking Area to Soledad
12 mi (19 km)*

Drivers note: California 146 is not a through road. No roads cross the park.

North Chalone Peak
3304ft
1007 m

1.6mi
2.6km

South Chalone Peak
3269ft
996m

CHERRY CANYON

Chalone Creek

Most of California 146 is winding and one and a half lanes wide (in some places only one lane wide) and **NOT** recommended for RVs, large vehicles or trailers.

North
↑

0   0.5   1 Kilometer
0   0.5   1 Mile

- - - - - Maintained trail

───── Unmaintained trail

········· Trail through cave

◥ 0.3mi
0.5km   Trail distance indicator

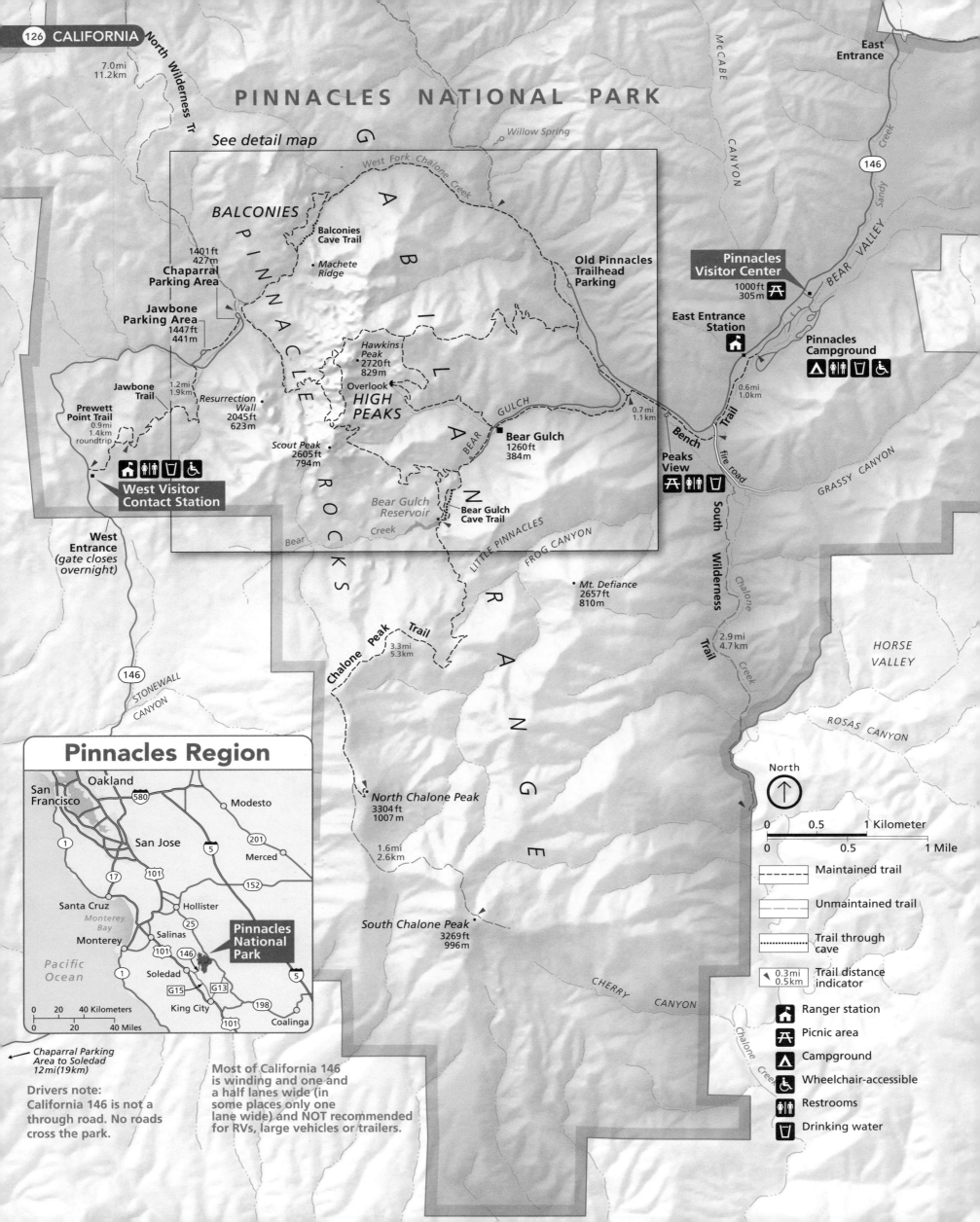 Ranger station

Picnic area

Campground

Wheelchair-accessible

Restrooms

Drinking water

East Entrance

McCabe CANYON

146

BEAR VALLEY

Sandy Creek

GRASSY CANYON

Pinnacles Basics

Tunnel Trail

(831) 389-4486 | nps.gov/pinn
Entrance Fee: $30/car
Lodging: None
Camping: Pinnacles*

*reserve at recreation.gov

Pinnacles Driving Distances

Pinnacles isn't an intensive driving park but it takes time to get to the other side.

San Francisco, CA ⟷ 2 hours / 120 miles ⟷ Pinnacles VC

Pinnacles VC ⟷ 75 minutes / 54 miles ⟷ West VC

West VC ⟷ 5 hours / 300 miles ⟷ Los Angeles, CA

Why Visit Pinnacles?

- To hike in the High Peaks!
- To tramp through two talus caves
- To spot California condor
- To climb some rocks

Pinnacles Favorites

Easy Hikes: Prewett Point (0.9 mile)
Moderate Hikes: Bear Gulch Cave (2.2), Balconies Cave (2.4)
Strenuous Hikes: High Peaks Loop (6.7), Juniper Canyon (4.3), Condor Gulch (5.3), Chalone Peaks (8/11)

What You Need to Know About Pinnacles

- The East Entrance is open every day, 24/7. The West Entrance closes overnight.
- Caves close due to flooding or resident bats from time to time. Check their status prior to arrival.
- Bear Gulch Cave's lower half is typically open from mid-July through mid-May. The upper half is usually only open in March and October. Don't forget two light sources.
- Spring through fall is busy, especially weekends and holidays. It's a small park, with most people congregating around the High Peaks, so it doesn't take too many people to feel like a crowd.
- Free shuttles run between East Visitor Center and Bear Gulch during busy weekends and holidays.
- If you want to escape the crowds, North and South Chalone Peak are good destinations.
- The park doesn't receive the Pacific's full cooling power. Triple-digit heat is common in summer.
- Spotting a California condor is pretty neat. Turkey vultures look eerily similar. Here's how to identify a condor. Condors are considerably larger. Their underwings have mottled white along their leading edges. They glide with their wings flat and they do not rock back and forth. They have a bright red head. And, if you get close enough, they all should have a numbered wing tag.

How Much Time Do You Have?

High Peaks

1 Day: Bear Gulch to High Peaks (and back via Condor Gulch or Bench) is one of the best hikes in the national park system (especially when the entire Bear Gulch Cave is open). Start with that.

2 Days: With another day, head to the west side to hike back to High Peaks but this time via Juniper Canyon Trail and complete the short loop with Tunnel Trail. If you have plenty of energy, there is a longer option. Instead of starting up Juniper Canyon, take Balconies Trail. Go through the cave and continue on Old Pinnacles Trail to High Peaks, returning to Chaparral Parking Area via Juniper Canyon. I'd still recommend looping through the High Peaks (doing Tunnel Trail twice) because High Peaks is awesome. (With another day, hike to Chalone Peaks.)

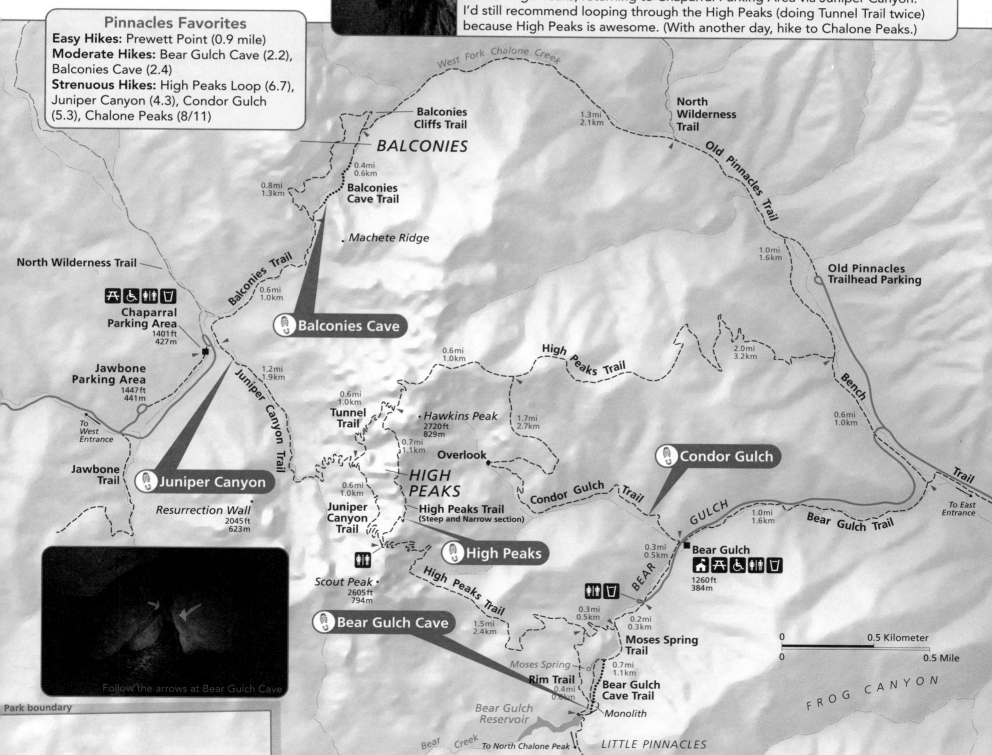

Follow the arrows at Bear Gulch Cave

Park boundary

Lida

Palmetto Mountain
8960ft
2731m

Mount Jackson
6411ft
1954m

45 mi
72km

Jackson Ridge

Gold Point

LIDA VAL

Mount Dunfee

Cottonwood Creek

266

FISH LAKE VALLEY

SYLVANIA MOUNTAINS

Palmetto

Wash

Magruder
Mountain
9046ft
2757m

SLATE

RIDGE

Deep
sand

Wyman Creek

168

Chocolate
Mountain
11123ft
3390m

Cucomungo Canyon

Last Chance
Mountain
8456ft
2577m

Last Chance Canyon

Crankshaft
Junction

Gold Mountain

To Big Pine

Deep Springs Valley

Deep
Springs
Lake

Death Valley / Big Pine Road

N Eureka Valley Road

Hanging Rock Canyon

11 mi
18km

8 mi
13km

Death Valley / Big Pine Road

NEVADA
CALIFORNIA

E U R E K A

23mi
37km

Joshua Flats

Cowhorn Valley

South Eureka Valley Road

14 mi
23km

LAST CHANCE RANGE

Sand
Dunes

⛺ 🚻

**Area temporarily closed
due to flood damage.**
🏠 🏕 ♿ 🚻 🚰

To Big Pine

8 mi
13km

Marble Canyon

In winter carry
chains. Road
may be closed.

North
Pass
7300ft
2225m

Jackass Flats

V A L L E Y

Eureka
Dunes

Deep
sand

Road conditions
require experienced
four-wheel drivers.

S A L I N E

🏔 **Ubehebe Crater**

Scotty's Castle
Visitor Center and Museum

3000ft
914m

Grapevine Canyon

🚗 **Eureka Dunes**

Waucoba
Mountain
11123ft
3390m

R A N G E

Ubehebe
Crater

5mi
8km

3mi
5km

Grapevine
📞 ♿ 🚻 🚰

Steel Pass

Mesquite Spring
⛺ 🏕 🚻 🚰

I N Y O

Waucoba Wash

Racetrack Road

Dry Mountain
8674ft
2644m

Tin Mountain
8953ft
2729m

INYO

25mi
40km

👍 **Warm Springs**

Sharp rock;
requires heavy-
duty tires.

20 mi
32km

Bighorn Gorge

NATIONAL

Willow Creek

S A L I N E

FOREST

Warm Springs
⛺ 🚻

White Top
Mountain
7607ft
2154m

🚗 **The Racetrack**

Saline Valley
Dunes

Teakettle Junction

Mount Inyo
11107ft
3385m

Saline Valley Road

V A L L E Y

Salt Lake

7 mi
11km

The
Grandstand

RACETRACK VALLEY

Hidden Valley

Sand Flat

🥾 **Marble Cany**

P A N A M

Marble Canyon

Cottonwood Canyon

New York Butte
10668ft
3252m

20 mi
32km

Ubehebe Peak
5678ft
1731m

The
Racetrack

Ulida
Flat

Dry Bone Canyon

To Manzanar, Bishop,
and Yosemite

Road conditions
require experienced
4-wheel drivers.

Homestake
Dry Camp
⛺

Lone Pine
🏨 🍴 ⛽ 🛏 🏕 ✈ 🚰

N E L S O N   R A N G E

11 mi
18km

In winter carry
chains. Road
may be closed.

Hunter
Mountain
7454ft
2272m

In winter carry
chains. Road
may be closed.

**Eastern Sierra
Interagency
Visitor Center**

136

O W E N S   V A L L E Y

18 mi
29km

Cerro Gordo Peak
9184ft
2799m

Lee
Flat

South Pass
5997ft
1828m

7 mi
11km

395

Keeler

Conglomerate
Mesa

Joshua
Tree
Forest

Santa

Los Angeles Aq.

21 mi
40km

Lemoigne

Death Valley

MOUNTAINS

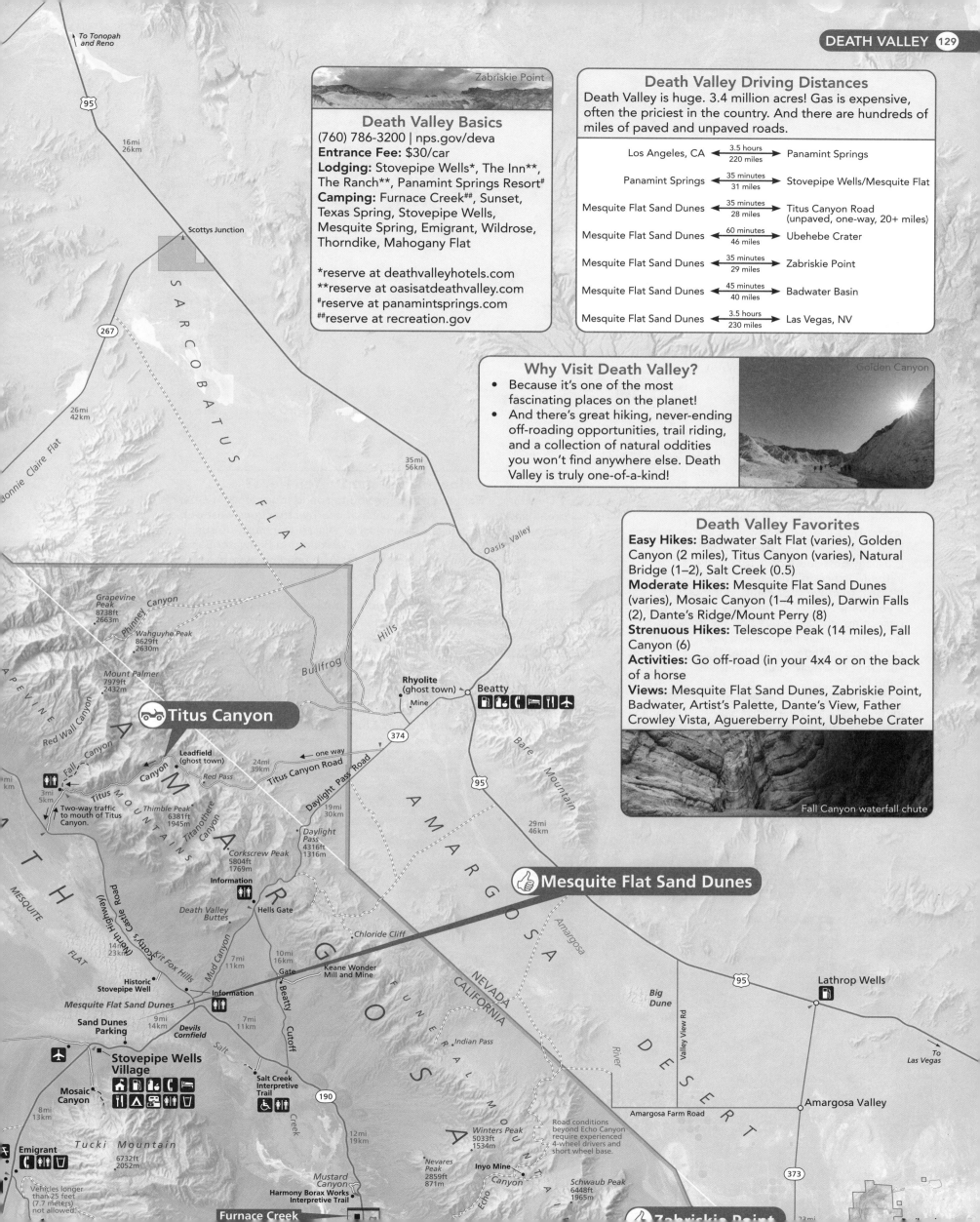

To Tonopah and Reno

95

16mi
26km

267

S A R C O B A T U S   F L A T

Scottys Junction

26mi
42km

Bonnie Claire Flat

35mi
56km

Oasis Valley

Death Valley Basics
Zabriskie Point

(760) 786-3200 | nps.gov/deva
Entrance Fee: $30/car
Lodging: Stovepipe Wells*, The Inn**,
The Ranch**, Panamint Springs Resort#
Camping: Furnace Creek##, Sunset,
Texas Spring, Stovepipe Wells,
Mesquite Spring, Emigrant, Wildrose,
Thorndike, Mahogany Flat

*reserve at deathvalleyhotels.com
**reserve at oasisatdeathvalley.com
#reserve at panamintsprings.com
##reserve at recreation.gov

Death Valley Driving Distances
Death Valley is huge. 3.4 million acres! Gas is expensive,
often the priciest in the country. And there are hundreds of
miles of paved and unpaved roads.

Los Angeles, CA	← 3.5 hours / 220 miles →	Panamint Springs
Panamint Springs	← 35 minutes / 31 miles →	Stovepipe Wells/Mesquite Flat
Mesquite Flat Sand Dunes	← 35 minutes / 28 miles →	Titus Canyon Road (unpaved, one-way, 20+ miles)
Mesquite Flat Sand Dunes	← 60 minutes / 46 miles →	Ubehebe Crater
Mesquite Flat Sand Dunes	← 35 minutes / 29 miles →	Zabriskie Point
Mesquite Flat Sand Dunes	← 45 minutes / 40 miles →	Badwater Basin
Mesquite Flat Sand Dunes	← 3.5 hours / 230 miles →	Las Vegas, NV

Why Visit Death Valley?
Golden Canyon
- Because it's one of the most fascinating places on the planet!
- And there's great hiking, never-ending off-roading opportunities, trail riding, and a collection of natural oddities you won't find anywhere else. Death Valley is truly one-of-a-kind!

Death Valley Favorites
Easy Hikes: Badwater Salt Flat (varies), Golden Canyon (2 miles), Titus Canyon (varies), Natural Bridge (1–2), Salt Creek (0.5)
Moderate Hikes: Mesquite Flat Sand Dunes (varies), Mosaic Canyon (1–4 miles), Darwin Falls (2), Dante's Ridge/Mount Perry (8)
Strenuous Hikes: Telescope Peak (14 miles), Fall Canyon (6)
Activities: Go off-road (in your 4x4 or on the back of a horse
Views: Mesquite Flat Sand Dunes, Zabriskie Point, Badwater, Artist's Palette, Dante's View, Father Crowley Vista, Aguereberry Point, Ubehebe Crater

Fall Canyon waterfall chute

Grapevine Peak
8738ft
2663m

Wahguyhe Peak
8629ft
2630m

Phinney Canyon

Mount Palmer
7979ft
2432m

Bullfrog

Hills

Rhyolite
(ghost town)
Mine

Beatty

374

95

Bare Mountain

Red Wall Canyon

Fall Canyon

Titus Canyon

Leadfield
(ghost town)
Red Pass

24mi
39km

one way

Titus Canyon Road

Daylight Pass Road

Two-way traffic
to mouth of Titus
Canyon.

Thimble Peak
6381ft
1945m

Titus Canyon

Titanothere Canyon

19mi
30km

Daylight
Pass
4316ft
1316m

Corkscrew Peak
5804ft
1769m

29mi
46km

Information

Death Valley
Buttes

Hells Gate

A M A R G O S A

Mesquite Flat Sand Dunes

Amargosa

Mud Canyon

Chloride Cliff

7mi
11km

Keane Wonder
Mill and Mine

Gate

10mi
16km

Kit Fox Hills

Scotty's Castle Road (North Highway)

14mi
23km

Information

NEVADA
CALIFORNIA

95

Big
Dune

Valley View Rd

Lathrop Wells

Historic
Stovepipe Well

Mesquite Flat Sand Dunes

Sand Dunes
Parking

Devils
Cornfield

9mi
14km

7mi
11km

Beatty Cutoff

Salt Creek

F U N E R A L

Indian Pass

River

To
Las Vegas

Stovepipe Wells Village

Mosaic
Canyon

8mi
13km

190

Salt Creek
Interpretive
Trail

Amargosa Valley

12mi
19km

Winters Peak
5033ft
1534m

Road conditions
beyond Echo Canyon
require experienced
4-wheel drivers and
short wheel base.

Amargosa Farm Road

D E S E R T

373

Emigrant

6732ft
2052m

Tucki Mountain

Vehicles longer
than 25 feet
(7.7 meters)
not allowed.

Nevares
Peak
2859ft
871m

Mustard
Canyon

Harmony Borax Works
Interpretive Trail

Inyo Mine

Echo Canyon

Schwaub Peak
6448ft
1965m

Furnace Creek

Zabriskie Point

Darwin Falls

What You Need to Know

- The park famously has no rivals when it comes to heat and drought. Still, there are plenty of good times to visit (even summer is a good time if you plan to climb 11,049-ft Telescope Peak). Fall through spring is best. Winter does get cool, especially at night.

- Most visitors simply drive-thru. Don't do this. The park is absolutely incredible.

- You need to come prepared. With that said, you'll find gas, food, and water at Panamint Springs, Stovepipe Wells, and Furnace Creek. I tend to refuel every possible chance while in the park.

- Superblooms are newsworthy events. They depend on winter rain, so they're slightly unpredictable. If you have some flexibility, monitor the park's social media feeds. They'll let you know what's blooming. The flower-stravaganza is usually best south of Artist's Drive in the March/April/May timeframe.

- It's best to move your camp, but if you want to have a stationary basecamp, choose Stovepipe Wells. It's fairly centrally located and you cannot go wrong with sunrise/sunset at nearby Mesquite Flat Sand Dunes.

- Badwater Basin is the lowest point in the Americas. Take about a 15–20 minute walk and you'll reach the flats where you can have fun with perspective.

How Much Time Do You Have?

1 Day: First, I want to encourage you to spend more time. The park is great, and there are a whole bunch of nearby attractions west of the park along US-395 (like Alabama Hills). Alas, if you must, do sunrise at Zabriskie Point, hike Golden Canyon, walk around Badwater Basin, and then hike trails near Stovepipe Wells before heading over to Mesquite Flat Sand Dunes an hour or two before sunset.

2 Days: If you enjoy horseback riding and know what you're doing, this is a pretty good place to get a private ride. Drive Titus Canyon Road. It'll take a couple hours. I've seen all kinds of cars make it but more ground clearance means less stress. And then continue up to Ubehebe Crater and Scotty's Castle.

3 Days: Depending on your vehicle you could head to The Racetrack. Jeep rentals are available in the park at Farabee's (farabeejeeps.com). But this is a park of exploration. Study the map and you'll find all sorts of things to seek out. And, like me, you'll eagerly await your next visit.

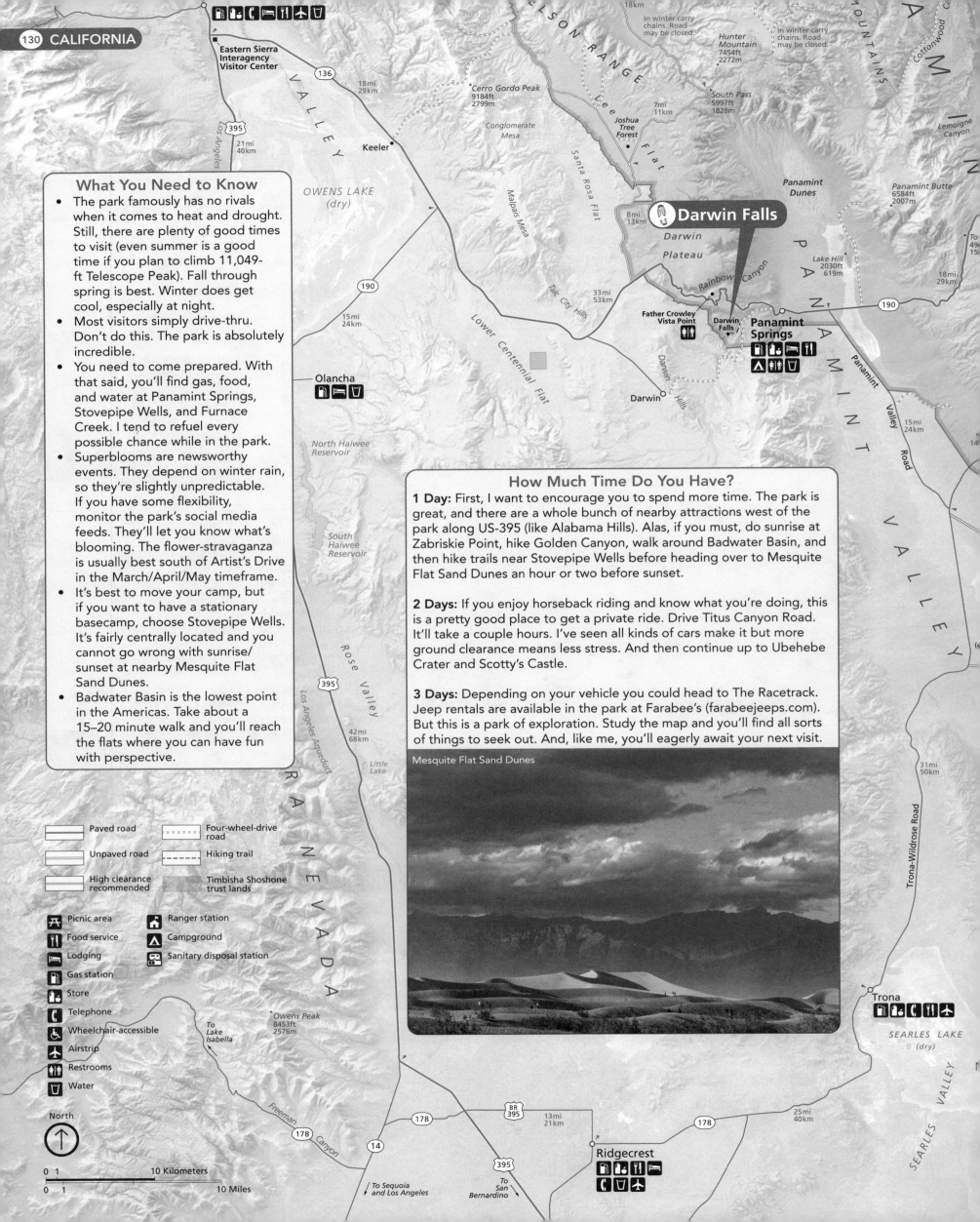

Mesquite Flat Sand Dunes

Legend

Paved road
Unpaved road
High clearance recommended
Four-wheel-drive road
Hiking trail
Timbisha Shoshone trust lands

Picnic area
Food service
Lodging
Gas station
Store
Telephone
Wheelchair-accessible
Airstrip
Restrooms
Water

Ranger station
Campground
Sanitary disposal station

North

0   1   10 Kilometers
0   1   10 Miles

Map labels:

Eastern Sierra Interagency Visitor Center

136
395

Keeler

OWENS LAKE (dry)

190

Olancha

North Haiwee Reservoir

South Haiwee Reservoir

395

Rose Valley

Little Lake

Los Angeles Aqueduct

SIERRA NEVADA

To Lake Isabella

Owens Peak 8453ft 2576m

Freeman Canyon

178
14
178
BR 395
395

To Sequoia and Los Angeles

To San Bernardino

Ridgecrest

18mi 29km
21mi 40km
18mi 29km
15mi 24km
42mi 68km
13mi 21km
25mi 40km

Trona

SEARLES LAKE (dry)

SEARLES VALLEY

Trona-Wildrose Road

31mi 50km

Panamint Valley Road

15mi 24km

PANAMINT VALLEY

Darwin Hills

Darwin

Darwin Falls

Father Crowley Vista Point

Panamint Springs

190

Rainbow Canyon

Darwin Canyon

Darwin Plateau

Lake Hill 2030ft 619m

33mi 53km

8mi 13km

Talc City Hills

Lower Centennial Flat

Malpais Mesa

Santa Rosa Flat

Conglomerate Mesa

Cerro Gordo Peak 9184ft 2799m

Joshua Tree Forest

South Pass 5997ft 1828m

7mi 11km

Hunter Mountain 7454ft 2272m

In winter carry chains. Road may be closed.

18km

Panamint Dunes

Panamint Butte 6584ft 2007m

18mi 29km

Lemoigne Canyon

Cottonwood C...

To 49...

NELSON RANGE

Lee Flat

VALLEY

PANAMINT

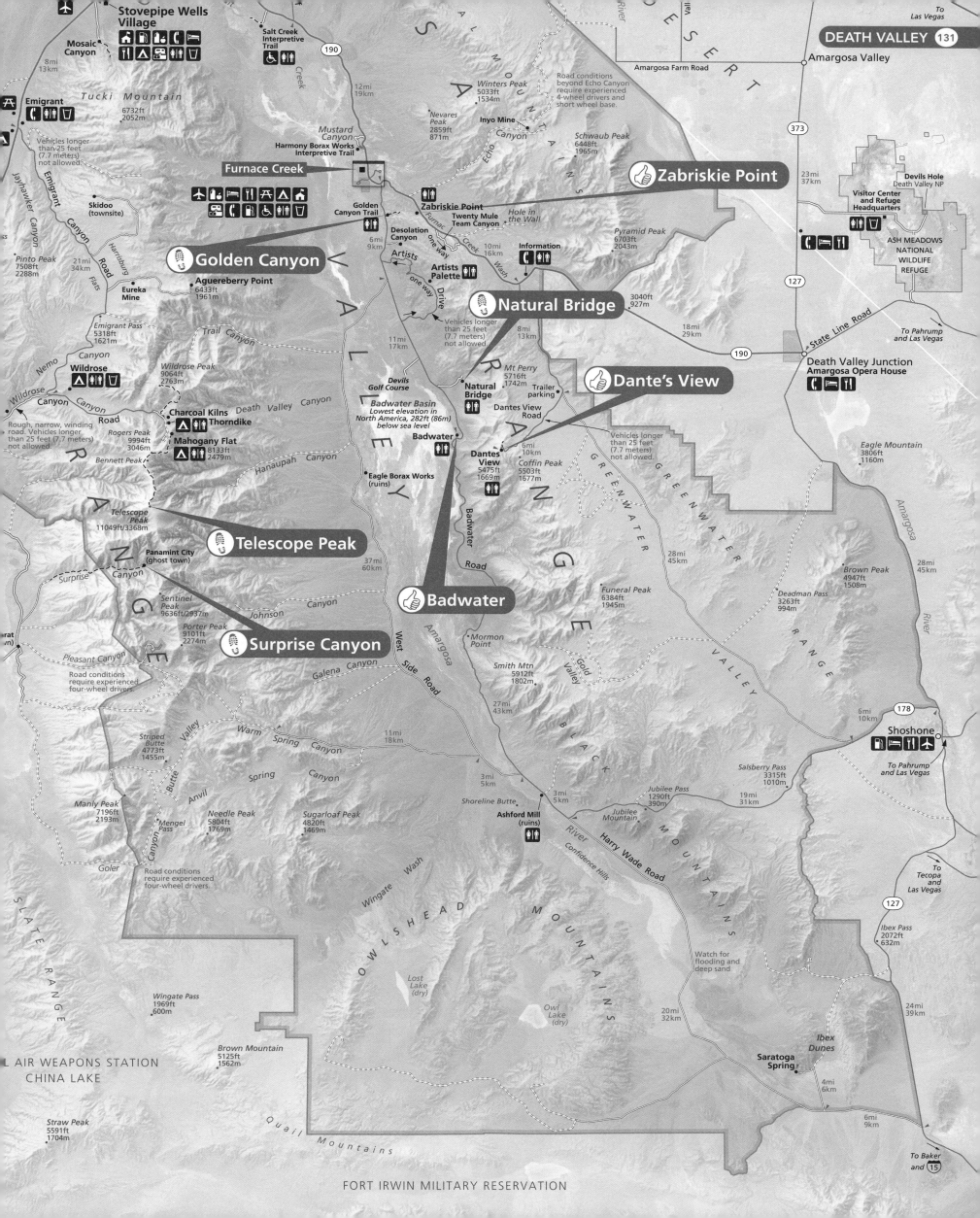

Stovepipe Wells Village

Mosaic Canyon

Salt Creek Interpretive Trail

8mi 13km

Emigrant

Tucki Mountain

6732ft 2052m

190

12mi 19km

Mustard Canyon

Winters Peak 5033ft 1534m

To Las Vegas

Amargosa Valley

Amargosa Farm Road

373

Vehicles longer than 25 feet (7.7 meters) not allowed

Skidoo (townsite)

Harrisburg Flats

Nevares Peak 2859ft 871m

Inyo Mine

Schwaub Peak 6448ft 1965m

Devils Hole Death Valley NP

Visitor Center and Refuge Headquarters

ASH MEADOWS NATIONAL WILDLIFE REFUGE

23mi 37km

Pinto Peak 7508ft 2288m

21mi 34km

Emigrant Pass 5318ft 1621m

Eureka Mine

Harmony Borax Works Interpretive Trail

Furnace Creek

Golden Canyon Trail

Zabriskie Point

Twenty Mule Team Canyon

Hole in the Wall

Zabriskie Point

Pyramid Peak 6703ft 2043m

18mi 29km

Golden Canyon

Aguereberry Point 6433ft 1961m

Desolation Canyon

Artists Palette

Artists

one way

Information

127

3040ft 927m

State Line Road

To Pahrump and Las Vegas

Wildrose Peak 9064ft 2763m

Natural Bridge

Mt Perry 5716ft 1742m

190

Death Valley Junction Amargosa Opera House

8mi 13km

Wildrose

Charcoal Kilns

Thorndike

Mahogany Flat 8133ft 2479m

Rogers Peak 9994ft 3046m

Devils Golf Course

Badwater Basin Lowest elevation in North America, 282ft (86m) below sea level

Natural Bridge

Trailer parking

Dantes View Road

Dante's View

Vehicles longer than 25 feet (7.7 meters) not allowed

Eagle Mountain 3806ft 1160m

Bennett Peak

Hanaupah Canyon

Badwater

Dantes View 5475ft 1669m

Coffin Peak 5503ft 1677m

6mi 10km

GREENWATER

28mi 45km

Telescope Peak 11049ft/3368m

Telescope Peak

Panamint City (ghost town)

Eagle Borax Works (ruins)

VALLEY

Brown Peak 4947ft 1508m

28mi 45km

Deadman Pass 3263ft 994m

Sentinel Peak 9636ft/2937m

Johnson Canyon

Funeral Peak 6384ft 1945m

Porter Peak 9101ft 2274m

Surprise Canyon

Galena Canyon

West Side Road

Amargosa River

Mormon Point

Smith Mtn 5912ft 1802m

Gold Valley

178

6mi 10km

Shoshone

To Pahrump and Las Vegas

Pleasant Canyon

Road conditions require experienced four-wheel drivers.

Striped Butte 4773ft 1455m

Warm Spring Canyon

11mi 18km

Salsberry Pass 3315ft 1010m

19mi 31km

Manly Peak 7196ft 2193m

Needle Peak 5804ft 1769m

Sugarloaf Peak 4820ft 1469m

Anvil Spring Canyon

3mi 5km

Shoreline Butte

Ashford Mill (ruins)

3mi 5km

Jubilee Pass 1290ft 390m

Jubilee Mountain

To Tecopa and Las Vegas

127

Mengel Pass

Goler

Road conditions require experienced four-wheel drivers.

Wingate Wash

River

Harry Wade Road

Confidence Hills

Ibex Pass 2072ft 632m

Wingate Pass 1969ft 600m

Lost Lake (dry)

Owl Lake (dry)

Watch for flooding and deep sand

24mi 39km

Brown Mountain 5125ft 1562m

OWLSHEAD MOUNTAINS

20mi 32km

Ibex Dunes

AIR WEAPONS STATION CHINA LAKE

Straw Peak 5591ft 1704m

Quail Mountains

Saratoga Spring

4mi 6km

6mi 9km

To Baker and 15

FORT IRWIN MILITARY RESERVATION

DINKEY
LAKES
WILDERNESS

JOHN MUIR

WILDERNESS

SIERRA NATIONAL FOREST

SEQUOIA NATIONAL FOREST

MONARCH WILDERNESS

MONARCH WILDERNESS

KINGS CANYON

SEQUOIA NATIONAL FOREST

KINGS CANYON NATIONAL PARK

JOHN MUIR WILDERNESS

INYO NATIONAL FOREST

OWENS VALLEY

CONVERSE BASIN GROVE

Grant Grove Village to Hume Lake

Gater road closed in winter!
Kings Canyon Lodge (closed in winter)

Kings Canyon Scenic Byway

Roads End Permit Station

180

395

WISHON RESERVOIR

COURTRIGHT RESERVOIR

Kings River

North Fork

Rancheria Creek

Kings River

Post Corral Creek

South Fork

San Joaquin River

LE CONTE DIVIDE

GLACIER DIVIDE

GODDARD CANYON

EVOLUTION BASIN

LE CONTE CANYON

DEVILS CRAGS

ENCHANTED GORGE

Goddard Creek

WHITE DIVIDE

KETTLE RIDGE

Blue Canyon Creek

Crown Creek

Middle Fork

Kings River

Kennedy Creek

Dougherty Creek

SIMPSON MEADOW

LOST CANYON

Kings River

South Fork Kings River

MURO BLANCO

CIRQUE CREST

Garlinda Creek

Cartridge Creek

Amphitheater Lake

Mather Creek

PALISADE CREST

JOHN MUIR TRAIL and PACIFIC CREST TRAIL

Palisade Creek

UPPER BASIN

DUSY BASIN

South Lake

Lake Sabrina

Middle Fork

Bishop Creek

South Fork Bishop Creek

Big Pine Creek

Woods Creek Trail

PARADISE VALLEY

Woods Creek

Bubbs Creek

Gardiner Creek

Mist Falls

The Sphinx

Charlotte Lake

Woods Lake

Bench Lake

Pinchot Pass 12050ft

Sawmill Creek

Owens River

To Bishop

Big Pine 3985ft

To Independence and Lone Pine

KINGS CANYON VALLEY

Spanish Mountain 10051ft

Obelisk 9700ft

Tehipite Dome 7708ft

TEHIPITE VALLEY

Kettle Dome 9446ft

Wren Peak 9450ft

Burnt Mountain 10608ft

Finger Peak 12404ft

Tunemah Peak 11894ft

Windy Peak 8867ft

Kennedy Pass 10900ft

Granite Pass 10673ft

Marion Peak 12719ft

Blackcap Mountain 11559ft

Mount Reinstein 12604ft

Hell for Sure Pass 11297ft

Mount Henry 12196ft

Mount McGee 12969ft

The Hermit 12360ft

Mount Goddard 13568ft

Charybdis 13091ft

Muir Pass 11955ft

Black Giant 13330ft

Le Conte Canyon 8720ft

Pavilion Dome 11846ft

Mount Goethe 13264ft

Mount Darwin 13830ft

Piute Pass 11423ft

McClure Meadow 9600ft

Mount Powell 13361ft

North Palisade 14242ft

Middle Palisade 14040ft

Mount Pinchot 13495ft

Split Mountain 14058ft

Striped Mountain 13160ft

Taboose Pass 11400ft

Mather Pass 12100ft

Pyramid Peak 12777ft

Arrow Peak 12958ft

Glacier Monument 11165ft

Mount Gardiner 12907ft

Mount Clarence King 12905ft

Rae Lakes 10596ft

Glen Pass 11978ft

Diamond Peak 13126ft

Mount Baxter 13125ft

Sawmill Pass 11347ft

Colosseum Mountain 12473ft

Kearsarge Pass 11823ft

Charlotte Lake

John Muir/Pacific Crest

Rae Lakes Loop

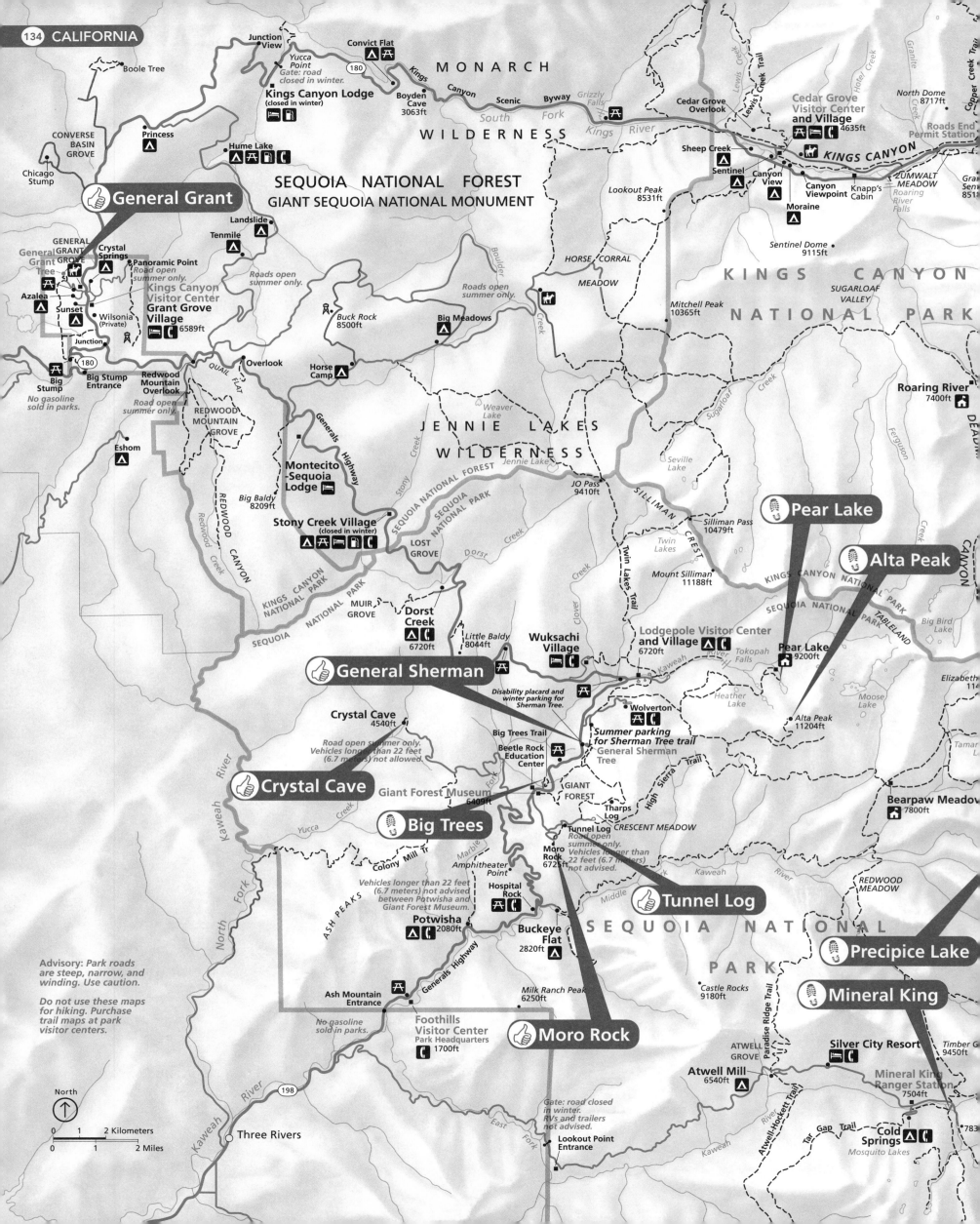

MONARCH WILDERNESS

Boole Tree

Junction View

Yucca Point
Gate: road closed in winter.

Convict Flat

Kings Canyon Lodge
(closed in winter)

Boyden Cave
3063ft

Kings Canyon Scenic Byway

Grizzly Falls

South Fork Kings River

Cedar Grove Overlook

Cedar Grove Visitor Center and Village
4635ft

North Dome
8717ft

Roads End Permit Station

Lewis Creek

Lewis Creek Trail

Copper Creek Trail

Granite Creek

Hotel Creek

KINGS CANYON

Sheep Creek

Sentinel

Canyon View

Canyon Viewpoint

Knapp's Cabin

ZUMWALT MEADOW

Roaring River Falls

Grand Sentinel
8518

CONVERSE BASIN GROVE

Princess

SEQUOIA NATIONAL FOREST
GIANT SEQUOIA NATIONAL MONUMENT

Lookout Peak
8531ft

Moraine

KINGS CANYON

Chicago Stump

👍 General Grant

Landslide

Tenmile

HORSE CORRAL MEADOW

Sentinel Dome
9115ft

NATIONAL PARK

GENERAL GRANT GROVE

General Grant Tree

Crystal Springs

Panoramic Point
Road open summer only.

Roads open summer only.

Roads open summer only.

Mitchell Peak
10365ft

SUGARLOAF VALLEY

Azalea

Sunset

Wilsonia
(Private)

Kings Canyon Visitor Center

Grant Grove Village
6589ft

Buck Rock
8500ft

Big Meadows

Boulder Creek

Sugarloaf Creek

Roaring River
7400ft

Junction

180

Big Stump

Big Stump Entrance

Redwood Mountain Overlook
Road open summer only.

Overlook

Horse Camp

JENNIE LAKES

Weaver Lake

DEADMAN CANYON

No gasoline sold in parks.

QUAIL FLAT

REDWOOD MOUNTAIN GROVE

WILDERNESS

Jennie Lake

Seville Lake

Ferguson Creek

Eshom

REDWOOD CANYON

Generals Highway

Stony Creek

JO Pass
9410ft

SILLIMAN CREST

Big Baldy
8209ft

Montecito-Sequoia Lodge

SEQUOIA NATIONAL FOREST

Silliman Pass
10479ft

👣 Pear Lake

KINGS CANYON NATIONAL PARK

Creek

Stony Creek Village
(closed in winter)

SEQUOIA NATIONAL PARK

LOST GROVE

Dorst Creek

Twin Lakes

Mount Silliman
11188ft

Twin Lakes Trail

👣 Alta Peak

SEQUOIA NATIONAL PARK

TABLELAND

Big Bird Lake

KINGS CANYON NATIONAL PARK

MUIR GROVE

SEQUOIA NATIONAL FOREST

Dorst Creek
6720ft

Little Baldy
8044ft

Wuksachi Village

Lodgepole Visitor Center and Village
6720ft

Clover Creek

Pear Lake
9200ft

Elizabeth
114

Moose Lake

👍 General Sherman

Crystal Cave
4540ft

Road open summer only. Vehicles longer than 22 feet (6.7 meters) not allowed.

Big Trees Trail

Beetle Rock Education Center

Disability placard and winter parking for Sherman Tree.

Wolverton

Summer parking for Sherman Tree trail
General Sherman Tree

Heather Lake

Tokopah Falls

Kaweah River

Alta Peak
11204ft

👍 Crystal Cave

Giant Forest Museum
6409ft

GIANT FOREST

Tharps Log

CRESCENT MEADOW

High Sierra Trail

Bearpaw Meadow
7800ft

REDWOOD MEADOW

Kaweah River

Colony Mill Tr

Yucca Creek

👣 Big Trees

Marble Fork

Amphitheater Point

Moro Rock
6725ft

Road open summer only. Vehicles longer than 22 feet (6.7 meters) not advised.

Kaweah River

Tunnel Log

Middle Fork Kaweah

SEQUOIA NATIONAL PARK

Kaweah River

ASH PEAKS

Vehicles longer than 22 feet (6.7 meters) not advised between Potwisha and Giant Forest Museum.

Hospital Rock

👍 Tunnel Log

North Fork

Potwisha
2080ft

Buckeye Flat
2820ft

Milk Ranch Peak
6250ft

👣 Precipice Lake

Advisory: Park roads are steep, narrow, and winding. Use caution.

Do not use these maps for hiking. Purchase trail maps at park visitor centers.

Ash Mountain Entrance

Generals Highway

Castle Rocks
9180ft

Paradise Ridge Trail

👣 Mineral King

No gasoline sold in parks.

Foothills Visitor Center
Park Headquarters
1700ft

👍 Moro Rock

Silver City Resort

Timber G
9450ft

ATWELL GROVE

North

Atwell Mill
6540ft

Mineral King Ranger Station
7504ft

0   1   2 Kilometers
0   1   2 Miles

198

Three Rivers

Kaweah River

East Fork Kaweah

Gate: road closed in winter. RVs and trailers not advised.

Lookout Point Entrance

Atwell-Hackett Trail

Tar Gap Trail

Cold Springs
7836

Mosquito Lakes

Death Valley–Sequoia–Kings Canyon–Yosemite Regions

Greater Yosemite Area

Yosemite Valley to Lake Tahoe and Reno
218 miles / 351 kilometers

North

0   10   20 Kilometers
0   10   20 Miles

STANISLAUS NATIONAL FOREST

YOSEMITE NATIONAL PARK
Road open summer only

Groveland (120)

Mono Basin Scenic Area Visitor Center
Lee Vining (395)

INYO NATIONAL FOREST

NEVADA / CALIFORNIA

El Portal (140)
(49)
Midpines
Mariposa
Fish Camp
Mammoth Lakes

DEVILS POSTPILE NATIONAL MONUMENT

SIERRA NEVADA

Yosemite Valley to San Francisco
195 miles
314 kilometers

(6)

INYO NATIONAL FOREST

Oakhurst
Merced (99)
(41)

SIERRA NATIONAL FOREST

Bishop

Big Pine

Fresno (180)

KINGS CANYON NATIONAL PARK

(395)

SEQUOIA NF
GIANT SEQUOIA NM
Road open summer only

DEATH VALLEY NATIONAL PARK

(33)
(5)

Independence
MANZANAR NATIONAL HISTORIC SITE
Eastern Sierra Interagency Visitor Center
Lone Pine

SEQUOIA NATIONAL PARK

Three Rivers

Visalia (198)

INYO NATIONAL FOREST

(136)
(190)

SEQUOIA NF
GIANT SEQUOIA NM

What You Need to Know About Sequoia & Kings Canyon

- Summer is the most popular time, but spring (wildflowers and super-charged waterfalls) and fall (smaller crowds and snow-free trails) are good too. Winter can be magical as well. Bring your tire chains and cross-country skis and have some fun.
- It's another park close to a fairly large population center, so weekends receive a considerable visitation boost. Try to travel mid-week.
- In summer the park runs four free shuttle routes between Dorst Campground and Crescent Meadow. Using it is a good idea.
- Sequoia Shuttle (sequoiashuttle.com) will get you from Visalia to Giant Forest Museum for $20/person. That includes the entrance fee.
- Nearby Yosemite National Park is great because you drive right into one of the most heavenly places on the planet. Sequoia and Kings Canyon are a little different. There are areas as stunning as Yosemite, but you have to work (backpack) to reach them.
- With that said, there are many worthwhile attractions for motorists and day hikers.
- Vehicles longer than 22 feet are not advised to travel between Foothills Visitor Center and Giant Forest Museum (or to Crystal Cave).
- Be sure to spend some time with the giant sequoias. General Sherman and General Grant are easily seen but there are other groves within the park.
- There are a bunch of great backpacking options: Mount Whitney, Rae Lakes Loop, and a bunch of options from Mineral King or Crescent Meadow (like up to Kaweah Gap).
- Sequoia Camp (sequoiahighsierracamp.com) and Bearpaw Camp (visitsequoia.com) offer backcountry tent cabins (including meals).
- Menacing marmots eat rubber seals, hosing, and electrical wiring at Mineral King. The current solution is wrapping vehicles with tarp (especially early in the hiking season).

How Much Time Do You Have?

1 Day: You don't need a whole lot of time here if you're staying near the roads. It's a whole different ball game heading into the backcountry. With one day, go to Giant Forest, checking out General Sherman. Head over to Crescent Meadow for Moro Rock and Tunnel Log. If you're looking for a good tough hike, drive to Mineral King (Mosquito Lakes or Eagle Lake) or spend the day at Wolverton (Lakes or Alta Trails). Those are full day hikes. An alternative option would be to book a night in the backcountry at Bearpaw Camp and explore that area, like hiking to Precipice Lake.

2 Days: Cross off a few more hikes in Sequoia or head over to Kings Canyon (Mist Falls, General Grant, and Big Stump Loop are good hikes).

3 Days: It'd be pretty easy to spend three days dayhiking, but this is a place to really think about backpacking. It's a special place. And then there's the Eastern Sierra too. You can hike around Lone Pine at the foot of Mount Whitney! CA-395 is fantastic too.

Black bear near Mineral King

Sequoia & Kings Canyon Basics

(559) 565-3341 | nps.gov/seki
Entrance Fee: $35/car
Sequoia Lodging: Wuksachi Lodge*
Kings Canyon Lodging: John Muir Lodge*, Grant Grove Cabins*, Cedar Grove Lodge*,
Sequoia Camping: Potwisha**, Buckeye Flat**, South Fork, Atwell Mill, Cold Springs, Lodgepole**
Kings Canyon Camping: Dorst Creek**, Azalea, Crystal Springs, Sunset, Sentinel**, Sheep Creek, Canyon View, Moraine

*reserve at visitsequoia.com
**reserve at recreation.gov

Sequoia & Kings Canyon Driving Distances

Sequoia is fairly accessible to motorists. Kings Canyon was designed with backpackers in mind.

From	Time / Distance	To
Fresno, CA	90 minutes / 83 miles	Foothills VC
Foothills VC	90 minutes / 27 miles	Mineral King
Foothills VC	55 minutes / 20 miles	Crystal Cave
Foothills VC	50 minutes / 18 miles	Crescent Meadow
Crescent Meadow	20 minutes / 7 miles	Lodgepole VC
Lodgepole VC	50 minutes / 26 miles	Grant Grove Village
Grant Grove Village	60 minutes / 34 miles	Roads End

Walk-through trees

Why Visit Sequoia & Kings Canyon?
- To enjoy a premier backpacking destination
- To look up at some of the most massive living organisms on earth, the giant sequoias
- To take in a good mix of caves and waterfalls and trees and wildlife

Sequoia & Kings Canyon Favorites
Easy Hikes: General Grant (0.7 mile), Big Trees (1.3), Sunset Rock (2)
Moderate Hikes: Monarch Lakes (8.4), General Sherman (1), Eagle Lake (6.8), Moro Rock (0.5), Big Baldy Ridge (4), Franklin Lakes (10.8), Mist Falls (8)
Strenuous Hikes: Mosquito Lakes (7.2), Lakes (Pear Lake) (12), Rae Lakes Loop (41 miles), Alta Peak (13.8), Crystal Lake (9.8)
Extreme Hikes: Mount Whitney (multi-day)
Activities: Tour Crystal Cave, trail riding
Views: Moro Rock, Tunnel Log, Tunnel Rock, Amphitheater Point

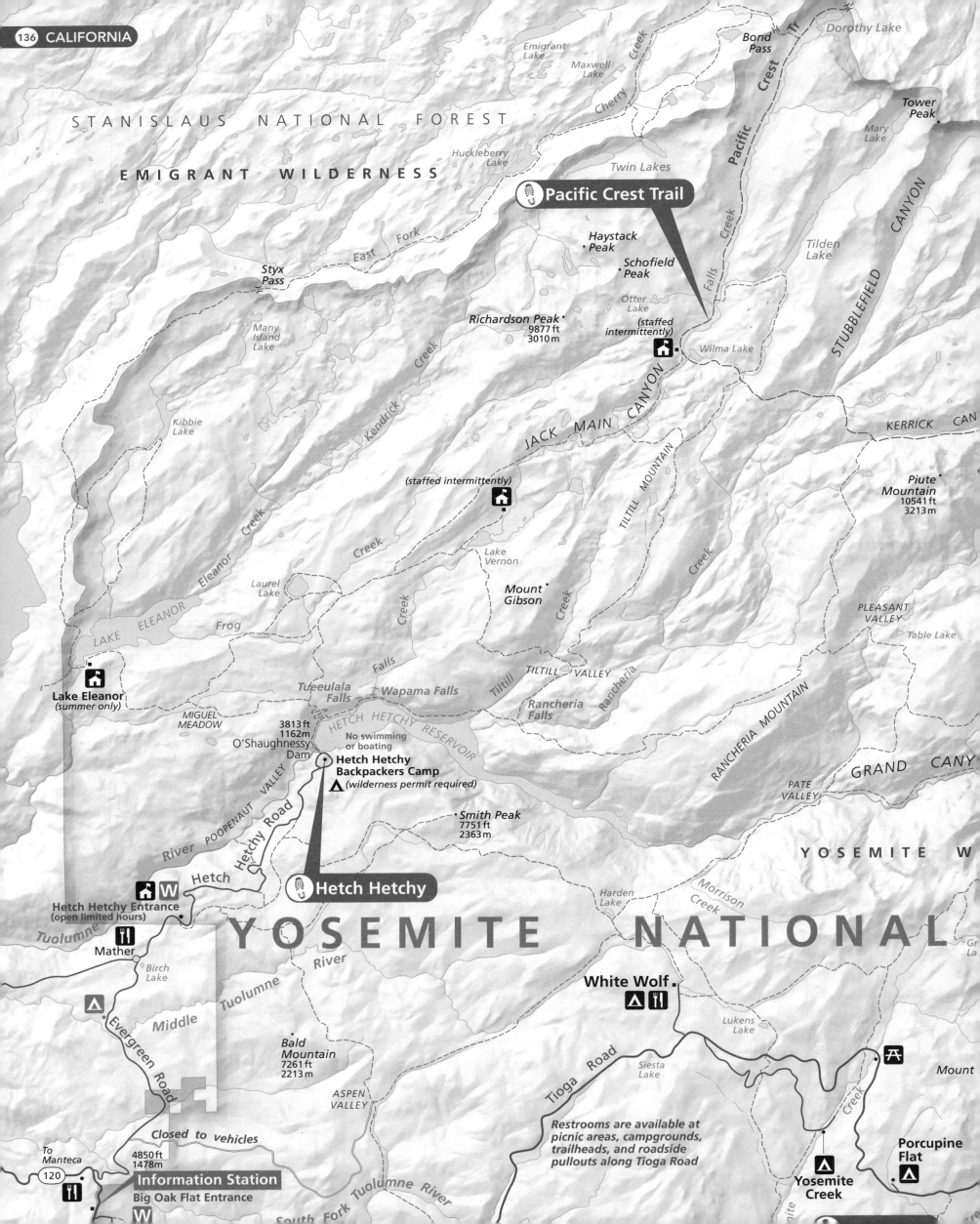

STANISLAUS NATIONAL FOREST

EMIGRANT WILDERNESS

Emigrant Lake

Maxwell Lake

Cherry Creek

Bond Pass

Dorothy Lake

Tower Peak

Huckleberry Lake

Twin Lakes

Mary Lake

Pacific Crest Trail

Haystack Peak

Schofield Peak

Styx Pass

East Fork

Richardson Peak 9877 ft 3010 m

Otter Lake

(staffed intermittently)

Wilma Lake

Falls Creek

Tilden Lake

STUBBLEFIELD CANYON

Many Island Lake

Kendrick Creek

JACK MAIN CANYON

KERRICK CAN

Kibbie Lake

Piute Mountain 10541 ft 3213 m

(staffed intermittently)

Eleanor Creek

Creek

Lake Vernon

Tiltill Creek

TILTILL MOUNTAIN

Laurel Lake

Mount Gibson

PLEASANT VALLEY

Table Lake

LAKE ELEANOR

Frog Creek

Creek

Rancheria Creek

Lake Eleanor (summer only)

Falls

Tueeulala Falls

Wapama Falls

TILTILL VALLEY

Rancheria Falls

RANCHERIA MOUNTAIN

GRAND CANY

Miguel Meadow

3813 ft 1162 m

HETCH HETCHY RESERVOIR

No swimming or boating

Tiltill

Rancheria

PATE VALLEY

O'Shaughnessy Dam

Hetch Hetchy Backpackers Camp △ (wilderness permit required)

Smith Peak 7751 ft 2363 m

River

POOPENAUT VALLEY

Hetchy Road

Hetch Hetchy

YOSEMITE W

Harden Lake

Morrison Creek

Hetch

Hetch Hetchy Entrance (open limited hours)

Tuolumne

Mather 🍴

Birch Lake

YOSEMITE   NATIONAL

Tuolumne River

△

Middle

Evergreen Road

White Wolf △ 🍴

Lukens Lake

Bald Mountain 7261 ft 2213 m

ASPEN VALLEY

Tioga Road

Siesta Lake

Mount

Creek

Porcupine Flat

Closed to vehicles

4850 ft 1478 m

To Manteca (120) 🍴

Information Station Big Oak Flat Entrance

W

South Fork Tuolumne River

Restrooms are available at picnic areas, campgrounds, trailheads, and roadside pullouts along Tioga Road

Yosemite Creek △

HUMBOLDT-TOIYABE
NATIONAL FOREST

H O O V E R   W I L D E R N E S S

Buckeye Pass
9572 ft
2917 m

Barney
Lake

Peeler
Lake

Crown
Lake

Rock Island
Pass

SAWTOOTH RIDGE

Matterhorn
Peak

Slide
Mountain

Burro
Pass

Whorl
Mountain

Virginia
Peak

Virginia Pass

Green
Lake

Summit
Lake

Virginia Lakes

167

395

Rancheria

Creek

Piute Creek

CANYON

Spiller Creek

Smedberg
Lake

Benson
Pass

Volunteer
Peak

Rodgers
Lake

Pettit Peak
10788 ft
3288 m

Virginia
Lake

MATTERHORN

VIRGINIA

CANYON

Creek

Return

Pacific Crest Trail

McCabe   Creek

McCabe Lakes

Upper
McCabe
Lake

Lundy
Lake

I N Y O   N A T I O N A L   F O R E S T

North Peak

Roosevelt
Lake

Mount
Conness
12590 ft
3837 m

HARVEY MONROE
HALL RESEARCH
NATURAL AREA

White
Mountain

Saddlebag
Lake

Gardisky
Lake

Tioga Peak
11526 ft
3513 m

Highway 120
closed in winter

OF THE TUOLUMNE RIVER

Virginia
Lake

Waterwheel
Falls

Tuolumne

Cold

Canyon

Creek

Young Lakes

Ragged
Peak

Conness   Creek

Creek

Granite
Lakes

Gaylor
Peak

Ellery Lake

Tioga Lake

120

 **High Sierra Camps**

Glen Aulin

River

Delaney

Dog Lake

Gaylor Lakes

Tioga Pass Entrance
9945 ft
3031 m

Tioga Road closed approx. November
to May west of this point

P A R K

Pothole
Dome

Lembert Dome

TUOLUMNE

MEADOWS

DANA MEADOWS

Dana

Fork

Mount Dana
13057 ft
3979 m

D E R N E S S

Tuolumne Peak
10845 ft
3306 m

Fairview
Dome

Medlicott
Dome

Cathedral
Peak
10940 ft
3335 m

Tioga Road

John Muir

Trail

Budd
Lake

Elizabeth Lake

**Tuolumne Meadows
Visitor Center**

W

Facilities along Tioga Road
available summer only

Mount Gibbs
12764 ft
3890 m

Mammoth
Peak
12117 ft
3693 m

Mono Pass
10604 ft
3232 m

May
Lake

...850 ft
...307 m

May Lake

Tresidder
Peak

Tenaya Lake

Cathedral
Lakes

Elizabeth Lake

Unicorn Peak

Johnson
Peak

Lyell

Fork

Creek

Rafferty

CATHEDRAL

LYELL   CANYON

KUNA CREST

Parker
Pass

Olmsted
Point

Sunrise
Lakes

Echo
Peaks

Nelson
Lake

Vogelsang

Evelyn
Lake

Potter
Point

Koip Peak
12962 ft
3950 m

Parker Pass

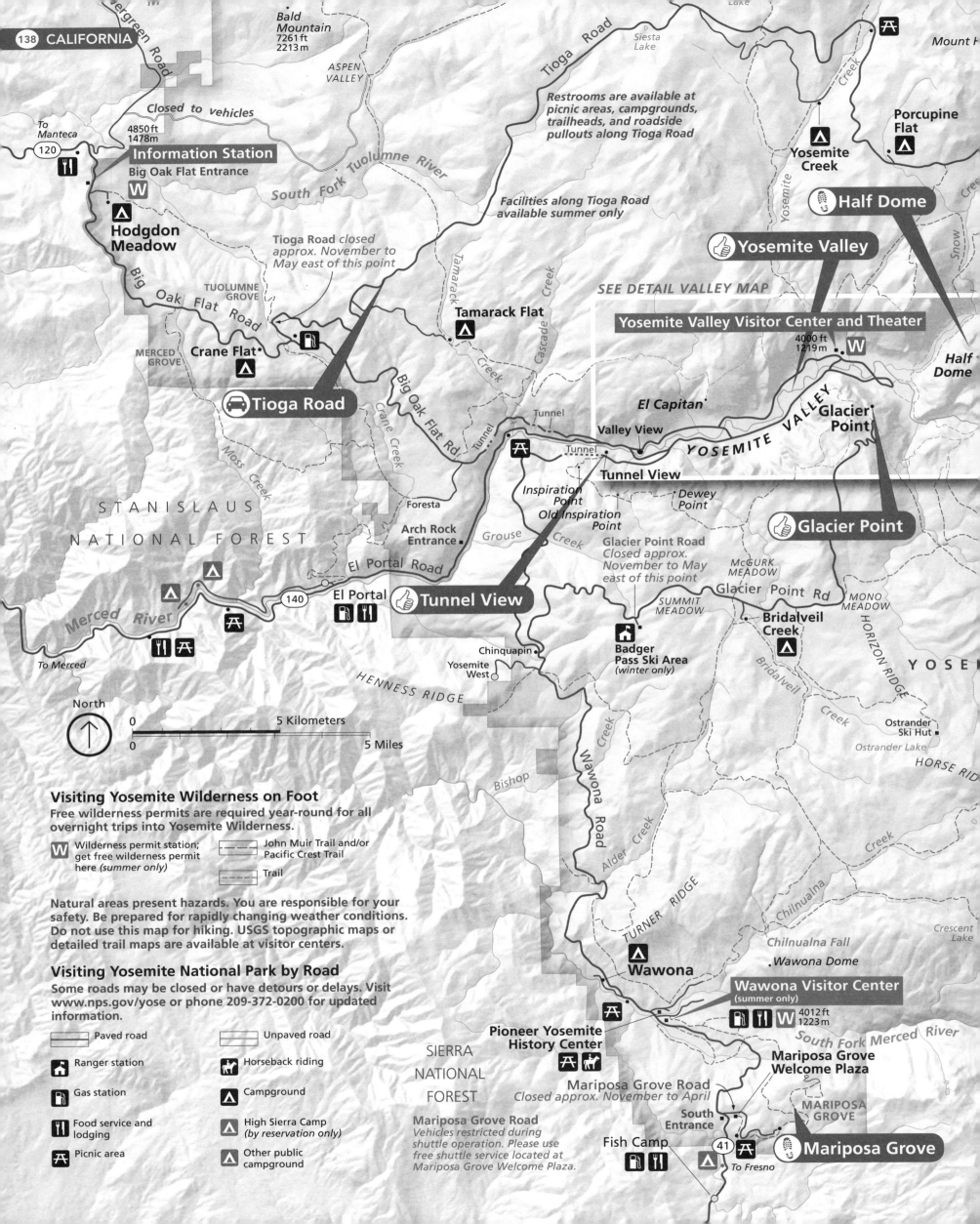

Bald Mountain
7261 ft
2213 m

ASPEN VALLEY

Porcupine Flat

Mount H...

Closed to vehicles

4850 ft
1478 m

To Manteca

120

Information Station
Big Oak Flat Entrance

W

South Fork Tuolumne River

Tioga Road

Siesta Lake

Restrooms are available at picnic areas, campgrounds, trailheads, and roadside pullouts along Tioga Road.

Yosemite Creek

Half Dome

Hodgdon Meadow

Tioga Road closed approx. November to May east of this point

Facilities along Tioga Road available summer only

Yosemite Valley

TUOLUMNE GROVE

Tamarack Flat

SEE DETAIL VALLEY MAP

Half Dome

Yosemite Valley Visitor Center and Theater

4000 ft
1219 m

W

MERCED GROVE

Crane Flat

Tioga Road

El Capitan

Valley View

YOSEMITE VALLEY

Glacier Point

Glacier Point

Tunnel

Tunnel

Tunnel View

STANISLAUS

Foresta

Inspiration Point
Old Inspiration Point

Dewey Point

Glacier Point

NATIONAL FOREST

Arch Rock Entrance

Grouse Creek

Glacier Point Road Closed approx. November to May east of this point

McGURK MEADOW

MONO MEADOW

Glacier Point Rd

El Portal Road

El Portal

Tunnel View

SUMMIT MEADOW

Bridalveil Creek

140

To Merced

Merced River

Chinquapin

Yosemite West

Badger Pass Ski Area (winter only)

Bridalveil Creek

Y

HORIZON RIDGE

HENNESS RIDGE

Ostrander Ski Hut

Ostrander Lake

HORSE RID...

North

0   5 Kilometers
0   5 Miles

Bishop Creek

Wawona Road

Alder Creek

TURNER RIDGE

Chilnualna Creek

Crescent Lake

Visiting Yosemite Wilderness on Foot

Free wilderness permits are required year-round for all overnight trips into Yosemite Wilderness.

W Wilderness permit station; get free wilderness permit here (summer only)

John Muir Trail and/or Pacific Crest Trail

Trail

Chilnualna Fall

Wawona Dome

Natural areas present hazards. You are responsible for your safety. Be prepared for rapidly changing weather conditions. Do not use this map for hiking. USGS topographic maps or detailed trail maps are available at visitor centers.

Wawona

Wawona Visitor Center
(summer only)

4012 ft
1223 m

W

Visiting Yosemite National Park by Road

Some roads may be closed or have detours or delays. Visit www.nps.gov/yose or phone 209-372-0200 for updated information.

Paved road

Unpaved road

SIERRA

NATIONAL

Pioneer Yosemite History Center

South Fork Merced River

Mariposa Grove Welcome Plaza

Ranger station

Horseback riding

FOREST

Mariposa Grove Road
Closed approx. November to April

Gas station

Campground

Mariposa Grove Road
Vehicles restricted during shuttle operation. Please use free shuttle service located at Mariposa Grove Welcome Plaza.

South Entrance

MARIPOSA GROVE

Food service and lodging

High Sierra Camp
(by reservation only)

Fish Camp

41

Mariposa Grove

Picnic area

Other public campground

To Fresno

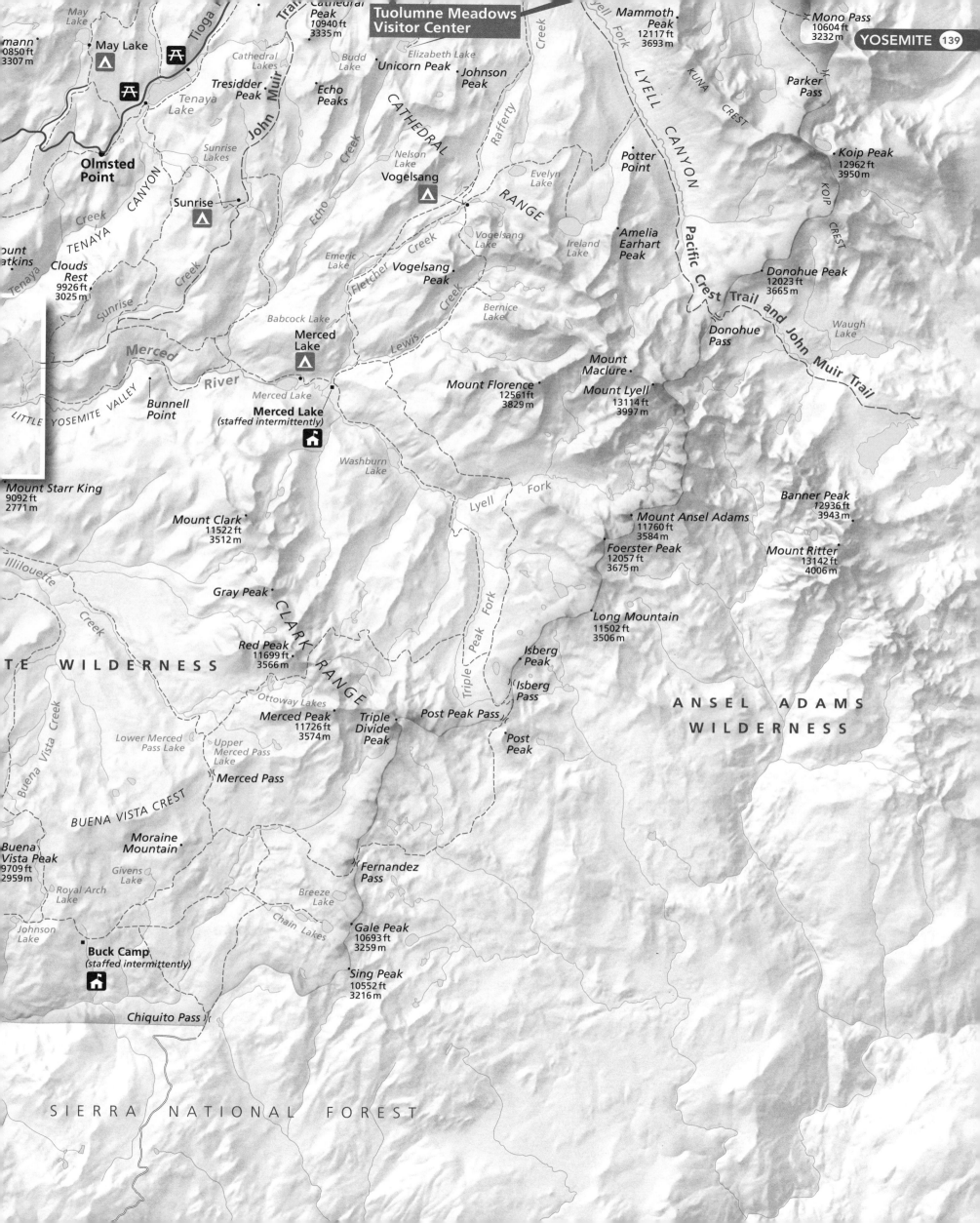

May Lake
mann
0850 ft
3307 m

May Lake

Tioga
Trail

Cathedral
Peak
10940 ft
3335 m

**Tuolumne Meadows
Visitor Center**

Mammoth
Peak
12117 ft
3693 m

Mono Pass
10604 ft
3232 m

Olmsted
Point

Tresidder
Peak

Cathedral
Lakes

Budd
Lake

Echo
Peaks

Elizabeth Lake

Unicorn Peak

Johnson
Peak

LYELL CANYON

KUNA CREST

Parker
Pass

Koip Peak
12962 ft
3950 m

Sunrise

Tenaya
Lake

John Muir Trail

Echo Creek

CATHEDRAL

Nelson
Lake

Vogelsang

Rafferty Creek

Evelyn
Lake

Potter
Point

KOIP CREST

Sunrise
Lakes

TENAYA CANYON

Creek

Emeric
Lake

Vogelsang
Peak

Fletcher Creek

Vogelsang
Lake

Ireland
Lake

Amelia
Earhart
Peak

Pacific Crest Trail

Donohue Peak
12023 ft
3665 m

ount
atkins

Clouds
Rest
9926 ft
3025 m

Sunrise

Babcock Lake

Merced
Lake

Bernice
Lake

Lewis Creek

RANGE

Donohue
Pass

and John Muir Trail

Waugh
Lake

Tenaya

Merced

River

Merced Lake

Merced Lake
(staffed intermittently)

Bunnell
Point

Washburn
Lake

Mount Florence
12561 ft
3829 m

Mount
Maclure

Mount Lyell
13114 ft
3997 m

LITTLE YOSEMITE VALLEY

Mount Starr King
9092 ft
2771 m

Mount Clark
11522 ft
3512 m

Lyell Fork

Lyell Fork

Mount Ansel Adams
11760 ft
3584 m

Banner Peak
12936 ft
3943 m

Illilouette

Gray Peak

CLARK

Foerster Peak
12057 ft
3675 m

Mount Ritter
13142 ft
4006 m

Creek

WILDERNESS

Red Peak
11699 ft
3566 m

RANGE

Triple Peak Fork

Long Mountain
11502 ft
3506 m

Ottoway Lakes

Isberg
Peak

Lower Merced
Pass Lake

Upper
Merced Pass
Lake

Merced Peak
11726 ft
3574 m

Triple
Divide
Peak

Post Peak Pass

Isberg
Pass

ANSEL ADAMS

WILDERNESS

Buena Vista Creek

Merced Pass

Post
Peak

BUENA VISTA CREST

Buena
Vista Peak
9709 ft
2959 m

Moraine
Mountain

Givens
Lake

Royal Arch
Lake

Fernandez
Pass

Johnson
Lake

Buck Camp
(staffed intermittently)

Breeze
Lake

Chain Lakes

Gale Peak
10693 ft
3259 m

Sing Peak
10552 ft
3216 m

Chiquito Pass

SIERRA   NATIONAL   FOREST

Sentinel Dome

Yosemite Basics

(209) 372-0200 | nps.gov/yose
Entrance Fee: $35/car
Timed-Entry Permits*: required spring through fall
Lodging**: The Ahwahnee, Yosemite Valley Lodge, Curry Village, Housekeeping Camp, Wawona Hotel, Tuolumne Meadows, White Wolf Lodge
Camping: Upper Pines**, Lower Pines**, North Pines**, Camp 4, Wawona**, Bridalveil Creek, Hodgdon Meadow**, Crane Flat**, Tamarack Flat, White Wolf, Yosemite Creek, Porcupine Flat, Tuolumne Meadows

*reserve at recreation.gov
**reserve at travelyosemite.com

Yosemite Favorites

Easy Hikes: Lower Yosemite (1 mile), Bridalveil Falls (0.5), Grizzly Giant (2)
Moderate Hikes: Sentinel Dome (2.2), Cathedral Lakes (7), Elizabeth Lake (4.8), Glen Aulin (11), Gaylor Lakes (2), Mono Pass (8), Taft Point (1.8), Lembert Dome (2.8)
Strenuous Hikes: Vernal & Nevada Falls (8), Yosemite Falls (7.2), Four Mile (9.6), Ostrander Lake (11.4), Panorama (8.3), Ten Lakes (12.6), Clouds Rest (7 from Tioga Pass Road, 13 from Happy Isles)
Extreme Hikes: Half Dome (14)
Views: Glacier Point, Tunnel View, Valley View, Washburn Point, Olmstead Point

Lembert Dome

What You Need to Know About Yosemite

- You may have to get a timed-entry permit from recreation.gov if you plan on arriving during peak hours. This pilot program was implemented due to increased visitation during the pandemic. They were going to roll it back but then decided to keep it around in 2022. Be sure to check on this if you don't have in-park lodging and want to visit. No one wants to waste a trip, even with so many other worthwhile destinations in the vicinity.
- Visitation peaks in July and August. About 75% of all guests arrive between May and October. The park is more peaceful in winter, and daytime highs usually reach the 40s°F at Yosemite Valley.
- It's highly recommended you stay in the park. If you miss out on lodging/campsites when they first become available, periodically check for cancellations. You'll be extremely thankful to go to bed and wake up in the valley.
- There are a couple free shuttles around the Valley and up to Glacier Point, Mariposa Grove, and Tuolumne Meadows. They're another great park resource.
- If you want to scale the back of Half Dome aided by steel cables and wooden slats, you need a permit (recreation.gov). The hike is no joke. Just getting up Subdome is a chore. Start early, possibly before sunrise, if you're dayhiking it.

Yosemite Driving Distances

Pavement leads into one of the most beautiful places this planet has to offer. It may be worth it to enter from the south so your first glimpse of Yosemite Valley is from Tunnel View, but views aren't shabby from the west either.

San Francisco, CA	← 4 hours / 190 miles →	Yosemite Valley VC
Yosemite Valley VC	← 70 minutes / 35 miles →	Mariposa Grove
Yosemite Valley VC	← 65 minutes / 32 miles →	Glacier Point
Yosemite Valley VC	← 80 minutes / 41 miles →	Hetch Hetchy
Yosemite Valley VC	← 90 minutes / 55 miles →	Tuolumne Meadows
Tuolumne Meadows	← 65 minutes / 49 miles →	Mammoth Lakes, CA

Why Visit Yosemite?

- Because Yosemite stands out among a collection of extremely special places
- While the hiking is top-notch, there's much more to do, including world-class rock climbing, trail rides, biking, floating, even skiing and skating
- It's a photographer's dream destination

Taft Point and a smoky valley

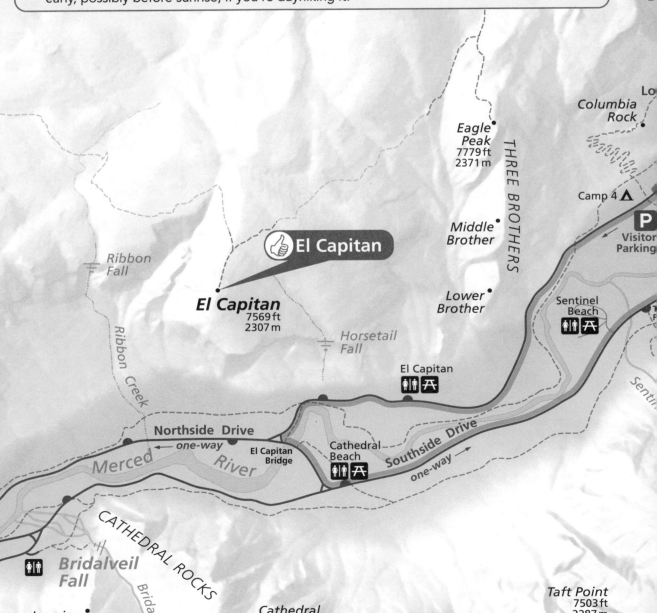

To Tioga Road, Tuolumne Meadows and Hwy 120; and Hetch Hetchy

El Portal Road

To El Portal and Hwy 140

Tunnel View

Valley View

Pohono Bridge

To Glacier Point, Wawona and Mariposa Grove; Hwy 41, Oakhurst, and Fresno

Wawona Road

Bridalveil Fall

Leaning Tower

CATHEDRAL ROCKS

Bridalveil Creek

Cathedral Spires

Taft Point
7503 ft
2287 m

Merced River

Northside Drive
← one-way

El Capitan Bridge

Cathedral Beach

Southside Drive
one-way →

👍 El Capitan

El Capitan
7569 ft
2307 m

Ribbon Fall

Ribbon Creek

Horsetail Fall

El Capitan

Eagle Peak
7779 ft
2371 m

Middle Brother

Lower Brother

THREE BROTHERS

Camp 4 ⛺

Visitor Parking

Sentinel Beach

Columbia Rock

Lo...

How Much Time Do You Have?

1 Day: Another park where this needs to be written... spend more than a day. But one day at Yosemite is better than no days. Start early. Sunrise at Glacier Point is a good idea. Stick around to hike Taft Point and Sentinel Dome while you can get parking. Walking/biking/shuttling around Yosemite Valley probably takes a day (or more) by itself. See as much of it as you can.

2 Days: Go for a big hike! Half Dome. Clouds Rest. Yosemite Falls (and on to North Dome). If you'd rather take it easier, head up Tioga Road, hang out at Tenaya Lake, hike to Cathedral or Elizabeth Lake. Lembert Dome is close by and not extremely difficult too.

3 Days: I could spend three days sitting in a lawn chair in Yosemite Valley and you'd never hear a complaint. Personally, I'd go for another big hike but Mariposa Grove (and Tunnel View along the way) are two spots to check out. You can also saddle up and let a horse do the walking for you at Wawona.

Another Dome, the cables up Half Dome

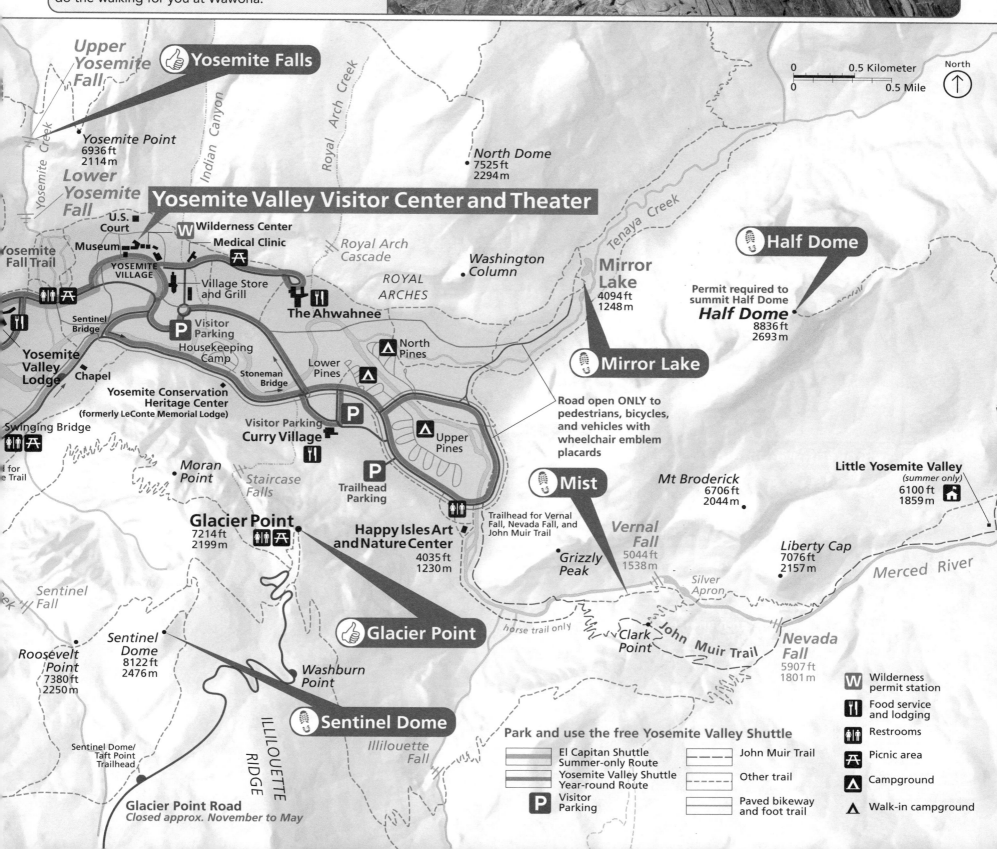

Yosemite Falls

Upper Yosemite Fall

Lower Yosemite Fall

Yosemite Point
6936 ft
2114 m

North Dome
7525 ft
2294 m

Yosemite Valley Visitor Center and Theater

U.S. Court

Museum

Wilderness Center

Medical Clinic

Royal Arch Cascade

Washington Column

Mirror Lake
4094 ft
1248 m

Half Dome

Permit required to summit Half Dome

Half Dome
8836 ft
2693 m

Yosemite Fall Trail

YOSEMITE VILLAGE

Village Store and Grill

The Ahwahnee

ROYAL ARCHES

Mirror Lake

Sentinel Bridge

Visitor Parking

Housekeeping Camp

North Pines

Yosemite Valley Lodge

Chapel

Lower Pines

Yosemite Conservation Heritage Center
(formerly LeConte Memorial Lodge)

Stoneman Bridge

Road open ONLY to pedestrians, bicycles, and vehicles with wheelchair emblem placards

Swinging Bridge

Visitor Parking
Curry Village

Moran Point

Staircase Falls

Upper Pines

Mist

Mt Broderick
6706 ft
2044 m

Little Yosemite Valley
(summer only)
6100 ft
1859 m

Trailhead Parking

Trailhead for Vernal Fall, Nevada Fall, and John Muir Trail

Vernal Fall
5044 ft
1538 m

Liberty Cap
7076 ft
2157 m

Glacier Point
7214 ft
2199 m

Happy Isles Art and Nature Center
4035 ft
1230 m

Grizzly Peak

Silver Apron

Merced River

Sentinel Fall

Glacier Point

Roosevelt Point
7380 ft
2250 m

Sentinel Dome
8122 ft
2476 m

Washburn Point

horse trail only

Clark Point

John Muir Trail

Nevada Fall
5907 ft
1801 m

Sentinel Dome

ILLILOUETTE RIDGE

Illilouette Fall

Sentinel Dome/Taft Point Trailhead

Glacier Point Road
Closed approx. November to May

0   0.5 Kilometer
0   0.5 Mile

North ↑

Park and use the free Yosemite Valley Shuttle

El Capitan Shuttle Summer-only Route

Yosemite Valley Shuttle Year-round Route

P Visitor Parking

John Muir Trail

Other trail

Paved bikeway and foot trail

W Wilderness permit station

Food service and lodging

Restrooms

Picnic area

Campground

Walk-in campground

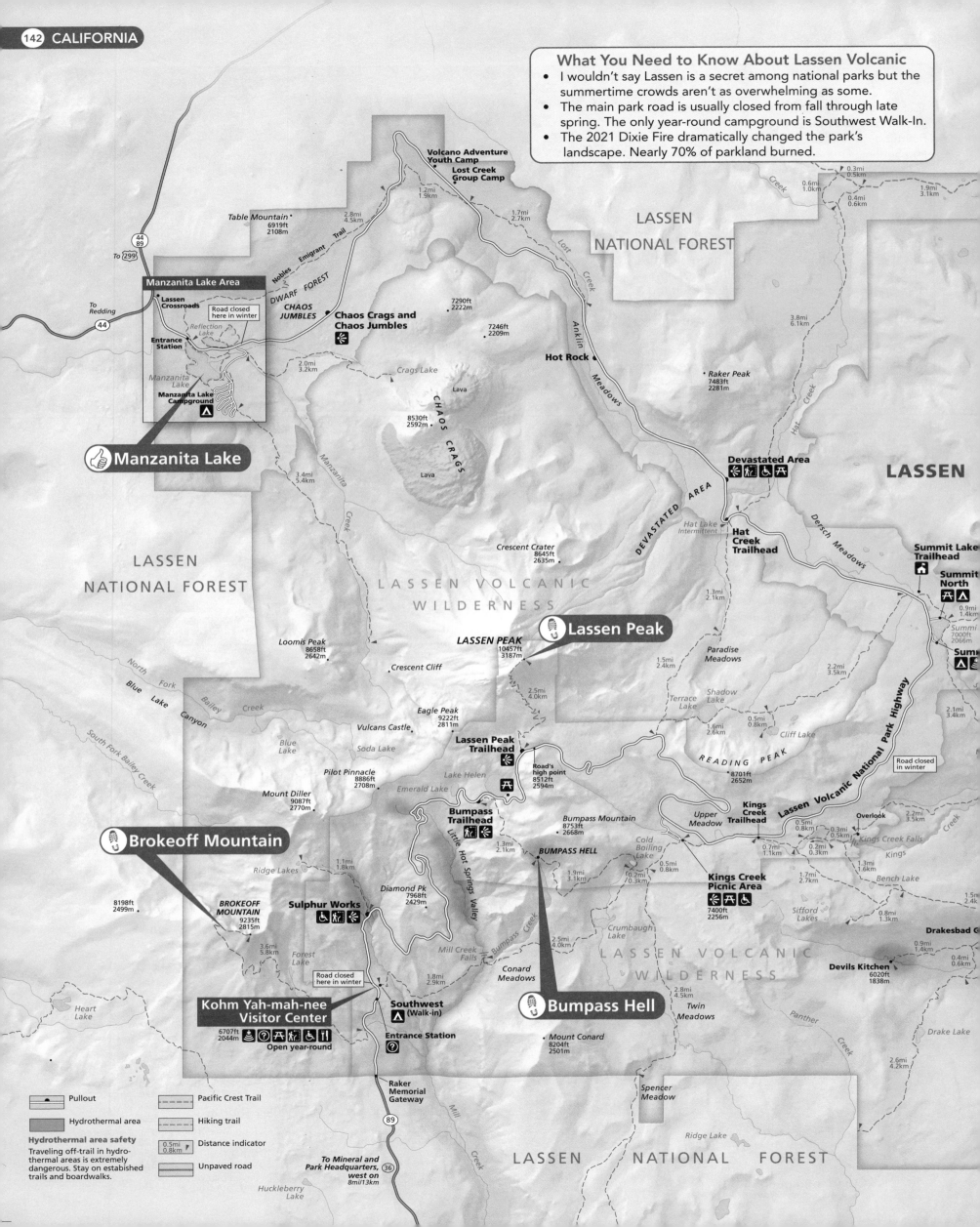

What You Need to Know About Lassen Volcanic
- I wouldn't say Lassen is a secret among national parks but the summertime crowds aren't as overwhelming as some.
- The main park road is usually closed from fall through late spring. The only year-round campground is Southwest Walk-In.
- The 2021 Dixie Fire dramatically changed the park's landscape. Nearly 70% of parkland burned.

LASSEN NATIONAL FOREST

44 89

To **299**

To **44**

Manzanita Lake Area
- Lassen Crossroads
- Road closed here in winter
- Entrance Station
- *Reflection Lake*
- *Manzanita Lake*
- **Manzanita Lake Campground**

Volcano Adventure Youth Camp
Lost Creek Group Camp

Table Mountain •
6919ft
2108m

Nobles Emigrant Trail

DWARF FOREST

CHAOS JUMBLES

Chaos Crags and Chaos Jumbles

Crags Lake

7290ft
2222m

7246ft
2209m

Hot Rock

Lost Creek

Anklin Meadows

LASSEN NATIONAL FOREST

Manzanita Lake

Manzanita Creek

8530ft
2592m
Lava

CHAOS CRAGS

Lava

Raker Peak
7483ft
2281m

LASSEN

Devastated Area

0.3mi
0.5km

0.6mi
1.0km

1.9mi
3.1km

0.4mi
0.6km

1.2mi
1.9km

1.7mi
2.7km

2.8mi
4.5km

3.8mi
6.1km

Hat Creek

Dersch Meadows

Summit Lake Trailhead

Summit North

0.9mi
1.4km

Summit 7000ft
2066m

Summ

3.4mi
5.4km

2.0mi
3.2km

DEVASTATED AREA

Hat Lake Intermittent

Hat Creek Trailhead

Crescent Crater
8645ft
2635m

LASSEN VOLCANIC WILDERNESS

Paradise Meadows

1.3mi
2.1km

1.5mi
2.4km

2.2mi
3.5km

2.1mi
3.4km

Loomis Peak
8658ft
2642m

LASSEN PEAK
10457ft
3187m

Lassen Peak

Crescent Cliff

Terrace Lake

Shadow Lake

Cliff Lake

Eagle Peak
9222ft
2811m

0.5mi
0.8km

1.6mi
2.6km

Vulcans Castle

Soda Lake

Blue Lake

Bailey Creek

North Fork

Blue Lake Canyon

South Fork Bailey Creek

Pilot Pinnacle
8886ft
2708m

Mount Diller
9087ft
2770m

Lassen Peak Trailhead

Lake Helen

Emerald Lake

Road's high point
8512ft
2594m

8701ft
2652m

READING PEAK

Road closed in winter

Lassen Volcanic National Park Highway

Brokeoff Mountain

8198ft
2499m

BROKEOFF MOUNTAIN
9235ft
2815m

1.1mi
1.8km

Ridge Lakes

Bumpass Trailhead

Bumpass Mountain
8753ft
2668m

Little Hot Springs Valley

BUMPASS HELL

1.3mi
2.1km

Upper Meadow

Cold Boiling Lake

Kings Creek Trailhead

0.5mi
0.8km

0.3mi
0.5km

Overlook

Kings Creek Falls

Kings

2.2mi
3.5km

Bench Lake

0.7mi
1.1km

0.2mi
0.3km

0.5mi
0.8km

1.7mi
2.7km

1.3mi
1.6km

Diamond Pk
7968ft
2429m

Sulphur Works

1.9mi
3.1km

0.2mi
0.3km

Kings Creek Picnic Area
7400ft
2256m

Sifford Lakes

3.6mi
5.8km

Forest Lake

Crumbaugh Lake

0.8mi
1.3km

Drakesbad G

Kohm Yah-mah-nee Visitor Center

Road closed here in winter

Mill Creek Falls

Conard Meadows

2.5mi
4.0km

LASSEN VOLCANIC WILDERNESS

0.9mi
1.4km

Heart Lake

1.8mi
2.9km

Southwest (Walk-in)

Entrance Station

Mount Conard
8204ft
2501m

2.8mi
4.5km

Twin Meadows

Devils Kitchen
6020ft
1838m

0.4mi
0.6km

6707ft
2044m
Open year-round

Bumpass Creek

Drake Lake

2.6mi
4.2km

Raker Memorial Gateway

Panther Creek

Spencer Meadow

1.5
2.4

89

Pullout

Pacific Crest Trail

Hydrothermal area

Hiking trail

Hydrothermal area safety
Traveling off-trail in hydro-thermal areas is extremely dangerous. Stay on established trails and boardwalks.

0.5mi
0.8km
Distance indicator

Unpaved road

To Mineral and Park Headquarters, west on 8mi/13km

36

Mill Creek

Ridge Lake

LASSEN NATIONAL FOREST

Huckleberry Lake

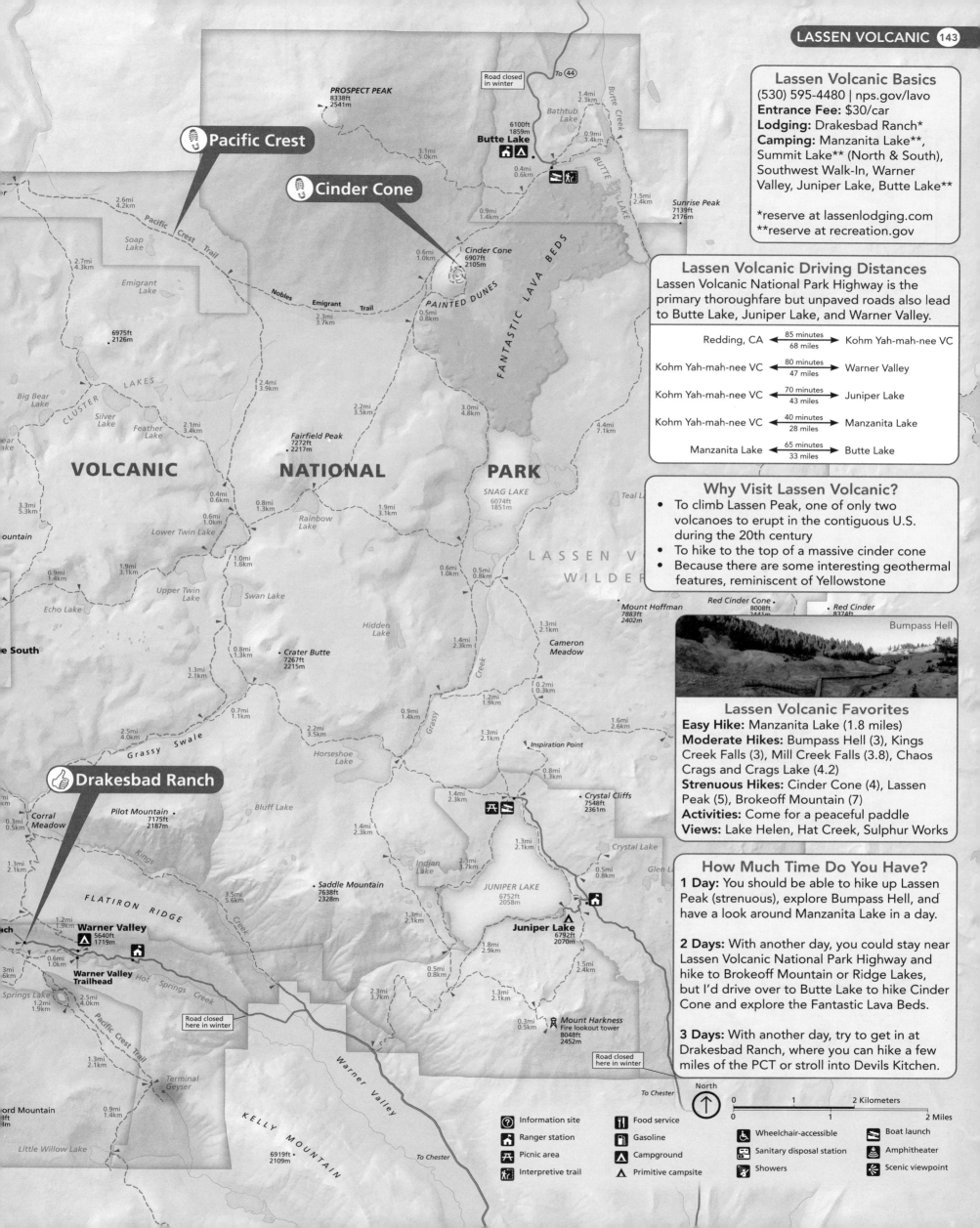

Pacific Crest

Cinder Cone

PROSPECT PEAK
8338ft
2541m

Road closed in winter

To 44

Bathtub Lake

6100ft
1859m
Butte Lake

1.4mi
2.3km

0.9mi
1.4km

0.4mi
0.6km

Sunrise Peak
7139ft
2176m

1.5mi
2.4km

Cinder Cone
6907ft
2105m

0.6mi
1.0km

0.9mi
1.4km

FANTASTIC LAVA BEDS

PAINTED DUNES

Nobles   Emigrant   Trail

2.6mi
4.2km

Pacific   Crest   Trail

2.7mi
4.3km

Soap Lake

Emigrant Lake

0.5mi
0.8km

2.3mi
3.7km

6975ft
2126m

2.2mi
3.5km

3.0mi
4.8km

4.4mi
7.1km

2.4mi
3.9km

CLUSTER   LAKES

Big Bear Lake

Silver Lake

Feather Lake

2.1mi
3.4km

Fairfield Peak
7272ft
2217m

VOLCANIC   NATIONAL   PARK

SNAG LAKE
6074ft
1851m

Teal Lake

LASSEN V
WILDER

0.4mi
0.6km

0.8mi
1.3km

1.9mi
3.1km

3.3mi
5.3km

0.6mi
1.0km

Rainbow Lake

Lower Twin Lake

1.9mi
3.1km

1.0mi
1.6km

Upper Twin Lake

Swan Lake

0.9mi
1.4km

Echo Lake

e South

Hidden Lake

0.6mi
1.0km

0.5mi
0.8km

Mount Hoffman
7883ft
2402m

Red Cinder Cone
8008ft
2441m

Red Cinder
8374ft

1.3mi
2.1km

Cameron Meadow

0.8mi
1.3km

Crater Butte
7267ft
2215m

1.4mi
2.3km

0.2mi
0.3km

1.2mi
1.9km

Inspiration Point

0.7mi
1.1km

2.2mi
3.5km

0.9mi
1.4km

1.3mi
2.1km

1.6mi
2.6km

2.5mi
4.0km

Grassy   Swale

Horseshoe Lake

0.8mi
1.3km

Crystal Cliffs
7548ft
2361m

Drakesbad Ranch

Pilot Mountain
7175ft
2187m

Bluff Lake

1.4mi
2.3km

1.4mi
2.3km

Crystal Lake

0.3mi
0.5km

Corral Meadow

1.3mi
2.1km

Kings

1.4mi
2.3km

Indian Lake

2.3mi
3.7km

JUNIPER LAKE
6752ft
2058m

0.5mi
0.8km

Glen Lake

1.3mi
2.1km

Saddle Mountain
7638ft
2328m

3.5mi
5.6km

FLATIRON RIDGE

1.2mi
1.9km

Warner Valley
5640ft
1719m

0.6mi
1.0km

1.8mi
2.9km

1.3mi
2.1km

Juniper Lake
6792ft
2070m

1.5mi
2.4km

Warner Valley Trailhead

Hot   Springs   Creek

Springs Lake

1.2mi
1.9km

2.5mi
3.9km

Pacific Crest Trail

Road closed here in winter

0.5mi
0.8km

2.3mi
3.7km

1.3mi
2.1km

0.3mi
0.5km

Mount Harkness
Fire lookout tower
8048ft
2452m

Road closed here in winter

1.3mi
2.1km

Terminal Geyser

WARNER VALLEY

ord Mountain

Little Willow Lake

KELLY MOUNTAIN

6919ft
2109m

To Chester

To Chester

North

Lassen Volcanic Basics
(530) 595-4480 | nps.gov/lavo
Entrance Fee: $30/car
Lodging: Drakesbad Ranch*
Camping: Manzanita Lake**,
Summit Lake** (North & South),
Southwest Walk-In, Warner
Valley, Juniper Lake, Butte Lake**

*reserve at lassenlodging.com
**reserve at recreation.gov

Lassen Volcanic Driving Distances
Lassen Volcanic National Park Highway is the primary thoroughfare but unpaved roads also lead to Butte Lake, Juniper Lake, and Warner Valley.

Redding, CA	← 85 minutes / 68 miles →	Kohm Yah-mah-nee VC
Kohm Yah-mah-nee VC	← 80 minutes / 47 miles →	Warner Valley
Kohm Yah-mah-nee VC	← 70 minutes / 43 miles →	Juniper Lake
Kohm Yah-mah-nee VC	← 40 minutes / 28 miles →	Manzanita Lake
Manzanita Lake	← 65 minutes / 33 miles →	Butte Lake

Why Visit Lassen Volcanic?
- To climb Lassen Peak, one of only two volcanoes to erupt in the contiguous U.S. during the 20th century
- To hike to the top of a massive cinder cone
- Because there are some interesting geothermal features, reminiscent of Yellowstone

Bumpass Hell

Lassen Volcanic Favorites
Easy Hike: Manzanita Lake (1.8 miles)
Moderate Hikes: Bumpass Hell (3), Kings Creek Falls (3), Mill Creek Falls (3.8), Chaos Crags and Crags Lake (4.2)
Strenuous Hikes: Cinder Cone (4), Lassen Peak (5), Brokeoff Mountain (7)
Activities: Come for a peaceful paddle
Views: Lake Helen, Hat Creek, Sulphur Works

How Much Time Do You Have?
1 Day: You should be able to hike up Lassen Peak (strenuous), explore Bumpass Hell, and have a look around Manzanita Lake in a day.

2 Days: With another day, you could stay near Lassen Volcanic National Park Highway and hike to Brokeoff Mountain or Ridge Lakes, but I'd drive over to Butte Lake to hike Cinder Cone and explore the Fantastic Lava Beds.

3 Days: With another day, try to get in at Drakesbad Ranch, where you can hike a few miles of the PCT or stroll into Devils Kitchen.

0   1   2 Kilometers
0   1   2 Miles

Ⓘ Information site
🏠 Ranger station
⛟ Picnic area
🚶 Interpretive trail

🍴 Food service
⛽ Gasoline
△ Campground
▲ Primitive campsite

♿ Wheelchair-accessible
🚽 Sanitary disposal station
🚿 Showers

⛵ Boat launch
🎭 Amphitheater
🌀 Scenic viewpoint

What You Need to Know About Redwood

- Weather is pretty good year-round. Summers are typically less foggy but also busy. Winter is wet. Migratory birds drop in during spring and fall.
- Don't fret too much about the fog. For starters, the trees need it to survive. And second, when it's just right, you'll feel like you've stepped into a fairytale.
- A few trails (like Fern Canyon) feature small seasonal bridges. They may be impassable or result in wet feet when they're out.
- State Parks have an $8 day-use fee. However, they honor national park passes.

How Much Time Do You Have?

1 Day: If you're just looking to drive through the park, that'll take an hour or two. Go on some hikes....two days should be fine. In a single day you could hike Fern Canyon (permit required via recreation.gov), Tall Trees (permit required), and Boy Scout Tree and/or Stout Grove. It'd be a full day, but it's definitely possible with an early start.

2 Days: Spread out the hiking from the other day and mix in a trail ride (mountain biking or horseback) or join a rafting trip down the Smith River. Spend the evening tidepooling at Gold Bluffs or Enders Beach, depending on which side of the park you're on.

Tall Trees

North

0 ____ 5 Kilometers
0 ____ 5 Miles

Old-growth coast redwoods

Redwood National and State Parks

State Park boundary

Redwood National Park and State Parks boundary

State Park boundary

Trail

Unpaved road

Campground

Backcountry campsite (free permit required)

Fishing

Wheelchair-accessible

Boat access

Interpretive trail

Picnic area

PACIFIC OCEAN

TRINIDAD STATE BEACH

To Eureka 21mi 33km

Trinidad

Patricks Point Drive

PATRICK'S POINT STATE PARK

101

HARRY A. MERLO STATE RECREATION AREA

Big Lagoon Beach and County Park

Big Lagoon

Dry Lagoon Beach

Stone Lagoon Boat-in Camp

HUMBOLDT LAGOONS STATE PARK

Stone Lagoon

Information

McArthur

Redwood Highway

Big Lagoon

Tall Trees

Big Lagoon

REDWOOD NATIONAL PARK

Rodgers Peak 2745ft 837m

Tom McDonald Creek

Tall Trees Grove

Tall Trees Trail

Emerald Ridge Trail

Dolason Prairie Tr.

44 Camp

Elam Camp

Redwood Creek Overlook 2100ft 640m

Redwood Creek

Bald Hills Road

Dolason Prairie

BRIDGE CREEK RIDGE

Bridge Creek

Childs Hill Prairie

Lyons Ranch

Schoolhouse Peak 3097ft 944m

Bald Hills Road

Redwood Creek

To Weitchpec

Creek

Kuchel Visitor Center

Stone Lagoon

Trailer parking

Redwood Creek Trail

Orick

Orick Horse Trailhead

Prairie Creek

Freshwater Lagoon

Redwood National Park boundary

GOLD BLUFFS

Gold Bluffs Beach

Davison Road trailers prohibited

Elk Meadow Trillium Falls Tr.

Coastal Trail

Berry Glen Trail

Lady Bird Johnson Grove

Redwood Creek Trailhead Permit required for overnight travel Trailer parking

Bald Hills Road motor homes and trailers not advised

HOLTER RIDGE

Elk Prairie

Prairie Creek Visitor Center

PRAIRIE CREEK REDWOODS STATE PARK

Fern Canyon

Coastal Trail

Big Tree Wayside

Newton B. Drury Scenic Pkwy.

May Creek

Lost Man Creek trailers not advised

Lost Man Cr.

Cal-Barrel Rd.

Cal-Barrel Road trailers prohibited

Ah-Pah

McG...

River

Fern Canyon

Big Lagoon

Tall Trees

Redwood Basics

(707) 464-6101 | nps.gov/redw
Entrance Fee: None
Lodging: None
State Park Camping*: Jedediah Smith, Mill Creek, Elk Prairie, Gold Bluffs

*reserve at reservecalifornia.com

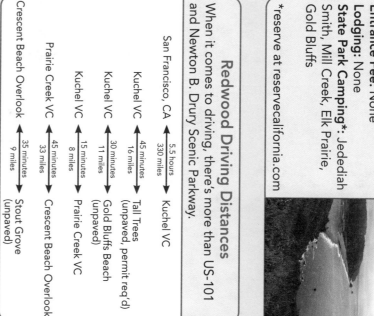

Klamath Overlook

Redwood Driving Distances

When it comes to driving, there's more than US-101 and Newton B. Drury Scenic Parkway.

From	To	Time	Distance	Notes
San Francisco, CA	Kuchel VC	5.5 hours	330 miles	
Kuchel VC	Tall Trees	45 minutes	16 miles	(unpaved, permit req'd)
Kuchel VC	Gold Bluffs Beach	30 minutes	11 miles	(unpaved, permit req'd)
Kuchel VC	Prairie Creek VC	15 minutes	8 miles	(unpaved)
Prairie Creek VC	Crescent Beach Overlook	45 minutes	33 miles	
Crescent Beach Overlook	Stout Grove	35 minutes	9 miles	(unpaved)

Why Visit Redwood?

- To look up at the world's tallest trees
- And walk through a Fern Canyon
- And to maybe see some whales!

Redwood Favorites

Hikes: Tall Trees (moderate, 4 miles), Boy Scout Tree (moderate, 5.6), Fern Canyon (easy, 0.7, permit required), Stout Grove (easy, 0.5), Lady Bird Johnson Grove (easy, 1), James Irvine (moderate, 8.4), Miner's Ridge (moderate, 8.2), Gold Bluffs (moderate, 4.8), Klamath (strenuous, 5.5), Rhododendron (moderate, 12.6), Crescent Beach (easy, 3.5)

Activities: Paddling Big Lagoon, rafting the Smith River, road biking the PCH or mountain biking, and horseback riding

Views: Howland Hills Road, Crescent Beach Overlook, Klamath Overlook

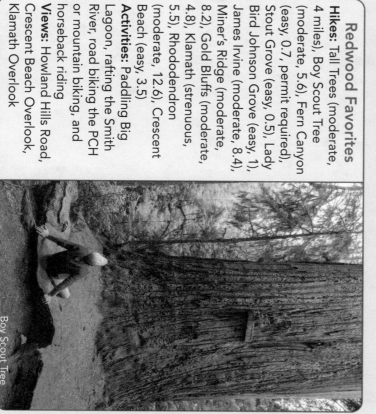

Boy Scout Tree

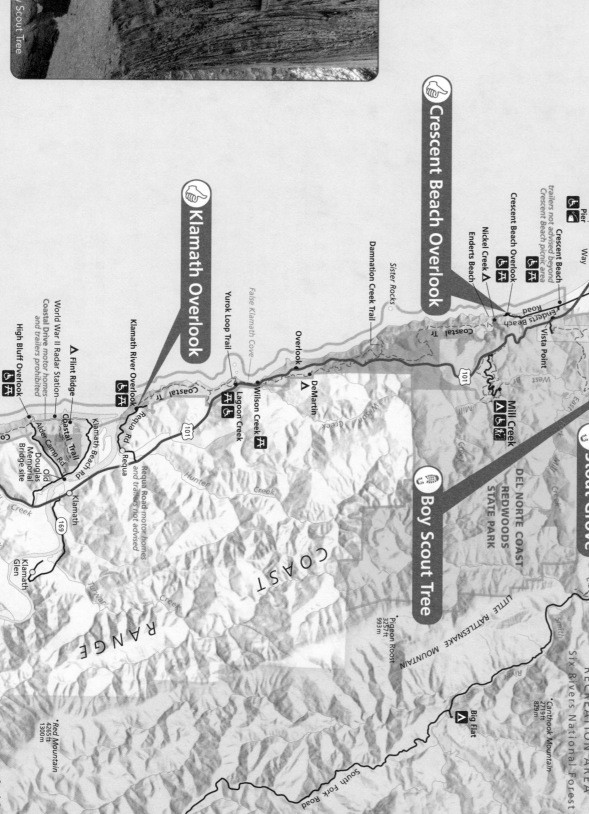

Crater Lake Basics

(541) 594-3000 | nps.gov/crla
Entrance Fee: $30/car
Lodging: Crater Lake Lodge, Cabins at Mazama Village
Camping: Mazama*, Lost Creek

*reserve at travelcraterlake.com

Phantom Ship

Boats ready to go

Crater Lake Driving Distances

You can access Rim Drive from the north and south. The drive itself circles Crater Lake for 33 miles.

Klamath Falls, OR	65 minutes / 54 miles	Mazama Village	
Mazama Village	15 minutes / 7 miles	Rim Village	
Rim Village	60 minutes / 17 miles	Pinnacles Overlook	
Rim Village	4.5 hours / 260 miles	Portland, OR	

Why Visit Crater Lake?

- To look down on an unbelievably beautiful lake and its deep blue water

Crater Lake Favorites

Hikes: Watchman Peak (moderate, 1.6 miles), Discovery Point (easy, 2), Mount Scott (strenuous, 4.4), Garfield Peak (strenuous, 3.6), Wizard Summit (moderate, 2), Cleetwood Cove (strenuous, 2.2)
Activities: Boat Tours!
Views: Sinnott Memorial Overlook, Watchman Overlook, Discovery Point, Cloudcap Overlook, Phantom Ship Overlook

How Much Time Do You Have?

1 Day: Crater Lake is a bit of a one-hit wonder. But the lake is quite special. If you only want to motor around 33-mile Rim Drive, stopping at a few choice viewpoints, an hour or two will do. Spending the night is better, to take in a sunset and sunrise (sunrise is often better).

2 Days: With two days, take a boat tour and hike to Watchman Peak and/or Mount Scott. There are many natural wonders in the area, so move it along and have fun.

What You Need to Know About Crater Lake

- Most roads and facilities are closed fall through spring.
- With that said, the road is typically plowed to Rim Village, and snowshoers and cross-country skiers explore this stunning setting when it's buried in snow.
- Roads typically fully open in July and August, when overlook parking when it's buried in snow.
- Drive the rim clockwise. Right turns are easier to make than left.
- Crater Lake Trolley (craterlaketrolley.net) offers 2-hour, ranger-guided tours of Rim Drive in summer for a fee.
- Another wintertime perk is the ability to camp along the rim. Just make sure you're properly prepared.
- You can reach the lake's shore via Cleetwood Trail. It's short but steep. This is also where boat tours depart from.
- It's a good idea to spend the night in the park. An even better one to spend it at Crater Lake Lodge simply for the setting.

Wizard Island

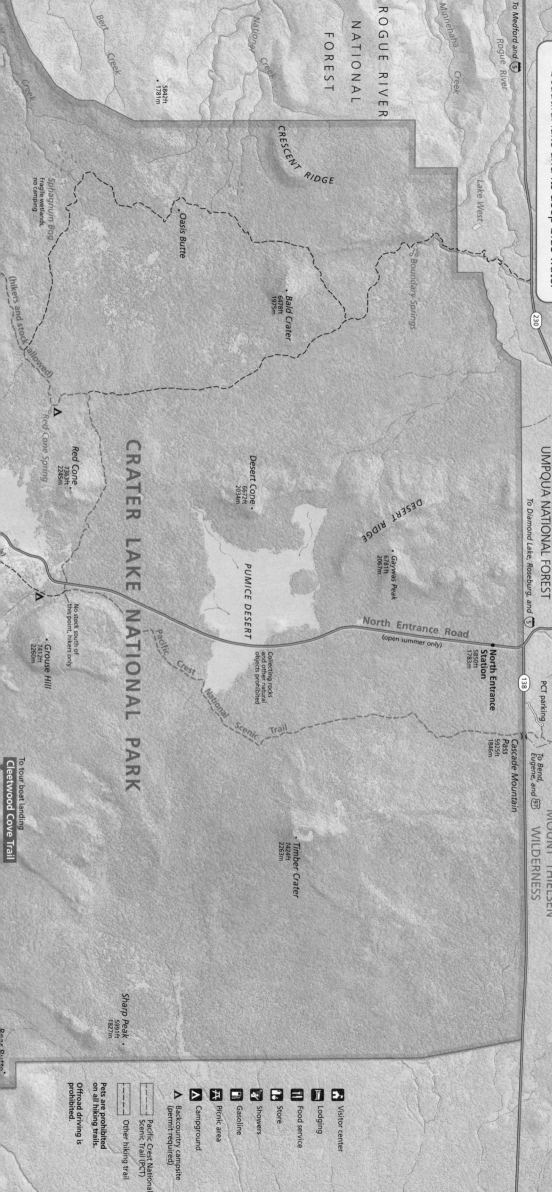

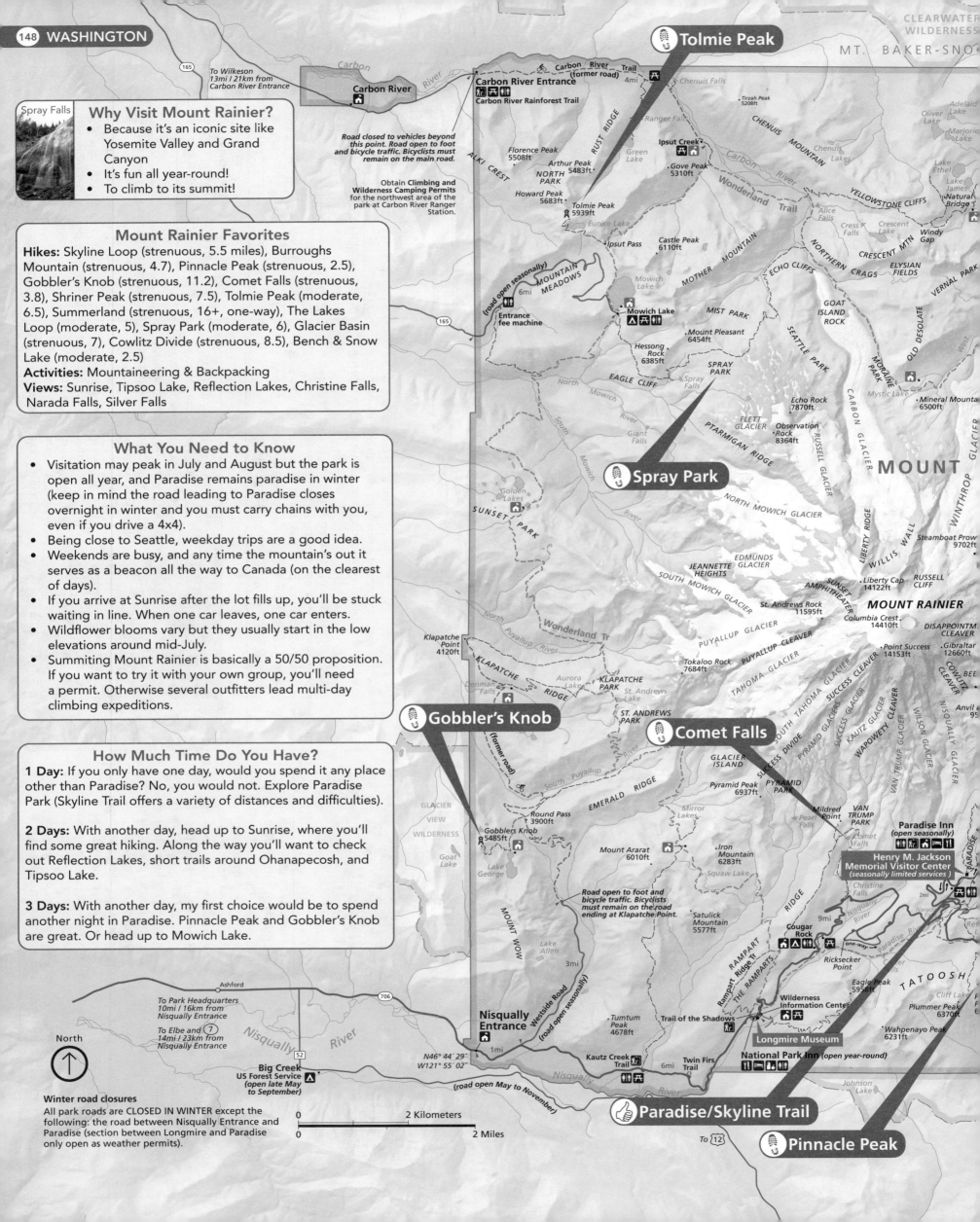

Spray Falls

Why Visit Mount Rainier?
- Because it's an iconic site like Yosemite Valley and Grand Canyon
- It's fun all year-round!
- To climb to its summit!

Mount Rainier Favorites

Hikes: Skyline Loop (strenuous, 5.5 miles), Burroughs Mountain (strenuous, 4.7), Pinnacle Peak (strenuous, 2.5), Gobbler's Knob (strenuous, 11.2), Comet Falls (strenuous, 3.8), Shriner Peak (strenuous, 7.5), Tolmie Peak (moderate, 6.5), Summerland (strenuous, 16+, one-way), The Lakes Loop (moderate, 5), Spray Park (moderate, 6), Glacier Basin (strenuous, 7), Cowlitz Divide (strenuous, 8.5), Bench & Snow Lake (moderate, 2.5)

Activities: Mountaineering & Backpacking

Views: Sunrise, Tipsoo Lake, Reflection Lakes, Christine Falls, Narada Falls, Silver Falls

What You Need to Know
- Visitation may peak in July and August but the park is open all year, and Paradise remains paradise in winter (keep in mind the road leading to Paradise closes overnight in winter and you must carry chains with you, even if you drive a 4x4).
- Being close to Seattle, weekday trips are a good idea.
- Weekends are busy, and any time the mountain's out it serves as a beacon all the way to Canada (on the clearest of days).
- If you arrive at Sunrise after the lot fills up, you'll be stuck waiting in line. When one car leaves, one car enters.
- Wildflower blooms vary but they usually start in the low elevations around mid-July.
- Summiting Mount Rainier is basically a 50/50 proposition. If you want to try it with your own group, you'll need a permit. Otherwise several outfitters lead multi-day climbing expeditions.

How Much Time Do You Have?

1 Day: If you only have one day, would you spend it any place other than Paradise? No, you would not. Explore Paradise Park (Skyline Trail offers a variety of distances and difficulties).

2 Days: With another day, head up to Sunrise, where you'll find some great hiking. Along the way you'll want to check out Reflection Lakes, short trails around Ohanapecosh, and Tipsoo Lake.

3 Days: With another day, my first choice would be to spend another night in Paradise. Pinnacle Peak and Gobbler's Knob are great. Or head up to Mowich Lake.

North

Winter road closures
All park roads are CLOSED IN WINTER except the following: the road between Nisqually Entrance and Paradise (section between Longmire and Paradise only open as weather permits).

Map labels:

To Wilkeson 13mi / 21km from Carbon River Entrance

Carbon River

Carbon River Trail (former road) 4mi

Carbon River Entrance
Carbon River Rainforest Trail

Road closed to vehicles beyond this point. Road open to foot and bicycle traffic. Bicyclists must remain on the main road.

Obtain Climbing and Wilderness Camping Permits for the northwest area of the park at Carbon River Ranger Station.

Chenuis Falls

Tirzah Peak 5208ft

Ipsut Creek

Tolmie Peak

Florence Peak 5508ft
Arthur Peak 5483ft
NORTH PARK
Howard Peak 5683ft
Gove Peak 5310ft
Green Lake
Ranger Falls
RUST RIDGE
ALKI CREST

Tolmie Peak 5939ft
Eunice Lake
Ipsut Pass
Castle Peak 6110ft

(road open seasonally)
MOUNTAIN MEADOWS
6mi
Entrance fee machine
Mowich Lake
Hessong Rock 6385ft
EAGLE CLIFF
Mount Pleasant 6454ft
MIST PARK
SPRAY PARK
Spray Falls
Spray Park

Wonderland Trail
CHENUIS MOUNTAIN
Chenuis Lakes
Alice Falls
Cress Falls
Crescent Lake
Windy Gap
CRESCENT MTN
ELYSIAN FIELDS
NORTHERN CRAGS
ECHO CLIFFS
OLD DESOLATE
YELLOWSTONE CLIFFS

MOTHER MOUNTAIN
SEATTLE PARK
MORAINE PARK
GOAT ISLAND ROCK
VERNAL PARK

Echo Rock 7870ft
PTARMIGAN RIDGE
FLETT GLACIER
Observation Rock 8364ft
Giant Falls

Mystic Lake
Mineral Mountain 6500ft

Golden Lakes
SUNSET PARK
North Mowich River
South Mowich River

NORTH MOWICH GLACIER
CARBON GLACIER
RUSSELL GLACIER
LIBERTY RIDGE
WILLIS WALL
Steamboat Prow 9702ft
WINTHROP GLACIER

MOUNT

EDMUNDS GLACIER
JEANNETTE HEIGHTS
SOUTH MOWICH GLACIER
St. Andrews Rock 11595ft
SUNSET AMPHITHEATER
Liberty Cap 14122ft
RUSSELL CLIFF
Columbia Crest 14410ft
MOUNT RAINIER
DISAPPOINTMENT CLEAVER

Klapatche Point 4120ft
Wonderland Tr
KLAPATCHE RIDGE
Aurora Lake
KLAPATCHE PARK
St. Andrews Lake
ST. ANDREWS PARK
Denman Falls
Tokaloo Rock 7684ft
PUYALLUP GLACIER
PUYALLUP CLEAVER
TAHOMA GLACIER
SOUTH TAHOMA GLACIER
SUCCESS GLACIER
Point Success 14153ft
Gibraltar 12660ft
SUCCESS CLEAVER
COWLITZ CLEAVER

Gobbler's Knob

(former road)
South Puyallup River
Emerald Ridge
GLACIER ISLAND
Pyramid Peak 6937ft
PYRAMID PARK
PYRAMID GLACIERS
SUCCESS DIVIDE
KAUTZ CLEAVER
KAUTZ GLACIER
WAPOWETY CLEAVER
VAN TRUMP GLACIER
WILSON GLACIER
Anvil 95..

Comet Falls

Mildred Point
VAN TRUMP PARK
Comet Falls
Pearl Falls

GLACIER VIEW WILDERNESS

Gobblers Knob 5485ft
Goat Lake
Lake George
Round Pass 3900ft
Mount Ararat 6010ft
Mirror Lakes
Iron Mountain 6283ft

Paradise Inn (open seasonally)
Henry M. Jackson Memorial Visitor Center (seasonally limited services)
PARADISE
Christine Falls
2mi

Road open to foot and bicycle traffic. Bicyclists must remain on the road ending at Klapatche Point.

Satulick Mountain 5577ft
Squaw Lake
Cougar Rock
9mi
THE RAMPARTS
RAMPART RIDGE
Rampart Ridge Tr
Ricksecker Point
Eagle Peak 5958ft
TATOOSH
Plummer Peak 6370ft
Wahpenayo Peak 6231ft

MOUNT WOW
Lake Allen
3mi

Nisqually Entrance
Westside Road (road open seasonally)

To Park Headquarters 10mi / 16km from Nisqually Entrance
To Elbe and (7) 14mi / 23km from Nisqually Entrance
Ashford
706

Nisqually River
52
Big Creek US Forest Service (open late May to September)

N46° 44' 29"
W121° 55' 02"
1mi
Kautz Creek Trail
Tumtum Peak 4678ft
Trail of the Shadows
Twin Firs Trail
6mi
Longmire Museum
National Park Inn (open year-round)
Wilderness Information Center
Nisqually River
(road open May to November)
Johnson Lake
Cliff Lake

Paradise/Skyline Trail

Pinnacle Peak

To 12

CLEARWATER WILDERNESS
MT. BAKER-SNO...
Oliver Lake
Adelaide Lake
Marjorie Lake
Lake Ethel
Lake James
Natural Bridge
Crescent Falls

0 2 Kilometers
0 2 Miles

ALMIE NATIONAL FOREST

RAINIER NATIONAL PARK

GIFFORD PINCHOT NATIONAL FOREST

TATOOSH WILDERNESS

WENATCHEE NATIONAL FOREST

WILLIAM O. DOUGLAS WILDERNESS

WILDERNESS

Mount Rainier Basics
(360) 569-2211 | nps.gov/mora
Entrance Fee: $30/car
Lodging*: National Park Inn, Paradise Inn
Camping: Cougar Rock**, White River, Ohanapecosh**, Mowich Lake

*reserve at mtrainierguestservices.com
**reserve at recreation.gov

Christine Falls

Mount Rainier Driving Distances
Roads circle the park, but they're only connected from the northeast corner to southwest corner.

Portland, OR	← 3 hours / 155 miles →	Paradise
Paradise	← 45 minutes / 23 miles →	Ohanapecosh VC
Ohanapecosh VC	← 60 minutes / 32 miles →	Sunrise
Paradise	← 190 minutes / 96 miles →	Mowich Lake (unpaved)
Seattle, WA	← 130 minutes / 62 miles →	Mowich Lake (unpaved)
Seattle, WA	← 140 minutes / 95 miles →	Paradise

Sunrise/Burroughs Mtn

Summerland (Wonderland)

Shriner Peak

Myrtle Falls

Grove of the Patriarchs

Sunrise Day Lodge (open July to late September) 6400ft
Sunrise Visitor Center
Emmons Vista
White River 4400ft
(road open July to early October)

White River Entrance
Wilderness Information Center 3500ft

Crystal Mountain Ski Area and Resort

Mather Memorial Parkway (road open seasonally)

Chinook Pass 5432ft
Cayuse Pass 4694ft

Shriner Peak 5834ft

(road open seasonally)

Box Canyon
(Stevens Canyon Rd open seasonally)

Grove of the Patriarchs Trail

Stevens Canyon Entrance

Ohanapecosh Visitor Center 1900ft
(open seasonally)

To Packwood via 12 11mi / 18km

Legend
- 🚶 Interpretive trail
- 🏠 Ranger station
- 🏠 Wilderness patrol cabin
- ⛺ Campground
- 🛏 Lodging
- 🍴 Restaurant
- 🔲 Picnic area
- 🛒 Groceries
- 🚻 Restrooms
- Fire Lookout

- Pacific Crest National Scenic Trail
- Wonderland Trail
- Other hiking trail
- Former road open to bikers and hikers
- Unpaved road and pullout
- Paved road and pullout

Mount Rainier Region
North

Seattle
SeaTac Airport
Tacoma
Olympia
Enumclaw
Buckley
Puyallup
Wilkeson
Morton
Packwood
Elbe
Ashford
Nisqually
To Ellensburg, Yakima, and Spokane
To Yakima
To Portland
MOUNT RAINIER NATIONAL PARK
Mowich Lake
Carbon River
White River
Stevens Canyon
CASCADE RANGE
0 — 15 Kilometers
0 — 15 Miles

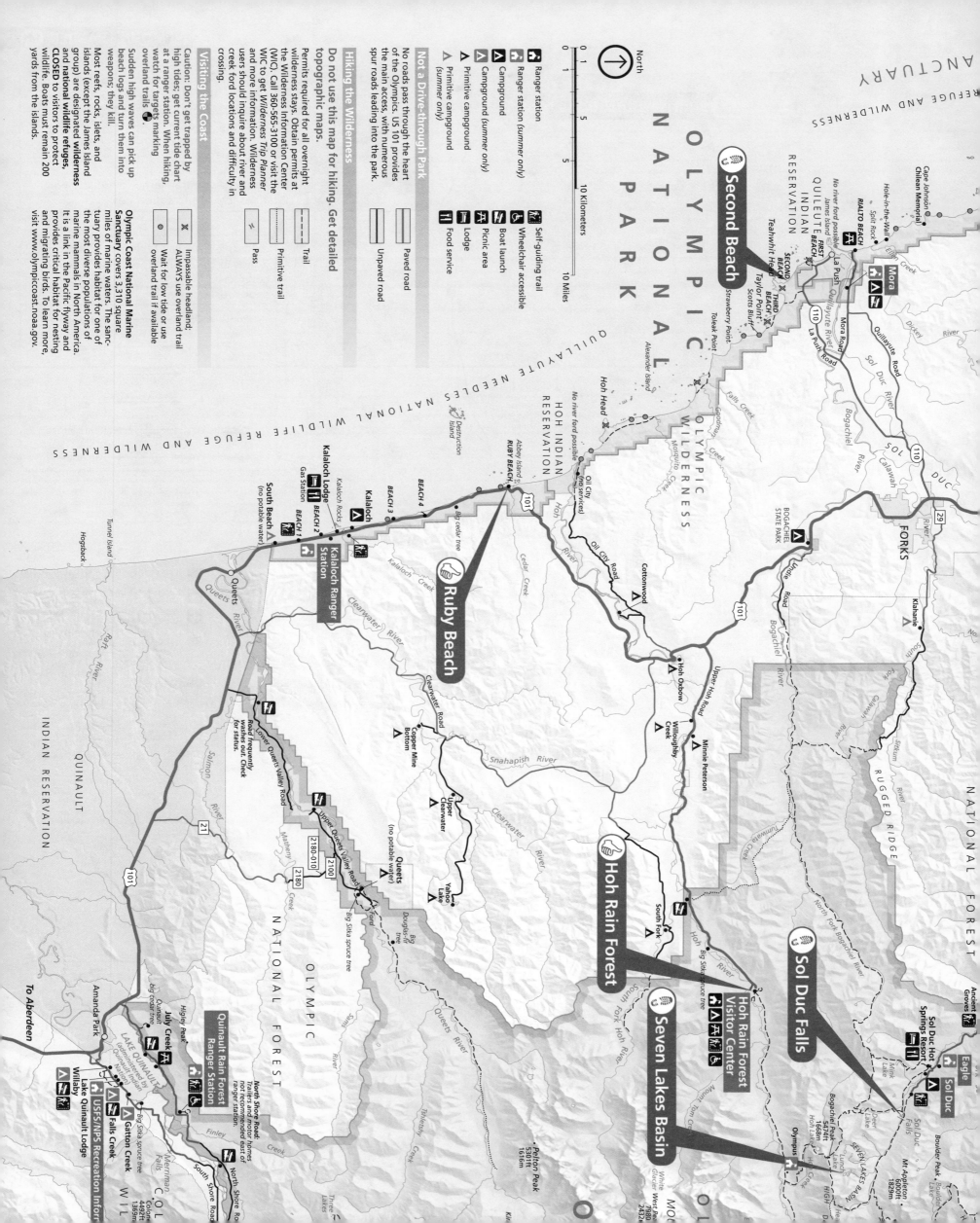

Olympic Basics

(360) 565-3130 | nps.gov/olym

Entrance Fee: $30/car

Lodging: Lake Crescent Lodge*, Sol Duc Hot Springs Resort*, Lake Quinault Lodge*, Kalaloch Lodge**

Camping: Heart O' the Hills, Elwha, Fairholme, Sol Duc#, Hoh, Queets, Graves Creek, North Fork, Staircase, Deer Park, Ozette, Mora#, Kalaloch#, South Beach

*reserve at olympicnationalparks.com
**reserve at thekalalochlodge.com
#reserve at recreation.gov

Mount Olympus from Hurricane Ridge

Olympic Driving Distances

No road crosses the Olympic Range but 12 separate roads penetrate the park's boundary.

From		To	Time	Distance
Seattle, WA	↔	Olympic Park VC (Port Angeles, WA)	150 minutes	130 miles
Seattle, WA	↔	Olympic Park VC (via ferry)	160 minutes	95 miles
Park VC	↔	Staircase	140 minutes	89 miles
Park VC	↔	Hurricane Ridge	35 minutes	18 miles
Park VC	↔	Fairholme (Lake Crescent)	40 minutes	27 miles
Fairholme	↔	Sol duc Falls	30 minutes	15 miles
Fairholme	↔	Ozette	80 minutes	59 miles
Fairholme	↔	Shi Shi Beach TH	85 minutes	61 miles
Fairholme	↔	La Push/Mora	50 minutes	42 miles
Fairholme	↔	Hoh Rain Forest	80 minutes	60 miles
Fairholme	↔	Kalaloch	75 minutes	63 miles
Kalaloch	↔	Quinault	45 minutes	35 miles

Why Visit Olympic?

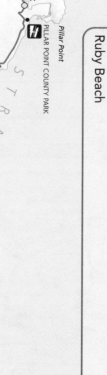

Mount Storm King

- To experience snow-capped mountains, ever-changing tidepools, isolated beaches, lush rain forest, and some of the best mountain hiking in the country, all in one fun-filled peninsula! (Unfortunately the Twilight craze has run its course. But maybe you'll spot a glistening vampire?!

- Olympic has a wide array of settings. Beaches? You bet. Mountains? Oh yeah! Rain forest? I don't see why not. And then the leeward side of the Olympic range is dry and a exploration destination for backpackers.

Olympic Favorites

Easy Hikes: Second Beach (1.4 miles), Marymere Falls (1.3), Rialto Beach (3), Third Beach (2.8), Hall of Mosses (0.8), Sol Duc Falls (1.6), Ozette Loop (9.2)

Moderate Hikes: Shi Shi Beach (4), Hurricane Hill (3.2)

Strenuous Hikes: Lake Angeles (6.8), Pyramid Peak (7), Klahhane Ridge (5.6, loop with Lake Angeles)

Activities: Paddle around Lake Quinault or Lake Crescent (rentals available)

Views: Hurricane Ridge, Rialto Beach, Obstruction Point, Ruby Beach

What You Need to Know About Olympic

- Mid-week trips are a good idea. Even then, if you're making summer plans, reserve things as soon as possible.

- It's not easy planning a trip to Olympic. Try to sample the immense geographic diversity (mountains, coast, and rain forest).

- With a vast range of topography, the park is pretty fun all year-round. Hurricane Ridge becomes a winter sports playground once it's buried in snow. While coastal temperatures rarely dip below freezing.

- If you want a base camp, Lake Crescent (Fairholme) is hard to beat. The drive to Hurricane Ridge isn't bad. You can reach the entire coast from Shi Shi to Kalaloch in under two hours (each way). It'd take some time to get to the eastern access roads but those destinations are primarily used as starting points for backpacking trips.

How Much Time Do You Have?

1 Day: Even though you could peer across the mountains to snow-capped Mount Olympus at Hurricane Ridge, paddle Lake Crescent, and tidepool at Second Beach in one action-packed day, you should spend more time here.

3 Days: With three days, spend one near Hurricane Ridge to hike to Lake Angeles. Another near Lake Crescent to explore the area as well as Sol Duc, and another along the coast. Rialto Beach. Second Beach. Shi Shi Beach. They're all great. You'll probably want more time (it's a recurring theme).

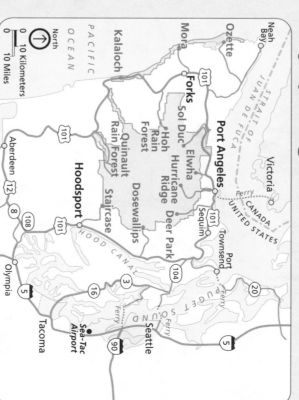

Sand Point Trail

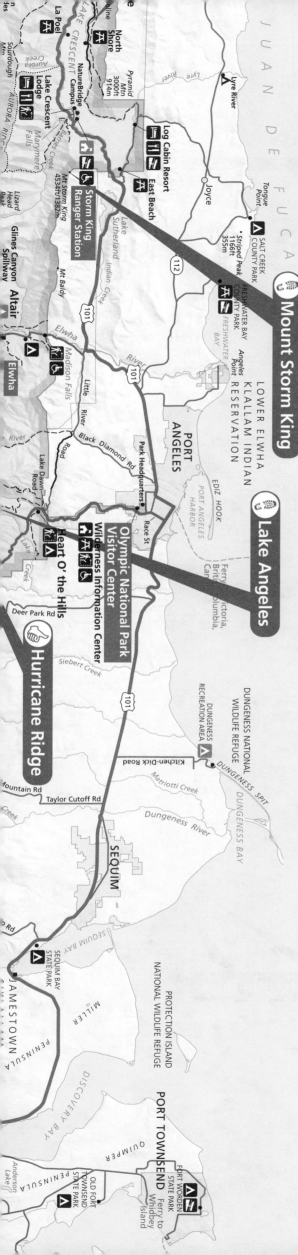

Olympic Region

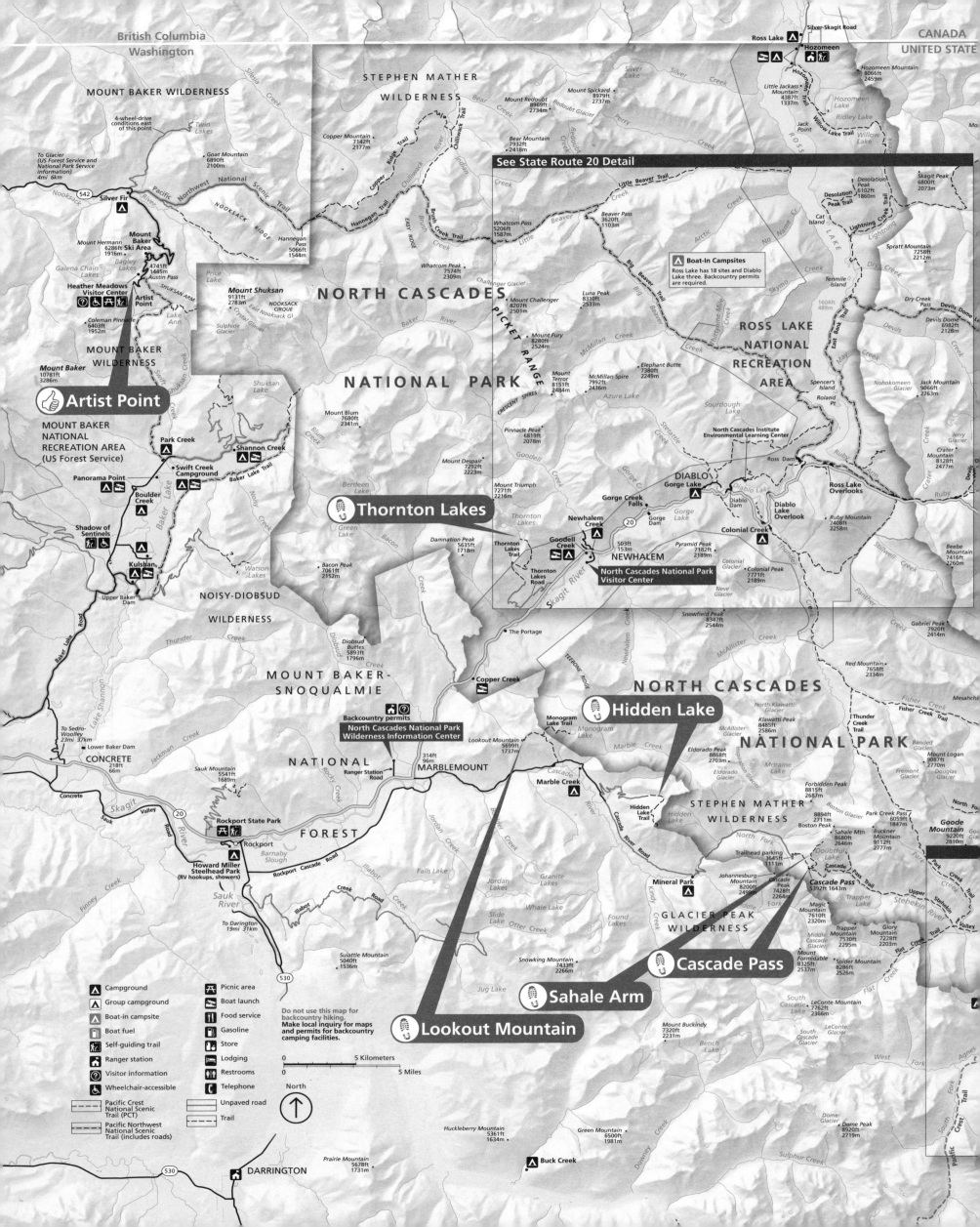

Blue Lake

North Cascades Basics

(360) 854-7200 | nps.gov/noca
Entrance Fee: None
Lodging: Ross Lake Resort (rosslakeresort.com),
Stehekin Lodge (lodgeatstehekin.com)
Camping: Goodell Creek*, Newhalem Creek*,
Gorge Lake, Colonial Creek*, Hozomeen,
Stehekin* (several, small camps)

*reserve at recreation.gov

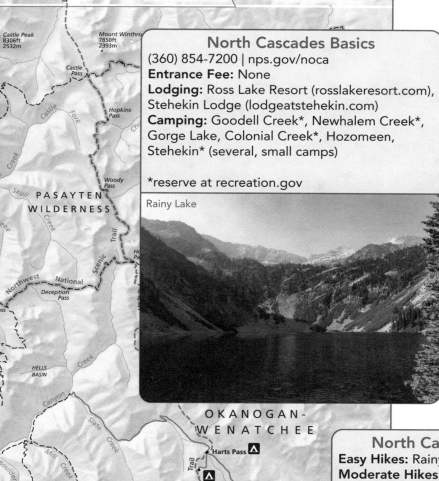
Rainy Lake

North Cascades Driving Distances

The park isn't straightforward. It's a National
Park Service Complex, consisting of North
Cascades National Park (North and South
Units), Ross Lake National Recreation Area,
and Lake Chelan National Recreation Area.
Most visitors only visit Ross Lake NRA because
WA-20 leads motorists right through it.
Cascade River Road (unpaved, seasonal, and
awesome!) heads to the southern half of the
national park. Lake Chelan NRA is mainly
reached by ferry from Chelan. The northern
half of North Cascades National Park is only
accessible by foot.

Seattle, WA	← 2.5 hours / 130 miles →	North Cascades VC
Seattle, WA	← 3.75 hours / 185 miles →	Chelan, WA (+ferry to Stehekin)
Seattle, WA	← 3 hours / 150 miles →	Heather Meadows VC
North Cascades VC	← 3 hours / 120 miles →	Heather Meadows VC
North Cascades VC	← 3 hours / 135 miles →	Chelan, WA (+ferry to Stehekin)

Why Visit North Cascades?

- To climb some mountains!
- Because you can paddle to your campsite
- To spend the night at two remote lodges, one along the shore of Ross Lake, the other nestled in remote Stehekin Village

North Cascades Favorites

Easy Hikes: Rainy Lake (1 mile)
Moderate Hikes: Blue Lake (4.4), Thornton
Lakes (10.4), Maple Pass (7.5), Hidden
Lake (9), Diablo Lake (7.6), Rainbow Creek
(19.4, can loop with Stehekin Valley Road)
Strenuous Hikes: Cascade Pass/Sahale
Arm (7.4/12), Purple Creek (16.2)
Activities: This is the mountaineer's
playground
Views: Diablo Lake Overlook, Rainbow
Falls

What You Need to Know

- Roads and facilities are generally open late April through November.
- Visitation is light by national park standards but almost all guests arrive between June and September.
- Most of the park is left to your imagination if you visit and don't spend a night in the backcountry (or Stehekin) or paddle Ross Lake.
- You'll need to do some planning for a trip here. It isn't exactly a park designed with motorists in mind.

How Much Time Do You Have?

If you only have a day, you need to sit down and decide which area you'd like to visit. If it's Stehekin,
that's a full day ferrying there from Chelan (and you should spend the night). If it's Ross Lake NRA,
you can drive through quickly, stopping at viewpoints, but there are several worthwhile trails (even
beyond the park boundary) and if you really wanted to enjoy Ross or Diablo Lake, you'd need more
time. Finally, you could head to Artist Point in Mount Baker Wilderness. It isn't in the national park
but you'd get a good view of Mount Shuksan which is. So, in short, it's at least a day for each area,
more if you're a backpacker or paddler or you intend to stay at one of the lodges. It's a difficult
decision, but take comfort knowing each region is gorgeous.

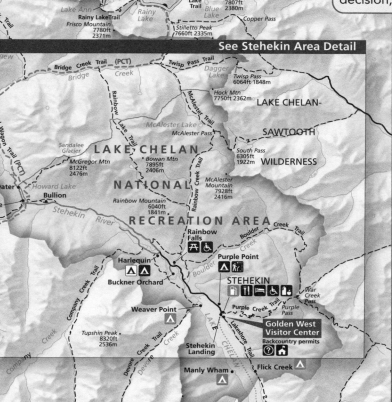

Maple Pass

See Stehekin Area Detail

North Cascades Region

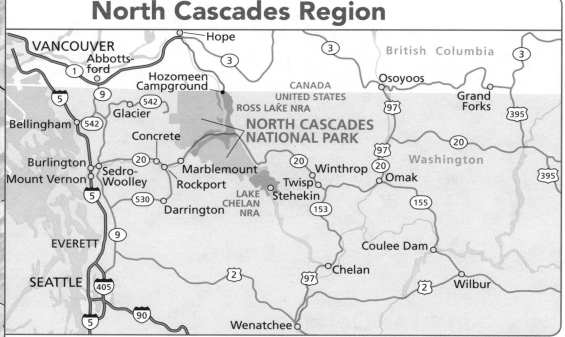

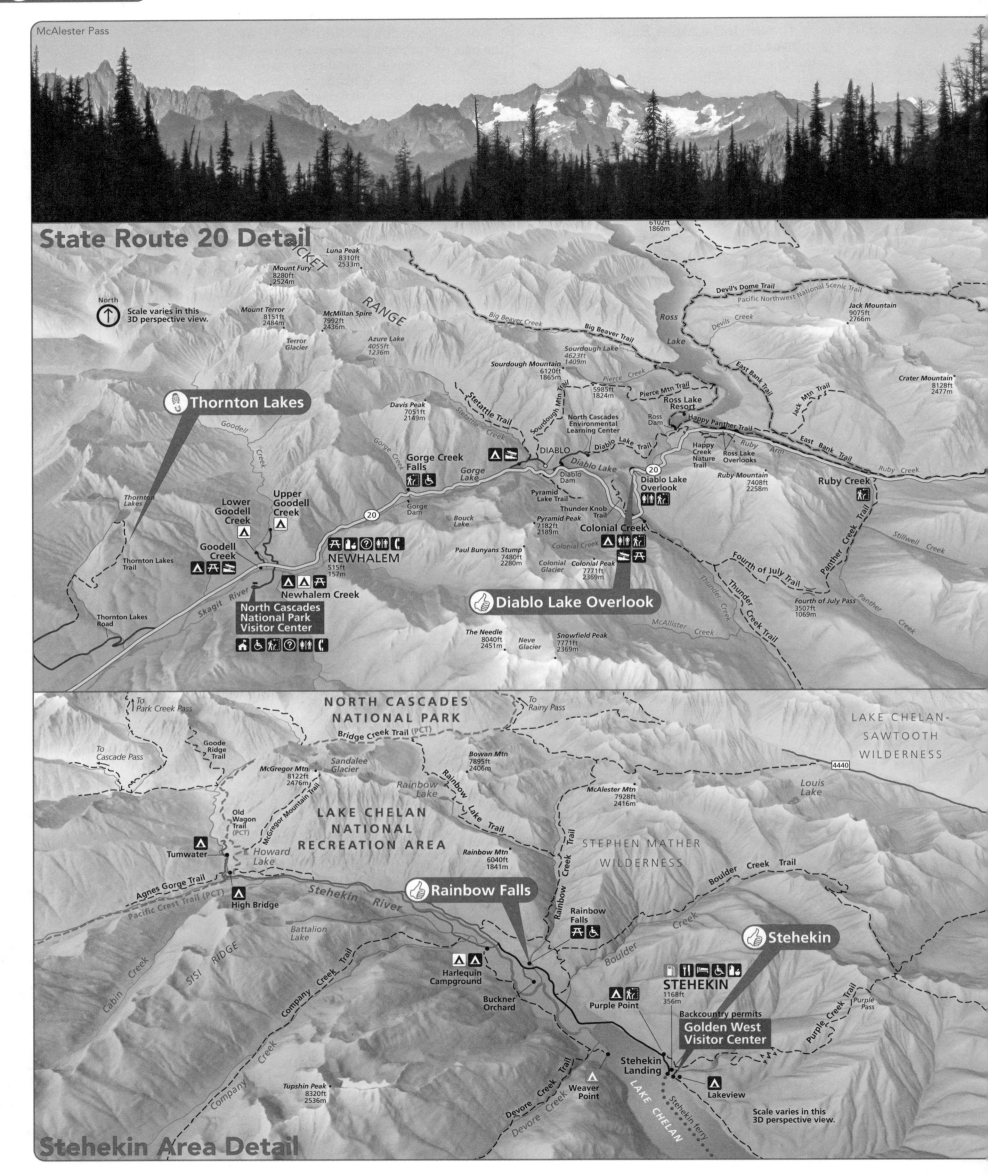

McAlester Pass

State Route 20 Detail

North — Scale varies in this 3D perspective view.

Luna Peak 8310ft 2533m

Mount Fury 8280ft 2524m

PICKET

Mount Terror 8151ft 2484m

McMillan Spire 7992ft 2436m

RANGE

Terror Glacier

Azure Lake 4055ft 1236m

6102ft 1860m

Big Beaver Creek

Big Beaver Trail

Ross

Devil's Dome Trail

Pacific Northwest National Scenic Trail

Devils Creek

Jack Mountain 9075ft 2766m

Lake

Davis Peak 7051ft 2149m

Stetattle Trail

Stetattle Creek

Sourdough Mtn Trail

Sourdough Lake 4623ft 1409m

Sourdough Mountain 6120ft 1865m

Pierce Creek

5985ft 1824m

Pierce Mtn Trail

Ross Lake Resort

East Bank Trail

Jack Mtn Trail

Crater Mountain 8128ft 2477m

👢 **Thornton Lakes**

North Cascades Environmental Learning Center

DIABLO

Diablo Lake Trail

Ross Dam

Happy Panther Trail

Happy Creek Nature Trail

Ruby Creek

East Bank Trail

Ruby Creek

Goodell

Creek

Gorge Creek Falls

Gorge Lake

Diablo Lake

Diablo Dam

20

Ruby Arm

Diablo Lake Overlook

Ross Lake Overlooks

Ruby Mountain 7408ft 2258m

🚶 **Ruby Creek**

Thornton Lakes

Upper Goodell Creek

Lower Goodell Creek

Pyramid Lake Trail

Thunder Knob Trail

Colonial Creek

Bouck Lake

Gorge Dam

Pyramid Peak 7182ft 2189m

Fourth of July Trail

Thornton Lakes Trail

Goodell Creek

Paul Bunyans Stump 7480ft 2280m

Colonial Creek

Colonial Glacier

Colonial Peak 7771ft 2369m

Thunder Creek Trail

Panther Creek Trail

Stillwell Creek

NEWHALEM 515ft 157m

Skagit River

North Cascades National Park Visitor Center

Thornton Lakes Road

Newhalem Creek

👍 **Diablo Lake Overlook**

Fourth of July Pass 3507ft 1069m

McAllister Creek

The Needle 8040ft 2451m

Neve Glacier

Snowfield Peak 7771ft 2369m

Stehekin Area Detail

To Park Creek Pass

NORTH CASCADES NATIONAL PARK

Bridge Creek Trail (PCT)

To Rainy Pass

LAKE CHELAN – SAWTOOTH WILDERNESS

To Cascade Pass

Goode Ridge Trail

McGregor Mtn 8122ft 2476m

Sandalee Glacier

Bowan Mtn 7895ft 2406m

McAlester Mtn 7928ft 2416m

4440

Louis Lake

Old Wagon Trail (PCT)

McGregor Mountain Trail

Rainbow Lake

Rainbow Lake Trail

Rainbow Creek Trail

STEPHEN MATHER WILDERNESS

Tumwater

LAKE CHELAN NATIONAL RECREATION AREA

Howard Lake

Rainbow Mtn 6040ft 1841m

Boulder Creek Trail

Agnes Gorge Trail

Pacific Crest Trail (PCT)

High Bridge

Stehekin River

👍 **Rainbow Falls**

Rainbow Falls

Boulder Creek

👍 **Stehekin**

Battalion Lake

SISI RIDGE

Cabin Creek

Company Creek Trail

Harlequin Campground

Buckner Orchard

Purple Point

STEHEKIN 1168ft 356m

Golden West Visitor Center

Backcountry permits

Purple Creek Trail

Purple Pass

Tupshin Peak 8320ft 2536m

Devore Creek Trail

Weaver Point

Stehekin Landing

LAKE CHELAN

Lakeview

Stehekin ferry

Scale varies in this 3D perspective view.

Brooks Falls (Katmai)

ALASKA

Alaskan Driving Distances
Only three Alaskan parks have road access. They're Wrangell–St. Elias, Denali and Kenai Fjords. The other five are usually bushplane-powered expeditions or a cruise ship destination in the case of Glacier Bay. Bushplanes are useful at the road-accessible parks as well, since roadways reach a tiny fraction of total park land (remember, Alaska is twice the size of Texas). But bundling these three is a very manageable vacation.

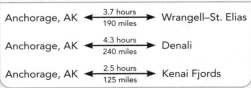

Anchorage, AK ⟷ 3.7 hours / 190 miles ⟶ Wrangell–St. Elias

Anchorage, AK ⟷ 4.3 hours / 240 miles ⟶ Denali

Anchorage, AK ⟷ 2.5 hours / 125 miles ⟶ Kenai Fjords

🕐 **ALASKA (Washington, DC, minus 4 hours)**

RUSSIA

Cape Krusenstern NM

Noatak N PRES

Gates of the Arctic NP & PRES

Kobuk Valley NP

Yukon-Charley Rivers N PRES

Bering Land Bridge N PRES

CANADA

FAIRBANKS

ALASKA

Denali NP & PRES

Wrangell-St. Elias NP & PRES

Lake Clark NP & PRES

ANCHORAGE

Klondike Gold Rush NHP

Alagnak WR

Kenai Fjords NP

Glacier Bay NP & PRES

JUNEAU

Katmai NP & PRES

Sitka NHP

Aniakchak NM & PRES

ALEUTIAN ISLANDS

| 0 | 200 | 400 Kilometers |
| 0 | 200 | 400 Miles |

Glacier Bay Detail

1925
1966
CANADA
UNITED STATES
Park boundary

Grand Pacific Glacier

Margerie Glacier
1907

Johns Hopkins Glacier

Topeka Glacier
1912
1907
1892

Jaw Point
1892
Mount Cooper
6780ft
2066m
1941
1892

Russell Island
1879

1879

Reid Glacier

Lamplugh Glacier

Gilman Glacier
1929
1966

Hoonah Glacier

Johns Hopkins Inlet

Tarr Inlet

Rendu Glacier

Mount Abdallah
5964ft
1818m

Rendu Inlet
1892
1966

CARROLL GLACIER

Gable Mountain
4780ft
1457m

Cushing Glacier

Sentinel Peak
4355ft
1327m

👍 **Margerie Glacier**

👍 **Johns Hopkins Glacier**

Composite Island
1892

1916
1966
1892

Queen Inlet

Wachusett Inlet
1966

BRADY ICEFIELD

Scidmore Bay

Gilbert Peninsula

Gloomy Knob
1331ft
406m

Mount Merriam
5083ft
1549m

Aurora Glacier

July Fourth Mountain
5007ft/1526m

Hugh Miller Glacier
1892

1892

-1416ft
-432m

Blue Mouse Cove

Tidal Inlet

1949

Hugh Miller Inlet

Chapentier Inlet
1892

Mount Bulky
3350ft
1021m

Geikie Glacier
1966
1948

GLACIER BAY

MUIR INLET

Muir Point

Tlingit Point

1892

Sebree Island

Muir Point

🏊 **Muir Inlet**

Blackthorn Peak
3789ft
1155m
1892

GEIKIE INLET

Wood Lake

Tlingit Peak
3274ft
998m

Marble Mountain
3365ft
1026m

Whidbey Passage

Drake Island

North Sandy Cove

North Marble Island

1860

Abyss Lake

Interglacial stumps

Serrated Peak
3327ft
1014m

Lake Seclusion

Francis Island

South Marble Island

Spokane Cove
1857

1845

Dundas River

Fingers Bay

Willoughby Island

Berg Bay

Beartrack Cove

White Cap Mountain
3299ft
1006m

Dundas Bay

Strawberry Island

BEARDSLEE ISLANDS

Narrows

Bartlett River

🎤 **Bartlett Lake**

North
↗

Sitakaday Narrows

1794

Point Carolus

Bartlett Cove

Trail

Bartlett Lake

0   5 Kilometers
0   5 Miles

Visitor Center
Glacier Bay Lodge

⛺ **Park Headquarters**

1860 Historic extent of glaciation

⛺ Campground

Park boundary

-198ft
-60m

Point Gustavus

Glacier extent
1750–1780

Lemesurier Island

ICY STRAIT

9.3mi
15.0km

Gustavus

Falls Creek

Airport ✈

Ice cave

Inside Passage

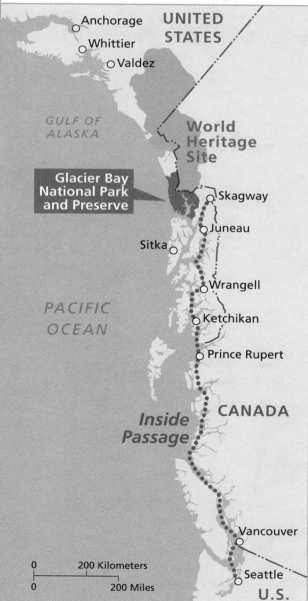

UNITED STATES

Anchorage

Whittier

Valdez

GULF OF ALASKA

World Heritage Site

Glacier Bay National Park and Preserve

Skagway

Juneau

Sitka

PACIFIC OCEAN

Wrangell

Ketchikan

Prince Rupert

Inside Passage

CANADA

Vancouver

0   200 Kilometers
0   200 Miles

Seattle

U.S.

SAINT ELIAS MOUNTAINS

ALSEK GLACIER

ALSEK RANGE

Tikke Glacier

Melburn Glacier

Hay Glacier

Mount Hay
8870ft
2704m

GRAND PACIFIC GLACIER

Alsek River

Alsek Lake

• Gateway Knob

Dry Bay

• Dry Bay Ranger Station
⛺ • Airstrip
• Airstrip
• Public use cabin

GLACIER BAY NATIONAL PRESERVE

East Alsek River

Doame River

DECEPTION HILLS

👍 Alsek River

Mount Lodge
10530ft
3210m

Ferris Glacier

Mount Barnard
8214ft
2504m

See Detail Map

ALASKA

BRITISH COLUMBIA

GRAND PLATEAU GLACIER

Mount Root
12860ft
3920m

Margerie Glacier

Tarr Inlet

GULF OF ALASKA

Ru Is

Mount Fairweather
15300ft
4669m

Mount Quincy Adams
13650ft
4161m

Johns Hopkins Inlet

Jaw Point

Lamplugh Gla

Mount Salisbury
12000ft
3658m

FAIRWEATHER

FAIRWEATHER GLACIER

CAPE FAIRWEATHER

Lituya Mountain
11750ft
3582m

Johns Hopkins Glacier

Mount Abbe
8750ft
2667m

PACIFIC OCEAN

Mount Orville
10495ft
3199m

Lituya Glacier

RANGE

North Crillon Glacier

Mount Crillon
12726ft
3879m

Mount Bertha
10204ft
3110m

Lituya Bay

Lituya

Crillon Lake

Mount La Perouse
10728ft
3270m

B IC

La Perouse Glacier

Glacier Bay Basics
(907) 697-2230 | nps.gov/glba
Entrance Fee: None
Lodging: Glacier Bay Lodge*
Camping: Bartlett Cove

*reserve at visitglacierbay.com

Beartrack Cove

Why Visit Glacier Bay?
• To paddle or cruise among glaciers
• To spot abundant sea life

Seals

Palma Bay

Icy Point

Astrolabe Point

What You Need to Know About Glacier Bay
• Glacier Bay is never filled with vessels because it's restricted to two cruise ships, three tour boats, six charters, and 25 private boats each day.
• Humpback whales are more commonly seen closer to the mouth of Glacier Bay around Baranof Island.
• Glacier Bay Lodge and Bartlett Cove are the most convenient accommodations but there are additional options in Gustavus.

Margerie Glacier

North
↑

Dixon

How Much Time Do You Have?
There's a 97% chance you see Glacier Bay from the deck of a cruise ship, so how much time you spend won't be up to you. However, that's also a good argument to plan your own trip, flying into Gustavus and spending your nights at Glacier Bay Lodge.

0   5   10   15 Kilometers
0   5   10   15 Miles

1860 Historic extent of glaciation

⛺ Campground

TONGASS
NATIONAL
FOREST

Haines

Mount Harris
5177ft
1578m

CANADA
UNITED STATES

T A K H I N S H A

Tsirku River

Takhin River

7

Taiya Inlet

Chilkoot Inlet

Chilkat Inlet

Morse Glacier

Muir Glacier

Cushing Glacier

Riggs Glacier

Mount Brock
4990ft
1521m

Mount Krause
6978ft
2127m

M O U N T A I N S

Sitth-gha-ee Peak
5870ft
1789m

Chilkat
Peninsula

CARROLL GLACIER

1976
1960
1972

White
Thunder
Ridge

1948

McBride Glacier

1966

Davidson Glacier

Sullivan
Island

ount
allah
964ft
818m

Rendu Glacier

Wachusett Inlet

Wolf Point

Interglacial
stumps

1929

Casement Glacier

Mount Rice
5658ft
1725m

Queen Inlet

1907

Mount Merriam
5083ft
1549m

1929

M U I R   I N L E T

1929
1907

Adams

Inlet

Endicott Gap
900ft
274m

Endicott River

L Y N N   C A N A L

Reid Glacier

Gilbert
Peninsula

B E A R T R A C K

Muir
Point

Mount
Wright
5139ft
1566m

Tlingit
Point

North Sandy
Cove

M T S.

C H I L K A T   R A N G E

GLACIER BAY
NATIONAL PARK

G L A C I E R   B A Y

Drake
Island

Interglacial
stumps

South
Marble
Island

Willoughby
Island

Beartrack Cove

Beartrack River

3759ft
1146m

Excursion

Excursion River

River

DY
ELD

GEIKIE INLET

Wood
Lake

Lake
Seclusion

Sitakaday

BEARDSLEE
ISLANDS

Bartlett River

5155ft
1571m

Abyss
Lake

Dundas River

Bartlett
Lake

E X C U R S I O N

BRADY
GLACIER

1794

Visitor Center
Glacier Bay Lodge

Trail

R I D G E

Bartlett
Cove

Airport

Excursion Inlet

1961

Point
Carolus

Narrows

Point
Gustavus

Gustavus

Icy Passage

Dundas
Bay

Pleasant
Island

Taylor
Bay

Lemesurier
Island

I C Y   S T R A I T

POINT
ADOLPHUS

Graves Harbor

Inian
Islands

Eagle Point

Graves
Rocks

CAPE
SPENCER

C R O S S   S O U N D

Elfin
Cove

Port Althorp

Idaho Inlet

Mud Bay

POINT
COUVERDEN

C H I C H A G O F   I S L A N D

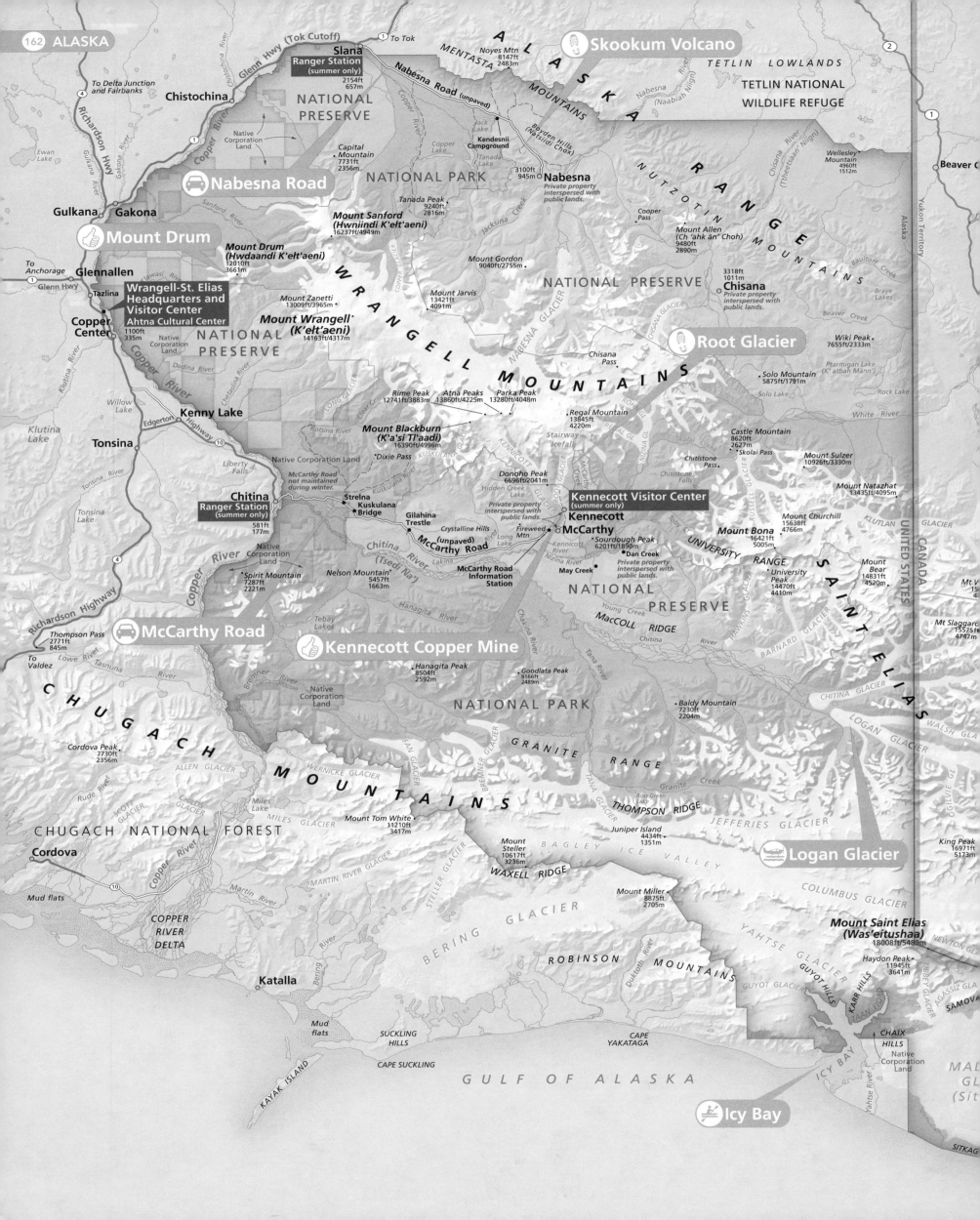

ALASKA

MENTASTA MOUNTAINS

TETLIN LOWLANDS

TETLIN NATIONAL WILDLIFE REFUGE

Skookum Volcano

To Tok

Slana
Ranger Station
(summer only)
2154ft
657m

Glenn Hwy (Tok Cutoff)

Nabesna Road (unpaved)

To Delta Junction
and Fairbanks

Chistochina

NATIONAL
PRESERVE

Native
Corporation
Land

Capital
Mountain
7731ft
2356m

Jack
Lake

Kendesnii
Campground

Beyden Hills
(Natsiidi Chox)

NUTZOTIN MOUNTAINS

Wellesley
Mountain
4960ft
1512m

Beaver C

Nabesna Road

NATIONAL PARK

3100ft
945m

Nabesna
Private property
interspersed with
public lands.

Cooper
Pass

Chisana
3318ft
1011m

Chisana
Private property
interspersed with
public lands.

Gulkana   Gakona

Tanada Peak
9240ft
2816m

Mount Sanford
(Hwniindi K'elt'aeni)
16237ft/4949m

Mount Allen
(Ch'ahk än' Choh)
9480ft
2890m

Braye
Lakes

Mount Drum

Mount Drum
(Hwdaandi K'elt'aeni)
12010ft
3661m

Mount Gordon
9040ft/2755m

NATIONAL PRESERVE

Glennallen

Mount Zanetti
13009ft/3965m

Mount Jarvis
13421ft
4091m

Wiki Peak
7655ft/2333m

Wrangell-St. Elias
Headquarters and
Visitor Center
Ahtna Cultural Center

Copper
Center

1100ft
335m

Mount Wrangell
(K'elt'aeni)
14163ft/4317m

WRANGELL MOUNTAINS

Chisana
Pass

Root Glacier

Solo Mountain
5875ft/1791m

Ptarmigan Lake
(K'atbah Männ')

Rock Lake

To
Anchorage

Tazlina

Native
Corporation
Land

Rime Peak
12741ft/3883m

Atna Peaks
13860ft/4225m

Parka Peak
13280ft/4048m

Regal Mountain
13845ft
4220m

White
River

Kenny Lake

Mount Blackburn
(K'a'si Tl'aadi)
16390ft/4996m

Stairway
Icefall

Castle Mountain
8620ft
2627m

Skolai Pass

Mount Sulzer
10926ft/3330m

Tonsina

Dixie Pass

Chitistone
Pass

Mount Natazhat
13435ft/4095m

Donoho Peak
6696ft/2041m

Chitistone
Falls

Chitina
Ranger Station
(summer only)

581ft
177m

Strelna

Kuskulana
Bridge

Hidden Creek
Lake

Private property
interspersed with
public lands.

Kennecott Visitor Center
(summer only)

Kennecott
McCarthy

Mount Churchill
15638ft
4766m

Gilahina
Trestle

Crystalline Hills

McCarthy Road
(unpaved)

Fireweed
Mtn

Long
Lake

Sourdough Peak
6201ft/1890m

Dan Creek

Mount Bona
16421ft
5005m

UNIVERSITY RANGE

SAINT ELIAS

McCarthy Road
not maintained
during winter.

Chitina River
(Tsedi Na')

Nelson Mountain
5457ft
1663m

McCarthy Road
Information
Station

May Creek

NATIONAL

Mount Bear
14831ft
4520m

McCarthy Road

Spirit Mountain
7287ft
2221m

Native
Corporation
Land

Kennecott Copper Mine

PRESERVE

MacCOLL RIDGE

University
Peak
14470ft
4410m

Mt
15

Thompson Pass
2771ft
845m

Hanagita Peak
8504ft
2592m

Goodlata Peak
8166ft
2489m

Mt Slaggaro
15575ft
4747m

To
Valdez

Tebay
Lakes

NATIONAL PARK

Baldy Mountain
7230ft
2204m

LOGAN GLACIER

CHUGACH MOUNTAINS

Cordova Peak
7730ft
2356m

GRANITE RANGE

THOMPSON RIDGE

JEFFERIES GLACIER

CHUGACH NATIONAL FOREST

Mount Tom White
11210ft
3417m

Juniper Island
4434ft
1351m

Logan Glacier

King Peak
16971ft
5173m

Cordova

Mount Steller
10617ft
3236m

BAGLEY ICE VALLEY

WAXELL RIDGE

Mount Miller
8875ft
2705m

Mud flats

COPPER RIVER DELTA

BERING GLACIER

Mount Saint Elias
(Was'eitushaa)
18008ft/5489m

Haydon Peak
11945ft
3641m

Katalla

ROBINSON MOUNTAINS

Mud
flats

SUCKLING HILLS

CAPE YAKATAGA

CHAIX
HILLS

Native
Corporation
Land

CAPE SUCKLING

GULF OF ALASKA

Icy Bay

KAYAK ISLAND

Approximately 750,000 of the 13+ million acres of land within the boundaries of Wrangell-St. Elias National Park and Preserve are non-federal lands belonging to Alaska Native Corporations, other private owners, and the State of Alaska. Significant amounts of these non-federal lands are located along the McCarthy and Nabesna roads and along the east bank of the Copper River. Please do not trespass. If you have questions, ask at visitor centers or ranger stations.

North
0   10   20   30 Kilometers
0   10   20   30 Miles

- Wrangell-St. Elias National Park
- Wrangell-St. Elias National Preserve
- Native Corporation Lands
- Unpaved road within park
- Other unpaved road
- Trail

Wrangell–St. Elias Basics

(907) 822-5234 | nps.gov/wrst
Entrance Fee: None
Lodging: Devil's Mountain Lodge (devilsmountainlodge.com), Ma Johnson's Historical Hotel (majohnsonshotel.com), Kennecott Glacier Lodge (kennicottlodge.com)
Camping: None*

*But you're allowed to camp in pullouts along McCarthy and Nabesna Roads

Kennecott Mill Town

St. Elias Range

Why Visit Wrangell–St. Elias?

- To view incomparable mountain scenery
- To drive McCarthy and Nabesna roads
- To fly above North America's "Alps"
- To paddle Icy Bay
- To tour Historic Kennecott Mill Town

How Much Time Do You Have?

For road-bound activities, spend at least one night each on the way to or at the end of Kennecott and Nabesna roads. There are 14 backcountry cabins for experienced backpackers. You'll also find nine of the sixteen highest peaks in the United States (in case you're into climbing mountains). Trips like this often require a bush flight and careful planning. If you aren't comfortable setting out on your own, several outfitters are available to help you out.

Mount St. Elias

Pure blue glacial lake

What You Need to Know

- Almost all park visitors arrive between June and September. It's a matter of climate. The park never closes, but you ought to be prepared for anything if you visit fall through spring.
- McCarthy Road is 60 miles from Chitina to Kennecott. It takes at least two hours each way.
- You can camp/sleep in pullouts along the road but it's a better idea to spend a night at one of the lodges in McCarthy beyond its eastern terminus.
- Spending the night is best because it's five miles from the end of the road into Kennecott National Historic Landmark (and then Root Glacier is another four miles). Spend a night (or more), you won't regret it.
- At Kennecott, you can also take a tour of Kennecott Mill with St. Elias Alpine Guides (steliasguides.com). They offer all kinds of other experiences as well.
- You'll find Nabesna Road up at Slana. It's 42 miles to Devil's Mountain Lodge. Along the way are a number of hiking trails, including Skookum Volcano (5 miles, Mile 36.2).
- While most vehicles can negotiate these roads, high-clearance is recommended by the park.
- The drives are scenic, but you'll need to come prepared. Carry a full-size spare. No fuel or services are available. There is cell coverage around Kennecott and McCarthy but pretty much anywhere else you'll need a satellite phone for assistance.
- Most major rental car companies do not allow their cars to be driven off-road. You'll have to decide if it's worth the risk. Or rent a more capable vehicle from a smaller company like Alaska 4x4 Rentals (alaska4x4rentals.com).
- If for some reason you come up here and don't want to drive the long unpaved roads, you can still get a good view of Mount Drum from Copper Center Visitor Center.
- If you can only pick one Alaskan national park to take a flightseeing tour at, this is it.

NISLIN

RANGE

Alaska

Highway

Kluane

KLUANE GAME SANCTUARY

Steele Creek

River

Donjek

River

Burwash Landing

Destruction Bay

KLUANE LAKE

Duke River

To Haines Junction

Macauly ft

Mt Steele 16644ft 5073m

Mt Lucania 147ft 26m

Mt Walsh 14780ft 4505m

DONJEK GLACIER

STEELE GLACIER

GLACIER

Slims River

KLUANE NATIONAL PARK AND RESERVE

ICEFIELD RANGES

McArthur Peak 14400ft 4389m

KASKAWULSH GLACIER

ALVERSTONE GLACIER

HUBBARD GLACIER

GLACIER

MOUNTAINS

ount ogan 9551ft 5959m

WARD GLACIER

Mount Vancouver 15979ft/4870m

Mount Augusta 14070ft/4289m

Mount Alverstone 14565ft/4439m

Mount Kennedy 13093ft 3991m

Yukon Territory Alaska

CANADA U.S.

NATIONAL PARK

Mount Cook 13760ft/4194m

Point Glorious 5000ft/1524m

VALERIE GLACIER

TURNER GLACIER

Mount Hubbard 15015ft 4577m

Mount Seattle 10070ft/3069m

LEWARD GLACIER

CANADA U.S.

Hubbard Glacier (Sit' Tlein)

YT BC

NA R

in)

Grand Wash River (Tsaa Héeni)

DISENCHANTMENT BAY

Haenke I.

Mount Jette 8460ft/2579m

RUSSELL FJORD

NUNATAK FJORD

Malaspina Lake

NATIONAL PRESERVE

TONGASS NATIONAL FOREST

YAKUTAT BAY

POINT MANBY

Yakutat Ranger Station (summer only)

Yakutat

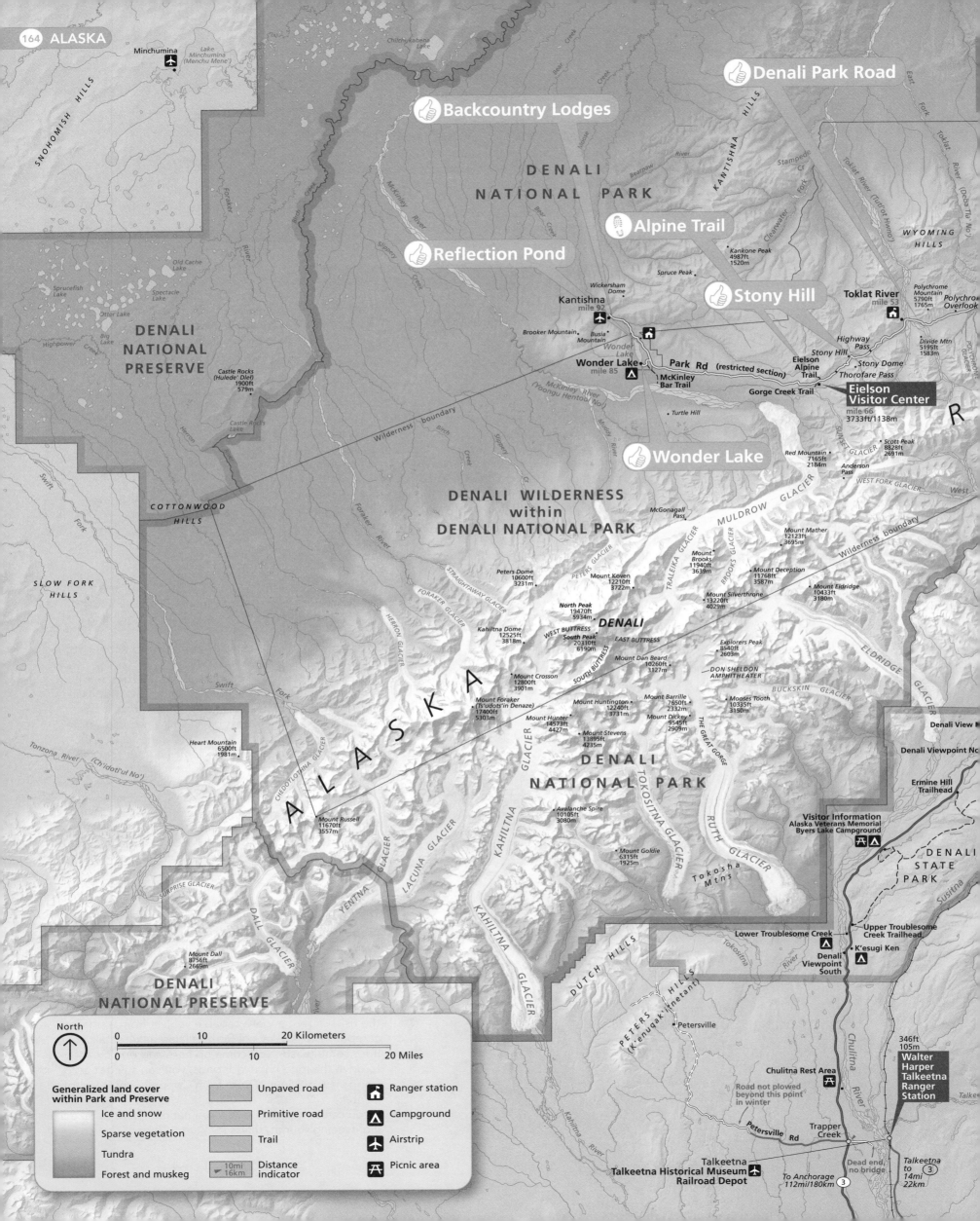

Minchumina

Lake
Minchumina
(Menchu Mene')

Chilchukabena Lake

SNOHOMISH HILLS

**DENALI
NATIONAL PARK**

👍 **Backcountry Lodges**

KANTISHNA HILLS

👍 **Denali Park Road**

WYOMING HILLS

Old Cache
Lake

Spectacle
Lake

Sprucefish
Lake

Otter Lake

Big Lake

👢 **Alpine Trail**

Kankone Peak
4987ft
1520m

**DENALI
NATIONAL
PRESERVE**

👍 **Reflection Pond**

Spruce Peak

Wickersham
Dome

Kantishna
mile 92

👍 **Stony Hill**

Toklat River
mile 53

Polychrome
Mountain
5790ft
1765m

Polychrome
Overlook

Castle Rocks
(Hulede' Diel)
1900ft
579m

Brooker Mountain

Busia
Mountain

Wonder
Lake

Wonder Lake
mile 85

Park Rd (restricted section)

Highway
Pass

Stony Hill

Eielson
Alpine
Trail

Divide Mtn
5195ft
1583m

Castle Rocks
Lake

Highpower

McKinley
Bar Trail

Stony Dome
Thorofare Pass

Gorge Creek Trail

**Eielson
Visitor Center**
mile 66
3733ft/1138m

Turtle Hill

👍 **Wonder Lake**

Red Mountain
7165ft
2184m

Scott Peak
8828ft
2691m

COTTONWOOD
HILLS

**DENALI WILDERNESS
within
DENALI NATIONAL PARK**

Anderson
Pass

WEST FORK GLACIER

West

McGonagall
Pass

MULDROW GLACIER

Wilderness boundary

SLOW FORK
HILLS

Peters Dome
10600ft
3231m

Mount Koven
12210ft
3722m

Mount
Brooks
11940ft
3639m

Mount Mather
12123ft
3695m

Mount Deception
11768ft
3587m

Mount Eldridge
10433ft
3180m

North Peak
19470ft
5934m

Mount Silverthrone
13220ft
4029m

Kahiltna Dome
12525ft
3818m

WEST BUTTRESS
South Peak
20310ft
6190m

DENALI

EAST BUTTRESS

Explorers Peak
8540ft
2603m

ELDRIDGE GLACIER

A L A S K A

Mount Crosson
12800ft
3901m

SOUTH BUTTRESS

Mount Dan Beard
10260ft
3127m

DON SHELDON
AMPHITHEATER

BUCKSKIN GLACIER

Mount Foraker
(Ts'udolt'in Denaze)
17400ft
5303m

Mount Huntington
12240ft
3731m

Mount Barrille
7650ft
2332m

Mooses Tooth
10335ft
3150m

Mount Hunter
14573ft
4427m

Mount Dickey
9545ft
2909m

THE GREAT GORGE

Denali View N

Heart Mountain
6500ft
1981m

Mount Stevens
13895ft
4235m

Denali Viewpoint

**Ermine Hill
Trailhead**

**DENALI
NATIONAL PARK**

TOKOSITNA GLACIER

RUTH GLACIER

Mount Russell
11670ft
3557m

Awalanche Spire
10105ft
3080m

Visitor Information
Alaska Veterans Memorial
Byers Lake Campground

**DENALI
STATE
PARK**

LACUNA GLACIER

KAHILTNA GLACIER

Mount Goldie
6315ft
1925m

Tokosha
Mtns

YENTNA GLACIER

DALL GLACIER

DUTCH HILLS

Lower Troublesome Creek

**Upper Troublesome
Creek Trailhead**

Mount Dall
8756ft
2669m

KAHILTNA GLACIER

**Denali
Viewpoint
South**

K'esugi Ken

**DENALI
NATIONAL PRESERVE**

PETERS HILLS
(K'enugak'tnetant')

Petersville

Chulitna Rest Area

346ft
105m

**Walter
Harper
Talkeetna
Ranger
Station**

Road not plowed
beyond this point
in winter

Talkeetna
to 14mi
22km

North ↑

Generalized land cover		

| 0 | 10 | 20 Kilometers |
| 0 | 10 | 20 Miles |

**Generalized land cover
within Park and Preserve**

Ice and snow

Sparse vegetation

Tundra

Forest and muskeg

Unpaved road

Primitive road

Trail

10mi
16km
Distance
indicator

🏠 Ranger station

⛺ Campground

✈ Airstrip

⛱ Picnic area

Petersville
Rd

Petersville

Trapper
Creek

To Anchorage
112mi/180km

Talkeetna

Talkeetna Historical Museum
Railroad Depot

Dead end,
no bridge

Talkeetna
to 14mi
22km

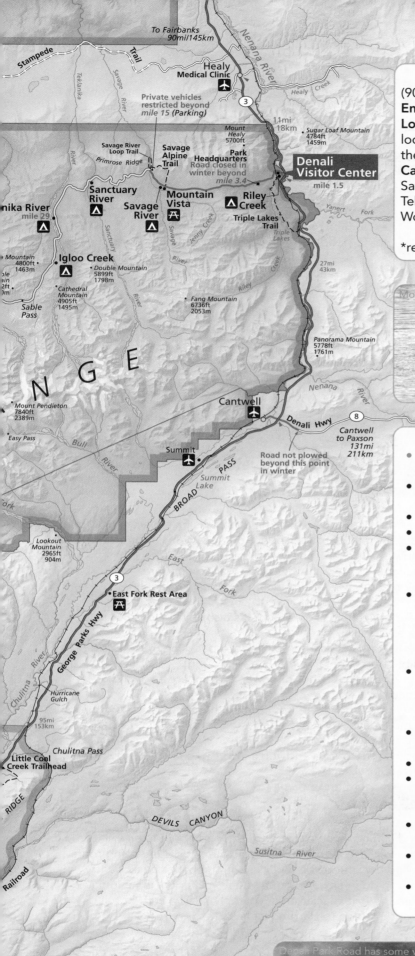

To Fairbanks
90mi/145km

Stampede Trail

Healy
Medical Clinic

Private vehicles
restricted beyond
mile 15 (Parking)

Mount
Healy
5700ft

Sugar Loaf Mountain
4784ft
1459m

11mi
18km

Savage River
Loop Trail

Savage
Alpine
Trail

Park
Headquarters
Road closed in
winter beyond
mile 3.4

**Denali
Visitor Center**
mile 1.5

Primrose Ridge

Sanctuary
River

Mountain
Vista

Riley
Creek

Triple Lakes
Trail

Savage
River

nika River
mile 29

Igloo Creek

Double Mountain
5899ft
1798m

Mountain
4800ft
1463m

Cathedral
Mountain
4905ft
1495m

Sable
Pass

Fang Mountain
6736ft
2053m

27mi
43km

Panorama Mountain
5778ft
1761m

N G E

Nenana
River

Cantwell

Denali Hwy

8

**Cantwell
to Paxson**
131mi
211km

Road not plowed
beyond this point
in winter

Summit

BROAD PASS

Summit
Lake

Lookout
Mountain
2965ft
904m

3

East Fork Rest Area

East Fork

George Parks Hwy

Chulitna River

Hurricane
Gulch

95mi
153km

Chulitna Pass

Little Coal
Creek Trailhead

RIDGE

DEVILS CANYON

Susitna River

Railroad

Denali Basics

Denali, "The High One"

(907) 683-9532 | nps.gov/dena
Entrance Fee: $15/person
Lodging: There are four lodges on private property in the park's backcountry
Camping*: Riley Creek, Savage River, Sanctuary River, Teklanika River, Igloo Creek, Wonder Lake

*reserve at recreation.gov

Moose and ducks at Wonder Lake

Why Visit Denali?

- To see "The High One" in person rising some 18,000 feet above its surroundings
- To land on a glacier during a flightseeing tour
- To join a bus tour, which is basically a safari, as you look to the distance trying to spot the big five: moose, grizzly, caribou, Dall's sheep, and wolves

What You Need to Know About Denali

- Denali Park Road is closed at Mile 43 until (at least) summer 2025 while a suspension bridge is built. Check with the park about status and if you can still fly into Kantishna.
- The park is open all year but Denali Park Road is first plowed beginning sometime in March and is usually accessible to vehicles sometime in April.
- You can drive the first 15 miles of Denali Park Road. The rest is open to park/lodge buses.
- Tour buses (reservedenali.com) begin in mid-may and run until mid-September.
- When the shuttle stops in September, there's a four-day window where the park opens Denali Park Road to motorists who win the "Road Lottery" (fee, apply through recreation.gov).
- There are two types of tour buses running the park road in summer. Narrated Bus Tours do exactly what you'd guess, provide a narrated tour of Denali Park Road. Shuttle Buses are also narrated by the driver but they're less formal, less expensive, and you have the freedom to hop off and hop on whenever you feel like it (as long as you aren't beyond the furthest destination of your ticket). There are also camper buses.
- There are very few maintained hiking trails. You'll find a few around the visitor center, Savage River, Eielson Visitor Center, Wonder Lake, and then there are a few near the private backcountry lodges. Alpine Trail (Thorofare Ridge) at Eielson Visitor Center should be your first choice. It's less than three miles but gains more than 1,000 feet.
- Climbing Denali takes considerable training and a permit. Or there are several outfitters leading summit trips.
- You can raft the Nenana River, which runs not too far from the park's entrance.
- Mountain biking is another great way to experience Denali Park Road. Rentals are available near the park entrance. Camper buses have room for two bikes. You must have a campground reservation or backcountry permit to reserve bike space.
- Everyone wants to see Denali. Unfortunately it's only fully visible about 1/3 of the summer. That number rises in spring/fall as the average high/low temperature differential decreases.
- There's a grill near Denali Visitor Center. Riley Creek Mercantile is stocked with essentials but you'll want to call to see if they stock a specific fuel type if you're relying on it.
- If you don't want to drive, the train (alaskarailroad.com) runs to Denali and the stretch from Seward to the park is about as scenic as a rail line can be.

How Much Time Do You Have?

Denali Park Road has some views

In a perfect world, you'd arrive with a flexible schedule so you could show up when the mountain's out, tour the park road (and maybe hop in a plane for a flight around Denali). But that isn't reality for most travelers, not to mention lodging and camping book very early here, often within minutes of becoming available. So, that's the catch with a trip to Denali. You could spend a mid-summer week here and not see the mountain or you could spend one day and it could be looming large the entire duration of your bus tour. I'd make some serious calculations before deciding how long to spend here.

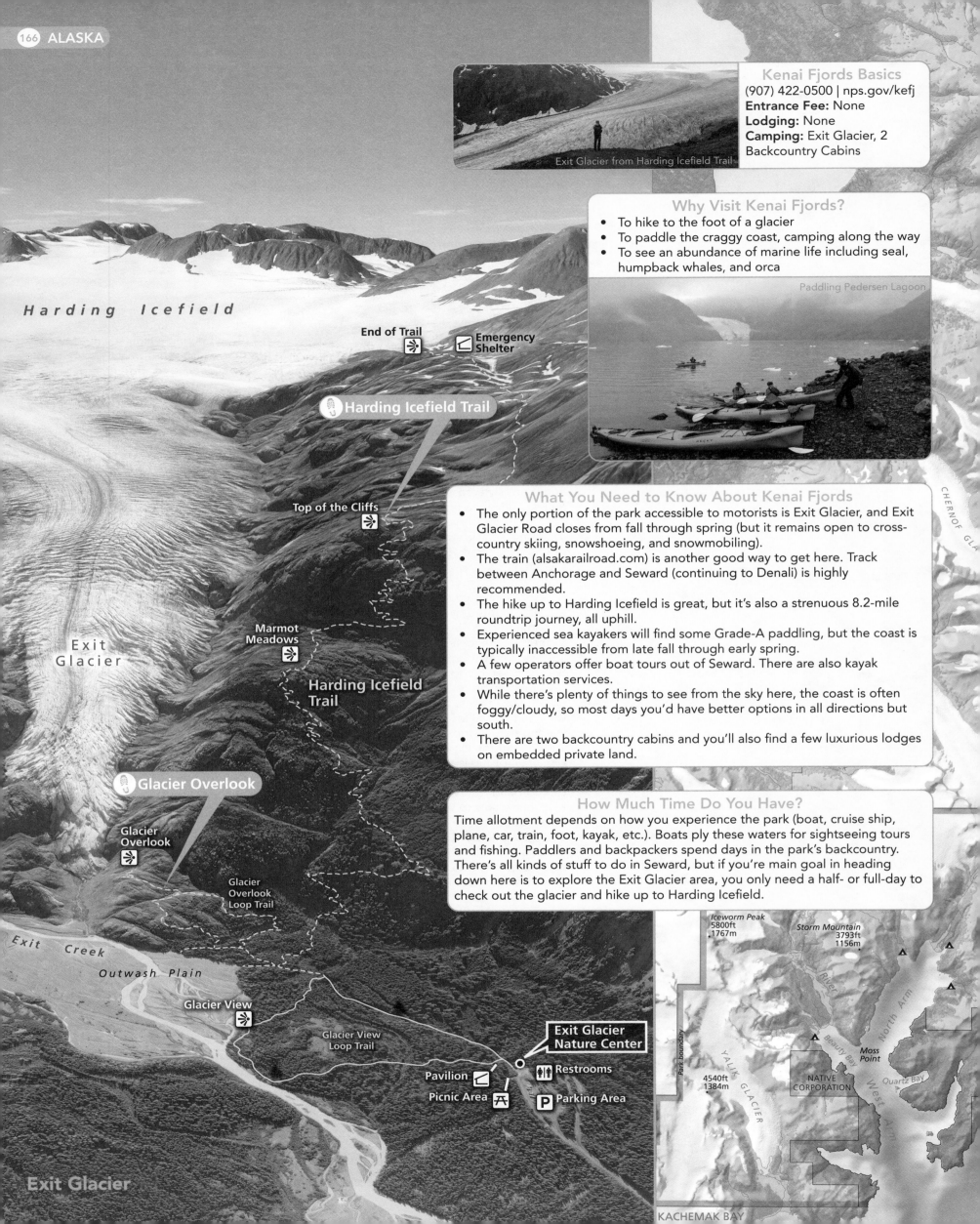

Exit Glacier from Harding Icefield Trail

Kenai Fjords Basics

(907) 422-0500 | nps.gov/kefj
Entrance Fee: None
Lodging: None
Camping: Exit Glacier, 2 Backcountry Cabins

Why Visit Kenai Fjords?

- To hike to the foot of a glacier
- To paddle the craggy coast, camping along the way
- To see an abundance of marine life including seal, humpback whales, and orca

Paddling Pedersen Lagoon

What You Need to Know About Kenai Fjords

- The only portion of the park accessible to motorists is Exit Glacier, and Exit Glacier Road closes from fall through spring (but it remains open to cross-country skiing, snowshoeing, and snowmobiling).
- The train (alsakarailroad.com) is another good way to get here. Track between Anchorage and Seward (continuing to Denali) is highly recommended.
- The hike up to Harding Icefield is great, but it's also a strenuous 8.2-mile roundtrip journey, all uphill.
- Experienced sea kayakers will find some Grade-A paddling, but the coast is typically inaccessible from late fall through early spring.
- A few operators offer boat tours out of Seward. There are also kayak transportation services.
- While there's plenty of things to see from the sky here, the coast is often foggy/cloudy, so most days you'd have better options in all directions but south.
- There are two backcountry cabins and you'll also find a few luxurious lodges on embedded private land.

How Much Time Do You Have?

Time allotment depends on how you experience the park (boat, cruise ship, plane, car, train, foot, kayak, etc.). Boats ply these waters for sightseeing tours and fishing. Paddlers and backpackers spend days in the park's backcountry. There's all kinds of stuff to do in Seward, but if you're main goal in heading down here is to explore the Exit Glacier area, you only need a half- or full-day to check out the glacier and hike up to Harding Icefield.

Harding Icefield

End of Trail

Emergency Shelter

Harding Icefield Trail

Top of the Cliffs

Marmot Meadows

Harding Icefield Trail

Exit Glacier

Glacier Overlook

Glacier Overlook

Glacier Overlook Loop Trail

Exit Creek

Outwash Plain

Glacier View

Glacier View Loop Trail

Exit Glacier Nature Center

Pavilion

Picnic Area

Restrooms

Parking Area

Iceworm Peak
5800ft
1767m

Storm Mountain
3793ft
1156m

4540ft
1384m

Moss Point

NATIVE CORPORATION

Quartz Bay

CHERNOF GLA

North Arm

West Arm

River

Beauty Bay

YALIK GLACIER

Park boundary

KACHEMAK BAY

Exit Glacier

KENAI NATIONAL WILDLIFE REFUGE

KENAI FJORDS

NATIONAL

PARK

KENAI MOUNTAINS

HARDING

ICEFIELD

5720ft
1744m

INDIAN GLACIER

KILLEY GLACIER

SKILAK GLACIER

5355ft
1633m

Park boundary

6197ft
1889m

TUSTUMENA GLACIER

FRIULI GLACIER

5269ft
1606m

5873ft
1791m

CHERNOF GL.

6340ft
1933m

MCCARTY GLACIER

NORTHWESTERN GLACIER

(Highest point in park)
6450ft
1996m

Striation
Island

Northwestern Fiord

4734ft
1443m

1900

Cataract Cove

Crater Bay

Paguna Arm

NATIVE
CORPORATION

Sandy
Bay

Harris
Point

-726ft
-221m

Taz Basin

-750ft
-229m

Surok Point

Harris Bay

HARRIS PENINSULA

4430ft
1351m

Quicksand
Cove

McMullen Cove

Bear Cove

Holgate Arm

Holgate Glacier

5641ft
1720m

AIALIK GLACIER

ADDISON GL.

PEDERSEN GLACIER

Holgate Cabin

Aialik Bay

SKEE GLACIER

BEAR GLACIER

5912ft
1802m

Slate
Island

NATIVE CORPORATION

Aialik
Public Use
Cabin

Pedersen
Lagoon

Coleman Bay

Aialik Bay Ranger Station

Holgate
Public Use Cabin

Three Hole Point

-972ft
-296m

Aialik Bay

AIALIK PENINSULA

Porcupine Cove

Agnes Cove

Three Hole Bay

3768ft
1149m

Bulldog
Cove

Bear Glacier
Point

Callisto
Head

Rugged
Island

Coleman Bay

Harding Gateway

-900ft
-274m

Cheval
Island

Glacier Lodge

1109ft
338m

No Name
Island

Aialik Cape

Chat
Island

-984ft
-300m

Harbor
Island

Dora Passage

-834ft
-254m

Natoa
Island

Pelfes Pass

CHISWELL ISLANDS

ALASKA MARITIME
NATIONAL WILDLIFE REFUGE

Matushka
Island

Lone Rock

Gulf of Alaska

-702ft
-214m

Exit Glacier
Nature Center

Willow Public
Use Cabin
(winter only)

EXIT GLACIER

Exit Glacier Road

Lost Lake Trail

To Anchorage

Salmon Creek

9

Mount Alice
5265ft
1605m

SEWARD

Nash Road

Marathon
Mountain
4603ft
1403m

Information Center

Chugach National
Forest Headquarters

Lowell
Point

Phoenix Peak
5155ft
1571m

Paradise Creek

Park boundary

Coastal Trail
Submerged
at high tide
south of
Tonsina Point

Tonsina
Point

-84ft
-26m

State Park
Cabins

Callisto
Peak
3223ft
983m

CAINES HEAD
STATE
RECREATION
AREA

Caines
Head

Resurrection Bay

Thumb Cove

-972ft
-296m

State
Park
Cabins

Humpy Cove

Fox
Island

Hive
Island

Eldorado Narrows

RESURRECTION PENINSULA

2904ft
885m

Driftwood Bay

Cape
Resurrection

Barwell
Island

McCarty Fiord

GLACIER

INGLESTADT

-876ft
-267m

Park boundary

1942

Taroka Arm

Two Arm Bay

1926

Desire
Lake

Thunder Bay

NATIVE
CORPORATION

Delight
Lake

1905

McCarty
Lagoon

James
Lagoon

Black
Bay

Black Mountain
2028ft
618m

Cloudy
Mountain
1810ft
552m

Moonlight Bay

Steep Point

PYE ISLANDS

ALASKA MARITIME
NATIONAL WILDLIFE REFUGE

Roaring Cove

Granite
Island

Granite Passage

1615ft
492m

Aligo
Point

Granite
Cape

Seal Rocks

North

0   5 Kilometers
0   5 Miles

Map warning
Do not use this map for
navigation or backpacking.
Use nautical charts and tide
tables for navigation.
Topographic maps and
area information are
available at the visitor
center.

Native Corporation land
Private lands owned by
Port Graham Corporation,
labeled Native Corpora-
tion, may be accessed only
on public easements or
with special use permits
issued by the village. Check
with the park for detailed
maps of boundaries and
easement locations before
venturing into the fjords.

Unpaved road
Trail
Historic extent of
glaciation

Campground
Landing/camping
beach

Generalized land cover
Ice and snow
Barren
Low vegetation
Cottonwood, alder, willow
Spruce, hemlock

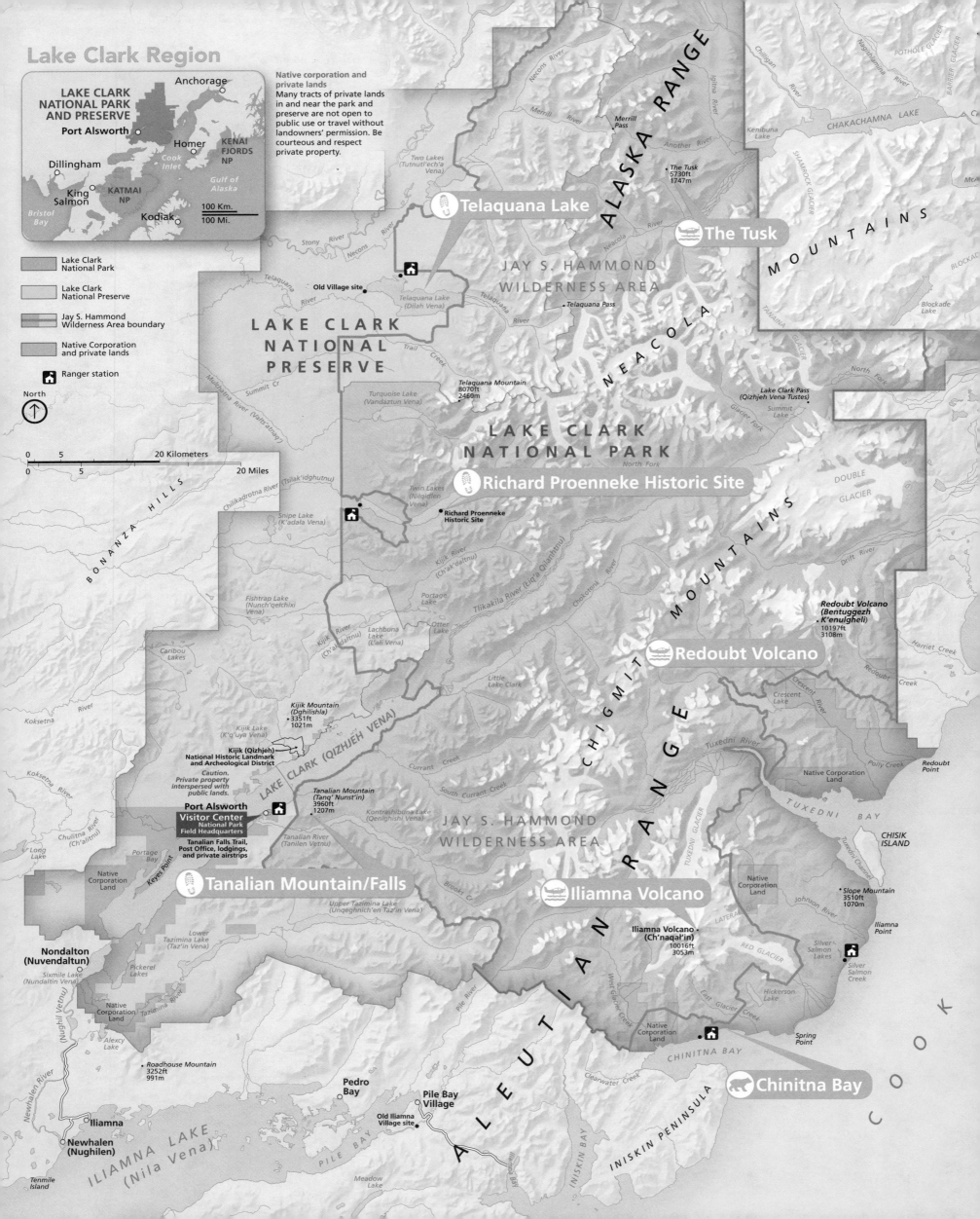

Lake Clark Region

LAKE CLARK NATIONAL PARK AND PRESERVE
Anchorage
Port Alsworth
Dillingham
Homer
KENAI FJORDS NP
King Salmon
KATMAI NP
Cook Inlet
Gulf of Alaska
Kodiak
Bristol Bay

100 Km.
100 Mi.

Native corporation and private lands
Many tracts of private lands in and near the park and preserve are not open to public use or travel without landowners' permission. Be courteous and respect private property.

Lake Clark National Park

Lake Clark National Preserve

Jay S. Hammond Wilderness Area boundary

Native Corporation and private lands

Ranger station

North

0   5   20 Kilometers
0   5   20 Miles

ALASKA RANGE

POTHOLE GLACIER

Necons River

Merrill River

Merrill Pass

Another River

Chilligan River

Nagishlamina River

BARRIER GLACIER

Kenibuna Lake

CHAKACHAMNA LAKE

Two Lakes (Tutnut'ech'a Vena)

• The Tusk 5730ft 1747m

SHAMROCK GLACIER

McA...

Telaquana Lake

The Tusk

JAY S. HAMMOND WILDERNESS AREA

Stony River

Necons River

Old Village site

Telaquana River

Telaquana Lake (Dilah Vena)

Telaquana River

• Telaquana Pass

NEACOLA

MOUNTAINS

Blockade Lake

TANAINA GLACIER

LAKE CLARK NATIONAL PRESERVE

Telaquana Trail

Summit Cr

Mulchatna River (Valts'atnaq)

Turquoise Lake (Vandaztun Vena)

Telaquana Mountain 8070ft 2460m

North Fork

Lake Clark Pass (Qizhjeh Vena Tustes)

Glacier Fork

Summit Lake

North Fork

LAKE CLARK NATIONAL PARK

DOUBLE GLACIER

Chilikadrotna River (Tsilak'idghutnu)

BONANZA HILLS

Snipe Lake (K'adala Vena)

Twin Lakes (Nilqidlen Vena)

Richard Proenneke Historic Site

Kijik River (Ch'ak'daltnu)

Richard Proenneke Historic Site

CHIGMIT

MOUNTAINS

Fishtrap Lake (Nunch'qelchixi Vena)

Portage Lake

Tlikakila River (Eiq'a Qilanhtnu)

Otter Lake

Chokotonk River

Redoubt Volcano (Bentuggezh K'enulgheli) 10197ft 3108m

Harriet Creek

Caribou Lakes

Lachbuna Lake (L'ali Vena)

Little Lake Clark

Redoubt Volcano

Crescent Lake

Crescent River

Redoubt Creek

Redoubt Point

Koksetna River

River

Kijik Mountain (Dghilishla) 3351ft 1021m

Kijik Lake (K'q'uya Vena)

Kijik (Qizhjeh) National Historic Landmark and Archeological District
Caution. Private property interspersed with public lands.

LAKE CLARK (QIZHJEH VENA)

Currant Creek

South Currant Creek

MOUNTAINS

Tuxedni River

Native Corporation Land

Polly Creek

Koksetna River

Chulitna River (Ch'alitnu)

Port Alsworth
Visitor Center National Park Field Headquarters
Tanalian Falls Trail, Post Office, lodgings, and private airstrips

Tanalian Mountain (Tanq' Nunst'in) 3960ft 1207m

Kontrashibuna Lake (Qenilghishi Vena)

Brooks Cr

JAY S. HAMMOND WILDERNESS AREA

TUXEDNI GLACIER

TUXEDNI BAY

CHISIK ISLAND

Long Lake

Portage Bay

Keyes Point

Tanalian Mountain/Falls

Tanalian River (Tanilen Vetnu)

Upper Tazimina Lake (Unqeghnich'en Taz'in Vena)

Pile River

West Glacier Creek

Iliamna Volcano

LATERAL GL

Johnson River

Slope Mountain 3510ft 1070m

Iliamna Point

Native Corporation Land

ALEUTIAN RANGE

Iliamna Volcano (Ch'naqal'in) 10016ft 3053m

RED GLACIER

Silver Salmon Lakes

Silver Salmon Creek

Nondalton (Nuvendaltun)

Lower Tazimina Lake (Taz'in Vena)

Pickerel Lakes

Native Corporation Land

Tazimina River

Sixmile Lake (Nundaltin Vena)

Newhalen River (Nughil Vetnu)

Alexcy Lake

• Roadhouse Mountain 3252ft 991m

Pedro Bay

Pile Bay Village

Old Iliamna Village site

East Glacier Creek

Hickerson Lake

Native Corporation Land

Chinitna Bay

Spring Point

CHINITNA BAY

Clearwater Creek

INISKIN PENINSULA

Iliamna

Newhalen (Nughilen)

ILIAMNA LAKE (Nila Vena)

Tenmile Island

PILE BAY

Meadow Lake

Iliamna Bay

INISKIN BAY

COOK INLET

Dena'ina Place Names

Present English	Dena'ina	Translation
Chilikadrotna River	Tsilak'idghutnu	Tongue stream
Chulitna River	Ch'alitnu	Flows out river
Iliamna Lake	Nila Vena	Islands lake
Iliamna Volcano	Ch'naqal'in	One that stands above
Kijik	Qizhjeh	Place where people gather
Kijik Lake	K'q'uya Vena	Red salmon lake
Kijik River	Ch'ak'daltnu	Animals-walk-out stream
Kontrashibuna Lake	Qenlghishi Vena	Boiling lake
Lachbuna Lake	L'ali Vena	Dead fall collapses lake
Lake Clark	Qizhjeh Vena	People gather lake
Mulchatna River	Valts'atnaq'	River
Newhalen River	Nughil Vetnu	Flows down river
Nondalton	Nuvendaltun	Lake extends below
Redoubt Volcano	Bentuggezh K'enulgheli	One that has a notched forehead
Sixmile Lake	Nundaltin Vena	Lake extends below
Snipe Lake	K'adala Vena	Birds fly out lake
Tanalian River	Tanilen Vetnu	Flows into water stream
Tazimina Lake - Lower	Taz'in Vena	Fish trap lake
Telaquana Lake	Dilah Vena	Fish swim into lake
Tlikakila River	Łiq'a Qilanhtnu	Stream where salmon are
Turquoise Lake	Vandaztun Vena	Caribou hair lake
Twin Lakes	Nilqidlen Vena	Flows together lakes
Tyonek	Tubughnenq'	Beach land

How Much Time Do You Have?

With these last four parks, "How much money do you have?" may be a more pertinent question. The parks are huge and almost entirely undeveloped. If you want to nearly guarantee a safe and enjoyable trip, you should rely on bush pilots, wilderness lodges, and/or adventure outfitters. Those things come with a price.

Silver Salmon Creek

Lake Clark Basics

(907) 781-2218 | nps.gov/lacl
Entrance Fee: None
Lodging & Camping: None*

*Several private businesses operate within park boundaries

Why Visit Lake Clark

- Bears!
- To see wilderness as Dick Proenneke did, you can even do so from the stoop of his cabin at Twin Lakes
- Unparalleled fishing and hunting
- Fly above volcanoes, Redoubt last erupted in 1966

Proenneke Cabin

What You Need to Know About Lake Clark

- Just about all visitation occurs between June and September.
- The park is almost exclusively accessed by air taxi. You can catch a commercial flight from Anchorage to Iliamna (30 miles outside the park) before flying over the park or to your destination. Or you can fly direct via bush plane from Anchorage, Homer, Soldotna, or Kodiak).
- There are a few hiking trails near Port Alsworth Visitor Center. Another trail connects Upper and Lower Twin Lakes.
- Proenneke's cabin is situated on the shore of Upper Twin Lake. The cabin is locked from late September through May. A float plane can get you there.
- Boat tours of Lake Clark are available.
- There are also a few rivers providing excellent packrafting opportunities.
- Hunting is allowed at Lake Clark National Preserve and it's quite popular. Several outfitters are available, just know many hunts must be planned more than a year in advance to take care of the logistics.
- Fishing outfitters are widely available too.
- Many companies offer bear-viewing tours. Popular spots to see grizzly include Chinitna Bay, Silver Salmon Creek, and Crescent Lake.

Katmai Basics

(907) 246-3305 | nps.gov/katm
Entrance Fee: None
Lodging*: Brooks Lodge, Kulik Lodge, Grosvenor Lodge
Camping: Brooks Camp**

*reserve at katmailand.com
**reserve at recreation.gov

Why Visit Katmai?

- To watch bears as they fish at Brooks Falls!
- To fish (with fly-fishing rods, not paws like the bears)
- To tour Valley of 10,000 Smokes

Valley of 10,000 Smokes

Touch your toes

What You Need to Know About Katmai

- The park is open year-round but services are only available from June through mid-September.
- Bear watching at Brooks Camp is best in July and September, and it's pretty good at Hallo Bay all summer long.
- Camping at Brooks Camp for prime bear time fills within hours of becoming available. Brooks Lodge distributes rooms via online lottery (about 1.5 years in advance) due to extremely high demand.
- Viewing bears in the wild may seem like a bad idea to you, but there are plenty of things to comfort humans at Brooks Camp, like bridges, viewing platforms, and even an electric fence around the campground.
- Similar to Lake Clark, Katmai is an exceptional destination for fishing, hunting, flightseeing, and paddling.
- Or you can hop aboard a bus at Brooks Camp to tour Valley of 10,000 Smokes (a byproduct of the 1912 eruption of Novarupta). Tours last about seven hours and can be booked through katmailand.com.
- You can get to know Katmai's resident bears by watching the park's webcams.

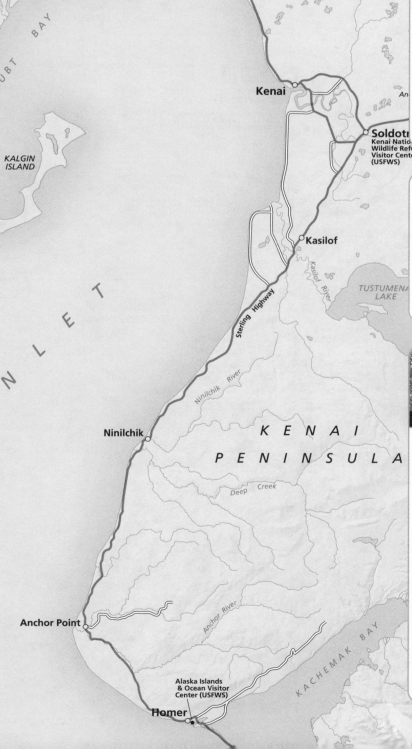

Mt Spurr
11,073ft/3374m

Chakachatna River

TRADING BAY

WEST FORELAND

Big River

REDOUBT BAY

KALGIN ISLAND

Harriet Point

C O O K   I N L E T

Kenai

Soldotna
Kenai National Wildlife Refuge Visitor Center (USFWS)

Kasilof

Kasilof River

TUSTUMENA LAKE

Sterling Highway

Ninilchik River

Ninilchik

K E N A I   P E N I N S U L A

Deep Creek

Anchor River

Anchor Point

Alaska Islands & Ocean Visitor Center (USFWS)

KACHEMAK BAY

Homer

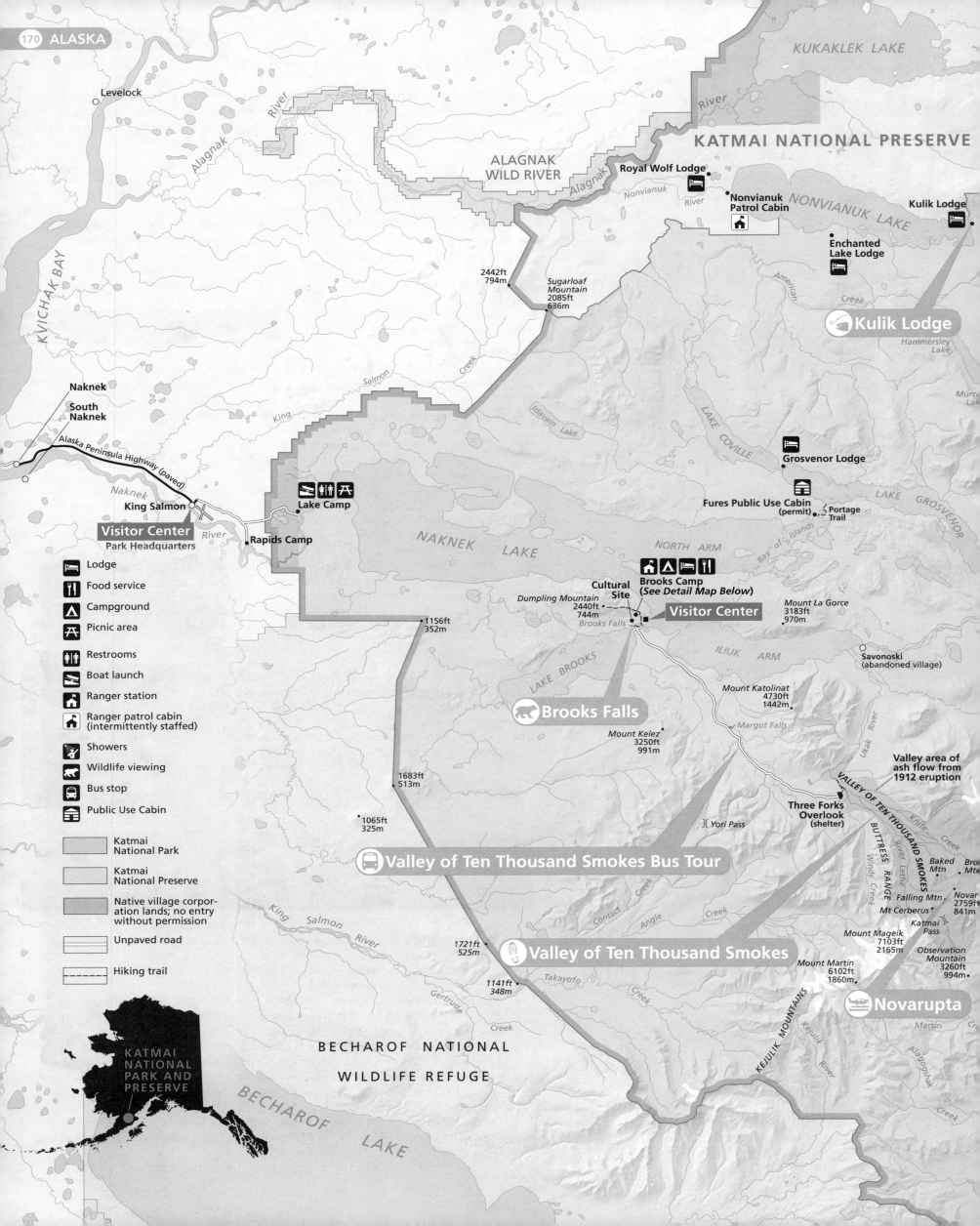

KUKAKLEK LAKE

Levelock

KATMAI NATIONAL PRESERVE

ALAGNAK WILD RIVER

Royal Wolf Lodge

Nonvianuk Patrol Cabin

Kulik Lodge

Enchanted Lake Lodge

2442ft 794m

Sugarloaf Mountain 2085ft 636m

Kulik Lodge

Hammersley Lake

Grosvenor Lodge

Naknek

South Naknek

Alaska Peninsula Highway (paved)

Naknek

King Salmon

Visitor Center
Park Headquarters

Fures Public Use Cabin (permit)

Portage Trail

Lake Camp

Rapids Camp

River

NAKNEK LAKE

NORTH ARM

Bay of Islands

Cultural Site

Brooks Camp (See Detail Map Below)

Dumpling Mountain 2440ft 744m

Visitor Center

Mount La Gorce 3183ft 970m

Brooks Falls

1156ft 352m

ILIUK ARM

Savonoski (abandoned village)

Lodge

Food service

Campground

Picnic area

Restrooms

Boat launch

Ranger station

Ranger patrol cabin (intermittently staffed)

Showers

Wildlife viewing

Bus stop

Public Use Cabin

Katmai National Park

Katmai National Preserve

Native village corporation lands; no entry without permission

Unpaved road

Hiking trail

LAKE BROOKS

Brooks Falls

Mount Kelez 3250ft 991m

Mount Katolinat 4730ft 1442m

Margot Falls

Ukak River

Valley area of ash flow from 1912 eruption

1683ft 513m

1065ft 325m

Yori Pass

Three Forks Overlook (shelter)

VALLEY OF TEN THOUSAND SMOKES

Valley of Ten Thousand Smokes Bus Tour

BUTTRESS RANGE

Windy Creek

Lethe River

Baked Mtn

Bro Mtn

Falling Mtn

Novar 2759ft 841m

Mt Cerberus

Katmai Pass

1721ft 525m

Valley of Ten Thousand Smokes

Mount Mageik 7103ft 2165m

Observation Mountain 3260ft 994m

King Salmon River

Contact Creek

Angle Creek

1141ft 348m

Takayofo Creek

Mount Martin 6102ft 1860m

KEJULIK MOUNTAINS

Novarupta

KATMAI NATIONAL PARK AND PRESERVE

BECHAROF NATIONAL WILDLIFE REFUGE

Gertrude Creek

BECHAROF LAKE

Martin

Kejulik River

Alagoshak

KVICHAK BAY

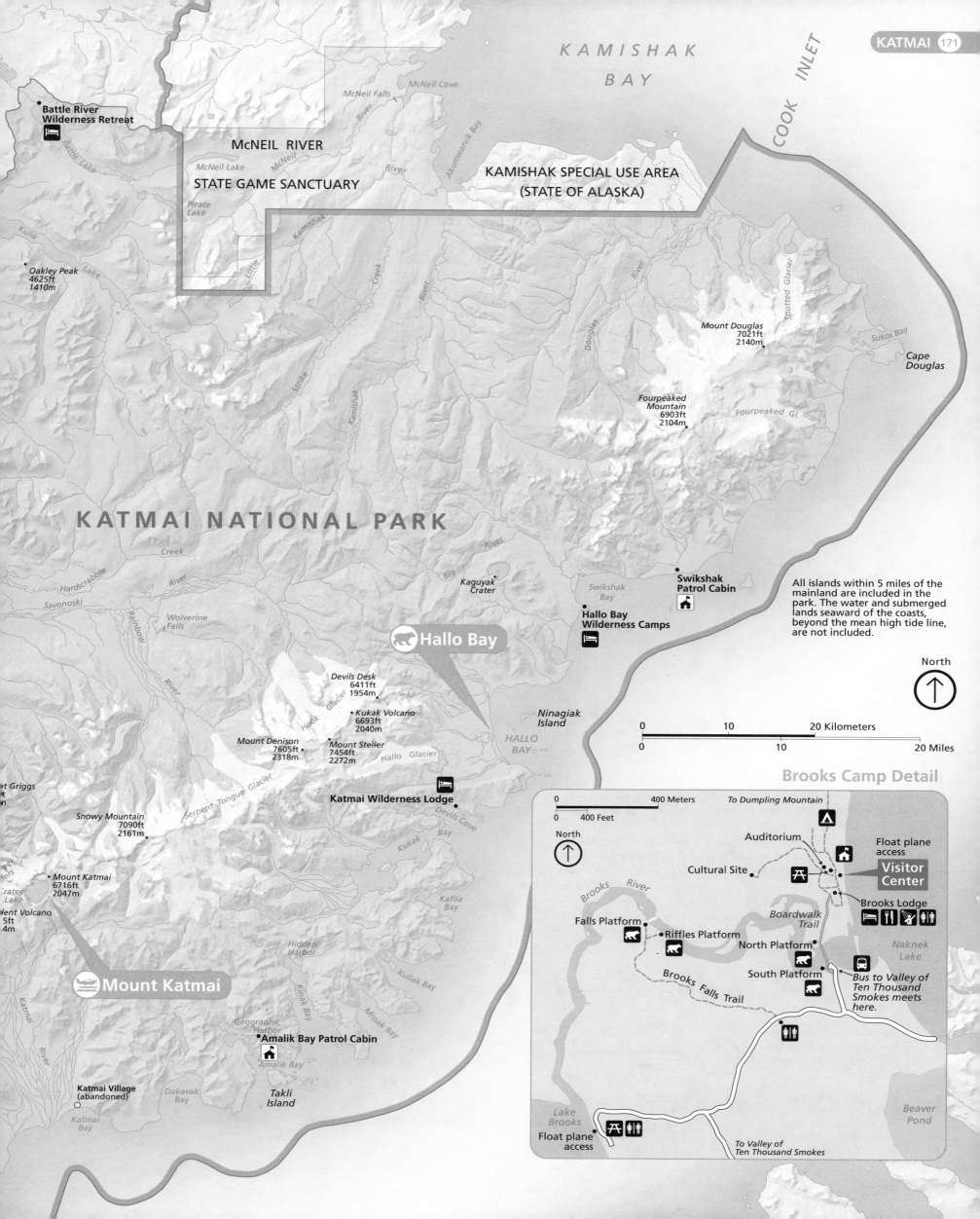

KAMISHAK
BAY

COOK INLET

McNeil Cove

McNeil Falls

**Battle River
Wilderness Retreat**

Battle Lake

McNEIL RIVER

McNeil Lake

McNeil River

Kulik Lake

Pirate Lake

STATE GAME SANCTUARY

KAMISHAK SPECIAL USE AREA
(STATE OF ALASKA)

Oakley Peak
4625ft
1410m

Little

Kamishak

Creek

River

Douglas River

Spotted Glacier

Mount Douglas
7021ft
2140m

Sukoi Bay

Cape
Douglas

Strike

Kamishak

Fourpeaked
Mountain
6903ft
2104m

Fourpeaked Gl.

KATMAI NATIONAL PARK

Creek

Hardscrabble

Savonoski River

Rainbow River

Wolverine
Falls

Creek

River

Big

Kaguyak
Crater

Swikshak
Bay

**Swikshak
Patrol Cabin**

**Hallo Bay
Wilderness Camps**

All islands within 5 miles of the
mainland are included in the
park. The water and submerged
lands seaward of the coasts,
beyond the mean high tide line,
are not included.

🐻 **Hallo Bay**

North

↑

Devils Desk
6411ft
1954m

Hook Glacier

Kukak Volcano
6693ft
2040m

Ninagiak
Island

Mount Denison
7605ft
2318m

Mount Steller
7454ft
2272m

Serpent Tongue Glacier

Hallo Glacier

HALLO
BAY

0   10   20 Kilometers

0   10   20 Miles

Mt Griggs

Snowy Mountain
7090ft
2161m

Devils Cove

Katmai Wilderness Lodge

Brooks Camp Detail

Mount Katmai
6716ft
2047m

Crater Lake

Kaflia
Bay

Kukak Bay

ent Volcano
5ft
4m

🌋 **Mount Katmai**

Hidden
Harbor

Kinak Bay

Kuliak Bay

Missak Bay

Geographic
Harbor

Amalik Bay Patrol Cabin

Amalik Bay

Katmai Village
(abandoned)

Dakavak Bay

Takli
Island

Katmai
Bay

Katmai River

Brooks Camp Detail

0   400 Meters

0   400 Feet

North

↑

To Dumpling Mountain

Float plane
access

Auditorium

Cultural Site

**Visitor
Center**

Brooks River

Brooks Lodge

Falls Platform

Riffles Platform

Boardwalk
Trail

North Platform

Naknek
Lake

South Platform

Bus to Valley of
Ten Thousand
Smokes meets
here.

Brooks Falls Trail

Lake
Brooks

Float plane
access

To Valley of
Ten Thousand Smokes

Beaver
Pond

Gates of the Arctic Basics
(907) 459-3730 | nps.gov/gaar
Entrance Fee: None
Lodging & Camping: None*

*at least one private business operates just outside park boundaries

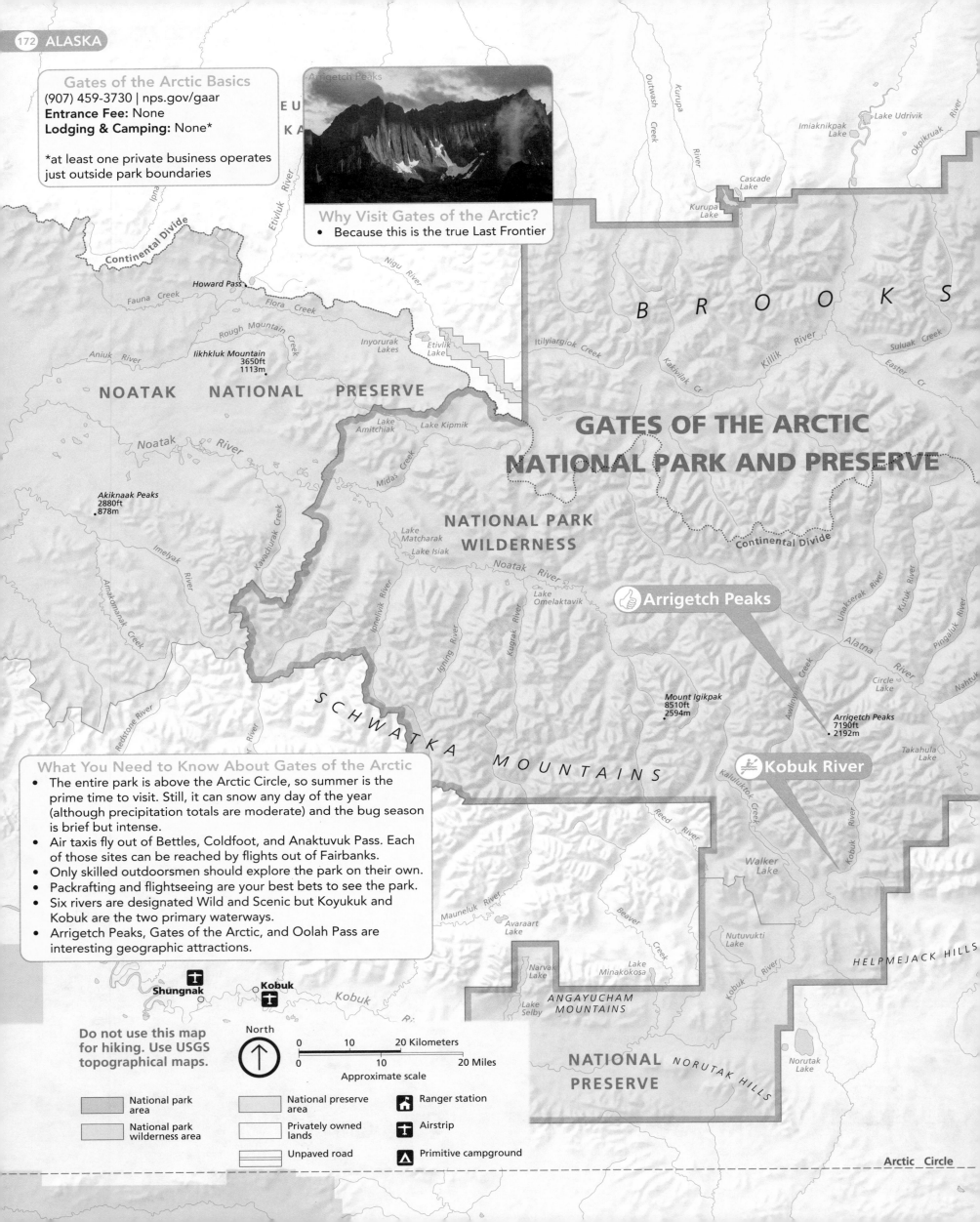

Why Visit Gates of the Arctic?
- Because this is the true Last Frontier

E U
K A

Continental Divide

Howard Pass

Fauna Creek

Etivluk River

Ipnat

Nigu River

Flora Creek

Rough Mountain Creek

Inyorurak Lakes

Etivlik Lake

B R O O K S

Outwash Creek

Kurupa River

Imiaknikpak Lake

Lake Udrivik

Okpikruak River

Cascade Lake

Kurupa Lake

Itilyiargiok Creek

Killik River

Kakivilak Cr

Suluak Creek

Easter Cr

Aniuk River

Iikhkluk Mountain
3650ft
1113m

NOATAK   NATIONAL   PRESERVE

Noatak River

Lake Amitchiak

Lake Kipmik

Midas Creek

GATES OF THE ARCTIC
NATIONAL PARK AND PRESERVE

Akiknaak Peaks
2880ft
878m

Kavachurak Creek

Imelyak River

Amakomanak Creek

Lake Matcharak

Lake Isiak

NATIONAL PARK WILDERNESS

Noatak River

Ipnelruk River

Lake Omelaktavik

Continental Divide

Unakserak River

Kutuk River

Pingaluk River

Arrigetch Peaks

Alatna River

Circle Lake

👍 **Arrigetch Peaks**

Igning River

Kugrak River

Mount Igikpak
8510ft
2594m

Arrigetch Peaks
7190ft
2192m

Takahula Lake

Nahtu

Redstone River

S C H W A T K A

M O U N T A I N S

Awlinyak Creek

Kalulukt Creek

🛶 **Kobuk River**

Kobuk River

What You Need to Know About Gates of the Arctic
- The entire park is above the Arctic Circle, so summer is the prime time to visit. Still, it can snow any day of the year (although precipitation totals are moderate) and the bug season is brief but intense.
- Air taxis fly out of Bettles, Coldfoot, and Anaktuvuk Pass. Each of those sites can be reached by flights out of Fairbanks.
- Only skilled outdoorsmen should explore the park on their own.
- Packrafting and flightseeing are your best bets to see the park.
- Six rivers are designated Wild and Scenic but Koyukuk and Kobuk are the two primary waterways.
- Arrigetch Peaks, Gates of the Arctic, and Oolah Pass are interesting geographic attractions.

Reed River

Walker Lake

HELPMEJACK HILLS

Mauneluk River

Avaraart Lake

Beaver Creek

Nutuvukti Lake

🏠✝ **Shungnak**

✝ **Kobuk**

Kobuk R.

Narvak Lake

Lake Selby

Lake Minakokosa

ANGAYUCHAM MOUNTAINS

Kobuk River

Norutak Lake

Do not use this map for hiking. Use USGS topographical maps.

North
⬆

0   10   20 Kilometers
0   10   20 Miles
Approximate scale

NATIONAL PRESERVE

NORUTAK HILLS

Legend
National park area	National preserve area	🏠 Ranger station
National park wilderness area	Privately owned lands	✝ Airstrip
	Unpaved road	⛺ Primitive campground

Arctic Circle

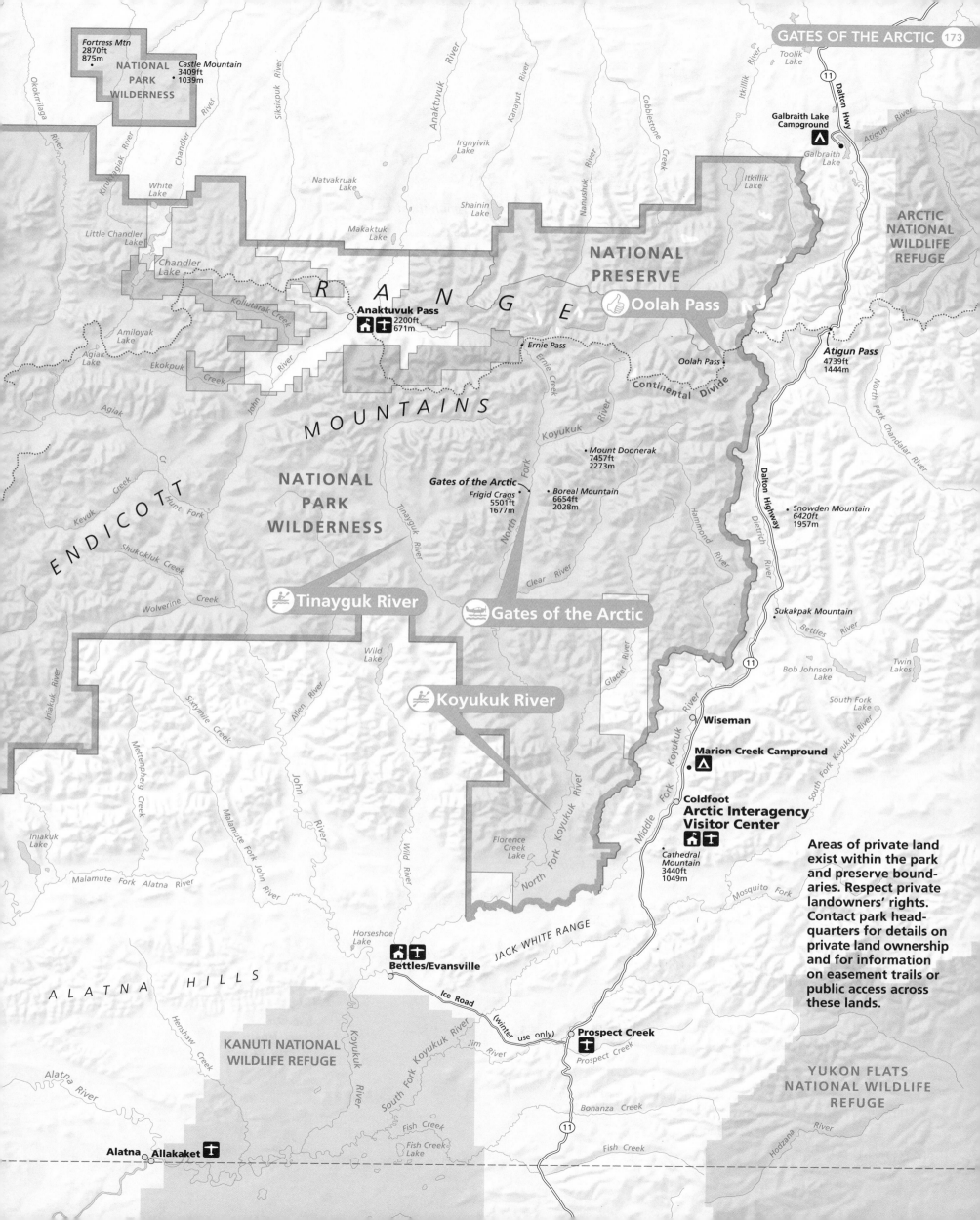

Fortress Mtn
2870ft
875m

NATIONAL PARK WILDERNESS

Castle Mountain
3409ft
1039m

Okokmilaga River

Kirukragiak River

White Lake

Chandler River

Little Chandler Lake

Chandler Lake

Kollutarak Creek

Siksikpuk River

Natvakruak Lake

Anaktuvuk River

Makaktuk Lake

Irgnyivik Lake

Kanayut River

Shainin Lake

Nanushuk River

Cobblestone Creek

Toolik Lake

Itkillik River

GATES OF THE ARCTIC 173

Dalton Hwy

(11)

Galbraith Lake Campground

Galbraith Lake

Atigun River

ARCTIC NATIONAL WILDLIFE REFUGE

NATIONAL PRESERVE

👍 **Oolah Pass**

Amiloyak Lake

Agiak Lake

Ekokpuk Creek

John River

Anaktuvuk Pass
2200ft
671m

Ernie Pass

Ernie Creek

Itkillik Lake

Oolah Pass

Continental Divide

Atigun Pass
4739ft
1444m

North Fork Chandalar River

ENDICOTT

Kevuk Creek

Hunt Fork

Shukokluk Creek

Wolverine Creek

R   A   N   G   E

M O U N T A I N S

NATIONAL PARK WILDERNESS

Koyukuk River

Mount Doonerak
7457ft
2273m

Gates of the Arctic
Frigid Crags •
5501ft
1677m

North Fork

• Boreal Mountain
6654ft
2028m

Hammond River

Dalton Highway

Dietrich River

• Snowden Mountain
6420ft
1957m

Bettles River

🛶 **Tinayguk River**

Tinayguk River

Clear River

🏞 **Gates of the Arctic**

Sukakpak Mountain

Iniakuk River

Mettenpherg Creek

Wild Lake

Allen River

Glacier River

(11)

Bob Johnson Lake

Twin Lakes

South Fork Lake

South Fork Koyukuk River

🛶 **Koyukuk River**

Sixtymile Creek

John River

Wiseman

Koyukuk River

Marion Creek Campround
⛺

Iniakuk Lake

Malamute Fork

Wild River

North Fork Koyukuk River

Florence Creek Lake

Coldfoot
Arctic Interagency Visitor Center
🏕 ⛪

Mosquito Fork

Hershaw Creek

Malamute Fork Alatna River

• Cathedral Mountain
3440ft
1049m

Areas of private land exist within the park and preserve boundaries. Respect private landowners' rights. Contact park headquarters for details on private land ownership and for information on easement trails or public access across these lands.

A L A T N A   H I L L S

Horseshoe Lake

🏕 ⛪
Bettles/Evansville

JACK WHITE RANGE

Alatna River

Koyukuk River

Ice Road

(winter use only)

Jim River

Prospect Creek
⛪ **Prospect Creek**

Prospect Creek

KANUTI NATIONAL WILDLIFE REFUGE

South Fork Koyukuk River

YUKON FLATS NATIONAL WILDLIFE REFUGE

Bonanza Creek

Fish Creek

Fish Creek Lake

(11)

Hodzana River

Alatna ● **Allakaket** ⛪

Fish Creek

Baird Mountains

Why Visit Kobuk Valley?
- To see hundreds of thousands of caribou on their annual migration
- To step foot on Great Kobuk Sand Dunes

LONG MTNS

INACCESSIBLE RIDGE

B R O O K

Bla
502

Mount
Bastille
4480 ft

*Amphitheatre
Mountain*
3528 ft

NOATAK NATIONAL PRESERVE

*IMIKNEYAK
MOUNTAINS*

KIN
MO

Red Dog Mine

Red Dog Mine

*Deadlock
Mountain*
2995 ft

*POKTOVIK
MOUNTAINS*

Lake Narvakrak

*ISACHELUICH
MOUNTAINS*

Iyikrok Mountain
2195 ft

Kelly River
(seasonal)

Kikmiksot Mountain
2285 ft

*MAIYUMERAK
MOUNTAINS*

*Tututalak
Mountain*
4474 ft

MULGRAVE HILLS

Noatak

**Red
Dog
Mine
Port
Site**

*Imik
Lagoon*

CAPE

B A I R D

KRUSENSTERN

*Kotlik
Lagoon*

NATIONAL

*NAGLATUK
HILL*

MONUMENT

IGICHUK HILLS

*Krusenstern
Lagoon*

**Cape
Krusenstern**

Mount Noak
2010 ft

*Aukulak
Lagoon*

KIANA HILLS

Anigaaq
(seasonal)

Kiana

Sheshalik Spit

Kotzebue
Park Headquarters and
Information Center

Noorvik

*BALDWIN
PENINSULA*

HOTHAM INLET (KOBUK LAKE)

HOCKLEY

What You Need to Know About Kobuk Valley
- Similar to Gates of the Arctic, Kobuk Valley resides north of the Arctic Circle, enjoys a short summer with 24-hour light, and it's primarily reached by bush plane and explored by raft (or plane).
- You can catch an air taxi to the park from Kotzebue (via flight from Anchorage) or Bettles (via flight from Fairbanks).
- The lowlands are swampy permafrost, which make for difficult travel.
- Each year a few hundred thousand caribou cross the park, traveling between their breeding and calving grounds.

Kotzebue

**KOBUK
RIVER
DELTA**

Arctic Circle

BERING LAND BRIDGE

For a detailed map of Bering
Land Bridge National Preserve,
please refer to its official map
and guide.

NATIONAL PRESERVE

SELAWIK LAKE

KOTZEBUE SOUND

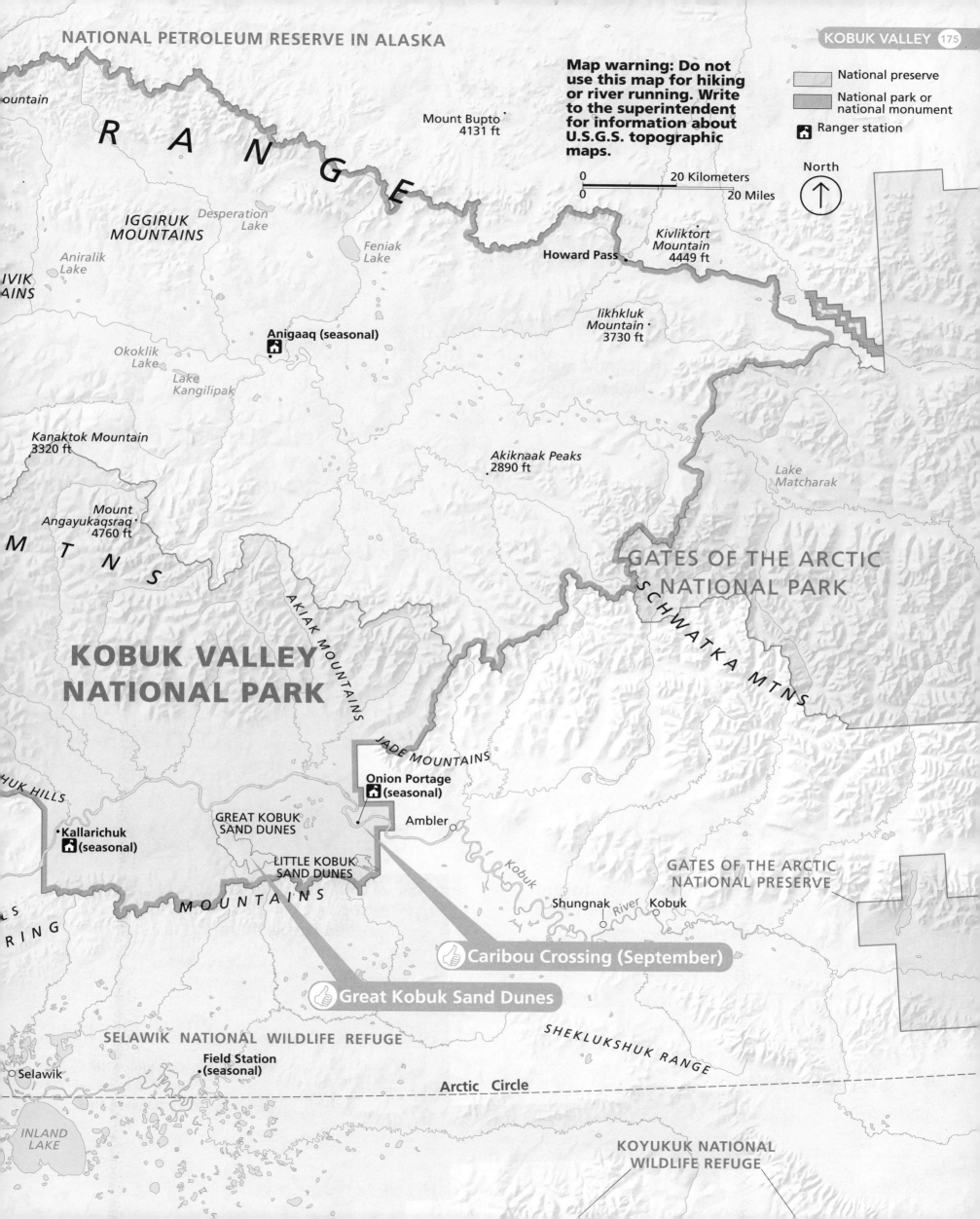

Map warning: Do not use this map for hiking or river running. Write to the superintendent for information about U.S.G.S. topographic maps.

National preserve

National park or national monument

Ranger station

North

0   20 Kilometers
0   20 Miles

R A N G E

IGGIRUK MOUNTAINS

Desperation Lake

Mount Bupto
4131 ft

Aniralik Lake

Feniak Lake

Kivliktort Mountain
4449 ft

Howard Pass

IVIK AINS

Anigaaq (seasonal)

Iikhkluk Mountain
3730 ft

Okoklik Lake

Lake Kangilipak

Kanaktok Mountain
3320 ft

Akiknaak Peaks
2890 ft

Lake Matcharak

Mount Angayukaqsraq
4760 ft

GATES OF THE ARCTIC NATIONAL PARK

M T N S

SCHWATKA MTNS

AKIAK MOUNTAINS

KOBUK VALLEY NATIONAL PARK

JADE MOUNTAINS

HUK HILLS

Onion Portage (seasonal)

Kallarichuk (seasonal)

GREAT KOBUK SAND DUNES

Ambler

GATES OF THE ARCTIC NATIONAL PRESERVE

LITTLE KOBUK SAND DUNES

M O U N T A I N S

Kobuk

R I N G

Shungnak   Kobuk
River

👍 Caribou Crossing (September)

👍 Great Kobuk Sand Dunes

SELAWIK NATIONAL WILDLIFE REFUGE

SHEKLUKSHUK RANGE

Field Station (seasonal)

Selawik

Arctic Circle

INLAND LAKE

KOYUKUK NATIONAL WILDLIFE REFUGE

HAWAII

🕐 **HAWAII (Washington, DC, minus 5 hours; minus 6 hours during daylight saving time)**

KAUA'I

NI'IHAU

O'AHU

World War II Valor in the Pacific NM

Honouliuli NM

HONOLULU

Kalaupapa NHP

MOLOKA'I

Haleakalä NP

HAWAII

MAUI

HAWAI'I

Pu'ukoholä Heiau NHS

Kaloko-Honoköhau NHP

Pu'uhonua o Hönaunau NHP

Hawai'i Volcanoes NP

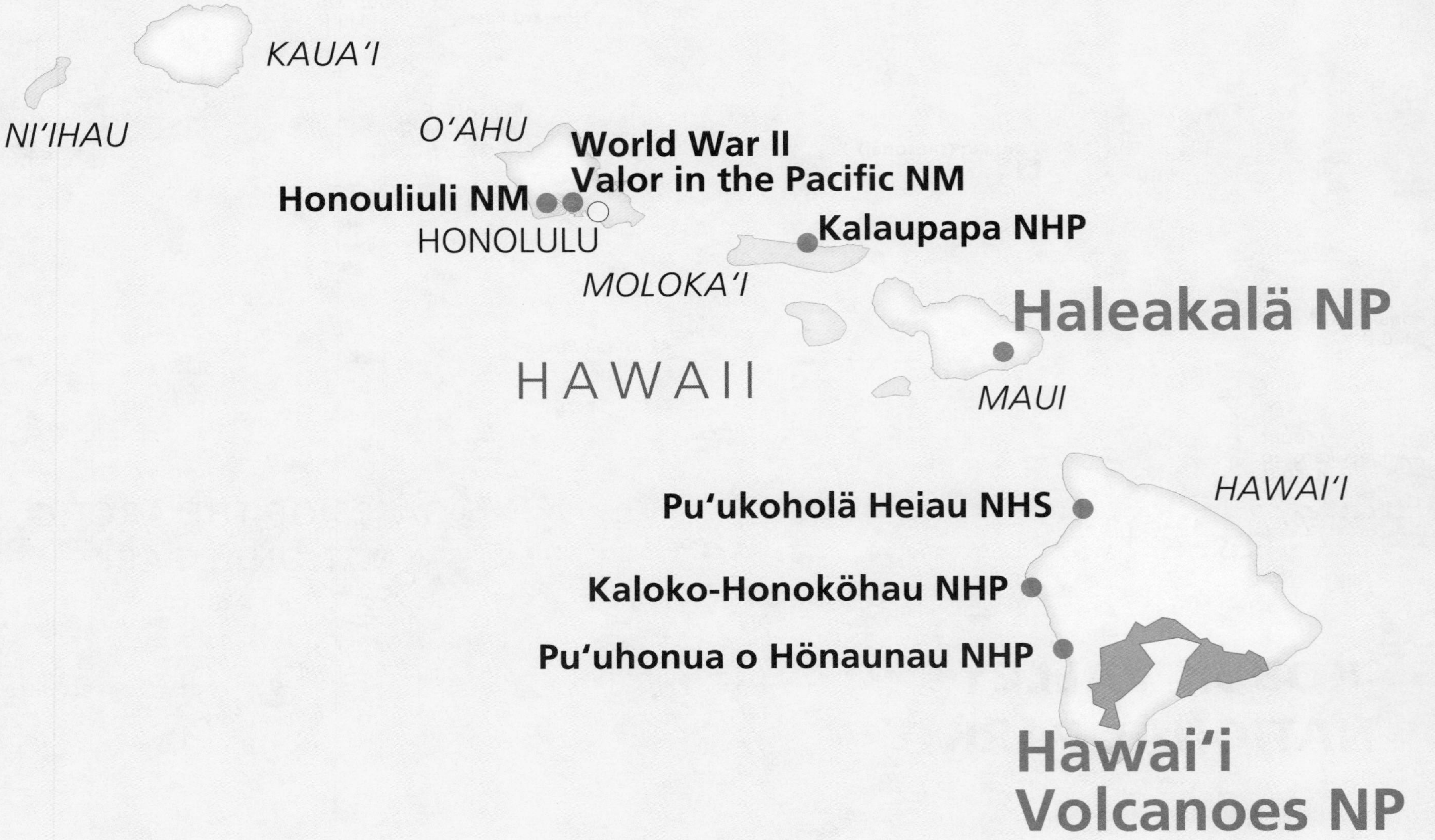

AMERICAN SAMOA

🕐 **AMERICAN SAMOA (Washington, DC, minus 5 hours; minus 6 hours during daylight saving time)**

National Park of American Samoa

TUTUILA

PAGO PAGO

OFU

TA'Ü

AMERICAN SAMOA

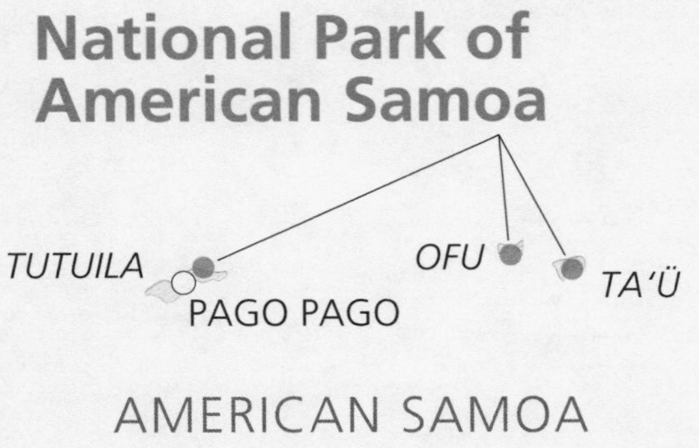

U.S. VIRGIN ISLANDS

🕐 **PUERTO RICO and VIRGIN ISLANDS (Washington, DC, plus 1 hour; same time during daylight saving time)**

PUERTO RICO   VIRGIN ISLANDS

SAN JUAN
San Juan NHS

Virgin Islands NP

CHARLOTTE
AMALIE

Virgin Islands Coral Reef NM

Buck Island Reef NM

Salt River Bay NHP and Ecological Preserve

Christiansted NHS

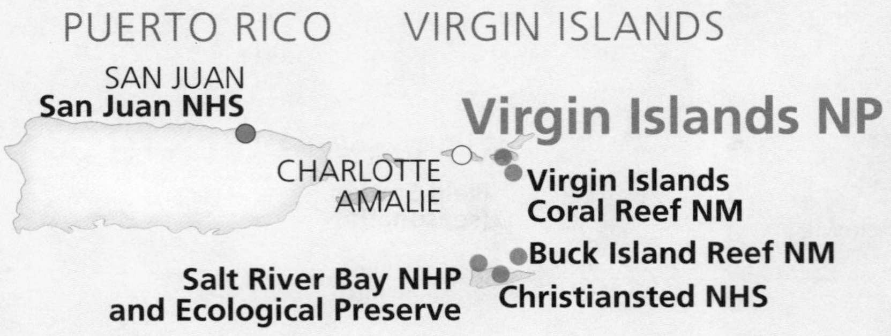

REMOTE ISLANDS

Trunk Bay's white sand

Virgin Islands Driving Distances

St. John is small and you can manage just fine without a car but it will take a few taxi rides to check out all the attractions.

Charlotte Amalie	25 minutes / 10 miles	→	Red Hook (ferry to Cruz Bay)
Cruz Bay	12 minutes / 3 miles	→	Trunk Bay
Trunk Bay	12 minutes / 3 miles	→	Annaberg Ruins
Annaberg Ruins	10 minutes / 3 miles	→	Coral Bay
Coral Bay	12 minutes / 4 miles	→	Saltpond Bay
Saltpond Bay	35 minutes / 12 miles	→	Cruz Bay

Salomon/Honeymoon Beach

Virgin Islands Basics

(340) 776-6201 x238 | nps.gov/viis
Entrance Fee: None
Lodging: Caneel Bay Resort*
Camping: Cinnamon Bay**

*Closed due to hurricane damage
**reserve at cinnamonbayresort.com

Why Visit Virgin Islands?

- For a change of pace from the typical national park vacation, a Caribbean beach holiday!
- To snorkel and sail and sunbathe, and you'll find some hiking too

Plantation remnant

Virgin Islands Favorites

Hikes: Lind Point (easy, 3 miles), Ram Head (moderate, 2), Reef Bay (moderate, 4.4)
Activities: Snorkel, SCUBA, SUP, all the fun water activities!
Views: Trunk Bay Beach (and overlook), Salomon/ Honeymoon Beach, Denis Beach

What You Need to Know

- Most visitors arrive between December and mid-April but the park is open year-round. Hurricane season is June through November.
- Trunk Bay features a bathhouse, snack bar, souvenir shop, and lifeguards. It also has a nominal entrance fee.
- Guests typically fly into Cyril E. King Airport on St. Thomas and then ferry (or water taxi) from Charlotte Amalie or Red Hook over to Cruz Bay on St. John.
- If you don't want to rent a car, a few companies offer driving tours of St. John.
- Rent a car and they'll likely be at the dock (be sure to confirm). Also, you drive on the lefthand side of the road.
- Friends of Virgin Islands National Park organizes a ranger-led Reef Bay Hike. There is a fee. Transportation (land and water) is included. Reserve your spot at the park visitor center in Cruz Bay (or give them a call).

Trunk Bay

View from Ram Head

How Much Time Do You Have?

1 Day: If it was a mainland park, a day would be fine to see the sights (Salomon Beach, Trunk Bay Beach, Annaberg Ruins, Ram Head). But since you flew all this way, stick around for a while (or spend time on St. Thomas, St. Croix, or the British Virgin Islands).

3 Days: If you're a beach person, you'll want to spend plenty of time at Salomon Beach and Trunk Bay. If you're into activities, go snorkeling or book a boat/sailing/SCUBA charter. There are a few hiking trails. Reef Bay heads down to the coast, passing petroglyphs. Ram Head leads to a scenic viewpoint. Or hike to Brown Bay in the park's northeastern corner.

0   0.5   1 Kilometer
0   0.5   1 Mile

North
↑

Private property exists
within the boundary of
the park. Please respect
property owners' rights;
do not trespass.

ATLANTIC OCEAN

Cinnamon Bay

CONGO CAY

Carval
Rock

Whistling
Cay

LOVANGO CAY

WINDWARD PASSAGE

Cruz Bay - British Virgin Islands Ferries

Johnsons
Reef

GRASS CAY

MINGO CAY

DURLOE CAYS

Trunk Bay

Underwater Trail

Rata
Cay

Ramgoat
Cay

Perkins
Cay

Trunk
Cay

Peter
Bay

MIDDLE

Henley
Cay

Hawksnest
Point

Denis
Bay

ruins

TRUNK
BAY

North Shore

Salomon/Honeymoon Beach

Turtle
Bay

Peace
Hill

Trunk Bay

PILLSBURY

PASSAGE

HAWKSNEST
BAY

Peter Peak
967ft

Smith
Bay

Shark
Island

Salomon
Bay

Caneel
Bay

Hawksnest Bay

Catherineberg
Sugar Mill (ruins)

Biosphere Reserve
Center

Honeymoon
Beach

Water
Catchment
Trail

10

Lind
Point

20

Community
Health Clinic
Emergency Care

Visitor Center

Lind
Pt Tr

Margaret
Hill
840ft

NPS dock

Caneel Hill Trail

H

ST THOMAS

32

Cruz
Bay

U.S. Customs
Police

10

CRUZ BAY

38

Cruz Bay - Red Hook Ferry   (20 minutes)

Steven
Cay

ferry dock

Gift Hill Road

RED
HOOK

Red Hook

Frank
Bay

Cruz Bay

Gift Hill
827ft

32

ferry
dock

REDHOOK BAY

Turner
Bay

104

GREAT BAY

Cruz Bay - Charlotte Amalie Ferry   (45 minutes)

GREAT CRUZ
BAY

FISH
BAY

Maria Bluff

Monte
Bay

Klein
Bay

Cocoloba
Point

JERSEY
BAY

ST JAMES BAY

GREAT
ST JAMES
ISLAND

Chocolate Hole

Boatman
Point

Cocoloba
Cay

Deck
Point

Hart
Bay

RENDEZVOUS
BAY

Devers
Bay

Dittlif
Point

ST JAMES CUT

Bovocoap
Point

CARIBBEAN   SEA

LITTLE
ST JAMES
ISLAND

Dog
Island

**User fees are charged at
Trunk Bay and Annaberg
Sugar Mill.**

For safe boating, use
NOAA nautical charts
25641 and 25647. These
charts show navigational
aids, such as markers and
buoys, and hazardous
areas in detail. Do not use
this map for navigation.

- - - - - Trail

→ One-way road

Unpaved road (4-
wheel-drive vehicles
may be needed;
check locally for
conditions)

National Park
Service land

Coral reef

Salt pond/mangrove

Ranger station

Picnic area
with pit toilet

Restaurant and/or
snack bar

Self-guiding trail

Campground

Showers and restrooms

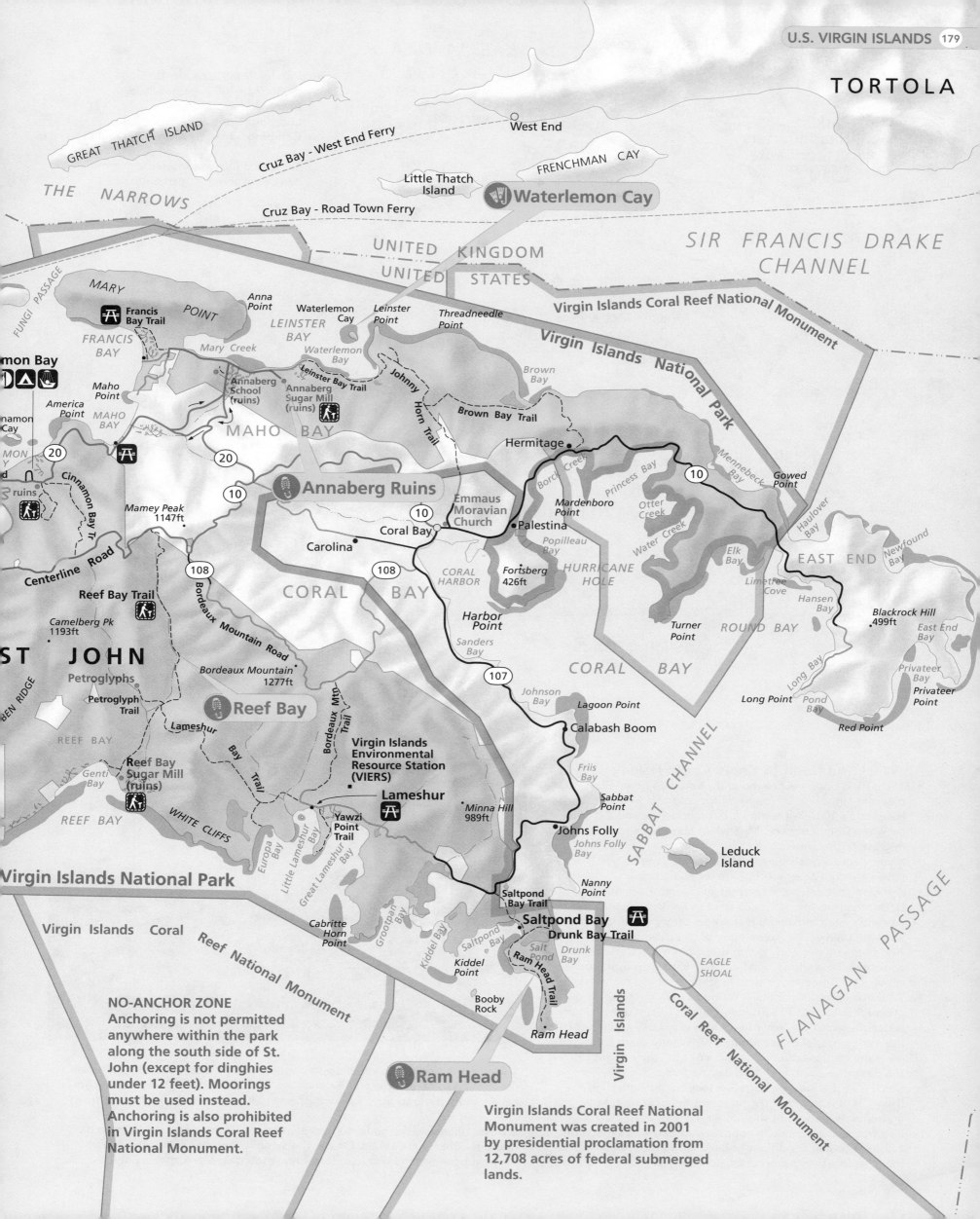

TORTOLA

GREAT THATCH ISLAND

Cruz Bay - West End Ferry

West End

FRENCHMAN CAY

Little Thatch Island

Cruz Bay - Road Town Ferry

Waterlemon Cay

THE NARROWS

SIR FRANCIS DRAKE CHANNEL

UNITED KINGDOM
UNITED STATES

Virgin Islands Coral Reef National Monument

MARY

Anna Point

Waterlemon Cay

Leinster Point

Threadneedle Point

Virgin Islands National Park

FUNGI PASSAGE

Francis Bay Trail

POINT

LEINSTER BAY

FRANCIS POINT

Mary Creek

Waterlemon Bay

Brown Bay

mon Bay

Maho Point

Annaberg School (ruins)

Leinster Bay Trail

Annaberg Sugar Mill (ruins)

Johnny Horn Trail

Brown Bay Trail

America Point

MAHO BAY

Hermitage

Gowed Point

20

Cinnamon Cay

MAHO BAY

20

Borck Creek

Princess Bay

Mennebeck Bay

MON d

Cinnamon Bay Tr

10

Annaberg Ruins

Emmaus Moravian Church

Mardenboro Point

Otter Creek

Haulover Bay

10

ruins

Mamey Peak 1147ft

10

Coral Bay

Palestina

Water Creek

EAST END

Newfound Bay

Centerline Road

Carolina

108

Popilleau Bay

Elk Bay

Limetree Cove

Hansen Bay

Blackrock Hill 499ft

East End Bay

Reef Bay Trail

Camelberg Pk 1193ft

Bordeaux Mountain Road

CORAL

BAY

108

CORAL HARBOR

Fortsberg 426ft

HURRICANE HOLE

Turner Point

ROUND BAY

ST JOHN

Petroglyphs

Bordeaux Mountain 1277ft

Harbor Point

CORAL BAY

Long Point

Long Bay

Privateer Bay

Petroglyph Trail

BEN RIDGE

Sanders Bay

Johnson Bay

Red Point

Privateer Point

Lameshur

107

Lagoon Point

Reef Bay

REEF BAY

Bordeaux Mtn. Trail

Calabash Boom

Virgin Islands Environmental Resource Station (VIERS)

Friis Bay

Reef Bay Sugar Mill (ruins)

Bay Trail

Sabbat Point

Genti Bay

REEF BAY

WHITE CLIFFS

Minna Hill 989ft

Lameshur

SABBAT CHANNEL

Leduck Island

Europa Bay

Little Lameshur Bay

Great Lameshur Bay

Yawzi Point Trail

Johns Folly

Johns Folly Bay

Virgin Islands National Park

Cabritte Horn Point

Grootpan Bay

Kiddel Bay

Saltpond Bay

Nanny Point

Saltpond Bay Trail

Saltpond Bay

Drunk Bay Trail

EAGLE SHOAL

NO-ANCHOR ZONE
Anchoring is not permitted anywhere within the park along the south side of St. John (except for dinghies under 12 feet). Moorings must be used instead. Anchoring is also prohibited in Virgin Islands Coral Reef National Monument.

Kiddel Point

Saltpond Bay

Salt Pond

Drunk Bay

Virgin Islands

Ram Head Trail

Booby Rock

Ram Head

Ram Head

Virgin Islands Coral Reef National Monument

Virgin Islands Coral Reef National Monument was created in 2001 by presidential proclamation from 12,708 acres of federal submerged lands.

FLANAGAN PASSAGE

Coral Reef National Monument

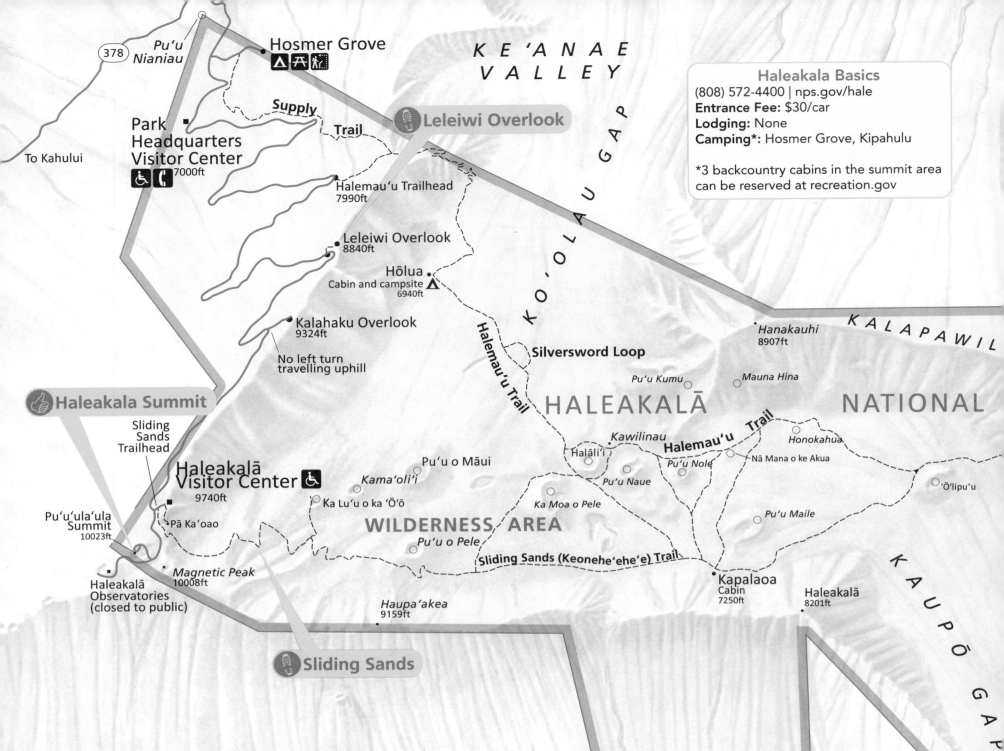

(378) *Pu'u Nianiau*

Hosmer Grove ▲🏕🥾

K E ' A N A E   V A L L E Y

Supply

Trail

👣 **Leleiwi Overlook**

To Kahului

Park Headquarters Visitor Center ♿🚻 7000ft

Halemau'u Trailhead 7990ft

Leleiwi Overlook 8840ft

Hōlua ⛺
Cabin and campsite 6940ft

K O ' O L A U   G A P

Haleakala Basics
(808) 572-4400 | nps.gov/hale
Entrance Fee: $30/car
Lodging: None
Camping*: Hosmer Grove, Kipahulu

*3 backcountry cabins in the summit area can be reserved at recreation.gov

Kalahaku Overlook 9324ft

No left turn travelling uphill

Silversword Loop

Halemau'u Trail

Hanakauhi 8907ft

K A L A P A W I L

👍 **Haleakala Summit**

Sliding Sands Trailhead

Pu'u Kumu

Mauna Hina

HALEAKALĀ

NATIONAL

Kawilinau **Halemau'u   Trail**

Haleakalā Visitor Center ♿ 9740ft

Pu'u o Māui

Kama'oli'i

Halāli'i

Pu'u Nole

Honokahua

Nā Mana o ke Akua

'Ō'lipu'u

Pu'u'ula'ula Summit 10023ft

Pā Ka'oao

Ka Lu'u o ka 'Ō'ō

Pu'u Naue

Ka Moa o Pele

Pu'u Maile

Haleakalā Observatories (closed to public)

Magnetic Peak 10008ft

Pu'u o Pele

Sliding Sands (Keonehe'ehe'e) Trail

WILDERNESS   AREA

👣 **Sliding Sands**

Haupa'akea 9159ft

Kapalaoa
Cabin 7250ft

Haleakalā 8201ft

K A U P Ō   G A P

What You Need to Know About Haleakala

- The park is open year-round and weather is generally pleasant (although be prepared for cold and wind at Haleakala's 10,023-ft summit). If forced to choose, I'd arrive between December and May, when humpback whales migrate to the area.
- If you want to catch sunrise at Haleakala summit, you'll have to secure a permit through recreation.gov
- A strong case can be made that sunrise at the summit is better than sunset, as clouds tend to bank up against the volcano's eastern flank, but sunset is pretty good too (and you won't have to wake up early or get a permit for it). And then you'll already be up there when the stars start to come out. They didn't build an observatory up there for show. It's a tremendous spot to stare up at the night's sky.
- When you go to Kipahulu, it's a good idea to spend at least one night in Hana. The Road to Hana is beautiful with many waterfalls along the way but it's also very busy and one of the most stressful drives around, with many sharp turns and one-lane sections. Spending the night will let you get to the desirable pull-offs before daytrippers arrive.
- Much is said about the unpaved section of Piilani Highway (Hwy 31). It is true that the fine print on most rental car agreements states you should not leave pavement. It is also true that that road is not nearly as bad as it's made out to be (of course conditions of unpaved roads change much more rapidly than paved ones).

Sliding Sands Trail

How Much Time Do You Have?

1 Day: For a single day, you have to choose: summit or Kipahulu? I'd choose the summit to take in the sunrise and hike Sliding Sands Trail. Technically, you'd have enough time to drive Piilani Highway to Kipahulu and hike Pipiwai Trail.

2 Days: Unless you're going to backpack to the backcountry cabins, two days is about right for Haleakala. One at the summit. Another at Kipahulu. The contrast between the two (rain forest and mountain Marscape) is unbelievable.

Haleakala Driving Distances

Maui isn't a huge land mass, but a 10,000-ft volcano makes for some interesting (and slow-going) roads.

Kahului, HI	←70 minutes→ 37 miles	Summit VC
Summit VC	←150 minutes→ 60 miles	Kipahulu VC (via Piilani Hwy)
Summit VC	←210 minutes→ 79 miles	Kipahulu VC (via Hana Hwy)
Kipahulu VC	←120 minutes→ 52 miles	Kahului, HI (via Piilani Hwy)

Why Visit Haleakala?

- To see the first rays of sun perched atop Haleakala's summit!
- To hike to towering waterfalls like Waimoku falls at Kipahulu
- To explore the inspiration for many of Maui's legends

Waimoku Falls

Honeycreeper at Hosmer Grove

Haleakala Favorites

Hikes: Sliding Sands (strenuous, 11.2 miles), Pipiwai (moderate, 4), Leleiwi Overlook (easy, 0.3)
Activities: Stargazing (dress for the cold)
Views: Haleakala Summit

△ Campground
△ Primitive campsite (permit required)
☎ Public telephone
✈ Airport
⛫ Picnic area
⌂ Ranger station
♿ Wheelchair accessible
🚶 Self-guiding trail

Cholla Cactus Garden

▭ Paved road
▭ Parking or overlook
▭ Unpaved road
▭ Trail
○ Cinder cone

0 0.1 0.5   1 Kilometer
0 0.1   0.5   1 Mile

North
↑

R I D G E

PARK

Kaluaiki

CLOSED TO ENTRY

• **Palikū**
Cabin and campsite
6380ft

Kaupō Trail

3880ft

Lower half of trail is on private land. Permission to pass is extended to hikers as a courtesy.

Kaupō ○

Narrow rough unpaved road

KĪPAHULU VALLEY
BIOLOGICAL RESERVE
CLOSED TO ENTRY

Kaukau'i Stream

CLOSED TO ENTRY

Alelele Stream

Lelekea Stream

Palikea •
2224ft

Pipiwai Stream

Palikea Stream

CLOSED TO ENTRY

🚶 **'Ohe'o Gulch**

To Hāna and Kahului

Wailua Falls

Narrow winding road

Waimoku Falls

Pipiwai Trail

🚶 **Pipiwai**

Falls at Makahiku

'Ohe'o Gulch

Pools
Kūloa Point

△ **Kīpahulu Visitor Center**

KUKUI BAY

Puhilele Point

PACIFIC OCEAN

Kahuku Unit

0.8mi
1.3km
1926

0.5mi
0.8km

● Forested
pit crater

Ka'u
Forest
Reserve

Pit Crater Trail

2.4mi
3.9km

ROD Quarantine Gate
(road closed beyond gate)

0.8mi
1.3km

← Hikers must
decontaminate
for Rapid 'Ohi'a Death

Pali o Ka'eo
trailhead

1.0mi
1.6km

HAWAI'I
VOLCANOES
NATIONAL PARK
Kahuku Unit

Pit Crater trailhead

Upper trailhead
Palm Trail

Palm Trail

0.8mi
1.3km

1.8mi
2.9km

Lower trailhead
Palm Trail

Lower
trailhead
Palm Trail

Kahuku Road

park boundary

1887

1868

1.7mi
2.7km

Pu'u o
Lokuana
trailhead

Kamakapa'a
trailhead
0.4mi
0.6km

Old Mamalahoa Highway

1.75mi
2.8km

**To Kilauea
Visitor Center
43mi / 69km**

Biking and
hiking trail

Hiking trail

North
↑

0   1 Kilometer
0   1 Mile

**To
Kailua-Kona
52mi / 84km**

11

🚻 🚻

0.4mi
0.6km

Mile marker 70

827
252

Kona International
Airport at Keahole ✈   1801

19   190

HU

Kaloko-Honokōhau
National Historical Park

Kailua-Kona

11

13677
4169

1949   1975

👣 Mauna Loa Summit

Pu'uhonua o Hōnaunau
National Historical Park

1950   1949

1950

1950

MAUNA LOA

1950

Kahuku Unit
HAWAI'I VOLCANOES NATIONAL PARK

7.5
12.

2.7mi
4.3km

Alanoa Trail

11

1926

Ocean
View

KAHUKU
(see detail
map above)

Kahuku Road

Park boundary

Ka'u Forest Reserve

1907

1887

6.4mi
10.3km

1868

South Point Road
Hawaii 11
to South Point
12mi / 19km

11

Great Crack

Southwest Rift Zon

Pāhala

Kilauea Visitor Center
to Kailua-Kona
via Hawaii 11
96mi / 155km
(2.5 hours drive)

Nā'ālehu

Park boundary   1823

1823

KA'Ū DESERT

Punalu'u
(black sand beach)

Island of Hawai'i

270   *KOHALA*   Honoka'a

Kawaihae

Pu'ukoholā Heiau
National Historic Site

Waimea   19

Kaloko-
Honokōhau
National
Historical
Park

MAUNA KEA

19   190   *HUALĀLAI*   200   Hilo

Kailua-
Kona

Kīlauea Visitor Center

Kea'au

Pu'uhonua o
Hōnaunau
National
Historical Park

MAUNA LOA   11   130

HAWAI'I
VOLCANOES
NATIONAL PARK   Volcano
Village   Pāhoa

11

Pāhala

North
↑

Nā'ālehu   VIEW

0   40 Kilometers
0   40 Miles

⌇ Pullout

⌇ Hiking trail

6.0mi
9.7km   Distance indicator

1974   Historic lava flow
and date

About the map

The computer-generated map above looks northwest across
Hawai'i Island. Because of perspective, areas in the foreground
appear larger than comparably sized areas in the background.
Vertical exaggeration is used. Map data courtesy
USGS/Hawaiian Volcano Observatory.

Refer to USGS topographic maps for exact trail locations.

⊞ Picnic area

🚶 Interpretive trail

♿ Wheelchair-accessible

🛏 Shelter

🍴 Food service

🚰 Drinking water

🚱 Water—must be treated
before drinking

🚻 Restrooms
(wheelchair-accessible)

🛏 Lodging

⛽ Gas station

☎ Emergency phone

⛺ Campground

△ Primitive campground

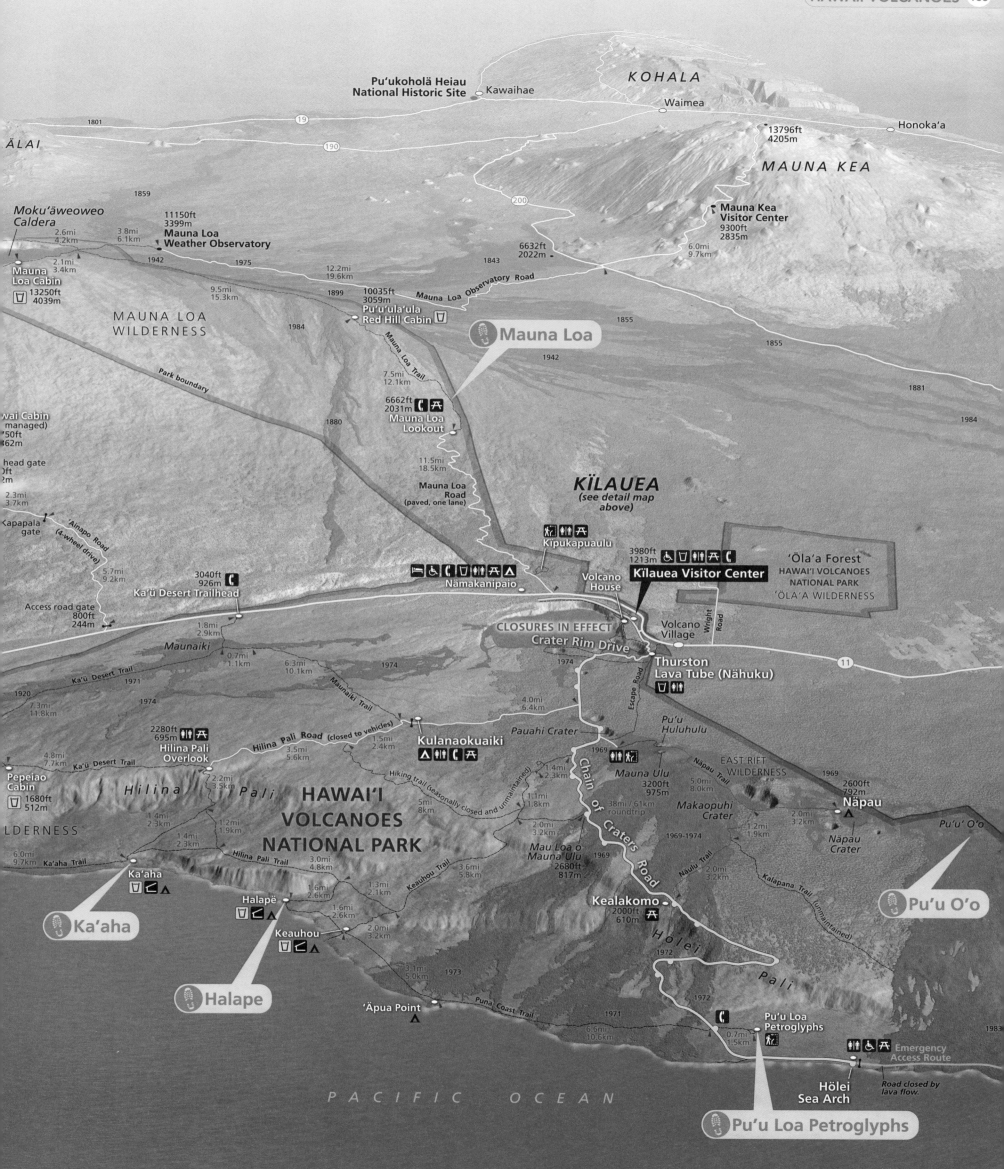

ÄLAI

KOHALA

Pu'ukoholä Heiau
National Historic Site ○ Kawaihae

○ Waimea

○ Honoka'a

13796ft
4205m

MAUNA KEA

1801

19

190

1859

11150ft
3399m
**Mauna Loa
Weather Observatory**

*Moku'äweoweo
Caldera*

2.6mi
4.2km

3.8mi
6.1km

2.1mi
3.4km

**Mauna
Loa Cabin**
13250ft
4039m

1942

1975

9.5mi
15.3km

1899

10035ft
3059m
**Pu'u'ula'ula
Red Hill Cabin**

200

Mauna Kea
Visitor Center
9300ft
2835m

6632ft
2022m

6.0mi
9.7km

1843

12.2mi
19.6km

Mauna Loa Observatory Road

1984

1855

**MAUNA LOA
WILDERNESS**

Park boundary

1984

1880

Mauna Loa Trail

👢 **Mauna Loa**

1855

1855

1881

1942

1984

wai Cabin
(managed)
750ft
362m

head gate
0ft
2m

2.3mi
3.7km

Kapapala
gate

5.7mi
9.2km

'Ainapo Road
(4-wheel drive)

3040ft
926m
Ka'ü Desert Trailhead

Access road gate
800ft
244m

7.5mi
12.1km

6662ft
2031m
**Mauna Loa
Lookout**

11.5mi
18.5km

Mauna Loa
Road
(paved, one lane)

KĪLAUEA
(see detail map
above)

Kïpukapuaulu

3980ft
1213m
Kïlauea Visitor Center

'Öla'a Forest
HAWAI'I VOLCANOES
NATIONAL PARK
'ÖLA'A WILDERNESS

Volcano
House

1.8mi
2.9km

Maunaiki

0.7mi
1.1km

6.3mi
10.1km

1974

Nämakanipaio

CLOSURES IN EFFECT
Crater Rim Drive

Volcano
Village

Wright Road

11

Ka'ü Desert Trail

1971

Maunaiki Trail

1974

1920

7.3mi
11.8km

1974

Hilina Pali Road (closed to vehicles)

1.5mi
2.4km

Kulanaokuaiki

4.0mi
6.4km

1974

**Thurston
Lava Tube (Nähuku)**

Escape Road

*Pu'u
Huluhulu*

EAST RIFT
WILDERNESS

1969

4.8mi
7.7km

Ka'ü Desert Trail

2280ft
695m
**Hilina Pali
Overlook**

3.5km
5.6km

2.2mi
3.5km

Hilina   Pali

1.4mi
2.3km

**HAWAI'I
VOLCANOES
NATIONAL PARK**

1.4mi
2.3km

1.2mi
1.9km

Hilina Pali Trail

3.0mi
4.8km

Keauhou Trail

1.4mi
2.3km

2.0mi
3.2km

1.1mi
1.8km

5mi
8km

Chain of Craters Road

Mauna Ulu
3200ft
975m

38mi/61km
roundtrip

5.0mi
8.0km

Näpau Trail

1969

1969-1974

2.0mi
3.2km

*Makaopuhi
Crater*

Näulu Trail

1.2mi
1.9km

2.0mi
3.2km

1969

Näpau
2600ft
792m

*Näpau
Crater*

Pu'u 'O'o

👢 **Pu'u O'o**

Pauahi Crater

*Mau Loa o
Mauna Ulu*
2680ft
817m

1969

3.6mi
5.8km

1.3mi
2.1km

Kealakomo
2000ft
610m

Kalapana Trail (unmaintained)

Pepeiao
Cabin
1680ft
512m

LDERNESS

6.0mi
9.7km Ka'aha Trail

Ka'aha
👢 **Ka'aha**

1.6mi
2.6km

Halapë

Keauhou

1.6mi
2.6km

2.0mi
3.2km

3.1mi
5.0km

1973

Holei   Pali

1972

1972

👢 **Halape**

'Äpua Point

Puna Coast Trail

6.6mi
10.6km

1971

**Pu'u Loa
Petroglyphs**

0.7mi
1.5km

1983

Hölei
Sea Arch

Emergency
Access Route

*Road closed by
lava flow.*

👢 **Pu'u Loa Petroglyphs**

P A C I F I C   O C E A N

Lava boat tour

Hawaii Volcanoes Basics

(808) 985-6011 | nps.gov/havo
Entrance Fee: $30/car
Lodging: Volcano House Hotel*
Camping: Namakanipaio, Kulanaokuaiki

*reserve at hawaiivolcanohouse.com

Hawaii Volcanoes Driving Distances

Most visitors arrive at Kona. A loop around Mauna   is a good idea but you don't want to miss the north coast's valleys either.

Kona Airport	130 minutes / 102 miles	Kilauea VC (via Saddle Road)
Kona Airport	140 minutes / 102 miles	Kilauea VC (via Hawaii Belt Road)
Kilauea VC	40 minutes / 22 miles	Holei Sea Arch
Kilauea VC	45 minutes / 14 miles	Mauna Loa Lookout
Kilauea VC	40 minutes / 30 miles	Hilo, HI

Why Visit Hawaii Volcanoes?

- Lava!
- Some pretty good backpacking!

Snow in Hawaii!

Hawaii Volcanoes Favorites

Hikes: Mauna Loa (strenuous, multi-day), Kilauea Iki (moderate, 3.3 miles), Thurston (Nahuku) Lava Tube (easy, 1.5)
Views: Wherever you can see lava if there's an active flow

Kïpukapuaulu
1.2mi / 2.0km

Highway 11 to Mauna Loa Lookout
11.5mi/18.5km

Mauna Loa Road

Park boundary

Tree Molds

🚗 **Crater Rim Drive**

1.5mi / 2.4km

Piʻi Mauna Dr

Kïlauea Military Camp

Steam

Nämakanipaio Campground and Cabins

Crater Rim Drive

Crater Rim Trail
1.0mi / 0.6km

0.6mi / 1.0km

Steaming Bluff (Wahinekapu)

(11)

Kïlauea Overlook ⬆

Lava flows before 1924

KÏLAUEA CALDE

To Kailua-Kona
96mi/155km

CLOSURES IN EFFECT
Check with rangers for current conditions

1982 lava

Halema'uma'u Crater

1971 lava

1971 lava

Keana
Ov

0.3mi / 0.5km

Southwest Rift Zone

Lava flows before 1924

1982 lava

KA'Ü DESERT

Holoholoakōlea

1971 lava

👍 Halema'uma'u Crater

What You Need to Know

- The park is open all year and visitation is steady, with marginal peaks in winter and summer.
- Weather is consistent too, although it varies greatly from point-to-point on the island. You'll need to pack for all conditions, especially if you plan to summit Mauna Loa or Mauna Kea.
- This is a dynamic place. An eruption began in 1983, continuing until 2018, culminating in the largest lower East Rift Zone eruption in the last two centuries. Then Halemaumau Crater began to fill with water. In 2020, the water started boiling. 2020 ended with a new lava lake at the crater's floor. It turned off and then on once more in 2021. Then Mauna Loa began erupting for the first time in 38 years. Kilauea and Mauna Loa eruptions ended before Christmas 2022, but Kilauea started back up May 2023 (then stopped). If lava is flowing, go see it. Check with the park/USGS for current information.

How Much Time Do You Have?

1 Day: Most visitors don't spend much time in the park. They show up, check out the lava (if there is any), maybe hike Kilauea Iki and/or Thurston Lava Tube, drive the road and continue on their way. Honestly, I can't fault that strategy. There's an awful lot to see and do on the island.

2 Days: Spending the night at Volcano House is definitely worth it if there's a lava lake at Halemaumau Crater. Lava glows after dark.

3 Days: With another day, consider backpacking to Mauna Loa or the coast. There's also a smaller region, Kahuku Unit, accessed near the road to South Point/Green Sand Beach.

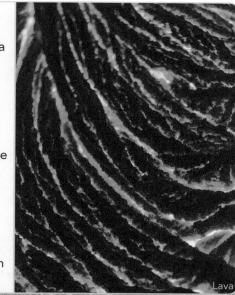
Lava

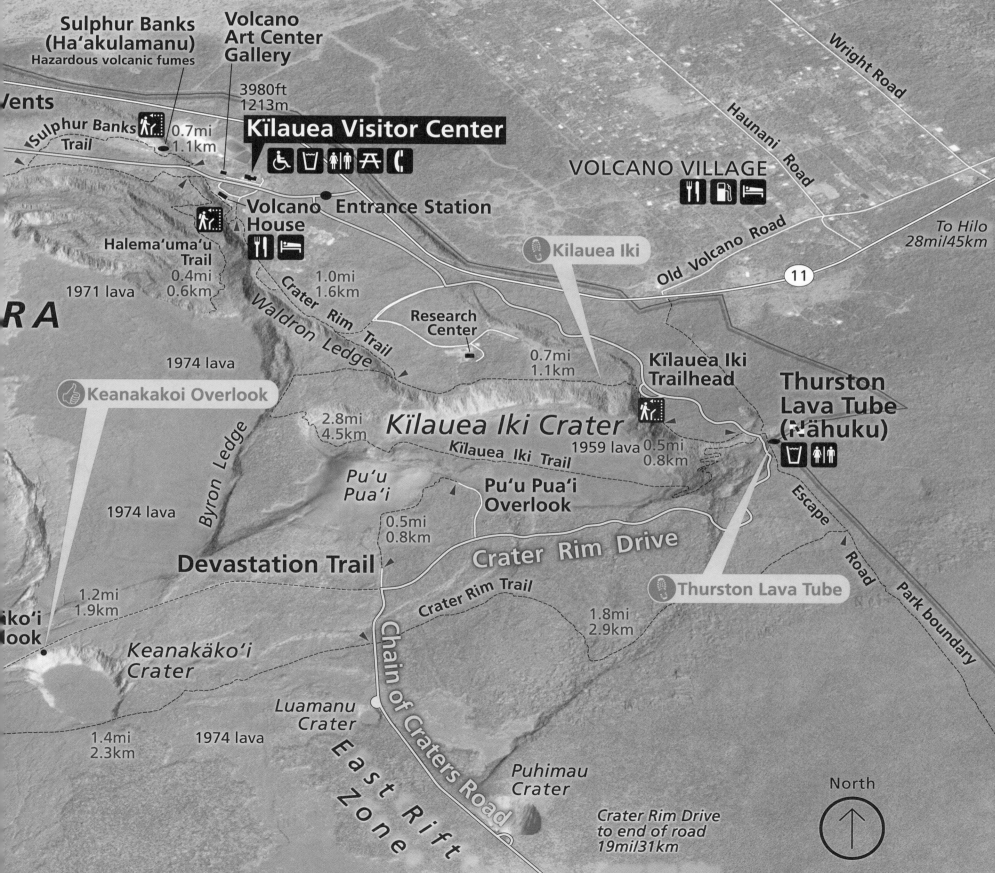

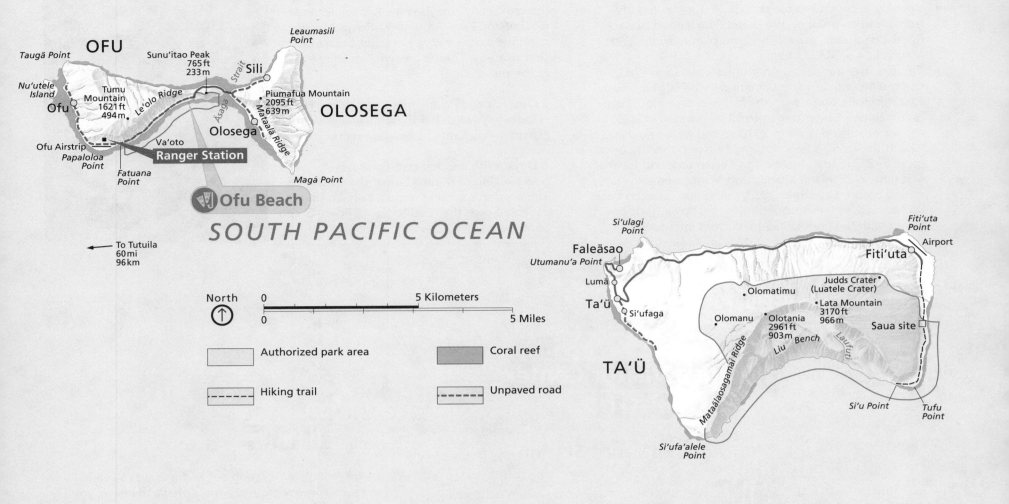

OFU

Taugā Point

Sunu'itao Peak
765 ft
233 m

Leaumasili Point

Sili

Nu'utele Island

Ofu

Tumu Mountain
1621 ft
494 m

Le'olo Ridge

Piumafua Mountain
2095 ft
639 m

OLOSEGA

Olosega

Matā'alā Ridge

'Asaga Strait

Ofu Airstrip

Papaloloa Point

Va'oto

Ranger Station

Fatuana Point

Magā Point

Ofu Beach

SOUTH PACIFIC OCEAN

← To Tutuila
60 mi
96 km

North ↑

0 ——————— 5 Kilometers
0 ——————— 5 Miles

☐ Authorized park area   ▨ Coral reef

--- Hiking trail   --- Unpaved road

Si'ulagi Point

Fiti'uta Point

Faleāsao

Airport

Utumanu'a Point

Lumā

Ta'ū

Si'ufaga

Fiti'uta

Olomatimu

Judds Crater
(Luatele Crater)

Lata Mountain
3170 ft
966 m

Saua site

Olomanu

Olotania
2961 ft
903 m

Liu Bench

Laufuti

TA'Ü

Mataālaocagamaī Ridge

Si'ufa'alele Point

Si'u Point

Tufu Point

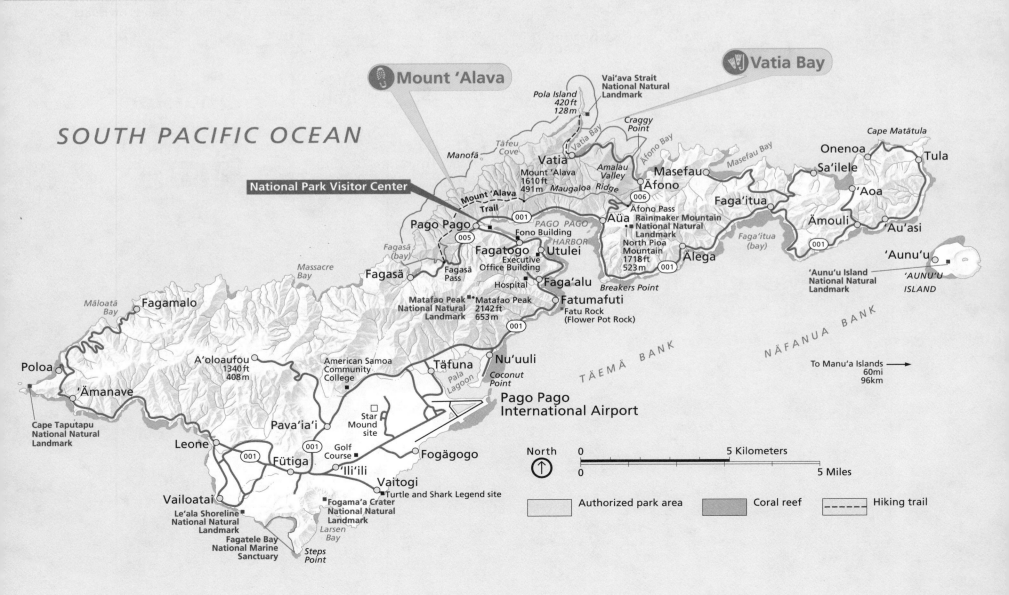

Mount 'Alava

Vatia Bay

SOUTH PACIFIC OCEAN

Vai'ava Strait
National Natural
Landmark

Pola Island
420 ft
128 m

Craggy Point

Tāfeu Cove

Manofā

Vatia

Vatia Bay

Āfono Bay

Masefau Bay

Cape Matātula

Onenoa

Tula

National Park Visitor Center

Mount 'Alava
1610 ft
491 m

Amalau Valley

Maugaloa Ridge

Masefau

Āfono

Sa'ilele

'Aoa

Mount 'Alava Trail

001

Āfono Pass

006

Faga'itua

Āmouli

Pago Pago

005

Fono Building

PAGO PAGO HARBOR

Aüa

Rainmaker Mountain
National Natural
Landmark

Au'asi

Fagasā (bay)

Fagatogo

Executive Office Building

Utulei

North Pioa Mountain
1718 ft
523 m

Faga'itua (bay)

001

Ālega

'Aunu'u

Massacre Bay

Fagasā

Fagasā Pass

Hospital

Faga'alu

Breakers Point

'Aunu'u Island
National Natural
Landmark

'AUNU'U ISLAND

Matafao Peak
National Natural
Landmark

Matafao Peak
2142 ft
653 m

Fatumafuti

Fatu Rock
(Flower Pot Rock)

Māloatā Bay

Fagamalo

A'oloaufou
1340 ft
408 m

American Samoa
Community College

Tāfuna

Nu'uuli

Coconut Point

TĀEMĀ BANK

NĀFANUA BANK

To Manu'a Islands →
60 mi
96 km

Poloa

'Āmanave

Cape Taputapu National Natural Landmark

Pava'ia'i

Star Mound site

Pala Lagoon

Pago Pago
International Airport

North ↑

0 ——————— 5 Kilometers
0 ——————— 5 Miles

Leone

001

Fütiga

Golf Course

001

'Ili'ili

Fogāgogo

Vaitogi

Turtle and Shark Legend site

☐ Authorized park area   ▨ Coral reef   --- Hiking trail

Vailoatai

Le'ala Shoreline National Natural Landmark

Fogama'a Crater
National Natural
Landmark

Larsen Bay

Fagatele Bay National Marine Sanctuary

Steps Point

American Samoa Basics
(684) 633-7082 | nps.gov/npsa
Entrance Fee: None
Lodging: Homestay Program*
Camping: None

*No longer available when we went to print

Ofu Beach

American Samoa Driving Distances
You'll fly into Pago Pago and "family" buses provide public transportation around the island (car rental is available). The other islands can be reached by boat or plane.

Pago Pago ←→ 28 minutes / 9 miles ←→ Visitor Center

Visitor Center ←→ 30 minutes / 9 miles ←→ Vatia

Why Visit American Samoa?
- To enjoy the peaceful seclusion of Ofu Beach
- To immerse yourself in Samoan culture

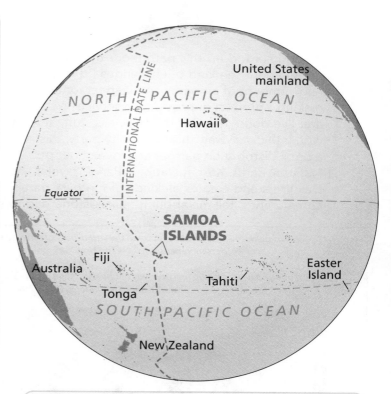

What You Need to Know About American Samoa
- It's always warm but winters are wet (typically October through April) and humpback whales are often seen in late summer/early fall.
- If you're collecting parks, you may as well add American Samoa to your itinerary when you're planning the Hawaii parks as flights are available from Honolulu. Other flights arriving at Pago Pago depart from Australia, Fiji, and New Zealand.
- Car rental is an option, but you'll also have family buses and taxis to get around Tutuila. (Buses do not run on Sundays.)
- Inter-island travel is complicated. A few optimistic airlines did, then didn't offer flights between islands. At print, Talofa Airways (talofaairways.com) was the only reliable airline between Samoa and American Samoa. Ships also make regular trips between islands (including Ofu), but it's best to contact the park for details.
- Ask for permission to walk in the village, take photographs, or use the beach.
- Remove your shoes before entering a home. Cross legs while sitting on the floor.
- Sunday is a day of rest (even swimming is prohibited).
- Each day around dusk villagers observe Sa (prayer). Stop and wait quietly until they're finished.
- The park can arrange for you to stay with a host family (you reach out to them to make sure it's a good match). Only stay with one host to avoid embarrassment.
- Avoid short shorts, bathing suits, and bikinis unless you wear a t-shirt over it. Dress modestly in public (long shorts, pants, skirts, sarongs).
- Excuse yourself when crossing someone's path. Lower your head and say excuse me ("tulou").
- Holding hands is acceptable, but other public displays of affection are discouraged.
- Disney offers a South Pacific cruise stopping at Hawaii, Fiji, and American Samoa. It's a lot of traversing the Pacific, but another way to get here.

American Samoa Favorites
Hikes: Tuafanua Trail (strenuous, 2.2 miles), Mount 'Alava (strenuous, 7), Tumu Mountain (moderate, 5.5)
Views: Ofu Beach, Vatia, Laufuti Falls (Tau)

How Much Time Do You Have?
Chances are you're flying halfway around the world to reach these remote islands. If that's the case, you should spend a decent amount of time (and you'll need it to reach Ofu and Olosega—transportation is difficult to pin down). Everything depends on boats or planes, and your travel plans should have some flexibility to arrange transport to Ofu, Olosega and Tau upon arrival. And, traveling this far, think about Fiji or New Zealand too.

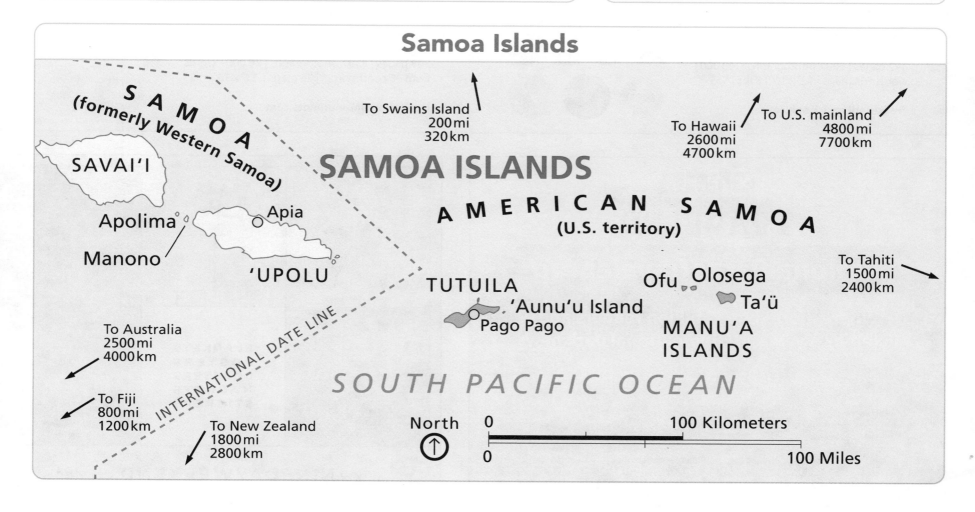

Samoa Islands

Supporting Park People...

When I started on this path more than 15 years ago, I thought it would be a significant challenge, but I was completely misguided (and naive) about the kind of challenges I'd face. Today I sit here, innocence lost, eyes wide open to the world of business and I've acquired a huge amount of empathy and respect for anyone who started and/or is running a company (honestly and ethically). Doesn't matter if you're making a product or providing a service. Working for yourself is hard. It's not to say there aren't challenges doing someone else's work. There are. I've done that. But this business stuff, at least from my point-of-view, requires superhuman amounts of discipline, mental strength, and work ethic. Anyway, this isn't a pity party, this is a celebration of others doing good work in the National Parks space. QT Luong and I share a book distribution partner and love of our public lands. He's spent 30 years and more than 400 park visits exploring and photographing our National Parks. Kurt at National Parks Traveler has been keeping people informed about the parks for nearly two decades. And Dan at Nine Day Weekend creates all kinds of fun park paraphernalia. If you or someone you know is doing positive work for the outdoor/public land communities, tell me about it (mike@stoneroadpress.com). I'll help if our missions align.

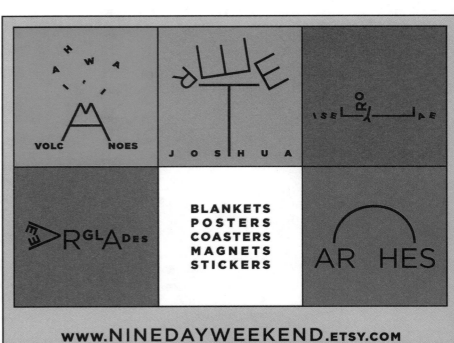